# The
# Theology
# of the
# Apostles

# The Theology of the Apostles

*The Development of New Testament Theology*

## Adolf Schlatter

Translated by
Andreas J. Köstenberger
1999

Original edition:
*Die Theologie der Apostel*
Stuttgart: Calwer Vereinsbuchhandlung
1922

Baker Books
A Division of Baker Book House Co
Grand Rapids, Michigan 49516

Published by Baker Books
a division of Baker Book House Company
P.O. Box 6287, Grand Rapids, MI 49516-6287

Printed in the United States of America

### Library of Congress Cataloging-in-Publication Data

Schlatter, Adolf von, 1852–1938.
    [Theologie der Apostel. English]
    The theology of the Apostles : the development of New Testament theology / Adolf Schlatter ; translated by Andreas J. Köstenberger.
      p.    cm.
    Includes bibliographical references and indexes.
    ISBN 0-8010-2189-8 (cloth)
    1. Apostles. 2. Theology—History—Early church, ca. 30–600. 3. Bible. N.T.—History of Biblical events. I. Title.
BS2618.S3313     1999
230'.0415—dc21                             98-53403

For information about academic books, resources for Christian leaders, and all new releases available from Baker Book House, visit our web site:
http://www.bakerbooks.com

# Contents

# Preface: The Reception of Schlatter's New Testament Theology 1909–23

*Andreas J. Köstenberger*

In light of the appearance of Schlatter's *New Testament Theology* in English, the question arises how Schlatter's work was received when it first appeared in print ninety years ago. It remains to be seen how North-American reviewers will assess Schlatter's contribution to New Testament scholarship from an end-of-twentieth-century vantage point. As this review process is just beginning to get underway, a look at the historical reception of Schlatter's two-volume *New Testament Theology* will prove to be instructive. After a brief biographical sketch, the present article will survey reviewer criticism, followed by a representative survey of Schlatter's own response (or that of his defenders) and a brief evaluation. A summary of reviewer praise and some final observations conclude the essay.

## I. Biographical Sketch[1]

Adolf Schlatter was born in St. Gallen, Switzerland, on August 16, 1852, as the seventh of nine children. After completing his theological studies in Basel and Tübingen (1871–1875), Schlatter served as pastor in several Swiss state churches (1875–1880). A brief tenure at the university of Bern where Schlatter

---

1. See esp. Werner Neuer, *Adolf Schlatter: Ein Leben für Theologie und Kirche* (Wuppertal: R. Brockhaus, 1996); *Adolf Schlatter: A Biography of Germany's Premier Biblical Theologian,* trans. Robert W. Yarbrough (Grand Rapids: Baker, 1995); and "Schlatter, Adolf (1852–1938)," in *Evangelisches Lexicon für Theologie und Gemeinde,* ed. Helmut Burkhardt with Otto Betz, vol. 3 (Wuppertal: Brockhaus, 1994); and the entries by Robert W. Yarbrough on Adolf Schlatter in *Historical Handbook of Major Biblical Interpreters,* ed. Donald McKim (Downers Grove: Inter-Varsity, 1998) and *Handbook of 20th Century Evangelical Bible Scholars,* ed. Walter A. Elwell (Grand Rapids: Baker, forthcoming).

submitted his dissertation on John the Baptist was followed by a post in Greifs-wald (1888–1893), a small town in the north of Germany. There Schlatter worked in close cooperation with the renowned Greek lexicographer Hermann Cremer. His next assignment led Schlatter to Berlin (1893–1898), where he was hired opposite the eminent historian Adolf Harnack who was at that time enmeshed in controversy for criticizing the Apostle's Creed.

In his last major career move, Schlatter went to Tübingen, where he lectured in New Testament and systematics for almost twenty-five years (1898–1922). The years following the death of his wife (1907) marked Schlatter's most pro-ductive as a scholar. In rapid succession, he wrote his two-volume New Testa-ment theology (1909/10, rev. ed. 1922/23) and no less than nine critical com-mentaries on all four Gospels, Romans, the Corinthian epistles, the Pastorals, and 1 Peter (published from 1929 until 1937). Schlatter's last major work was a daily devotional called *Kennen wir Jesus?* (*Do We Know Jesus?*; 1937). He died the following year on May 19, 1938, just prior to the outbreak of World War II.

# II. Schlatter's New Testament Theology[2]

## A. Composition

Soon after the death of his wife, Schlatter decided to write a two-volume New Testament theology. In it, he strove for "pure perception, perception that penetrates to the heart of the matter, to what really happened, to who he [Jesus] was."[3] According to Schlatter, the major obstacle to such a procedure was the "fog" created by the opinions and hypotheses of his scholarly colleagues.[4] Schlatter's own goal was the presentation of Jesus' message as Jesus himself had conveyed it rather than how it was interpreted by others. To this end, Schlatter affirmed the following three fundamental methodological convictions.[5]

First, he distinguished categorically between historical exegesis and "dogmat-ics." New Testament theology, conceived as a historical discipline, must come first; only then can the teaching of Scripture be presented systematically. Hence Schlatter devoted two volumes to lay out the theology of the New Testament, with a third volume devoted to dogmatics.

Second, Schlatter pointed out that historical research must confine itself to the exploration of available sources. He refused to go beyond the evidence, and as a result gave little weight to source-critical questions which, in his view, must of necessity remain speculative.

Third, he portrayed Jesus' teaching in relation to his actual work rather than focusing exclusively on Jesus' proclamation. In this Schlatter broke decisively with the so-called *lehrbegriffliche Methode* ("doctrinal concepts")[6] practiced by

---

2. Cf. esp. Neuer, *Schlatter* (1996), 464–80.
3. *An Christine, 15. 10. 1908,* quoted in Neuer, *Schlatter* (1996), 465. Translations from the German in this essay are the present author's.
4. Ibid.
5. On this, see Neuer, *Schlatter* (1996), 467–70.
6. Cf. Gerhard Hasel, *New Testament Theology: Basic Issues in the Current Date* (Grand Rapids: Eerdmans, 1978), 46.

most of Schlatter's contemporaries such as B. Weiß, H. J. Holtzmann, or P. Feine. For Schlatter, Jesus' word and work constitute an inseparable unity, and both are rooted in Jesus' messianic consciousness. According to Schlatter, Jesus' major purpose was not the impartation of dogmatic or ethical instruction (a *Heilslehre*) but the establishment of the saving, kingly rule of God (Jesus' *Heilswille*).[7]

Immediately after completing *Das Wort Jesu*, Schlatter devoted himself to writing the second volume of his New Testament theology entitled *Die Lehre der Apostel*. Underlying this work is the observation that there exists a close relationship between Jesus and the New Testament witnesses. The continuity between the message of Jesus and apostolic teaching provides the New Testament with a salvation-historical and theological unity that is not merely accessible by faith but can also be investigated historically. This conviction set Schlatter's work apart from that of many of his contemporaries who, according to Schlatter, presented the relationship between Jesus and the New Testament writers as "torn by a thousand contradictions."[8]

In his attempt to exhibit the continuity between the New Testament witnesses and the word and work of Jesus, Schlatter started with "the convictions represented by Jesus' followers" (that is, Matthew, James, Jude, John, and Peter), then treated Paul and the theology of the "coworkers of the apostles" (Mark, Luke, Hebrews, 2 Peter), and finally discussed the "convictions prevailing in the churches." One of the most pervasive characteristics of Schlatter's work is his effort to demonstrate common ground in the thought of the various New Testament writers. At the same time, original elements in an author's contribution are acknowledged as well, so that New Testament theology emerges as a "unity in diversity."[9]

## B. Reception

The years from 1909 until 1923 saw the publication of a total of eleven reviews of one or both volumes of Schlatter's *New Testament Theology*, all in Germany.[10] Nine reviews are of one or both volumes of the first edition (1909/10),

---

7. Cf. Neuer, *Schlatter* (1996), 469, referring to Schlatter, *Das Wort Jesu*, 358–429.

8. Cf. R 233f., quoted in Neuer, *Schlatter*, 477.

9. Cf. Neuer, *Schlatter* (1996), 477–78. Note the commendation by M. Kähler in *Kähler an Schlatter, 14. 11. 1909*, quoted in Neuer, *Schlatter* (1996), 479.

10. The reviews are listed here in order of publication: Ernst Kühl, Review of *Das Wort Jesu*, in *Die Theologie der Gegenwart* 3 (1909): 57–65 [response by Adolf Schlatter in *Evangelisches Kirchenblatt für Württemberg* 71 (1910): 25–27]; Johannes Leipoldt, Review of *Das Wort Jesu*, in *Theologisches Literaturblatt* 30 (1909): 363–66; Christian Römer, Review of *Das Wort Jesu*, in *Evangelisches Kirchenblatt für Württemberg* 70 (1909): 157–58 [response defending Schlatter in *Evangelisches Kirchenblatt für Württemberg* 71 (1910): 137–39]; Heinrich Julius Holtzmann, Review of *Das Wort Jesu* and *Die Lehre der Apostel*, in *Theologische Literaturzeitung* 35 (1910): 299–303; Hans Windisch, Review of *Das Wort Jesu* and *Die Lehre der Apostel*, in *Zeitschrift für wissenschaftliche Theologie* 52 (1910): 219–31; Rudolf Bultmann, Review of *Das Wort Jesu* and *Die Lehre der Apostel*, in *Monatsschrift für Pastoraltheologie* 8 (1911–12): 440–43; Schöllkopf, Review of *Das Wort Jesu* and *Die Lehre der Apostel*, in *Monatsschrift für Pastoraltheologie* 8 (1911/12): 18–24; Martin Dibelius, Review of *Das Wort Jesu* and *Die Lehre der Apostel*, in *Die christliche Welt*

two are of the first volume of the second edition. Notably, *Die Theologie der Apostel* elicited not a single review. Of these eleven reviews, four are positive (Leipoldt, Römer, Schöllkopf, Beck), three are mixed (Windisch, Bultmann, Dibelius), and four are negative (Kühl, Holtzmann, Knopf, Bauer). Following is a list of reviews in chronological order of publication.[11]

### Reviews of *Das Wort Jesu* (1909)

| Year | Reviewer | Background of Reviewer | General Assessment |
| --- | --- | --- | --- |
| 1909 | Ernst Kühl | Professor of NT in Göttingen | Mostly negative |
| 1909 | Johannes Leipoldt | Professor of NT in Halle | Very positive |
| 1909 | Christian Römer | Dean at Tübingen | Very positive |

### Reviews of *Das Wort Jesu* (1909) and *Die Lehre der Apostel* (1910)

| Year | Reviewer | Background of Reviewer | General Assessment |
| --- | --- | --- | --- |
| 1910 | H. J. Holtzmann | Professor emeritus of NT | Very negative |
| 1910 | Hans Windisch | Privatdozent of NT in Leipzig | Mixed |
| 1911/12 | Rudolf Bultmann | Privatdozent of NT in Marburg | Mixed |
| 1911/12 | Schöllkopf | Württemberg pastor | Very positive |
| 1913 | Martin Dibelius | Privatdozent of NT in Berlin | Mixed |
| 1913 | Rudolf Knopf | Privatdozent of NT in Marburg | Mostly negative |

### Reviews of *Die Geschichte des Christus* (1920, 1921)

| Year | Reviewer | Background of Reviewer | General Assessment |
| --- | --- | --- | --- |
| 1921 | G. Beck | Württemberg pastor | Very positive |
| 1923 | Walter Bauer | Professor of NT in Göttingen | Mostly negative |

### Reviews of *Die Theologie der Apostel* (1923)
None

---

27 (1913): 938–41; Rudolf Knopf, Review of *Das Wort Jesu* and *Die Lehre der Apostel,* in *Theologische Studien und Kritiken* 86 (1913): 634–40; G. Beck, Review of *Die Geschichte des Christus,* in *Monatsschrift für Pastoraltheologie* 17 (1921): 230–34; Walter Bauer, Review of *Die Geschichte des Christus,* in *Theologische Literaturzeitung* 48 (1923): 77–80.

11. Only the authors of reviews will be mentioned in the following discussion. For complete bibliographic references, see the list of reviews in the previous note.

## 1. Reviewer Criticism

Only a brief summary of the major criticisms of Schlatter's work can be provided here, followed by Schlatter's response.[12] One notes six recurring criticisms, three each directed at substance and style. Regarding matters of substance, critics take exception to Schlatter's approach to history, his dogmatic bent, and his overemphasis on the will in relation to the cognitive domain of faith. With regard to style, Schlatter is faulted for the way he deals with his opponents, his alleged lack of humility, and his difficult style of writing.

### (a) His approach to history

One of the most frequent charges advanced by Schlatter's critics is that he unduly neglects *Einleitungsfragen* (introductory matters), history-of-religions issues, and literary tools such as source criticism.[13] Schlatter's opponents contend that he glosses over the critical issues pertaining to the Gospels rather than facing them head-on. Many consider Schlatter to be unduly hostile and reactionary toward the historical-critical method and the history-of-religions school and feel that he stereotypes those who hold differing views.[14] Also, his critics contend that he intermingles the christologies of the Synoptics and John indiscriminately without adequately differentiating between them. According to those critics, the distinction between older material and portions that were added later is part of historical research, so that it is not irrelevant which of the Synoptic texts is given priority.[15] Indeed, it is charged, Schlatter himself operates under the assumption of a source theory, and a dubious one at that: the notion of Matthean priority, defended on the basis of scholarly convenience rather than historical considerations.[16]

Bultmann, though not unappreciative of Schlatter's work, is one of his most incisive critics. He finds the historical element "entirely missing" in Schlatter's presentation, faulting him also for his total neglect of source criticism and his consequent leveling of the Synoptics and John. Bultmann also charges Schlatter with naivete regarding his own presuppositions, commenting that Schlatter only deceives himself[17] when he claims to see nothing but what is in the sources and to be able to manage entirely without inferences and hypothetical reconstructions of his own. Or is it not an inference, Bultmann asks, when Schlatter claims that Jesus' consciousness of his birth was an essential part of his self-understanding, or when Schlatter hypothesizes that Jesus' realization of the failure of his call to repentance convinced him that he had to die? Where is this

---

12. The following survey focuses primarily on the reviews of Schlatter's work published between 1909 and 1923 as listed above. Only occasional reference is made to the reception of Schlatter's work in recent scholarship. On modern Schlatter reception and relevance, see the essay by Robert Yarbrough at the end of this volume.

13. Cf., e.g., Bultmann, 442; Holtzmann, 302. Note the discussion by Neuer, *Schlatter* (1996), 472.

14. Holtzmann, 300–301; Bultmann, 442.

15. Kühl, 61–62.

16. Dibelius, 939; Holtzmann, 300.

17. Cf. Bultmann, 443; the term "self-deception" is echoed in the review of *Die Geschichte des Christus* by W. Bauer, 78.

borne out in the sources? Bultmann queries. Or where does it say that the disciples considered the offense of the cross to be not primarily the Messiah's suffering but his rejection by Israel? "Overall," Bultmann writes, "one parts with this work that contains so much good with a feeling of pain: how can a mind so receptive to the purely religious, so unclouded by prejudice, be so incapable of historical work?"[18] Some also fault Schlatter for his conservative stance on the authorship of disputed New Testament writings such as 1 Peter, the Pastorals, the Gospel of John, or the Apocalypse.[19]

### *(b) His dogmatic bent*

Schlatter is charged with an arbitrary selection of texts leading to an artificial unity. Some of his critics allege that Schlatter simply discusses his favorite passages of Scripture in form of meditations. This, they claim, proves that Schlatter acts as a dogmatician after all. Knopf speaks for many when he says, "The dogmatician speaks to us in the book from the first page to the last, the systematician who flaunts a peculiar thought world and rediscovers it in the thought world of the New Testament."[20] Holtzmann flatly states that Schlatter's work is Christian dogmatics (*christliche Glaubenslehre*) rather than New Testament theology.[21] By choosing a few select themes (such as the cross and the regal will and status of Jesus, the relationship between grace and judgment or between repentance and the kingdom) and by stressing them in his discussion, Schlatter creates the appearance of a certain unity in the New Testament writings, but the coherence achieved by Schlatter is artificial and of his own making, a product of Schlatter the dogmatician rather than a reflection of New Testament teaching.[22] His is an exercise in unhistorical biblicism that glosses over discrepancies, diversity, and contradictions.[23]

### *(c) His overemphasis on the will in relation to the cognitive domain of faith*

Some critics take exception to Schlatter's emphasis on the will over against the cognitive domain of faith. This is frequently considered to reflect an over-reaction against the unilateral focus on Jesus' teachings by the *lehrbegriffliche Methode*. Bultmann in particular feels that Schlatter's polemic against intellectualism is overdone.[24] Holtzmann likewise charges that Schlatter unduly demands for everything to reach the will. But what, he asks, are we to make of 1 Peter 3:19–20 or John's discourse about the Logos?[25] These passages seem to be aimed primarily at the cognitive domain.

18. Bultmann, 442–43.
19. Holtzmann, 300.
20. Knopf, 635–36; similarly, the New Testament scholars Bauer, Bultmann, Dibelius, Holtzmann, and Windisch.
21. Holtzmann, 299.
22. Kühl, 63–64; Bauer, 78.
23. Holtzmann, 302.
24. Bultmann, 442.
25. Holtzmann, 302.

### (d) His failure to interact with other scholars

Schlatter's critics fault him for his lack of interaction with other scholars, his stereotyping of those who hold differing views, and his polemic tone. Schlatter's lack of explicit interaction with his opponents' views is judged to be "an indulgence unbecoming of a first-rate theologian."[26] Schlatter should name his opponents and cite their respective works for the benefit of his readers. As it is, Schlatter's work is removed from the mainstream of New Testament scholarship.[27] Again, it is Bultmann who complains that Schlatter often mocks and injures his opponents.[28] Bauer, too, is offended by Schlatter's denunciation of those who engage in "speculations," have "confidence in their own conclusions," and are "dreamers who give themselves to speculative reconstructions."[29]

### (e) His false sense of confidence

Some critics observe Schlatter's absolute use of language; words such as "always," "never," "certainly," etc. prevail. They conclude that Schlatter operates on the basis of the certainty of faith rather than in the realm of the relativity of historical scholarship. Bauer, for instance, points out how Schlatter seems to know precisely why the sources are silent regarding a particular issue or why they say what they say, or why one apostle depicts a given matter in one way and another New Testament author in another. With thinly veiled sarcasm, he comments how issues that have eluded definitive solutions for centuries present no problems for Schlatter who solves them with enviable ease. A case in point is Schlatter's explanation of Jesus' use of the term "Son of Man" in terms of Jesus' effort to accentuate his commonality with man. Schlatter's use of absolute language and his simplistic solutions seem naive and a product of faith rather than being the result of a judicious use of the historical method.[30]

### (f) His difficult style of writing

Some find Schlatter's style to resemble that of "delphic oracles."[31] They lament that his expressions are frequently awkward, even obtuse, and that his idiosyncratic style makes it difficult to follow his line of argument.

### 2. Schlatter's Response and Evaluation

The cumulative force of these charges weighed heavily on Schlatter. Often he felt at a loss as to why his work met with such serious criticism.[32] In particular, he found it difficult to defend himself against the various charges leveled against his work since these tended to be general rather than taking the form of concrete objections. "I will not be able to enter into dialogue [with my critics]," Schlatter

---

26. Kühl, 64, echoed by Holtzmann, 300.
27. Holtzmann, 301.
28. Bultmann, 442.
29. Bauer, 78.
30. Cf. esp. Bauer, 77–80.
31. Kühl, 65.
32. Cf., e.g., in the foreword to the second edition of *Das Wort Jesu* entitled *Die Geschichte des Christus*, 6.

lamented, "unless I am told, 'here you overlook something or this or that view is wrong.'"[33] Nevertheless, while Schlatter took these charges seriously, he insisted that when his rationale for his chosen procedure was taken into account, it constituted a marked advance over against competing contemporary models. Here is a sketch of Schlatter's response (or that of his defenders) against the above listed criticisms accompanied by brief comments of evaluation.

### (a) His approach to history

To his critics' charge that he neglects *Einleitungsfragen* and literary questions such as source criticism, Schlatter responds that these matters are a prerequisite for New Testament theology rather than its proper subject. He therefore feels no need to defend his views on these matters at length but rather asserts his conclusions at the outset of his work. Moreover, Schlatter notes that, just because we are not able to solve the riddle of the exact nature of the interrelationships between the Synoptic Gospels, this does not mean that we lack certainty concerning the history of Jesus. For the Gospels mutually confirm each other in this regard. Jesus' teaching is straightforward and univocal, so that the interpreter of Jesus should not speak of the "words of Jesus" but of "Jesus' word." Only what turns out to be genuinely in doubt owing to the diversity of the Gospel accounts may therefore be set aside.[34]

Moreover, Schlatter rightly points out that his opponents' skeptical stance toward the sources' reliability is rooted in the Enlightenment thinking of Descartes (the "atheistic method").[35] For Schlatter, historical work applied to the Gospels means to illumine the inner logic, dynamic, and connections underlying the events portrayed in these writings. But because he does not buy into Cartesian thought and thus does not share its epistemological skepticism, Schlatter steadfastly refuses to pit the Jesus of history against the Christ of faith, as Bultmann and many others did in the tradition of D. F. Strauß.[36] Rather, he affirms the New Testament writers' continuity with the thought of Jesus. In this, Schlatter has been followed by much of recent evangelical scholarship. Thus the Tübingen scholar Peter Stuhlmacher self-consciously sees himself as operating in the tradition of Schlatter, taking his cue from him.[37]

### (b) His dogmatic bent

Ironically, while Schlatter himself claims to be a historian, emphasizing the priority of historical exegesis over dogmatics, he is frequently charged by his critics with being oblivious to the true nature of historical research and with operat-

33. *An Lütgert*, 15. 1. *1910,* cited in Neuer, *Schlatter* (1996), 474.
34. Schlatter, "Response to Kühl," 26–27.
35. Besides Schlatter's essay on "Atheistic Methods" referred to above, see also his *Die philosophische Arbeit seit Cartesius. Ihr ethischer und religiöser Ertrag,* in Beiträge zur Förderung Christliches Theologie 10 (1906).
36. This is rightly noted by Bauer, 78.
37. P. Stuhlmacher, *Jesus of Nazareth—Christ of Faith,* trans. S. Schatzmann (Peabody, Mass.: Hendrickson, 1993), 1–7, 38. See also Markus Bockmuehl, *This Jesus: Martyr, Lord, Messiah* (Edinburgh: T. & T. Clark, 1994), 21–23. On Stuhlmacher, see further R. Yarbrough's essay at the end of this volume.

ing as a dogmatician. Among those defending Schlatter against this charge was Römer, at that time dean at Tübingen.[38] He contrasts Schlatter's work with treatments where a scholar's general reconstruction becomes the schema into which details are fitted whether they suit this overall pattern or not. A total impression is abstracted before the work is studied in detail; what does not cohere is declared corrupt or interpolated, and it is alleged that Paul (or other New Testament writers) were themselves unaware of breaks in their logic. With fine irony, Römer observes that such interpreters would rather charge Paul with inconsistency than suspect incongruencies in their own thinking. So-called "contradictions and inner tensions" are found to characterize Jesus or Paul, simply because no effort is made to look at *all* the evidence first; and this is called "scientific method"!

To the contrary, Römer charges, this method is riddled with problems of its own, creating yet further difficulties. Indeed, Schlatter himself, in his treatise on New Testament theology and dogmatics, asks the question whether the "scientific method" can truly comprehend its subject in the practice of New Testament theology.[39] As Römer points out, one who, like Schlatter, seeks to challenge a conventional method that claims to be "scientific" will of course be called "unscientific" by those who are proponents of this traditional approach. Some people's difficulty in understanding Schlatter thus related to the unconventional nature of his method. But to charge Schlatter with dogmatism merely because he fails to conform to commonly accepted scholarly procedures in his day begs the question and betrays a defensive posture rather than doing justice to Schlatter's work.

Indeed, it may be argued that, contrary to the charges made by his critics, the approach underlying Schlatter's *New Testament Theology* is not dogmatics but biblical theology. The practice of biblical theology, of course, still involves the selection of major themes in the respective New Testament writings. Yet while one may differ with Schlatter's particular reconstruction, the charge that "the dogmatician is speaking to us from the first to the last page" seems unfair and overblown.

### (c) His overemphasis on the will in relation to the cognitive domain of faith

Schlatter is convinced that New Testament scholarship focused unduly on Jesus' sayings and teachings at the expense of his appeal to the will. Not merely right belief, but repentance and trust were the intended results of Jesus' ministry according to Schlatter. In this Schlatter feels vindicated by the Gospels themselves when read open-mindedly. The foremost task of the New Testament theologian is therefore "a pure, sincere listening to Jesus." But this was not the Jesus taught at most religion faculties of Schlatter's day. "We must not make Jesus a Professor of Theology and answer-man to all questions currently moving the church," Schlatter writes. "We must allow Jesus to say what he himself wanted to say rather than burdening him with our modern questions, construing an answer to our

---

38. Römer, 137–39.
39. Cf. Adolf Schlatter, "The Theology of the New Testament and Dogmatics," trans. Robert Morgan, in Robert Morgan, *The Nature of New Testament Theology*, SBT 2/25 (London: SCM, 1973), 117–66. Now also in Neuer, *Schlatter* (1995), 159–210.

modern questions from his words."[40] In this, Schlatter felt further confirmed by A. Schweitzer's then recent work on nineteenth-century life of Jesus research.

In hindsight, Schlatter's consideration of Jesus' work alongside his word and his effort to look at Jesus' life holistically clearly constitutes an abiding contribution to New Testament scholarship. Many recent interpreters have sounded similar calls to consider Jesus' acts together with his words. By emphasizing Jesus' appeal to the will, Schlatter did in no way mean to minimize the contribution made by Jesus' verbal proclamation. He rather opposed the tendency of characterizing Jesus primarily as a teacher of content to be believed rather than of commands to be obeyed. Charging Schlatter with neglecting the cognitive domain of faith therefore seems to misrepresent his true intentions.

### (d) His failure to interact with other scholars

To his critics' charge that he fails to make explicit reference to his opponents in his writings Schlatter replies that he does not want his work to be distracted from the apprehension of Jesus and the New Testament writings themselves. Indeed, "hearing [the text] is imperiled when at the same time we are stormed by a jumble of voices. Stillness is the condition for hearing: it demands restricting our communion to the one who now speaks to us."[41] According to Schlatter, the major sources for Jesus are the Gospels, so that the historian's primary task is to read the Gospels. And these Gospels are available for everyone to read, so that everyone can judge for himself whether Schlatter interprets them accurately or not.[42]

Generally, it is indeed helpful to refer to one's opponents. But it is also the case that constant interaction with opposing views can cloud the issues. Schlatter is right: the primary source for an understanding of Jesus *are* the Gospels, and the one who seeks to construe a New Testament theology must read *the Gospels.* This is the standard by which any New Testament theology should be judged: how does it measure up against the primary texts, and does it reflect a thorough reading of the New Testament writings? It is precisely the fact that Schlatter focuses his work on Scripture rather than on interaction with contemporary scholars that dates his *New Testament Theology* significantly less than the works of most of his colleagues.

### (e) His false sense of confidence

Schlatter devoted an entire essay to the issue of faith and scholarship in which he took to task the "atheistic" character of contemporary biblical scholarship.[43] He excoriated theological scholarship for its rootedness in Cartesian doubt and skepticism that led to a dichotomy between faith and reason and between his-

40. Schlatter, "Response to Kühl," 25.

41. This reference is from W. Neuer, *Schlatter* (1996), 435, quoted in Yarbrough, "Schlatter, Adolf" in *Historical Handbook of Major Biblical Interpreters,* ed. Donald McKim (InterVarsity, 1998), 518–23.

42. Schlatter, "Response to Kühl," 26.

43. Originally published in *Beiträge zur Förderung Christlicher Theologie* 9 (1905), this essay is most readily accessible in translation in Neuer, *Schlatter* (1995), 211–25.

tory and theology. The only way to overcome this chasm, according to Schlatter, is to question the legitimacy of the Cartesian model in the first place. When he frequently sounds confident in his conclusions, this is in part a function of his confidence in the reliability of his sources which enables him to attain secure results in his understanding of Jesus and the early church.

The tone of assurance in Schlatter's writing could indeed convey the notion of arrogance. To be sure, while part of the confidence pervading Schlatter's work doubtless arises from his thorough study of Scripture, a certain dogmatism and polemic thrust are undeniable. Apart from his pietistic background, however, Schlatter's idiosyncrasy in this regard may at least in part be explained by his personal circumstances. In many ways, he was virtually alone in his day in defending a more conservative theological position. More than once he expressed dismay at the notion that he had to contend with an entire phalanx of interpreters who opposed his views.[44] The competing paradigm, the history-of-religions approach practiced by Holtzmann, B. Weiß, and later Bultmann, studied Jesus and the emergence of New Testament teaching largely from an evolutionary perspective rather than the vantage point of divine revelation.

Finally, some of Schlatter's contemporaries were also provoked by Schlatter's self-acknowledged stance as a *believing* scholar. Again, however, Schlatter's approach has begun to find support in recent years through the work of G. Maier and M. Noll.[45]

### (f) His difficult style of writing

Schlatter contends that the issue is not primarily his awkwardness of expression but the element of mystery attached to his subject matter. The coexistence of Law and grace or of temptation and forgiveness of sin are difficult to explain by anyone, because these matters are complex and spiritually appraised. Launching a counter-offensive of his own, Schlatter charges that scholarship in the wake of the Enlightenment has undertaken to remove every element of mystery in order to master its subject; but rationalism, according to Schlatter, is the antithesis of historical scholarship.[46]

But Schlatter's protestations notwithstanding, the difficulty of his style has indeed proven to represent a major stumbling block for the modern reception of his thought. Curiously, Schlatter's style is quite uneven, and passages of great simplicity, clarity, and beauty alternate with convoluted sentences whose meaning is difficult to discern. It remains for the translator to alleviate this potential obstacle as much as possible by choosing appropriate renderings.

### 3. Reviewer Praise

One of the curious features of the reception of Schlatter's *New Testament Theology* is the mixed nature of reviews. Even those highly critical of his work

---

44. Cf. *An Theodor, 22. 1. 1910,* quoted in Neuer, *Schlatter* (1996), 475. Cf. also Neuer, *Schlatter* (1996), 479–80.

45. Cf. Gerhard Maier, *Biblical Hermeneutics,* trans. Robert W. Yarbrough (Wheaton: Crossway, 1994); Mark A. Noll, *Between Faith and Criticism: Evangelicals, Scholarship, and the Bible in America,* 2nd ed. (Grand Rapids: Baker, 1991).

46. Schlatter, "Response to Kühl," 25–26.

do not offer wholesale denunciations of Schlatter's writings but combine harsh criticism with high praise.[47] Four positive features of Schlatter's work are mentioned with particular frequency: his consideration of Jesus' work as well as his word; his emphasis on the Jewish background of the Gospels and the life of Jesus; his intuitive grasp of the essence of Pauline or Johannine theology; and the spiritually nurturing character of Schlatter's writing.

### (a) His consideration of Jesus' work as well as his word

Schlatter contends that Jesus was not primarily a teacher, and that his message did not merely constitute a system of new concepts, doctrines, or religious insights. Rather, the Gospel presents Jesus' ministry primarily in active terms: he seeks to effect repentance, foster a decision of the will, offer forgiveness (rather than merely provide instruction regarding God's gracious disposition), and grant divine forgiveness (rather than merely teaching or defining it). Thus Schlatter does not merely gather similar passages and then condense them as aspects of Jesus' theology. This is frequently considered to be an improvement over against earlier studies of Jesus even by Schlatter's opponents.[48] Interestingly, Bultmann faults Holtzmann here precisely for failing to do what Schlatter does. According to Bultmann, Holtzmann places too much weight on the intellectual aspects of spiritual life in the New Testament. But the driving forces of history, Bultmann contends, are not theoretical ideas but religious and ethical forces.[49]

### (b) His emphasis on the Jewish background of the Gospels and the life of Jesus

Leipoldt commends Schlatter for his excellent refutation of the "modern legend" that early Christianity was something entirely non-Jewish, and many others agree that Schlatter was successful in demonstrating the essentially Jewish background of Jesus, Paul, and early Christianity.[50] In an age when the history-of-religions school related early Christianity primarily to Hellenism, Schlatter was a lonely voice. But his stance has been abundantly vindicated in recent scholarship. A case in point is Schlatter's advocacy of the Palestinian provenance of the Fourth Gospel (now supported decisively by the Qumran discoveries) at a time when it was widely interpreted in Hellenistic terms.

### (c) His intuitive grasp of the essence of Pauline and Johannine theology[51]

Windisch calls Schlatter "one of today's most thoughtful and perceptive theologians," commenting that the section on Jesus' piety is "particularly profound and beautiful" and that the chapter on Paul's theology is among Schlat-

---

47. Cf. Neuer, *Schlatter* (1996), 470, who cites as examples the reviews of Bauer, Bultmann, Holtzmann, Knopf, and Kühl.
48. Cf. Römer, 157. This is noted also by Neuer, *Schlatter* (1996), 471.
49. Bultmann, 434.
50. Leipoldt, 366; cf. Dibelius, 940; Knopf, 635.
51. Apart from the reviews referred to below, see also Neuer, *Schlatter* (1996), 470.

ter's most valuable and penetrating scholarly contributions.[52] Bultmann sees the greatest strength of Schlatter's work in his grasp of the religious substance of the New Testament; he especially commends Schlatter for his treatment of ethical questions, such as his discussion of the "new commandment" in the chapter on Jesus' call to repentance.[53]

### (d) The spiritually nurturing character of Schlatter's writing[54]

Even Schlatter's harshest critics are virtually unanimous in commending him for the profundity of his theological insight and the spiritually nurturing character of his writing. This suggests that it may have been primarily Schlatter's defiance of existing paradigms that led to his scholarly isolation in his day. Notably, Schlatter's harshest critics were part of the German theological establishment while his most grateful readers were local pastors and laymen.[55]

## III. Final Observations

The mixed nature of reviews Schlatter received for his *New Testament Theology* is evidence for the difficulty his contemporaries had in evaluating Schlatter's work. Was Schlatter "incapable of historical work" (a)?[56] Did "the dogmatician speak to us . . . from the first page to the last" (b)?[57] Was Schlatter an anti-intellectual fideist (c)? Is that why he failed to interact explicitly with his opponents (d)? Does this also explain the absolute tone characteristic of Schlatter's writings which was regarded as naivete at best or arrogance at worst by Schlatter's opponents (e)? And do Schlatter's writings resemble "delphic oracles" (f)?[58]

It is not the primary purpose of the present essay to adjudicate between Schlatter and his critics. After all, more recent responses to Schlatter's work must be considered before a more definitive assessment of his contribution to New Testament scholarship can be made.[59] At a preliminary level, however, the survey of reviewer criticism and Schlatter's response suggests that Schlatter repeatedly and very effectively countered the charges brought against his work.

---

52. Windisch, 225, 228; similarly, Knopf, 635–36, 639; Bauer, 80. Still, Windisch sides with Kühl's critical review (230, n. 1).

53. Bultmann, 441–42; cf. also Holtzmann, 302.

54. Cf. for further examples Neuer, *Schlatter*, 471.

55. To the above cited commendations of Schlatter's *New Testament Theology* may be added the comments made by the British scholar P. T. Forsyth in "The Faith of Jesus," *Expository Times* 21 (1909–10): 8–9 (cited in *Evangelisches Kirchenblatt für Württemberg* 71 [1910]: 94 by Eberhard Nestle), who compares Schlatter's work with Holtzmann's as follows: "I remark in passing how I am struck with the moral and historic insight of this book in contrast with the intellectual acumen and fertility of combination of Holtzmann. It is all the difference between *sympathetic interpretation* and analytic construction. The one seems *written from within*, the other from without; the one *with radiance*, the other with brilliance; the one *so steadying*, the other so illuminating; the one *so grave*, the other so keen; the one *so full of grace*, the other of truth" (emphasis added). I am indebted to W. Neuer for this reference.

56. Bultmann, 443.

57. Knopf, 635.

58. Kühl, 65.

59. This is the subject of the essay by Robert Yarbrough at the end of this present volume.

But a more conclusive evaluation of the legacy bequeathed by Adolf Schlatter to modern scholarship will be possible only as part of a survey of reactions to Schlatter's writings in recent scholarship.

It is done. Translating almost eleven hundred pages of Schlatter's difficult prose from German into English has proved to be a tedious yet exceedingly rewarding task for this translator. My daily regimen of translating Schlatter almost took on the form of second devotions, so spiritually nurturing are many of Schlatter's insights. Now that the project has been completed, I will need to look for a substitute—perhaps Schlatter's own daily devotional *Kennen Wir Jesus?*

Once again, I want to say a hearty "thank you" to my friends at Baker Book House for their courage and vision to publish this work in English translation decades after its initial release in the German original. Robert Yarbrough, too, has poured himself into this project with great enthusiasm. He has carefully read and edited the entire manuscript and significantly enhanced the quality of this translation.

Martin Hengel recently ranked Adolf Schlatter (together with F. C. Baur) as "the most significant evangelical theologian in Tübingen during the past two hundred years," calling him "a towering intellect, the kind of which German theology has produced only precious few in the past one hundred and fifty years."[60] May the second volume of Schlatter's *New Testament Theology* continue to bless and stimulate those who read it. *Soli Deo gloria.*

---

60. Martin Hengel, "Vorwort," in *Paulus und das antike Judentum,* ed. Martin Hengel and Ulrich Heckel (Tübingen: Mohr Siebeck, 1991), vii–viii.

# Foreword to the First Edition[1]

I ask that my readers, especially those engaged in formal scholarship, free themselves from the usual presupposition that they have long since mastered the religious content that the New Testament makes palpable to us. In this view the call to serious observation of that content is regarded as unnecessary and perhaps even insulting. This attitude has a long history, stretching back to the beginnings of the discipline of New Testament theology as such. The discipline arose as the rational interpretation of history separated itself from history as passed along in church tradition. Both sides, the rational and the ecclesiastical, saw in the knowledge of Christianity a long-standing possession. Both also viewed the new scientific task solely as "explaining" Christianity's rise as a whole and in its parts. That is why what New Testament research needs today is a breakthrough, a bold thrust through the maze of explanatory constructions and conjectures. This would enable us once more to bring an eye capable of genuine apprehension to those events and words of which the New Testament documents are witnesses. In view of this most pressing and fruitful task I made a conscious decision. When framing and delimiting what follows in this volume, and when the question arose: statistics or etiology? (that is, the passing along of the New Testament's statements, on the one hand, or of suppositions regarding the events and words out of which those statements grew, on the other), I often opted for the former—the simple presentation of the content. This greatly simplified the task of interacting with dissenting theories, since many of them become untenable once the true state of affairs surrounding the data is genuinely apprehended.

---

1. The first edition had the title *Die Theologie des Neuen Testaments. Zweiter Teil: Die Lehre der Apostel* (1910).

# Foreword to the Second Edition

Gladly, very gladly indeed would I have completed a considerable number of other projects before producing this second edition of my New Testament theology. But the years pile up, and I have not lost the hope expressed in the 1910 edition that my presentation might help this or that person to personal appropriation of the contents of the New Testament through clear, genuine apprehension. The more shaky the structure of the church becomes, speaking now first of the German church but also of the structure of the church everywhere as events take their inevitable course, the more vital it becomes that we find access to the New Testament. We must recover a keen eye for grasping what it was that created New Testament history. The calamities that weaken our church are not, in my view, the result of the word given to the apostles; they are due rather to the promiscuous intermixing of that word with pre-Christian traditions that are causing the entire thought and action of the church to depart from the New Testament. History pronounces a devastating verdict on this intermingling. In order to avoid falling prey to it, and instead to transform the calamities into a powerful movement forward, we all require knowledge and understanding of the New Testament—clergy and laity, clergy of every persuasion, laity of every congregation. I am not talking here about that interpretation of the New Testament that makes a book of divine legislation out of it and then works at pressing the church back into the mold of its beginning decades. In my view this interpretation of the apostolic word distorts its basic ideas. What the word of the apostles says to the church is rather this: what weakens her is overcome, and the work she is entrusted with is completed with growing strength, only as she remains united with her Author and Perfecter. But no other access to Jesus exists than the one which the apostolic word opens up to us.

Of criticisms leveled by my colleagues at the first edition, none hit me harder than the charge that my presentation distorted history by failing to make clear Peter's key role in early church formation. Perhaps this new edition will correct that impression, less through the expanded discussion of Peter's letters than by the initial overview of the standpoint shared by Jesus' disciples at the outset of their work based on the work accomplished by Jesus. These introductory sections are intended to ensure that the reader will not see merely isolated phenomena as he regards individual men and their writings.

D. A. Schlatter

# The Disciples' Vantage Point at the Beginning of Their Work

The work of Peter and Jesus' other disciples flowed from that which the history of Jesus had brought into being. In the wake of the Easter events they reflected on Jesus' lordship with that certainty which genuine apprehension of the Risen One had imparted to them. From that time on, faith in him was their firmly established conviction, determining their conduct. But this also meant that Jesus' combining of his regal status with his divine sonship guided their entire thought and volition. The foundation of what they believed was now that Jesus was the Christ because he was the Son of God, that his lordship over the world was rooted in his union with God, and that it revealed God's rule. Because Jesus had transformed their association with him into their religion, their ministry created history of religion from the beginning, and the community gathered by them was a true community from its first day, united by the consciousness of God it derived from its knowledge of Jesus.

## A. The Disciples' Consciousness of God

### 1. The One

The will to unity arose victoriously from the concept of God Jesus had made his disciples' central conviction. One foundation supports everything, and everything moves toward one goal. There is one who is the founder, and one who is the perfecter, and contemplation of him immediately produces a desire for the whole. For he proves himself to be the One by pervading everything and transforming it into a whole. In being Jesus' disciple all thoughts and goals were shaped decisively by the movement toward the One and the Whole. The one Father is united with the one Son in complete unity. All Israel, all the nations are called; his kingdom comprises all that is in heaven, on earth, and under the earth, everything that exists. The living and the dead belong to him. He is exalted over all, above every heavenly power, and God's entire work is accomplished through him; creation and its consummation are his doing. Man is wholly his and has no

27

other Master. His victory is total, involving complete removal of guilt and death, bestowal of life that is abundant life, but also complete loss of life when his wrath arises. Man unreservedly departs from evil, judges himself completely, and destroys all self-reliance, trusting him fully, and refusing to doubt, loving wholly, so that he lives and dies for him. He creates a community, and one alone, one that comprises all who belong to God, in all ages and among all peoples.

The contrasts of the present situation found clear expression through the power of the will to unity. They were not obliterated by it; rather, everything that presents an obstacle to unity is now recognized most distinctly and resisted most vigorously. God and the world stand in complete opposition to one another, and faith and unbelief part company like life and death. Perception of Satan is heightened, consciousness of guilt gains force, and the ethical struggle acquires a depth unknown in the earlier history of religions. The divine demand and the divine gift, and the Law and the Christ are distinguished as never before, and the distinctiveness of faith over against work and of believing over against seeing and knowing reveals its profundity. But the power of these antitheses merely reveals the glory of the One, who transcends all these opposites and brings everything to completion. Thus these powerful opposing realities evoke the resolve to resist, and the disciple enters his struggle as the victor, carrying the palm branch in his hand even when the world crushes him. For he believes that "One is God."

## 2. The Creator

The One whose possession Palestinian Judaism knew itself to be was the Creator. Therefore, in those who now knew the revealed Christ, every movement of their inner life was pervaded by the recollection of the effective power of the divine creation.

Being God means being the Creator. Because the disciples' concept of God was identical with the concept of the Creator, the disciples immediately transferred it to Jesus. The completeness of the One's communion with Jesus did not result in the pronouncement that God had accomplished the creative work and ruled over all things through him merely as the product of peculiar speculation in the case of individual teachers. It was rather found in the community (John 1:3; 1 Cor. 8:6; Col. 1:17; Heb. 1:2), which believed that he possessed total power to guide them from within and from without and to make both their heart and their destiny the locus of his work. Since nothing is too hard for God, and since nothing happens without him, nothing occurs without the Christ. The conviction that he was in all and that they were in him (namely, Peter, John, and Paul) therefore became the foundation of the community from the beginning. This took place without any mystical effort, because the conviction was implicit in the idea that God's presence is creative activity and extends to everything.[1]

---

1. Those theories that seek to explain how Jesus' disciples gradually elevated Jesus to the level of divinity and reached the consciousness of living in him as the product of a logical process or of a mystical self-manipulation of their consciousness fail to understand the nature of the Jewish consciousness of God.

Now, after the disciples had come to value the work of Jesus, including his cross as the work of the Christ, their faith was no longer, as in Jewish piety, mere trust in divine providence. Now their inner condition of life, no longer merely their destiny but their abject need in willing, working, and knowing, was placed under divine grace. But looking toward the One who is the Creator did not allow their destiny to become meaningless in light of the concerns arising from their internal condition of life. It rather bestowed completeness and steadfastness to their confidence in the hand that assigned them their destiny. Thus they began their work as men free of concern, exhibiting this aplomb, which was rooted in their concept of God, even when events imposed severe suffering on them. Since the greatest concern, the weight of their guilt, had been removed, this liberation from worry extended to all of life, even to those natural and historical processes that intruded into it. They warded off worry empowered by the certainty that everything that happened to them was salvific because it occurred in keeping with God's providence. The disciples started their work therefore not merely resigned to whatever befell; through their assurance of the divine rule they rather possessed the capacity for resolve and the power for action. This gave them liberty in their dealings with nature[2] and active joy in their work with people.

In pursuit of their calling they were dependent on more or less favorable circumstances. Since these are, however, encompassed within the divine government, they did not fear that circumstances would bring to naught the mission they were charged with. They rather expected that the circumstances would result in their mission's success. Therefore they continually honored the providential ordering of circumstances as divine guidance and did not consider it hard or unworthy to accommodate their work to them. Rather, in dependence on them they experienced their dependence on God. To hallow this dependence in word and deed comprised the task of Christendom, a task to be fulfilled with joy.

For this reason the disciples did not derive from their commission the necessity of struggling against the natural order of life. To the contrary, they assigned to it an even stronger role in their midst. Since Jesus had established a perfect community among them that left no aspect of human existence out of consideration, they, too, practiced table fellowship and made it not merely the sign of their brotherly closeness and the expression of festive joy, but linked with it the care for those who were unable to provide for themselves. They extended this care first of all to widows (Acts 2:42, 46–47; Jude 12; 1 Cor. 11:33; Acts 6:1; James 1:27; 1 John 3:17; 1 Tim. 5:3–16). This they did not out of a sense of grudging compulsion, but because they reckoned the provision of food for the needy to be part of their service. At the same time, however, the perfection of their fellowship excluded the possibility of economic concerns becoming the

---

2. One does not, however, find in the early church an intentionally cultivated immersion into nature, be it with poetic sentiment or with knowledge gained by penetrating observation, because love directed toward others and concerned with the needs of mankind made itself known with overwhelming force, which did not permit the contemplation of nature to gain independence. In this the New Testament continued the outlook of contemporary Judaism.

most important task of the new community, since their compassion extended also to the whole range of their members' inner concerns.

Among the disciples, marriage is not merely preserved as established by the creational will of God; it is elevated to the paradigmatic human relationship, in that the rule of chastity took on inviolable status with all who joined them. From the beginning, the community was therefore formed out of "households." It was thereby given a constitutive principle that determined its entire structure.[3]

The disciples were separated from the political organization of Judaism by their religious separation from it. For this reason the founding of the church entailed immediately the distinction between the religious and the civic community. Within their own circle, the disciples achieved unity by their common allegiance to Jesus, consciously and powerfully subordinating all other relationships to the acknowledgment of their heavenly Lord. Since what is God's, according to Jesus' rule, stands above all other concerns, they possessed unshakeable resolve to deny obedience to any authority, if that obedience necessitated disobedience to God (Acts 4:19; 5:29; John; Paul: Rom. 8:36). This did not, however, lead the disciples to anarchic, revolutionary thoughts and enterprises. For to become certain of their most important possession and their first obligation was to acknowledge the ethnic and civic union by which the Jews were bound together. This was seen as no less important than the family (cf. the "countrymen" in Paul: Rom. 9:3; 16:7). On the part of the Jews, admittedly, this approach was not considered satisfactory. They rather perceived it as a profound affront to the existing order, because up to that point the national and religious communities had been identical and the former had received its living power from the latter. The merger of the national with the religious community on the part of the Jews did not, however, induce the disciples to destroy the Jews' national order. They kept their call to repentance completely free of any political theories or attacks on the Jewish authorities and situation.

The more the impact of a decision for or against the Christ was revealed, the greater significance the fact became that the One who transcended all such choices was the Creator and Cause of all things. Since the time when the Jews had sealed their opposition to Jesus by nailing him to the cross, the disciples' judgment of the situation manifested itself in powerful antitheses, in which the Spirit was contrasted with the flesh, the saints with the world, the children of God with the children of Satan, and the Christ with the Antichrist. But above all such statements made by the disciples, which may be called dualistic, towered the thought of the Creator, and any ultimate dualism was rendered impossible in Christianity, because it stood by the conviction that all things derived from the creational will of God (John 1:3, 9–10; Acts 4:11; 5:13; James 1:18; Rom. 8:19–22; Acts 14:17; 17:25–28).

Therefore the disciples remained linked with all people through an inner communal bond that continually guided them in their work. Just as their vision

---

3. Peter's community was thus fundamentally distinguished from a sect such as that of the Essenes. Here too (see previous note) the community preserved its Jewish character.

of the Creator made them at home in nature, which they dealt with without fear, the idea of the Creator gave their dealings with others transparent courage and public visibility that were plain for all to see. The question could not arise whether there were people for whom ethical norms did not exist, so that their blameworthy behavior was not to be condemned as sin, or those for whom the promise was invalid because they were incapable of the knowledge of God. All are creatures and stand in an unalterable dependence on God. Thus the universal call did not first need to be justified by the formation of a "natural" ethic or religion, since the concept of creation already provided the certainty that no one was in complete darkness but that the divine word illumined everyone who came into the world. No one was free from obligation; everyone knew the divine Law, and no one's goal lay elsewhere than in God who had given him life (John 1:9; Rom. 1:19, 32; 11:36).

For this reason the new community also did not become home to a mysticism that merely turned man inward in an effort to find the divine work solely within himself. True, the assurance of God given to believers by their attachment to Jesus determined their whole inner lives. They found refuge within themselves, had Christ with them, were in him with their thinking and willing, and thus received an entirely personal religion. But this never caused them to write off nature or history, the body or human community, as religiously irrelevant. For these existed solely by God's creating power. Therefore, while their will was distinguished from the body, since the latter incites sinful passions, at the same time the will also focused on the body, for it is to be used as a weapon of righteousness in the service of God. On this account the world was simultaneously the cause of their suffering, because it was evil and stood in the power of Satan, and the cause of their joy, because everything in it became reason for thanksgiving. For this reason what they longed for transcended the present condition of life, because human existence was tied to the earth. Yet at the same time they affirmed that the earth with all it contained belonged to God. This is indicated by their continuation in Jewish custom with an even stronger conviction that recognized in every natural gift an occasion for thanksgiving. They considered the use of nature to be pure because and when it led to thanksgiving (Rom. 14:6; 1 Cor. 10:30; 1 Tim. 4:4).

Because the whole course of the disciples' thinking was based on their consciousness of God, it did not stop at the boundaries of the visible and present condition of the world but rather was supernatural. The Christ inaugurates the new age, the perfect world, and thereby reveals completely that the Creator is at work through him. Thus the disciples' consciousness of God also entailed the expectation of miracle. But because "miracle" carried within it the idea of the Creator who sanctified and subjected nature to them as God's work, the disciples were protected from the danger posed by cutting ties with the natural conditions of life. They could not fight against nature or yield to anything contrary to it, because God's power had created the natural just as it produced the miraculous. This enabled the disciples to shape their account of Jesus' miracles as we find them in the Gospels: miracles revealed both a boundless confidence in God's power and the complete obedience by which Jesus submitted to the order of life given to us. Moreover, the significance of a Creator concept extended to the disciples' entire view of Jesus, because they recognized in him the ultimate miracle and exalted him above the earth in his origin and aim; for he exists through God. Still, this recognition never issued in an attack on the natural form of his human life or on the truth of his suffering. For it was clear that God's rule was revealed through the man Jesus and that God's grace was rendered effective through Jesus' death; what is natural is God's work as well. Therefore in their eschatology they spoke not of the world's destruction but of its perfection. By directing their hope to the new heavens and the new earth, the richest possible substance was conferred on their recollection of the creating power of God.

### 3. The Righteous Father

In Palestinian Judaism's concept of God, righteousness, together with the boundless glory of divine power, was the essential characteristic of God. God's will reaches for man's will and action with absolute, compelling power, giving him the Law, opposing any breaking of it, and transforming the work done in obedience to God into the salvation of man. This certainty likewise received its complete confirmation through the disciples' communion with Jesus. For them there was no work of God that was not also the revelation of his righteousness, no hope in God that did not long to see God's righteousness, no adoration that did not praise God's righteousness (Rom. 1:17; Matt. 6:33; Acts 16:5). Therefore for them every religious will carried in it at the same time ethical decisiveness, renunciation of all evil, and readiness for every good work. Their proclamation of Jesus as the Christ became the continuation of his call to repentance, which demanded separation from evil from all who followed him. The disciples never wavered at this point, particularly since Jesus had showed them in God's will and work something still greater than that righteousness which orders our human activity and leads it to its goal according to truth. He had shown them God's grace, his goodness that makes anew and freely gives, by which he becomes the Father for them. Human merit perished with the knowledge of the giving God.

But the divine commandment did not thereby disappear; it was rather infused with power. Nor did the compelling power of the divine will vanish, nor the utter despicableness of rebellious self-will. Gone was merely the synergism that placed human work beside or even above the divine activity. Instead there arrived that obedience which perceives and does God's will. For God's grace was revealed in Jesus' work, as he created the community set apart for God and liberated from Jewish and human guilt. Therefore the disciples' message united the testimony to the divine law with the offer of complete grace, and there was no place for the notion of an abundance of grace manifesting itself by freeing people from ethical norms. God's will is seen rather as good, as separated from all evil and separating people from it, and the work of grace consists in subjecting the person's will to the good will of God. God's grace engenders righteousness. The disciples' ability to rise above the conventional concept of righteousness (represented by the school of thought that never overcame the dichotomy between law and grace and that was never able to frame both as the unitary characteristic of the divine work) was not a product of their own mental efforts. Nowhere are there traces of an attempt to demonstrate that grace has limits beyond which judgment will fall, or that the validity of the Law is limited by the fact that grace ultimately preempts it, or how the believer's obligation arises out of divine grace, and why grace is unshakeable.

The healing of the rupture in their concept of God and the union of righteousness and grace in God were not effected by theories but by the story of Jesus. The disciples possessed this unified concept of God because they knew Jesus. Therefore the completeness of divine grace and the sanctity of the divine commandment were for them tied to each other in such a way that no tension could ever arise between them. The uniform will of the one God found expression in both norms, since both were revealed in the life and the death of the Christ. This grasp of the Christian goal vividly reveals how strongly that which Jesus had imparted to the disciples continued to live in them.

# B. The Christ of God

Initially, the disciples' message inevitably gave the impression that they idolized a human being, since they offered their faith, love, hope, and worship to the man Jesus. Therefore their success depended completely on their ability to transcend the notion that they worshipped the man Jesus in place of God or beside God. If they could not utterly discredit this charge, their work would disintegrate. The clarity and coherence characteristic of the disciples' work from the beginning is demonstrated by the fact that we do not have a single saying from the apostolic community that approximates a Christian polytheism separating God from Jesus and oscillating between the two in prayer and faith. The early Christian message in all its forms focused on Jesus' oneness with God as a result of the integration of Jesus' work in the divine activity. Since this conception of God unwaveringly controls the entire proclamation, Jesus is not preached as a substitute for God, but in relation to God, because God sent him and worked through him. Because Jesus belonged to God, the disciples believed in him, that through him they might arrive at assurance of God, love for God, and obedience toward God. It stood decisively established that Jesus had been of godly character; through him, his disciples, too, became godly, and this spread through them to the entire community. As a result all their work was permeated by the principle that each must truly apprehend that he thought and acted out of love for God.

This rendered phrases that described Jesus' communion with God as complete and eternal indispensable for them, because it was thereby realized why and how they obtained communion with God by following Jesus: not because they idolized the man Jesus, but because God had revealed himself in him. This, however, did not lead the disciples to that conceptuality that the later church called "Christology," which sought to explain by which processes God was present in Jesus and how he united his humanity with his divinity. For the disciples' conviction that Jesus participated fully in the divine work arose from his regal commission and from the completeness of his love for God. Therefore they expressed Jesus' complete oneness with God by way of two traditional concepts: he had been made by God's Spirit (Matt. 1:20; Luke 1:35; 1 Peter 1:11; Rom. 1:4) and by God's Word (John 1:1).

The fact that now the messianic idea no longer had the uncertainty of a hope but was related to the work accomplished by Jesus resulted in the pronouncement that God's final aim had now been revealed and his complete grace was perceptible. This injected from the beginning a powerful tension into the disciples' work, instilled into their actions by the idea of the Christ, a tension that had already been evident in Jesus' ministry. The Christ is the one who leads the community to its eternal fulfillment. Therefore his proclamation demanded from the disciples that they use absolute terms for the things inaugurated by him to describe what was complete. They had to show that omnipotent grace was the causative force in what they had become through Jesus and what they brought to humanity. The exposure of the rebellion with which man opposed God, however, now stood revealed with a clarity that far transcended their earlier state of consciousness. God's gift had been rejected, and the Christ had been killed. The proclamation of the Christ became therefore the attestation of the world's blameworthiness and at the same time entirely the offer of divine grace, because Jesus, through his death, had entered into his rule by which he revealed God's glory to mankind. The disciples' message once more became the proclamation of grace not through a feat of ratiocination, nor through discovery of a didactic formula, but by the weight of the fact that God had given the Christ for mankind even though it crucified him. And since Jesus was the Christ also on the cross, the result was not the curse of Israel and of the world, but their call to God's kingdom.

Since the disciples must proclaim Jesus as the one who seeks and leads Israel to life even now, despite her guilt, whoever is called by him receives complete forgiveness through his death. The repentance awakened by Jesus' crucifixion in those who believe is immediately transformed into love, because it consists in the realization that God's grace had been spurned and God's gift despised. The disciples subjected the result of Jesus' death immediately to teleological considerations by claiming that Jesus had died precisely in order to be able to forgive. Therefore they venerated his blood as the means of their salvation; it rendered them pure and righteous. Because their entire thought was controlled by the concept of God, they saw in the facts the revelation of the divine will. What occurred through Jesus' cross was intended by God; for he had brought it about. This way of thinking was confirmed in the disciples, because Jesus himself had shared this perspective on his destiny and because they vividly remembered his interpretation of the cross at the Last Supper.

The Christ concept, however, rendered it impossible that Jesus brought about merely the assurance of forgiveness. His followers saw in him the Perfect One who brought perfection, and perfection had entered human history in such a way that it seized believers' own life experience. This placed all terms that had earlier carried eschatological connotation into direct connection to the present, giving them new meaning. The procurement of complete communion among those ruled by Christ, the gathering of the nations into a holy community, their government and revitalization by the divine Spirit, rebirth, divine sonship, justification, perfection, resurrection, eternal life, glorification—all of these had up to this point been eschatological terms, which now surged into the present and gave full meaning to the relationship established between the disciples and God.

The disciples maintained the dual opposition, against evil and against death, into which God's rule placed Jesus. Thus they saw sin and death subjected to them. In their assessment of the present, however, a distinction between these two aspects gained ground, since victory over evil became a part of believers' experience differently than victory over death. The latter was expected with a certain hope that seized the thing hoped for as one's sure possession. Redemption from evil was hoped for as well, because it transcends what is possible for human experience in the present. But at the same time it became visible already in the here and now, in the will and behavior of believers. Now they could serve God with a pure will. Paul was not the first one who placed redemption from evil above liberation from death; this development in Christendom was from the beginning based on the fact that Jesus' death was the event that controlled all of believers' thinking and willing. Before Jesus' resurrection, which guaranteed eternal life, stood his cross, with the realization of guilt and liberation from it. Therefore the Christ's forgiveness was not merely hoped for but received; reconciliation with God was not merely expected but obtained, and the individual's separation from evil was thereby achieved. Thus the followers of Jesus are transformed into the community of the sanctified and justified.

By making the church into the communion of the saints, the disciples went beyond what Jesus had explicitly taught them before his death.[4] It remains, however, entirely transparent why they did not consider this to be a new kind of piety that separated them from him: their confidence of being saints arose directly from the religious dimension with which Jesus had invested his own idea of rule. Since he exercised his rule by leading the individual to God, those who know him and belong to him are, by virtue of their communion with him, God's own possession and possess holiness themselves.

The disciples' statements regarding the Christ would have been impossible without a mechanism linking man with Christ even now that he is invisible. The disciples identified this mechanism as faith, and they were unaware of creating thereby their own, new form of piety in place of the one given to them by Jesus. They rather acted in the conviction that Jesus effected faith in them, that he required it from them, and that he had given unlimited promise to faith. Therefore the disciples gave priority to faith above all other religious achievements and made it the hallmark of godliness, so that they used faith also as the designation for the community they brought together. Faith took on such significance because it produced union with the Christ because he placed all who

---

4. The concept of holiness recedes into the background in Jesus' words. Nevertheless, by presenting himself as the enduring temple in contrast to the old sanctuary, he had already assigned a priestly calling to the disciples (Matt. 12:5–6; John 2:19). See also the name given to Peter as a "stone" in God's temple.

believed in him under his promise. But faith also became a new experience with regard to its conscious side, which was destined to become the characteristic of the new community. For compared with the assurance of God and the confidence in him arising from the proclamation of the Christ, the disciples considered their earlier piety to be uncertainty and doubt, as fear and reliance on their own achievement in taking the initiative to seek after the gracious God. Only then, only with the knowledge of Jesus, did those who accepted his word receive that assurance of God which turned their confidence to him, and by being able to believe, they now truly apprehended that the Christ had called and sanctified them.

Faith in Jesus, however, could not arise without hope in him, since Jesus' regal aim transcended what could be achieved in the present. The disciples' prophecy by which they grounded their hope in him remained entirely subjected to the prophecy of Jesus. The genuine, resolute hope that was established by the anticipation of the coming revelation of Jesus was intent on two aims: that Christ would come for the salvation of his community in order to unite it with himself; and that he would come as the Lord of mankind for its purification and perfection. No tension arose between these two goals, because the disciples did not set the aim that elevated them in opposition to the salvation of everyone else. Their hope was not subjected to a selfish concept of blessedness. It rather desired Christ's appearing, because he would bring about the revelation of God's rule and thus fulfill his commission.

The work of the Returning One consists in the execution of justice whose absolute validity is expressly attested by prophecy. He acts as a judge, not merely on the world, but first of all on his community. Jesus' words utterly prohibited the disciples from embracing the notion of a partisan distortion of the divine norms in favor of their own community. They must not fail to uphold standards that were equally valid for all. In their confidence in him and in his salvation of all who believed on him, they did not expect him to overlook their own sins but maintained that his opposition toward evil was comprehensive and that the guilt of precisely those who knew him was greater than that of others when they sinned.

For this reason their hope never served merely as a means to enjoyment. It rather became a mind-set that strengthened them for their work. It provided them not merely with comfort but equally with energy. With the Christ's return, the power of death comes to an end and life begins; thus the resurrection is tied to it. People's state after death, on the other hand, and the place where death leads them remain concealed. The disciples were content to know that they would continue to be with the Lord (thus already in Stephen's prayer: Acts 7:58; cf. 2 Cor. 5:1; Phil. 1:20; 2 Tim. 4:18). Hope was grounded solely in the idea of the Christ, which made Jesus the Giver of divine grace and thus of eternal life. The disciples did not resort to physiological theories that adduced the special substance of the soul and the like to substantiate their hope. Life arises out of union with God, and believers rest assured of their final destiny, because eternal life has been revealed in Jesus. By being united with him, they are united with the One who lives and are set free from death. In all of these basic contours of eschatology, there remained a firm connection between the prophetic words of Jesus and those of the apostles.

## C. The Spirit's Presence with the Disciples

The first condition, without which the expansion from Jesus' circle of disciples to the church would not have been possible, was that the disciples possessed certainty regarding Jesus' regal status. This was given to them through the Easter events. The second condition consisted in the events instilling in them the conviction that God's Spirit would be with them from now on. This conviction confronts us everywhere in their writings, which grant us a glimpse of the community with such vigor and consistency that the conviction proves to be an essential characteristic of apostolic piety. Jesus' community consists of those moved by the Spirit; it is, because he lives in it, God's temple. Whoever is united with it through baptism receives the gift of the Holy Spirit. Therefore whoever has not heard of the Spirit is not a Christian. Through the Spirit those who believe in Jesus possess life, and in the Spirit their conduct has its ground and reigning principle (Rom. 8:9, 14; 1 Cor. 3:16; Acts 2:38; 19:2; Gal. 5:25).

This assurance was not confirmed in the disciples merely by deduction from the promises of Scripture and Jesus. It rather was tied to particular experiences and had a historical rationale. At the feast of Pentecost, subsequent to Jesus' death, the disciples experienced the Spirit's coming in Jerusalem.[5] They apprehended it truly by way of signs, which in part happened in the realm of nature and in part proved their internal lives to be moved by the Spirit.[6] While these events were not considered to be the abiding and necessary visualization of the Spirit, they retained continual significance for the community, because they became the basis for the conviction that the Spirit had been given to it.

Thus it became clear to the disciples that they could not judge the presence to be devoid of divine grace and revelation. God did not only demonstrate his grace to them in former days when Jesus walked the earth, nor would he do so solely in the future at the time of his return. Otherwise they would have been

---

5. Paul did not consider the community to have originated in the gathering of about five hundred men who were all granted the appearance of the Risen One (1 Cor. 15:6), so that we should consider this to be the original form of the Pentecost narrative. For a glimpse of the Risen One was never made a requirement for every community member. Similar to the Gospels, Paul conceives of the Easter story as that process which established the apostolate, but not yet the church, and he considered the sending of the Spirit to be a new divine act that occurred subsequent to Jesus' cross and was grounded in it (Gal. 4:6).

6. The account of the miracle at Pentecost probably shows a certain similarity to the Haggadic presentation of the proclamation of the Decalogue at Sinai. According to this account, the Decalogue was not proclaimed merely in Israel's own language but also in the languages of all the nations. It was also heard by the Gentiles, but they rejected it. The distance between the account of Pentecost and the Sinai narrative, however, remains, so great that Pentecost cannot be understood as merely a construct in competition with Sinai. For the proclamation of the Christ occurs at Pentecost merely to those gathered in Jerusalem, and there is no formulation of the preaching of the divine word to all the nations. In any case, the Haggadic parallel indicates that the Pentecost narrative does not represent a free composition on the part of Luke but is based on an existing tradition in the Palestinian church.

able to give to the new community only history and eschatology, mere reminiscences and hopes. But now God's grace received ever-new attestation by the Spirit. This attestation determined the community's own experience, since it occurred internally in believers. They perceived God's rule in their own inner being, whereby they experienced that the Christ was with them and guided them. Those prerequisites by which alone the thought of an internal activity of God in man is made possible, and is preserved ethically pure without succumbing to excessive arrogance, had been created in the disciples by Jesus' work. Jesus brought an end to their internal rebellion against God; he reconciled them to God, thus bowing them entirely before God, liberating them from arrogance, and placing them into the love of God, which prevented them from any attempt to make God's gift subservient to their own selfish will. From an ethical perspective, it is no surprise that the idea that the Spirit was present with the disciples could take root in them only after Jesus' dealings with them had been concluded.

Through the pronouncement of the Spirit's presence the disciples' confidence in Jesus attained its completion. He himself was active in his community through the Spirit. What the Spirit told them was said by the Christ, and they lived in Christ in that they lived in the Spirit (Rom. 8:9, 10; Rev. 2:7). This provided their hope in him the power to persevere. Even now, when the community is separated from Christ, he gathers and rules them through the Spirit. But this occurs for the purpose of uniting them completely with Christ in the world to come.

By Christendom's faith and hope being directed toward Jesus, its thinking and willing were pointed to the word received from Jesus' messengers. By virtue of the fact, however, that this word was tied to the assurance of the Spirit, believers were turned inward and alerted to what occurred within them personally. The revelation and guidance granted to them by Jesus' story was supplemented by the instruction given to them from within. The former provided their faith with the firmness that stems from complete, established fact. The latter accompanied their actions, clarified for them their task, awakened their energy, and gave them strength for the execution of their service.[7] From the conviction that both mediators of divine revelation and grace, the Christ and the Spirit, worked together, arose the essential characteristics of Christianity.

Since the Spirit was considered to be Christ's gift to his own, it was impossible for his disciples to believe that the Spirit's presence related merely to their own salvation. That presence was rather immediately placed in connection to their work. The disciple needed the Spirit because he was Jesus' messenger. The community needed him, since it must reveal his lordship to the world. A self-centered view of the Spirit, which expected from him merely the enhancement of one's own power and blessedness, can nowhere be found. It would only have been possible by a conscious turning away from Jesus' word.

For this reason the promise of the Spirit is also universally conceived. His arrival does not occur merely for the disciples but for the world, in order that ac-

---

7. Not only every pagan omen (divination) but also the "divine voice" of the synagogue and the casting of lots now vanished.

cess might be granted it to the Christ and to God. The Spirit's presence was immediately and invariably linked with the universal conception of the divine grace that related its revelation to all. The sending of the Son and the sending of the Spirit remained therefore parallel to one another in the universal conception of their aim. Thus there is never any doubt in the course of the apostolic work whether the Spirit had come for all or merely for a privileged few. This resulted not merely from Old Testament prophecy that had promised the Spirit to the messianic community in its entirety, but even more so from the Spirit's relationship to the ministry of the Christ, who successfully implanted in the disciples consciousness of the universal scope of divine grace. He had brought all into complete communion with himself and with one another and had destroyed the idea of distinctions in rank before God. The "universalism" advocated by Jesus himself consequently led to the confidence that the gift of the Exalted One, likewise, was given to all believers, just as he had died and risen for them all.

## D. The Office of Jesus' Messengers

By aligning themselves believingly with Jesus' kingly aim, the disciples also had confirmed that word of Jesus that granted them commission as his messengers. They knew that they should not merely wait for him in quietness until he himself established his rule, but that they must proclaim him. It was through their message that Christ now revealed his presence and rule.

They strongly felt the mysterious greatness of their undertaking. Did it not amount to an insurmountable contradiction to human consciousness? Their goal was not to move their listeners merely to wait, whether joyfully or fearfully, to see how Jesus would reveal himself; they rather summoned them to believe in him and thus be united with him in an effective and complete communion, as he had granted it to the first disciples themselves by uniting them with him in faith (1 John 1:1–4).

But could they yield themselves to the one they could not see with the complete trust that subjects one's entire life to him (1 Peter 1:8; John 20:22; Heb. 11:1)? The disciples overcame these considerations by viewing the proclamation of the Christ as God's work in the same way as the sending of the Christ itself had been. They considered it to be God's work, in which their own position was merely that of slaves. Their ministry was encompassed by God's activity that revealed the Christ and created faith in him. This was confirmed by their ability to speak as those whom God had given their word and work by his Spirit. Therefore the disciples' appreciation for the word that had made Jesus an "evangelist" remains undiminished. They likewise saw in Jesus' message not merely a set of teachings that helped their listeners to arrive at certain insights but the effective bestowal of divine grace extended through their proclamation.

Alongside the proclamation of Jesus' message, prayer constituted a significant portion of the apostles' activity. "They devoted themselves to prayer and to the ministry of the word" (Acts 6:4; 10:9); Paul ministered similarly. Thereby they set their work into a conscious, continual relationship with the divine will and showed that the aim of their work lay not merely in man but first and foremost in the glorification of God. Through prayer their activity took on its cultic, priestly character. Their ministry thus accomplished its purpose by producing in congregations the prayer by which God is praised by petition and thanksgiving (2 Cor. 1:11; 4:15).

Their work was characterized by their role as witnesses. This is what made their ministry valuable. The fact that they were witnesses to Jesus' historical ministry rendered their office irreplaceable. This was emphasized at the occasion of the selection of a twelfth apostle and is also shown by the discussions regarding Paul's apostolic office. It is required for an apostle to have seen the risen Christ; otherwise, he cannot be his messenger (Acts 1:21–22; 1 Cor. 9:1; 15:7–8). The pneumatic giftedness unique to an apostle did, of course, confirm his commission; but the most important element always remained the fact that he vouchsafed the historical pronouncements of the gospel as an eyewitness of the outcome of Jesus' life.

This did not, however, limit the apostles' work to providing the community with a knowledge of its beginning by sharing the recollection of their dealings with Jesus. The relationship into which they entered with others as Christ's messengers rather received its depth from the present connection with God that arose for their listeners through them. God's grace and judgment became effective for other people through their word and work. They open and close access to God's rule. Whoever deceives them lies to the Holy Spirit, and the Holy Spirit made his decision jointly with them (Acts 5:3; 15:28). This consciousness of power, which is evident both with the Jerusalem apostles and with Paul, did not arise from their individual giftedness or greatness, but was based solely on their union with Jesus, which continued in the present as he ruled them through his Spirit.

## E. The Disciples' Commission to Israel

In relation to Israel, the disciples saw their immediate task in retaining fellowship by continuing to participate in its temple ritual and house of prayer.[8] They were able to do this because Judaism encompassed a variety of religious groups, parties who had particular customs and teachings without separating from the community. From a Jewish perspective, the community gathered around the apostles was a Jewish sect (Acts 24:14). They were this, however, only in the eyes of their opponents. Although it is said today that the first Christians were a Jewish sect, this merely reiterates the judgment of their antagonists, which the disciples never accepted as accurate and which never became part of their self-understanding. They rather retained the universal scope of their mission, which addressed itself to all of Israel, in obedience to Jesus' command. Their community was, of course, now organized more firmly than the circle of disciples had been prior to Jesus' death. But since the Christ is the creator of the

---

8. The rupture of community was not initiated by Christendom but resulted from Judaism's ban of Christians.

community called to eternal life, those who believed in him were not a single group within Judaism, but the community of God, the one group set apart for him but therefore also open to all.[9]

The disciples saw the task of the community gathered by them in being what Israel was supposed to be: God's community, God's house and nation, the saints and chosen ones. This resulted in two statements regarding their relationship to Israel according to the two pronouncements that unified the call to repentance. Positively, it was said that Israel was preserved and fulfilled in Christianity. Negatively, the fact that the call to repentance pronounced judgment on Israel led to a stress on the newness of the Christian community, which replaced Israel now that it had come under God's judgment. Both pronouncements complemented one another, since the preservation of Israel had always been considered by the Christian community to be a new creation, and the creation of the new community the fulfillment of the previous one.

It was an existential issue for Christians to retain this self-understanding and to reject the formulation that its opponents sought to impose on them. For an effort to close off the community would have twisted self-preservation into a selfish desire. Rejecting others is a way of elevating oneself; contempt and self-admiration are the result. A person learns and practices hatred and fights for himself. In this way the community would have destroyed itself internally. From the very beginning it constituted a great temptation for the disciples to configure themselves as a sect. Since Judaism rejected them with brutal opposition, they had to retain their fellowship with the Jews against the Jews' will. They bore within themselves the highest self-consciousness regarding the gift given to them: they, and they alone, were called of Christ; for them the glory of the last days had been prepared; they alone had God's Spirit and were separated from the world through him. If the apostles had instructed the community to draw back from others and to admire itself on account of its Christian privilege, this could have resulted in a harsh separatism. It would, however, have precipitated the same collapse which, according to Jesus, led to the demise of Pharisaism.

But the disciples began their struggle with Judaism in faith, and they preserved this faith during the long and heated controversy. They led the early Christians to the understanding that in Christ lay the ground of their existence and greatness. Therefore they did not seek to acquire greatness or power for themselves. The Spirit's presence with them meant that they allowed themselves to be drawn by him to God, which, to be sure, resulted in separation from the world, but which also separated them from collective egotism. Through the Spirit, they were connected with all others, since he placed them into the service of divine grace. The disciples obeyed Jesus' commandment, which united love for God and one another, and they tolerated no hatred among themselves except hatred of sin. The struggle against sectarian temptations had implications for the entire state of Christendom. Everything depended on the fact that Christians victoriously suppress any bitterness toward Judaism, that they allow

---

9. That this was already the case in the first months in Jerusalem is shown by Gal. 1:13=1 Cor. 15:9: "the church of God."

themselves to be hated and banned without hating in return, that in their fellowship with Christ, they become free from the old community without forsaking fellowship with it. The New Testament writings maintain that the early community won this victory over itself.[10]

In this Jesus' initially severe attitude bore fruit for the disciples. If he had invested his call to repentance with pride and his regal actions with arrogance, this would have inevitably resulted in a sectarian church. Only by completing his way to the cross with unblemished selflessness did he make it possible for the community to separate from the world without rancor, to unite firmly without self-centeredness, to remain within Judaism without weakening the call to repentance, and to proclaim this message to all without smugness. It was able to do this only in connection with Jesus' own conduct. Since his call to repentance that he directed to them had its aim in the offer of reconciliation, and since it revealed the Christ's grace which desired to save Israel, it did not engender hatred but was itself love and did not separate the one who called to repentance from those whose guilt he exposed, but was itself an act of genuine, complete fellowship.

The Greeks could be told Jesus' message only after two prerequisites had been fulfilled: first, particular divine instructions that had for its recipients the certainty of revelation and that gave them the assurance of doing this work in obedience to God's will; second, an intellectual synthesis which proved that the introduction of the Gentiles into God's grace was compatible with the gospel. Without this second condition, a forced obedience would have resulted from those experiences that revealed the commission to the Gentiles to be Christ's will. Such an obedience would have amounted to the attempt to overcome countervailing notions by suppressing them and to executing God's will without understanding it. Thereby, and to its detriment, the mission to the Gentiles would have been different from the rest of Christian conduct, which was always predicated on clear assurance able to clarify its justification. If the mission to the Gentiles had proceeded without such assurance, it would have continually remained impeded by an internal deficiency. Yet without the experiences that assigned to the agents of the Christian work the mandate to the Gentile mission in a particular form, it would have appeared to be a human enterprise, usurping the divine government. However, logically such conclusions could have been deduced from firm convictions; they were no abiding ground for the good conscience of those who called the nations to the Christ. For they did not accomplish their work as philanthropists with the Gentiles, appealing to their good will out of mercy. Rather, they spoke in God's name as his messengers who had been commanded to bring the divine grace to the nations. This commission entailed more than an understanding of the necessity and rightness of the matter. The first question remained: was the Gentiles' introduction into the community of the Christ really God's will and the Christ's own work?

The Lucan account is most instructive in this regard. Through the story of the Ethiopian eunuch, Luke alerts us to the fact that the attractive force of Ju-

---

10. This accounts for all those features denounced as "Judaism" in Matthew, James, Paul, Peter, John, and Luke.

daism was far-reaching and that it led many to Jerusalem. Old Testament prophecy presented the picture of the dying servant of God as a mystery that captured the attention of many. However, this is not what Luke considers to be the most significant element. For Christians, it rather was the clear guidance that led Philip as Jesus' messenger to the Ethiopian. That Scripture and the contact with the synagogue had prepared many for the gospel, and that those also offered points of contact for an understanding of the cross, would not by themselves have justified the mission. Justification is provided only by the positive divine command. This train of thought is entirely determinative for the Book of Acts (cf. chap. 10; 13:1, 2; 16:6, 9). It was not the particular possession of Luke, but reveals competently the ultimate motivations of apostolic history.

The task with which Christian theory was presented in order for the Greek mission to be made possible did not arise from the concept of the kingdom or the Christ but from the Law. Calling the Gentiles into the community would, of course, have been impossible if the disciple had seen in the Christ merely the one who brought Israel to completion and in his kingdom merely God's good work for Israel. Jesus became the one who would awaken the Gentiles and receive their faith only when his commission pertained to all of humanity and when it elevated him to lordship over all. But the concepts of the kingdom and of the Christ directed everyone's view toward the act of God that would bring fulfillment to the world. No one, not even the most daring Zealot, spoke here of an antithesis, a choice, as if the Christ were to be sent either for Israel or for the world. Rather, one aim confirms the other and leads it to its completion. By transforming Israel into the sanctified and perfected community, the Christ reveals God's glory to the world, and by gathering the nations around himself he accomplishes the fulfillment and the glorification of Israel. It therefore required neither a new Christ nor an altered Christology to call the nations to him. What was needed, however, was a clear answer to the question whether the Law did not prohibit their call. The objection that arose regarding the Law possessed particular power because it appealed to norms that were absolutely valid and whose violation was to be rejected as sin. The notion that it did not constitute sin to suspend or to transgress the Law was a lofty pronouncement that initially appeared entirely paradoxical. What was clear was that sin was an unbearable, entirely blameworthy act, which completely destroyed fellowship with the Christ. This reveals that the church's expansion in the Greek region elevated the disciples and the entire community far above those kinds of deliberations that otherwise move a religious community when it seeks to enlarge its field of operation. Since the Greek question was inseparably linked to the issue of the Law, it touched in all who were affected by it their innermost, most personal relationship with God.

Every pious person in Judaism looked back to the "elders," who towered in incomparable height above later generations and stood completely elevated above the present. They looked up to Moses as the one who was exalted above all. But for the disciples, this was a thing of the past. They looked forward, because they knew the Christ, the Perfecter predicted by Moses, who creates what is to come (Acts 3:22). The old community looked up to Moses because he had brought it the divine Law. Does God's will change, then? Is it not immutable? Jesus had elevated his disciples above this thought, too. For through him the new act of God had occurred, and the new gift of his grace had been received. This new gift, in turn, brought the new ministry, the new obligation, the new commandment. What the Law provided for the community—love regulated by the Law; purity produced by the Law; the temple, the altar, and priests granted to the community by the Law—was not what God gave to his perfected community. Jesus had abrogated the old order. At the same time, he treated it by his call to repentance in all sincerity as God's obligatory Law. Therefore the disciples were not to sink below the Law nor become its transgressors. They must rather transcend it and demonstrate its fulfillment in what the Christ made them to be. This lent a greatness to the task to be carried out by Peter that supersedes all that later had to be accomplished by the church. It was clear and had to remain clear that the Law was God's express will. Whoever doubted this had no place in the community of the Christ. What was likewise clear was that circumvention of holy ordinance had to occur, not with evil conscience and inner wavering, but only in such a way that the one who was free from the statute acted in obedience to God and knew himself even in its "transgression" to be God's servant. Only a clear stance of faith provided the ability to remove the community's old constitution and effective order of worship freely and joyfully with a view toward the cross and toward Jesus' rule. That this faith existed in Peter and John was the fruit of Jesus' ministry. It was confirmed at the present time by the events that gave them the divine commission for their work.

## F. Baptism in Jesus' Name

Proclamation of the Christ occurred initially by calling the Jews again to baptism. For this reason Greeks were subsequently led to the Christ by the same means.[11] Thus the disciples repeated the act by which the proclamation of the divine rule had begun with the Baptist. The renewed exhortation to the Jews to submit to baptism had become necessary because they had rejected and killed the Christ, and because their call to God's kingdom fell to pieces in light of this guilt. Yet the new offer of divine grace was possible because the Christ had died for them as one who forgives. The new element in this baptism was its explicit relation to Jesus; it was offered and received in his name. This resulted directly from the Christ concept. Israel's return to obedience toward God occurred through conversion to the Christ, its reconciliation with God through the forgiveness granted by the Christ.

This did not constitute a departure from the original meaning of the preaching of baptism, because the announcement of God's rule retained full significance for the disciples. This is confirmed by the Gospels. The Pauline epistles likewise attest that the phrase "God's rule" depicted the promised goal and the

---

11. Matthew shares his conception of the origin of the church with Luke, since in his Gospel the Risen One commands the disciples to baptize. Paul, who knew all of Christendom, did not know any unbaptized segment of it.

gift granted in its entirety at the present time even in the Greek communities.[12] Thus baptism could at all times also be considered to be the call to share in God's rule. But now the proclamation of Jesus as the Christ provided the content for the act of baptism and not merely the announcement of God's rule. The latter was suited to express what Christianity and Israel had in common, but it did not make recognizable the elements separating the community of Jesus from Judaism. What these had in common was the expectation of God's rule and the confidence of being chosen for it. What separated them was the confession of Jesus and the implicit statement regarding how and for whom God rules and what procures participation of the individual in his grace. The disciples dealt with this issue by replying that God's eternal gift was received by following Christ Jesus, so that the baptismal preaching consisted in the proclamation of his name.

Even now baptism remained what it had been with the Baptist: active repentance. By grounding the community in baptism, the disciples transformed the church into the community of those who returned repentantly to God. They thus continued Jesus' struggle against Israel's sin. However, repentance now received its content from being brought about by the proclamation of the Christ. The first thing the Jew had to change was his verdict regarding Jesus. Whoever was ready for baptism separated himself from those who crucified him and still rejected his rule, and he confessed Jesus' regal status. As a call to repentance, the baptismal preaching was therefore always at the same time a call to faith in Jesus. This rendered a sharp distinction or temporal separation between the preaching of repentance and the call to faith impossible. Whoever obeyed the call to repentance and desired baptism did away with his unbelief in Jesus and affirmed Jesus' messianic office. Precisely for this reason the Christ was proclaimed expressly, initially in the offer of baptism, and then in the act of baptism itself. The washing was given, not merely by calling to God in God's name, but by appealing to Christ in Jesus' name. This exposed the difference between this baptism and other religious washings, even the baptism of John. The confession of Jesus was initially the duty of the one who baptized, who could have denied Jesus' name only by denying his own office as a messenger. His first obligation was the task of illumining the relationship between baptism and the grace of Christ, whose name was proclaimed by the act of baptism.[13] The proclamation by the person administering the baptism corresponded to the answer of the person baptized, not merely by a silent submission to the rite, but by his active confession of the Christ. At this important juncture it becomes clear that Jesus freed his disciples entirely from casuistry. We find no statutes or regulations which require or regulate the baptized person's confession. Likewise, there are no pre-

---

12. Regarding the present share in God, see Rom. 14:17; 1 Cor. 4:20; Col. 4:11. Regarding the final aim, see 1 Cor. 6:9–10; Gal. 5:21; 1 Thess. 2:12; 2 Thess. 1:5. The Apocalypse presents the same picture regarding Asia.

13. The idea that a baptism in the name of the Father, the Son, and the Holy Spirit was not a baptism in the name of Christ or that baptism in the name of Christ was not a baptism in the name of God or the Spirit belongs to an entirely different conceptual world than that of the New Testament. For this objection works with a magic phrase that is effective by the invocation of a particular formula.

cepts concerning the confession of guilt by which repentance is expressed. The essential requirement stipulated by the community was that the relationship between baptism and Christ remain crystal clear.

The conversion enacted in baptism was, however, not exhausted by the baptized person's change of attitude toward Jesus. It never consisted merely in the correction of error, now replaced by the more correct verdict regarding Jesus, for Jesus' crucifixion was never explained as deception but always viewed as the result of the nation's guilt. Jesus' struggle against sin, the ethical objective of his ministry, and the illegitimate rationale for his rejection were clearly attested by the baptismal preaching. Whoever was called to baptism was told that Christ's work meant liberation from all evil. He died because of sin and brings to the community redemption from it through his revelation in glory. He was confessed as the adversary of all sin in his pure separation from all disobedience toward God. Thus the conversion expressed in baptism took on an ethical dimension. By baptism, the baptized person judged his evil conduct and attained, not merely a new way of thinking, but a new will. He did not merely reject his previous intellectual views but pronounced a guilty verdict against his entire person.

This understanding of the act of baptism, which relates it to the condition of one's entire life, finds support in the prevailing religious circumstances. Judaism felt keenly, and lent explicit expression to, the close relationship between our convictions regarding God and our conduct. Every sincere Jew was convinced that Jerusalem, were it to have rejected the Christ, would not merely have succumbed to deception but have sinned with no possibility of restoration. Such a rejection of God's will and work was not merely a calamity but resulted from existing guilt. It issued in new guilt that was immeasurably weighty. Therefore repentant turning to Jesus amounted to sincere self-condemnation by which the baptized person lent personal expression to his own guilt. In this respect, the disciples' ministry found antecedent support in Pharisaism, since the Pharisaic movement had provided a serious formulation of guilt. The new element the baptized person could not import from Pharisaism but was able to receive only from Jesus was that baptism offered him a state of faith. This condition of faith provided him with the confidence that the Christ would forgive his as well as the nation's entire guilt and redeem him from evil.

At the point of baptism it was not yet recognized, and in many instances probably hardly suspected, what all in the individual's conduct was affirmed and denied by the repentance entailed in baptism. Likewise, it was subject to further clarification to what extent his activities up to that point must be discontinued and the will currently inhabiting the person must die. This only came to light through life within the community, by continued obedience to the apostolic word and as the effect of brotherly contact, whose conscious purpose was mutual assistance in the struggle against sin. Nevertheless, what was achieved by the repentance resulting in baptism was the admission that the baptized person had sinned. It signaled the decisive renunciation of all evil and the willingness to receive God's forgiveness. The righteous who did not need conversion were denied entrance into the community, because baptism brought it about. Within the Christian community, all those who clung to their evil disposition were denied the right to receive it. When Paul told those who contemplated sinning that they would thereby violate their baptism (Rom. 6:2–3), his judgment was no different than that of Christendom at large.

Baptismal preaching remained faithful to Jesus' word not merely by rejecting evil and demanding conversion, thus honoring God's Law. It also united the offer of divine grace with the acknowledgment of divine Law. The promise implied in baptism likewise took on new shape by being tied to the confession of the Christ. For now it was by his commission and as the demonstration of his grace that Christ's messengers proclaimed forgiveness of sins. By uniting in baptism the call to repentance and the offer of divine grace, they caused the baptized person at the same time to be repentant *and* to believe in Jesus. For by exercising repentance in baptism, he would at the same time receive Jesus' forgiveness. The baptized person recognized Jesus' messianic authority by acknowledging that Jesus could forgive and that he exercised his prerogative with respect to those who accepted his word. On this account the baptized person also received all the benefits bestowed on the community by Jesus: not merely hope of sharing in his glory but also God's Spirit, that gift he now grants his own by which he transforms them into saints. By the ministry of the Spirit, the repentant person experienced personally the removal of his guilt and the bestowal of divine grace.

## G. The Lord's Table

From the church's earliest beginnings, the baptized person was brought to Christ's table. This constituted a second act that powerfully moved believers' thoughts and desires and bound them together as a united community. According to Luke, table fellowship immediately became an important part of the disciples' communal life (Acts 2:42, 46; 20:7; cf. Jude 12). Paul's comments regarding the significance of "the Lord's table" shed light on this practice. They reflect the community's belief that Jesus had not given the gift he gave to his disciples at the Last Supper to them alone but to all. With the bread he gave his body, and with the wine his blood, not merely to those who ate with him at that time but to all (1 Cor. 10:16–22; 11:23–34).[14] Each of the three statements— that Jesus gave his body and his blood to his disciples before his death (Matthew); that the table fellowship constituted a continually exercised concern for Christendom (Luke); and that the community on the occasion of its own meal was obliged to do what Jesus had done on the night he was betrayed unto death (Paul)—indeed possesses particular emphases transcending the other accounts. Nevertheless, they converge into one straight line and cast bright light on the course of events.

The assumption that the Last Supper described by Paul was particular to him without being celebrated elsewhere, or at least without being celebrated elsewhere in such a way, flies in the face of Paul's explicit assertions. With reference to the

14. The phrase "table of the Lord" is found regarding the altar also in Palestinian tradition in connection with Mal. 1:7: see, for example, the statement, "Do not let your table be full and the table of your Lord [that is, the altar] empty." The use of the phrase for the table of the Last Supper was a natural choice, since it was an actual "table."

customs instituted by him in Corinth he distinguished between practices open to the community's discretion and subject to alteration and directives he had received from the Lord. The latter did not originate with Paul and were therefore not to be altered or corrupted. This holy, inviolable core of the entire ritual was the Last Supper. Whoever claims that Paul freely invented Jesus' words ventures a conjecture unsupported by Paul's statements elsewhere. Paul never spoke in a way that obscured the boundaries between his own words and those of Jesus.

This second celebration, which issued in action by which the church achieved its community with Christ, effectively supplemented baptism. For the celebration of the Lord's Supper did not merely draw a demarcation line between the time of one's ignorance and a person's newfound condition of faith by way of a one-time act. Rather, it was constantly repeated and lent visibility to the church's continual union with Jesus. The celebration of the Lord's Supper also did not merely associate individuals with him but took place in the gathered community and thereby further strengthened its union.

It was of decisive significance for the church's entire existence that its major act of worship focused on Jesus' work on the cross. Both Matthew and Paul maintain that the community did not suppose that the exalted Christ gave it a heavenly body to eat and glorified blood to drink. Its celebration rather commemorated what Jesus had done for his disciples through his death. Believers thought of the body that had been hung on the cross and of the blood that was shed at Jesus' death. The introduction of a heavenly substance into the Last Supper was based on the conviction that the words would be unintelligible without it. But what is more important than so-called necessities is the fact that we cannot find anywhere a distinction between the body eaten at Jesus' table and the body given into death nor between the blood drunk in Jesus' cup and the blood shed at his death. The words used at the Last Supper direct the view of celebrants to the events at the cross. His memory, however, is not evoked merely to relive his pain nor solely to provide an occasion for repentance. Rather, the meal is transformed into a celebration of thanksgiving by making Christ's crucifixion an occasion for faith. This shows that Jesus' death provided for the disciples reconciliation with God. In him they found the perfect expression of God's grace. This presentation does not in any way conflict with Luke's portrayal of Peter's ministry in Jerusalem. There Jesus' cross serves indeed as proof of Jewish guilt. But this would clash with the understanding that the disciples obtained the material for thanksgiving from their memory of Jesus' cross only if the proclamation of the cross were designed to provide a rationale for the rejection of Israel. However, since it took place in order that Israel receive God's kingdom through the Crucified One, Jesus' death becomes the demonstration of God's grace. For this reason the disciples made the reenactment of their final time with their dying Lord a never-ending giving of thanks.

## H. The New Church

The formation of a community with unified convictions, a common will, and a joint work, is always a profound process, and this applied particularly to the community established by the disciples. For Jesus' concept of religion, formulated in personal terms and resulting in boundless truth and liberty, demanded the utmost from the newly emerging brotherhood. Present were the common conviction uniting its members, faith, personal assurance of God, and the common will producing the community's actions; here also was love liberated from selfish desires. Had the disciples established the community on a different foundation, they would have fallen short of their commission.

While Jesus had not yet taken those who had responded to his word out of their real-life circumstances, the ones baptized in the name of Christ now united with the apostles and one another to form a permanent union. For the Christ's crucifixion had accentuated the separation between Jesus' disciples and the old community more deeply and visibly than before. Moreover, the public confession of Jesus' lordship produced in them a union that oriented everyone's conduct toward the same goal, and the Spirit's presence invested the community with a thoroughly spiritual dimension. Baptism did not result in a multitude of autonomous congregations but the one church, because baptism called its recipients to the Christ. Likewise, the table around which the community gathered was not the table of a teacher or baptizer or bishop but Christ's table. By receiving their share in Christ, they simultaneously entered into communion with all other believers. The concept of the church thus took on a universal dimension from the start that remained undiminished, just as the individual local Jewish congregation had always been considered to be part of the one Israel.

The establishment of the church effectively confirmed faith in Jesus' regal status. Since the messianic name designated him as the Creator of the holy community, the disciples truly apprehended in the emergence and growth of his new community the revelation of his lordship and fulfillment of his promise.

Since entrance into the community was effected by baptism, the community's unity was established by that faith which acknowledged Jesus' commission. This entailed the struggle against sinful desires and the readiness for service and obedience to Jesus. A uniform will arose in all which found its aims, not in selfish passions, but in God's will, and which therefore possessed its constitutive principle in the rule of love.

The men who speak to us in the New Testament documents did their work in the context of this united church and for its sake. Their writings provide a glimpse of two events, one occurring in authors' inner lives, the other resulting from the work and struggle of the church in and for which they lived. The historian needs to pay attention to both elements: the personal character of the men who are speaking here and the common possession of the community addressed in their writings.[15] Both events, the history of the apostles that shaped each of their distinctive outlooks *and* the common life of believers that molded them into one fellowship, took place simultaneously and stood in continual

---

15. The contents of the New Testament are not given comprehensive expression when it is divided into individual doctrinal units that are biographically determined. Neither is justice done to the New Testament when one seeks to find in it a doctrinal system comparable to later ecclesiastical tradition. The former procedure obscures the connection between the apostles and the community, the latter the nature of their convictions as conditioned by their own personal history.

contact. The community came into being through what it was given by the apostles. At the same time, events in the community moved and enriched the thought of its leaders. The same combination of simultaneity and commonality linked the work of those who conducted the dispute with Jerusalem and led the church there with the ministry of Paul and his associates, who planted the Gentile church.[16]

In the movement leading from Jesus to the Gentile church the leading role belongs to the men who had received Jesus' commission and produced Jewish Christianity. The historian should first of all seek to understand their writings. Then he should listen to Paul, and subsequently to those who shared with the apostles in the work of teaching. This furnishes the requisite equipping for formulating what early Christian "doctrine" consisted of, for clarifying those convictions which embodied the community's shared beliefs and which gave it its unifying commonality.

---

16. Whatever arrangement the interpreter may choose, neither he nor his readers can be spared the task of grasping the simultaneous nature and interdependence of what can only be examined and described successively.

# The Convictions Upheld by Jesus' Followers

## A. The Aim Set for the Church by Peter

During the first phase of their ministry in Jerusalem, the apostles in Jerusalem carried out their work solely by the spoken word. Only later, toward the end of their ministry, they began to produce written documents which spread their message to the entire church. From Peter, we possess such a document only from the period when the church of Asia Minor had already grown considerably beyond that which Paul had established. Peter wrote after he had left Palestine because the call to repentance had been directed to Israel in vain.[1]

### 1. The Christ

#### a) Material from Jesus

Much of the material found in Peter's first epistle at once proves to be material from Jesus. Peter calls Jesus by the regal name "Christ," thus depicting him as the Creator of the community which is God's possession. Jesus establishes the community by issuing God's call which entitles them to call upon God as Father. He thus leads them out of darkness, because God dwells in marvelous light. For this reason Jesus' word is "the good news of God": it does not merely promise the divine gift but also confers it and grants man new birth. Thus a person receives life produced in him by God and becomes one of God's chosen people. Those who resist the word, however, incur God's judgment. They are rejected, because they refuse to believe (1 Pet. 1:15; 2:9; 3:9; 5:10; 4:17; 1:12, 23; 1:1,17; 2:8). The cornerstone of the community, Jesus, is at the same time

---

1. Only the first epistle can be used as a source for Peter's preaching, and even its Petrine origin is hotly disputed. The Petrine authorship of 1 Peter is, however, supported by the accounts concerning Peter provided by the Gospels, Paul, and Luke.

*part of it* and exalted *above it* as Lord. Since he exercises his lordship according to the norm of grace, his lordship can be depicted by the image of the shepherd (2:4, 6–8; 5:4). As the Anointed One, Jesus has the Spirit, so that the designation of those who believe as "Christian" entails the promise of the Spirit (1:11; 3:18; 4:14).

His demise towers above all other events of Jesus' history. He suffered death while carrying out his mission in accordance with his will, and by dying he redeemed the community, removed its sins and led it to God. In keeping with the overall hortatory character of the epistle, direct ethical prescriptions are intertwined with assertions regarding divine grace. The idea that this might be a distortion of religion was foreign to Peter. He did not consider the forgiveness acquired for the community by Jesus' cross to be a substitute for its good will. Likewise, he did not have in mind a forgiveness that failed to liberate a guilty person from evil and did not sanctify him. By moving and ennobling the community's resolve, Jesus' cross proves its redemptive power. The cross does not merely set the community free from punishment; it turns it away from evil, providing it with the norm to which it must remain obedient. For Jesus showed believers by his death how they too should serve and suffer (1:17–20; 2:21–24; 3:18).

Jesus' resurrection provides hope for believers. For his gift is life, so that they themselves are born again on account of his resurrection (1:3; 3:7; 4:6). Now he is at God's throne and thus exalted above all heavenly powers. Nevertheless, he is not separated from the community, because he is its shepherd and overseer of their souls. Since his call causes the community to draw near to him, it receives from him the enablement for its priestly work. Its prayer is thus the glorification of God. He can answer it, because it arises from his own activity (3:22; 2:25; 4:5).

Soon he will be revealed to the community once again, and God's people delight in this hope. At his new revelation, the execution of justice will be connected with the perfection of grace, because he comes in order to judge the community, each one according to his own work. For the unity of grace and righteousness is an essential characteristic of God's work. The most precious gift the community received from Jesus is the privilege of calling upon God as the one who as Father judges righteously. The epistle's eschatology does not extend beyond the moment at which Jesus will be revealed to the community. Even the designation "aliens and strangers" for the community draws on a motif from Jesus' prophecy, who considered the gathering of the community to be the purpose of his coming. The concept of resurrection is further revealed by the statement that the dead will come back to life (1:7; 4:5–6; 1:17, 1).

Thus the epistle contains all the characteristic features of Jesus' messianic consciousness. Peter conceives of following Jesus as religion, as acceptance of the divine work, as the reconciliation of man with God. Because he directs faith and love toward *Jesus*, he draws all images for the actions and suffering of Christendom from the life of Jesus. Thus the entire mindset of Jewish piety vanishes and is not somehow replaced by new and corresponding constructs.[2] Peter

---

2. Greek religiosity has vanished entirely. There is no mention of gods, mysteries, Greek mysticism, asceticism, or the exercise of virtue.

knows nothing of theology that in itself grants salvation; he acknowledges no casuistry, church order, sacramental regulations, or moral efforts apart from union with Christ. Rather, he derives everything he needs to tell the community about its calling from the things Jesus did for it. Union with Jesus is not the result of a mystical experience; it is rather grounded in the outcome of Jesus' earthly life: his cross, resurrection, exaltation, and return. What the congregations possess, perform, and suffer is determined by Jesus' life and suffering. Christendom consists here in participation in the history of Jesus.

For this reason the epistle nowhere attempts to show ways in which the people of Asia Minor can be connected with Jesus. For their share in Jesus derives from his possession of regal status. The community belongs to him because he is the Christ. Believers are granted liberation from sin on account of his death, and the hope of eternal life on account of his resurrection. This is the message that his word brings to them, and it is full of the living power of God's grace (1:3,18–19; 2:24–25; 1:25).

### b) Distinctive Characteristics of Peter's Christology

Since the religious content of the doctrine of Christ—that the Christ possesses his lordship through God—powerfully shapes the axiom on which Peter's entire course of thought is based, a trinitarian designation of God stands as a heading over the epistle (1:2). Together with the Spirit Christ is related to the Father as the one through whom God's predestined will is carried out and to whom the Spirit leads people by sanctifying them. However, the trinitarian framework of Peter's conception of God does not lead to elaborate attempts to explain or defend Jesus' relationship with God by some theological construct. The only foundation Peter needs to show the comprehensive salvific power of Jesus' death is the concept of predestination: as the Lamb of God, given over to death for the sake of mankind, Jesus was foreknown by God before time (1:20–21). By thus de-emphasizing the concept of pre-existence, the epistle directs attention to the true basis for faith: the only proper object of faith are the events of Jesus's life, the work he accomplished in his humanness. But because God's eternal will was accomplished through him, his death has imperishable power and thus grants the community faith in God. The Spirit, on the other hand, through whom God was present in Jesus, is conceived of in terms of pre-existence, since the Spirit belongs to God and did not originate in time. Therefore Jesus is also related to Old Testament revelation: Christ's Spirit was active in the prophets (1:11). Nevertheless, the epistle contains no statement regarding the Christ's part in the work of creation.

Regarding the removal of guilt by Jesus' cross, Peter provides formulations that transcend those found in the Gospels. God's gracious gift consists in the fact that the community obtains its share in the sprinkling of Christ's blood (1:2).[3] This theology is derived from Israel's cult in one of two possible ways: the reference may be to the sprinkling of blood on the altar and in the sanctuary.

---

3. Hebrews 12:24 contains the same formulation, evidence that it was widespread in the church.

In this case Peter describes Jesus' death as the sacrifice and his blood as presented to God. Or it may frame the benefits of Jesus' death for the community in terms of the ritual of purification, by which a priest had to be consecrated by sacrificial blood and impure persons had to be sprinkled with cleansing water. In that case, the analogy pertains to his ability to remove our guilt. God sanctifies the community by the Spirit, so that death occurred on its behalf and believers can be granted forgiveness of their sins. Thus it is said regarding sins that Jesus carried them in his body to the cross, so that they are removed by his death (2:24). Similar to Paul, Peter links a believer's dying and awakening to new life with the cross. He thus depicts the change of will resulting from his devotion to Christ (2:24).

A notable feature of Peter's Christology, not attested in the same way in other documents, is the reference to Christ's departure and proclamation to the spirits (3:19–22; cf. 4:6). If the author had presented this as an idea of his own making, by which he sought to demonstrate to his readers his greatness as a teacher or prophet, the segment would suffice to reject the epistle's authenticity. But the passage does not contain any gnostic coloring, as though the writer immersed himself passionately into a mystery which brought delight to his own imagination or spurred the community on to similar speculation. The section rather forms part of an argument by which the community is enjoined to suffer. Christ's example therefore serves as an example of the blessedness of suffering. For him it led to the expansion of his ministry far beyond what he would have been able to accomplish in the flesh. After having suffered, now alive in the Spirit, he was able to go to the spirits in prison. Suffering did not result in loss of ministry; it rather provided him with power greater than the one he had in the flesh. Now his messianic work had become so universal that it also encompassed the spirits. But this had grave importance for struggling Christendom because its struggle can also bring it death. But Christ's saving power also extends to the dead.

Peter does not formulate this statement in general terms; he refers merely to the generation taken away by the flood. The Palestinian rabbinate stated that this generation was definitively judged and excluded from the resurrection. But everything, even the first humanity taken away by the flood, waited for Christ's work. Even those spirits had merely been imprisoned, where they still must wait for the divine verdict. But now Jesus appeared also before those who belonged to a different generation, not the one living presently but the one confined to prison by God's judgment. This was possible in the power of his death, because he had yielded his flesh to death and received life by the Spirit. That this way of thinking is not indebted to gnosticism is apparent from the complete absence of any fascination with the mystery of what had happened to the spirits. All attention is focused on Christ and directed solely toward that which Jesus did in his comprehensive salvific power, not toward the spirits and their conduct and destiny. Consequently, the passage does not elaborate on the success of Jesus' proclamation. Merely the *fact* of proclamation is noted. Likewise, no information is given regarding the exact *time* of proclamation, apart from the statement that Jesus accomplished it after having been brought back to life by the Spirit.

The epistle sets Jesus' universal salvific power, which led him even to the spirits in prison, alongside the fruit of his cross manifested in the course of earthly history: the availability of the saving waters of baptism. The significance of baptism is that it amounts to the offering up of a good conscience toward God (3:21).[4] The gift given to man by baptism is described as purity, which baptism is able to provide because God in baptism invites him to have a good conscience. The description of baptism as the saving act entails a rejection of all symbolism; Peter acts as baptizer by the authority of God's grace. But magical conceptions are excluded with equal resolve. The matter involves renewal of the conscience, and the sincere offer of divine grace given to man in baptism leaves open whether or not the one baptized allows himself to be given a good conscience or not. If he truly has what he is supposed to receive in keeping with the intention of baptism—a good conscience—his baptism has become his salvation. For he who has a good conscience is enjoying the fruit of God's grace.

## 2. The Apostolic Office

The epistle's conception of the apostolic office is of decisive historical significance. Because the status of being a child of God is granted through God's word, and salvation through baptism, the apostle stands before his listeners as the mediator of God's perfect gift (1:23; 2:2; 3:21). He looses and binds according to the authority given to him by Jesus. However, he is thereby not given ruling power but remains dependent on God. His ministry is not an end in itself but is subordinate to God's work, so that his success is tied to the "visitation" granted to his hearers by God (2:12). Likewise, his office does not give to him power to rule the church. Peter does not speak as a lawgiver but as an exhorter who urges the community to courageous, joyful obedience. He interprets and applies the name given to him by Jesus, the "rock," by showing that every believer is called to become part of God's temple as a living stone. His privilege thus becomes a unifying bond that links him with all others, just as his name links him to Jesus, "the cornerstone," and makes his ministry part of Christ's work (2:4–5). The term "elder" adequately conveys his official authority, a term by which he places himself alongside all those who work on behalf of local congregations (5:1).

The epistle assumes that the eyes of the entire church are directed toward Peter. The apostle expects that all are prepared to receive Jesus' instruction through him, even though his word is not directly occasioned by his personal relationship with the recipients of his letter (although such is not entirely lacking).[5] This does not mean, however, that he was the sole bearer of Jesus' message, and the church in Asia Minor is not shortchanged for not having received the gospel from Peter. By his Spirit, Jesus also enabled others to proclaim his

---

4. Ἐπερώτημα is an established term for the motion presented to an assembly for acceptance or rejection.

5. Silvanus's trip to Asia Minor occasioned the letter (5:12). Also, Mark's presence with Peter provided a personal connection between him and those in Asia Minor.

message (1:12).[6] Nevertheless, Peter's office remains distinct from those who planted churches in Asia Minor. The difference that sets Peter apart from all others results from his role as a witness of Jesus' sufferings. These sufferings, seen in the light of Jesus' divine sonship and glory, are the surprising and wonderful truth which must be defended by eyewitnesses against any efforts to dispute them. Peter is fit for this task because he accompanied Jesus to Jerusalem and Gethsemane.[7] It is not exotic knowledge or spectacular spiritual experiences that qualify Peter for leadership in the church. Rather, it is his ability to speak as a witness which lends to his word indispensable and authoritative power. For he saw Jesus, while the church in Asia Minor places its faith and love in Jesus without having seen him. His personal relationship existing between him and Jesus makes him Jesus' compatriot with whom the Lord will share his glory (5:1; 1:8, 12). Yet his special relationship with Jesus does not result in Peter stepping forth as the most expert narrator of the life of Jesus. Indeed, Peter's first epistle does not refer to it in any detail. The knowledge of Jesus' earthly sojourn and faith in him remain clearly distinct, and God's call is shown to aim at producing inner union with Jesus by faith.

Still, significant intellectual labor is devoted to explicating the community's preparation for obedience to Christ. This sets the epistle miles apart from the chatty verbosity of Greek literature. In its condensed richness, it bears the mark of a worker who knows how to make maximum use of his time. Sentences follow one after another like measured hammer blows, every one substantial, issuing from an active ministry without which such discussion of ethical issues would be inconceivable. Nevertheless, Peter's entire intellectual effort remains focused on the question of how the church is to accomplish God's will.[8] Even the apostles' exegesis of Scripture is not conceived in intellectualistic terms, even though the author is obviously engaged in active reflection on it. For the epistle is replete with Old Testament allusions, and the author expects even the churches of Asia Minor to gauge the epistle's importance from the way in which its major motifs connect with Scripture. Allusions to Old Testament figures such as Noah or Sarah will be immediately transparent to Peter's audience. Nevertheless, the exegetical task does not in itself give Peter's word its purpose. While the apostle does not even remotely compare him-

6. Since the churches of Galatia and Asia came into being through Paul, we find out here how Peter thought of Paul. The dual apostolic office, that of Peter for the Jews and Paul's for the Gentiles, does not appear. Peter places Paul among the larger number of Spirit-equipped evangelists. This was required by the particular circumstances, since the church of Cappadocia and that of Pontus and Bithynia were connected with the Pauline churches. This also coheres with Galatians 2:9, where Paul and Barnabas stand side by side. The characteristic of being a "witness," however, is also conceded to these messengers of Jesus, for Peter addresses the church as ἐπιμαρτυρῶν, that is, as the second witness, who confirms the testimony of the first (5:12).

7. Only the innermost circle of Jesus' followers witnessed Jesus' death. The circle of witnesses of the resurrection, on the other hand, was far greater (1 Cor. 15:6; Acts 1:22). Barnabas and Paul, too, belonged to this group. There is no reference to Peter's unique role in the Easter account.

8. Regarding the brilliance of the Petrine statements, issuing from a well-focused mind, one should remember that the apostles spent a considerable part of their time in prayer, which confers clarity and depth on thoughts which comprehend the divine will. The same is true of James's epistle.

self to Jesus, to whom the community owes everything it has, Peter places himself alongside the prophets. He claims to have a similar calling, both Peter and the Old Testament prophets being witnesses of the Christ, particularly of his sufferings. The prophets are witnesses of Christ's sufferings in that God's Spirit spoke through them. Because the Spirit knows what lies within God's will, he enabled the Old Testament prophets to proclaim Christ, even prior to his actual coming, in terms that are valuable as testimony. But now their witness is supplemented by that of the apostle who saw the Lord (1:10–12). In all of this, not a single foreign element is introduced into the teachings Jesus imparted to his followers.

No miracles are adduced as support. In the portrayal of Jesus, miracle recedes in comparison to the importance of his demise. The apostle does not ground the life-giving power of his word in signs. This, too, marks no deviation from Jesus' own conviction that only an evil and adulterous generation looks for signs, because it wishes to evade the impact of the message of repentance on the conscience.

## 3. The Shape of Christian Existence

### a) Injunctions Derived from Jesus

The community receives from Christ both God's gift and her obligation, and these are inextricably linked. As in Jesus' word, celebration and labor are one. The stance of believers toward God is now one of faith, and faith claims Jesus' promise, because Jesus, when he judges, intercedes for those who believe in him (1:21,5–9; 2:7; 5:9). Their stance toward others consists of "doing good," which is one way of summing up the entire duty assigned to believers by God's will. Thereby they achieve the pinnacle of achievement: the praise of God. The community demonstrates to be Jesus' own possession by works of genuine kindness. Behavior rooted in love receives its law by the truth; the juxtaposition of truth and love proves that the concept of truth is not influenced by Greek thought but rather derived from Jesus' pronouncement that both truth and love are God's gift to man (2:12; 4:19; 1:22). Love enables the community to pour all of its energy into the smallest service. What appears to be small and inconspicuous constitutes the foundation for Christians' pure conduct and fruitful work. Moreover, love is supported by patience that endures injustice. In Peter as in Matthew, patience is boundless (5:5; 2:15, 23; 3:8–9). Since suffering results from righteousness which respects and abides by ethical norms, the community must not fear or avoid it. For it experiences God's grace in its suffering. Thus victory in suffering is elevated to the lofty position Jesus' word assigned to his disciples. Suffering comports with the reception of this blessed power, because the one who suffers for the sake of righteousness is one who receives Jesus' promise. The Spirit is with those who suffer for Jesus' sake; suffering is the way by which they follow Jesus as his disciples (3:14; 4:14; 2:20–21).

Being a Christian requires therefore the sincere resolve Jesus' word calls watchfulness. By its resistance to fleshly lust and its courageous acceptance of suffering, the community cares for its soul, or better, for its life whose bearer is the soul (1:9; 2:11). It can be enticed by neither gold nor honor. It is free from the quest for gold; for gold perishes, and the revelation of Christ will transform its current shame into honor (1:7).[9] The seriousness of believers' condition is heightened by the opposition of the accuser who invokes God's righteousness against them. Christians are reminded of the devil in view of the testing that suffering brings. But the severity of the struggle need not lead to fear or doubt. Rather, the community may free itself from anxiety because God cares for it (5:7–8). Strength for action and suffering is drawn from its hope, which it appropriates correctly when it girds its loins with it. Its share of salvation is guarded for it by God, so that it is rich even now, while still involved in the work of love and suffering for Jesus. For its heavenly inheritance has been set aside and is kept for it (1:13, 3–5).

The commandments Jesus issued to his followers are thus preserved without attenuation. Yet they are not merely proclaimed as his legislation or commandments but rather live in the apostle and the community as the energy that empowers them.

### b) Aims Derived from the Present Circumstances

Since the community is the work of the Christ, who has brought and will bring her God's grace, she is called to worship God. Only a single element is chosen from among the entire scope of statutes and institutions provided by Scripture to characterize its religion: the Temple. Circumcision, holy days (including the Sabbath!), holy offerings, purity, altar, and priests have vanished. The epistle no longer looks back to these features of the old community.[10] But one element cannot disappear: the Temple, the place where God lives and reveals himself. This, however, does not mean that the subject is holy sanctuaries, Christian church buildings, or other topics—the construction of the Temple rather occurs by the establishment of the community. The community itself is the place where God is present and worshipped. It is into this edifice that every individual must be integrated as a "living stone" in order to accomplish what Jesus granted to and commanded Peter. For an individual does not participate in the great work of God's revelation and glorification by focusing on himself or in separating from the fellowship, but as a member of the community. Thus the distinction between the priesthood and the rest of the community has been obliterated. God's house, the throng of children brought into life by God, the living temple, is at the same time his priesthood able to bring sacrifices, so that God's purpose for Israel is realized in the new community. Jesus now enables his community to bring genuine sacrifices, because the Spirit empowers it for worship. The praise of God's glory is the es-

---

9. Resistance to the enslaving power of possessions is elsewhere not made the subject of exhortation. Wildly incited lust is considered to be the more powerful and dangerous opponent. In this the epistle concurs with John and Paul, while the writings composed for Jewish Christians, that is, Matthew, James, and the source of Luke, strongly emphasize the dangers of material possessions.

10. The tie between worship and natural elements, such as physical location or times, has been completely removed. This is repeated again and again in all the epistles and is the characteristic of the earliest era of the church.

sential act of this priestly service. But this does not result in separation between ritual and morality, between love for God and man. For the good work the community must accomplish in its given, natural circumstances is grounded in the love offered to God and united with the highest aims, similar to what Peter calls "spiritual sacrifices" (2:5, 9, 12; 4:11).

What the community receives results in an irresistible movement toward a goal that has no end. Apart from the term "building," which is related to the term "temple," Peter also uses the phrase "growth," when he depicts the word as the nourishment that sustains believers' lives. Mindful of the fragility of human life and the powerful contrast between our present condition and our final destiny, Peter calls the word the milk that promotes a newborn's growth (2:2). Through this assemblage of terms, a rich, impressive foundation had been created for the necessity of continual striving. Thus Peter also includes a metaphor related to athletic competition, when he directs the attention of those ministering in the community to the laurels they are to obtain (5:4). This image, which was clearly widespread in the early community, likewise provided a powerful illustration: those who stand in Jesus' service must make a persistent effort to give visible and fruitful expression to what has been entrusted to them.

The concrete phrases of exhortation spurring the community on to good works remain free from all elements that would indicate a distinct approach to holiness and to what it means to be a Christian. Obedience and love rendered to God by the community in Christ are not merely proven in the brothers' dealings with one another procured for them by their participation in the community. This is, to be sure, to be their first priority. But they are manifested as well in the natural forms of community, in the service of slaves, in marriage, in subordination to the government, and in dealings with non-Christians. Thus these forms of community are entirely confirmed and protected from any violation (2:13,17; 3:1–7).

One misses any particular means for spreading the gospel. It is everyone's duty to be prepared to give an account for the Christian hope. Believers' ethical purity and industry are considered to be the most important factors commending the Christian community to Gentiles. Suffering takes on special value from this vantage point as well (2:12; 3:16). From Judaism is expected nothing but opposition, but those who refuse to believe in Christ are themselves caused to stumble by him. But nothing is said about Judaism, either regarding the claims it makes for itself or concerning the peaceful union of Greeks and Jews in the new community. The hostility of the Greeks and the Roman state are an even more powerful threat to the community than the wrath of the Jews. Peter does not conceive of the possibility of "winning the world" and softening the nations' rage. Rather, he leads the church into suffering and death. With courageous resolve, the community's view is turned inward toward what she must accomplish among her own while loving and suffering. The imposing situation is judged to be a necessity ordained by God as the revelation of his judgment, until Christ's return changes everything by manifesting God's grace (2:7–8; 4:17; 1:13).

## 4. Peter in Relation to Other Religious Groups

### a) Peter and John

The content of the letter coheres closely with the information provided by both Paul and Luke that no one among the Twelve stood closer to Peter than John in the work to be accomplished in Jerusalem. John's Gospel likewise features Peter and John side by side. While there are also formal similarities with the epistle of James, there are no such similarities to John owing to the distinctness and peculiarity of Johannine style. The epistle's ethical presentation, however, evinces strong similarities with John. Both John and Peter fully terminate fellowship with Judaism. For both, the sole reason for such separation is Judaism's persistent refusal to believe in Jesus. Neither's separation was motivated by a fear of suffering or a desire to escape death. Because they judged the danger presented to Christendom by Rome to be very serious, both assume leadership over the Gentile church in the full awareness that they are leading it into death.[11]

Both Peter and John viewed Israel's refusal to believe not merely in terms of stubbornness of human will but in terms of God's sovereignty over all obstacles, including human resistance. Both considered the fall of Judaism as ultimately brought about by God (cf. 2:8 with John 12:37). Their separation from Israel ties them only more closely to the prophets. Regarding these, Peter maintained that they were indwelt by Christ's Spirit who testified through them to Christ's sufferings and subsequent glory. John claims that Isaiah saw Christ's glory. These two statements constitute a peculiar parallel, since both embody the seed of a fertile approach to biblical interpretation that interprets Old Testament revelation in terms of the work of the pre-existent Christ. Both statements, however, remain mere hints that are not developed (cf. 1:10–12 with John 12:41).[12] For both Peter and John the originating and controlling conviction underlying these passages is that the prophets' communion with Christ is important because Christendom uses their writings as canon. It does not thereby incorporate foreign elements; rather, by obeying Scripture, it remains exclusively and completely subject to Christ. Thus this idea led neither for Peter nor for John to an approximation of gnostic theory.

Peter and John both portray Jesus simultaneously as Lamb and as Shepherd. Likening the community to a flock results for both in the phrase "tending Jesus' flock" for the apostolic office and the ministry of elders in the community (cf. 1:19; 5:2 with John 1:29; 10:12). Peter calls Jesus "chief shepherd," one who appoints shepherds for the flock and gives it leaders and nurturers. In John, Jesus, as the Door, leads the shepherd to the flock and commissions Peter to feed his "lambs" (cf. 5:4 with John 10:7–9; 21:16). Both apostles link Jesus' care for the community with his power over the dead. Just as Peter portrays the Exalted One as going to the spirits, John has the dead hear the voice of the Son of

---

11. The commonality would be even greater if Babylon in 5:13 refers to Rome. For this would also signify Peter's transfer of the prophecies directed toward Babylon and Edom to Rome. But Babylon can also be the name of the country.

12. These parallels also extend to Paul: see 1 Cor. 10:1–4.

God from now on (cf. 3:19 with John 5:25). Both Peter and John consider Jesus' ministry among the living and the dead as of one cloth, the unified fulfillment of Jesus' messianic vocation.[13] The final statement of Peter's epistle portrays Christians as those who are in Christ (cf. 5:14 with 1 John 2:5–6). His characterization of Christians as those who do not see Jesus but still believe concurs with the concluding statement of the main body of John's Gospel (cf. 1:8 with John 20:29).

Both portray the Spirit as the One who knows and therefore speaks as the Witness, naming it as one of his characteristics that he gives life (cf. 1:11 with 1 John 5:6; 1 Pet. 3:18 with John 6:63).[14] The Spirit's presence is traced back to his being sent from heaven. A connection between the concept of the Spirit and internal processes of individuals is absent from the writings of both (cf. 1:11–12 with John 15:26; 1 John 5:6). The Spirit's close union with Christ's work, foundational in Johannine teaching on the Spirit, finds expression in Peter's trinitarian formula, where the Spirit's work is placed between the Father's predestination and the gift of Christ to the community. Peter maintains that the community will obtain her share in the removal of guilt procured by Jesus' death and that she will attain obedience to Jesus by being sanctified by the Spirit (1:2). Both Peter and John express the assurance that evil has been overcome for Christians, and both derive from this assurance the same consequence: resolute obedience that keeps Jesus' commandment. Here both Peter and John use Jesus' death as the great controlling norm for Christian conduct (cf. 2:21–25; 3:17–18 with John 15:13; 1 John 3:16; 4:9–11).

Both writers find in Exodus 19:6 a description of the Christian community which is thus awarded priestly dignity. Believers' adoration and petition is described as the true sacrifice by which Israel's temple worship is brought to fulfillment (cf. 2:9 with Rev. 1:6; 5:8, 10; 8:3–4). Brotherly love is the will that shapes the community. Neither Peter nor John thinks in terms of a contrast between love and faith. Peter's portrayal of his preeminence in Christendom concurs entirely with John's assessment of himself. Both assume the church's leadership as witnesses and followers of Jesus who had seen the Lord, exhorting Christians to believe in Jesus without having seen him. Nowhere does John insist on his function as eyewitness more emphatically than with regard to Jesus' suffering. This is paralleled by Peter's insistence that he can and must testify to Jesus' sufferings. Both apostles are content to assert their authority in the church by the term "elder," in contrast to the status of younger members (cf. 5:1; 1:8 with 1 John 1:1; John 1:14; 19:35; 2 John 1; 3 John 1). Since both conceive of the church's establishment and its religious privilege exclusively as a result of Christ's work, they consider any discussion of Israel's national situation unnecessary. The community chosen and sanctified by God is for both the one created by Christ, so that they do not address the issue of the Law. Neither Peter nor John cites apostolic commandments ordering the constitution of the church. They do, however, challenge the church with equal vigor to suffer joy-

---

13. See also Paul in Rom. 14:9.
14. These parallels also extend to the rabbinate and Paul.

fully for Jesus' sake. Peter also relates the community's persecution to the execution of divine justice, which must precede the revelation of the Christ and which shows the sinful world that God resists it (4:17–18 contains the fundamental thought of the Apocalypse). But both express the prior and overarching conviction that the community experiences God's grace even when being subject to persecution.

Both draw from the Old Testament the formulations by which they portray the community's final God-given destiny. If Peter calls the community's present, still incomplete state a "diaspora," John holds that the ultimate goal of God's work is the city of God (cf. 1:1; 2:11 with Rev. 21).

These points of contact—for example, the similar use of Lamb and Shepherd imagery—are in part explained by memory of the Lord, for whom both lived. However, these converging theological motifs transcend the Gospel tradition available to us, pointing to the working relationship the two men enjoyed.

### b) The Opposition to Greek Thought

The number of Greek forms of expression is somewhat larger in Peter than in the writings of other authors from Palestine.[15] This does not, however, lessen his distance from Greek thought. His formation of ideas does not take on a life of its own, as if doctrine should become the means of producing the church's unity. Although Peter's intellectual achievement by far transcends that of subsequent ecclesiastical literature, his epistle does not evidence the pursuit of knowledge for knowledge's sake nor betray tendencies toward a systematic or scientific approach. For his thought is controlled entirely by his commitment to do Jesus' will. When doctrine started taking on a life of its own, ethics by itself became an important part of Christian instruction, which now considered its essential task to be the development of moral ideas. Peter's epistle, however, does not aim at imparting moral concepts to the community; it rather seeks to urge the church to action, assisting it in overcoming obstacles to living the Christian life. The epistle does not develop the concept of love in terms of a new moral idea but assumes that the community knows what love is, and moreover possesses love as the will that moves it. The letter takes as its theme that the community is to exercise love even in the face of suffering. It is impossible to separate the doctrinal element from the epistle's ethical pronouncements, since Peter relates God's grace closely to norms for Christian conduct. Neither Peter's concept of God nor his description of Christ nor his substantiation of Christian hope draws on analogies from nature, an important device in Greek philosophy. The phrase "excellencies of God," whose proclamation is part of the community's calling, is taken from Isaiah 43:21. The term "excellencies" is used in the epistle in reference to proofs of divine grace and power without revealing any influence of Greek ethical teaching (2:9).[16] Psychological concepts such as the terms "spirit," "soul," "body," "flesh," "desire," and "will," likewise occur in

---

15. Συνείδησις θεοῦ: 2:19; cf. 3:16, 21; ἐπερώτημα: 3:21; ὑπογραμμός: 2:21; ἀντίτυπος: 3:21; συσχηματίξεσθαι: 1:14; λογικὸν γάλα: 2:2.

16. This use of ἀρεταί has affinities with Gentile linguistic usage through the Greek synagogue.

their Palestinian form. The term "reason" is entirely absent, while "conscience" is that process in one's inner life which determines the nature of a person's relationship with God.[17] The Christian message is therefore directed toward the conscience and aims at its normal condition. This meant for the entire evangelistic effort among the Greeks that the Christian message was framed once again as a call to repentance. Thus the listener's acceptance of a message does not occur merely through his mental faculties and the concepts found in the individual but through those processes denoted by the term "conscience." While every person, by his own work and lively joy, participates in the benefits provided by Christ for the community, Greek ethical thought, elevating the desire for happiness to the status of normative will, was completely rejected.

### c) The Jewish Heritage

Peter's epistle provides evidence for Jesus' successful liberation of his disciples from the Jewish way of handling the Scriptures; both halakhah and haggadah have perished. The letter is even further removed from the affectations of Hellenistic biblical interpretation. This critical approach toward conventional ways of interpreting Scripture, however, did not destroy the contribution of Palestinian teaching to Jewish devotion. Indeed, one finds points of contact with Palestinian tradition even among Christians who were raised in Palestinian Judaism. These converging elements in Peter's letter resemble those found in Matthew, John, and James. For Palestinian Judaism, the Temple was the place of God's presence, considered to be the most glorious gift ever given to the Jews by God. Thus Peter conceives of God's work for humanity in terms of the establishment of a Temple, a place where God is present and worshiped. The epistle does not describe the glory of the Christian message merely by claiming that the prophets desired to know it but also by maintaining that the angels longed to look into it. This represents a further development of the synagogal praise of Torah: the angels longed to know it. The exhortation addressed to the community that its Father is at the same time its Judge, and its Judge also its Father, is also found in the homiletical tradition of the rabbinate. The divine name "the Living and Abiding One" has Palestinian parallels, as does the use of Genesis 18:12 as an example for women's obedience to their husbands and the use of the term σκεῦος (thing, object) for the body with respect to sexual intercourse. The phrase "to gird one's loins" does not merely repeat a biblical expression but also has points of contact with contemporary Palestinian usage, and the statement that "angels and authorities and powers" dwell in heaven evidences material and formal similarities with synagogal terminology. "The one who is ready to judge the dead" was part of the doxology spoken by the people of Palestine at the grave. The divine name "Creator" likewise was current in those circles. Peter's use of the expression remains distant from Greek thought in that he does not employ the phrase to represent God's relationship with the entire world or with

---

17. Διάνοια in 1:13; cf. 1 John 5:20; similarly ἔννοια in 4:1 and συνείδησις in 3:16, 21 and 2:19. The use of συνείδησις is found analogously in Paul in Hebrews. Prototypes for this usage were provided by the Greek synagogue. Both Philo and Josephus are instructive in this regard.

nature but in order to describe God as the Giver of life to man. Consequently, whoever is called to die may assuredly entrust his soul to him as the "faithful Creator." The use of the term "creature" for authorities, likewise, is not strange from the vantage point of Palestinian Judaism, since "creature" was used freely for the individual person (1:12, 17, 23; 3:6–7, 22; 4:5, 19; 2:13).

### d) The Relationship with Paul

Paul claims that his meeting with Jerusalem's apostles added nothing to his message (Gal. 2:6). For them, in turn, it was crystal clear that their gospel could not be supplemented or enriched by Paul, since it received its content through the history of Jesus. Peter's epistle provides corroborating evidence in this regard. For Paul adds nothing essential to its underlying convictions. The focus of a person's entire religious commitment on Jesus; the elevation of the remembrance of his cross above any other element; confidence perfected to the extent of full assurance; unbroken trust in his lordship by which the community is set free from guilt and granted eternal life; faith issuing in love; believers' separation from Judaism, so that the Mosaic Law ceased to be the controlling norm for their relationship to God and no longer prevented the gathering of all believers into a single church—these are the underlying axioms of the epistle and at the same time the characteristics of Pauline Christianity.

At the same time, while some elements may be missing in Peter owing to the epistle's brevity, one notes the absence of prominent theological motifs that occupy a powerful place in the Pauline version of the gospel. This observation contradicts the effort by some to account for the commonality between Peter and Paul by Paul's overpowering influence on Peter. Set beside Paul's statements regarding Christ and the Spirit, Peter's statements appear antiquated. Paul's pronouncements regarding the Law are missing. The phrases "Law" and "commandment" are entirely lacking, and the redemptive power of Jesus' death is not set in relation to the rule of the Law, which explains why the epistle can call believers in Asia Minor a "holy community" without addressing their relationship to Israel. The term "righteousness" is used by Peter only in ways that are not Pauline (3:18; 4:18; 2:24; 3:14). The expressions "justification" and "reconciliation" are missing, and the concept of "being a child" is not related to adoption but to the new birth. There is no felt tension between faith and works. These differences point to the new elements worked out by Paul in the course of his apostolic ministry.[18]

These observations must be balanced by a discussion of the strong similarities between the ethical formulations of both writers. Both demand that love be unhypocritical. Paul's "inner man" corresponds to the "hidden person of the heart" in Peter. Paul speaks of accommodation to this world, Peter of accommodation to former passions. For both "soberness" bespeaks the seriousness that thinking and willing call for. Freedom in relation to others is based on slavery in relation to God, so that freedom cannot be construed as authorization

---

18. The distance between Peter and Paul resembles that between Peter and John, in whose case it is even more apparent owing to the greater compass of his writings.

to do evil. Both view Christian suffering as participation in Christ's suffering; suffering is no contradiction of divine promise. Slaves and women are enjoined to subordinate themselves willingly to the will of others. The marriage of believers and unbelievers is not dissolved, and government is justified by pointing out that law protects against evildoers and upholds doing good.[19] Paul fought for the same norms that Peter mandated for the community: the voluntary nature of service and the elimination of any authoritarian or money-hungry approach to leadership.[20]

It is entirely impossible to determine the respective contributions made by individual co-workers in the development and confirmation of ethical norms, because these were applied and current throughout the church. The unity between Peter's epistle and Pauline ethics provides telling testimony to the emergence of a strong common will in the community: believers were to act according to a unified set of norms, and this is how Jesus' reign comes to full fruition.

The observer of Peter's relationship with other first-century Christian documents will perceive, not without admiration, the considerable originality of Peter's thought. One is also struck by the way in which the leaders of the church lived entirely among the community of believers without being separated from other Christians by a hierarchical concept of power, nor by a mystically conceived view of religion walled up within itself. Rather, leaders with their own intellectual vitality were active in the give-and-take of what all believers shared. A strong commonality of thought and action thus co-existed with a personal coloring of ideas, which brought the rule of freedom to full expression, so that none of these documents is merely a copy of the other.

# B. The Establishment of Recollections about Jesus by Matthew

## 1. The Message Regarding the Christ

### a) The Message's Aim

Peter's epistle shows how Jesus' lordship was proclaimed by the disciples.[21] They emphasized those elements of Jesus' life that they believed to reveal his regal commission. The listener subsequently chose to follow Jesus or to reject

19. Cf. 1:22 with Rom. 12:9; 2 Cor. 6:6; cf. also James 3:17; cf. 3:4 with 2 Cor. 4:16; Rom. 7:22; cf. 1:14 with Rom. 12:2; cf. 1:13; 4:7; 5:8 with 1 Thess. 5:6, 8: cf. 2:16 with Gal. 5:13; cf. 4:13 with Phil. 3:10; Rom. 8:17; cf. 2:18 with Eph. 6:5; cf. 3:1 with Eph. 5:22; cf. 2:14 with Rom. 13:1–5. One may speculate that the author knew not merely James but also Romans and Ephesians. But a literary dependence with the latter writings is less secure than in the case of James. The basic forms of human community were sanctified for the church by Jesus' own word, and the instruction to observe these basic forms constitutes a constant subject of pastoral care from the start. First Peter 5:12–13 refers to a fact that was even more important for the relationship between Peter and Paul than the Pauline epistles: the fact that Paul's co-workers Silvanus and Mark were at the same time co-workers of Peter.

20. Cf. 5:2–3 with the epistles to the Corinthians and Timothy. There is also a very strong correlation between 1 Peter 3:3 and 1 Tim. 2:9 (the three prohibitions given to women regarding proper attire).

21. Luke's and Paul's accounts essentially concur with Peter's presentation.

him. Jesus was described to him as sent by God, crucified, risen, and exalted to God, which was tied to the promise of Christ's return. The Christian message issued to the listener the call to faith, which he either obeyed or refused. Christian preaching thus did not become a history lesson that sought to impart Jesus' words and deeds to one's audience as comprehensively as possible. For the disciples did not view knowledge as the thing that vouchsafed salvation. The listener, to be sure, can know Jesus only by being told about his works, and the message always consisted of historical material regarding Jesus' life. Apart from such information, Christian preaching ceased being a message. The gospel remained, however, markedly different from the kind of instruction that merely imparts knowledge. It confronted the listener with Christ in order to elicit his acknowledgment of Jesus' lordship. This, in turn, took place in that faith in Jesus arose in the listener.

This form of proclamation was supplemented by another approach. We find evidence for this in Matthew and similar writings collecting individual words and deeds of Jesus. This approach did not antedate the other one but existed in the community alongside it from the beginning (Luke 1:2).[22] This form of instruction about Jesus remained linked with the other kind of proclamation by maintaining the same basic outline into which particular reminiscences were inserted. For the events recalled in the epistles as God's mighty acts revealing his rule also constitute the core of this kind of presentation. The focus is the final outcome of Jesus' life; what is told is the story of Jesus' crucifixion. Earlier events in Jesus' life show that he was the Christ and explain why he was rejected; the resurrection narrative makes entirely clear that this history is the history of the Christ. But concrete reminiscences are inserted into this fixed basic pattern of proclamation, through which the community learns what Jesus said and did. This form of proclamation was occasioned by the desire of receiving a clear picture of Jesus. Because the community's faith, love, and hope clung to him, the traditions that made him known and intelligible took on utmost significance. Had this been the only or even the predominant motivation, however, the accounts would have taken on greater sophistication and embellishment. But their terse formulation, which provides little material for mere knowledge or sheer speculation, reveals that their purpose was not merely to keep alive reminiscences about Jesus but to establish obedience toward him.[23] Since the community only believes in Jesus when it also obeys him, Jesus' words are passed on to it in order that it may live as he demanded. His works are recounted so it may know how Jesus relates to it and how it should relate to him. The point of reference is always the Christ; at work here is a religious concept demanding for Jesus resolute faith and obedience from the listener.[24]

<hr>

22. The information that took on significance in the church of Asia regarding the acceptance of Mark into the canon, that is, that Mark was indebted for his material to Peter's stories, indicates that Peter had an important role, not merely in the former but also in the latter form of proclamation.

23. The earliest citations of Jesus' words (1 Cor. 7:10; 9:14; 11:23; Acts 20:35) provide clear evidence for the presence of this motivation.

24. For this reason the term "gospel" was also transferred from the proclamation of Jesus' rule to these portrayals.

This made reminiscences of Jesus similar in form to the traditions by which the rabbinate preserved the memory of the fathers.[25] The rabbinate preserved the fathers' sayings and words by faithfully recording essential elements, yet omitting many details that would be valuable for us such as time, place, or sequence of events. The rabbis retained with reliable clarity the deed or action that made the idea intelligible. Christians passed on their tradition regarding Jesus by the same means: by sayings that express his will, and by the narration of individual events developed only to the extent necessary to illumine Jesus' underlying intentions. The individual accounts are not linked by way of chronology or a scheme that explains the development of the events. The constitutive principle is rather the unity of the will of Jesus, who reveals his regal office in all his words and deeds. Just as Jewish tradition brought unity to a multitude of details by subordinating them to the interpretation of the Law, the disciples' presentation of Jesus conveys a unified message, since every aspect of their writings reveals the Christ.

In order to provide the listener with comprehensive knowledge of Jesus despite the limited amount of information, the disciples give priority to those actions of Jesus that indicate the boundaries he set.[26] The beginning of the Sermon on the Mount, for example, immediately bestows a promise on all who are aware of their need for God's help. Thus people's sense of need for God's mercy is presented as the measure of greatness. Subsequently, the love commandment is issued in a form that requires love even for one's enemies. Thus it is preserved from any demeaning self-centeredness. Matthew's account of Jesus' signs does not begin with the healing of the leper because he considered this to be the first gracious act of Jesus. Rather, Matthew juxtaposed leper and Gentile because both stand outside the community. Now we know the full compass of Jesus' help. John the Baptist's and Jesus' call for all to repent are illumined and made intelligible by being directed to the righteous. The forgiveness granted by Jesus to the guilty is portrayed when he makes a tax-collector his disciple. Thus these events are described in their full import. Jesus' involving the disciples in his own work is illumined by their call to martyrdom, while Jesus' refusal to succumb to pressure to reveal and exercise his regal status prematurely is given expression by Jesus' reply to John the Baptist. Any claim upon Jesus on the part of his followers is ruled out by Jesus' response to the request of his mother and brothers. If Jesus did not even acquiesce to the desires of John the Baptist or his mother, we know his attitude toward all other such claims. Desire for greatness is excluded by Jesus' dismissal of the question of who was the greatest among his disciples. This desire is now annihilated. The disciple's need to extend complete forgiveness is illustrated by Jesus' threat of imprisonment when Peter was prepared to forgive only seven times. Judaism's inability to guard people from evil is demonstrated by Jesus' exposure of the sins of the rabbinate and Pharisaism; thus all of Judaism stands condemned.

25. In Matthew, on the other hand, one looks in vain for influences of Greek biography.

26. In this, too, the parallelism between gospel tradition and the synagogue is preserved, since the latter, likewise, preserved such works of the fathers that represented a boundary marker in one way or another which the pious person may approach, be it upward in the greatness of his achievements, be it downward in the lessening of the commandment.

This procedure entails the frequent use of contrast as the means of illumining the thrust of Jesus' word and work. The Sermon on the Mount juxtaposes the beatitude with the announcement of the disciples' suffering, and the announcement of the disciples' suffering with their glorious calling on behalf of the world. Jesus hallows the entire Law while at the same time freeing the disciples from everything God had commanded the ancients, subjecting his followers solely to his own will. The disciple's righteousness consists in love, yet his worship is performed in secret. He has no treasure but is also free from concern; he is prepared to perform any service in his dealings with all and yet walks the narrow way as part of a tiny flock. Matthew presents the Sermon of the Mount in stark contrast with his narration of Jesus' signs. While the Sermon spells out Jesus' demands, Jesus' signs portray what Jesus grants. Jesus' aim in the Sermon was the disciples' complete obedience; his signs call for complete faith. Again, Matthew inserts statements pertaining to the renunciation required by Jesus in his account of the help granted by Jesus. Jesus, the one who gives everything, does not possess anything and frees the disciples from everything (8:19–22). The condemnation of Capernaum is linked with Jesus' prayer of thanksgiving for the illumination of little children and his call to all who are heavy-laden. Jesus, having just freed his disciples from purity regulations, proceeds to affirms Israel's privilege to the pleading Gentile woman. The miraculous feeding is followed by the rejection of demands for a sign, and Peter's appointment to the apostolic office by a reminder of his call to martyrdom. The unlimited promise for the believer, which grants him power over all things, gives way to instructions regarding the avoidance of giving offense when dealing with Jews. This is accomplished by the disciples' renunciation of privilege and the removal of the notion of greatness among the disciples. Their renunciation of all possessions, in turn, is followed by Jesus' assignment of thrones for them to participate in his work of judgment.

The woman who sacrifices everything for Jesus is placed alongside the disciple who betrays him for money; the Last Supper is followed by the struggle in Gethsemane; Jesus' confession before the priest is contrasted with Peter's denial; Jesus' confession of his regal status before Caiaphas and Pilate yields to Jesus' dying prayer that represents him as God-forsaken; finally, the disciples' call to martyrdom on account of Israel is balanced with the risen Lord's commission to disciple the nations. According to the evangelist, these contrasts do not render Jesus' conduct inscrutable. Matthew rather detects in these events an underlying unity, an expression of Jesus' regal will in perfect grace and righteousness. This will becomes visible to us by the boundaries set by Jesus' word and work: his gifts and his demands, his fellowship with the Jews and his commission for mankind, and his union with God and his share in the human predicament.

Since conventional forms are capable of being transformed into new constructs, the method used by the rabbinate to form and recite tradition may well have exerted influence on the mode of instruction practiced by the Christian community. But similarity of purpose accounts even more for the convergence of traditions than imitation. Just as Jewish instruction sought to regulate the conduct of later generations by way of remembrance of the fathers, the Gospel record served the purpose of enabling the community to obey Jesus. That the imitation of Jewish methods of instruction thereby played merely a subordinate role is confirmed by the fact that similarities are limited solely to the *form* of certain accounts. However, not a single pericope in Matthew or elsewhere in the Gospels has a halakhic purpose or is given to the community for the purpose of encouraging it to imitate Jesus.[27] The interpretation of Matthew as a Book of Law or a textbook of ethics, according to which the evangelist sought to show the community how to act in every circumstance by a collection of examples gathered from Jesus' life, completely misunderstands the Gospel. All aspects of Matthew's account are controlled by the idea that Jesus, as Lord, stood *above* Christendom rather than *beside* it, so that it could learn through his word and work what to expect from him and how they were to obey him.

Matthew's Gospel does not function as a Book of Law; this reveals that it was not composed in opposition to that development of the church which arose through the apostles' work. Since the fruits of apostolic labor were not injected into Matthew's portrayal of Jesus, the messages of the Lord and the apostles were placed side by side. The church received instruction from a dual message: that of Jesus and that of his disciples. Thus the foundation had been laid for the division of the canon into the Gospel and the teaching of the apostles. In addition to this, the community was keenly aware that it said and did many things that had not yet had room in Jesus' own history. This included the collection of Jesus' words, since Jesus did not pass on a holy book to the disciples. The Christ of the Gospels does not proclaim his own regal name: it is apostolic preaching that proclaims Jesus as the Christ. Jesus neither gathers a community nor leaves a blueprint for organizing the church. Rather, the apostles establish and regulate the church. Jesus does not embark on a mission to the Gentiles: the apostles do. Since the experiential and intellectual possession of the early church was not injected back into the portrayal of Jesus, Matthew did not purge his reminiscences of Jesus of the local coloring lent to all of Jesus' words and deeds by his particular circumstances.

Historical analogies may suggest the theory that the collection of reminiscences of Jesus was influenced in part by a desire to keep the community close to Jesus' own teaching and the original state of discipleship. In this case, however, the Gospel would inevitably have taken shape as a Book of Law commanding the church's obedience. But Matthew clearly tells us why such motivation could not exert any influence on the Gospel record. For he closes his account with the risen Lord's promise to the disciples assuring them of his presence and guidance at the time he issued the commission to disciple the nations. Thus the remembrances of Jesus are tied to the anticipation of a new era taken up with the disciples' work, and the preservation of material about Jesus serves the purpose of establishing rather than obstructing their new ministry.

The evangelist's own contribution to his account consists of the selection and arrangement of Jesus' sayings and works. The preeminence given to Matthew's

---

27. The only thing resulting in an imitation of an act of Jesus by the disciples would be the Last Supper, if Paul had not told us that the repetition of the Last Supper is based on Jesus' command.

Gospel among the books of the New Testament is a result of his compilation of Jesus' discourses. The man who arranged and connected Jesus' sayings in such a way belongs, together with Paul and John, to the great religious teachers of mankind. Particularly in the case of Matthew's discourses, parallel accounts reveal that both their chronological order (by which they constitute a carefully considered course of instruction) and the framing and arrangement of individual sayings represent not merely the possession of the entire community but also the work and judgment of the first evangelist. The narrative portion of his account, on the other hand, hardly permits a definitive verdict regarding the extent to which it owes its form to Matthew's own work.[28]

It would have occurred to no one in the early church to limit the portrayal of Jesus merely to his words.[29] Only Greek thought would have led to the separation of words and works due to its failure to understand the effective power of history. For this mind-set, the concept of the Christ was no longer intelligible. It therefore sought abiding value in Jesus' word as the only thing able to provide a link between Jesus and the community. Because Matthew proclaims Jesus as the Christ, he sees in him the Lord, not merely the teacher, the Creator of the eternal community, not the propounder of the eternal theory. He seeks from him neither psychology nor morality nor physiology, nor the description of heaven and the divine nature, but rather God's actualization through the granting of life on account of redemption from evil. Jesus' works bear witness to God, so that Jesus becomes the Creator of a new humanity brought into being by God's grace. Matthew thus preserves Jesus' understanding of God's revelation to man and concurs both with the claims of Scripture and with patterns of Palestinian Jewish piety. Precisely for this reason, however, the evangelist's work challenged his capacity to understand to the highest degree, because he did not merely seek to narrate what occurred in the past but to portray Jesus in order to elicit faith in him and to issue to his audience an effective call to God. The history of Jesus is related to the reader so that he may realize God's attitude toward him and receive from that history instruction regarding his share in God's grace. The evangelist does not report mere events but deeds that have their basis in the will and are thus laden with understanding. He recounts deeds of the Christ, which originated in God's will and therefore embody the highest teaching. Thus narrative became at the same time mental and didactic labor of the highest order.

### b) The Judgment of Israel

Matthew's selection of material reveals that he considered providing a clear answer to the question of Israel's destiny an important part of the evangelist's

---

28. As is well known, the question of literary history regarding the priority of Matthew or Mark in the case of the pericopes common to them is disputed. Both documents are preceded by the oral teaching carried out in the churches. It is this teaching that provided both Matthew and Mark with their material.

29. Matthew's text does not permit a separation between discourse and narrative material. The significance of the Papias fragment, which occasioned such attempts, can no longer be determined. The collections of sayings preserved from Egypt do not belong to the early period. The numerous accounts of Jesus known by Luke (cf. 1:1) were not sayings collections.

calling. He related Jesus as the conclusion of Israel's history. His message makes clear that Jesus called Israel to God but that his call had been issued in vain. Israel thus had incurred God's judgment, but God's rule was realized nonetheless. All of Jesus' discourses selected by Matthew serve the purpose of developing this insight: the Sermon on the Mount, because it is based on the rejection of Jewish piety; the commissioning discourse, because it portrays Israel's opposition to his messengers; the discourse regarding God's kingdom, because it shows how Israel could have had access to it and why it was excluded from it. Thus it happened that Jesus demanded and received the confession of his regal status only from his disciples. Thereafter Jesus showed to his disciples the governing norms of their community. He did so, not by placing them in a universal framework that features them as the leaders of humanity and the creators of the universal church, but by directing their entire energy toward separating themselves from the sin of Judaism and serving the weak and lost in obedience to Jesus. The final discourse condemns Israel's pious ones and turns the disciples' attention beyond Jerusalem's judgment to Christ's return. The conclusion of Matthew's Gospel consists in the disciples' sending to all nations by the risen Lord, whereby the national question receives its definitive answer.[30]

We find here a clear presentation of Jesus for Jewish Christians. Following Jesus is considered to be impossible, unless clarity is achieved concerning God's verdict regarding Israel's destiny and Jesus' attitude toward the nation: the nation's place in God's plan, its Law and Temple, the rabbinate and Pharisaism. Matthew answers the national question unambiguously: the truth and validity of God's revelation to Israel are solemnly and emphatically confirmed. Jesus is one with the entire Law and considers its fulfillment his calling. For that reason the rabbinate's calling to teach and judge is not disputed; it occupies the seat of Moses. Israel's fall is not caused by deficient revelation or insufficient instruction but by its transgression of the divine commandment. For Israel's justification is not a matter of her possession of the authentic sanctuaries or of the true Word of God. Her conduct is rejected as sinful, and the community is exhorted to repent. Since this admonition is issued in vain by both Jesus and his messengers, Israel falls on account of her own guilt. Her time has come to an end, and Jesus' messengers, like Jesus, must announce her imminent demise. The kingdom is inherited by Jesus' community.

The new community gathered in the present by Jesus' messengers is sharply distinguished from the old. It occupies a place totally separate from the former community and remains in comparison with them a small flock that is trampled upon and destroyed by them. But this separation does not result from a polemic against the old community's national constitution. Rather, the ethical founda-

---

30. Even some of Matthew's unique historical material relates to the national question: the genealogy and Joseph's marriage to Mary assigns to Jesus a place in the house of David; since Jerusalem is the city of Herod, Israel's struggle against the Child begins immediately at his birth; the saying regarding the temple tax orders the relationship of the new community to the old; the events at Judas's death, the Jews' declaration that they assume full responsibility for Jesus' death, and the proclamation of the resurrection by the guards at the tomb to the high priests all show how the Jews opposed the Christ.

tion of its religious devotion is honored together with its entire religious heritage as a divine institution. The contrast between "national religion" and "individual piety" plays no role in Matthew.[31] Christians' separation from the old community is brought about solely by Jesus' word of repentance, solely by the condemnation of Judaism's sin. The old community does not die because it is a nation, but because it does not obey God.

### c) Ethics

For Christian devotion, Israel's judgment results in an emphasis on repentance. This consists in Jesus' disciples judging their evil and doing the good will of God as Jesus had presented it to them. In his preservation of numerous sayings of Jesus and his arrangement of these in form of cohesive discourses, Matthew was led not solely by historical interests or literary considerations, but by his intention to reveal that will which determined his religious commitment. For Jesus' community is distinguished from the community he rejected by its obedience to the call to repentance. If it too gave room to sin, its very basis of existence would be destroyed. There is no doubt that Christians are subject to the same norms that apply to Israel.[32] For if partiality were involved in the judgment of Judaism's sin, the call to repentance issued to Israel would lose all power, Jesus' purity would be compromised, and faith in him would wither. Since the community separates itself from Israel because it does not want to share in her sin, its duty consists of doing God's will in obedience to Christ.

This goal is already continually revealed by the form of individual pericopes, since Matthew never speaks of the gift of the Christ resulting in his community's wealth and privilege without immediately adding a warning against the abuse of God's grace. The calling of the tax-collector, a testimony to Jesus' complete forgiveness, introduces one of the harshest words of indictment by which Jesus refused to call the righteous. The transferal of their high calling to the disciples is immediately followed by a warning that impresses on them the obligation which that call entails: they are the salt of the earth, but they know what happens to salt that has lost its taste. The first portrayal of Jesus' future glory does not employ the motif that his disciples will receive thrones beside him but rather condemns those who achieve great things in his name but exempt themselves from God's Law. Jesus' intercession securing God's favor for his own is not discussed apart from his warning that he would deny them if they denied him. God's Spirit, who would be the disciples' advocate, is first mentioned at

---

31. Since the view is widespread that the religious progress sparked by Jesus or at least by Paul consists in the opposition to national religion, Matthew's pronouncements honoring Israel's national constitution as given to it by God appear to be a polemic against Jesus or at least against Paul (Matt. 5:17–19; 10:5–6; 19:28; 23:2–3). But this perspective is historically unusable. No one thought during the early period of opposing national religion merely because it was national religion.

32. What Matthew makes Jesus' final word to the disciples is very telling in this regard: he concludes with those who hope for the Christ in vain and who receive his offer in vain. The parable of the tares amidst the wheat, likewise, is typical for Matthew: the thought that membership in the church infallibly guarantees salvation is emphatically rejected.

the time when they are strengthened for martyrdom and protected against that discouragement and unfaithfulness to which persecution may lure them. The Spirit's presence in Jesus is mentioned because the blasphemy of the Spirit incurs eternal damnation. The portrayal of the divine dominion revealing God's perfect grace is cast simultaneously as an act of judgment, dealing substantially with God's execution of justice. The prediction of the cross does not lead Matthew to choose words that praise its liberating and reconciling effect; the announcement is rather accompanied by the disciples' call to martyrdom. The statement regarding the value of the cross serves the purpose of countering the disciples' own craving for power in human terms. Peter is shown the greatness of forgiving grace when he must realize the sinfulness of his refusal to grant complete forgiveness to another person. The account concludes with the solemn threat that Peter would lose God's grace if he refused to forgive. The depiction of the wedding feast prepared by the king for his son ends with the rejection of the one who came without festive garments.[33] This frequent pattern is also borne out by the balance between the solemn passion narrative and the no less sober Easter account, in which the disciples' appointment to their apostolic office takes center stage.

Matthew's selection of major discourses serves the same purpose. Both the Sermon on the Mount and the commissioning discourse seek to sensitize the disciples regarding their own proclivity to sin and to inoculate them against temptation. The discourse on the kingdom of God likewise aims at the removal of potential stumbling blocks for the disciples. The regulations given to the community of believers occupy Matthew exclusively with respect to his ethical agenda, and the word of farewell does not portray God's glory and Christ's regal ministry but provides the disciple with weapons for overcoming temptation while separated from Jesus. Parables also show him how he can use hope for his advantage or to his detriment. Consequently, the final pericope makes baptism and obedience to Jesus' commandment the hallmark of the new community, which thus consists of those who have received forgiveness from the Christ and therefore do his will.

The repentance that Matthew urges is not painful but joyful; for it removes evil and makes room for love. Matthew deliberately alternates images of work and celebration, which are both applicable to the community. What moves it to total commitment to God's lordship is its rejoicing at the discovery of the great treasure. It does not sacrifice its life reluctantly but willingly, because such sacrifice leads to the gaining of life. Possessions are given away because the community thus becomes rich toward God. This is how the disciples attain to participation in God's kingdom. Christ's work of judgment rejecting Israel and expelling all evil from his community is surpassed by his positive aim: God's glorious rule establishing the perfect community.

The hallmark of the devotion Matthew advocates, however, is seen in the priority he gives to negative pronouncements focusing on the disciples' need to

---

33. See Matt. 9:13; 5:13; 7:21; 10:32–33, 19; 12:28, 32; chap. 13; 16:24–27; 20:28; 18:23–35; 22:11–14.

renounce all worldly goods. It can be stated more clearly that anger, hate, and the unwillingness to forgive must disappear than how we should show love toward one another. Love's perfection is expressed by its being extended to the enemy. This assures the complete removal of hate; its positive, constructive contribution, however, is thereby not yet shown. It is portrayed more clearly how we are serving Money than how we must serve God. Rather than being anxious we are to believe: but only the negative pronouncement showing how we can avoid unnecessary worry receives extensive formulation. Similarly, the commissioning discourse receives its substance in terms of what the disciple is not to do: he should neither pursue gain nor defend his life nor be afraid of men. The parables emphasize the elements corrupting the seed rather than the great harvest. They focus on the presence of evil men in the community rather than on the birth of sons for the kingdom. They stress the need for complete renunciation for the acquisition of the great treasure rather than the treasure's value itself. It is clearer that the net also catches what is thrown away than that all are now offered the kingdom.

The discourses addressed to the disciples reveal the same orientation. Attention is directed toward the need for alertness, not toward the value of help we grant one to another. Emphasis is placed on the loss of forgiveness by a person's unwillingness to forgive rather than on the greatness of the grace given to us. In the final parables given to the disciples, the evangelist's prophetic vision assumes astonishing lucidity concerning that which threatens the church. The bearer of the religious office who craves power and gratification, the person enamored with eschatology who contemplates his view of the future with joyful excitement and thereby turns into a fool, the one who possesses Jesus' word but thinks only of himself and renders his wealth unproductive with regard to others: these are figures we encounter frequently in the church in later years, people under whose corrupting influence Christendom must suffer greatly. But even here the images of the foolish virgins and the unmerciful servant are depicted with greater vigor than the alert and faithful. Matthew views the church's major work to be the resistance against our reprobate will, the recognition and accomplishment of what is good by means of the eradication of evil.

This conception of ethics manifests itself in Matthew's practice of juxtaposing conversion, which rejects selfish conduct and decides for love, and faith, giving unconditional promise to the latter. The positive content of the call to repentance can be summed up in one statement: following Jesus, discipleship, which preserves closeness with him. What the person ready to serve Jesus must do will become clear in his respective circumstances, assigned to him by Jesus' rule over all things. Therefore Matthew entertains no doubt regarding the possibility of fulfilling the commandment given by Jesus, although his opposition to natural ways of thinking and people's passions is in no way diminished or concealed. Whether it is possible to love one's enemies, exercise complete patience, and live without anxiety or possessions, and whether it is possible for the community to be expelled from national life without perishing, these are questions Matthew does not entertain. Jesus commanded these things, the one who opens the kingdom of heaven to everyone who believes in him. And Jesus does not issue an empty summons but adds to his commandment the power of God. The disciple will not fail if he follows Jesus.

Therefore there is no limit to the help granted to faith. Matthew has gathered abundant examples of what faith is and how Jesus responded to it with omnipotent help. No other topic is developed to the same extent. Neither the origin of repentance nor its mastery of evil nor the nature of how love does its work is spelled out in as much detail. The community must know above all how to approach Jesus in faith and how he responds to such faith.[34] Matthew's field of vision does not extend to the possibility that the use of one's entire will for the sake of obedience toward Jesus' commandment could disturb or hinder faith. Likewise, he does not take up the problem that obedience may become a substitute for faith, or that the Sermon on the Mount could be made into a substitute for the gospel. How could man seek within himself what the Christ alone is able to accomplish? And how will he find and retain confidence in Jesus' help when he denies to Jesus obedience?

This religious devotion stands in noticeable harmony with Matthew's own experience.[35] The first part of his life concludes with his rejection of his life up to that point as a time of selfish godlessness. He arrived at this verdict through his encounter with Jesus, who by his call granted him his all-forgiving grace. This issues directly in a type of Christianity whose primary intention is directed toward the rejection of evil. Repentance cannot be faithless nor polluted by the idea of merit or the doubt of God's grace. For he was granted conversion by Jesus' extension of fellowship and apostleship. Such a conversion experience surely leads to a lasting opposition toward that kind of evil that had caused guilt prior to conversion: harshness, lust, greed for money, misdirected love that craves not the things of God but the things of man. This is now replaced by love toward God that does good to one's neighbor. Thus the doer of God's will has been born. It was not Matthew alone who had experienced this with Jesus. Rather, Jesus had shown the resolute seriousness of conversion and the guilt-removing power of his grace to the entire nation of Israel. Thus Matthew had been set free from Pharisaism and all authorities of the old community. They had not helped him, nor were they able to do so. They merely despised and judged him and kept him in his sin. Solely Jesus had opened to him the way to God, and his unbroken faith had been placed in the Christ alone. This, however, did not result in a rejection of Scripture or of Israel's religion. For his sin was condemned by Scripture, and his conversion was simultaneously a declaration of allegiance to Scripture. Jesus had once again made him an Israelite, but

---

34. Thereby Matthew confirms the claim of 1 Peter that it was not Paul, but the Palestinian community, which first esteemed faith as the component of its devotion that procured for it the gift of Jesus.

35. Of course, the objection may be raised against this view that it transcends the boundaries of observation. On the other hand, I cannot consider the thesis to be a vain theory that different types of devotion always have historical grounding. If this principle is valid, the question becomes unavoidable, at least in the case of the New Testament documents, how the history ascribed to its authors relates to the type of devotion they advocate.

in such a way that he now belonged to that Israel which has Christ as its Lord and recognizes no other Israel.

### d) The Christ

Where national and ethical questions come to the fore, the concept of Christ has supreme significance in Matthew's consideration of Jesus. How he is related to the community, what he requires from it and makes of it, are central topics. In this the concept of lordship remains completely safeguarded from any irreligious, selfish distortion. Matthew demonstrates the rootedness of Jesus' rule in God not through an abstract depiction of God, nor by a "Christology" made up of Jesus' words describing his dealings with God; he rather narrates Jesus' deeds. Because Matthew proclaims Jesus as the one who receives his rule from God rather than acquiring it himself, he begins with the birth narrative: Jesus is conceived by the miraculous act of God.[36] And since Jesus receives his authority because God exercises it through him, Matthew places him right from the start beside two powerful figures: Herod, who ruled Jerusalem while passionately craving power for himself, defending it even against God; and the wise men, who subdue others by their mysterious knowledge and magical powers. The king's plans fail, and the wise men kneel before the child created by God. The miracle story is thus an essential part of Matthew's message. For Jesus' regal commission is revealed by the power given to him by God. Jesus' universal promise to all who act in love and long for God, attested together with Jesus' special promise to his disciples, stems from the same basic idea. For Jesus does not preach himself but works exclusively for the purpose of seeing God's will accomplished. Matthew lends no credence to the idea that Jesus' kingdom was thereby concealed. By extending God's grace to all those who are poor in Spirit and merciful, Jesus makes clear that he does not represent his own interests but rather seeks to reveal the greatness and grace of God. For this reason he requires no one but his disciples to honor him as king, his disciples to whom the Father chooses to reveal his name. He bears his cross in obedience to God, who makes him the Christ by raising him up and promising his return. Jesus' ruling authority derives from his dependence on God, a function of his divine sonship. Matthew considers this proof for the legitimacy of Jesus' reign. Thus the agreement of Matthew's account with Scripture, portrayed in part by the evangelist's own quotations, in part by adaptation of his narrative to scriptural language, takes

---

36. This is the foundation for Matthew's religious material in chap. 1. There is no trace of docetism, rejection of marriage, a tendency toward imaginative poetry, or theologizing composition. The suspicion that the statement regarding Jesus' miraculous conception represents a particular theological creation of Matthew which only he popularizes in the community is excluded by the fact that Mary's experience is not related at all; it is determined only why Joseph nevertheless entered into marriage with her. Luke's report likewise opposes this suspicion. Whoever seeks and believes to have found the key to the Christ's secret exposes it with a detailed substantiation of its necessity and appropriateness. A more plausible theory is that Matthew wanted to make room for an apologetic concern, seeking to show why Jesus, while having been miraculously conceived, was nevertheless Joseph's son and Mary was Joseph's wife. In that case, however, the former statement likewise existed in the community and is not only spread by Matthew but merely protected by him against possible objections.

on religious significance. For this convergence makes God's sovereignty in the history of Jesus palpably visible.[37]

Therefore Jesus' poverty and humility become a major part of Matthew's presentation, not merely because the evangelist seeks to accentuate the contrast between Jesus' regal aim and the outcome of his earthly ministry, but because Jesus' lowliness magnifies that it is God who leads the Christ. Matthew deliberately places the statements regarding the completeness and miraculous nature of Jesus' divine sonship in the midst of a reference to his will to exercise his reign in hiddenness and ministry to the weak (11:25–30). The one conceived by the Spirit must flee from Herod and is brought to Nazareth, and the one revealed by the Spirit is subsequently tempted by Satan. Matthew does not record one word of John the Baptist's praise of Jesus' commission. He rather shows us the offense Jesus' path of suffering created for John, just as he also tells us only after John's arrest that Jesus withdrew to Galilee without noting events prior to John's arrest. In Matthew, Jesus sets foot in Jerusalem solely for the sake of the crucifixion. Of Jesus' final hours, Matthew records only the prayer expressing Jesus' forsakenness. No hint at Jesus' glory, be it by word or deed, detracts from the solemnity of Jesus' suffering. Matthew's Easter account is characterized by the same restraint. Just as Jesus had called people to conversion while based in Galilee rather than gathering them in Jerusalem, the Risen One now leads his disciples back into hiddenness from Jerusalem to Galilee. Matthew did not believe that this would render knowledge of Jesus more difficult; he rather considered it an important incentive to faith.

Thus God's hand is revealed in Jesus' history, and God's greatness manifests itself in Jesus' lordship. Matthew's passion narrative therefore juxtaposes the suffering Christ with the visible demonstration of God's providence which proves the legitimacy of Jesus' kingship even when Jesus is forsaken by God through all the circumstances of the crucifixion. Likewise, the heavenly powers do not intervene in the Christmas story for the purpose of preventing Jesus' hiddenness: they rather promote it, albeit in such a way that he accomplishes the regal work even in his lowliness. The same train of thought is also revealed in the selection of Scripture citations, because Matthew appeals to Scripture whenever he wants to make visible Jesus' poverty and humiliation.[38] Since Jesus is and does what Scripture predicts on account of these traits, they no longer constitute an offense but rather become the reason for faith. In the same manner, Matthew is attracted by Jesus' selflessness: "Come to me, for I am humble." Neither the beatitudes of the Sermon on the Mount nor Jesus' answer to John

---

37. Chap. 2 has Moses' birth narrative in view, probably in the form found in Josephus, whereby Moses' birth is prophesied to Pharaoh, so that he wants to deal with Moses directly through his bloody command. In the story of the cross, words of Scripture and narration are continually interwoven (cf. 26:15; 27:9, 34–35, 39, 43; cf. also 21:7). A parallel to the proof from Scripture is the conviction that God's providential will was revealed in all circumstances of the crucifixion.

38. Escape to Egypt: 2:15; slaying of infants: 2:17; home in Nazareth: 2:23; work in Capernaum: 4:14; mercy with those who suffer: 8:17; Jesus' hiddenness: 12:17; discourse in parables: 13:35; betrayal by Judas: 27:9.

the Baptist (describing him exclusively in terms of helping those in need) nor Jesus' statement that God alone is good (rendering everyone accountable to God's commandments) cause Matthew to doubt Jesus' commission. He rather recognizes Jesus' greatness in his humility and the truth of his divine sonship in his selflessness. For these attributes reveal that Jesus wants nothing but God's will, honors nothing but obedience to God's commandment, and includes all of those in his community who obey God.

The legitimacy of Jesus' kingship is revealed by his work: his creation of the community obedient to God. This is why Matthew gives us his Christology by describing the disciple both in terms of his religious authority to loose and bind and in his lofty ethical position by which he is able to love and serve. The greatness of the position assigned to him by Jesus is expressed powerfully by Matthew's emphasis on the disciples' great distance from Jesus and their inability to free themselves from their selfish thoughts. This includes the stories featuring Peter that are peculiar to Matthew, where Peter is unable to believe or forgive, asks for reward, and is afraid of the Jews.[39]

Regarding Jesus' own relationship to God, Matthew contents himself with referring to God's Spirit, by whom Jesus receives the power to carry out God's will. Jesus is conceived by the Spirit, revealed by the Spirit's descent upon him, and empowered by the Spirit to do his work. This is why baptism is administered in Jesus' name as well as in the name of the Spirit; for Jesus exercises his authority by giving his Spirit to his community (1:18; 3:16; 12:28; 28:19). These statements are not unique to Matthew in the sense that they originated with him rather than having been received from Jesus. Characteristically, Matthew considers Jesus' anointing with God's Spirit a sufficient explanation for his sonship and lordship. He sees Jesus' uniqueness in the completeness with which he possessed the Spirit's power that had conceived him body and soul. Since he lived completely by the Spirit, he stood alongside the Father and the Spirit: on the same level as God rather than man.

This kind of Christology results in a community characterized by selfless humility. Matthew cannot conceive of a boastful, prideful Christendom or of a self-glorifying apostolate. Otherwise, the condemnation of Israel's arrogance would need to be revoked, and there would no longer be any basis for separating the community from the "righteous" members of the synagogue. This characterizes the evangelist's entire method. He foregoes any rhetoric, apologetic skill, or melodramatic efforts to influence his reader. The calmness of Matthew's entire account is striking. The evangelist predicts death for his own people whom he loves as well as the destruction of the Temple. He sees in Pharisaism the opponent he must discredit and in Jesus the Lord before whom everything must bow. But the account's calmness is never interrupted by strong emotion. It results from the priority of Matthew's ethical agenda over all other concerns and his firm assurance of faith. Matthew desires only one thing: that the community

---

39. There is no trace of hierarchical ideas in these narratives. The exaltation of the greatness of the apostolic work (cf. 16:18) is completely protected from human craving for power by the immediately following word to the "Satan" who eludes the service of God.

conduct itself in righteousness. Since what matters is its work, it needs sobriety in carrying it out. Its work has its basis in faith, which grants it carefreeness even in its gravest concerns. God himself will establish his rule, and the way he brings it about will demonstrate his perfect grace and righteousness.

Thus there is no need for the Christian community to pride itself on or parade its newfound faith in Jesus. At the same time, it must not deny its Lord (6:1–18). Matthew's trinitarian concept of God was from the start taken as evidence that he considered it to be the essential feature of Christianity and the reason for separation from the synagogue, so that the two religions and communities were divided by their differing concepts of God. But if Matthew wanted to separate Christianity from Judaism because it had a fuller developed understanding of God and used the trinitarian formula, his entire account of Jesus is rendered unintelligible. To be sure, its knowledge of God as a Trinity and its ability to address him thus are Christ's gift to the community. This is what invests its baptism with salvific power and provides the basis for its faith, just as Israel's sin and her fall consist in her rebellion against the Father, her rejection of the Son, and her contempt for the Spirit. But Christ's will is not already done by a disciple's calling upon God as Trinity; he must obey what Jesus' commandments require of him.

The same consideration shapes Matthew's Christology. Matthew believes that Christ is present in his community. This does not cause him to engage in Christological speculation. He does not attempt to identify individual experiences as the occasion for the manifestation of Christ's presence. His justification lies in doing what he has been commanded to do, not in knowing that Christ is with him or experiencing his presence in a particular way. Matthew thus renders his separation from Judaism both complete and yet free from sectarian strife. His separation is complete, for it possesses the unyielding sincerity of ethical necessity and therefore provides the rationale for the disciples' readiness for martyrdom. Whoever denies Jesus commits apostasy against God. At the same time, separation from Judaism remains free of sectarian pride. For it is not based on Christendom's special knowledge or giftedness but on the will of God, binding on all and accomplished by love, so that any form of religious arrogance is excluded.

Christ's poverty and suffering, paralleled by the humility and suffering of his community, can give rise only to a faith that requires, possesses, and cultivates hope. The glorious picture of God's promise is therefore at the heart of Matthew's Christology.

## 2. Matthew's Relationship with the Gentile Church

What unites Matthew and Peter is the fact that for both the ethical aim determines their entire framework of thought. For the hallmark of Christendom is right action; on it depends their share in salvation. The major commonality in Matthew's and Peter's calling the community to unlimited love and patience can be traced to their common dependence on Jesus' word. But they also remain aligned with one another in the way in which they describe Jesus' communion with God. To express this, the term "Spirit" is sufficient for both, and both view this communion as so complete that they formulate a trinitarian concept of God, to the effect that Jesus stands to the Father in the same kind of relationship as the Spirit (cf. Matt. 28:19 and 1 Pet. 1:9).

The commonality of Matthew and Peter helps explain why Matthew's Gospel, which is in its form and content entirely a product of Palestinian Christianity, was also received by the Gentile church. On its part, it observed that Paul and the men who gathered her did not embark on any religious missions of their own but were led by Jesus' history and word. Matthew himself rooted the universality of the gospel in the fact that, by recording Jesus' word to Israel, he provided Gentile Christians with everything they needed for the establishment of their own faith. It will not do to argue along negative lines that Matthew merely left room for the emergence of Gentile Christianity. Church arises from community, not from a mere tolerance that leaves the other person alone. The Gentile church's use of Matthew's Gospel for the purpose of reinforcing this fellowship is not adequately accounted for by Matthew's mere tolerance, but only by the fact that Matthew's Gospel contained convictions indispensable for their Christian existence.

Paul helped Gentile Christians understand that the meaning of Jesus' commission for national Israel represented a major concern for Jewish Christians. Paul himself had a religious interest in the future destiny of Israel and required even born Greeks to respect the call issued to Israel and to acknowledge the connection between Christ's commission and Israel's destiny. Thus Matthew was not separated from Gentile communities by his portrayal of Jesus' ministry as the conclusion of Israel's history. Still, his presentation made a difference in the church's proclamation: the subject was the purpose of Jesus' coming for mankind rather than merely for the Jews. By describing Jesus' relationship to Israel in terms of Jesus' rejection of Israel's sin and his establishment of a new community made up of those who followed him in faith, Matthew provided Gentile communities with justification for their faith. They proved to be converted to Christ only by forsaking everything the Lord had judged and by doing what he had required. If they obeyed Paul, Gentile Christians were ready to do this earnestly. They saw the aim of Jesus' sending to be the liberation of mankind from evil by their reconciliation to God, through which man comes to obey God and do his will. Still, Matthew subsumed all theological and ecclesiastical concerns occupying Gentile communities under one purpose: that the transformed will issue in good works of obedience to Jesus' commandment. Nevertheless, the Gentile church did not consider Matthew's message to be a threat to its faith, since Matthew placed the work of God above the community's obligation and did not deem an unbelieving will capable of repentance and love. For the Gentile church was for its part prepared to use God's insight and provision for the purpose of accomplishing good works in Christ.

The attempt to unite essentially incompatible elements in one religious system is often called syncretism. It is sometimes argued that not merely Gentile communities but also Matthew yielded to syncretism and exposed his portrait of Jesus to contradictions he set side by side without attempting to reconcile them. Matthew's Gospel, it is argued, shows Jesus obeying the Law, refusing to obliterate even the most minute detail of Scripture, fulfilling it perfectly, while nevertheless exempting himself and the disciples from the Mosaic laws pertaining to worship and everyday life. Also, it is said that Jesus retained the notion of Israel's privilege to the extent that he limited the apostle's work entirely to Israel. Still, Matthew's account ends with the Risen One's commission to disciple all nations.[40] Our assessment of this issue depends initially on how we conceive of Jesus' own convictions. If both allegiance to Israel and to Scripture as the transcending principles of liberty characterized Jesus, being founded in an integrated way on his filial consciousness, these principles shaped his disciples' attitudes as well. But even if we limit our discussion to Palestinian Christendom, Matthew's statements cause no difficulty. His Gospel could not do without either of the two following convictions: that Jesus found himself nowhere and never in conflict with the Law; and that his legacy for the new community surpassed the state of the old community as his new, free, and perfect gift. Christendom's separation from Israel was justified only when even Pharisaic righteousness fell short, not merely when Pharisaic sin was judged, which was recognized as sin even by the Pharisee himself. Whoever labels Matthew Jewish because he argues that Christendom did not separate from the rabbinate because of its false teaching commits a severe historical misjudgment. To the contrary, it would never have come to the church's separation from the synagogue, if the reason for this separation had been seen in the realm of doctrine and if both communities had compared each other from the vantage point of which of them possessed the more perfect orthodoxy. This might have resulted in a theological dispute exercising people for a while, but never in a church which endured the great pressure exerted upon it by her separation from the nation of Israel and had the strength of sustaining the Gentile mission. The Palestinian Christian community attained its independence, not by attacking the rabbis as theologians, but by knowing itself to be separated from them by an absolute contrast separating sin from righteousness and man's righteousness from the righteousness of God.

It was no less important for the state of the Palestinian community that it held unwaveringly to the notion of Israel's election, honoring it with undying faithfulness. Matthew showed this both by Jesus' cross and by the commissioning of his messengers. The evangelist's depiction of Christ as the Judge and Lord of the nations was equally indispensable for the Palestinian community. This also has important implications for the commission and work of his messengers, since without this universal scope Jesus' regal aim would have been compromised. Also, God's kingdom would not have been revealed and the fulfillment of the promise would not yet have occurred, because the Christ's judgment marked the end of the old community. No one in Jerusalem believed that God's revelation ended with Israel's demise, and certainly no one believed that this represented the success of the Christ's commission. There the indispensable prerequisite for faith was the formation of God's community, and not merely despite or through Israel's fall but in a form that reflected the glory of God.

---

40. Cf. 5:17–20 and 23:2–3 with 12:1–13; 15:1–20; 17:24–27; 19:8. Cf. further 10:5 and 15:24 with 28:19.

It is therefore wrong to derive Matthew's statements merely from the consideration of Pauline communities, as if Matthew fused incompatible aims that divided the church. What these portrayals call "Matthean inconsistencies" are rooted in the very religious core of early Christianity. Jesus' new community made its appearance as the true Israel but separated itself from those who did not acknowledge Jesus as the Christ. Whoever yields either of these two elements denies that an early Christian community existed, and that an apostolic office founded on Jesus' regal claim had come into being.

## C. The Purification of Jewish Devotion by James

### 1. The Tradition Received from Jesus

#### a) Statements Regarding God

If we understand "repentance" as resistance of evil by active removal of it, James's message is also a message of repentance. For he writes as one who exhorts, one who stands in the struggle against evil. His exhortation, however, is based on the assurance that access to God remains available to Israel; for God is completely good, and he is recognized when it is seen that everything good comes from God. This is why James, like Jesus, condemns Jewish perfectionism. For perfection does not come about by human effort; all that is perfect is God's gift. What God bestows is perfect, undiluted, irrepressible goodness (1:17).

God's goodness is already evident in nature. In James the designation "Father of lights" is parallel to Jesus' characterization of the sun as belonging to God. But the perfect divine gift, encompassing all of God's good gifts to us, is the sonship of God. God is the Father, and he makes a man into the person he wants him to be. This is described as birth from God. James gives particular flavor to this concept by illustrating God's activity with the role of a mother by which the child is completely formed and brought into the world rather than conception. Thus a special relationship with God develops which elevates the sons of God above all created beings. James, like Jesus, calls the turning of God's love toward man "election." Election, like divine sonship, does not pertain to Israel or Christianity as a whole; it relates to individuals. The prior existence of God's love and gift above all human desire is expressed by both concepts, birth and election. The idea of "God's will" takes on decisive significance with regard to God's goodness. God's will is the basis for his giving us life, himself being the author of it (1:18; 2:5).

Therefore the individual can believe God, and faith is characterized as that experience which provides the individual with a share in all of God's gifts. Like Jesus, James represents faith as certainty in contrast to internal division and wavering. Faith makes it possible for God to grant a request, so that prayer receives unlimited promise (1:3, 5–8; 4:8; 5:13–18). But God is not only the one who saves; he is also the one who gives people over to death. Justice is just as much a divine attribute as grace and is the eternal characteristic of God's work. Nevertheless, a guilty person may return to God. God forgives, and this forgiveness manifests itself also in the removal of sickness and the preservation of life. God draws near to all who draw near to him in repentance (4:12; 1:5; 5:15; 4:7–10).

## b) Statements Regarding the Christ

Jesus' relationship with Israel is expressed by his regal name. Because he is the Lord, his disciple is his slave and serves God by belonging to Jesus and serving Jesus. The confidence of those who know him is in him. Thus James's relationship with Jesus can be termed religion. But once again there is no trace of a Christian polytheism. James nowhere places Jesus beside the Creator as a second God or treats him as a substitute for God. James has only one God, and his assurance of God controls his thoughts and actions. Jesus has been given lordship by "the glory": this designation for God deliberately points to God's greatness, at a time when Jesus is portrayed as the legitimate object of the community's faith (1:1; 2:1; 5:7). Jesus' lordship will be manifested at his second coming, which will occur soon. It is the ground of joy, the aim of a genuine hope. But hope works patience. As in Jesus' parables, the harvest becomes the image of the work to be accomplished by the Christ. But help is granted not merely to those who patiently wait for him. Albeit only by way of faint allusion, James also refers to the other motif connected with this goal in Jesus' prophecy: that he would bring the entire world to completion. When he calls the sons of God "the firstfruits of creation," this requires that God's impending harvest be greater than the number of those whose Father God became by his word of truth. Like Paul, James expected that Christ would reveal God's glory in the realm of creation and that it would take effect for all to whom God's creative power had given life (cf. James 1:18 with Rom. 8:19–23).

James sums up what Jesus brings to those who wait by the single concept of "life." But God's gracious, life-giving act is coupled with the execution of justice, because Jesus will act as the judge, not merely in relation to the world, but also with regard to those who wait for him and believe in him. Nevertheless, the anticipation of Jesus remains a *joyful* hope. For when he judges, he intercedes for the merciful and thereby transforms the execution of justice into the revelation of God's mercy. Still, the seriousness of Jesus' warning returns in the pronouncement threatening tongues which ignite great blazes in Gehenna, a place of judgment where fire seizes the tongue (5:7–9; 1:12, 21; 2:12–13; 3:6).

The phrase "God's kingdom" accompanies the messianic idea as a depiction of what is to come. Participation in God's kingdom is the essence of God's promise. This motif is characterized by the same dual reference to the future and the present found in Jesus' thought. For participation in God's rule is already granted in the present. Believers' relationship with Jesus is therefore more than mere hope: it is rather a relationship of faith, by which the community avails itself of God's eternal gift. This is also why hope in Jesus is no apocalyptic theory but rather a rule for one's conduct. It purges any ill-treatment of one's fellowman. In the same way, when a poor man knows himself to be exalted, receiving full honor and love from his brothers in Christ because he is joint heir of God's rule and believes in Christ, or when the rich are charged with the foolish accumulation of treasures in this life while they live in the "last days," practical daily life conduct is ordered by those norms which hope in Jesus confers on the readers. Christ is not far from them even in their present condition: he hears their prayer, taking note when they groan against one another, and saving from guilt and death (2:5, 1; 5:9; 5:3, 15).

Reference is also made to the work of the Spirit. God gives wisdom to the one who asks for it. He illumines him in his inner being, so that wisdom is not merely a human trait but a gift from God. Wisdom is therefore heavenly rather than earthly, spiritual rather than metaphysical, divine rather than demonic. By calling a person's ethical thoughts metaphysical and subordinating them to notions arising from God's work in man which renders a person's entire inner life clean and fruitful, James arrives at the concept of the Spirit.[41] But neither Jesus' omnipresence nor the Spirit's work in man compels James to construe a theory.

The greatness of the divine grace given to man becomes apparent when one considers transcendent threats to man. Satan approaches him; but he flees when a person draws near to God. The demonic present in a human being is not conceived of as merely a pathological disorder, but in terms of rebellion against God. For arrogant wisdom can be demonic, and through dead faith the assurance of God becomes similar to the fearful prospects that make the demons tremble (4:7; 3:15; 2:19).

The means of divine grace is the word with which God's gift is inextricably linked. The word's power is based on the fact that it is the truth. God gives life to man by "the word of truth." Departure from the truth costs a man his life, while return to the truth restores it. The word can be likened both to a seed that has been sown into a man's heart and is at work in that individual and something that is brought to that person by an act of external proclamation, so that man becomes a hearer of the word (1:18, 21; 3:14; 5:19). While James does not elaborate on how man is able to hear God's word, he clearly had Scripture in mind that "does not speak in vain." Still, Jesus did not think of God's word as audible solely through Scripture. For the epistle does not see its task as explicating Scripture's words. Jesus' word, too, is part of the powerful, life-giving word of truth, because James speaks as the servant *of Jesus.* Christ's community bears his name and is in need of his presence, and the power of its prayer is based on Jesus' name. Thus the name that designates Jesus' office remains at the heart of the word that testifies to him (4:5; 2:7; 5:14).

James's readers know God's promise through God's word. But God's word also tells them his Law that needs to be done. James conceives of the Law here primarily in terms of what God requires of us with regard to others. James follows in Jesus' footsteps when using the second tablet of the Decalogue to explain how one transgresses or fulfills the Law (1:25; 2:10–11; 4:11–12).

James's relationship to Scripture thus parallels that of Jesus. James esteems Scripture as the divine word that guides the community in the way it should go while steering clear of the order of worship prescribed for Israel. For James says nothing of Sabbath, purity, the tithe, circumcision, the Temple, or the priest-

---

41. See 1:5; 3:15, 17. The difficult statement of 4:5 apparently refers to the spirit that has indwelt man since creation.

hood (see already 1 Peter). But James's lack of reference to the Old Testament for the purpose of regulating pious conduct does not by itself provide us with a perspective on James's attitude toward the Old Testament. Rather, his designation of the Jews as the "twelve tribes" acknowledges Israel to be God's work that cannot be harmed by the destruction that had fallen on the nation since that time. When James calls those who live outside of Palestine "those who live in the Diaspora," he reveals a preference for Jerusalem as the "mother city," drawing further attention to the fact that he speaks from Jerusalem to those who live in the Diaspora. James compares the community's suffering with the suffering of the prophets and shows believers by the example of Job how God helps those who persevere. Elijah provides an example of how believers must pray. The example of Abraham shows believers what faith does and how it justifies before God. Abraham's name, "friend of God," helps Christians perceive the glory of God's gift, and Rahab's example teaches believers how to help fellow-believers. Scripture makes clear that God's grace extends particularly to those of low esteem, and Scripture gives believers the royal Law of love and condemns partiality. Similar to Jesus, James's use of Scripture is determined by the love commandment (5:10–11, 17; 2:21–25; 4:6; 2:8–9).

### c) The Community's Obligation

The word aims at the creation of doers of God's will. By its work the community readies itself for the Lord's arrival. The good work consists in that which love does. It is offered to God; he gives life to those who love him. But James does not permit a distinction between love rendered to God and love rendered to one's fellow-man and thus a separation between religion and morality. Caring for widows is worship; not merely the work of Abraham, who gave his son to God, but also that of Rahab, who rescued the brethren, shows how justification is obtained. God's promise is for the merciful, the peacemakers, those who bring their brothers back to the truth (1:22, 12, 27; 2:21–25, 13; 3:18; 5:19–20).

Loving God requires a person's entire will, a rejection of all divided loyalties, and a desire of nothing beside God; this is how the perfect work comes about. Regarding the community's worship, by which she reveals her love for God, only prayer is discussed, including blessing and psalm. Oaths, however, are done away with, and there is no mention of Old Testament sacrifice and sacrament nor of baptism and the Lord's Supper. The guilty one approaches God by confessing his sin. But confession, too, remains entirely free from regulation, as was the case with Jesus (4:4; 1:4–5; 4:8; 5:13–15; 3:9; 5:12). The community's gatherings only attain the status of service to God when elders are given the authority and obligation for intercession that overcomes people's guilt and sickness, and when these gatherings become the place where the poor are no longer put to shame and the rich are no longer given preferential treatment in view of the impending righteous judgment of the glorified Lord (5:14; 2:2).

The community is called to a persistent struggle. It defends itself against external persecution; its fate resembles that of the prophets. Nevertheless, it should enter this struggle with joy, since it can overcome temptation (5:10;

1:2). The epistle devotes even greater attention to the struggle arising from within by which the community separates itself from sin. The impulse toward evil proceeds from within man himself, from his own desires, but also from outside, from the world. All are placed in this struggle, those who believe in Jesus as well as Israel, the "righteous" as well as those who strayed from the truth. All violations of love are sin; thus unrighteous anger is rejected. Particularly great is the danger arising from wealth, so that the poor are pronounced blessed on account of their poverty. James does not promise them a change in their condition. Like Jesus, he promises the sick that God will save them, but not the poor that God will make them rich. Precisely because they are poor, their honor and wealth consist in the fact that they have God on their side (1:14–15, 27; 4:4; 1:20, 9–11; 2:1–7; 5:1–6, 14–15).

The epistle gives even more attention to the struggle against arrogance by which piety becomes sin. In this regard, too, it does not distinguish between Christians and pious people among the Jews. The hearer of the word can easily derive false confidence from his hearing of the word; but mere hearing does not save his soul. A teaching office can lead to arrogance, which fails to consider how easy it is to fall by the word. The community possesses wisdom that makes arrogant and therefore stirs up strife, manifesting a tendency to judge one's brother. Even prayer can turn into temptation and lose its effectiveness. The warning against oaths belongs here as well, since the oath violates God's majesty (1:21–25; 3:1–2, 13–16; 4:11, 3; 1:6–7; 5:12). As serious as the call to repentance is, however, the grace God offers to the community is never in doubt. For no one approaches God in vain. As with Jesus, the call to repentance and the offer of the kingdom are inseparable.

## 2. New Material

Although the epistle's content stands in closest relationship with what Matthew and John portray as Jesus' own thought, James's letter also contains new pronouncements. For James, like Peter, did not consider it his task merely to reiterate Jesus' words. By not merely quoting a dominical saying even when his own formulations cohere entirely with those of Jesus but by addressing the community by a word of his own, James brings this word into an effective connection to that which their present circumstances demand of them. James's conceptual work transcends what can be documented from the Gospels in that he pays close attention to inner spiritual processes. Religious psychology is emerging.

### a) The Depiction of Sin

Resolute obedience to Jesus' call to repentance leads to a sharpened understanding of the perverse and the right course of action in a given situation. Sin is the result of the alluring power of passion over an individual. When he obeys it, sin is conceived, and the sinful action ensues, and out of this comes death. James holds a person fully responsible for his passion, sin, and death. He subsumes ethical norms under his concept of God, so that man may not attribute these processes to God but must distinguish between the things originating from within himself and the things coming from God. The general principle is that only that which is good comes from God. Passion is rooted in lust located in the members of one's own bodily members. Thus right conduct takes on the characteristic of a struggle led by an individual against himself. Lust originating in the members of his own body attacks him; the person's own inner struggle leads to that strife which tears the community apart. James devotes special attention to the tongue as the organ which reveals a man's ethical dilemma and obligation with particular clarity. Thus the control of one's body becomes the aim toward which one should strive, and from the impossibility of complete control of the members of one's body arises the renewed need of repentant turning back to God (1:13–15; 4:1; 3:2–12).

Parallel to this is the attention given to a person's divided loyalty, "the double-minded soul." James conceives of this as man's ability to fix his will on two contrary aims at the same time. This is compared to unchastity. The abnormalities resulting from the division of one's will are noted perceptively: whoever prays and wavers between confidence in God and reproach against him; the hearer of the divine word who forgets it when time for action has come; the believer who sees human honor alternately in relationship with Christ and in wealth; and the one who perverts faith into an authorization to evil, his piety oscillating between praising God and cursing others and simultaneously seeking to be friends with God and the world—all of these portray the same phenomenon: a divided, confused will (1:6–8, 22, 25–26; 2:1, 14; 3:9–12; 4:1–8). Thus James does not single out individual commandments of the Law and rejects the Pharisaic theory of compensation. The unity of God renders a partial transgression or fulfillment of the Law impossible. Whoever breaks one commandment breaks the entire Law, because lawbreaking amounts to rebellion against God (2:10–11; 4:10–11).

The will that gives in to passion is contrasted with the will that affirms the Law. When man yields his will to the perfect Law that expresses God's complete will, so that in fulfilling that will complete obedience takes place, he experiences the therapeutic nature of the Law. Liberty is emphatically portrayed as the result of the Law (1:25; 2:12). While man may fear the Law as robbing him of his freedom, liberty is rather the reward granted by the Law to those who do it. Whoever stands the test of the Law enters a sphere of freedom. This reflects an eschatological reality, because perfect liberty is obtained when the danger of corruption is removed and life is received. Nevertheless, this concept is also relevant for the present and helps guide one's conduct. Liberty is not acquired by struggle against the Law but by fulfilling it. For freedom cannot be attained by prevailing against God; it rather must be received from God. It is one of the good and perfect gifts that come from above, and therefore it can only be received by the doers of the divine will. This explains James' own liberty in relation to Scripture, the community, and its authorities: such liberty is not disobedience toward God but the mark of "perfection" on the part of the one who does the perfect will of God in complete obedience.

Love stands in danger of breaking the Law, because it seeks to treat others in a way that is suitable and pleasing for them. James assumes that preferential treatment given to the rich will be defended as the fulfillment of the love commandment. But he considers love and injustice to be incompatible. Favoritism apart from ethical norms is condemned by the Law, just as love is commanded (2:8–9). The antithesis between love and justice is however treated in the same way as the antithesis between obedience and freedom and between God's sovereignty and man's free will. A theoretical, speculative discussion of these questions is avoided; James merely notes the assured certainty that must regulate the proper course of action for the community. All good things come from God, while sin and death proceed from man; the Law entirely obliges our will, and this results in freedom; we fulfill God's will by love issuing in good done to others; but love carries ethical norms within it and remains therefore integrated with justice.

### b) Instructions Regarding Faith

The special attention directed by James toward faith reveals what is already recognizable in Peter and Matthew: that Christendom viewed faith as the process that determined people's relationship to God. Faith renders every temptation meaningful, because faith is tested by temptation and attains perfection by resolute obedience. Through faith comes the steadfastness that overcomes suffering; faith brings freedom from the blinding influence of wealth that blurs one's judgment and leads to injustice; faith provides the ability to offer pure and answerable prayer. Thus there is no question whether faith is optional for the community or not, because it obtains wisdom and all of God's good gifts only by faith (1:3; 2:22, 1, 5; 1:6; 5:15). If it is divided in its attitude toward God and wavers, it sins. Still, the questions of how the community has faith, the purpose for which faith is used, whether or not believers have faith adequate to procure salvation and justification, are discussed with profound sincerity. The customary verdict regarding wealth and poverty destroys faith, because the believer sees great benefit in Christ's gift and great calamity in hostility toward Christ, a judgment that is compromised when honor is assigned to people according to their possessions. This is what James considers double-mindedness, which causes faith to disintegrate. Since he conceives of faith as confidence in God that has become assurance and conviction, faith exists for him only when it controls a person's actions, and the selected example shows that, for James, faith's power to shape one's actions encompasses an individual's entire conduct (2:1–4).

While the corruption of faith results here from denying a brother his due, it can also arise from refusing God what is rightfully his. This happens when the community is complacent in her assurance of faith, declaring the question of salvation as already taken care of by virtue of mere faith. Since faith is the assurance of divine grace, the believer is confronted with the danger of complacency or false self-confidence in his faith, as if everything had been won by it, so that he fails to act on his faith, thus refusing obedience to God. This condition of faith that rationalizes one's failure to act is entirely discouraged by James. This does not result in a lack of clarity or a shift in his concept of faith, as if faith is now no longer confidence in God as in James's other pronouncements but merely opinion and theory. Confidence in God lies to the highest degree in one's claim to be justified by faith. The lack of faith excoriated by James does not consist in a lack of assurance but in man's separation of his will from his assurance in an effort to restrict his relationship to God to faith alone. This danger can be overcome solely by supplementing faith by works. The danger cannot be removed by a change in faith itself, such as by more extensive instruction, but solely by the believer's obedience to God and his obedient action toward God and his fellow-believers. Now his faith is no longer dead, ineffective, and comparable to a corpse; the believer is rather complete and receives what he as a believer desires from God: salvation and justification (2:14–26).

In this regard it is also significant how we can lend visible expression to our faith. Mere confession cannot be considered to be a sufficient demonstration of faith but only works, since words do not yet reveal the essential characteristic of faith: that a person's beliefs move and direct him. Whether or not someone who claims to have faith really believes can be seen in only one thing: works (2:18).

### c) The Indictment of the Rich

Conditions in Judaism indicate that the struggle against the rich became the holy duty of a man who struggled for the preservation of Israel and attacked the dynamics that led to its demise not merely at the symptoms but at the root. The incitement of Zealot passion was strongly promoted by the hedonistic exhibition of wealth, together with the harsh exploitation of the lower classes. Whoever gave up his possessions for God's sake because he honored him alone as his Lord, going into the wilderness as a bandit, despised the one who, in order not to be without his property and enjoyment, subjected himself to pagans. The bandit did not merely despise the affluent man but knew himself to be called to be the avenger of such godlessness. If Jerusalem was to be saved, the rich finally must wake up, and whoever worked for her salvation needed to do everything in his power to arouse them. The epistle's view, of course, is directed, not toward Jerusalem, but toward the Diaspora. But even there rich Jews were those who evoked the wild anti-Semitism that provided a ubiquitous threat for Christian communities, and this external danger was accompanied by inner corruption. The greedy and violent rich man polluted Judaism everywhere by making it subservient to his own selfish will, and he was everywhere the one who ridiculed faith in the crucified Christ, rejecting membership in the community of the poor as lunacy.

When James seeks to reverse the current verdict regarding wealth and poverty, he therefore stands in close proximity to Jewish history. Being rich is not glorious but lowly; for the rich person will wither away. This is not deplored, it is inevitable: the flower of grass must pass away. This process is a result of the transitory nature of human existence. On its account man's desire to accumulate wealth, with its presumptuous plans regarding the future, turns into boastful arrogance. This proud denial of human lowliness leads to rebellion against God. Men deny their need for God. A drive toward the acquisition of worldly goods is accompanied by sluggishness unable to do what is good even when it knows what should be done. Wealth gives rise to the selfish will, which accumulates treasures as an end in itself and allows them to corrode without having

used them. This is the rich person's guilt. Moreover, wealth results in the shaming of the poor, harshness toward those who work for the rich, the lawless abuse
of the power that wealth brings with it, and rebellion against the Christ. The
rich are blind toward God's work. Their use of even the final days given to them
to accumulate riches for themselves further compounds their guilt. The poor
man, on the other hand, is exalted on account of his lowliness. He is chosen by
God, so that he is in truth the one who is rich. He is rich by virtue of the fact
that he believes. The popular judgment regarding the rich and the poor therefore contradicts God's own judgment, because it honors the one who is rejected
by God and shames the one whom God chose (1:9–11; 2:1–7; 4:13–5:6).

Did James violate here the norms stated by Jesus in his dispute with the
wealthy? It is clear that James at the same time considers poverty to be undesir-
able and wealth a blessing. But because lack constitutes need, man should rejoice in it, in keeping with the principle that every trial should be counted all
joy, because the one who keeps trusting God when in need has stood the test.
He thus gives to God what is God's and has the love of God. Conversely, the
rich man's blessing results in his corruption, because he appears to himself as
the great one who has no desire to submit to God. The concepts of merit and
virtue are both entirely absent from James and in no way tied to poverty. His
judgment arises exclusively from the ethic of love. Possessions are assessed entirely from the vantage point of how they affect a person's will, whether they
confirm someone in his selfish and thus godless will or whether they turn him
toward God. James's statements appear to be harsher than those in the Gospels,
since he omits any positive instruction as to how the rich person may be able to
use his wealth in a way that yields eternal gain for him. Because James does not
include any parallels to Jesus' pronouncement, "Sell what you have," the impression arises that he excludes the possibility of repentance for the rich, considering them to be lost at the outset. James merely reiterates Jesus' own judgment
that the rich person is subject to God's rule like the camel seeking to pass
through the eye of a needle, albeit without including the statement that omnipotent grace is able to save even the rich. Thus he ties wealth solely to the fear
that a man of wealth plunges into his corruption without remedy. Still, James's
recognition that wealth makes godless and evil does not nullify the universal appeal of Jesus' call to repentance. The principle remains that whoever draws near
to God will find him. Like others, the rich person is shown his sin in order that
he may find salvation, and he is shown the path to it by recognizing where
wealth becomes guilt for him.

### d) The Goal of the Community

Since believers should not wait in idleness for the reception of Christ's perfect gifts at his return, their task is pictured as a competition: they are to win the
wreath God has prepared for them. This image coheres well with the perfection
of God's present rule, because Christ brings the community to fulfillment. For
those who know Christ, "perfection" does not mean that they are spared need
and death, but that they are perfectly and resolutely committed to serving God
(1:12, 4; 2:22). The epistle uses the concept of life to describe a man's necessary

aim. This concept encapsulates the eschatological notion inherent in the simple contrast of life and death. It envisions Christ's future work in his giving man life through his judgment. But this does not lead to a discussion of the resurrection, by which the epistle might have developed the idea that at some point in the future life will be restored to the dead. Hope is rather individualized, albeit without taking on an eudaemonistic coloring or being subjected to an egotistic desire. For since death is placed in a causal relationship with sin, everyone must overcome evil in order to escape death, and the struggle for life becomes an ethical struggle. From this vantage point the concept of justification takes on a central place in James's teaching on salvation. Like sin and death, righteousness and life belong together. The "righteous" person, namely, the one who has sown the fruit of righteousness, has served God's righteousness and performed it through his own actions, is the one who obtains God's gift. Whoever is considered righteous by God receives the crown of life. Since the wrestling for the goal does not entail any uncertainty, because the assurance of God's grace produces and guides all efforts, the concept of justification takes on the same relationship to the present as do the terms "kingdom of God," "life," and "salvation." The one who has been transformed into a doer of God's word by faith is justified (5:16; 3:18; 1:20; 2:21–25). In this way the absolute terms describing God's perfect gift are already applied to the present.

## 3. James's Relationship with the Jews

### a) Christians' Fellowship with the Jews

One of the striking characteristics of the epistle is the fact that it does not draw on Jesus' earthly life in order to substantiate the need to strive for the crown of life. While James calls himself a slave of Jesus, he addresses his readers merely in terms of their Jewish status as Israel living in the dispersion (1:1).[42] That this is not merely an allegorical description of the church is revealed by the fact that pronouncements labeling James's readers as Christians are accompanied by numerous other statements describing the religious process in a way that was easily intelligible for every Jew. For neither the cross nor the resurrection of Jesus is mentioned, nor are there any quotations of Jesus' words. The characterizations of God's gift as adoption of God, election, salvation, justification, and the bestowal of life closely follow characteristic Jewish terminology. The Spirit, whose presence provides Christendom with its most distinctive mark, is only alluded to while the sons of God are described as the firstfruits of creation and thus God's possession; the term "saints," by which Christianity expressed its share in God in contrast to Judaism, is missing. Yet the phrase "righteous one," a term frequently used in the synagogue, is applied. Mention is made of "the word," but without indication that the community heard it through Jesus. That "truth" to which the brother is brought back is spoken of,

---

42. The limitation of the word to the dispersed communities may indicate the judgment that Jerusalem and Palestinian Judaism had been told the saving word amply but in vain. The fall of Jerusalem should not also result in the ruin of the Diaspora.

without any indication that this occurs by confession to Jesus. Justifying faith is discussed without relating it to the Christ. Zeal for the teaching office is another subject that is treated without any reference to the Christian character of the community. The teacher is enjoined to instruct it concerning God's will and on how to approach God without an indication that this consists in following the Christ. Mention is made of the rich who slander Christ and will be judged without acknowledgment that they do not belong to the community spoken of by James (cf. 2:1; 5:7, 14 with 5:16; 1:18; 5:19; 2:14; 3:1; 4:8; 2:2, 6–7; 5:1–6).

This is in harmony with the epistle's introductory statement where James does not merely address Christians but all of Israel. By this he makes clear that he sees much common ground between Jews and Christians. Both are under the perfected blessing of divine grace, so that it applies to the Jew as well that God gives to all who ask of him, and that God grants him life through the word of truth. Both, on the other hand, also are confronted with the same dangers: corrupt piety, dead faith, ineffective hearing, pious arrogance, and the allure of riches. The task of Jesus' servants thus consists in the purification of Israel's devotion and the conforming of her faith and love to truth. Even when the offense of Jesus' cross cannot be removed from Israel and she cannot be persuaded of Jesus' resurrection, there remains room for Christians to work with Israel. For Jesus' promise is to all who do God's will. This, however, does not imply that James's allegiance to Jesus was somewhat loose. He rather did the will of Jesus, who did not agitate for his messianic name but poured all his strength into helping Israel recognize and forsake her evil ways. Thus James proved that he had received love from Jesus, love striving for the purification of Israel's piety from sin.[43]

In the introduction to his epistle James affirms Israel's election and expresses his commitment to preserve fellowship with the synagogue as long as it is ready to do so. He expects equal readiness from his Christian readers when he exhorts them not to give preferential treatment to those who persecute them on account of their wealth. Because these rich persons, who blaspheme Jesus, are still Jews, separation from them has not yet occurred. Moreover, believers are in danger of concealing these internal disputes in their dealings with them. James opposes this alleged "love," seeking to make explicit believers' internal separation from Jesus' enemies. This exhortation became inevitable when Christendom saw its task in the preservation of fellowship with the Jews. But the judgment that this was a true mark of Judaism misjudges the situation. Nothing would have brought about the Judaization of early Christendom more surely than Christians' formation of an exclusive sect beside Judaism. When they later allowed themselves to be pushed into this position owing to the pressure of Judaism, they irredeemably turned into a second synagogue, albeit with other rituals and teachings than the old one while resembling it internally, and Jesus' work was destroyed. The only way the Jerusalem church could preserve its internal difference from Judaism during the initial period was irrepressible love. This love al-

---

43. In Jerusalem it was not forgotten that Jesus himself did not avoid obscurity, and his pronouncement forbidding the display of one's piety was in effect, as Matt. 6:1–8 indicates.

lowed itself to be hated and expelled without wavering, holding fast to its universal vision, and continuing its fellowship with all in Israel who served God earnestly. It thereby preserved its inner distinction from Judaism.[44]

The epistle's exhortations to believers to be doers of the word, to prove their faith by works, to renounce the vain exercise of the teaching office, and to avoid a judgmental attitude and all religious pride, do not merely serve the purpose of preserving fellowship with Israel but grow out of James's earnest desire to link each man's salvation with the keeping of ethical norms. But even these exhortations affect Christians' relationship with Israel, because it is the word, faith, and knowledge that separate the two communities from one another. Thus everything that corrupted faith, in Judaism as well as in Christendom, rendering the word empty and worship sinful, deepened and hardened the rift between these two movements. This is why the contrast between the two communities failed to find clear expression. Moreover, no solution was achieved that could produce peace between them.

Not a single pronouncement in the epistle seeks to alleviate this contrast by artificial means. Not does the letter derive the antagonism from the particular historical circumstances of Judaism. No mention is made of the rabbinate and Pharisaism. These are in view only in that aberrations caused by them in one's conduct are combated. According to James, the pervasive, definitive division between men arises through internal processes by which conversion to God is received or rejected. James thus completely concurs with Jesus' verdict regarding Israel. He does not distinguish between the holy nation and the Gentiles but between the world and those whose faith and love are directed toward God (1:27; 4:4). What makes a Jew a Jew does not yet separate him from the world, and the same can be said with complete justification regarding Christendom. James pronounces judgment on the adulterous generation that seeks to combine friendship with the world with friendship with God, subjecting even prayer to its own lusts, and that kills the righteous in its arrogance. Whoever draws near to God, however, receives grace from God. This is how the community of the elect is distinguished from those who perish in God's judgment. But this separation does not coincide with the boundaries of ecclesiastical denominations or confessions. It will rather be revealed when the Lord comes as a judge. In order that everyone can look forward to his judgment with confidence, James instructs believers to do away with anything that contaminates the pure service of God.

### b) James's Break with Jewish Tradition

All of the things rejected by James as sin are extensively attested in Palestinian Jewish literature: the tendency of making one's occupation with Scripture a matter of mere study and doctrine; the worship of wealth; the dissection of the Law into individual regulations, of which one may be kept while others are transgressed; the separation of faith from work, whereby each meritorious deed receives its own value; the tendency to excuse what is sinful by appeal to reli-

---

44. This is not the sole characteristic of James's epistle: see pp. 74–75.

gion, since monotheistic teaching placed one already into the realm of God's favor; the desire to use one's teaching office to rule others; the use of wisdom which facilitates profitable activity to further one's prestige and indulge in strife; and the ability to unite the praise of God with the cursing of man. The terms used by James to promote the will he seeks to produce likewise originate in part in Palestinian piety. Such piety considered man's will to be a causal force, which led to the question of how God's omnipotence relates to human decisions. Such piety deemed victory over temptation to be among the most important tasks of the pious, understood lust to be the origin of sin, saw in humility a focal point of piety, and held poverty borne in confidence to God in high esteem.[45] It strove for freedom with a glowing desire, but did not seek it beyond the Law. Rather, freedom was expected *from* the Law, so that the rabbis concurred that the Law grants liberty. The relationship between faith and the uniqueness of God was fundamental doctrine of Palestinian Judaism. Other expressions with parallels in synagogal exhortation include the use of the term "image of God" for the purpose of ordering the dealings with one's neighbor; the reluctance to take an oath; and the illustration of the power given to prayer by the request for rain exercised by Elijah.[46]

James's separation from the rabbinate is nevertheless profound, as deep as the rift created by Jesus' call to repentance.[47] Not a single statement uses the halakhic method, seeking to determine the correctness of an action by its measurable success. And since there is no mention of cultic regulations, the major characteristic of pious Jews in Palestine is set aside as insignificant.[48]

The individual is confirmed in his relationship with God by being assured that God will give wisdom to the one who asks, forgiveness to the one who confesses, the kingdom to the one who believes, and justification to the one who obeys. This relationship releases the believer from the community and its teachers, so that the level of understanding possessed and admitted by the rabbinate in the community is surpassed. The rabbinate does not know the assurance of victory with which James encounters every temptation; it would have considered such confidence arrogance. The absolute validity of ethical norms that demands everyone to renounce all excuses before God destroys Pharisaic perfectionism. For the judgment of our evil and the assurance of justification are possible only when the concept of merit has been removed. As long as it is held, the assurance James attributes to one's relationship with God cannot be reached, because faith cannot attain assurance as long as each is referred to his

---

45. James has a point of contact with Zealotism in his struggle against the rich. But the Zealots' use of the sword has entirely disappeared in James and is replaced by the perfect patience of Jesus.

46. On the other hand, not a single saying has a close connection to Alexandrinism. One expression that may reflect ideas is the term "the course of life" in 3:6. If it has a more involved prehistory, however, it does not derive from Alexandria but from the Orient, and it is the only term of this kind in the entire epistle. The knowledge of heaven required for 1:17 was available everywhere, even when παραλλαγή τροπῆς ἢ ἀποσκίασμα is preferred.

47. The verdict that claims that the epistle may be placed within Judaism with a few small deletions misunderstands the actual situation.

48. Haggadah is missing as well; the use of the phrase "friend of God" for Abraham is based on Isa. 41:8.

own work in relation to God. The means by which the concept of merit is overcome is not a theory concerning the achievements of the human will but, as in Jesus' case, the word of repentance. This word acknowledges ethical norms and testifies to the giving God who alone is good and by whose work alone the individual is placed in a position where he can serve God.

Thus the restriction of faith in God to belief in providence is transcended as well, because James conceives of God as the Giver of wisdom and righteousness. This renders the Jewish theory of recompense not only unnecessary but impossible; it now is considered to be ill-conceived. Thus every use of faith as a means of making excuses is dispensed with. Underlying the promise of wisdom from above is the Christian conception of the Spirit, a conception foreign to the synagogue: the rabbinate did not call its wisdom spiritual. Likewise, it is impossible to remove the Christian component from James's protest against the shaming of the poor. For the demand that faith determine our dealings with one another to the extent that fellowship is denied or granted on the basis of faith transcends the religious fellowship produced by the synagogue. It separated people into "righteous" and "sinners," not into believers and unbelievers, and the standard by which the righteous man was distinguished from a sinner was always only works.

The final reason for the pervasive difference can be found in the conception of God: grace is understood as that will of God which determines his entire dealings with us. For this reason, not in spite of it, ethical norms become absolute, so that there is no part of God's promise where they are not in operation. The Jewish antithesis between righteousness and goodness, however, has disappeared from James, because man's obligations are surpassed by God's goodness in all of its perfection. This shows that James's epistle has its origin in Jesus' words and deeds.

## 4. James's Place in the Apostolic Circle

### a) Peter and James

The difference between the epistle to the church in Asia Minor and the letter sent to the Jewish Diaspora is readily apparent. Peter points continually to Jesus and derives the motivation for believers' works exclusively from the identity of the Christ. In James's epistle, on the other hand, Jesus stands in the background. Nevertheless, both letters are closely parallel, because Peter's epistle likewise is based on the differentiation between faith *in* Jesus and knowledge *about* Jesus. Just as Peter encourages the church to realize and perfect its faith by good works—which, as in James, also entails the joyful acceptance of suffering as a central component—James leads the Jews to Jesus by showing their pious among them the reprehensible aspects of their piety, thus cleansing them and exhorting them to pious works. For both, the condition of the world loses significance in comparison with the concern for the community's ethical condition. Peter's message to Christians addresses the state of the Roman Empire as little as James's exhortation of the Jews. Moreover, even church politics, the burning question regarding the relationship between Judaism and Christendom and the relationship between Jewish and Gentile Christians in the church is dwarfed in light of both men's central concern: that that Israel might arise to which God draws near (James), and that God's Temple might be built among the nations (Peter).

The convergence in the basic orientation of the two epistles corresponds to several points of contact in the conception of individual norms. Both authors cast temptation as a means of proving one's faith, so that every struggle should be faced with joy. Peter's depiction of the war led by one's fleshly passions against the soul is reminiscent of James's description of the inner wavering of the will. For both, the concepts of chastity and purity are turned inward, while the Jewish external means of attaining purity disappear entirely. For the soul is purified by obedience to the truth. The community receives the new birth through the Word and thus obtains the salvation of the soul which is life. This is the crown placed before it by God, and in light of this reward all other goods that sparkle alluringly in apocalyptic Judaism vanish. Believers are given freedom by sharing in God's grace, but this freedom is the result of their complete submission to God. Peter likewise urges submission to God and considers the fear of God to be part of that normal religious conduct by which the community is kept from sin. But this does not result in a lessening of confidence: for both know the unity of justice and grace and of judgment and the fatherly will that is in God.[49]

### b) Common Ground with Matthew

The way in which James conceives of God's will and of believers' struggle with evil brings him into close proximity with Matthew. Therefore an interpretation of Matthew is doomed to fail that transforms Jesus' commandment into Matthew's own ideal present nowhere but in his book.[50] James's epistle confirms the claim made by the Gospels that these norms were alive in the community. Like Matthew, James directs the word of repentance toward the righteous: not toward obvious sinners who were condemned already by the Law, but toward that kind of godlessness that portrayed itself as piety. He addresses himself not to those who were not able to hear the word but to those who heard it eagerly without doing it; not to those who failed to believe but rather to those who had high praise for faith, but a corpse-like faith lacking obedience; not to those who lacked wisdom but to the wise; not to those who never prayed but to those whose prayer was despicable in the sight of God. In this way, Matthew thereby continues Jesus' struggle against transforming religion into rebellion against God, which constitutes the essence of Jesus' call to repentance in Matthew. Only the words to the rich condemn what was commonly rejected in popular thought. But these words had a clear basis in the fact that everyone considered

---

49. Cf. James 1:2–3 with 1 Peter 1:6–7; 4:12; James 4:1 with 1 Peter 2:11; James 4:8 with 1 Peter 1:22; James 1:18 with 1 Peter 1:23; James 1:21 with 1 Peter 1:9; James 1:12 with 1 Peter 5:4; James 1:25 with 1 Peter 2:16; James 4:10 with 1 Peter 5:6; James 4:7 with 1 Peter 5:9. The points of contact between the epistles of James and Peter are so considerable that the conclusion is reasonable that Peter knew James's letter and that he expected the church in Asia Minor to be reminded of James's epistle by his own words.

50. This kind of interpretation is also incompatible with 1 Peter, since there, too, Jesus' commandment encounters us as the power living in the community.

wealth to be a blessing desired of God, so that many became blind to, and covered up, sins related to riches.

Nevertheless, James's epistle should not be considered to be a mere copy of Matthew. In fact, several important principles preserved by Matthew are missing in James. Since James does not refer to Jesus' earthly life, he also does not include any of Jesus' pronouncements that go beyond Scripture. Jesus' new order is not featured, which uses even holy days for the purpose of doing good; this brings an end to conceiving impurity as primarily the effect of external influences, and makes free from rendering payments owed to God. Thus all potential stumbling blocks that might compromise a Jew's Jewishness are removed. Likewise, James has no parallel to Jesus' words regarding the protection of women, love for one's enemy, unlimited forgiveness, the removal of piety from the public view, or the obligation to martyrdom.[51] These elements are certainly not missing because James seeks to evade these obligations. Perhaps he does not mention them because all these pronouncements transcend the measure of devotion given to the community by Scripture and show the community tasks that could be accepted solely by faith in Christ. That which becomes the special duty of Jesus' own disciples is not addressed for the same reason that the removal of guilt is not traced to the cross of Jesus nor life to his resurrection.

James also agrees with Matthew in that for both, relationship with Jesus is determined entirely by the Christ concept. Therefore neither James nor Matthew uses Jesus' sayings or earthly life to construe a Christian Law, a new Christian halakhah. It is not self-evident why an epistle urging people to do good as strongly as James does would fail to draw on Jesus' example. James, like Matthew, does not present Jesus as the community's example but places him in relation to God who rules and judges through him.

Both documents also show strong agreement in their assessment of Israel. James agrees with Matthew in his opposition to any form of Christian fanaticism that uses Jesus' word to argue about its greatness. In Matthew, too, Jesus' promise takes on a universal scope, including all who need and obey God. And in Matthew, too, the call to repentance, which helps Israel to regard sin and righteousness the way Jesus did, precedes the proclamation of Jesus' regal status, because Jesus' commission and particularly his cross would otherwise remain unintelligible. James's limitation of his word to Israel does not set him apart from Matthew, who includes the disciples' commission to Israel as part of his Gospel. The impossibility of tying the work in Jerusalem simultaneously to the evangelization of the nations was evident to both.

### c) The Agreement with John

James does not share common ground merely with Matthew but also with John. No epistle is closer to James's than John's, for both speak out against

---

51. The exhortation to suffer like the prophets comes close to martyrdom, for the prophet was considered to be a martyr. But it is not said explicitly to die like the prophets die. The lack of a statement regarding the carefreeness of the poor is parallel to the absence of exhortation to the rich to give.

pious self-deception, boastful arrogance, and religious pretense. Both demand that faith prove itself in conduct. This commonality stems from the convergence of their deepest convictions. For both, the perfection of divine love is the foundation of all their judgments. John and James both characterize the gift of grace by way of the simple phrase "gift of life." Thus both sum up the wealth of eschatological conceptions in the pivotal statement that the Christian community will be confronted with Jesus as the judge, receiving life by his judgment. For both this fact controls Christians' entire conduct. For the community is then set free from death, if it does not commit sin (cf. James 1:12, 21; 5:8–9 with 1 John 1:1–2; 2:28; 4:17). On this account both consider the idea that God is the originator of evil a severe danger for true devotion (cf. James 1:13–17 with 1 John 1:5–6).

As in James, where wisdom is related to the life given by God, John juxtaposes light with life (cf. James 1:5; 3:17 with 1 John 1:7).[52] Both writers therefore do not merely speak of illumination ordering our thoughts, nor merely of guidance granted to us, but of the birth from God that issues in man's unified condition of life from God. For both the granting of life occurs through the Word, and for both this is rooted in the fact that the Word is the truth, so that a person's stance toward the truth leads to life or death. Thus in John truth leads to freedom, just as it arises in James from the Law that cannot be separated from the Word of truth (cf. James 1:18 with 1 John 3:1; 1:1; James 1:18; 5:19 with 1 John 3:19; and James 1:25 with John 8:32). Both epistles trace conflict in the community to the fact that not all within man comes from God. James and John state emphatically that lust is not from God. This conflict makes all historically conditioned differences disappear by comparison. Both subject the entire human existence to God's wrath and contrast the children of God with the world.

James's exhortation not to desire the world's friendship and to avoid contamination by the world corresponds to the Johannine exhortation not to love the world (cf. James 1:14, 27 with 1 John 2:15–16). For both even Israel is nothing more than part of the world. John likewise is closest to the Zealots, albeit not by exhortation of the rich, but by his judgment of the "ruler of this world." But like James, John distinguishes himself from the Zealots completely by his patient resolve to suffer. The determinative will controlling the actions of both is perfect love which gives everything to God. Both deduce from Jesus liberation of love from all limitations and the completeness of his love that Jesus is the Christ and the perfecter of the community. Both emphasize that even the capacity to have faith in God depends on right action (cf. James 2:22 with John 3:21). Since both ground their ethic in the concept of love, they know nothing of a person's limitation to his own needs or perfection. They rather find the basis for action in the community. Still, neither writer depicts the community by itself or speaks of its condition, office, sacrament, or worship. The only act

---

52. The difference in phraseology reveals the constantly evident difference in the piety of the two writers. "Wisdom" enables a person to act; "light" grants him sight. Since man is called to work, he needs and receives wisdom; since he is called to faith, he needs and receives light.

of worship addressed by both is prayer. The man praying in James for the sufferer's forgiveness of sins and restoration corresponds in John to the one praying for the sinning brother; and both pray in Jesus' name (cf. James 5:14 with 1 John 5:16; this instance again reveals the difference between both writers: John refers only to intercession for the sinner, not the sick). The entire external formation of conduct, on the other hand, is completely conformed to the constitutive processes of a person's life.

The powerful contrast between James's thought, as far it is apparent from his epistle, and Johannine piety results from the fact that John determines his entire thought and will from the Christ while being almost entirely devoid of any religious psychology, while James directs his observation toward the religious process as it occurs in man, sharply portraying the community's ethical condition. Thus in John the ethical decision is a direct part of one's faith, while James ascribes independent significance to the processes by which evil is rejected. On this account works take on for James a different place than they do for John. John, too, knows that one must be warned against love that merely consists of lip-service. But the internal term "love" remains for him the main concept even for Christians' actions; with it he summarizes all exhortations. These pervasive differences can be traced back to the fact that John is completely separated from Judaism, speaking solely to those who believe in Christ, while James had gained his thoughts in the work for Israel and maintained communion with Israel even in his letter.

#### d) James and Paul

James's epistle, too, was quickly used by the Gentile congregations (I consider the use of James in 1 Peter to be assured). This fact shows, no less than the use of the first Gospel by the Gentiles, how firm the link was between both parts of the church. Similar to Matthew's Gospel, James's epistle expected Christian Gentiles to understand why Jesus' disciples preserved fellowship with the Jews, and that they should first of all seek to perfect devotion themselves but then as much as possible strive to purify Jewish devotion through energetic repentance. Other demands on the maturity of the Gentile churches included the great challenge for insight represented by the difference in the terms used for justification.

A particularly telling testimony to the power by which the first Christian generation loved and believed and therefore also thought is the development of diametrically opposed phrases for justification and the community's ability of using them both in conjunction with one another. If the concept of God receives its form from confidence in God, two issues arise: first, what God does for us, and second, what we want to do for God. Both questions were posed and answered with perfect clarity by the men in charge of the community. "God does everything for us," says Paul. "He forgives us perfectly, redeems entirely, he is our complete salvation; therefore it is already faith alone, and only faith, but it completely, that is our righteousness." With equal veracity and resolve, James responded to the other question of what we want to do for God by saying, "We want to give him everything, faith and work, and all of our love without division; therefore faith is not yet our righteousness, if we merely believe and refuse God the work, and thus obedience and love." Perfect love is generated by the collaboration of both movements of the will, which find expression in both terms for justification. This love protects the gift of the one to whom it yields, praises his goodness, and rests in it, while simultaneously providing our will with the full power for giving everything we are and have to him.

Therefore the two terms for justification are not restricted to different groups within the church and to its leading figures but are found everywhere. They already occur in Jesus' own word, where the promise for faith and the call to repentance coexist with the promise for love. They are also found in John's first epistle, as well as in his Gospel, and they are present in both Paul and James. James does not point the sinner who mourns and humbles himself before God by confession to his works but to God's forgiveness which he receives because he believes. He points that person to the fact that God draws near to him because he draws near to God and that God will exalt him because he humbles himself before God. This, however, is not yet the ultimate form of faith, for complete confidence in God has been gained only when evil inaction has been overcome and obedience has been rendered. Paul, on the other hand, also knows the time when that person places himself with complete resolve into God's service, and this occurs precisely by the believer's justification, not in spite of it, and because he already stands in God's grace as a believer, not in spite of that standing. Now he may and can act, because God's grace is righteousness. Paul teaches this in the clear consciousness that good works are the indispensable condition for a believer's share in God's grace. Far from diminishing God's grace, this constitutes its reception. Because it removes his entire guilt and completely ends his rebellion against God, liberating him from all evil and declaring him to be righteous, he can neither persist in evil nor consider himself to have a part in his own justification, since this would constitute a denial of what he has been given in the person of Christ.

It is no coincidence that the concept of justification serves the precise purpose of rendering both aims of love entirely clear. It is suited for this purpose because it expressed the unity between grace and ethical norms, maintaining that God gives us his grace as the Righteous One through the execution of justice. Therefore Paul affirms the completeness of grace by his formulation of justification without which the guilty cannot believe in it: that God forgives entirely and removes any obstacle from our relationship with him, so that it already receives its rightness by the fact, and only by the fact, that he is gracious toward us and that we believe in him. But the concept of justification at the same time assigned full weight to the question of how also on the part of the individual his conduct toward God would receive its rightness and possess the mark of righteousness. This is not the case as long as the person refuses God his actions, and this refusal is entirely culpable if it appeals to faith and thus to God's kindness.

Both formulas of justification stood in relation to the direction pursued by both men's work. All pronouncements of James express those kinds of convictions that Christianity and Israel had in common and by which they were able to cultivate fellowship with one another: that there is one love and one faith which are pleasing to God even without being directly related to Jesus; that the assurance of God also included the assurance of his grace, since he only gives what is good and since he draws near to everyone who submits himself to him; that the Law judges those who transgress it while providing liberty to those who do it; and that the individual is placed into God's grace and has justification only by faith united with obedience. All the elements of the Pauline pronouncement regarding justification express the new possession belonging to Christianity alone, thus revealing what separated it from Jewish piety, so that Paul severed Christianity from Judaism: that the Law was the legal code directed against our sin which rendered us guilty; that we arrive at divine forgiveness and the good work solely by faith in Jesus; and that we are not to seek the basis for it in ourselves, because we are unable to cover our sin with our work. Thus we have our righteousness by faith, since it is ours in the Christ, with whose death and life we are connected by faith. James kept Judaism and Christendom side by side; Paul freed Christendom from Judaism.

The question of whether James took into account the Pauline version of the gospel in the formulation of his own pronouncements cannot be decided by any clear proof but remains in the realm of the uncertain weighing of probabilities. For his words do not contain any clear references to Paul. The tendency of failing to perform works for the sake of faith is foreign to Paul. The depiction of faith as the assurance of God's oneness has no connection to Paul. The appeal to Abraham as proof for the justifying power of faith does not originate with Paul but is caused by the passage of Scripture that had already been the subject of much debate in the pre-Christian community.[53] The contrast between faith and works, likewise, is not original with Paul; even less is the concept of justification. The tendency of transforming faith into an orthodoxy capable of evil can be found in the synagogue, and the danger that the proclamation of Jesus had no effect other than mere faith threatened Christendom from the beginning, as soon as and since it constituted itself as the community of those who believed in Jesus, separating itself from the synagogue for the sake of its faith. It is, however, not inconceivable, and it may be probable, that the phrase "justification by faith" became the mark of Christendom through Paul's work. The attitude of the Gentile church may have caused James to illumine the point at which godlessness may tie itself to this formula. He would have done so with a view toward Israel, whose verdict regarding Christendom would be entirely distorted if it did not remain clear how Christians had faith: not in such a way that they thought their faith saved them, but as Abraham had it who gave everything to God, and even more with a view toward Jesus' word, from whom Christendom would separate itself entirely if it sought to reject Israel's confidence in God while failing to struggle against a form of "faith" that supported evil within its own ranks, considering itself righteous even while remaining without works.

53. Jewish tradition contains few concrete reminiscences of the teachers of the first century before Christ. To these belong, however, statements regarding the power of faith, whereby Gen. 15:6 was not forgotten. I have commented on the interesting collection of proofs on behalf of faith in the Mekhilta regarding Exod. 14:31 in my treatise regarding faith, III:609.

The prevailing will in a community will never emerge more clearly than where opposition arises. At this point its claim that its Lord had given it love and had commanded it to love is proven completely. For the contrast in the formula of justification has nothing to do with selfish passion. It rather reveals how love wrestles for its completion. Love moved Paul to unite all who believe in Jesus completely, so that the community was made up, not of righteous Jews and guilty Gentiles, but only of those justified by faith. The same love moved James to preserve fellowship with all pious people in Israel, so that Christians justified by faith did not stand beside Jews judged by the word of repentance, but so that all receive justification in the same way from the God who judges impartially, namely, in such a way that they accomplish what he requires *by faith*. Love gave Paul a clear eye for the way in which zeal for works regularly was the death of faith and how trivialization of divine grace resulted from reliance on one's own achievements. No less clearly, love supplied James with the observation that confidence in God's kindness may lead to inaction. The interplay of both desires, of which one sought to free God's gift to men and the other man's gift to God from any limitation or imperfection, shows that the thinking and willing of Jesus' disciples arose from love.

The accounts available to us of Paul and Luke (Gal. 2:9, 12; Acts 21:21) regarding the contrast between Paul and James can easily be reconciled with James's epistle. From Paul, we learn that James sent men associated with him to the Gentile congregations whose task it was to preserve the Jewish Christians in a connection with Jerusalem and to confirm them in the preservation of Jewish custom. On this account Peter refrained in Antioch from transgressing the food laws after the arrival of those sent by James. This shows that James was not entirely in agreement with Paul regarding the teaching on justification. For Paul possessed complete liberty from the Law by which he transgressed it without misgivings, uniting Jewish and Gentile believers completely to the point of table fellowship by his pronouncement regarding justification. From James's epistle it can be gleaned without difficulty that James opposed the separation of Jewish Christianity from Judaism, demanding that the former should not place an unnecessary offense in the latter's way by removing the Law also for the Jews that confessed Jesus. For James, this belonged to the work of love, which renounces its own right and grants others what helps them, omitting whatever distances them from Christ. Such an attitude did not prevent the justification of Christianity but secured it for it; it did not weaken its faith but perfected it. For it was comparable to the work of Abraham who gave everything, even his most cherished possession, to God, and to Rahab, who risked her life for the brethren.

In James, too, the events that had decisive significance for his own experience cohere seamlessly with those convictions expressed by his epistle. He was the brother of Jesus and the witness of his work, but he did not receive faith until the appearance of the Risen One. From that time on, he led Jewish Christianity together with Peter and John, advocating the preservation of fellowship with Israel during the church's growth, and remaining in Jerusalem until the Jews killed him. Through these experiences and work James could never become a theoretician or a gnostic. The outcome of Jesus' life had shown him that he had been in the wrong with his thoughts and that Jesus did God's will rather than he, even when Jesus went to the cross. Then Israel had decided to resist Jesus, since its teachers rejected him on account of their understanding of how God would send the Christ. Thus James experienced with particular clarity how the claim of knowing God can lead to wrong paths. What James received from Jesus, in contrast, was not a theory, but the word of repentance that confronted Israel's religious hypocrisy and pride and offered it divine grace. The concept of repentance was retained by James in the form given it by Jesus also in his formulation of justification. Because conversion to God consists in the action that rejects the reprobate will and thus obtains God's grace, repentance does not cause James to doubt whether the individual is able to obey. This, after all, he is told by the very fact that he is called to repent, and by this it is simultaneously affirmed that he enters into God's grace when he decides to act. Only in such a way does Christendom furnish an effective proof for Jesus before Judaism, and only in such a way does it gain life at the revelation of God's rule. The resolute turning of the will toward the ethical aim; the rejection of merely theoretical questions, even questions that related directly to the events that revealed God and particularly of questions hankering to penetrate into the mystery of the Christ and of God; the expectation that Jesus would soon reveal himself and thus settle the dispute between those who believed in him and those who rejected him; the use of the present as a time to prepare for the return of Jesus— all these characteristics of James's epistle result from his fellowship with Jesus and at the same his fellowship with Israel.

# D. The Refutation of Gnosticism by Jude[54]

## 1. The Gnostic Threat

Jude concurs with what Matthew and James tell us regarding Palestinian Christendom since he, too, focuses on the call to repentance. Jude writes because he opposes evil. In his case, however, the subject of discussion is not the sin by which Israel fell. The struggle is now directed against an aberration that originated from within Christianity.

Jesus' verdict regarding the Jewish "righteous" had revealed how piety can result in sin and how an appeal to God's grace may lead to rebellion, so that religion may turn into irreligion if man uses it for the purpose of strengthening his own selfish will. Jesus' disciples were thus equipped to pay attention to such processes in their community and to resist them. In that community the urge arose of transforming piety into self-admiration and of transforming Christendom into the struggle for one's own greatness. This was done by presuming on those absolute statements by which Christians portrayed their share in God.

---

54. The preservation of the epistle is based on the tradition that Jude, who calls himself a brother of James, was Jesus' brother. Thus he belongs to those who were in charge of the Palestinian church (1 Cor. 9:6). The first author in whom we encounter an esteem for this letter as the testimony to apostolic teaching is the writer of the second epistle of Peter. Whoever rejects this tradition as uncertain will integrate this portion of Scripture elsewhere in his historical reconstruction.

They claimed that their knowledge of Christ secured for them God's rule and granted them God's Spirit. Both convictions could easily be used to provide great power to the selfish will. By doing this they no longer founded their faith on God and on love devoted to him. Thereby the clear contrast between Christian and pre-Christian piety was done away with, and the obstacle was removed that resisted the resurgence of pre-Christian traditions.

Because the community claimed that God's Spirit was at work in it in such a way that it was granted freedom from evil and was thus able even in its dealings with the world to use without sin whatever it contained, it was only a short step to a form of piety that had the satisfaction of human desires as its aim with a proud sense of one's own importance. This was coupled with an appeal to God's grace which granted men divine powers and insights. These Christian tendencies found appeal and support among the Hellenized forms of Judaism that transcended the Law by religious speculation, mysticism, and ascetic conduct. The use of such examples becomes visible within Christian movements when they form their central tenets, their concept of God and their image of Christ, their self-concept and the instructions regarding the reception of redemption, using conceptions taken from nature. In that case, faith is replaced by the possession of certain concepts as the essential characteristic of Christianity, whereby a salvific theology develops. Separation from evil is then conceived of as a natural process that produces its result with infallible certainty. Ethical norms thus become secondary for those who are united with God and are replaced by special regulations that qualify one for the reception of rites that provide grace.

In the brand of Christianity addressed by Jude, the presence of the Spirit was taken to provide unrestricted permission to erotic pleasure. This introduced a form of piety into the church whose roots go back far into the pagan Orient. At the same time, the Spirit's work is understood in terms of providing the pious with communion with heavenly powers (vv. 4, 8, 14). This is the kind of Christianity against which Jude warns the community, for he sees in a piety that rejects Jesus' rule and produces license not God's work, but rather godlessness. Which spirits were appealed to by these gnostics is not discussed. But the decisive feature of this heresy is for Jude that it does not make room for the Christ concept. This is also proof that its proponents do not have the Spirit. For the Spirit's work consists in subjecting the community to the Christ. Because these men also described God's will in terms of grace, they desired fellowship with Christianity. While in their case, however, divine love did not receive its content by ethical norms, these have absolute validity for Jude and are integrated with the concept of God. He therefore confronts the grace proclaimed by gnostics with the doing of righteousness which always accompanies divine revelation and which was directed in particular against the deeds indulged in by the gnostics. These included disbelief and unchastity, even among those who had been the recipients of the greatest blessings, such as Israel after its rescue from Egypt, or the angels (vv. 5–7). Thus assurance of God is used as the motive for the fear of God. Conversely, faith in God that is merely concerned with his grace while ignoring his absolute opposition toward evil is rejected as erroneous.

Since competing conceptions existed in the community, one may have expected that the concept of faith would have received general formulation, so that this new form of piety, too, might have been considered a form of faith, albeit another kind than the old one. But the confrontation with gnostic teaching did not take this turn. Jude does not detect any faith in it, and even his opponents did not call the religious conduct they desired "faith" but "knowledge." "Faith" had not yet dissipated into a vague idea that can comprise contradictory notions. Rather, it designated the confidence the community has in Jesus, in particular, that he is its Lord. To recognize other masters beside Jesus was therefore to forsake the faith. But faith is the essential characteristic of Christendom, determining its entire relationship with God. It derives its importance from the fact that it comes into being, not as the believer's own accomplishment, be it by decision or insight, but as the gift given to him by God. Therefore faith is exceedingly holy, because it links the community directly with God. The greatness of divine grace received by the community by the gift of faith is revealed by the fact that it is received only once. It needs to be preserved by the one who possesses it. If he forsakes it, he is not given the gift he despises once again (vv. 3, 5, 10).

The two aims for which Jude fights against gnostic teaching, purity of desire and the acknowledgment of Jesus' rule, clearly stand for him in complete unity. Jesus' will is one with the good will of God, one with the divine justice that Jesus executes by his rule. No other Law, be it one of doctrine or of ritual, is revealed beside the ethical norms whose observance was the task of the community. gnostic teaching is combated not because of its distinctive ideas, in which case its individual theories would have been considered and judged. Jude uses the concept of "orthodoxy" as little as Matthew or James. He does not fight for a body of fixed doctrines whose possession made one a Christian and whose denial was the gnostics' sin. He measures solely the orientation of a person's will. Religion is not theory but action, and an individual becomes guilty or righteous by his deeds. What matters is how he conducts himself toward others and toward Jesus.

Jude considered the knowledge offered to the community by gnostic piety to be worthless, since he judged the speculative element in its ideas to be perverted. The gnostic leads a dream life, cut off from reality, because, in spite of his speculation, the supernatural powers remain unknown to him. Apart from his insights derived from special revelations, he does, of course, possess all kinds of knowledge that has been acquired by natural means. But this cannot be claimed as salvific knowledge. Even animals receive knowledge by way of nature; this knowledge brings gnostics only destruction (v. 10).

The reprehensible nature of their conduct is also revealed by the arrogance by which they slander supernatural powers and criticize the existing condition of the world. They may slander; but for Jude, as for James and Matthew, this is a fundamental sin. Selfish will is given free rein, the meal of the community is transformed into an orgy, the community is torn apart, dealings with one another are corrupted by the admiration of men, and financial gain is craved. Thereby this religious movement is rendered fruitless, and thereby it is refuted (vv. 8–10, 12–13, 16).

But even this call to repentance entails the offer of reconciliation. Jude's primary aim is the protection of the community and its preservation in the faith. But beyond this it is also capable of saving those who had been trapped by gnostic teaching. It was to attempt such salvation, however, with fear and trembling, since it did not know whether or not those who had fallen were still capable of returning, and since it needed to take precaution lest it itself be infected in the attempt to save others (vv. 22–23). Attention is directed solely toward those internal aims that extend to the core of personal devotion. There is no mention of legal regulations or actions by which discipline can or should be preserved in the community against this "knowledge." In Jude, as in Matthew and James, there is no ecclesiastical Law.

## 2. The Religious Possession of the Community

Beside the evil-resisting energy and the accompanying fear of God's judging activity stands the assurance of his love, not merely as a general idea, but as the grace granted to the community. It has love, because Jesus is its Lord. Therefore it belongs to him and is preserved for him, and it will experience his goodness when it sees him (vv. 1, 21). The epistle contains no backward glance at Jesus' earthly life; like James, Jude refers neither to the cross nor to the resurrection. While gnostic teaching, by neglecting faith, also forsakes hope, Christians are exhorted to focus on what lies ahead.

At the present time, the community experiences Jesus' rule by possessing the Spirit. Since it has him through its union with Christ, the Spirit is not available to those who separate from the Christ and whose internal life remains limited to what the soul is able to produce. Participation in the Christ, on the other hand, provides Christians with more than merely what people naturally generate from within. The process by which the Spirit's presence is truly apprehended is prayer. In the case of the apostles, this is supplemented by prophecy. The Spirit's ministry stands in clear contrast to fleshly desire, and separation from the latter is the mark of the believer (vv. 19, 20, 17, 8, 23). Because the community belongs to the Christ, and because it has the Spirit, it consists of the saints, and for this reason the faith by which it is united with Christ is holy as well (vv. 3, 20).

The fact that Palestinian Christians called themselves saints is not yet visible in James but is confirmed by the information provided by Paul and Luke. By this designation they portray themselves as God's possession, sharing in the invincibility and dignity possessed by all that belongs to God. Not merely the community as a whole, but all of its members are authorized to claim holiness as the property personally granted to them. This would not have been possible if holiness had been derived from the performance of the human will; it rather is based on the fact that God's communion with the individual makes him holy. Thus he receives holiness by God's call. Since this holiness, however, separates him from evil and subjects him to God, the concept of salvation necessarily takes on an ethical dimension. Sin and holiness become utterly incompatible. By calling itself holy, Christianity expresses, together with the assurance of God, also the consciousness of its ethical power which is able to overcome evil. Therefore the concept of holiness is coupled with the obligation of resolute resistance toward everything that is blameworthy, and on this account gnostic piety is denied any fellowship.

The conviction that the firmness of believers' relationship with God would not be shaken even by the kinds of events taking place in the congregations at that time is confirmed by the fact that these things have already been predicted both by Scripture and by Jesus' messengers. The possibility of stumbling and falling is considered to be real even within Christendom. Thus believers are equipped for the struggle evoked by this possibility, because they cannot be surprised by it but have been warned. Since those who fell into the gnostic sin are said to never have been genuine members of the community in the first place but rather covertly to have crept in, the perfect grace of God, which is free from any wavering, is cast as manifesting itself in the divine call. Therefore those who succumb to a debased will through their Christianity turn out to be intruders seeking to secure their share in the community by unlawful means (vv. 4, 17; Paul has the same phrase in Gal. 2:4; it was used both in combating Pharisaic and gnostic Christians).

The reception of divine grace produces a striving toward a goal whose sincerity and power Jude as well as Peter portray by the images of athletic contest and construction work (vv. 3, 20). Thus Jude likewise obliges the community to a persistent and progressive movement that must not stop at what it has already been given at its inception, as if it were enough merely to wait for Jesus' appearance. The present is rather filled with a task that is judged both necessary and productive. Since it is based on what the community has been given, faith provides believers with the ability for their contest and constructive work.

It is not in the realm of knowledge that Jude seeks the tasks by which the community's strength must be tested. Believers "possess all knowledge," so that the epistle's word of exhortation is presented as merely reminding them of what they already know (vv. 5, 17). All theological concerns are subordinated to ethical requirements. The word of those who lead the community serves the purpose of its salvation rather than of its knowledge. It draws its knowledge from Scripture, which is related seriously and directly to the present events. Even recent apocalyptic literature is used to the extent, and only to the extent, that it directs the call to repentance to Israel, announcing divine judgment (vv. 9, 16, 14, 15).[55] Alongside Scripture, the community has its foundation in the word of Jesus' messengers. Jude thinks of a closed circle of such messengers and does not include himself among them. Their special authority is obviously based on their special relationship to the Lord.

Another characteristic of the community is the common meal (v. 12). This reveals that its fellowship embraces all concerns, both what affects its internal life and what results from its natural condition. It practices prayer fellowship as

---

55. The emphasis on apocryphal literature is probably related to the fact that gnostics read it zealously and found support in it. The step from the intellectualism of meditative apocalyptic to gnosticism was a small one.

well as table fellowship. The genuineness of its love is proved by the fact that it does not separate religious processes from the rest of life but grants fellowship to others with everything that matters to them. But the closer the community, the more indispensable discipline becomes as well. For the secure closeness of the community also provides an impetus to unethical forms of Christianity that may become a threat for all.

One should not conceive of Jude's epistle as an imitation of James, for Jude's letter is a warning against gnostic teaching while James's epistle is an exhortation to pious Israel. Still, both writers concur regarding the general framework of authentic devotion. God is conceived of as the Father in his perfect love, but love is one with justice. His gift to the community is eternal life, and he illumines the fellowship; the wisdom given to everyone who asks for it in James corresponds in Jude to the confidence that the community has been equipped with everything it needs. It confesses Jesus as its Lord, and this provides it with the hope of his revelation. The major element in the community's cultic life is prayer. Its inward property is faith, which is the basis for a striving with which the community as a whole and individuals in it press toward their goal in the continual straining of their energies. Both writers use the term "undefiled" to express this thought. By this goal everything is measured that takes place in the community. Every new idea is rejected that puffs up, makes unchaste, or is unfruitful. Ethical norms apply with complete impartiality to all, including those who are Christians. The crass appearance of transgressions in the community is therefore in no way viewed as a surprising mystery. The community's struggle is not directed only outward toward others but is turned with equal decisiveness against the things arising from its own passion. If we compare all this with the tradition about Jesus left to us by Matthew, we will observe the congruent basis from which the thought and will of both men derive their form.

## E. Jesus' Message to the Greeks According to John

### 1. John's Prophecy

#### a) The Aim of Prophecy

Through the Gospels and epistles we know that Jesus powerfully simplified Jewish expectation by tying his disciples' hope to his new revelation. Thereby he laid all further questions to rest, since Christianity with a resolved desire now keenly desired this one aim. This is also confirmed by John's prophecy, because it likewise sums up the promise in the one statement that Jesus will soon come, and sums up its desire in the single request that he might come soon (1:7; 22:17, 20). John did not prophesy in order to describe the blessings of the time of salvation more clearly than it had previously been done or in order to announce Jesus' return for the purpose of protecting it against doubt. For the brief final portion of the book receives its significance from its connection with the preceding visions which express the conviction that the world joined with the Roman state had begun a fight against Christianity that would threaten it severely as long as it considered merely the visible aspects of events.

John did not expect toleration for the community of Jesus from the Roman world. He did not seek to find the reason for resistance against the church in the nations' religions, be it in their faith in gods or in their priesthood, for he nowhere speaks of gods. Even less did he blame the state for the coming struggle, and he assuredly did not think of what we today call culture. The nations' religions do, of course, rest upon them as a severe guilt; in this judgment John concurred with all Jews. He saw the guilt of Gentile religion in the veneration of religious images and in the worship of spirits (9:20; 13:14). Accordingly, he charged Rome with the weighty guilt of perverting sensual desires. The great city drives the nations into a frenzy of pleasures, so that their chastity was compromised by that whore Rome (chap. 17).

But the already existing evil is not the final one; it rather reveals evil at work by indicating that the most severe sin still lies in the future. This evil arises from the will that craves for power for the sake of power, deifying itself (13:4–8). That is why the world possesses no tolerance for Jesus' community. For the person who strives for world rule and others' worship cannot bear Jesus' word and wages war against his rule. On this account it becomes the prophet's calling to testify to the community regarding the necessity of this struggle and thus to equip the community for it. In this way Christ grants to the community his protecting grace by the service of his messenger (1:1; 22:6): for it is grace that gives to the community the seeing eye that perceives the imminent struggle, freeing it from vain hopes and granting it the power to forsake success, not to desire blessedness and rule for itself, and to enter the fight with the assurance that it will bring death, but that it will be transformed into victory through Christ.

Since Christian prophecy began directly after the foundation of the church in Jerusalem, and since it developed in all Pauline communities, Johannine prophecy is preceded by a long series of Christian prophecies, by which the expectation of the Antichrist had long since been firmly established in the church. Paul likewise passed on the expectation to the communities that prior to the Lord's return sin would be revealed and the Christ's opponent would attain dominion (2 Thess. 2:3–12). Those forms of this expectation that were older than Christianity have not been preserved for us by clear tradition. Moreover, in the view of Christians, Daniel's vision received more weight, in which the appearance of the Son of Man is linked with the judgment of the final beast that dares to fight God. And no less weighty was the surprising and powerful revelation of sin that had occurred by Jesus' cross and Israel's fall.

The new heritage provided for the church by the Johannine prophecy should particularly be found in the things it says regarding the part Christians play in this struggle. In any case, this emerges more clearly in John than in Paul. The church shares in the coming struggle not by procuring Christ's victory for him but by being subject to the seduction of the Antichrist, from whom and from whose worshipers it must remain separate with that kind of faithfulness that knows how to die (13:15–17; 20:4). John sees in the anti-Christian period not merely an event that needs to take place before the Christ can come and that the church can merely passively observe. He rather pits one community against the other, the worshipers of the ruler of the world against the worshipers of the heavenly Lord. The Antichrist demands even Christians to serve him and to worship him. They are therefore directly affected by his rule with its seduction and oppression, so that it becomes an existential question for the church whether or not it is up to the task. Associated with this is the fact that the Antichrist is here not related to the sin of Israel, because his rule is not merely the culmination of Israel's rebellion against God; rather, the community's attention is clearly directed toward Rome (17:9, 10, 18; 18:2). This is where the attack is coming from, and how the church overcomes this opponent is the question to which John furnishes the answer.

John considered the prophecy necessary not merely owing to human aversion to suffering, which shivers in the face of torment and death. John, of course, also aids the church in this regard; he equips the martyrs. But the temptation accompanying the final confrontation is more profound. There were, after all, ways by which it could have been avoided, alterations of Christianity that satisfied the needs of the Greeks and thereby removed or at least softened the contrast between Hellenism and Christianity. Syncretistic constructs that intermingled Greek thought with Christianity had already been formed by the gnostic movement, and the book begins with the order to exclude them from the churches. Thus the church was confronted with danger not merely from the outside but also from within, since gnostic prophecy fought Jesus in the name of the "Spirit," despising Jesus' promise and thereby dispensing with the Christ's victory over the world, creating in its place a religion by which man glorified himself and elevated himself to unlimited power. Thus the same will was revealed in it from which the self-deifying dominion arose outside the church. For this reason John prophesied that the world rulers would unite with false prophets, thereby bringing sin to completion and providing it with the power that seduced all (13:11–17). For now the Spirit and the miracle confirm man's claim to rule. Therefore the community is shown the impossibility of an intermingling of Jesus' word with the Roman way of life by a depiction of the contrast in its final, mature form by which the Antichrist subjects the world to himself, and the Christ comes in order to judge him. There is no middle ground between the Christ and the Antichrist. There is only one correct choice, and the contrast is absolute.

John linked with the call to resistance one explanatory thought that subjected this turn of history to a divine necessity and thereby counteracted the objection to it. This necessity arises from the fact that God's judgment of the world is an essential part of his government. The church needs to have a picture of the divine execution of justice that demonstrates its terrible scope. By this, too, John opposed the transforming of Christianity into worldliness as it was practiced by the gnostic, who had little esteem for Jesus' cross, who denied his own sin, and who dispensed with hope in the proud consciousness of his religious achievements. The illusions that promise a person complete salvation already in the present and that expect a period of affluence and world peace forget the guilt resting on mankind from which a calamitous harvest must result. God's Lamb was slaughtered, the Christ was killed, and that religion was founded which consists of the deification of those whose power is based on the sword and the spirit powers. This does not remain without consequences. Therefore God's judgment comes with bitter pain and massive death, sweeping away old humanity, and establishing God's rule.

However, the portrayal of the coming confrontation and the testimony to the necessity of divine judgment constitute only the penultimate emphases of the prophecy, which are not significant in and of themselves but in relation to their final outcome: in this way the Christ comes and establishes his kingdom and brings humanity fulfillment in eternal life. By depicting the world as the place where divine wrath is revealed in its full magnitude, John shows the church how great things are given to it by its calling to Christ, and with its separation from the world its gratitude is deepened for the fact that it is saved.

### b) The Difference between Johannine Prophecy and Jewish Expectation

Christianity placed its prophets beside the Old Testament prophets and recognized in both the same Spirit-caused process. This gave Old Testament prophecy and its interpretation by Palestinian Judaism, which we know from the exegetical collections that developed in it, great influence on the content and form of Christian prophecy.[56] What developed therefore was a unique prophetic style that required the prophet to prophesy in symbols, because he could not recognize the invisible and the future in their actual form but only in the form of an image derived from the larger world. This was considered to be a characteristic of the prophetic word to such an extent that John identified even present persons and events not by their actual names but merely by symbols. The symbol easily gives rise to a symbolic act, because the prophet does not see in front of him merely a static image which he observes. Rather, the figures act, and he himself is made a part of their action. But Christian prophecy was given not only its form but also its content in part by Old Testament prophecy, since Christian prophecy did not seek to replace Old Testament prophecy but rather to repeat and thus renew it by incorporating it into the knowledge of the Christ.[57]

Only one standard is suitable for recognizing what in prophecy should be considered to be a new Christian element: if Jesus' history, his cross and his res-

---

56. The interpretation of the prophets, publicly presented in congregations and repeated over the centuries, produced much greater historical effects than the apocalyptic tractates, which attracted attention only in the later church through their false titles.

57. John assumes that the framing of prophecy in symbols would not bother the congregations he addressed. This permits the conclusion that Christian prophecy cultivated a symbolic style already before him, whereby the prophetic images were handed down from one prophet to the next. It is impossible, however, to identify how many of the images used in Johannine prophecy had become part of Christian prophecy already before him. John's Gospel, which gives an indication of how John related to the Synoptic tradition, raises the expectation that he had a rich part in prophetic tradition, while at the same time using it with considerable independence. Moreover, the question of how far individual images can be traced backward and from which sources they are finally taken, and whether or not myth, such as the Babylonian creation myth, had an influence on the development of images, must be completely set aside, since it is here our task to consider what John prophesied. It is certain that he thought in the case of the seven lampstands, not of planets, but of the seven churches of Asia, and in the case of the dragon and the beast, not of big reptiles, but of Satan and the ruler of this world.

urrection, determines the content of prophecy, it is a new acquisition of Christianity. Old Testament prophecy and the tradition that served as its interpretation and supplement constituted a common property of Judaism and Christianity. But when it is allegiance to the Crucified and Risen One that determines the outlook for the future, the one who prophesies is doubtless a Christian.

There can be no question regarding the Christian nature of the first vision, namely, Jesus' address to the seven churches of Asia (1:9–3:22). The Christ stands in heavenly glory among the churches resident in Asia. He treats them as his property, pronounces his judgment over them, obligates them to confess him, and promises them victory and God's eternal gifts in their conflict with the world. This sequence of thought was possible only subsequent to Jesus' resurrection, for it provides us with the Christ concept in the form it had received from Jesus' history. Only after Jesus died was there a Christ who reigns invisibly, to whom Gentile congregations belong, whose connection with him consists in the fact that they confess him. This vision is entirely John's and does not use any Jewish source. By its form and content, however, it is linked with the major section of the book, for this portrait, like the subsequent one, is made up entirely of symbols. Thus the Christ's judgment on the churches is pronounced not directly but through angels who mediate the churches' communion with the heavenly Christ (I reject the interpretation of the angels as bishops). And here, too, the action is based on the world's rebellion against the Christ and on the judgment he executes upon it. The announcement of the end gives rise to the call to repentance to the churches. For the Christ does not merely judge the sin of the world but also sin in his churches, so that they gain victory and glory by forsaking evil. John seeks to assure the church that it is secure, but this does not constitute an authorization to do evil. It is secure because it belongs to the Christ, who does not tolerate any evil.

The second vision, that is, the opening of the seals of the book in God's hand, is Christian, since the place where the Christ acts is the throne of God (chaps. 4–5). John initially does not see the Christ among the circle of heavenly powers. Until he appears, God's verdict remains sealed. Then the Lamb appears with the reminder of his death, and he opens the scroll. Here it is not merely the Lamb and its slaughter that refer back to Jesus' cross, but the entire event is conceivable only on the basis of the outcome of Jesus' life. For every Jew, even those who applied the concept of preexistence to the Christ and cultivated it with strong devotion—for they used it as a measure of Christ's connection with God and his power which was superior to the world—the place where the Christ accomplishes his work was never heaven but always the earth. A Jewish apocalyptist could perhaps begin his depiction of the Christ with a heavenly act through which the Christ would receive his commission and might before God's throne; but now the Christ exercises his rule over the earthly church and the nations. John does not report, however, how the Christ is revealed and commissioned. Rather, he is already present, already known to those in heaven, and not merely to them, but to all of creation (5:13). He does not receive in heaven the commission for his work but executes it in heaven by breaking the seal of

God's book. Without this act, for the sake of which those surrounding God's throne are depicted first, the entire image collapses. Therefore it is not possible to argue that the vision is actually a Jewish form if one simply makes a few minor changes, such as removing the name "Lamb" from the Christ. From its very root, the vision is controlled by the conviction that Jesus is the Christ, since it allows the Christ in heaven to exercise his rule. The concept of God expressed here is the trinitarian one, since God's will is accomplished by the work of the Son who possesses the Spirit. But clearly the trinitarian concept of God was not Jewish.

Together with the first vision, this portrayal of the Christ expresses the two convictions that jointly issued in the disciples' faith: Christ's presence with the church and his divine authority to rule the world in God's presence (Matt. 18:20; 28:20). The second vision provides the key for the first and shows how Jesus is omnipresent in the midst of the churches. Since he accomplishes the divine work at God's throne, he both possesses the seven spirits of God and holds the seven angels in his hand, who provide the churches with the heavenly gift and guidance.

The corresponding element to the opening of the seals are the events on earth by which judgment occurs upon the sinful world. But it is not the portrayal of divine punishments that constitutes the new element in the Johannine vision. This was rather borrowed in part from Old Testament prophecy, in part from synagogal traditions, and in part from Jesus' prophecy. If the vision of the Rider is removed from the action, this renewal of Zechariah's vision would, of course, find room even in a Jewish portrayal. By contrast, the fifth seal contains an appreciation of martyrdom. This would be uncharacteristic for Judaism while it is common in Christendom, because it resulted from the conviction that the Crucified One was the Christ (6:9–11). Already the fact that the souls of many are poured out at God's altar casts the concept as an aspect of the teaching of the cross. Christ's death was worship, sacrifice; the same is true for the death of his own. Thus they are told when appealing to God's righteousness that God still grants time to the world until even their brothers would be killed. Dying for the sake of the divine word is here made the community's calling. It is not merely considered to be a temptation or a calamity by which their love for God must be tested; it is rather love's obligation, inseparable from the rendering of their testimony.

The calling of God's servants is here described in terms of what Jesus did. Nevertheless, he is elevated above those who died in God's service, totally exalted, since he is not placed beside those souls who are poured out at the altar and who appeal to God as their protector but rather stands above all heavenly beings as the only one who knows and is able to execute God's judgment with great power. If this seal were removed from the older vision as a later Christian accretion, however, we lose the number 7, which is essential for the shape of the visions. The parallel to this vision, in which likewise war, hunger, pestilence, the persecution of the church, and the cataclysmic end of the world follow one another in preparation for Christ's coming, is Jesus' word of farewell to the disciples as given to us by Mark and Matthew. In John, Jesus first effects the inauguration of those signs he announced to his disciples prior to his death. Regarding Jesus' prophecy, we know both that John was familiar with it and that it is not Jewish.

Now the church is described—first, how it remains secure from encroachment and is rendered inviolable by God's seal, so that not a single person is lost from among the number determined by God, that is, twelve times twelve thousand. We are told how it already possesses the victory, how it is transported into heaven and given the palm branch and the white robe, an innumerable multitude from all the nations (chap. 7). This vision transcends Jewish hope already by virtue of the fact that it addresses itself solely to the contemporary community without looking back to previous generations, calling it God's possession, which God secures by his seal and to which he grants invincibility. This is all the more certain as the sealing does not preclude the possibility of the death of God's saints, since God's servants continue to be killed. Nevertheless, God's seal has made them indestructible. This is victory over death, a state of faith that does not fear its own demise and knows itself to be protected in testing by omnipotent grace. This kind of faith cannot be interjected back into the synagogue but arose from the Christ who had returned, from the community's celebration of him as the one who had overcome. From this it derives its assurance that it too had overcome, even though it had lost, while in Judaism the approaching conflict inevitably gave rise to the depressing thought that the benefit of living is cast in doubt. That the community is described in two parallel images, one with Israel's name, the other depicting an innumerable multitude from all the nations, is assuredly not Jewish. For Judaism required Gentiles who wanted to participate in God's kingdom to become a part of Israel. To such Gentiles the rabbinate extended a friendly dispensation; it did not award them, however, the praise of overcomers.

The main section of the Apocalypse transposes the community into heaven and describes it as God's indestructible possession that praises him together with the heavenly host. No other depiction exists. This already confounds the idea that it might have been indebted largely to a Jewish document. From such a book John could have taken no more than the depiction of the punishments inflicted upon the world. For these it is, however, not immaterial how the contrast is conceived between the part of humanity that is rejected and the part that is chosen by God. The Johannine contrast between the community that has its place in heaven and the world that is controlled by Satan and confronted with God's judgment is, however, not rooted in Judaism.

To be sure, one of the Johannine images relates to Jerusalem's destiny (chap. 11). However, the demise of the Temple and the city is cast there merely in preparation for the image that is developed more richly, the appearance of both witnesses in apostate Jerusalem. Notably, their fate is portrayed as identical to that of Jesus. God's witnesses are killed in Jerusalem, resurrected, and exalted into heaven. But if the section on God's witnesses is separated from the larger picture, it disintegrates completely.

A new vision depicts the birth of a boy who is described as the Christ by the application of the second psalm to him (chap. 12). This may initially be understood as a Jewish segment, since this represents a prophecy of the birth of Christ. But subsequently the boy is persecuted by the dragon and therefore snatched up to God's throne. Thereby a Jewish train of thought is broken once again. For according to it Christ is not born for the purpose of being chased from the earth by Satan and returning to heaven. This depiction is not possible except as a backward glance at the cross.[58] The accuracy of this contention is confirmed by the fact that Christ's rapture to God leads to the accuser's ejection from heaven by Michael. Christ's exaltation thus results in Satan's rejection and in the community's vindication in the face of his accusation. In characteristic fashion, this vision graphically portrays here nothing else than the pronouncement of Jesus' disciples that the community had been given justification through Jesus' death and exaltation. Of course, John has already told us that Jesus' blood had taken away the guilt of an innumerable multitude of pagans in all their godlessness and unrighteousness (7:14). But this is an exclusively Christian conviction.[59]

The prophecy regarding the Antichrist brings him into a clear connection with the Roman imperial power. This could also take place in the synagogue, but there it always had the effect of setting Israel and the emperor, Jerusalem and Rome, in contrast to one another. In John, on the other hand, this concept is entirely absent, for his thought world transcends all national boundaries. The place of conflict is humanity, and at issue is not the continuation of Jerusalem and Judaism but world rule. This rule belongs to the Exalted One, although the Antichrist has secured power over mankind. Only religious conflict is emphasized as the driving motivation for this struggle. The Antichrist craves worship for himself and for his image, while Christ's rule leads to the adoration of God. Thus the issue of which city is dominant becomes irrelevant, and the other question of who would receive humanity's adoration, God or the beast, alone receives full attention. Now the beast secures worship by being wounded unto death but coming to life, whereby it earns the nations' admiration (13:3; 17:8, 11). By this means the Antichrist is depicted as the counterimage of the Christ.

58. The idea of being translated to heaven is applied to the Christ also by the synagogue, together with the community's retreat into the desert also found in the present vision. But this always constitutes only a short testing of its faithfulness and ends with the Christ's renewed appearance and the establishment of his rule. That the Christ would be translated to God's throne while the community lived and suffered without him on earth was claimed by no one before Jesus in the Judaism known to us. The rapture of the alleged Christ Menahem ben Hiskija relates to the events of the year A.D. 66 and does not belong here. Our historical picture is, however, limited by the fact that no tradition has been preserved regarding the Jews living in Persian territory. The tradition preserved by Judaism started in Jerusalem and was developed by the Palestinian school. Whether Eastern Judaism, in contact with Persian war religion, developed an interpretation regarding the divine government that used the image of war, making the Christ a warrior against the dragon, and whether, and if so, how, a piety influenced by the Persians affected Palestinian Zealotism so that it was in turn able to influence John, cannot be recognized by the tradition that is extant, at least as far as I can tell.

59. That Satan makes his appearance in heaven as an accuser was also affirmed by the Jewish teachers according to Job's story. They also claimed that Michael and the other high angels invoked God's grace regarding Israel and that God rejected the accuser. But that the accuser's rejection resulted from the Christ's exaltation to God's throne, this is the Christian teaching regarding the cross and not Jewish tradition.

For just as Christ establishes his power by death and resurrection, the Antichrist gains it by appearing to be doomed to death while triumphing over it.[60] And when the Prophet stands beside the world ruler and confirms his legitimacy by his miracles, this likewise provides a counterimage to the Christ whose rule is attested by the Spirit until he returns. The Antichrist appears to overcome everything that serves to prove Jesus' regal honor.

### c) The Refutation of Judaism through the Prophecy

The hope given to the community by John is not based in the Law. The Law no longer features in the prophecy at all.[61] The churches of Asia, whose freedom from the Law cannot be doubted, are Christ's property. When he admonishes and judges them, this is based on the fact that he created and ruled them and that he intends to redeem them into glory. Their separation from the synagogue is complete. The synagogues persecute them but must convert and unite with the churches if they want to be freed from the rule of Satan, whose communities they now are (2:9; 3:9). The distinction between Judaism and Christendom could not be depicted in sharper terms. The churches maintain their separation from the Gentiles by avoiding sacrifices brought to the gods as well as temple prostitutes (2:14, 20). Whoever is not prepared to do this breaks fellowship with Christ. The boundary thereby erected between paganism and Christendom is declared immovable, not by Judaism, but by all of Christendom (1 Cor. 5, 6, 8, 10; Acts 15:29). Because the triumphant certainty that is unafraid of contact with pagan ritual or sexual lust is founded on the possession of the Spirit and is proclaimed by prophecy, we are clearly confronted with a gnostic movement.

The expulsion of gnostics from the community, however, is not a characteristic of Judaism (cf. our comments on Jude). In the case of those whose souls lie at the altar and whose death God avenges, we hear nothing regarding their faithfulness to the Law. We are, however, told that they possessed and upheld God's Word and testimony (6:9). This term, "testimony," with its reiteration of the facts witnessed to by the community in its conflict with all who deny them, is a Christian concept. Thereby the community's call to God's service, in which it is to sacrifice its life, is removed from the concept of merit and from a person's own righteousness. It is entirely separated from the possibility of acquiring the divine grace by the power of human will. For the witness is not the creator of his own values; he rather does not deny what he has seen, and he confesses the one who revealed himself to him. The community's calling arises from the divine act done for it. Thereby the powerful commandment of the book is placed entirely on the footing of faith.[62]

---

60. The hopes of those Jews who did not believe in Nero's death but who waited for his return do not constitute a parallel. They did not hope for Nero to rise from the dead but merely that he had fled to the Orient, where he would find an army by which he would avenge himself on Rome.

61. We already know from Peter and James that the Law completely disappeared once it had been overcome. Those who transcended the Law saw before them nothing but Jesus alone.

62. It is the mark of Christendom that it keeps God's commandments and holds to the testimony of Jesus (12:17); that it keeps God's commandments and upholds faith in Jesus (14:12).

No Law-keeping achievements, whose merits might preserve them in the final, great struggle, are attributed to those gathered from the twelve tribes. When John sees the same number for the second time, he is told that they did not touch a woman (14:4). While false prophecy glorified the prostitute and had frequent contact with her, and while the city of the world procures its magic by which it entices all people by inciting erotic passions, the insurmountable strength of the community rests on those who overcame natural lust. The closest parallel is found in Paul, who was concerned for Christians' marriages in light of imminent persecution (1 Cor. 7:26–31). Conversely, this idea is not taken from Judaism, since the renunciation of marriage ran counter to Israel's national constitution. The depiction of the final judgment in Revelation likewise nowhere speaks of circumcision or Sabbath or other parts of the Mosaic Law. The complete absence of the Law already excludes that the substance of the visions was pre-Christian, and it also refutes the verdict that their piety is that of Judaism.

John calls the day on which he was infused with the visions, or at least the first vision, "the Day of the Lord" (1:10). Thus we hear that John brought Sunday to Ephesus, and since he explicitly names this day as the day of revelation, he seeks to establish a connection between what he experienced and saw and what happened on Sunday. On the day set aside for worship on which the churches everywhere gather around Jesus' table, albeit in such a way that he remains invisible for them, John sees Jesus as the one who is present in the midst of his churches and hears how he pronounces his judgment over them. Thereby the churches' need for a firm custom ordering their worship is recognized as legitimate and fulfilled. The constitution given to the church by Paul, of course, was thereby altered significantly. For Paul completely removed the religious calendar and called the church to perfection by not giving it any "holy days," rather instructing it to live in unceasing fellowship with God. But the introduction of Sunday was not Judaism; to the contrary, it represented a deliberate public separation of the new from the old community. Moreover, John does not speak of a legislation that proclaims the celebration of Sunday as the new obligation of Christians instituted for believers in place of their earlier liberty.

The religious esteem for the holy land, a matter tied to the validity of the Law, is completely absent from Johannine prophecy. Christ does not come to Jerusalem. The community is not gathered there, and it is not the place where the dead rise.[63] The fact that John's final vision depicts the descent of the heavenly Jerusalem does not elevate Judaism but may rather reflect resolute opposition to it, as is shown by Paul (Gal. 4:26; cf. Heb. 12:22; 11:10, 16; 13:14). If there is a heavenly Jerusalem, the earthly city is, of course, likewise described as God's city, and God's Old Testament work is granted believing affirmation similar to John's portrayal of Jesus as the Son of David. But this does not imply a transformation of earthly Jerusalem, of that "Sodom," into an eternal city, nor

---

63. Therefore the term "Gehenna" is likewise not repeated, but the place of judgment is depicted as the lake of fire. The reason for this is probably that Gehenna was still associated with the memory of the place near Jerusalem.

the establishment of a connection between the divine aim and the old nature of the community. Rather, the tie to the earthly city is severed as believers' longings are directed solely toward the heavenly city of God.

Equally complete is the removal of the community's limitation to the national state of Israel. John sees Jerusalem solely as a place of rebellion against God, as the location where God's witnesses are killed (11:1–13). The theme of his prophecy is not the relationship between Israel and the Christ but the relationship between the world and the Christ. Israel is also missing from the depiction of heaven. There is no mention of Abraham sharing a meal with his sons in God's kingdom; likewise, there is no reference to Moses.[64] The establishment of an Israel from the twelve tribes in complete conformity to it clearly involves symbolism (7:1–8; cf. 14:1–5 and 9:4). The symmetry assigning the same number to all tribes, even to those who had long since disappeared, is symbolic. The ten lost tribes are sealed, not because they are hidden at an unknown location, but because they are facing a time of great testing and conflict with the Antichrist. Thus they live in the world known to John. But no Jewish Christian would have assumed that Reuben and Manasseh would be represented in Christendom in equal proportion to Judah and Benjamin. When the two descriptions of the community in chapter 7 juxtapose the remnant chosen from Israel with the church gathered from the Gentiles, this yields a parallel to the statement in the Gospel that some of Christ's sheep are found even in Israel, and that his community would be gathered both from within and beyond the flock of Israel (John 10:2–5, 16). The image also corresponds to Paul's promise of preservation and renewal to Israel (Rom. 11:25–27). Characteristic sayings of Paul, however, can hardly be claimed as representative of Judaism.

The symbolic nature of presentation does, however, not guarantee that Israel is promised national continuation only to that extent. The two depictions of the saved stand rather in antithetical relation. Protective sealing from misery corresponds to the palm branch, the sign of attained victory, and the predetermined number of believers from whom no one is lost is juxtaposed with the countless number of those who overcome. The preservation of every tribe in the indestructible community is linked with the image of all nations before God's throne. Are those who are preserved different people than the ones who overcome? Is protected, perfect Israel an entity other than those who are gathered from all mankind? Moreover, the number 144,000 is used also of those who separate themselves from all earthly ties by renouncing marriage and who thereby provide the community with insuperable strength, there, however, without any reference to their origin from the twelve tribes of Israel. Since in the eternal Jerusalem a perfected Israel will be united with God and with the Christ, its gates bear the name of the twelve tribes and thereby proclaim that the

---

64. Similar to the Palestinian teachers, John interpreted Exod. 15:1 as a promise that Moses' song would be sung once again in the last days. Now, however, Moses' song is no longer sung by Israel, but by Jesus' community. The two witnesses provided for apostate Jerusalem by God (11:3) are reminiscent of Moses and Elijah, but since no name is mentioned it remains uncertain whether an identity of persons or a similarity of characteristics in office and work is in view.

work begun in Israel here came to completion, while the nations who obtain eternal healing in the city reside in the area surrounding it (21:12, 24, 26; 22:2). By describing even the perfect, eternal community according to the old constitution of Israel, John makes clear that the eternal state is the fulfillment of God's acts during the course of earthly history. This, however, is not the same thing as saying that only born Jews live in the heavenly Jerusalem. The promise given by the first vision to the churches of Asia excludes such interpretation.

By John's measuring of the Temple, the Temple itself, the altar, and the worshipers are confirmed as God's possession. At the same time, a boundary is established between them and the courtyard, since only they remain while the courtyard is obliterated (11:1–2). If we remove the symbolic dimension from the scene even though the act is manifestly symbolic, John may be viewed as teaching the miraculous preservation of the Temple and of the priests and thus as attributing a value to the Old Testament ritual that could be judged as evidence of a Judaistic tendency. This, however, would result in a peculiar Judaism. What belongs to God, that is, the house, the altar, and the priests, is retained; the place where the community gathers, namely, the courtyard, on the other hand, is done away with. A Jewish Christian, however, cannot do without the courtyard of the Temple, since he hopes for God's almighty protection of the Temple, in order that the ritual may be carried out for which the courtyard was needed. A Temple without a courtyard is a Temple without a community, without ritual, and without Israel. This amounts to a complete denial of the hope of Judaism. And the Temple makes an appearance only here, although it is miraculously preserved. The heavenly altar and sacrifice are frequently mentioned. Temple sacrifice, Aaronic priests, or feasts in the Temple, however, are not referred to at all.

Regarding the holy city that is discussed in chapter 20, we hear merely that it is the home of the saints, but not that it is the home of the eternal Temple; the heavenly Jerusalem has no Temple, since God and Christ himself are the community's Temple (20:9; 21:22). Now, in order for the community to stand in God's presence, it no longer needs any mediation. Thus the preservation of the pieces of the Temple that are exclusively God's property is a simile that expresses the same conviction that John also expresses in the Gospel, that is, that the loss of the Temple through the fall of Judaism and the victory of the Romans did not affect Jesus' community, since it is given God's gracious presence, granted to the old community by the Temple, in powerful truth in the Christ. This corresponds to the statement of prophecy that in Christ's community, the Israel created by God would not merely be preserved but attain its perfection. By the condemnation of the Caesars, whose government is rejected as the complete contradiction to God's rule, and by the rejection of Rome, which is depicted as corrupting the nations, John shares a common element with those who dared to conduct holy war with Rome in Palestine.[65]

65. I regard it as impossible to locate the vision of the measuring of the Temple in a time when it no longer stood. In A.D. 68 and 69 Vespasian's slack pursuit of the war lent powerful strength to faith in the Temple's inviolability, so that it was discussed at that time everywhere in Judaism and Christendom with passionate zeal.

Arguably, this common element also extends to the Temple vision, since the Zealots, who defended the Temple against Titus, believed in its indestructibility until the end. In order to interpret this vision not as the refutation, but as the confirmation of Zealot thought, we would need to forget that John does not equip the community with the sword but rather prepares it to die. His maxim, "Here is the patience and faith of the saints," separates him completely from the rebellious presumption that sought to establish God's rule with the sword. John, too, believes in the indestructibility of the sanctuary built by God: but this was not the building in Jerusalem. Equally deep is the chasm that separates him from Jewish pacifists who proclaimed the indestructibility of the empire and who therefore acquiesced to Roman rule. John also believed in the invincibility of the world ruler who will not be overcome by human strength. But he did not bow to his power. If, with his symbolically depicted preservation of the Temple, he had really wanted to testify to more than the indestructibility of the true sanctuary, seeking to extend God's protection also to the Jerusalem Temple, its salvation throughout the entire prophecy would take on the significance of an accusing sign, confronting Jerusalem that now had come to resemble Sodom with the genuineness and eternal nature of its sanctuaries, while it itself stood in rebellion against God and killed his witnesses.

The use of the ark that appears in the heavenly sanctuary and of the hidden manna in the imagery of the visions is completely unsuited to prove a "Johannine Judaism," since those elements, precisely like the establishment of the community from equal parts of the twelve tribes, do not point to religious values still held by Judaism, but merely to ones it possessed at one time but lost a long time ago (11:19; 2:17). John completely condemns the Judaism of his day, counting it as part of the world and describing its rebellion against God and judgment by God.

## 2. The Norms of the First Epistle

### a) The Condemnation of Gnostic Teaching

According to the epistles, gnostic Christians had left the community. John confirms that this separation had indeed been necessary. Religiously, he considers it to be their sin that they sought to dispense with Jesus. They did, of course, claim to have the Spirit, but they did not want to confess the flesh of Jesus, refusing to believe in the man that once bodily walked the earth. Like Jude, the present epistle considers the confession of Jesus to be the act that creates the community. There is no room in it for an assault on Jesus. Where such occurs, John breaks fellowship.[66] This is supplemented by the ethical reproach that the gnostic denied sin which, ironically, led him into sin. The mark of Christianity, on the other hand, is the confession of sin, which makes Christians unable to sin. The gnostic proves his capacity for evil by being able to hate, just as Christians prove their lack of capacity to evil by loving. The perpetration of sin ac-

---

66. On the other hand, John does not enter into discussion with the gnostics' speculative beliefs regarding the origin of the world, the nature of matter, or other issues. Fellowship is not broken owing to such theories, but merely for the reason that the gnostics had become indifferent to Jesus the man.

companied by its denial results in a lie, while the confession of sin places Christians in the truth. Thus the gnostic hides in the dark, transforms his insight into a secret doctrine, and excludes the uninitiated from his fellowship, while Christians prove their union with God by walking in the light. John, likewise, links the ethical errors of this brand of piety to the gnostic's turning away from Jesus. The gnostic lacks high regard for the death of Jesus, so that he denies the cleansing power of his blood. Christendom, on the other hand, possesses the veracity that confesses sin, because it appreciates Christ's blood as what cleanses it and places hope in his intercession with the Father. It possesses love, because it perceives God's love in the fact that the Christ provided forgiveness for it by his death. Thus the community possesses in hope an incentive that leads it to purity. gnostic piety, on the other hand, already believes to have achieved its goal and consequently forsakes hope in Jesus (2:18–19, 22–23; 4:1–6; 1:6–2:2; 3:7–10; 4:10; 2:28; 3:3; 2 John 7–10).

### b) The Christian Commandment

The epistle's challenge to the community receives its substance from the contrast between God and the world, light and darkness, love and hate. By framing his commandments consistently in both negative and positive terms, John depicts the community's task as a struggle, since it can only have the right will through the denial of the wrong will. The need to choose between two ways of life, of walking in the light or walking in darkness, of keeping or rejecting Jesus' commandments, and of loving or hating, by no means arises merely from the particular assault mounted by the community's gnostic opponents. The gnostic sin rather simply crystallizes for the community the pervasive contrast that exists in particular instances between it and the world, because it exists between the world and God. The community does not face this choice with indecisive wavering. Its position is entirely determined by the Christ. Through him it knows God; therefore it cannot deny its sin, nor can it do evil or hate. We love the brethren, for we know God (1:6, 8–10; 3:6–10; 4:7–8). But the fact that the decision posed for the community by this ethical alternative is already predetermined by the Christ does not remove the clear consciousness that it can retain its position only by continually denying the opposition with which it is confronted. Whether it reaches the positive aims resulting from the knowledge of the Christ or not depends on the persistent and complete realization of this denial.

The ethical question is decided for the community because the Christ has brought it the gift of being children of God. They consist of those who are begotten of God (2:29; 3:1, 9–10; 4:7; 5:1–4, 18). They are connected with the Christ in such a way that they are in him and are able to remain in him. The depiction of the nature of Christian existence is thus placed on the basis of a decisive act of faith. The phrase "born of God" relates the divine love and gift to the human person in its unity and entirety. The person is thereby granted, not isolated gifts, such as individual true thoughts or good volitional impulses, but he himself is now God's work, possessing a vitality conferred by God. What he is is what God makes him to be. This results in the abiding consistent conditionedness of his choices and actions, since being born of God introduces the individual to communion with God as a person and therefore includes the person's will. The individual who is born of God wants God's will in such a way that he does it.

The community's resulting separation from sin, darkness, and death, however, is not described by natural analogies. It does not result in a physical impossibility. Sin rather remains for the community something it has to fear. Its will needs to be directed toward not sinning. This is indicated not merely by the passages that show what must happen when sin has been committed by Christians (2:1; 5:16). It becomes even more evident by the entire forceful exhortation of the epistle, which would be pointless unless separation from evil were conceived of as the natural property of believers.

The impossibility of desiring and doing evil is grounded in what God is and what has been revealed by Christ. Since God is entirely light, it is impossible for the community to lie by denying its own sin and by refusing to confess it. Since the Christ is righteous, the community does righteousness, and since Christ has come to destroy Satan's works, the community cannot receive its will from Satan; for being a child of God and a child of Satan are mutually exclusive. We love, because God is love, and because Christ has first loved us (1:5–10; 2:29; 3:5–10; 4:7–8).

Because the community wants what God has prepared for it in the Christ, its will transcends the wavering, immature conditions it finds itself confronted with. Its will is not overcome or made insecure by these circumstances. If the believer sins, this does not yet irrevocably tear his communion with God, for God forgives and Christ died for the purpose of providing forgiveness for every sin. Therefore Christ also functions as the believer's advocate. The liberation from evil possessed by the community has its basis in the forgiveness of sins and therefore transcends even sins themselves (5:16; 1:8–10). There is, of course, a boundary beyond which communion with God is destroyed by sin; there is a sin leading unto death. Access to God would be lost if sin were denied; for thus the sinning person would refuse to separate himself from his sin and choose to persist in it. Thereby he would lose Christ, because he cannot at the same time remain in the Christ and in sin (1:9; 2:1, 2, 12; 3:19–20).

Similar to its depiction of the ethical question as decided, the epistle also issues a complete promise to the community's understanding. In this area, too, the divine gift completely covers its need. It is not handed over to seduction, nor does it depend on human help, so that the teaching of others is indispensable for it. It rather has "the anointing," the Spirit, and in him the one who teaches it all things, granting it the opportunity to recognize its way, even when it lacks the apostle's instruction and is beset by the Antichrist (2:20–21, 27).

### c) Love

The characteristic of the will, in which the word of the Christ has its aim and which Christ's word creates as its fruit, is love. What is evil is hatred, which destroys others and which stands in a causal connection with passions produced by the flesh, the eyes, and the desire of boasting of one's own achievements. Love is made possible by the liberation from these impure and selfish longings. It is that will by which we act for the sake of others, be it God or the brethren. Man

does not find it in himself; for not man but God, and God alone, is love. Therefore it also coheres entirely with the knowledge of God. Because we truly apprehend God's love, our love is turned toward God, and now we also extend love
toward the brethren, since we cannot separate God and the brethren from one
another. Love is not merely conceived of as a heightened emotion, nor merely
as an act of the will apart from action, which would produce merely the internal
longing for God. It is rather the will to the generous deed. One cannot love
merely with the tongue. John is convinced that this norm confers justness on the
entire conduct of the community. It does not have other obligations besides
love; for love is not merely a part of what is good, but is all of it. Since it is what
God is, it also is what he gives us. It is the characteristic by which he is known
and by which communion with him is produced. Where there is love, there also
exists the other great norm which John urges with absolute sincerity; then truth
is the power that controls our actions. Things by which the individual seeks to
protect himself, such as pretense, flight into darkness, craving for secrecy, breaking of fellowship, all come to an end when he has love. Now he moves in the
light, and now he also does righteousness. John knows nothing of a tension between love and righteousness, just as hatred and unrighteousness likewise go
hand in hand. The evil will is the lawless will that has no other norm but its arbitrary selfishness (3:11; 4:7; 2:16; 4:20–5:3; 3:18; 1:7; 2:10–11, 29; 3:7, 4).

Regarding the concrete ethical norms that designate what is righteous, John
believes that the community will find them step by step itself. His exhortation
therefore has a starkly visible peculiarity in that it entirely omits any formulation
of obligations depicting assorted individual tasks of Christendom. John specifies
such tasks neither for the church's worship, by which it acts out its love for God
and for the Christ, nor for the tasks that are necessitated by our natural circumstances. The particular circumstances that occasioned the epistle likewise did not
move John to provide particular regulations by which individual ideas or actions
of the gnostics were identified in terms of what required separation from them.[67]
The community's relationship to the Greek cult which became uncertain by the
gnostics and which, even apart from such offense, always had utmost importance
for them, is regulated by the sole verse that exhorts John's readers to "flee idols"
(5:21). John sees in the internal process compared by the awakening of love the
complete guarantee for the fact that one's actions would now be pure and fruitful.

John directly unites the concept of community with the entirely personal
framing of the relationship to God, since we, after all, love one another. Everyone is born of God and receives the divine grace individually. But this does not
render community secondary, because the individual believer's experience consists in his allegiance to the Christ which thus unites him with the brethren.
Christ makes them one. In the Christ, the community possesses together with
its firm union also protection against sectarian self-centeredness. For Jesus did
not provide forgiveness of sins for it alone but for the entire world (2:2; 4:14).

---

67. John does not even touch any of the concrete ethical issues by which Paul exposes the difference between gnosticism and Christianity, such as celibacy, foods, prostitution, payment of
teachers, women's prayer, liberation of slaves, or idol worship.

Just as its sin does not preclude God's grace but is overcome by his forgiveness, love toward those in the world likewise must not capitulate in the face of human sin, since Christ made forgiveness available for it as well.

The absolute contrast with the world, which renders believers unrecognized in it and unintelligible to it, does, of course, affect the exercise of love very profoundly. The community does not have room for successful work directed toward the outside in its present circumstances. The Johannine exhortation is characterized by the fact that it conceives of the act arising from love primarily in negative terms as sacrifice to the point of giving one's life. The situation of Christians requires from them first of all that they be able to suffer and die. Thus their calling remains parallel to the way of Jesus, since his love likewise revealed itself in his giving of his life for his own. As the shepherd died for the flock, brother dies for brother (3:1, 13, 16, 17; 4:10). Thus the exhortation produces the community's liberty, without questioning the admonition's absolute validity, but rather by an unconditionally necessary obligation. Its internalization excludes any compulsion by law that is merely external and breaks entirely with synagogal casuistry. The term "Christ's commandment" possesses unrestricted validity for John. Because it has its sole content in love, however, it does not result in human bondage as would be the case if his activity were prescribed in external terms (2:3–4; 3:22; 5:2–3). The ordering of external relationships constitutes the area in which the individual and the community exercise their freedom.

The epistle's ethic may be called "spiritual," because all external means of obligation retreat completely into the background that might provide uniformity for the community's actions by way of specific regulations. The formulas of confession given by John merely express the basic idea that effects allegiance to Jesus, that is, that he is the Christ, the Son of God, without any basis for the formulation of an extensive doctrinal system that could serve the community as a means of unity (3:23; 4:15; 5:1, 5). No order of repentance or confession results from the ethical contrast whose incompatibility and danger is clearly exposed, nor does one find any regulation of conduct that could be called "methodical." The point at which sin becomes so sinful that it produces death is not determined by a legal norm. The cult, likewise, remains free from any legislation. The community's unity has a firm foundation and all-sufficient power by having received love through its common union with the Christ.

### 3. The Establishment of Faith through the Portrayal of Jesus

The agreements between John's Gospel and the epistles, both in substance of thought and form of expression, are so persistent and complete that their common authorship is secure.[68] One does not detect in John an effort to dis-

---

68. Whoever separates the Gospel from the first epistle does so at the expense of attributing to the author of one document, not merely a skillful, but a cunning imitation of the thought and style of the other. Those who consider the Gospel to be a compilation of pieces by different authors are confronted with the same difficulty. The lexical affinity of the Apocalypse with the remaining Johannine writings, likewise, is so great that those who attribute them to different authors cannot do so without assuming a conscious accommodation of one document to the other.

tinguish Jesus' word from his own by a particular coloring. This reveals the extent to which he considered himself to be Jesus' disciple. He did not sense any difference between what he received from Jesus and what he himself acquired in the course of his work for the community but rather applies the parable to himself that the branch owes everything it has to the vine.

Nevertheless, the Gospel, when viewed from the perspective of the first epistle, assumes a surprising stance that would never be derived from the epistle, even though now that we have both documents available it is certainly possible to unite the aims underlying them both. The same resolve with which the epistle advocates ethical norms is in the Gospel made subservient to the presentation of Jesus for the purpose of establishing faith. John elevates faith above everything that can otherwise be considered to be the work of Jesus, and he relates Jesus' entire ministry to it.

### a) Focusing Faith Solely on Jesus

Two prerequisites must be met for trust to be directed toward the man Jesus. To begin with, his communion with God must be apparent in its completeness, because consciousness of God alone is able to give conclusive certainty and unbroken confidence. If God reveals himself in the man Jesus, and if God's grace is received from him, then, but only then, faith is turned toward him. Therefore John's first words express Jesus' unity with God, and among Jesus' sayings it is those which demonstrate the perfection of his divine sonship that have the power of establishing the resolve of faith. But faith would not turn toward Jesus but rather elevate itself above him if Jesus were merely dependent on the Father without also receiving, on account of his dependence, his own authority and rule. Such faith might be *caused by* him but would not be *directed toward* him. But because John trusts in Jesus, and because he wants to impart a confidence directed toward Jesus to the community, he makes Jesus' glory, which is in turn a function of his divine sonship, the center of his presentation. Jesus himself embodies the virtues by which he reveals the wealth of divine love to humanity. Thus John frames all sayings pertaining to Jesus' gift for his community as statements by Jesus regarding himself. John never separates Jesus' promise from his own person. He rather expresses by it what Jesus has within himself as his own essential characteristic and what he makes available to us and effective for us.

Because faith is directed entirely toward Jesus, no one is placed beside him, neither God's messengers who were sent to Israel nor the disciples and the church.[69] For John, the glorification of the disciples is entirely excluded by the

---

69. John said expressly that Jesus' uniqueness was revealed also in the fact that John the Baptist bowed completely before him, attributing only to Jesus, not to himself, complete fellowship with God (1:15, 30; 3:30, 31). The theory that certain events in Ephesus, such as the activities of a gnostic group that venerated the Baptist as the highest messenger of revelation, caused John to make these statements, cannot be confirmed by concrete observations. What is clear, however, is that Jesus' superiority over all preceding messengers of God could be demonstrated upon the Baptist with particular clarity, since he immediately precedes Jesus' ministry, himself intervening significantly and receiving highest testimony from Jesus. But also the one among the Old Testament men who is linked directly to Jesus' work remains separated from him by the contrast that divided the one who is from the earth from the one who is from heaven.

goal of his account. Their obligation to serve, according to which Jesus gave them his word, so that the community might be established through them, is not concealed. The Christ is the door that leads the shepherds to the flock, and the vine that produces the branches that bear fruit. The gift given to Peter by Jesus consists in being given charge over Jesus' flock (10:2, 7; 15:1–2; 21:15–17). The disciples' power is based on the fact that Jesus gives to them his word and that he makes them to be his witnesses. Thus they do not bring about faith directed toward themselves but toward him. The portrayal of the church as the work by which Jesus' kingdom is revealed retreats entirely into the background.

Neither is the sacrament placed beside the Christ, as if it were a separate object of faith. John clearly has high esteem for it; for he sees Jesus' gift in the fact that he allows us to eat his flesh and to drink his blood, and he cites the water along with the Spirit when stating how man is born from God (6:53–56; 3:5). But this esteem does not apply to the sacramental act in and of itself, because the latter is not mentioned at all, either the Lord's Supper or baptism. All that is mentioned is what the Christ gives, not how the church is to act. Thus the idea is effectively ruled out that the community possesses in the sacraments the means of salvation that are effective apart from Jesus and that could serve as his substitutes.

The same motive determines the manner in which the promise of the Spirit is tied to Jesus' proclamation. The Spirit grants the life which comes from God to the believer. But even more emphatically John emphasizes the other perspective, that is, that the Spirit as the advocate of his disciples represents Jesus' cause while exposing the world's unbelief in him. Attention is directed, not toward the rich relationships to all aspects of the internal life into which the Spirit enters, but toward the fact that the Spirit assists the disciples in their witness to the Christ in their struggle with the world. The Spirit thus enables the disciple to effect faith in Jesus (3:5; 7:38–39; 14:16–17; 15:26; 16:7–15).

Because Jesus' proclamation has its aim in the establishment of faith within people, John does not portray a perceptible phenomenon, by which a change in the course of the world is produced, as Jesus' work. The subject of the message is rather solely Jesus himself, solely what he is in and of himself by his share in God and by his union with the disciples. The means by which he reveals himself are, of course, his works, without which faith in him would be inconceivable. In order for them to give rise to faith, John emphasizes their eternal, spiritual substance by which they have significance for all, not merely for their recipients. Thus the past event also impacts the readers, since it reveals to all that Jesus is the bread, the light, the life, and the resurrection. The account of the cross is therefore cast entirely from the perspective that Jesus' death represents his return to the Father, so that the cross not only presents no obstacle to faith: it rather engenders it. And the account of the resurrection extends only to the point at which the disciples, even the last one, believe. Likewise, Jesus' return is discussed to the extent that it relates to the establishment of faith. Because Jesus promises to the disciples that his communion with them is eternal and that he will come and take them with him, they trust in him. Thus it was that the richest eschatological portion of the account consists in the indictment of the inhabitants of Jerusalem, by which Jesus promises the fulfillment of Jewish expectation while no longer speaking to the disciples about the dead coming out of their graves nor sketching a depiction of his judgment (14:3; 5:28–29).

### b) The Elevation of Faith above All Other Activities

Since the aim of this portrayal of Jesus lies in faith, strong emphasis is placed on the fact that the perfection of divine love elevates his ministry above the execution of justice. It is his vocation to give life. He did not come to judge and does not stand before God as the accuser of those who reject him. Whoever believes in him is not judged, so that the final promises portray him merely as the one who comes to his own and unites himself with them. This should not be construed as a protest against the execution of justice. It rather indicates that judgment belongs to the work of the Father and the Son, because the Father has delegated judgment entirely to the Son. His presence also brings with it immediate execution of justice, because the one who does not believe is judged by that unbelief; thus he is denied God's gift. But it is divine love that provides Jesus with the aim of his commission by which he is able to give life to everyone who believes (3:17–18; 5:45, 22, 27, 30).

This is further paralleled by the fact that Jesus' call to repentance is in John entirely made part of the offer of the divine gift. John does not start by leading people to the realization and rejection of sin and thus to fellowship with the Christ and to faith. He rather *begins with faith,* since God's gift enters humanity from above, bearing in itself the basis for faith. His initial statements begin with God and then turn to the contrast between the world and God, and this same movement shapes the historical account. John does not present John the Baptist's preaching of repentance. Rather, he shows how John reveals Jesus' glory and how he brings the disciples to faith. Regarding Jesus, he demonstrates how he opens access to the divine gift both to Nicodemus and to a Samaritan woman. Now there arises hostility against him and crucifixion.

On the other hand, John was able to relate Jesus' word to faith alone in such a way that Jesus' opposition toward evil, which was characteristic of him and which he also imparted to his own, remained completely clear. Thus he demonstrates the antithesis between light and darkness, love and hate, truth and lie, life and death, God and the world. Where one element of these contrasts is present, the other is excluded. But separation from the world and its ungodly passions is gained in John by taking Jesus as starting point, and John grounds separation from below in one's allegiance to above. The power of John's position derives essentially from the fact that he expresses the resoluteness of rejection in no weaker terms than "following Jesus," so that believers gain union with the Christ at the same time as they separate themselves from sin and death. That is why John considers the Jews' opposition to Jesus a major theme of the Gospel, because it reveals unbelief which also exposes more profoundly the basis for faith and the kind of faith that is required. The genesis of unbelief also reveals how faith comes about, and the fall precipitated by unbelief also highlights the believer's possession. John casts in sharp relief the ethical basis of this struggle, contrasting those who plot murder with the one who gives life, those who lie with the one who speaks truth, the sons of the devil with the Son of God. But their reprobate will results in death, for it renders them unbelieving.

John contains little material regarding the positive content of Jesus' call to repentance, which provides instruction to good works. But the idea of a passive faith cannot arise for him, since whoever believes in the Christ belongs to the circle of those who love one another. Nevertheless, he omits any specific instruction to perform works. Jesus' commandment pertains exclusively to the internal condition of proper action, solely to love that arises directly from faith. Love is also emphatically portrayed as enabling a person to renounce greatness and even one's life (1:13, 34, 15; 12:25–26). Those norms, on the other hand, by which Jesus helped his disciples arrive at a proper evaluation of money, the institutions of marriage and the church, or the discharge of the apostolic office, are completely absent.

The relationship between faith and knowledge, likewise, proves that the controlling motive of this portrayal of Jesus is that of faith. John gives greatest emphasis to knowledge, because he does not merely present us with sayings by which Jesus ordered his disciples' conduct (as do the older Gospels) but renders visible Jesus' inner life, his dealings with the Father. But the knowledge that John associates with Jesus and seeks to impart to the church, receives its forms through love. Love wants to know the one for whom it lives; love liberates thinking from fear and does not permit intellectual labor to cease prematurely before a perfected knowledge is reached, that is, the assurance that grants us the resolved will. At the same time, love also endows knowledge with its opposition to those selfish desires which push its object far away and make out of it a thing to be used, in order to violate it and bring it under control. Instead, love wants to know only one thing: how the one to be known grants it communion. This sets limits to thought, because it is now tied closely to what it is given, to that by which the one who wants to know it reveals himself to it.

Knowledge in John has therefore each of the following two characteristics: assurance, which is entirely unaffected by doubt or anxiety and does not need theodicy or apologetic; and restraint, which seeks to possess merely what it is given and respects things that remain unrevealed. For John considers knowledge of God to be the gift of God based on the life-communion with God granted to man by God. Because the relationship with God into which man enters by knowing him is not achieved by man but is granted to him by God, the basis for all assurance regarding God is the witness borne by God regarding himself. This testimony is mediated to the believer not merely by the community and its doctrine and Scripture; it rather emerges from within him. Whoever listens to God and learns from God and is drawn by him truly apprehends his work (5:37; 6:44–45). This also comes to expression in John's concept of truth. Just as the actuality that makes us conscious of the truth is not produced by man but is the work of God, truth likewise is not a product of his conceptual efforts, as if it did not exist until it arose in his consciousness. It rather possesses objective reality and power given to it by God. It offers itself to man for the purpose of being accepted by him, and only by his receptive attitude does it become his. This is why John unites the Spirit with the truth. Since truth is God's possession and gift, it becomes part of man's knowledge by the activity of the Spirit. For this reason John did not portray Jesus as an originator or innovator but as the witness, because truth requires nothing but the witness who advocates it against those who oppose it.[70] And for this reason John uses the metaphor of light as an illustration of what truth is and provides. It radiates from God into the world and is not the production of man. Man receives the capacity to see by being illumined by light from God and the capacity to hear by being laid hold of by God's word.

By uniting knowledge with love John also clarifies its relation to faith. The esteem granted to faith by John is also transferred to knowledge, particularly to that process with which knowledge begins, that is, seeing, since faith receives its basis and substance from true apprehension. John ties that vision which apprehends the working of God immediately and indivisibly to the possession of life. There is no longer any death for the one who knows God (17:3; 6:40; 12:45). Since selfish longings are, however, completely separated from knowledge, answers are denied to questions that hanker after no more than knowledge. How the Word that is God came into being, how that darkness originated in which the light shines, how the Word and the flesh of Jesus coexist, by which processes the birth of the Spirit is experienced, how Jesus' flesh and blood can be enjoyed by us, such questions are neither posed nor answered. It is merely stated what, in John's judgment, is able to effect believing allegiance to Jesus, while the entire Gospel does not feature a single speculative sequence of thought, however childlike or fantastic we may suppose that John would have sounded had he attempted speculative thought. For this reason theological speculation has always gratefully appropriated Johannine knowledge but always supplemented it with its own ideas. This was true in the case of Origen, who found his doctrine of the Logos in John, and applies to those who in our day find in John parallels to Philo's pronouncements regarding the Logos or discover in him a form of dualism or the doctrine of transubstantiation. All these theories fail to stop where John does, because his statements do not satisfy their intellectual curiosity. John considered what he wrote sufficient, since he wrote in order to establish faith, not speculative theories.

## 4. New Christological Elements

### a) The Sonship of God

As the reason why faith should be placed in Jesus, John names the fact that Jesus is the Son of God. The concept of the Son is his major expression, and his theological achievement, as far as one can speak of such, consists in the development of this concept. For the Son concept provided him with both conditions of faith: Jesus' dependence on God by which he speaks the divine word and performs the divine work, and his independent authority by which he provides hu-

---

70. John's doctrine of knowledge, through being determined by the concept of "witness," retained a Jewish form far removed from Greek logic, which was syllogistic. The rabbi sought and valued nothing but eyewitness proof. This was because as theologian he was a legal specialist, and as a teacher a judge, and therefore was intent on assessing evidence. But evidence was evaluated by means of witness.

manity with the divine gift. Thereby, however, John neither forsakes nor weakens the Christ concept. For since Jesus brings the divine gift to humanity, he becomes its Lord by creating the community of believers. Nevertheless, John determines that the Christ concept does in fact require an explanation and substantiation. How is it that the king of the Jews is the one with whom all are to unite in faith? John uses the Son concept to delineate the basis, manner, and extent of Jesus' rule. It is based on the fact that he has his life from God and for God. From the perspective of Jesus' divine sonship John directly derives the universal scope of Jesus' mission. By it Jesus signifies the decisive turning point, not merely for Israel's history, but for that of humanity. Because God is known in him, he is for all the one they need, the one who provides the fulfillment of the fundamental relationship in which all created beings stand with God (1:3, 9).

Jesus possesses sonship of God in the personal realm of his being that is illumined by consciousness, not by a transfer of power or a communion of substance with God, which might tie him to God beneath or alongside God's personhood without actually touching it. On this point, John's pronouncements have a deliberate clarity, because he seeks to distance the concept of a God-man, which he shows Jesus to be, entirely from gnostic, magical connotations. Jesus' sonship provides him with a share in God's love and thus also in his power, and the uniqueness of his sonship results in the fact that this share amounts to perfect communion. God's love that is given to him provides him with the ability of co-laboring with God to an unlimited degree, and, since it is based on God's love, this collaboration is predicated upon the fact that the Son truly apprehends and does the Father's will and brings his work to completion. He has sonship because his love is matched by identical obedience. Now there is no work of God that the Father does not hand over to the Son (5:19–30; 4:34; 8:28–29; 12:49; 14:10).

Therefore Jesus' glory does not consist merely in his future rule; it is also entailed by his sonship and is truly apprehended with every bit of knowledge Jesus acquires. For the communion of willing and working with God in which he stands is glory, so that he promotes God's glorification by his earthly life (1:14; 12:28; 13:31; 7:4, 22). At the same time, John manages to describe Jesus' glory in such a way that any appearance of selfish motivation or self-exaltation is excluded. He achieves this by revealing Jesus' complete subordination of all the activities of his will to his consciousness of God. Jesus desires nothing but communion with the Father, places his glory in no one else's hands, and does not seek glory from things or people, but rather stills his longing completely by knowing the Father and by having him at his side. He conceives even of his relationship with the Father in such a way that his communion with him consists in his dependence on him. His possession therefore arises from his receiving, his power from his selflessness, and his rule from his obedience.

Thus the depiction of Jesus also reflects a concept that may be called "spirituality." John frames the concept of God in personal terms, placing Jesus' communion with God in his knowledge and love of the Father and considering it to be his all-encompassing possession and his entire glory. In these internal, spiritual processes consists for John the essential characteristic of Jesus' life. Thus Jesus' messianic ministry merges entirely with his function of revealing

God. From this John gains both the complete separation from all forms of piety opposing Jesus and the power of his union with him. There cannot be any share in the love of God that is not rooted in union with the Son. A claim on God in opposition to the Son is futile and unattainable, for God never breaks the bond of love with his Son. Whoever separates himself from the Son has forsaken God (3:18; 8:19, 36, 45; cf. 1 John 2:23). Following Jesus, on the other hand, brings about inclusion in the love of God, and thus one has passed from death into life. Since believers perceive Jesus to be in the Father, they know that his fellowship with them grants them union with God. Those who believe in him therefore consider it to be the highest good that they know him, remain in him, and are where he is (5:24; 6:56; 15:4–7; 17:24). By uniting them with himself, he exercises his regal authority over them. His messianic activity does not consist in the subjection of the world or the transformation of the community but in the fact that he imparts to it the knowledge of his sonship. The essence of what Christendom possesses is therefore of purely spiritual substance and does not consist of visible effects or powers, or material possessions. All elements of thought here cohere as parts of a whole: as the Father relates to Jesus as Father by his love and commandment, Jesus performs the work of the Son in love and obedience, and the community has his gift by believing and loving.

John does not, however, conceive of Jesus' spirituality in such a way that he neglects the visible actualization of what is internal or spiritual, thus depreciating the natural part of human life. Rather, internal realities must be made manifest. For the will of Jesus is love, which, in turn, brings about fellowship. The external act, as far as it consists in a *work,* remains a *sign* that points beyond itself to an internal reality, and insofar as it consists in a *word,* a *testimony* that confirms his concealed relationship with the Father. Even the dealings of the resurrected Jesus with the disciples are viewed from the perspective of "signs" (20:30). Still, it would be erroneous to conclude that John derives the concept of resurrection only reluctantly from tradition, merely visualizing the idea of immortality. The Easter account shows clearly that John with his faith is a serious participant in those processes. But they remain somewhat limited and isolated beside the constant presence of the Christ with his own and his future eternal reunion with them. The individual encounter receives value from the fact that it establishes and reveals a person's abiding relationship with Jesus.

Thus there also is no discernible effort to relate the Gentile church (as whose member and for whom John wrote) directly to Jesus' earthly work. We do not even read in John a commissioning along the lines of Matthew.[71] Jesus' concluding prayer gives thanks for the successful accomplishment of his work without concealing its limited scope. The disciples united with him at that time are, however small and weak, what the Father gave him. And this is what Jesus praises God for, because thereby God glorified both himself and his Son. For even the few who remained with Jesus serve the purpose of revealing the Father and of accomplishing the work the Father had given to the Son; through them

---

71. John 12:20–24 is merely used to show that Jesus' concern for the Greeks did not keep him from the cross, and the same principle is expressly affirmed for his disciples as well.

he shows who he is and what he gives. The community of disciples becomes the sign by which the abiding, perennially effective will of God is made manifest. What he gave to them, he gives to all believers. By drawing them to himself, and by preserving them with himself by virtue of his death and exaltation, he reveals his messianic office to the world.

This provides John with the freedom he exercises in respect to the individual events that made up Jesus' earthly life.[72] John's account is based on the conviction that Jesus' ministry cannot be reduced to the individual events of his earthly work. For John, Jesus' works were not primarily significant because of their immediate results but because they revealed and made effective Jesus' inner being that makes him visible as the Son. John proclaims Jesus in the conviction that the gospel is completely expressed by the statement "Jesus is the Son." John's elevation above individual events is also reflected in his depiction of the historical particularity and uniqueness of the history which to later generations can never become so clear as it was for John. As apostolic preaching grew further removed from its point of departure both temporally and spatially, this knowledge was bound to come to the fore. Nevertheless, John portrays Jesus from the vantage point that what occurred in his earthly life is what introduced all to God's presence and gives them life. He answers the question of what constitutes the abiding and essential element in Jesus' life by maintaining that it was not individual *sayings* or single *acts* but the *person* in its complete and therefore eternal communion with God. This assurance corresponds directly to the concept of God that he affirmed. God's life does not merely consist in individual acts or temporally limited effects. He is. The same is true of Jesus. What he is gives shape to what he does. He does not acquire sonship and rule through his individual acts but possesses them on account of what he is in his continual relationship with God. And when this relationship comes to light, it is revealed to all that their faith can and should be directed toward Jesus.

### b) Jesus' Eternity

Since John affirmed God by the expression denoting the perfection of God, "He is," his consciousness of God rejects any change, oscillation, or process, that is, the intrusion of time into God's will and work. What is done by God in history and time contains a *being*. His word was in the beginning: it did not merely originate when the world began and man heard it; it is not a product of history. Truth does not come about through human thought and speech; *it is,* and the calling of the one who expresses it consists in his articulating it as its witness. The Son does not come into being but *is* before Abraham was, and his relationship with God is immutable. Christ's unique status does not first arise when he aspires to it, acquires it, and appropriates it: it is his because it is God's. The shepherd knows his own, and the sheep do not become his property for the first

---

72. The freedom with which John places his account beside the older writings is at present customarily compared to that of the poet who shapes his material according to his own judgment and sentiments. But faith is never tied to poetic images but rather to the clear consciousness that the poetic construct lacks reality.

time when he enters his sheepfold; that is why they hear his voice (1:1; 18:37; 8:58; 10:3–5). The entire portrayal of time and history is subordinated to the conviction that God's will is unshakeable and comes to pass inexorably.

From this John did, however, not conclude that history was futile or, as he was interpreted by the Greeks, that it merely revealed what had long existed in God's invisible realm. Rather, he also attributed productive, causal effectiveness to the temporal process. God does his works, gives the Son to the world, and possesses in him a presence that pervades his temporal existence. Likewise, he works in the believer, draws him to himself, gives Jesus to him, and brings him to life (5:17; 10:38; 6:44–45; 17:6, 9; 3:3), so that God's love, directed toward the believer, is completed in what the believer experiences and does. Jesus' "nature" would not exist apart from these acts; his works do not merely reveal his nature but render it effective, so that it has its existence and its reality by them and in them. From Jesus' "I am" result his knowing and loving, his bearing of witness, and his ministry. His obedience is not merely a manifestation of his sonship but exists and is preserved by it. Likewise, the community's inclusion into the eternal knowledge and love of God results in that communion with him that fulfills its existence. Therefore the power of the human will that is effective toward God does not disappear in John, even though his attention is primarily devoted to the eternal nature of the divine life. As the Son does not sink into a will-less passivity on account of God's work but rather himself becomes the worker of the divine works, so the doing of truth, the keeping of Jesus' words, and the fulfillment of the divine commandments possess for man the complete seriousness of a causal act by which communion with Jesus comes into being and is preserved (3:21; 8:51; 14:15; 15:10, 2). Conversely, man becomes a slave to sin by doing it and is separated from the light by loving the darkness (8:34; 3:19). The refusal to believe to which the individual is led by his lying, hatred, and evil deeds effects his separation from God.

More accurate than the thesis that John's consciousness of God depreciated the course of the world to mere appearance is that interpretation of his words which found in it elements of the doctrine of predestination. For what is God's own and what he does not recognize as such are separated from one another by a boundary drawn by God himself. John, however, nowhere elevates the divine counsel above the course of history, erecting a dichotomy between these two elements by placing God's eternal decree on one side and the course of history on the other. Rather, God's relationship to the world that orders all human experience and activity is at work in the present. John does not contrast the past and the present but distinguishes between what is above and what is below, what is divine and what is human, and what is above and divine exists forever and possesses effective power.

John makes the testimony to Jesus' eternal life in God a central part of his proclamation, because it reveals the perfection of Jesus' communion with the Father. John did not call Jesus eternal merely in the sense that he brings about the future consummation but also in the sense that he participates in the work of creation. This secures Jesus' complete supremacy above all and the universal scope of his commission. Humanity came into being through him, and nothing was created apart from him. Man's relationship with him does not originate for the first time from the proclamation of his message; it precedes all events of individual or general history. He is the light of all who come into the world (1:3, 9–11).

This makes unbelief all the more severe, because it ruptures the relationship to Christ that is rooted in creation. Whoever does not accept him, does not know the one by whom he came into being. He disputes the right of the one whose possession he is. His own did not receive him. By the same token, faith thereby comes to completion. As the Jew preserves by faith in Jesus what he was given through Abraham and Moses, the Greek, too, possesses by faith in Jesus the completion of that relation to him that shaped the course of his life from the beginning. Since he belongs to Jesus' sheep, the shepherd calls him to himself (1:10–11; 11:52; 10:16).

The messianic idea always entailed the expectation that the Christ would complete what God had begun in former times. Initially it was Israel that presented itself as what had been begun but remained incomplete, yet awaited fulfillment. Israel's fall into judgment, however, does not jeopardize Christ's aim of completing what God had begun. It rather reveals that the beginning to which his work harks back is not merely the calling of Israel or the giving of the Law, but truly the beginning, that is, the coming into being of creation and humanity's origin. The appearing of the Christ in time and his work in history bring to completion what had been established at the very beginning.

This resulted in a severe problem comparable to the one that arose from the rule of the Law prior to the Christ. John now knew a dual revelation, the illumination of all by the Word that exists with God, and the calling of the community to God by the man Jesus. He united both in such a way that he did not conceive of Christ's supernatural work as a substitute for his earthly ministry but as the foundation from which it receives its authority. He did not base Jesus' worthiness merely on the fact that he had a part in the work of creation, but first and foremost on the fact that he possessed and revealed sonship in his human form of life. By leaving this mystery intact, John does not intend to obscure what has been revealed; he rather seeks to show its profundity. Since he derived from Jesus' eternal existence not the depreciation of history but its effective power by which it produces eternal results, the knowledge of the earthly Christ does not enable us merely to be aware of the existence of the eternal Christ. Rather, he becomes the Christ for us only by coming into the world and calling us to himself through his message. For history is not necessary merely for our sake, so that we might obtain a knowledge of God's gift; it is also effective before God, is made by him, and is brought to its eternal completion by him.

The rootage of Christ's work in his identity as the Creator corresponds to its extension to all of humanity, which it will receive by his new revelation. For "on the last day" he is the judge of all, and he also is the one who brings everyone to life, since the judgment of the dead presupposes their resurrection. The conclusion, however, that a logician might have derived from Christ's creative power, that is, that the latter's salvific activity might pertain to all of mankind so that all would be led into eternal life, was not drawn by John, since the concept of justice possessed immovable firmness in his concept of God. John testified mightily to the divine necessity of the execution of justice by pointing to the fact that, while everything came into being through Jesus, not everyone is his possession, and that, even though God had given the world to him, the world in its entirety does not possess life, but believers have life in him. Yet not all believe. John affirms this with profound sincerity, without, however, formulating a theory to explain this phenomenon. He was content to show to the believer the firmness of his union with Christ and to the unbeliever the guilt and destructive power of his rebellion against Christ by allowing the individual's share in God which stems from creation to be established in Jesus.

### c) The Word

Eternity and the causal power of history exist side by side in John. This corresponds in his concept of Christ to the fact that the divinity of Jesus does not suspend his humanity. It rather produces and guides it. If, for John, Jesus' work were not tied to his humanity, he would not portray his human life for us. He wants to show us that Jesus was the Son of God in such a way that the man Jesus came into being through the divine Word, so that it may be said regarding the man Jesus that he had descended from heaven (1:1; 3:13; 6:33, 38; 16:28). This affirmation is profoundly altered if it is said that John's interest is devoted merely to Jesus' body, but not to his humanity. This is excluded by his use of the term "flesh" in contrast to deity. The term "flesh" never directs attention merely to corporeality, a concept that has absolutely no independent significance in John's thought, not even in his ethics. Jesus' greatness also does not consist in the fact that deity provided for itself with a body a kind of vessel. The subject of John's proclamation and of his faith is rather Jesus' person, with its internal knowledge and actions, and that is what he portrays as human.

When he speaks of the Word that had been prior to creation with God and that shares in everything God is, John provides an explanatory statement that indicates how eternity and creative power became the characteristic of the man Jesus who came into being by his birth. Therefore he is the one who brings the world into being. The fact that the Word becomes flesh ensures that the human being that originates in such a way stands in complete communion with God and possesses God's glory. Jewish tradition that completely unites effective, creative power with the divine Word, and Jesus' statements regarding the power of the Word, which does not merely describe but is able to give, ensure that John conceived of the Word in terms of the causal power by which Jesus' humanity came into being and by which it was determined and led. This is confirmed by Jesus' own words regarding the foundation of his individual actions, of his words and works in God. In John's view, Jesus proceeded in his human life, will, and thought from the divine Word, and Jesus' humanness was for him not merely a temporary shell but an abiding, integrated whole.

Thus John prevented any wavering in devotion between Jesus and God, uniting the remembrance of Jesus completely with the consciousness of God. The older christological formula that has Jesus live and act in the Holy Spirit was insufficient in this regard, and it is not unduly daring to suspect John to have felt this. If the Christ was conceived of as eternal, an eternal man easily took his place in the community's conception beside the eternal God.[73] John refutes such ideas: the Word is eternal, and Jesus is eternal, because he is the Word. As long as Jesus' proclamation has its subject in his work for humanity, the concept of the Spirit was sufficient to ground his right to rule, since he is able to act according to God's will and in God's power because he has the Spirit. Once Jesus' earthly work, however, had been supplemented in the community by the portrayal of his heavenly activity, resulting in the trinitarian framing of the concept of God, a formula became desirable that distinguished God's presence in Jesus from that possessed by the church. John achieved this by saying of believers that the Spirit was with them, and of Jesus that he was the Word. And even in the portrayal of Jesus' earthly ministry, the concept of the Spirit did not completely prevent the notion that what was in view was merely a limited, isolated movement by a divine impulse, an inspiration by which individual words were received from God and individual works done with God. For the concept of the Spirit was easily emptied to denote mere "power." In John, however, Jesus' majesty does not consist of individual deeds he performs, but of the continual unity of his personal life with God. Among existing terms to describe the persistent presence of God in Jesus, by which he shaped him in his conscious existence and revealed himself through him, John knew none so apt as that of "the Word."[74]

Even this designation, however, did not provide a completely secure protection against the interpretation of Jesus' aim in terms of material conceptions. There was still speculation that John might have meant the world's elemental power. He rendered such speculation, however, difficult for his readers, because the Word in itself entails a conception different from power and immediately suggests the conscious, personal life of God. Moreover, John stresses that the Word is nothing less than God and does not rank below him in status; rather, it embodies the complete vitality and power of God. John never called the world's elemental power "God." Such interpretations intermingle the Johannine message with Stoic concepts of God and other similar ideas that are not found in John at all. By this use of "Word" he grounded the human person of Jesus not in nature or God's power but in the wisdom and love of God.

Why the Word became flesh—this is not discussed in terms of a necessity inherent in God. John answered this question only by indicating the purpose of its commission, because he conceived of the Word in terms of God's spirituality. For the ground of the will is revealed in that which it creates. By Jesus' proclamation of the message of the Father whom no one has seen, and his conferral of eternal life which no one has, it becomes clear why the Word became flesh and why God gave his Son to the world (1:18; 5:37; 6:46; 3:16). The will of God who sends him is recognized by the gift he brings, and this makes evident that his commission has its basis in the love of God.

---

73. One is reminded of the modern interpretation of Paul's statements regarding the Christ that finds an eternal primal man even in Paul. If Christians, whose thought was less clear than Paul's, spoke about Jesus' eternity, their statements may easily be taken to imply that they placed an eternal man beside the eternal God.

74. John also knew the term "Shekinah," which was used by the rabbinate for God's presence with Israel (1:14). He rightly considered it, however, less clear than "Word."

## 5. New Anthropological Elements

What did John consider to be the essential characteristic of man, to whom the Christ was sent and whom he unites with himself through faith, the characteristic by which his relationship with Christ is determined? The answer to this question centers around the term "world," another one of the convictions that shaped John's entire presentation of Jesus.

### a) The Jewish World

The demonstration of Jesus' divine sonship and his close association of people with "the world" constitute a close unity, because the universal scope of the message that is grounded in sonship is brought to completion by the concept of the "world." What God does is done for all; because it was God's love that sent Jesus, he is given to the world, and therefore faith, which is not tied to the particular characteristics of an individual but can be granted to all, becomes the means by which Jesus creates his community.

The central significance of Christ in John's thought caused his concept of the world to receive its form through the contrast existing between Jesus and man. This contrast is caused not by the caprice of individuals or the particular circumstances of Judaism but by the pervasive condition of mankind. For this reason it exposes the nature of the world. What opposes Jesus and is opposed by him is in John not merely an individual aberration, such as Pharisaism, but the joint will of all, which comprises human character everywhere. Therefore Jesus' cross exposes the world's separation from God, and it is not simply Caiaphas or Gamaliel who are judged: judgment is rather executed upon the world (12:31).

The orientation of Jesus' mission toward the world arises in John not from the fact that he considered the Jewish way of life and that of the world to be antithetical, but rather from the observation that the Jew in fact follows the ways of the world and thus belongs to it. If John had set Jesus' Jewishness in contrast to his universal aim in the opinion that Jesus could not have been a Jew if he wanted to fulfill his universal calling in its positive and negative dimensions, he would have removed himself far from the original perspective of Jesus and his disciples. John, however, in no way obscured Jesus' embeddedness in Judaism; neither did he treat it as an embarrassment that required justification. He does not perceive any tension between Jesus' Jewishness and his rule over all but considers him to be the Savior of the world, because he is the King of the Jews (1:49; 12:13; 18:33; 19:19). For John, like all the other disciples, held Israel to be the religious community established by God. Like the other apostles, he does not place Israel beside the other nations as a nation like them, nor does he set Israel's temple beside the other temples. Neither does he place Israel's Scripture beside other books as of equal or comparatively greater value. He rather regards as settled God's calling of the fathers and his sending of the prophets.[75] Therefore Jesus' entire work is devoted to Israel and receives its

---

75. The fathers and prophets: 4:22; 5:45–47; 7:22–23; 8:39–40; 12:41; Scripture: 5:39; 10:35. Since John considers the prophets to be witnesses of the Christ, he certainly did not have them in mind in 10:8. The desire to secure for themselves rule over the community and to exploit it for their own ends, John found in Jesus' opponents, not in the prophets.

world-historic significance from the fact that he performs it upon the Jews and is rejected by them. Because Israel rejects him, his death is the judgment of the world and of its princes, and Jesus' glorification is the revelation of life for all who believe. For in John, the representative of mankind who possesses what epitomizes good and evil is neither the Greek, be it a philosopher or artist, nor the Roman as world ruler—it is the Jew who occupies this lofty place, not owing to his natural attributes, but because he is the recipient of God's revelation. Therefore it is also not in polytheism or in pagan vice but in Israel's unbelief that the sin of the world and the resulting judgment appear. Israel's privilege is completely realized by the fact that Jesus comes to the nation and lives and dies among its people. But this does not result in a glorification of Israel; John rather sees the significance thereby awarded to the Jew in the fact that he reveals the world's godless nature.

This train of thought stands in connection with the feature that may be called the pale and abstract manner of Johannine narration. John viewed the events occurring in Jerusalem in view of humanity at large, both regarding what was divine in this history as well as its human and reprehensible elements. For this reason he was not concerned with a colorful narrative style that would reflect the local and individual characteristics of that drama but with the demonstration of its implications for all, so that all might recognize that they are here cast aside and called.[76]

### b) The World's Corruption

Jesus' presence and destiny reveal the world's darkness. John derives its neediness not from the condition of nature but pays attention solely to the things that determine man's personal existence. Man is cast by the concept of the "world" as receiving his condition from what is characteristic of all and as being placed into an existence from which issue his thinking and willing. Therefore the sin of the individual reveals the moral corruption of all, because the moral state of all determined the state of his life with its profound sinfulness. John did not acknowledge this interdependence as normal. Man needs the liberation that severs his bondage to the condition of the entire human race. God's grace for man consists in the fact that God takes him out of the world, so that he is no longer from the world and no longer has what it injects into him. Instead of receiving the things that fulfill him from the world, he now receives them from God (15:19; 17:6, 14).

Through the conception of "the world," Jesus' call to repentance receives a virtually universal framework. In this form, it encompasses all stages and varia-

---

76. Therefore John does not linger over the particular Jewish or Pharisaic sins; he is solely concerned to expose the Jews' opposition toward God. For this reason he also places no value in a distinction between the subsequent stages in Jesus' work. True, John indicates that Jesus performed a large portion of his work in Galilee; but his attention is devoted to the final outcome, which results from the fact that Jerusalem rejected him. The city has this importance as the center of Judaism in its entirety, whose actions determine the destiny of all. What happened in Jerusalem was done by all the Jews, and the entire narrative focuses on the way in which the ancient community related to Jesus as a unified whole. James provides the same assessment of the Jewish condition.

tions of human development and renders all distinctions between wise and fool-ish, righteous and sinners, Jews and Gentiles insignificant. The basic form of human life is the same in all, so that it provides a common element. Therefore all are at an equal distance from Jesus, who is elevated above all through his communion with the Father. Nicodemus, the Teacher of Israel, bears the mark of worldliness no less than the Samaritan woman who had sunk to the lowest level of her nation.[77]

The world's alienation from God is shown by the fact that there is neither light nor life in it. It is dark, because it does not know the truth, walking in delusion and therefore being ignorant of what it does and where it is going (1:5; 8:12; 12:35). Therefore its end is death (3:16; 5:24; 6:49; 8:21, 24). Since God, how-ever, is the Giver of life, Christ's gift to believers consists in the fact that they live. The couching of Jesus' promise in terms of "life" constitutes another characteristic feature of the Johannine conception of the Christ. It also lends expression to John's "universalism." For through the term "life," Jesus' gift is defined in such a way that it provides help for the need of all, independent of any particular situa-tion. But there is always still a second idea that John links with the term "life." This results in the following conceptual pairs: life and light (1:4; 8:12), life and truth (14:6; cf. word and life in 6:68), spirit and truth (4:23; 14:17; 15:26; 16:13), grace and truth (1:14), freedom and truth (8:32; cf. work and truth in 1 John 3:18). By itself, the concept of life would at least not exclude a physically oriented doctrine of salvation. But John's understanding of spiritual devotion receives its personal nature in a comprehensive way from the sonship of God toward which faith is directed. John secures this personal dimension by a second term designat-ing God's relationship to our consciousness and will. By proving to be the Light of the World, Jesus moves our consciousness and creates the possibility of faith. But because formulations that remain in the realm of our volition and sight are insufficient, and because he needs a word that relates God's work to man's entire existence, designating its absolute scope, he selected from among the phrases that expressed Israel's hope and Jesus' promise the term "eternal life."

### c) The Prince of the World

The human inability to see and experience life is rooted in the fact that Satan rules man as the Prince of this world (12:31; 14:30; 16:11).[78] This name does not assign him a relationship to nature but designates human existence as his domain. The fact that man is ignorant of this dependence demonstrates that he lives in darkness. As he does not know God above, he is ignorant of the lower

---

77. This likewise influenced the shaping of the narrative. Those reports are missing that reveal Jesus' compassion for those who had fallen; the tax-collector is not featured; the image of the shepherd is well developed, but the account of the lost sheep does not occur. The distinction be-tween the righteous who do not need repentance and those who had fallen vanishes.

78. The title "Prince of the world" with its Jewish connotation will stand in connection with those "princes" whom God places as rulers over the nations. If we ponder the unity of mankind, we arrive at one prince who presides over all. For John, however, we cannot show that the respec-tive references to "the accuser" and "prince of the world" point to two different spirits. Since he says of the accuser that he is the father of those who lie and hate (8:44), it is certain that he rules the world. For the world lies and hates, and fatherhood is always the basis for ruling status as well.

powers from which he receives his impetus and guidance. It was only Jesus who told the world this; and he did not merely tell it but simultaneously revealed the evil one's rule to the world by the fact of his own existence. Belonging to the Jewish nation provides no protection from Satan; in the case of the Jews it becomes rather particularly evident how dark and in bondage to evil people are. This reveals Jesus' calling and the value of faith in him even more fully. He comes in order to destroy the devil's works. He draws to himself out of the world those who are God's rather than Satan's property (16:33; 12:31; 8:47; 18:37).

This is probably the reason why John's account of Jesus does not stress demon exorcisms. The attention to the ethical process is not diverted by referring to physical maladies as the work of supernatural corrupters. Mankind's misery does not consist merely in the fact that delusion and other calamity overtakes it with inexplicable power, but that it obeys the satanic impulse in its reasonable and religious conduct.

John does not comment on the origin of mankind's alienation from God, its fall into darkness and death: he merely pronounces the fact. He rejects the theories of gnosticism that somehow derived what is dark and evil in the human being from God, for God is pure light and thus does not have any darkening effect on man. Therefore darkness does not arise from one's share in God but from alienation from God. It arises not from God's influence, but from the loss of the divine gift (1 John 1:5). Moreover, he made expressly clear that God's majesty operates in such a way that no one can see him (1:18; 6:46; cf. 1 John 4:12, 20). This is a boundary rooted in the nature of God which therefore cannot be overcome, separating the world from God. For John, this is the reason why we need the Son for true apprehension of God. He rejects all gnostic assurances claiming to have attained to a vision of God. But this does not account for the world's opposition toward God. The canon ensures that he has the fall of the first man in view, which is also evidenced by the fact that he calls Satan "the murderer from the beginning" (8:44). But no attention is drawn to the connection between the world's present condition and the events at the beginning. John did not yield to an impulse that led away from the fact of man's predicament to the exploration of its origin, certainly not in the way which is alleged by the popular attribution of a gnostic dualism, by which he might have assigned to the world a physical quality that separated it from God. Not a single one of John's pronouncements uses naturalistic categories. Ethical categories appear rather precisely when the contrast is delineated in the starkest terms. They lend John's opposition to the world its irreconcilable sharpness, because he does not conceive of truth and lie or love and hate as relative difference but irreconcilable contrasts from which, based on his concept of God, results man's destiny.

### 6. The Interpretation of Jesus' Cross

The understanding of Jesus' sonship on the one hand and the concept of the world on the other also determine the necessity and appropriateness of Jesus' will to the cross. The Son has his place with the Father; he returns to the place from which he came (13:1, 3; 16:28; 17:13). In death he proves to be the one who lives, because it represents his departure to the Father. His departure lessens neither his own nature nor his calling on behalf of the world; it rather elevates both. This outcome becomes necessary, because the world can neither love nor understand him and therefore has no room for him.

John therefore does not view the cross as a mystery that renders faith more difficult for him, although he gained his relationship with Jesus entirely from the cross. His entire presentation of Jesus is a *theologia crucis,* since he places Jesus' aim from the beginning in his death. He diligently develops his conflict with Judaism and collects the entire message given by Jesus to his disciples as the Farewell Discourse, because Jesus here expresses his conviction that his death does not separate him from believers but rather unites him with them. But the teaching of the cross does not become for John a principal theme in the sense that he wrestles with a mystery whose exploration requires an unusual amount of theory: the gospel consists for him in the teaching of the cross precisely because it is in his *death* that Jesus reveals his sonship and thus his glory and his grace for the community.

The overall thrust of John's portrayal of Jesus is that John does not engage in furnishing proof for the necessity of Jesus' death apart from the demonstration of his purpose and success. Because Jesus acts on his own accord in his death, but his will is obedient and carries out God's will, God's and Jesus' wills are once again known by what they give us. For Jesus, the value of the cross arises not merely from the glory to which it leads him; rather, the suffering itself has that value which obedience always possesses. By the deed of the cross he proves love to the Father and acts out his commandment, thus evidencing that conduct that constitutes his sonship and therefore bears absolute intrinsic value. Seen in this light, his death is an act of worship (10:18; 13:31; 14:31). In relation to the disciples, it renders his love perfect. He does not leave his own even when he must die. His love and fellowship with the disciples are of absolute value owing to the Son's communion with them (10:12; 13:1; 15:13). Therefore, as the Crucified One, he becomes the one who awakens faith. Faith is only possible in that which "is lifted up," just as ancient Israel believed in the raised serpent (3:14; 12:32). By his death, Jesus provides faith simultaneously with enormous tension and a firm foundation.

In relation to the world, the cross carries out Christ's office as the judge; for by it the world is judged and its ruler rejected (12:31; 16:11). Because Jesus perfects his union with the Father by way of the cross, he thereby frees himself from all that is satanic. He achieves this victory over the world and Satan by his death. By eluding their attacks unyieldingly, however, Jesus enacts his separation from the world, and this is judgment. Thereby its claims are rebutted and its power abolished. Its separation from the Son, which is completed by his rejection, death, and exaltation to the Father, is itself already executed judgment (3:18).

This *theologia crucis* renders Jesus' life and death a perfect unity. John does not refer to any single effect of his death. Jesus himself is God's gift, and in order to be such he must enter the world, die through the world, and depart from the world to the Father. One and the same will is revealed in his life and death:

Jesus' will to be the Son of God and the Savior of man, in a uniform, indivisible act. His death is therefore his entire work, just as it is only his life that sanctifies him in death and renders him effective. The claim is therefore wrong that John rooted Jesus' ministry solely in his suffering. And it is equally wrong to maintain that John based it solely in his work. Rather, he remembers Jesus' work as a great unity, for which Jesus' ministry was equally essential as his suffering, and vice versa, where living is impossible without dying and dying impossible without life. For Jesus' ministry and suffering issue from who he is. Because he is the Son whom God has given to the world, he lives by his obedience and love and likewise dies through them.

The reconciling effect of his death, on account of which Jesus is able to forgive sin, John does not attribute to a particular divine intervention; it rather results from the fact that the one who dies possesses divine sonship. Because Jesus endures sin, but only endures and does not commit it, he has overcome it. Consequently, he may and can give his fellowship to his own by placing them in God's love and peace. They are also granted forgiveness of sins through communion with him; now they are clean by the word that unites them with him (15:3; 13:10; 14:27; 20:23).

For John, the pardoning effect of Jesus' death coheres without tension with its compelling power. Jesus' demise serves for the disciples as a rule for what love does and for what it suffers by the world. Therefore his cross frees his own from false concepts of rulership and readies them for service, liberating them also from the desire to preserve their own souls, and enabling them to give their lives for one another (13:15; 12:25–26). The effect of his death, an effect intent on faith and action, leads to a uniform result, because faith determines action.

## 7. Statements Regarding the Spirit

### a) The Characteristic of the Spirit

John distinguishes the internal possession of the church from what the disciples received through their fellowship with Jesus by the following pronouncement: at that time the Spirit was not yet with us, but now he has come. But even this pronouncement does not give rise to a religious psychology: the topic of how the Spirit unites himself with human consciousness is not dealt with at all. Since he is God's possession, he exerts divine power over man and is known like the Father and the Son by what he provides for the one who believes. Since the Spirit effects life, his potent activity produces man's birth from God (3:5). This, however, remains a mystery, a matter of faith, which is assured by the certainty of communion with God while remaining inaccessible to human exploration. John rather names the Spirit's bringing of truth to reign in him as the effect entering into the consciousness of man. He nowhere stresses the special forms of prayer that were found in Christendom. The essential mark of Christian worship, on which everything depends, is that it possess the truth, which is brought about by the Spirit. John calls prophecy a gift of the Spirit, but he considers it neither the only nor the primary gift. The disciples' ability to remember Jesus' word is no lesser gift of the Spirit. The Spirit invests Jesus' word with the power by which it rules the disciples. But he also grants new, progressive insight, because he "leads them into all truth" (14:17, 15, 26; 4:23; 16:12–15).

By shaping his conception of the Spirit in such a way, John remains opposed to all intellectual theorization. He directs his view solely toward the goal of the disciples' ministry, that God's work may be done and the Christ be glorified. To this the disciples are enabled, because the Spirit speaks for them as their advocate and preserves Jesus' regal prerogative. By tying the term "Paraclete" (in the God-related turn of phrase according to which the advocate represents the disciples before God and procures for them God's grace) not to the Spirit, but to Jesus (1 John 2:1), John expresses the completeness of faith he possesses through his knowledge of Jesus. In Christ his relationship with God is secure, and his establishment in God's grace a fait accompli. He needs no other advocate before the Father but Jesus. Insofar as any legal issues arise—and they arise when the believer sins—the Christ intercedes for him as his advocate. The community needs help in relation to the world; for it cannot carry out its ministry by itself; it is aided here by the Spirit. John does not render him insignificant for the religious conduct he envisions because he receives life solely in the accomplishment of his calling (15:2). As Jesus has his sonship in the accomplishment of the divine will, the disciples have theirs in the accomplishment of their ministry. Therefore the Spirit's presence keeps them, because it helps them carry out their work, even in communion with Christ and in life.

### b) The Trinitarian Formulation of the Concept of God

Since the Spirit's roles—his witness regarding Jesus, his conviction of the world, his teaching and guidance of the community—differ from human conduct, the Spirit receives in John clearly the characteristic of personhood. He exercises his own unique functions, which are not identical with those of Christians or the Christ. John, however, said nothing of the Spirit's coming into being in the movement of life within the Godhead but merely spoke of the Spirit's presence with humanity and thus of the event that occurred on account of the exaltation of Jesus. In the Spirit's sending, the will of the Father comes to pass, but not in such a way that the Son retreats passively beside him; his sending is uniformly the act of the Father and the Son. Both are stated: that the Father gives the Spirit, and that the Christ sends him (14:16; 15:26; 16:7). This corresponds to his office as the Paraclete, since he can only serve effectively as the disciples' advocate if he comes from the Father and performs God's work upon the individual, so that God renders witness through him. Moreover, the Spirit becomes Christ's witness only because Christ sends him to his own, and his presence represents the distinguishing mark of Jesus' disciples whose message he confirms.

John conceives of God's collaboration with the Christ and of Christ's collaboration with the Spirit as a genuine unity. The idea that the Spirit replaces the Christ does not cross his mind. He does not tolerate any desire that elevates itself above the Christ, just as he does not tolerate any that would elevate it above God. The Spirit is present so that the Christ in his invisible communion with them may give to his disciples everything they own, and so that he may create everything they are. Even when the Spirit leads them to new insight, this is Jesus' possession, according to the principle that everything that belongs to the Father also belongs to the Son. Thereby the relationship between the Spirit and the Son remains completely analogous to that existing between the Father and the Son. The idea that the Christ replaces God finds no room in John, any more than does the thought that the Spirit replaces the Christ. Not merely in his inner life, but also in his actions and his success, the Son is always enveloped by the activity of the Father, which precedes the Son's work and subsequently follows it. Through God man is led to Jesus; for this reason he is received by him, and, because he has been accepted by the Christ, for this reason God bestows on him his love and presence (6:37–39, 44–45; 14:23). As the Father's and the Son's ministries are continually intertwined, the Spirit's work likewise has its ground and goal in the work of Christ. Because the Christ died and lives for man, the Spirit is with him, and because he is with him, he truly apprehends Jesus' divine sonship. Moreover, truth is powerfully at work in the believer, so that he believes it, whereby he stands in fellowship with the Christ. Thus John's concept of God takes on a trinitarian form without reflecting a formulaic use of the three divine names.

## 8. The Evangelist's Hope

In the case of the fourth evangelist, one cannot speak of a waning of hope, since he expects from the Christ the perfect gift in the clear consciousness that it will transcend the present condition of life. The Christ will reappear not merely to the disciples but to all, even to the world that crucified him. Thus a final day is approaching for the world, those who remain in their sins, the day on which they die, or, in the case of those who believe in Christ, the time at which they will live through him. Moreover, the expectation is not merely directed toward the perfection of individuals but is combined with that of the community and the world; for the concept of resurrection is maintained. The idea that Jesus' renewed appearance may follow shortly after his earthly ministry has not receded, because the final word of the account, the Risen One's instruction to John, places the fulfillment into a possible, albeit not certain, relation to the present. But the community is expressly admonished that Jesus' prophecy does not entitle it to any dogmatic conclusions. Jesus alone determines how he fulfills his promise (19:37; 6:39; 8:21, 24; 11:24; 12:48; 17:24; 21:22).

Through the faith established by John through his presentation of Jesus, the accompanying hope is strengthened as well. While gnostic piety did without hope, because it no longer appeared necessary for it at the lofty height of its religiosity, John did not go along with this trend; for he concluded that the gnostics had lost hope because they had forsaken faith in Jesus. As hope and faith perish together, the establishment of faith also produces hope. For the communion with Christ that is rooted in faith is not yet the final and complete gift Jesus gives to his own, even though it makes it visible and renders it secure. The strengthening of hope results in John at the same time in its reassurance. What Christendom currently possesses in faith and what the end will bring for it do not stand here in opposition to one another, as if an empty, dark space were wedged between the two. The Christ is known, not merely expected; he is present rather than being merely the Coming One; death has passed away rather than merely being expected to pass away at some time in the future; life has been revealed rather than being expected to be revealed at some future point in time. This relieves hope of its passionate and painful longing. Whoever can imagine desire merely as passion and hope merely as strained longing caused by pain will therefore judge that hope fades from view in John. But this does not adequately capture the matter. John achieves a strong unity between faith and hope, and this unity also strengthens hope.

The quiet assurance thus injected into hope restricts all questions pertaining to the future. No Johannine parable requires an eschatological ending in order to find its proper conclusion. The image of the shepherd portrays the community as it is currently established by the Christ; the vine is bearing its fruit at the present time. The connection between the general resurrection and the consummation of which the individual is assured, between the disciples' exaltation to see Jesus' glory and the conclusion of world history, is not made by any prophetic parable or other figure. The question of why the Christ does not reveal himself to the world is rejected; the disciple is to be grateful and to strive to stand in complete communion with God himself (14:22–24). Therefore John reproduced none of Jesus' words regarding the destiny of Israel nor concerning the glorification of the world or nature. Hope shares in the internalization and simplification accorded here to whole-hearted devotion. The object of hope consists in our seeing in the Son of God his communion with the Father.

## 9. The Unity of the Gospel and the Epistle

Because the two writings cannot be attributed to different men, we need to understand the respective aims to which John devoted his message at the exclusion of any other concerns—in the Gospel the establishment of faith in Jesus, in the epistle the fulfillment of his love commandment—as his uniform will.

### a) The Directing of Faith Solely on Jesus

In the Gospel, faith is rooted solely in the One, in Jesus alone. This exclusive reference of faith to the Christ is, however, also characteristic of the epistle. For the separation from evil it assigns to the community is derived solely from what God is and what he reveals in the Christ. One could expect from a discussion of the ethical substance of Christianity that it portray the ethical value of brotherly relations, by which the individual possesses strong protection against sin and an effective awakening to love. But the epistle's predominant theme does not point to multiple sources from which the pure will of Christendom arises. And it does not juxtapose Jesus and the church. The only thing mentioned in this regard is intercession, by which the one participates in the preservation of the other in the divine grace (1 John 5:16). This is the community's upward function, which achieves success through God's activity.

Nor did John's consciousness of his apostolic authority lead to a condition where the community's faith clung to him. Of course, it is true only of him, not also of the community, that he can testify to what he saw and heard. Thus the community receives its communion with Jesus and God through *his* word and listens to God by listening to *him*. The community's break with the apostle separates anyone who makes the attempt also from God (1 John 1:1–3; 4:6). His office consists, however, in connecting the community with Christ through his word, and therefore its faith is devoted exclusively to Christ. The assurance that they act in the truth does not result from having the apostle and receiving his epistle, but from the fact that the Spirit teaches them (1 John 2:20–21, 26–27). As faith is not placed in the church, it is likewise not directed in the epistle toward the sacrament.

The epistle's statements regarding the water and the blood, by which God's testimony comes to man, are paralleled in the way in which the Gospel links water with birth of the Spirit and the blood of Jesus is praised as the drink by which we receive life (John 3:5; 6:53–56; 1 John 5:6–8). Just as, according to the Gospel, the life-bestowing power of Jesus' flesh and blood is based on the fact that his word is Spirit and therefore is powerfully manifested in man, it is, according to the epistle, the water and the blood that bring God's testimony to man. For the Spirit speaks as Jesus' witness, and God's testimony consists in the fact that eternal life is received, just as in the Gospel life is granted through the water and the blood. This reveals an absolute appreciation for the sacraments, but one that is directed solely toward Jesus' gift that comes through them to the community. The community's act does not become the basis for its faith, and therefore neither does the form of the sacrament, about which the epistle has as little to say as the Gospel.

The same parallelism is found in the concept of the Spirit. One might expect of a presentation that becomes a didactic statement about love, and of love particularly devoted to Christ, that it focus primarily on the Spirit. But the boundaries set for such a treatment in the Gospel remain in force in the epistle. The Spirit is decidedly distinguished from believers' own experience and stands above them in divine majesty. In this regard no distinction is made between the anointing that provides teaching for the community and the advocate who guides them in all truth. Therefore the work of the Spirit is brought into a strict unity with that of the Christ. We are told in both writings that the Spirit is the witness, indeed, he testifies to the Christ's flesh: not merely to union with the exalted Lord, but an understanding of Jesus' earthly ministry and trust in his humanity (1 John 2:20, 27; 5:6; 4:2; 2 John 7). By virtue of the fact that faith in the Incarnate One becomes the mark of the divine Spirit, strong expression is given to the reality that the Spirit does not grant elevation above the Christ but that he is present in order to bring Jesus' earthly ministry to completion. Faith is directed by him indivisibly and solely to the Christ.

### b) The Elevation of Faith above All Other Activities

The Gospel gives absolute promise to faith. Since death is a thing of the past for the believer and the eternal communion with the Christ has been obtained, there is no conduct that could be placed above or beside faith. The epistle's absolute ethic is based on the same perfected assurance of faith. Its pronouncements gain their absolute validity not from what the community desires and brings about, but solely from what God effects in the Christ. The depiction of Christian existence yields therefore a clear parallel to the statements regarding the Christ; in both instances priority is given to the pronouncements pertaining to *being* over those that describe what took place. Through what God *is,* Christian existence likewise takes on the mark of perfect *being.* But in both instances this does not result in a depreciation of action. Action rather becomes significant because the nature given to the believer effects corresponding actions and preserves them. The Christian's sin does not disregard merely a commandment; it severs the real union in which he stands with God. Therefore it results in death. Likewise, love is rooted in the effective union with God in which the believer lives, and because love preserves this union, it grants him eternal life.[79]

Thus the vigor with which John poses the ethical demand does not effect a renewal of the idea of merit; for the ethical obligation results from what God is for us. That we love him because he first loved us provides the deed of Christendom both with unconditional necessity and the impossibility of crediting works to the one who does them, which would transpose faith away from Christ to man's own achievements.

We can therefore observe in the epistle the same limitations of knowledge that are characteristic of the Gospel. This is particularly manifest in the treatment of the concept of "birth from God," because the expansion of the way the question is posed becomes particularly pressing and useful for clear self-assessment when the divine work seizes our own life. John does not provide a description of the process he calls generation from God; he merely depicts its result. His train of thought goes back to the birth and the beginning, not for the sake of the beginning itself, but for the sake of what originates from it, for the sake of the life that begins with the birth. The birth receives its significance from what it produces. The community knows therefore everything it needs to know, when it is told by which kind of manifestations the life granted to it by God is revealed (1 John 2:29; 3:9–10; 4:7).

The epistle like the Gospel recognizes in Jesus the Eternal One and calls him the Word, the one who does not merely speak the Word but who is the Word, the Word that possesses life-creating power (1 John 1:1). But the formulation of Jesus "being" the Word is used in the epistle not for the purpose of explaining Jesus' unity with God but in order to point out to the community what Jesus provides for it. Whoever is able to think of faith merely in terms of a recitation of a theological formula may consider distinguishing the epistle from the Gospel because it does not reiterate the doctrine of the Logos. But the difference between the introduction to the epistle and the Gospel's Prologue merely reveals that John distinguished between theology and faith, a distinction that is also clearly seen in the Gospel. For also according to the Gospel, faith does not consist in the ability to explain Jesus' generation from God but in the assurance that grasps that purpose for which Jesus was sent into the world. But this is revealed

---

79. God is light, and he is love; therefore, we walk in the light and in love. Whoever lies and hates does not know God (1 John 1:5–6; 4:8).

by the fact that he is for them the Word of Life, the one who gives life to them through his word.

Both writings also equally include repentance in faith, which is a characteristic of Johannine devotion. Since the epistle combats religious conceit and arrogance that boasts of God but is devoid of truth and power, it would not be surprising for it to assign independent significance to repentance. But the form of admonitions preserves that found in the Gospel. The contrast between the two possible ways is stressed, and it is shown what leads to the one or the other and where they lead us. It is the task of the reader himself to determine the nature of the powers that drive him and on whom he depends, if he is a child of God or of Satan. As the believer must not find the basis for his love and faith in the power of his own will, John does not create the illusion that he can manufacture what only God is able to produce by virtue of his own admonition.

The epistle attributes causal significance to man's actions; for his salvation or doom depends on whether he denies or confesses his sin, whether he keeps or refuses fellowship with others, and whether he loves or hates (1 John 1:6–10; 2:10–11, 13; 3:17, 24). But this is neither a deviation from the Gospel nor a violation of faith. By assigning to faith the power to make someone a child of God, faith is not made the sole act of the community so that it does not need to obey, love, or keep Jesus' commandment but instead must merely believe. The idea that there was a legitimate devotion which consisted merely in believing did not exist for Jesus' disciples and would have separated them from him completely if it had entered their minds. The Gospel likewise does not consider the actions that comprise a disciple's life to be dispensable but as desired by Jesus and granted to the disciple. Therefore he must devote himself to these deeds with the same commitment that transforms his trust in Jesus into complete assurance (John 3:19–21; 13:34–35; 14:21–24; 15:2, 10). These functions assume their causal power from the same source from which faith receives its impetus: that God, because he is light, overcomes darkness and, because he is love, brings an end to hate, so that we live in him by loving, just as we believe in him for the same reason. Therefore the power by which the community is confronted with Jesus' commandment is itself a direct sign and mark of the power of the faith with which John takes hold of God in Jesus.[80]

The aversion to gnosticism, which did away with hope, accounts for why eschatological motifs are more prominent in the epistle than in the Gospel. The epistle alone speaks of the Antichrist. The community had learned that he would come; it thus expects an adversary of God who would attain world rule. But this prophecy would be perverted if for its sake the events would be neglected that currently take place in their own midst. The present does not reveal one but many antichrists, and the Antichrist not in the way in which the community expected him, but still in such a way that what prophecy alluded to,

---

80. The antithesis stems again from the following two issues: what God does for man and what man does for God. The fact that John placed the faith of the Gospel beside the moral obligation of the epistle and the fact that James and Paul kept fellowship, and the fact that the church acknowledged both James and Romans to be apostolic, all point in the same direction and complement one another.

that is, the substitution of Christ through others, transpired before their very own eyes (1 John 2:18). They should not underestimate Anti-Christendom, even less aid and abet it, because the image cast by prophecy deviates from the things that are taking place at the present time. This yields an important parallel to the manner in which John interpreted the prophetic words in the Gospel, by which the Risen One revealed to Peter and John the contrasting outcomes of their apostolic ministries. There he took his interpretation of the word directed toward Peter that initially was open to a variety of possible fulfillments from history and found its fulfillment in Peter's crucifixion. The word addressed to him, on the other hand, had already found fulfillment by virtue of the fact that it had not been given to him, as to Peter, to glorify God on a cross, but that it had become his calling to wait for Jesus; but since he does not yet stand at the end of his "remaining," he leaves the prophecy's significance open. The interpretation of the prophecy announcing the Antichrist likewise demonstrates that he has the limited figurative nature of prophecy clearly in view. Its purpose is not to replace the careful observation and examination of current history with a passive waiting for the fulfillment of the predicted events. It rather is designed to furnish the community with an alert perception of the present and the standards by which it is to evaluate the present circumstances. Thereby John exercises the same liberty concerning prophecy that his historical account reveals in relation to his reminiscences of the life of Jesus. Just as he did not tie the community's possession of salvation to the knowledge of individual words and actions of Jesus, because Jesus envelops and guides the community by his effective presence, so the value of prophecy did not consist in individual statements regarding the future but in revealing the world's antagonism toward God in all its profundity and thereby to assign the community its proper place in all stages of this struggle.

The fact that John concluded from the emergence of gnostic anti-Christianity that it was the last hour reveals that the original form of hope possessed for him a firmness that could not be shaken, a firmness that he neither wanted nor was able to dissolve or reconfigure. The objections of gnosticism did not weaken this foundation for him. To the contrary, they prove by their opposition against Jesus that he is about to reveal himself, which in turn corresponds to the final word of the Gospel, which makes waiting for Jesus' return the characteristic and calling of John.

Still, the epistle features a conflict between faith and hope as little as the Gospel. Its practice of drawing attention toward Christ's return and his verdict as the judge (1 John 2:28; 4:17) does not shake the absolute statements that we are born of God, have overcome the world, are not touched by the evil one, and cannot sin. For hope arises from God's gift and is here not merely an unbelieving result of pain. It is commensurate with the ethical thrust of these pronouncements that the execution of justice belongs emphatically to the office of the Christ, because the anticipation of Christ's judgment aids one's will in its resolve to do good. That he will execute his office as judge reveals completely that he removes the ability to do evil from the one whom he unites with himself.

## 10. The Prophet and the Evangelist

Since prophecy serves the substantiation of hope with the same resolve by which the Gospel requires faith and the epistle ethical industry, the three writings preserved by the church because it considered them to come from John jointly stress the three constituent activities of the community's piety: faith, love, and hope. This "systematic" approach does not provide occasion for deriving it from a deliberate plan, say, that of a literary artist who spins reality out of his pen. It rather resulted from the fact that John in his dealings with the community was continually led to strengthen its hope, faith, and love. His apostolic commission required that he give it whatever it needed, and for this reason he served it as evangelist, teacher, and prophet. The church's conviction that John combined the hope proclaimed by his prophecy with faith as established by the Gospel and love as revealed by the epistle is confirmed by the fact that the same motifs, which are decidedly characteristic of a given individual, represent the constitutive elements of all three documents.

### a) The Personal Conception of Religion

Prophecy depicts only people in their ethical dimension. The course of history culminates in the battle of the Antichrist against the Christ. God stands above the latter, Satan above the former. To the person with his will moved from below or above is added the city, the organization of the many for the purpose of joint life. Beside the Antichrist stands Rome, beside the Christ the future city of God. The entire web of relationships that we call history, state, and culture is beyond the purview of this book. Even nature retreats almost completely into the background in light of the activity of God's heavenly servants. A depiction of the glorification of nature, by which nature is brought into conformity with the eternal life of the risen ones does not become the subject of prophecy. Since Scripture promises a new heaven and a new earth, John repeats this promise. But the meaning of "a new heaven and a new earth" is not the focus of the vision. The powers for whose struggle John seeks to open Christendom's eyes are found in the realm of the will.

The other Johannine writings share this personal conception of religion. All John needed for his teaching regarding the Christ were the terms "Father" and "Son." For his teaching of what it means to be a Christian he needed nothing but the term "child of God." His concept of the world is devoid of any consideration of the manner and effect of natural processes. It takes shape through human desire and action, and behind the world stands the evil one. Jesus' work consists of uniting those who believe on him with himself; the work of the church consists in loving one another. John pays no attention to the natural and historical processes that accompany and influence personal conduct. There is no word of institutions, customs, or doctrines that support internal decisions and serve the church as means in its work. This is no longer Jewish: while the Jew also elevated his share in God and thus his ethical aspirations above all other concerns, natural life circumstances always occupied a significant place in his spiritual life. Jesus was the one for whom such things amounted to nothing compared to man, because the world seemed insignificant for him in comparison to God and because God unites himself with man.

John's prophecy expresses the personal conception of the idea of God by the fact that the theophany introducing its major portion uses a human figure to depict God (Rev. 4:2). On the other hand, John conspicuously avoided anthropomorphic statements regarding God in the actual discourse. With these two methods of rendering the recollection of God strong and accurate John followed the practice of Jesus. In his statements regarding God, he used exclusively those kinds of conceptions provided for us by our personal life acts and thus applied the categories of knowing and willing consistently to God. For this reason he also created parables that illustrate God's behavior by what man himself does and experiences. His relationship with God bore the mark of firsthand knowledge. But this intimacy never suppressed the consciousness of God's unsearchable transcendence. Rather, every remembrance of God also evoked the notion of his "glory," so that he avoided risky formulations that would project our human image directly on God.[81] Therefore he saw in the figurative nature of the word an indication that the disciple's knowledge was still clouded and thus the word still hindered, and he promised his disciples that he would one day speak to them without parables (John 16:25).

When the prophetic experience therefore created in one of his disciples a vision of heaven, this gave him of necessity also a vision of God. He could see in heaven not merely animals, elders, angels, or even solely the Christ: this would have entirely separated him from Jesus' proclamation and the Gospel's concept of God. For heaven is heaven through the presence of God, and the Son lives in the Father. To see heaven without seeing God was for John a contradiction in terms. He did, however, protect himself from dogmatic anthropomorphism by simultaneously seeing the Christ as a lamb with seven horns and the Spirit as seven spirits through seven flames of fire and seven eyes (Rev. 4:5; 5:6). Using a human figure to depict the exalted Christ would have been an obvious choice; but it is avoided, because it was used for God. John did not see in heaven two men who reigned side by side, or three, Father, Son, and Spirit. The gradation of the images—the use of the human form for the Father, the figure of the animal for the Christ, and of the eye and the flame for the Spirit—is perfectly compatible with the Gospel's statements regarding the all-surpassing majesty of God who sends the Son, just as the Son now sends the Spirit. However, as the depictions of the Son and of the Spirit are not conceived of dogmatically, neither is the human form of God. Therefore the contention that no one has seen God, found in both Gospel and epistle, is not compromised by prophecy but rather confirmed, because it can show us nothing more than a human figure, since the prophet cannot see God in any way other than a figurative one even when he is led into heaven in the Spirit. John also lends powerful expression to God's exaltedness not drawing God himself into the action. He describes him

---

81. "God's face" is mentioned only in Matt. 18:10. "God's hand" occurs only in John 10:29; it was a widely used expression. "God's foot" only occurs in dependence on Isaiah's terminology in Matt. 5:35, similar to the "throne" in Matt. 5:34; 22:44; 26:64 and, following Jewish usage, in Matt. 23:22.

as the will which reigns over all, which comes to fulfillment through the Christ and his heavenly messengers. As a being in the midst of humanity, the vision places God only into the image of the new Jerusalem; for only in the final state does humanity not require any mediation of his presence but live in his light (Rev. 21:22–23).

Only the vision continually involves the heavenly spirits in the events, while the Gospel says that angels ascend and descend upon Jesus without linking the perceptible occurrence with a heavenly act, such as that an angel descended and revived Lazarus at his resurrection or an angel assisted the Samaritan woman in her confession or an angel brought the community's intercession for sinners before God. This merely preserves the distinction between vision and experience, between what is seen in the Spirit and with the eye, and this is not incompatible with prophecy but is required by it. Prophecy does not hold that natural eyes will ever be able to see what the prophet sees in the Spirit. This does not happen even when the prophecy is fulfilled. Neither should we merely think of aesthetic or artistic impressions, if John did not intermingle his prophetic and didactic style of presentation and used in prophecy exclusively figurative language and in historical narrative and exhortatory discourses merely the word taken from perception. Rather, in this he obeyed the principle of truthfulness, which bound him to the facts of history. For its sake he portrayed merely himself but not Jesus as the recipient of visions, since Jesus did not speak of visions even when he prophesied but used for prophecy the same means of expression he employed in his teaching. Even when he revealed what was to come, he spoke in sayings and parables. John distinguished his own prophecy from that of Jesus by casting it exclusively and completely in the form of visions, even though he esteemed Jesus' prophecy as a gift given to him by Jesus.

When John in the Spirit views world history as the work of angels, he is moved by one thought that always emerges in the eschatological outlook, even in the prophecy of Jesus: that the community will through its consummation also attain fellowship with angels.[82] By seeing Christ's rule, the eyes of the prophet, once opened, also see the heavenly host busy in its service. The living view of heaven, however, does not result for John in a division of faith, so that another divine messenger beside Jesus might receive comparable significance. The community's faith is in John everywhere devoted indivisibly to the Christ. Thus there arises also at this point no distance from the things Jesus gave to his disciples. For Jesus placed the spirits by whom his rule is carried out in proximity to God, and his living portrayal of heaven was not insignificant for his concept of God. The Son's joy and power had its basis also in the fact that the heavens were open for him and "legions of angels" stood ready for his defense, and that at his return God's glory will be revealed through him by the fact that angels will accompany him. In heaven he saw God's glorification, not his obfuscation. The Son needs nothing but the Father, since he has everything in him. Similarly, there is no other way for man to enter into fellowship with angels

---

82. The fourth evangelist prayed the Lord's Prayer, too: he sees in the Apocalypse how "the will of God is done in heaven and therefore also on the earth."

than the worship of God, no means of procuring their assistance other than obedience toward God. Heaven was important for Jesus solely under and through God, not on the same level with him. John also acknowledged this principle expressly by not attributing any work to angels in his vision beside God's and Jesus' work, but by assigning to angels entirely the carrying out of God's will in the world.

The Apocalypse's teaching regarding angels stands in tension only with that interpretation of the Gospel which finds in it a mystical piety. In this case, the tension can rise to the point where one feels compelled to separate the two writings from one another. Does not that kind of inwardness and completeness of one's union with Christ disappear which characterized the piety of the disciples "who remained in him" when the Christ's dealings with the world, including those with John himself, are mediated by angels? Two thoughts that use this theory as a premise require careful investigation. Is it really the purpose of the prophecy's complex depiction of angels to expose the weakness of God and Christ? Is it based on the idea that God is unable to intervene directly in the world so that he needs angels, and that the Christ sends his angel because he himself is not present? Or was it the prophet's view that the number and greatness of the heavenly host revealed the richness and power of the divine life and thus also the glory and omnipresence of Christ who reigns together with God? Then is the union believers enjoy with Christ as it is portrayed in the Gospel indeed based on mystical processes? Are these pronouncements not rather an expression of faith in the Christ's unlimited share in God's presence and effective power, benefits that remain completely independent from any religious moods or spiritual developments in the believer, because they result from Jesus' boundless divine sonship? If the latter interpretation correctly grasps who John was, the only thing added to prophecy's depiction of heaven for the understanding of faith is colorful illustration. Such illustration shows in a manner commensurate with our sense perception that Christ possesses the power to receive believers into his presence and to envelop them in any situation and with their entire history. In any case angels do not vanish from the first vision of the Apocalypse merely because Christ is present among the churches. Rather, it is precisely because Christ holds their angels in his hand that he is the one who reigns.

The teaching on angels in both Johannine writings also concurs in the fact that there is no mention of a notion according to which princes or special spirits rule over nations and historical events, even though such an understanding has a basis in Scripture, was widespread in the synagogue, and was emphasized by Paul. None of the angels featured in the prophecy has autonomous ruling power.[83] This can be accounted for by the unmitigated contrast with which John relates humanity either to Satan or to God. As the Gospel features Satan

---

83. An allusion to the "princes" may be found in the reference to the "angels of the churches" in 1:20. Following Daniel, Michael is described as an angelic prince in 12:7, but not as prince over Israel. On the other hand, John perceives the relationship between nature and God as established by creation in the fact that angels preside over the regions and elements of nature: the angel of the abyss (9:11), of fire (14:18), of water (16:5). Parallels can be found in the tradition of the synagogue.

as the prince of the world, the Book of Revelation casts him as the one who gives power to the world ruler.

### b) Johannine Dualism

The Book of Revelation upholds the antithesis characteristic of the other Johannine writings with equal vigor. It distinguishes between what is above and what is below, not according to a gnostic developmental scheme, so that what is below possesses less life, reality, or divinity than what is above, with the result that various regions are construed which are closer or farther from God. There rather rages a war between those who are above and those below, and in this conflict John sees the midpoint of history, a mystery, but one regarding whose solution he has full assurance.

It is instructive in this regard that not only are there no references to "princes" in the material from which John construes his vision but there is also no mention of the seven heavens. Since he uses a multitude of antecedent conceptions, the expectation seems reasonable that he might find the seven heavens useful already on account of the number seven, which he uses purposefully as a sign that everything is ordered by God. But he contrasts the one heaven with the one humanity and does not violate the complete contrast by differentiating between several stages in the heavenly sphere. Parallel to this is the lack of any depiction of the subterranean spheres: we do not receive any description of the dwelling of Satan or the dead.

The contrast that renders human history a struggle with God is in Revelation as well as in the Gospel transcended by the motif of the Creator, which in both writings prevents the contrast from escalating into a metaphysical dualism (Rev. 4:11; 5:13; 10:6; John 1:3). It finds its resolution through the Judgment. What the vision illustrates by way of repeated calamities, the historical account portrays by making the unbelief and fall of the Jews a major element of the good news. Here a clear causal connection can be drawn from one writing to the other. Because the history of Jesus and Jerusalem unfolded as the Gospel presents it, the future of the world and of Christendom is as prophecy describes it. Here the world hardens itself against the one who came to visit it; there it rebels against the one who is in heaven. Here Jesus' work is limited to the creation of faith in the ones given to him by the Father, there to the provision of the seal and the palm branch to those who are not of the world in order to save them in the course of the cosmic struggle. As little as Jesus was able to win the world for himself is this the calling of his community. As he came to die, it also is the calling of the community to lay down its life in confession of him, and as he went to the Father by dying, the community likewise, by dying, gains eternal life.

On this account the same kind of criticism is directed against both writings. The oft-voiced verdict, the Apocalypse breathes hatred, is thirsty for blood, and longs for the world's demise, is paralleled by the opinion that the Gospel mocks the Jews, rejoices in their obduracy, and declares them to be a despicable race. But the alleged hatred motivating the visions of the apocalyptist cannot serve as proof that the Johannine writings stem from different authors. For John's opposition to the world, its unbelief, and darkness are always equally clear. We also know through the epistle and the Gospel that John was completely convinced not merely of the reality of the judgment that links death with sin but that he also embraced it with a resolute will. In his view evil meets this end by God's justice.

It is equally false to detect in the Gospel animosity toward Jerusalem or in the epistle animosity toward gnostics and Greeks or in the Apocalypse animosity toward Rome. For the rejection which John claims to be absolutely valid possesses universal significance in all his writings. Jerusalem, gnosticism, or Rome are not rejected on account of their particular Jewish, Greek, or Roman background, but as components of the world, which are singled out because the course of history causes them to come into contact with Jesus. In Jerusalem, Jesus works in vain; the gnostic devastates Jesus' community; and Rome declares war against it. Therefore this battle cannot be moved to the side by replacing Rome with another world capital. John expected nothing different from a new emperor, just as he did not think another high priest would have responded more favorably to Jesus' work; nor did he have a more positive view regarding another gnostic teacher. Everywhere, attacks upon Jesus reveal to John's eye man's antagonism toward God. This lent absolute resolve to John's protest against the world's condition; for his protest did not arise from arbitrary, selfish aspirations, but from his ethical judgments. In all his writings, John rejects nothing but godlessness, nothing but what he considers to be Satanic about mankind. Nowhere can we escape the phrase found in the epistle: the world must perish, and people are not to love it, because what is in it is not from God. For John, the refusal to love what he cannot consider to have come from God was one with the love of God. But neither in the Gospel nor in the Apocalypse has the refusal universal validity in the sense that all the Jews or all the nations were handed over to final condemnation. For Jesus seeks and finds his own among the Jews, and an innumerable multitude belongs to him among the nations, even in Rome, to whom he has given white garments and whom he has placed in heaven before God. The crisis does not pertain to these natural constructs as such but divides them into what is God's and what is Satan's. The promise on one side is as absolute as the rejection on the other.

What attests to the honorableness of the will which renders judgment here is that he always subjects Christendom to the same norms that inform his opposition to the world. Christians are in no way glorified in their entirety as a human entity, despite the absolute promise that lends assurance to their relationship with God. The shoots that do not bear fruit are thrown away, and whoever does not walk in the light does not know God. Accordingly, John's prophecy begins with Christ's judgment of his churches; for it is possible for the lampstand to be removed.

In all his writings, John describes grace and judgment as a unified divine work, and this in such a way that grace reigns and through its operation also secures the execution of righteousness. The sending of the light is a merciful act that gives life; but the light simultaneously has a judging effect. Jesus' death renders the forgiving grace of God effective and covers the guilt of the entire world; but at the same time it is the judgment of the world (1 John 2:2; John 12:31).

Likewise, the calamities expected by John bring about the revelation of the Christ for the perfection of mankind. He does not describe the world's destruction but its introduction into God's eternal communion, and all destructions are but means to an end, not obstacles for the divine purpose but in fact the means by which the Christ establishes his rule and creates the humanity that is glorified in God. John portrayed this in his prophecy by placing heaven with its worship above the dark earthly sphere, not cut off from earthly matters, not absorbed in the blessedness granted to the heavenly beings, but rather full of adoration because something is underway on earth which to the human eye looks like nothing but misery and death. John hears all of creation thanking God for the execution of justice that begins with the opening of the book (Rev. 5:13).

John's verdict regarding Israel's relationship to the world remains entirely the same. The fate of all the Jews is tied to what Jerusalem did. As the Gospel does not linger over Jesus' ministry in the Galilean villages, the great vision of prophecy does not speak of the conduct of the Jews spread among all the nations but portrays solely the sin and final destiny of Jerusalem. Both writings show the basis for Jerusalem's privilege: it was the city of the Temple, the one city of God.[84] Therefore Jerusalem's rejection of Jesus brought death for all of Judaism. Now the synagogue of Smyrna, the persecutor of local Christians, is a community of Satan, as the priests and teachers of Jerusalem who crucified Jesus had been sons of Satan. Neither the Gospel nor the Apocalypse reserves special grace for Jerusalem or the Jews. At the same time, the Old Testament canon possesses unlimited divine validity in both writings. The Apocalypse likewise operates on the basis of the pronouncement that "Scripture cannot be broken," whatever the Jew may do (John 10:35).[85] This also brought John into extensive spiritual communion with the interpretation of the synagogue. In both interpretive schemes the permanent validity of Scripture and the Jews' rejection of Jesus concur in the conviction that Christ's rule amounted to the completion of God's work for Israel.

### c) Johannine Metaphysics

In the Gospel, everything that proves to be true and good for man is grounded in that which comes from above. Light and life come into the human sphere from above and become ours because they are eternal. This axiom also entirely shapes John's prophecy. The devastating blows and saving divine acts originate from above. What happens on earth reveals what takes place in heaven. This is already typified by the beginning of the great vision: in order to understand what is and what is about to come, John must enter heaven. Only then does he see the operating forces, only then does he see the true meaning of

---

84. This is also transferred to the worldview of Revelation. While it is understandable that Ephesian and Alexandrian Jewry pale by comparison with Jerusalem, it is not as clear why the other world cities—Ephesus, Antioch, Alexandria—vanish in comparison to Rome. But since there is only one city of God, the vision also features but one city of the world, only one city of the antichrist.

85. All the scriptural quotations found in the Book of Revelation stand therefore also within the purview of the evangelist; he also knew the Scriptures, including their Palestinian interpretation.

the events taking place upon the earth. The end of the prophecy vigorously confirms this once again. As the Christ is the man descended from above, the eternal community is the city of God descended from above.

The Book of Revelation likewise presents the relationship between essence and action, eternal and temporal occurrence, in John's characteristic style. The eternal is the first and immovable. Yet the temporal is not depreciated but rather originates from the eternal and belongs to it. Therefore John's prophecy is based on the doctrine of predestination in exactly the same way as the Gospel. As the Shepherd calls the sheep because they are his possession, the Lamb has bought through his death men as God's possession because he has written their names in the book of life from the beginning of the world (Rev. 13:8; 17:8; 20:12; 21:27). Thus the first beginnings bring to light the final outcome of the events in the Gospel as well as in prophecy. Since God is the First and the Last, the final form of God's work is contained in its beginnings.

What is the final hope in Paul, that is, that all creation in heaven, on earth, and under the earth worship the Christ, occurs in John at the very beginning of the plot, even before the seals of the divine book are opened (cf. Phil. 2:10 with Rev. 5:13). Parallel to this is the statement made by the Baptist, placed at the very beginning of the Gospel, which sums up Jesus' entire achievement on behalf of mankind. This view of history that does not distinguish between subsequent steps and interprets everything from the vantage point of the final destiny is particularly striking in the Apocalypse, since its focus is on temporal, historical events, seeking to explain what becomes of mankind and how it reaches its destiny. But we will not receive the answer to this question if we do not come to terms with our own current condition. Victory will be celebrated in heaven not merely at some point in the future; it is already being celebrated at the present time. Not merely in the future, but already now does the innumerable multitude stand before God, clad in white garments. The statement that Jesus was in the bosom of the Father and in heaven while on earth, and the statement that the community is already found before God's heavenly throne, are truths pertaining to the same man; for they issue from the peculiar, vigorous formulation of his concept of God. But this does not even in the Apocalypse lead to escape into another world. The earth is not surrendered; human history not rendered devoid of meaning. Rather, because the events are effected from heaven, they emerge from the divine sphere with invincible power and thus accomplish their purpose. Because the Christ became the Lamb that was slain, he opens God's book, and because he opens its seals, the riders set out. Because believers did not stain their garments and did not become the possession of the Antichrist by receiving his mark, they are invited to the Supper of the Lamb.

Therefore the prophecy also directs an urgent exhortation to the community. As the Gospel seeks to establish faith and the epistle desires to achieve the keeping of Jesus' commandment, prophecy aims at strengthening commitment to God, at liberating the community from the world, and at providing it with the weapon with which it will win the victory. By having their source in the divine being and activity, these commandments receive their absolute validity. John does not acknowledge unclear circumstances in which good and evil or divine and devilish elements are intermingled. He rejects every form of compromise and demands complete commitment. Unholy alliances are simply impossible. God takes that which is his own completely to himself and removes whatever is not his own completely from himself. This finds expression not merely in the letters of the Apocalypse, such as in Christ's rejection of the lukewarm; this conviction also stands at the root of the great vision.

### d) The Portrayal of Christ

As in the Gospel, so also in the prophecy, the community's union with God is based solely upon the Christ. He holds the stars in his hand, and because he opens the seals of God's book, the world moves toward its destination. No human witness of God is placed beside Jesus in any way, neither Abraham nor Moses, much less any of Jesus' already deceased disciples, not even a heavenly spirit. Jesus stands above all as the Only One with the Father; he is also in the prophecy in the strict sense "the only Son." While God's will is an inscrutable mystery for all, he is the one who finds out what it is and executes it with omnipotent power. And because he reigns with God, he also receives everyone's worship together with God. He himself, on the other hand, is not among the multitude of those who cast themselves down before God and worship Him.

Since the prophet sees what the divine judgment has assigned to the world and the community that lives in it, not merely the types of natural life but also representatives of the community are placed beside God and characterized as participants in his reign by assigning them thrones and crowns. This, however, is not done in such a way that they are awarded an active share in the divine work. The execution of the divine judgment takes place solely through the Christ, not also through the elders. Even less is there a consultation between them and God. Their privilege consists of being witnesses of the divine work, so that they are the first who praise his greatness and offer worship to Christ.

John expresses Jesus' union with God in both texts by calling him "the Lamb." Thereby his divinity is rooted in his selfless love that obeys God completely. And so Jesus' earthly work is summed up in both presentations as his deed on the cross. By dying, he realizes his kingly calling. As the dying Christ is the glorification of God in the Gospel, the universe praises the Crucified in the Apocalypse. But the Lamb is in both portrayals simultaneously the Lion: for the defenseless one who dies for God's sake is the one who acts in God's omnipotence. Therefore he also is in both writings simultaneously the Shepherd and the Lamb. The prophecy explains how God's power is at work in him by the same phrase used also in the Gospel and the epistle, namely, by the designation "the Word of God": he does not merely know it or speak it—he is the Word.

That he reveals this in the Gospel through his incarnation, in the epistle through the gift of eternal life, and in Revelation through his return demonstrates that John recognizes God's coherent, comprehensive will in all stages of Jesus' work. At the revelation of his glory, however, he is the Word in the ultimate sense, because he expresses at that time what God thinks and actualizes what he wants done. Since Jesus is "the Word" according to the Apocalypse, the Gospel's claim that creation was mediated through him coheres neatly with the

Christology of the Book of Revelation. For every Jew bore the conviction that the Word of God embodied the power of the Creator. Correspondingly, the creation of the new heaven and earth are part of the work of the Coming One. The notion of preexistence, however, is shaped analogously in both texts, because the Christ claims eternity for himself, yet does not provide a description of his eternal communion with the Father. Both take their point of departure from the "beginning" and derive from Jesus' eternity his authority over creation.[86] The prophecy too expresses the thought by which the Gospel lends practical significance to the doctrine of preexistence: that the Christ illumines every man, and through this his community becomes greater than the number of those who entered into a conscious, historically mediated encounter with him. For the innumerable number from all the nations, which John designates already at that time as Jesus' possession, did not arise merely through the apostolic mission, nor merely through the addition of small congregations that confess him now, but only by virtue of the fact that, to use the Gospel's own diction, all who are from the truth are God's. As in the Gospel, the Spirit is again called Christ's possession. It is not a coincidence that it is the Lamb that has seven eyes and not the Spirit. While the Gospel states that Jesus received the Spirit "without measure," he possesses him in the Apocalypse sevenfold, that is, in his totality. He possesses him in order that he might send him, and the sending of the Spirit bears the mark of a deed that has been accomplished once for all also in the Apocalypse; for the Spirit has been sent into all the earth (John 3:34; Rev. 3:1; 5:6).[87]

It corresponds to the difference in purpose of the two books that the Apocalypse centers around the Christ motif and thus is linked with Synoptic tradition while the Gospel shows us the Son of God. Jesus' reign provides hope with its content, Jesus' sonship does the same for faith. A rupture between these two portrayals of Jesus, however, would arise only if the Apocalypse described his rule as no longer based on his unity with God and no longer aiming at God's glorification. But no attentive reader can imagine that the Apocalypse severs Jesus' authority over the world from God. It cleanses hope from all selfish, eudaemonistic desires and makes the revelation of God's rule the sole object of our longing. The one who, according to the Apocalypse, reigns independently of God for the purpose of self-glorification is not Jesus but the Beast. The introduction to the main vision already makes clear that Jesus' rule is the service of God and is based on his dependence on God's will. The Lamb does the will of God, for it opens God's book.

Another foundation of the Apocalypse is the concept of life. The Christ is the one who was dead and lives. The fact that he lives characterizes him completely in his glory as the Christ. This results in the promise for the community that it gains life when it must surrender to death in its struggle with the world (Rev. 1:18; 2:8; 20:4). There is a difference between the Johannine writings in that the Gospel and the epistle use the phrase "life or death" as a description of

---

86. Shepherd: Rev. 7:17; Word: 19:13; Spirit: 5:6; eternity of Jesus: 3:14; 22:13.
87. Regarding the plural "spirits of the prophets," cf. the plural of "spirits" in 1 John 4:1.

the contrast between the world's destiny and the believer's aim, while the Apocalypse also adds torment to death. Before Christ hands over to death those who wage war against God on account of his sword-like judgment, there is a long series of subsequent plagues which immerse mankind in torment and pain; the final verdict, the casting into the Lake of Fire, likewise results in eternal agony. The prophet thus evokes people's instinctual aversion against pain more strongly than the evangelist, who characterizes man's choice merely by way of the fundamental contrast "life or death." But the Gospel also describes the end of the world in terms of "perishing" and "being killed" (John 3:16; 10:28), not merely as the extinction of life but as violent loss of life effected by God's judicial verdict.

Nevertheless, the fact that Jesus' message centers in the promise of life does not result in an immortality doctrine in either document. To have life means to be with Christ, to know God. This is neither expanded nor changed in the Apocalypse. John did not desire revelation regarding the place and destiny of souls. Not even where he hears the souls call upon God for their vindication does he transport us into the world of the dead. The souls are "below the altar." On the other hand, both writings feature resurrection in a universal sense. The judgment does not decide whether or not someone will rise but merely distinguishes between those who have risen. Therefore John adopts the phrase "second death" from the tradition of the synagogue. The first death is the one at the end of one's earthly life; the second death occurs when the final resurrection has taken place. The death that denies eternal life to the one who has risen but is condemned is the second death (Rev. 6:9; 2:11; 20:6, 14; 21:8; John 5:28–29).

Life comes to man through Jesus' word. The relationship between his word and the Word of God is characterized in both writings by the term "witness." "The Word of God" and "the testimony of Jesus" is one and the same. This means that Jesus knows God, listens to God, and transforms God's Word into his own discourse. Through him it comes to man, and he champions it in the world which denies it. Therefore it constitutes the calling of the community that it "has the testimony of Jesus" (John 3:11, 32; 18:37; Rev. 3:14; 1:5, 9; 6:9; 12:11, 17; 19:10; 20:4). For all three writings, the major emphasis in his word is the name of Jesus, because his testimony reveals what has been given to him as his office and work, and this, in turn, is expressed by his name. Thus, according to the Gospel, a person believes in his name, according to the epistle receives on account of his name the forgiveness of sins, and according to prophecy holds fast to his name (John 1:12; 3:18; 1 John 2:12; Rev. 2:3, 13; 3:8). In the Gospel, John describes Jesus as the one who knows, maintaining that the inward-flowing power of his knowledge ties the disciples to him as a strong motive to faith. Likewise, the first statement of the Christ to the churches in the letters of the Apocalypse claims that he knows their works. By this John preserves the connection with an idea zealously cultivated by the synagogue: for it cherished the conviction that God knows everything a person does as a particularly strong incentive to piety.

The power of Jesus' death by which he cleansed the innumerable throng is also in the prophecy not depicted in priestly terms, even though it uses priestly imagery abundantly for the heavenly host and the community dwelling on earth. But the Christ does not officiate at the heavenly altar as a priest, and his death likewise is not seen from the perspective of sacrifice. The slaying of the Lamb does not imply that it was offered on the altar but that it exposed itself to the world's hatred and allowed itself to be killed for God's sake. The Christ is exalted to heaven because the dragon wanted to destroy him. Analogously, the shepherd is killed in the Gospel because the wolf, the prince of the world, is about to come. The Apocalypse describes what the community received through Jesus' death as "its having been bought for God," just as Jesus' confidence regarding his disciples is based in the Gospel on the assurance that "they are yours." Thus the idea of "being God's possession, belonging to God" is made in both writings the comprehensive characteristic of the state of grace. The community's liberation from guilt is expressed equally and everywhere not by the concept of justification but of purification. Because he dies, the Christ washes the disciples in the Gospel, purifies the community through his blood in the epistle, and provides it through his blood with clean garments in the Apocalypse (Rev. 5:9, 12; 7:14; 13:8). His blood acquired forgiveness for an innumerable multitude from all nations, just as the Christ covers the sins of the world in the epistle, and as he takes away the sin of the world in the Gospel.

Because the book which the Lamb is able to open because he was slain contains God's judgment of the world, grace, which grants forgiveness to humanity, and the execution of justice are also here linked in Jesus' death to form a complete unity, parallel to the pronouncement in the Gospel that the world is judged through Jesus' cross. Moreover, as Satan is cast out as a result of Jesus' death in the Gospel, he is driven from heaven subsequent to Jesus' exaltation in the Apocalypse (John 12:31; Rev. 12:7–10). It is no mere coincidence that we find both of the following statements in both writings: that Jesus' death broke Satan's power in its judicial effects, and that his rule over mankind has not yet been lifted but will only come to an end through the coming judgment. The first pronouncement is borne out by the fact that there is a purified community that has been made God's property among men, and the second pronouncement receives its confirmation by the world's condition, which "lies in the power of the evil one."

Although the categories depicting the religious process are framed strictly in personal terms, it remains a self-evident premise of the entire train of thought that Jesus' aim is the establishment of the community purified in him. Therefore the Apocalypse does not place Christ before individual souls but before the churches, and his goal is not the bringing of blessing to individuals but the city of God. None of John's writings knows of an individualization of persons, each of whom stands in separate, isolated relationships with God. As in the Gospel the shepherd knows every sheep and calls it by name, yet calls the sheep together and creates the one flock of God, in the Apocalypse it is not souls but the people of God that is brought to its full number and completion. Thus both texts describe the eschatological process similarly in its dual aim: Jesus comes for the glorification of his community, and he comes in order to establish God's reign over the world. The idea that the parousia effects the salvation and exaltation of the community is portrayed by the first vision, the concept that it executes God's will upon mankind is shown in the second one. Whoever separates both visions by positing differing eschatological aims errs in judgment, just as the one who attributes John 5 and 13–17 to different authors.

It would be unobjectionable if a work such as the book of Revelation, which considers the divine government in its entirety, were to link its beginning and end, creation and fulfillment, paradise and the city of God, and the fall of Adam and the Antichrist. But the Apocalypse looks back as little as the Gospel. The name "the old serpent" for the accuser, borrowed from synagogal tradition, connects his accusing power with the temptation in paradise the same way in which the Gospel does when it calls him the "murderer from the beginning" (Rev. 12:9; 20:2; John 8:44).

A new element in relation not merely to John's Gospel but also Synoptic tradition is the use of warfare imagery with regard to Jesus' revelation, which presumably goes back to older traditions, since it is linked with the Antichrist. But warfare imagery is not developed in such a way that it results in a struggle between Jesus and his adversary. His authority above all that rises up against him on earth is in no way obscured. Likewise, Rome's destruction is not made the aim of Jesus' return; it already takes place at an earlier time. As Jesus does not come in Matthew for the purpose of punishing the Jews and in order to destroy the temple, he here does not come for the purpose of destroying Rome. God's judgment is announced as necessary to both cities, because guilt will not go unpunished. But this punishment is carried out within history through mediating elements provided by it and therefore can be subsumed under predictive signs of the final act. What remains decisive for John is how humanity relates to God in its worship and love, whether it serves the devil or God, and only as part of this contrast does the Christ receive also the form of the general who sets out to make war.

### e) Faith

The Apocalypse, too, sees the task of Christendom in faith alone. When it "holds fast to Jesus' name," it has done everything it is required to do, because it is God's possession, as long as his name is the authority under which its thoughts and actions stand. This does not mean that the community does not consist of those who do good. The Christ "knows their works." If the prophecy judged differently, if it counseled the church to rely on its Christian conviction and to rest assured in the knowledge of possessing the Christian confession, it would not be Johannine, because we know how John assessed the kind of Christianity that claimed to know God but did not carry out his commandments. Thus Revelation likewise declares unambiguously that the church can preserve its communion with God only by refraining from doing evil, instead observing God's commandment. After all, this is the root of the struggle into which Christians are placed. They must be able to die because they are, as the epistle puts it, unable to do evil.

But it is not Christians' work within mankind that decides the course of history. It is not their works that bring about God's reign. This John attested with a glowing passion, calling it a delusion to hope for the victory of the church.

What he predicts is Christ's victory over the world. We hear nothing of the church's mission, of its work which leads the nations to repentance and faith. Of course, it is privileged not merely to serve but to receive open doors in order to be able to carry out its work, and it must faithfully exercise its power even when it is small. But this is not followed by a discussion of the work it needs to do. It has Jesus' testimony, keeps it until death, and shares it with all who are ready to hear it. Thereby it gains life for itself; but it is not the church itself which establishes Christ's reign through its own work. True, Jerusalem is promised that the divine word will not be taken away from it even during the rule of the Antichrist. Even then there will be God's witnesses in it who will be equipped with God's power until they complete their work. But it is neither the disciples nor Christendom who are called to tell Jerusalem God's message with overpowering might. For this hope is not based on an esteem for the evangelistic work of the community and its successes but clings to the prophetic words that place prophets such as Elijah and Moses prior to the Day of God. On John lay a clear consciousness of powerlessness, both when he thought of the apostles' work in Jerusalem and when he considered the nations' slavery to Rome. But precisely this realization that renounced everything, that had in view the impossibility of obtaining the apostolic aim and of bringing about the condition desired by Jesus, gave rise to Revelation; for it evoked hope and tied it solely to Jesus. From where does man's help come? From above! Christ alone achieves progress and the completion of his work. There is only one way by which the community shares in the final, greatest things, and that is that act emphasized by the epistle alone, the act by which the Christ completes his work on earth in the Gospel: the community's prayer, which rises to heaven as an incense offering and brings about the demonstrations of divine power (Rev. 5:8; 8:3–4). The supreme value of faith comes to light in the elevation of prayer as the community's allotted share in the divine work.

According to Jesus' word as repeated by John, the disciple has nothing on his side but the truth, and through it he overcomes the world. According to the prophecy, the community has nothing but the word of God, and it dies for it and overcomes through it. The same assurance communicated by the phrase "born of God" comes to expression in the prophecy by the fact that it does not portray the community as endangered or shaken but transported to the Christ on heavenly Zion and to God before His throne. Being sealed and crowned by God is no less than being born of God. In John, believers are always God's possession, which cannot be jeopardized by any man. Therefore the prophecy of the Apocalypse differs from the prophecy of Jesus preserved by the Synoptic tradition in the same way as the promise of the Gospel. The older Gospels link prophecy with the task that needs to be carried out by the community within its own circle, since it has in hope the means which makes it faithful in its work and diligent in its readiness for God's rule. Only the first introductory vision of the Apocalypse provides a parallel to the Synoptic parables; the main body of the book, however, does not contain any description of the community that depicts how it waits for the Coming One and readies itself for him. Because it has communion with the Christ, John portrays it as heavenly and pure. But even the first vision, which exhorts the churches emphatically to do away with all evil, introduces no element of uncertainty in its relationship with the Christ: they are his and remain his as they remove what he judges. In John, complete faith always stands above hope, faith which is conscious of its possession and gives thanks for it. In the Apocalypse, Christ is also not depicted as the one who goes after the lost sheep, but as the one who protects his flock against the wolf. It is not shown how he gathers his community, strengthens it inwardly, and presents it before God, but how he removes from it the pressure of the world and leads it to eternal life.

Love is in the Apocalypse as complete as elsewhere in John. As John in the Gospel esteems as glorious grace Jesus' promise to Peter that he will at last be allowed to follow him and that he will likewise be crucified, the community proves its love to Christ also according to Revelation's commandment by dying joyfully for him. Without a hint of complaint, the Gospel recalls the inexpressibly great sacrifice of blood Palestinian Christendom had to bring and the horrible events in Rome, because the cross of Peter is illumined by that radiance which is cast on us when we are able to "glorify God," to give visible expression to God's greatness. Likewise, the Apocalypse does not view dying Christians with a sigh; "from now on those who die in the Lord are blessed" (John 13:36; 21:18–19; 16:2; Rev. 14:13). That love is measured less by what it achieves than by what it suffers and sacrifices is a common characteristic of all the Johannine writings. Regarding the Ephesian church it is said that it exercised proper discipline, was unable to tolerate evil in its midst, and was not afraid even of the name of an apostle, not giving room to a false apostle just because he had the affrontery to claim such status. With the vigorous exercise of discipline, it connects the ability to suffer; it has the courage to martyrdom. But this is accompanied by the admonition: "You have forsaken your first love." The simultaneous validity of that praise and of this exhortation does not obscure the historical picture, since the vigorous exercise of discipline and of confession easily went hand in hand with an increase in the drive toward self-preservation, which led to a weakening of personal closeness and a certain hardness and coldness toward one's brothers. But the return to love cannot be replaced by any other virtue but lends absolute urgency to the call to repentance. Love stands above, and its absence devalues, all other Christian virtues (Rev. 2:4). The norms by which the letters in Revelation differentiate between genuine and reprehensible Christendom are the same as those used by the epistle: any Christian piety is rejected that surrenders love and allows intermingling with the world. The guilt arising from such conduct is doubly severe, if it is done with an appeal to God and his Spirit.

What is new in the Apocalypse is that the Christ's address to the communities is cast in terms of a call to repentance. Thereby the concept of repentance merely reappears, however, in its original form in which it was well known to the entire church since the days of the Baptist and of Jesus. For repentance is conceived of in terms of a change in behavior, by which evil is removed in view of the approaching rule of God. That John reiterated the call to repentance at a time at which he renewed the promise of the divine rule merely proves that he knew the history of Jesus.

Even the new element found in the Apocalypse that transcends the scope of prophecy contained in the rest of the New Testament stands in close proximity to what we know to be apostolic. The expectation of the Antichrist belongs to the image of the future established in the community also in the epistle and there is affirmed by John as well, and the evaluation of gnosis as the anti-Christian sin in the epistle is paralleled in the Apocalypse by the fact that it allows the world ruler to come to power by joining forces with the false prophet. The manner in which John's prophecy ties the revelation of the Christ to the present differs from the widely attested type of apostolic sermon found elsewhere and also does not differ from the first epistle (1 John 2:18), cohering with the latter also by virtue of the fact that we find no calculation of the end. Only the final portion of Daniel's weeks of years, the three and a half years, is repeated, whereby a calculation of the end by means of the seventy weeks of years is excluded. The differentiation between the Christ's arrival and the world's completion, Chiliasm, has a parallel in Paul. The insertion of the war against the Christ led by Gog and Magog between the parousia and the end of the world is hardly original with John, since Ezekiel's prophecy against Magog is continually attested in eschatological tradition. Moreover, the differentiation between the Antichrist and Gog, which is significant since the Antichrist is thereby linked with the conflict that currently needs to be endured by Christendom and that is related to Roman imperial power, is prepared in tradition by the fact that it offered the interpretation of Daniel's fourth beast as Rome as entirely fixed and thereby distinguished it from Gog's struggle against Jerusalem. The depiction of the eschatological community by way of the new Jerusalem descending from heaven likewise is hardly the exclusive property of John: the motif of the "heavenly Jerusalem" had long before John's prophecy been transferred from Jerusalem to Christendom.

The Apocalypse does not constitute the prophet's entire religious possession: for it is inconceivable that a Christian prophet's whole life's work of proclamation consisted solely in the description of the Antichrist. The assumptions on which the first vision is based, that is, that Greeks are brought to Jesus and that they live together as his community, yield that religious understanding which had to be supremely cultivated in the present. Equally unusable is another idea: that the fourth evangelist placed himself in opposition to the entire rest of Christian tradition, and that he rejected everything that he himself did not say, because he wanted to replace all other Christian convictions through his own writings. This interpretation of the Johannine text sacrifices not merely the epistle, which develops a motif that differs significantly from that of the Gospel, but also the message of the Gospel, which does not isolate John from the remaining disciples but rather describes him as one of Jesus' disciples, linking him particularly with Peter in equality and collaboration. The contention that John designated himself alone as the bearer of Christian tradition and witness of Jesus' word nullifies his message. It is therefore inaccurate to call conceptions such as those ranging from Christ's parousia to the judgment of the nations as foreign to John while they are notoriously established in the community, upholding the entire apostolic work. John did not stand apart from the community but was a part of it. If his prophecy shows us that he had a rich share in the community's religious tradition beyond what is revealed by the Gospel, this coheres with the fourth evangelist's statements regarding himself.

## 11. The Greek Element in John

John wrote for the churches of Asia, which were subject to Greek culture and tradition and which had received their first Christian form through Paul. The significant fact that Jesus' word had been removed from Jewish soil and been made the property of the Greeks had occurred. That it impacted John's entire thought and action is certain from the start, since his ethic consists of the rule of love, and love opens our eyes for what others are, providing our will with substance in the form of what others need. We merely need to ask how this fact impacted John.

### a) Openness toward Greek Thought

Greek Christians' share in God was completely and exclusively Jesus' work. In John's view, this is the way it is and should be. In order for their religion to have a firm foundation, they need the assurance that Jesus enjoys complete communion with God and that he grants it to all. Therefore John makes Jesus' divine sonship the central message of his Gospel. Thereby the Greek learns how God proves to be his Father and allows him to become his child. John considered that he had thereby completely expressed what was entailed by the promise of God's rule (John 3:3; 18:37).[88]

In addition, the elevation of faith above repentance and the subsuming of repentance with the state of believing clearly relates to the fact that it is Greeks who are addressed at this point. For the Greek did not approach the gospel with a pronounced consciousness of sin, while the Jew possessed it from reading the Law and felt its full impact all the more when he recognized the Christ in the one who had been rejected by his own people. The Greek, on the other hand, as a result of the ambiguity of his ethical understanding, had evil within himself but was not conscious of it; he took pleasure in evil and did not feel its sting. He is therefore presented with the good he is given by the knowledge of the Son of God, in order that he might gain the renunciation of evil from this knowledge and realize his own guilt. In his case, it was not consciousness of his own guilt that moved him toward faith. Rather, he understood through faith that the world was evil and perceived darkness by being brought into fellowship with the one who is light. John's concept of "the world" is therefore related to his Greek mission, because, for Greeks, the first realization that clarified for them God's relationship with them was not the personal attribution of guilt but God's verdict regarding the entire sphere of human existence.[89] Here the individual found himself to be ignorant of God without any doing of his own, put in this

---

88. The Apocalypse, which consists entirely of the announcement of God's rule, likewise does not use the phrase "kingdom of God" in a formulaic sense; but of course it is familiar with the term (Rev. 11:15).

89. John's concept of "the world" does not reveal any influence from Greek interest in nature, just as Greek political thought did not impact the Apocalypse.

state by the common condition of all. Only by being called to Jesus was he set free from his dependence upon the powers that separated him externally from God. Thus sin received its full seriousness for him only in light of the knowledge of Jesus, and John expressed emphatically that guilt arose in its full sense only when Jesus was rejected. From a Christian perspective, Greek life proceeded under the rule of delusion, without guidance, direction, or purpose, as a stroll in the dark. The Greek needed light, and John told him that Jesus was and will give him light, because he will receive through him the message regarding the Father whom he did not know. At the same time, the Greeks often had a painful sense of death as being the world's final destiny. They received the message as good news that proclaimed eternal life as attainable for them, and the promise of life became altogether indispensable because the call to Jesus entailed the obligation of preparing to die for his name's sake. This the community is able to do because life has appeared in the Christ.

### b) The Opposition toward the Greek Church

The consideration of the particular needs of John's Greek audience, however, is merely one part of the process. Equally significant is the way in which John felt and combatted his opposition toward the Greek way of life. John nowhere quotes or refutes Greek ideas, not even in places where his refutation of them is categorical. The Greeks' ideas about the gods and sexual pleasure are nowhere confronted head-on. The Johannine writings are based on the assumption that Christendom had made a complete break with pagan norms. Nevertheless, the struggle between Greek thoughts and the norms relevant for Jesus' disciples did continue in Christendom, for which the gnostic movement was the most visible indication, and in this regard John carved out his position with great determination. For he resolutely opposed the Greek tendency of seeking to bring about communion with God by means of religious objects, rendering any equating of Christian piety with such devices impossible. He thereby kept Christianity in its original form as it existed in the disciples' fellowship with Jesus, where it amounted to their entire possession by virtue of their personal allegiance to him and their trust in him. This is not caused by a later situation but rather stands in such sharp contrast to it that we must not deny John an awareness of its basis and necessity.

The second Christian generation did not immediately think of the possibility of entering into a personal relationship with Jesus nor conceive of the fact that this represented its central religious process. It rather directed its faith to the religious elements present in its midst. People looked, not toward whom they neither saw nor knew, but toward the messengers of the divine word who were speaking to them at the present time. They turned to the means of divine grace now available, toward the church and its office-bearers, the Bible and the sacraments. Therefore communion with Jesus was now replaced by a combination of religious institutions, doctrines, and means of grace. Not only did John not join this movement—which transcended gnosticism but also manifested itself in the gnostics' new teaching office and means of grace—he represented the contrary conviction that the Christian religion was faith in Jesus so strongly that we must believe that he knew what he was doing.[90] He lifts Christians' gaze *above* the church, the bishop, the sacrament, and theology *to Jesus*. But this also meant that Jesus' divine sonship became the centerpiece of his message. For it alone makes a relationship with him possible that is independent of space and time and is attainable by all; it alone transforms allegiance to Jesus into the universal religion.

In terms of ethics, Greek tradition provided the concept of virtue, which immediately came to the fore when faith in Jesus had been transmuted into "Christianity." John again resolutely expressed his opposition toward the kind of ethical ideal that esteems the acquisition of virtues through which we increase our own knowledge and ability. For Johannine ethics consist solely in the concept of love, albeit a love with categorical urgency. Not that the believer should enrich and develop himself and elevate himself to some kind of perfection, but that he should live for Jesus and the brothers, is proof of his communion with God. In his description of that work and effort needed for the perfection of one's own life, John did not even appropriate the concepts of fight, growth, and building, which were used not merely by Paul but also by Palestinian Christendom. For another writer, the apocalyptic image would easily have provided the occasion of depicting the church as the one who fights or runs for the prize. But John incorporated this idea only when he placed the palm branch into the hand of the church. Similarly, Greek longing for good fortune was given no influence whatsoever on the development of Christian norms. Since John did not move beyond the original terminology of the promise of "eternal life," he does not encourage a hope that occupies itself narcissistically with its own condition but one directed toward the future work of God. Prophecy likewise avoids any sensual depiction of the future blessedness, so that its promise portrays a desirable aim only for the one who longs for the reign of God.

The clarity with which John expresses his opposition toward Greek norms finds its corollary in the fact that he does not use any Greek forms of thought. The "Word" has its prefigurations in the synagogue but no longer relates to the ground of reason which creates the world in Stoic thought.[91] For John does not think of an integration of the world with God and does not occupy himself with a dualism of ideal and rational or material and fiery creative power. The Johannine conceptual pair of light and life is completely distinct from the Stoic conceptual pair of fire and thought, because it does not pertain to the difference between natural and spiritual processes and is not designed to explain how the constellations of nature come into being but exclusively deals with what man needs for his personal life and what he receives from God. It would be utter nonsense to claim that John taught that primordial fire became flesh in Jesus. For John conceived of God as a person, especially when he distinguished be-

---

90. The community should abide in what it has heard from the beginning: 1 John 2:7, 24; 3:11.

91. The presentation of relationships that developed between Platonic ideas, Aristotelian reason, and Stoic thought on the one hand and the teaching on God on part of the Greek and Jerusalem synagogue on the other does not belong to a discussion of the Johannine message but to the history of Judaism.

tween God and his Word and ascribed to the Word the undiminished entirety of the divine life and complete divinity. On the other hand, the supposition may be correct that John expected he would illustrate Jesus' union with the Father for the Greeks by way of the term "Word" and to aid their understanding of the reason why their access to God occurred by way of faith in the man Jesus. For those who took part in Greek education were able to link the term "Logos" with the concept of the pervasive divine government and express by it what was divine in nature and in man.[92] John protects his thought from Greek influences by defining the Word solely in terms of Jesus' history. The community is to realize, not in nature or spiritual processes, but in Jesus what God has with himself as his eternal Word, by which he created the world and by which he rules it and leads it to himself. Thereby John was able to fend off Greek ideas that posited a unity between God and human reason and natural law.

### c) The Refutation of Gnosticism

Similar lack of evidence prevails regarding John's use of gnostic ideas. He accused this kind of piety of having neither faith nor love nor hope and saw its guilt that separated it from God in its attack upon Jesus. For this reason he went beyond Paul in his condemnation of gnostic teaching, although Paul already judged the danger it represented for the community to be grave and expected from it the ethical wreckage of the church. But Paul did not yet place the movement into a world-historical context but dealt with it as an internal Christian matter; it made him fear for his own work, for the congregations he had gathered. John, on the other hand, relates false prophecy to the Antichrist. In his view, the struggle far transcends the scope of an internal rift or a theological discussion within the church, so that it cannot merely be adjudicated by the teaching of sound doctrine. One finds here a conflict of opposing wills which is decided by God's powerful deed.[93] Therefore John does not believe that the church can be protected from gnosticism merely by a discussion of individual gnostic ideas. What was needed was rather the establishment and strengthening of the foundational features of Christian piety: faith, love, and hope. In this sense, every word in John, in the Apocalypse and the Gospel as well as in the epistles, is influenced by his opposition to gnosticism. This influence, however, should not be understood as having operated in such a way that John received his own religious beliefs only by his struggle against gnosticism, for we cannot

92. The use of the Johannine pronouncements regarding the Word in the church of the second century goes in this direction.

93. Of certain portions of the Fourth Gospel it can be said that they are partially determined by apologetic considerations. But in every case those portions lie on a far higher level than the views distinctive to gnosticism. In John 6, John has in mind the offense caused by the community's practice of eating Jesus' body and drinking his blood. But this offense was as old and widespread as the observance of the Last Supper, just as prominent a feature of Christian practice in Jerusalem as in Ephesus, and for a normal Christian as for Christians whose piety was gnostic in nature. The struggle of the Jews against Jesus and his cross is explained by their conflict with God; but the question, Why was Jesus executed by his own people?, dogged the Christian proclamation everywhere it went. Pilate's case shows that with contempt for truth and knavish cynicism he condemned Jesus. But the struggle with Roman magistrates was under way everywhere.

dispute John's claim that he defended the legacy of Jesus. The energy John invested in the refutation of this heresy stemmed from the power by which he appropriated and preserved what he had received from Jesus.

Every fight always brings with it positive results, since it leads to the establishment and deepening of convictions held to be true. These positive yields have come down to us in the clarity and vigor with which John was able to clarify faith and love, the essential features of Christian devotion for the community. On the other hand, John did not create any conceptualities that dealt with the issues addressed by gnosticism from his vantage point; nor did John seek answers for them, precisely because he resisted the confusion of faith in Jesus with a speculative way of thinking that seeks to establish communion with God. John's assertions regarding God that he is spirit and love, have nothing to do with gnosticism but rather are designed to refute it, because the Spirit engenders truth, not speculative imagination, as the basis for devotion. Moreover, gnosticism, which deems to possess a share in God by its knowledge, is rejected because of love, because only the one and already the one who knows God has love. This is also borne out by the fact that the trinitarian conception of God in John neither leads to a fixed formula nor becomes the food for speculation as well as by the total absence of any speculative or practical discussion of the spirit world.[94] One looks in vain for a discussion of the relationship between God and matter or nature. The Creator concept is sufficient for John in his treatment of our relationship with nature. Not even those mysteries which he uses consistently as the basis for Christian piety, the presence of the Christ and birth from God, lead him to theories of any kind. The gnostic efforts to animate the concept of God through ideas provided by nature did not incite John to parallel constructs. He speaks merely of personal life and remains focused on aspects of human life even when he uses the physical functions of conceiving, eating, and drinking to describe Jesus' gift. The portrayal of the Christ by way of the fruit-bearing vine planted by God is not based on gnostic stimulus but uses an image that is provided by Scripture and therefore widespread. John is not affected by that idea of restoration by which gnosticism tied creation with redemption to a speculative unity in that it allowed creation to be damaged or even brought into being by a fall and then assigned to the Christ the task of removing any vestiges of flaws or ungodly elements in creation. We find in John no traces of ascetic regulations or any methods of self-healing, although he considers the power of love that overcomes natural drives to be the element that secures victory for the community, providing it with communion with the Christ (Rev. 14:4). However, John transformed this neither into a theory of asceticism nor into an instruction of how a person may raise himself to perfection, just as he portrays martyrdom as every believer's obligation without making it the basis for special honor or a means for the attainment of higher glory. While gnosticism usually has an immortality doctrine as its salvific theory, John does not have such a doctrine and does not consider it to

---

94. The angelic name "Michael" was supplied to John by Scripture. Abaddon (Apollyon) in Rev. 9:11 is not the proper name of a spirit but stands beside death and Hades (6:8; 20:13–14).

be his calling to instruct Christians regarding what the soul will encounter and its duty after death.

Adjudication of whether John wanted to accommodate gnostic piety and to show the community that the convictions held by it also granted it what gnosticism sought to achieve with its own means is possible only in what may be called John's metaphysics: in the subordination of temporal processes to the eternally existent, and with the summary of Jesus' promise by means of the terms "light" and "life." It might then be argued that John confronted gnosticism with the statement that Christians are given true reality, in preexistence and afterlife, though Jesus and that man's true nature is revealed by one's proximity or distance from him, because gnosticism derived the religious process from a metaphysic that connected it with the basic elements of the cosmos. It might further be argued that John confronted the gnostic concepts of light and life with the light and life the community received from Jesus, because the gnostic considered delusion and death to be the evils he sought to remedy by his religion, finding redemption in the change of consciousness brought about by the impartation of proper knowledge, and the benefit of its dogma and method of healing in the attainment of immortal life. This, however, would be to interpret everything as a refutation of gnosticism that constitutes a parallel between the Johannine message and Greek thought. It was not in the first instance the founders of gnostic religion who gave Greeks the desire for knowledge and life, and the desire to reveal God entirely and exclusively in Jesus provided the answer to the first question continually and invariably addressed by the Greek to the proclamation of Jesus: the Greeks always confronted John with the question where this history touched them and how it aided them in their effort to be religious. But from the religious assessment of Jesus (which John possessed and represented not merely out of polemic motives) also arose the Johannine metaphysic, the power by which he applied the concept of eternity to God's relationship with Jesus and with the believer. Because God is manifest in him, what was in the beginning and what is permanent reality is revealed in him. Since John's statements nowhere deal directly and clearly with gnostic theories, it completely eludes observation to what degree certain gnostic objections motivated his presentation of Jesus and not merely the consideration of perennial Greek religious need.

## 12. The Jewish Heritage in John

### a) The Separation from Judaism

By describing Jesus as the eternal Word and revealing the perfection of his divine sonship, John distinguishes himself and the church completely from Judaism. The significance of these pronouncements is based not only on the fact that they call the Greeks to Jesus; they point simultaneously to the fact that they show the Jew his guilt and misery and substantiate the verdict pronounced against him. As the Greek gained communion with God through faith in Jesus, the Jew has lost it by his rejection of Jesus; for Jesus is the Son. Therefore John does not merely stand apart from individual Jewish groups and particular forms of their worship but from Judaism as a whole, because the rejection of Jesus, which John considers to be the act of the entire nation, renders everything else the nation otherwise possesses useless. Therefore John reckons the Jews as part of the rest of the world and demonstrates by this in particularly convicting clarity the world's alienation from God. This demonstration was necessary not merely because he himself had come out of Judaism and because the churches were opposed by Judaism, but particularly because the canonical validity of the Old Testament required proof of how and why Israel came to an end. Consequently, John, regarding his relationship to the Law, had merely to point out that the Law had been given, not through Jesus, but through Moses, whereby its significance ends for those who believe in Jesus. For believers in Christ are united with him completely and solely through their faith and find in him the grace and truth they were not yet given by the Law (John 1:17).

### b) The Contrast with Philo

His separation from Judaism also set him apart completely from the Alexandrian form of Jewish theology, from which he was removed even further than from Jerusalem's rabbinate, since the reasons for his opposition to gnosticism also separated him from the Alexandrians. He therefore shares nothing in common with the concepts that were decisive for Philo, so that it was foolish to speak of the influence of the Philonic commentaries on the Pentateuch upon John, or in indeterminate terms of the influence of a Philonic tendency or school. John does not deal with the contrast between nature's corporeality and the purely intelligible nature of God's being at all, while this constitutes the foundation of Philo's theory. Since John disavows any knowledge of virtue and knows nothing of ascetic methods, he shares nothing with the entire Philonic morality. That the Gospel places faith above all other religious functions and that the epistle places love above works and that the Apocalypse demands from the community that it be able to die for God—none of this is taken from Philo. If John ever did read Philo, the Johannine pronouncements deny Philonic piety as completely as they do gnosticism.

Philonic logic is equally foreign to John, the esteem for abstract ideas as pure insight, which causes history to be dissolved into ideas. In John's view regarding both Old and New Testament history this amounts to the destruction of the element that renders them revelation for him. For John, Moses is not the presentation of an idea but the one who spoke with God, probably also the one who still lives before God (John 9:29; 5:45). Likewise, he does not represent Jesus as an idea, but Jesus is the Savior of the world owing to the fact that he lives, speaks, and works. John is not aware of the concept of an "idea" at all; he contrasts his concept of truth with the lie, which is distorted when the contrast is reinterpreted in terms of the Philonic antithesis between the idea and the physical world. Accordingly, John advances not even a single allegorical interpretation of Scripture. His interpretations are rather based on the absolute validity of the words of Scripture and are in form akin to Palestinian interpretation.

John's incompatibility with Philonic logic also extends to Philonic mysticism. In Philo, the dissolution of history into allegory results in the fact that religion arises for him in the internal course of one's spiritual life in which moments occur at which a person is moved by God. Johannine faith stands in complete contrast to such a notion, because faith does not originate within the human self but by the acceptance of the testimony regarding Jesus. As a mystic, Philo is a religious hermit; he does not need the community for the completion of his communion with God. In John, the work of the Christ consists of his creation of the community. Philo's idealistic philosophy and mysticism result in the disintegration of his concept of personhood. He prefers neutral categories as designations for God, such as "the one who is" or similar terms, while downplaying the will in his concept of God. Regarding self-consciousness, he strongly jeopardizes the unity of personal life by a pluralism of forces and processes. There exists great tension between sensual, rational, and suprarational elements. In John, the concept of person is the prevailing category in his message regarding God, the Christ, and Christian existence. His God wills, his Christ acts, his Christian has been born of God in the unity of his existence. Conversely, the phrases "the Word became flesh" or "children of God born of God" have no room in Philo, because in both instances God's community is attributed to a genuine human life in its entirety and unity, which Philo cannot tolerate. This difference manifests itself significantly in eschatology. John teaches the resurrection; Philo, on the other hand, has an immortality doctrine, which is interwoven with physiological theories, with the ethereal nature of reason and souls' descent and ascent in the air. In John, we find nothing of this kind. The Philonic pronouncement that the angels are souls acknowledges no higher existence than that possessed by man. The Johannine angel, however, is not a soul, but has another and higher existence than man, and the unity of the universe is not achieved by limiting all existing forms of life to a human dimension; it rather arises from the pervasive power of the divine will.

When Philo speaks of the divine Logos, he thinks of God's mental activity. His Logos is the idea of the world and thus the creator of those ideas which shape souls and nature with a molding power. He thereby stands in close connection with Greek notions of the Logos. The Johannine pronouncements regarding the Word do not take their starting point from the question of how nature takes on its intelligible dimension and how reason receives its thought forms which may be applied to the material world. For him, the Word is rather the mediator of the divine work at the creation of the world as well as at the calling of the community. John knows nothing of the Philonic "second God," which is needed for Philo because God's abstract being obtains contact with reality merely by way of a mediating being, since reality is separated from God by virtue of its corporeality. Even the linkage between Logos and image, frequently found in Philo, is absent in John, although it has an exegetical basis and belongs to Philo's Jewish inheritance. Among all of Philonic pronouncements it could therefore be reconciled with Christian convictions most easily. But not even this idea, which already finds a parallel in Paul, can be found in John.

Philo's use of the Logos concept is therefore *not* valuable for an understanding of John because John derived this notion *from Philo* (he did not) but because we have precious little of the rich work of Greek synagogues except for the

Philonic tractates, so that they provide us with a glimpse of the piety and theology of Greek-speaking Jews not given us by any other source. Through Philo we more or less catch a glimpse of how one spoke of the divine Word even in the Greek synagogues of Jerusalem and Ephesus, and this, in turn, is not without significance either for the pronouncements of the Palestinian rabbinate regarding the divine word or for the Johannine presentation of Jesus. The complex history of the concept of the "Word" makes clear that the introduction of the Johannine Gospel is misinterpreted when it is regarded as a private speculation of John, as an attempt to acquire a theology of his own. The rule which pertains to the entire apostolic work applies also in this case: it used such conceptualities that established commonality and communication between Christian teachers and their listeners precisely because they were not construed arbitrarily but had developed historically.

### c) The Use of Palestinian Tradition

In his style and thought, John retained significant common ground with Palestinian tradition. The doxology "Praised be the one by whose Word everything came into being," heard continually in Palestine, stands in much closer proximity in both form and content to the sentence with which the Gospel begins— "Everything came into being through the Word" (1:3)—than all Philonic deliberations. The Gospel's first pronouncement links Genesis 1:1 with Proverbs 8:30: this combination stems from Palestinian interpretation.[95] The way in which John speaks of the world and its prince, the Father and his love for the community, the advocate who acquires before God the forgiveness of sinners, the glory of God we are to seek, eternal life and resurrection on the last day, clearly continues Palestinian usage.[96] John knows nothing of a need to create a distinct Christian language different from the Jewish one, and neither did any other of Jesus' disciples, after Jesus himself had carried out his ministry within the terminology and conceptual framework found in the synagogue.

The standard by which the Apocalypse determines the acceptance or rejection of Jewish ideas can be clearly seen in its relationship to Scripture.[97] The terms that are used always have their roots somehow in Scripture. Therefore

---

95. Tradition also brought the merger of both scriptural passages to Philo. But it required great perceptiveness to find it in him, since he comments exclusively on the Pentateuch.

96. A statement by Akiba provides a close parallel to the praise of the love of God who called us his sons (1 John 3:1); the term "Paraclete" was not infrequently used by the rabbinate in similar ways as by John. The rabbi likewise says regarding the bronze serpent that it granted healing to the one who looked at it in faith, and he considers it to be the mark of the prophet that he sought "the glory of the Father and the son" (of God and of Israel).

97. Traditional are: the old serpent, the second death, the repetition of the Song of Moses in eternity, the appearance of the ark of the covenant, the feeding of the glorified community with manna, the existence of the heavenly Jerusalem and of the heavenly service at the altar, the repetition of the Egyptian plagues and the blowing of the trumpet prior to the parousia, the renewed sending of the two witnesses to Jerusalem, the portrayal of the rescue of the community as an escape into the desert, the expectation of the Parthians as the power punishing Rome, the interpretation of the prophecy directed against Babylon and Edom with reference to Rome, the use of the term "bride" for the community. Here one finds everywhere at the same time an exegetical motive that supports the use of existing concepts.

these commonalities with Judaism did not present themselves to John's consciousness as something foreign beside the things he received from Jesus. For
Scripture and the Christ were not authorities in tension with one another for
Jesus' contemporaries; they rather are built on the same foundation and serve
the same purpose. But as in his own prophecy, John proved also with regard to
Scripture that he had the freedom given by Jesus to his disciples. Although it
clearly constitutes a goal of the Apocalypse to renew Old Testament prophecy
by being placed into contexts that have importance and intelligibility for the
community in the present, it nevertheless nowhere evidences anxious literalism.
It does not have any explicit quotations and freely modifies the Old Testament
images it uses. The animals Ezekiel places at God's chariot do not recur in the
same form in the Apocalypse, but every animal figure is a being of its own. John
features only one of Daniel's four beasts and introduces a new one not occasioned by Daniel's prophecy. The measurement of the temple is based on Ezekiel but transcends it, since John distinguishes by the measurement between
what is destroyed and what will remain while Ezekiel predicted, not the destruction, but the building of the temple. Correspondingly, the heavenly Jerusalem
does not have any temple, while the river flowing through the city again is based
on Ezekiel. In Christendom, prophecies were made in the assurance that the old
prophetic word needed to be renewed after the Christ's coming had brought its
fulfillment. But this was also an expansion that completely transcended the
frame of reference of the pre-Christian community.

## 13. John and Matthew

John stays close to the older form of the Gospel record in that he, too, uses
sayings and works of Jesus to provide the community with knowledge of Jesus.
But his account already differs from the older one in form in that the sayings
and narratives no longer express their own ideas in isolation from one another
but are subsumed under a purpose that uniformly determines the whole. This
purpose encompasses together with Jesus' discourses also the historical materials, since John reveals in Jesus' works the same will which is also attested by way
of Jesus' words. The new form of presentation resulted from the transition of
the gospel proclamation from the Jewish community to the Greeks. The composition of the account using individual sayings and works remained an effective method as long as the community continued to find itself in the same circumstances in which Jesus' work had been accomplished: as long as the
community had direct knowledge of Pharisees and sinners, lepers and demon-
possessed, adversaries and disciples, and thus heard directly through the gospel
what Jesus' work showed them to be the will of Jesus; and as long as the interpretation of these abbreviated accounts could at any point be derived from its
living memory. It is not surprising that on Greek soil greater emphasis was
placed on the interpretation of a given event. John offered this to the community by making the individual pieces elements of a coherent train of thought, so
that in his Gospel events and discourses mutually explain one another.

The inner difference between the communities, however, also exercised great
influence on the content of the Gospel. Matthew wrote on the assumption that

his readers had a firm assurance of God because they did not receive their religion only from Jesus and his messengers but already knew God. The Jew merely needed to be asked by John whether or not he obeyed God, and John needed to tell him that he did not in fact obey but that he could learn to obey God through Jesus. The Greeks, whose thought and love were directed toward God only by the knowledge of Jesus, were no longer addressed by John in this manner. He showed them why they knew God through Jesus and why knowledge of God was given to them through Jesus alone.

The impetus that the labor of a man gives to his thinking, and the impetus provided for him by his own internal history and peculiarity, unite to form a coherent result.[98] John too was mindful of the significance the course of his own life had for his entire apostolic work: for he began his account with the narrative of how he himself became a follower of Jesus and concluded with the information that the Risen One assigned to him in contrast to Peter not martyrdom but waiting for him (John 1:37; 21:20–22). The manner in which he describes his coming to Jesus show that he had not struggled with the community and God the way Matthew had. Jesus had already encountered him at the time he still was with the Baptist, and now he believed and loved. But now also arose for him the break: for in following Jesus he separated himself, as he claims without exaggeration, from the world, from everything. In a strictly historical approach, it can easily be seen that men like Matthew came to Jesus, men who had a hardened, firm will, active men, whose highest possession consisted of ethical formulations, as they are given to us in Matthew through Jesus' sayings. But it is equally clear that there were among Jesus' followers those who esteemed the consistent direction of their internal lives toward him, their faith in him, as the highest good they owed to him. The separation of devotion into work and faith, which differ so sharply from one another and are still so indispensable for each other, is an essential component of the difference between the two accounts of Jesus. The two basic forms of the Christian will, however, manifested themselves among the disciples neither separately, consecutively, nor alternately, nor did they stand in conflict with one another. The norms preserved by Matthew as his legacy arose from Jesus' kingly will, his office, and his work for his own people; John's faith arose from what Jesus possessed within himself, his joyful and quiet assurance of God, to which he also introduced those whom he called to himself.

By placing his account beside the older books he knew, the same contrast revealed itself in increased clarity which is already manifest in Matthew who fol-

98. The attempt to isolate both the impetuses for the purposes of observation would far transcend what is achievable for historical observation. The presentation of relationships that books sustain with their authors' life experiences are easily distorted by ideas brought to us by modern analogies. One should not think of an intention, strengthened by skillful reflection, to express oneself and to bring to bear one's own individuality. The norms which were binding for the disciples precluded such aspirations. Therefore the evangelist never becomes the subject of his own account, and his personality does not push into the foreground. The connections between the man and his thoughts, between history and his book, did not arise from selfish considerations but found direct expression. On the other hand, a conscious effort was made to pay attention to the situation and need of the community for which the work was written.

lowed the Sermon on the Mount with an account of Jesus' works, the commanding Christ with the gracious one, and the disciple obliged to obedience and work with the believing leper and Gentile.[99] The idea that a theoretical balancing statement is required for such a contrast did not exist for John, as he also places the theology of his epistle beside his presentation of Jesus without attempt at resolution. His method is determined by the assumption that those who receive faith in Jesus will acquire everything characteristic of a Christian. He considered disobedience and faith to be incompatible: whoever believes in him obeys his word.

In Matthew, Christology shapes the narrative, because the Jew obeys God by obeying the Christ; in John, it is the motif of the Son, because man knows God by knowing the Son. Therefore Matthew picks up on Jesus' self-renunciation, because it shows the purity of motive by which Jesus desires and obtains his rule. John focuses on Jesus' glory, because his glory is his communion with the Father by which he reveals God. For this reason the promise of Jesus' return is Jesus' most important word for Matthew, because Jesus will reveal himself at that time as the Christ, while for John it is his present union with the Father and with believers, because it is by this union that he leads all to God. The promise that the disciple will be the doer of the divine will therefore comes first in Matthew: for the new information received by the Jew is how he becomes subject to God. In John, on the other hand, Jesus' message centers on the fact that we receive life, because life is God's gift and God is revealed in his gift. For this reason Christian existence consists for Matthew in conversion, by which man carries out, not his own evil will, but the good will of Jesus. In John, it is faith, by which Jesus' word becomes valid for man. For this reason Matthew reveals in the case of the disciple what Jesus wants and produces, while John focuses his discussion on Jesus' own dealings with God; for that is the means by which faith in him develops.

In Matthew, Jesus is an Israelite, and Matthew is one, too. He tells Israel that the Christ was in its midst and died for its sake. Since Christian existence consists for him in action, Jesus also fulfills his calling by action. He acquires a share in God's rule for himself and his own. From this stems his will to the cross and similarly the significance of his resurrection. Dying, he pays the price, sets the prisoners free, and provides for them forgiveness from God. Through his resurrection, he is able to send his messengers into the world, to be with them always, and to return in glory. To the causal power of his activity corresponds the reality of his suffering. He is tempted, calls upon God to deliver him, and bears in his

---

99. The method of revealing the depth of events by way of contrast without providing a resolution between them also determines the details of the presentation. Beside the Synoptic assertion that even John the Baptist doubted stands the Johannine statement, "The Baptist proclaimed Jesus' office and we followed Jesus on account of his testimony"; beside the Synoptic information that Jesus did his work in the privacy of Galilee, we find the Johannine claim that Jesus facilitated decision for Jerusalem in complete openness; beside the Synoptic "in Gethsemane Jesus wrestled for and obtained certitude" is the Johannine "in Gethsemane he protected us." Here also belongs the relationship between John 1:1 and Matt. 1:1. Both Gospels relate their account of Jesus to ultimate beginnings: Matthew to Gen. 5:1, John to Gen. 1:1; Matthew to the beginning of mankind, John to the beginning of the world. The perfecter of mankind is contrasted with the perfecter of the universe.

consciousness the entire gravity of pain. In John he has everything; for he has God. Therefore his cross is also the revelation of his glory, because he proves by his death that he is from God and therefore leaves the world, yet without forsaking his followers. While Matthew brings the Christ close to the community because he acts, struggles, and suffers as it does, Jesus' union with the Father, as it is portrayed by John, elevates him above the human condition.

The connection established by Matthew between Jesus and Israel at the same time reveals and magnifies the alienation between Jesus and Israel. Jesus' wrath becomes evident and rejects human will, and fear of his judgment becomes an essential characteristic of Christian devotion. John neither conceals Jesus' opposition toward the human will nor softens his Christology. But because he places above Jesus' words of judgment concerning man the pronouncements that express its necessity and basis—because the one who is in the Father cannot love what man loves but creates the person born of God—the individual conflicts with their acerbic sharpness are transcended by the great, fundamental contrast which at the same time reveals the good for whose sake Jesus is entitled to demand any sacrifice. As the one by whom we recognize God, he is, on the other hand, close to man and not separated from him by anything. For the one who exists in God stands in the most direct relationship with man's internal being and draws him to himself with an indissoluble tie. And since his claim on men can be summarized by the one commandment of acting in love, liberation from fear is achieved as well, for perfect love casts out fear. Here there is not merely power and breadth on the one hand and weakness and narrowness on the other, but every state of faith possesses together with its limitation also its strength.

## 14. John and Paul

### a) Common Elements

The unity between John and Paul is extraordinary. It extends to the most profound personal thinking and willing. The prerogative of being considered first belongs to the emphatic claim on the part of both men that their religious tradition stems from Jesus. To those who cannot put to rest the corresponding messages of both men, the coherence between them reveals with glorious lucidity the manner and extent of Jesus' impact on the circle of his first disciples.

John and Paul give their faith and love one sole point of reference, that is, Jesus, and they view his significance for them as based on his oneness with God. Their religion is their relationship with Jesus. They consider Jesus to be the one through whom God created the world and through whom he will perfect it. From this they derive the certainty of his presence with them, so that they live "in him." For both, the decisive focal point in Jesus' earthly life is his departure, so that the proclamation of Jesus becomes the attestation of his death. The Gospel of John, too, claims to know only the Crucified One. Of course, the heavenly world, with its multitude of spirits and with the irreconcilable contrast dividing it into two armies and making Satan the adversary of divine grace and the corrupter of the work accomplished by that grace in humanity, constitutes an important aspect of the convictions of both men. At the same time, however, the subjection of all transcendent powers to the rule of God and the rule of the Christ is completely assured. Therefore neither of the two makes reference to the spirit world a substitute for the clear comprehension of the human condition and obligation. Just as Paul describes the calling of Christians in his epistle to the Romans without referring to angels or devils, John confronts Israel with Jesus in his Gospel apart from the manifestation of spirits. Neither Paul nor John contains a parallel to Matthew 4:1–11. The reconciliation effected by the dying Christ comprises for both also a process that occurs in heaven. As, in Paul, God displays his triumph over the rulers and principalities through the cross of Jesus, in John, Satan and his armies are defeated in heaven on account of Jesus' exaltation to God (cf. Col. 2:15 with Rev. 12:1–9). But in neither author does the transcendent consequence of Jesus' death cast a shadow on the image of the cross. John, like Paul, portrays the Crucified One before Christians' very eyes (cf. Gal. 3:1 with John 18:19). Both assign the community a place in the heavenlies, for it is Christ's possession (cf. Eph. 2:16; Phil. 3:20 with Rev. 7:9; 14:1; 15:2; even the pre-Christian community already bears heavenly adornment: Rev. 12:1). But this does not detract from the sober assessment of the things happening in their respective fields of service.

Both consider faith to be the attitude that procures for them communion with Jesus, and both link faith with the assurance that with Jesus they are given the entire grace of the Christ. Therefore it is in faith that they possess liberation from guilt, separation from evil, and eternal life. The Johannine "born of God" does not have lesser weight than the Pauline "declared righteous by God." If in Paul "the old man" is handed over to death and the believer becomes "a new creature," in John a person's old name passes away and he is given a new one (Rev. 2:17).

Paul and John combine repentance with faith to result in one uniform will, so that in laying hold of Christ they at the same time effect repudiation of the flesh and the world. With faith, they are given liberation from the passion embedded in every person, and by faith love is established in them, from which they derive strength for their actions. They also expect from the Christ the complete satisfaction of their quest for knowledge by a guidance that moves and fills their thinking, and they thank him for liberating them from handed-down, human thoughts. Paul says of the world's wisdom that it is judged by Jesus' cross, just as John says of the world that it languishes in darkness.

Both unite with the perfection of divine grace the inviolability of ethical norms, thus uniting with assurance the ethical claim that requires from the believer attention to his conduct. They did not say that the greatness of the divine grace rendered it impossible for the believer to stumble. While Paul speaks of branches of the olive tree that will be cut off again, John talks about branches of the vine that will be cut off. If Paul tells those who die in Corinth that this was the punishment for their contempt of Jesus' body, in John Christ threatens licentious members of the community with death (cf. 1 Cor. 11:30 with Rev. 2:22–23). Both approximate predestination in their statements regarding the perfection of the gracious and righteous divine work. But their thinking and willing are not diverted from the present communion with God.

According to the judgment of both, Israel's destiny has been decided. Both Paul and John maintain that Israel had fallen and that it had incurred God's judgment. For both, it becomes therefore an important part of their didactic work to illumine the reason for the fall of Judaism, and both find it in God's glory resulting in the assertion that faith must remain the only way by which man can achieve union with God. Just as Paul sees God's majesty revealed in the way in which he creates vessels of wrath and vessels of mercy by his own sovereign choice, Jesus in John effects the separation of his community from Israel by setting apart those who belong to him from those whom he does not acknowledge as his own possession. As a result both do not base their share in the Christ in the Law but they see in Jesus the final, autonomous foundation for their communion with God. They do not conceive of liberty from the Mosaic Law in terms of a simple swapping of the Mosaic for a Christian Law. This liberty rather consists of complete subordination to the leadership of the Christ as their only Lord, and they have confidence that his guidance will prove effective for them in rendering their entire conduct righteous. This makes them free and capable of giving liberty to their communities.

For both, Jesus' community is gathered from all of mankind, so that all national and social differences and all distinctions of education or status become secondary as soon as the tie with Jesus is established. For both, this tie brings God's work begun in Israel to completion, so that they are also able to say of the community that it began with the establishment of Israel. The olive tree in Paul parallels the twelve tribes preserved for the Lamb in John, just as the synagogue of Satan is matched by the vessels of wrath (cf. Rom. 11:17–24 with Rev. 7:4–8; Rom. 9:21–23 with Rev. 2:9; 3:9). In similar terms, they avert the community's danger of exchanging their confirmed community for a sectarian exclusiveness by the pronouncement that forgiving grace has been given to the world. As Paul maintains that God in Christ did not count the world's sins against it, John claims that the Christ has effected forgiveness for the sins of the world. Neither writer considers the present level of attainment to be the ultimate aim of individual Christians or the community; both require them to grow (cf. 1 Cor. 3:10 with Rev. 2:19). Both see in gnosticism not the church's growth but its corruption. They separate the church completely from gnostic teaching since they declare any knowledge of God unfruitful that is not rooted in love and does not determine practical behavior. Both judge Christians' situation in a Greek environment to be perilous and identify the imminent rule of the Antichrist. Nevertheless, being a Christian remains for both complete joy; for suffering and death have been overcome. Just as Paul expected, regarding the day of his execution, that Christ would be magnified in his body, John said of Peter's crucifixion that God would be glorified by it. According to both, believers will participate in the judgment at the time of Christ's return, by being judged as well as by judging and ruling with the Christ. In view of his death, Paul thinks of the eternal building prepared for him in heaven, while in view of the demise of humanity John thinks of the heavenly city. If for Paul the rule of the Christ has its aim in the fact that now all are completely the work of God, it ends in John with the fact that now God comes to the community with the

Christ and that he is present in its midst (cf. Phil. 1:20 with John 21:19; 1 Cor. 6:2–3; 2 Tim. 2:12 with Rev. 2:26–27; 2 Cor. 5:1 with Rev. 21; 1 Cor. 15:28 with Rev. 21:22; John 14:23).

### b) John's Independence

Just as peculiar is the distance John keeps in a number of respects from Paul. Whoever finds in what John has in common with Paul the measure for Jesus' legacy, in which both writers have a part, recognizes in the distance existing between John and Paul the measure for the new yields of Pauline instruction. Pauline teaching concerning the Law is entirely missing in John. John does not speak of the relationship between sin and the Law. He does not relate his worldview to the Law. This has the important consequence for the basic act of devotion that John contains no parallel to the Pauline antithesis between works and faith. Paul leads the individual to the true apprehension of God's righteousness by way of the condemnation of one's own self and to the appropriation of the life made available through the Christ by the recognition of one's own death. In no weaker terms than Paul, John develops the pronouncement that faith in Jesus alone is what unites us with God. This faith, however, originates for him in what Christ is, from the uniqueness and completeness of his divine sonship. Therefore it is only faith, by which the individual turns to Christ, that provides a share in God. For this reason there does not arise in John any tension between faith and works. Faith causes us to walk; faith in God causes us to walk in the light. The terms by which Paul describes the power of sin are therefore absent from John: the flesh and its opposition to the Spirit, and Adam's fall and its power over mankind. The Johannine contrast between the world and God does not arise first of all from observation of the individual life but from the assessment of the general condition which is revealed by Jesus' departure and by the destiny of his community. The Pauline antithesis, on the other hand, pierces discerningly through the personal consciousness of the individual.

Since John neither repeats nor develops Paul's anthropological statements, the concept of justification is quite absent. The term "righteousness" remains in John simply what it was in Jerusalem's piety. One does righteousness. The act of God by which he takes away a person's guilt John calls forgiveness or cleansing. The Pauline parallels to justification, that is, reconciliation, calling, election, adoption into sonship, are missing as well.[100] John describes God's fatherly activity upon us not as "adoption" but as conception. The expression "sanctification" in its Pauline sense is likewise missing in John.[101] This can be explained by the fact that the Pauline teaching on the cross is also not used. The thought that Jesus' death and resurrection pertain to all and that all are crucified and risen with him is missing. For this reason there is also no trace of those statements by Paul regarding the Spirit that portray him as the root of all religious

---

100. The concept of calling as the act that grants grace is found solely in connection with the image of the shepherd and the meal (John 10:3; Rev. 19:9). The terms "called" and "chosen" in Rev. 17:14 do not go beyond the traditional use of Jesus himself.

101. That Jesus' community consists of the saints also in John corresponds to the confirmed self-designation of Christians.

activity. The Spirit is placed over the disciples and above the world with divine power, but he is not discussed in terms of internal experience.

Regarding the richly developed Pauline doctrine of the church, neither the statements clarifying God's dealings with Israel nor the statements regarding the newness of the Christian community in which Jews and Gentiles are united find any parallels in John. The entire rich material of Pauline ethics, all the concrete instructions by which Paul regulates the life of the community, remain unused.

This fact reveals the freedom of the early period with particular clarity. John was linked with Paul not merely by the tradition regarding Jesus but also by his area of ministry. In Ephesus, he was continually reminded of the fruit of Pauline labor, and all of his writings are based on the presupposition that he did not have to impart first-time faith to believers. Rather, he wants to preserve them in faith. His portrait of Jesus seeks to show that the community's faith was precisely what Jesus sought to establish during his earthly ministry. In this limited sense it is correct that the Johannine Gospel as well as John's prophecy and exhortation presuppose Pauline preaching. Yet this does not result in an accommodation to Pauline statements.[102]

John's claims regarding his relationship with Jesus are thereby confirmed, and the converse theory becomes implausible that his inner fellowship with Paul was based on a discipleship relationship with Paul, a "Paulinism."[103] For a Paulinism that avoided the majority of the convictions characteristic of the Pauline documents is inconceivable, and the thoughts common to Paul and John are the fruit of Jesus' own dealings with his followers. These common elements are therefore the assured property of the entire community and not Pauline in the sense that Paul alone possessed them as his own discoveries which only he injected into Christendom.

When disciples deviate from their master, one normally thinks of followers who "misunderstand," be it through inattentiveness or through exaggeration of the thoughts moving their master. The attempt to bridge the theologies of Paul and John by way of misunderstanding is doomed to fail. John expresses the conviction regarding rebirth as strongly as Paul does regarding justification. Just as Paul calls himself dead with reference to sin and the Law, John is able to protect the ethical resolve that knows itself incapable of sinning both against libertine softening and against perfectionist tendencies. Jesus' divinity obscures or dethrones God in John as little it does in Paul. His agreement with Jesus' cross unites our inclusion in God's forgiveness and our sealing against evil with the same resolve as it does in Paul. Some argue that John would sink below Paul if the ethical judgment against sin were less resolute than in Paul; the Paulinist was not able to repeat the complete repentance Paul embodied, because it was grounded in Paul himself by his own unique life experience. That is why, they argue, the doctrine of justification is missing in John, together with the terminology of "flesh" and the teaching on original sin. But the Johannine conscious-

---

102. The corresponding observation that John shares significant common ground with James is demonstrated on pp. 97–99. Regarding John's relationship with Peter, see pp. 60–62.

103. This theory is rendered implausible by the fact that it treats John's claims regarding his relationships with Jesus and Peter—which are not matched by a single reference to Paul—as false.

ness of guilt bears at the same time his concept of the world and is therefore no less sharp than Paul's, even though it is configured differently than Paul's regarding the movement of one's inner life, because John derives the verdict regarding what man is from who Christ is. A misunderstanding would result in a deviant use of the concept of the Spirit, if John had fearfully avoided the Pauline connection of the Spirit, with all that it provides the community in terms of sanctified activity, lest the human element be deified. At the same time, however, he places us with this intimacy of love into the Christ. If he had had scruples of a psychological or of an ethical nature against the Pauline confidence in the Spirit, would these not also have been directed toward the Christ in whom we are? He reveals nothing of the concern that our inclusion into Christ's presence would dissolve our will and work or even deify our evil. If John possessed a clear eye for what Paul calls pneumatic, how could he be incapable of understanding his doctrine of the Spirit?

That John's impact on the later church was equal to Paul's is based on the fact that he does not merely provide the concept but a portrayal of Jesus' oneness with the Father (the portrayal is more powerful than the concept), and that he illustrates the sonship of God for us by the life of Jesus, of course without obscuring his cross, but still by a life whose glory is revealed even in Jesus' death: but the life is more powerful than the death. And thus some suggest: Is it not conceivable that the concept of development is applicable to John's relationship to Paul, perhaps in the manner that the Johannine Gospel was motivated by a sense for the boundary that Pauline Christology was not able to surmount by its conceptual nature and its concentration on the final outcome of Jesus' life? Is it not possible that John recognized that a Gospel would be valuable for the church that took the didactic formulas of Paul and condensed them into a graphically illustrated image of Christ? And this, the argument runs, is what rendered the complete repetition of the Pauline formulations impossible. But to this we must reply: Such a further development of Paulinism would not merely have left the Pauline convictions unused but would have destroyed them.

How a Pauline follower could write a Gospel becomes apparent in Luke. He did not do this by his own constructs but by way of traditional material. John, on the other hand, on the basis of this presupposition, is supposed to have transformed Paulinism into an account of Jesus' history, even though an innovative faith, which claims to have the ability of forming its Christ according to its own desire, would have lost everything on which Paul based the development and the salvific power of faith. Paul did not forego the composition of Gospel narratives merely by accident; he could not do so, since he thereby would have given up faith in Jesus. That faith does not create for itself according to its postulates a Christ of its own. It rather exists because it has what happened as its content and is based on the accomplished act of God. The Paulist who at the same time evangelizes as pseudo-John by way of a work of religious fiction is a muddled misconception, since a Pauline follower may be led by his faith to be a thinker, a scholar, or a teacher, but never a creator of his own Christ. For the Pauline faith stands and falls with the reality of the Christ. Moreover, John did in no way "develop" the faith in such a way that he sacrificed the concept of truth and cut that concept loose from its object. The absolute validity of the principle of truth to which the development and the value of the concept are tied, is a certainty with John, since it depreciates every account of the Christ that is not testimony. It becomes therefore an irresolvable mystery, not merely from Paulinism, but also from John's own condition of faith, how the latter should have produced a fictional Gospel.

The verdict regarding the Johannine writings and their place in early Christian history depends primarily on whether we consider the faith expressed in these documents to be genuine and the man's true conviction, or illusion and invention. The judgment regarding his faith also pertains directly to his hope and love. Whoever allows him to be a religious dreamer also will not consider his hope and love directed toward the Christ to be a genuine will but rather mere words. Conversely, whoever concedes that he kept himself separate from the world with a sincere will, that he longed for the Christ, and that he was prepared to give his life for him and for the brethren, will also judge his faith to be genuine, since hope and love which stem from a genuine will require more than mere fantasies: they require certainties. I cannot consider it probable that sincere historical research, however it may assess the value of Johannine theology, will doubt that we are dealing here with a man, not merely with books; with a will, not with phrases, and therefore also with faith, not with fantasy bordering on lie.

## 15. John and Jesus

John desires nothing but God, and him above all, and nothing apart from him. He desires Jesus for God's sake, the brethren for God's sake, and not the world for God's sake. This comes from his allegiance to Jesus. Where would there be a process that gives power to the assurance of God, subjecting to it one's entire will so profoundly that it is turned into love for God, if the encounter with Jesus was not able to do so? His desire is filled with gratitude and assurance. It is not mere longing, nor is it mere asking. He does not explore but testifies, does not hope but prophesies, does not regret but loves. He does not require any further mediation in order to enter into fellowship with God. He already enjoys fellowship with God and makes all of his decisions and orders all of his relationships in the context of this fellowship. Whatever else provides for the desire directed toward God the characteristic of mere longing, whatever attaches to it any wavering of uncertainty, has been overcome by him. The fact that he cannot see God now does not present an obstacle to him, for God has been made manifest. Sin does not separate him from God, because God purifies from all sin. Death does not frighten him, for life has been revealed. The world's objection and opposition do not confuse him: they have been overcome.

This is the mind-set and commitment of the one who has understood and experienced Jesus' friendship in terms of being related to the Son of God. This lent his relationship to God its directness and completeness. It reaches back all the way to his conversion, which John does not portray as a struggle in which conviction was born by the overcoming of doubt, love by wrestling with hate, forgiveness from wallowing in guilt, or life from internal dying. He rather maintains that the testimony regarding the Christ had come to him, and he had become one of his by accepting it and by extending his friendship to Jesus. This corresponds to the manner in which he permanently unites faith and repentance, fellowship with God and separation from the world, religion and morality. At the beginning stands God's initiative, which places man in fellowship with God. From this arises the struggle against all that is not divine. This also issues in the difference between John and Paul. Looking back to the benefits of fellowship with Jesus it becomes clear why he did not become a Paulinist.

John considers the contrast between God and the world's will and work to be irreconcilable and thoroughgoing. All it takes to understand this is an appreciation for John's own experience, that is, first of all the Jews' opposition to Jesus from which those words and actions of Jesus originated which liberated the disciples completely from it, and then Judaism's struggle against Jesus' messengers, and finally the struggle of Greek society and of the Roman state against Greek Christendom. He stood at the feet of Jesus' cross, saw his brother beheaded to the joy of Judaism, experienced Peter's cross and dying of Roman Christendom. He was aware of James's murder and the dying of Christians in Palestine and the smashing of the mother church. He saw Vespasian leading Roman legions to Judea and the sacking of Jerusalem, and experienced that Greek Christendom split and that gnostic quasi-churches wrestled with it. Historically it is entirely plausible that he did not love the world but that he viewed it from the perspective that it had to be overcome while at the same time being convinced that it had been overcome.

Therefore he did not become a dualist nor make room for a Satan who created the world. For someone who knew Jesus, it was impossible that the contrast in which he found himself put, however intense it might become, would ever break the universal requirement of love. Jesus' God is above all. The hope derived from Jesus transcends everything else. John's own life experience provides rich substantiation for the idea that Jesus sent word from the Father which guaranteed God's judgment in all its fearfulness while at the same time promising his rule. His dealings with Jesus also constitute the basis for the liberty with which he fres himself from Israel. After all, he had experienced how Jesus rejected all the claims of Judaism and how he allowed it to fall. This did not first require an especially reasoned liberation from the Law. For the Christ transcends the Law.

We must seek at the same place the foundation that provides John's ethics with its inner direction. Wherein should someone who knew Jesus see his commandment if not in the requirement of love? Those who had encountered Jesus could not develop the desire to transform the church into an entity that stood in competition with Israel, so that the old law, sacrament, and office would be replaced by other similar institutions. John knows nothing of this. He maintains, however, that Jesus conferred his promise on love, and John claims that, by obeying this commandment, the community did everything it could do in the service of God. Loving and dying, dying in such a way that God would be glorified by death, these are the two Johannine commandments by which he describes the community's obligation. How did this ethic come into being if it did not arise in the one who accompanied Jesus to his cross?

# The Calling of the Nations through Paul

## A. Paul's Task

### 1. The Apostolic Office in Paul

Paul's attainment of the reputation of being one of Christ's messengers constituted a strong test of the church's solidity and of the unity of its apostolic office in view of Paul's independence and vitality. Would his ministry likewise submit to Jesus' principle that power consists in service? Would his authority, too, produce liberty and his prominence establish equality? In the end, the form of doctrine Jesus gave to the church was confirmed by the test which Paul's apostolic office constituted for the church. For he assumed without reservation and with complete devotion that position prescribed for him by the apostolic office as it existed prior to and during his rise to prominence.

#### a) Selflessness

Paul dealt a fatal blow to his innate selfish craving for power. He cannot perform his task without assuming and confirming his role as a messenger of the Lord. But he himself forms part of his message only as a servant of the church: his message proclaims Jesus' lordship and no one else's. His trademark claim is not that the church is his, but to the contrary, that he is the possession of the church. It is not that his listeners are obliged to him: rather, he is accountable to them. Because he does not desire to manifest his own power, he is able to rejoice that he stands as the least of all, not exercising his power as he urges the church on to the single task of proving itself strong by judging its own evil and by doing what is good. He rejects any violation of the church's liberty as an unfaithful discharge of his office. He considers it an impossibility to be lord over someone else's faith. If his administration of baptism had created even the appearance of baptizing people in his own name, tying those he baptized to himself, he sincerely regretted this. Therefore he thanked God for the fact that his administra-

187

tion of baptism in Corinth made clear that he did not claim any lordship over the church for himself (2 Cor. 4:5; Rom. 1:14; 1 Cor. 3:21–23, 5; 2 Cor. 13:7–9; 1:24; 1 Cor. 1:13–16).

He also does not tolerate any violation of liberty in his dealings with his younger co-workers, who owed him everything they were. His desire for Titus to return to Corinth shortly after arriving from there does not keep him from careful consideration of Titus's own preference, and he is glad when Titus makes up his own mind. Of course, he is also able to command absolute obedience. But the obedience he requires is always complete and thus voluntary, never forced. He is entirely free from the tendency of using another person, particularly those God gave him as his co-workers, merely as means for his own ends. A man like Apollos makes his own decisions regarding his ministry, and Paul, in dealing with him, must resort to a request. Paul's request, in turn, is denied if the one so petitioned judges the request not to be according to God's will (2 Cor. 8:16–17; 1 Cor. 16:12).

Therefore the idea did not exist for Paul that his churches must or could stay the way he planted them. He laid the foundation, nothing more. Now follows the subsequent construction, which is accomplished by the hands of others. Paul dismisses the notion that he somehow incurred loss, such as diminished stature or authority, if others ministered effectively beside him in the church (1 Cor. 3:5–10).

For this reason he carefully distances himself from anything that would make him a hero. He would have considered it sin to use his superior intellect to captivate and persuade his listeners. Correspondingly, he does not pervert what he considers to be a special gift of divine grace as an instrument of self-glorification. We do not have from him a single record of a miracle he performed. To the contrary, he assigns positive value to his weakness and counts it among the means by which he fulfills his office. He exults in the fact that he performed his work in Corinth burdened by fear. For in such a way it remains pure and finds true success, because thus he is prevented from appearing to be the one who is successful, drawing others' admiration and wooing others to faith for his own sake. The continual suffering he undergoes provides him with the benefit of turning the eyes of all away from him to the one from whom he receives the power by which he acts. Thus he can boast in his weakness. He is fully aware that this clashes with Greek sentiments, which esteem glorious manifestations and are ready to admire strength while contemptuously turning their back on weakness. But this is precisely what keeps Paul from minimizing his own weakness, for by acknowledging his weakness Paul prevents others from exalting him to the status of hero, demonstrating to all that the power manifested through him belongs to God (1 Cor. 2:1–5; 2 Cor. 4:7; 6:4–5; 11:30; 12:5, 10; Gal. 1:10; 4:13–14).

He therefore also submits to the principle by which the disciples in Jerusalem exposed their own sin—Peter's denial, James's unbelief, and John's impetuousness—to the whole church. For Paul likewise shows the congregations he plants what he judges as sin in himself, not reluctantly, but freely and openly. It was known in Galatia as well as in Corinth that he had initially taken offense at the

Christ and persecuted him. His profound word regarding the extent and gravity of sin before the Roman church Paul framed in the form of a personal confession. His share in the Christ is no different in kind than that of the church: he is united with it in the same faith by the same guilt-covering grace (Gal. 1:13–14; 1 Cor. 15:9; Rom. 7:7–25).

The grace granted him results therefore, for him as for the Twelve and for every church member, in a categorical obligation. He says nothing of the glorious nature of his office, nothing of the grace given to him to discharge his commission without deriving from his mandate the obligation which subjects his entire conduct to ethical norms. Consequently, he considers his purity of motive to be an indispensable characteristic of his apostolic office. The questions of how he obtains salvation and how he discharges his ministry thus converge: if he fails in his ministry, he forfeits his share in the gospel. He submits unreservedly to the rule by which Jesus united participation in life and the obligation to serve for those he had called (2 Cor. 4:1–2; 6:3–10; 1 Cor. 9:23–27; 10:33).[1]

### b) Authority

While Paul discharges his apostolic office with complete selflessness, he was not afraid to exercise the will to power and acknowledges the loftiness of the office Jesus had created for those he called into apostolic service. Through that will comes knowledge of God, which Paul does not conceive of as a development of a concept of God or the appropriation of a formula descriptive of God, but as the true apprehension of the divine activity in its revelatory glory. Therefore men's response to Paul results for them in life or death, and he loosens or binds with no less effective authority than Peter, because God's forgiving and judging work is performed upon men through him. He issues the call to God to those who receive his word and grants them thereby righteousness and the Spirit. With equal effectiveness, he pronounces over the guilty a verdict that separates them from the Christ and subjects them to Satan's power (2 Cor. 2:14–16; Gal. 4:9; 2 Cor. 3:6, 9; 5:18, 20; 1 Cor. 5:5; 1 Tim. 1:20).

His claim to power and his rejection of any form of leadership that enslaves the church originate in Paul as in Jesus' first followers from the realization that his own power is rooted, not in himself, but in God. Therefore his authority does not elevate him above the church but subjects him to God's will in the same way as it does them. In this way, the apostle and the church are on equal footing, and they are free in their relationship with one another.

If a church tends to consider itself superior to Paul and seeks to subject him to its own views, Paul lends daring expression to his own liberty. Its judgment is of no account to him, because he is accountable only to God. And yet the bond between them has a firmness that transcends any other form of communion, because he has become the father of those for whom he has procured life by calling them to God. He keeps requests directed to them free from any dictatorial compulsion. Yet such requests are nonetheless always accompanied by the absolute obligation which binds them completely to Paul: "You owe me

---

1. Regarding the role of the Twelve, see *The History of the Christ*, pp. 127–28.

your very life" (1 Cor. 4:3–4, 15; Phlm. 19). If the churches break fellowship with Paul, this constitutes their demise; for thereby they separate themselves from Christ and oppose God. In his dealings with the Corinthians he subjects any other concern to the one goal: that they accept and obey him as Christ's messenger. Although he needs to discuss with them the central planks of his gospel—the difference between the aim of the Law and the gift of the Christ, the reconciling power of Christ's death and the bestowal of life by him—the ordering of their relationship with Paul now takes on decisive significance; for on it depends their share in the Christ.[2]

### c) The Means of Paul's Ministry

The call to God takes place through the transmission of Jesus' message, which Paul distinguished from "tradition" in a manner similar to teachers in Palestine.[3] The message consists in the account regarding Jesus, particularly the outcome of his life, by which Jesus' messianic name receives content and substantiation for the listeners and they understand the purpose of his coming. Here a comparison of the Pauline statements with the Gospel accounts reveals that Paul did not even in one instance change traditional information regarding Jesus. This is all the more remarkable as Paul vigorously derived new ideas and ambitions from the history of Jesus. Because he came to significant new insights regarding the Law, Paul made a vital contribution to the meaning and results of Jesus' death. Yet not a single one of Paul's statements regarding Jesus' work is Paul's own, gained, as it were, by extrapolation from Paul's teaching on the Law. All of these statements already existed in the community independent from Paul's teaching on the Law. In Paul's writings, the Christ comes from heaven and receives by his birth a genuine human existence. He is an Israelite, a son of David. His brothers are known by everyone: he did not live apart from natural family ties. He stands before God as his Son and is led by the divine Spirit. Thus the regal activity of God, by which he extends his perfect grace to mankind, has become present in Jesus. As the Son, Jesus renders complete obedience to God, free from sin, and desiring authority only as God gives it to him. He limited his ministry to Israel, seeking to show to it God's covenant faithfulness; he himself stood under the Law. He called Israel to repentance, particularly its "righteous ones," the Pharisees. That Paul knew Jesus' dispute with Pharisaism can be seen in his appeal to Jesus' prohibition of divorce (which was part of Jesus' dispute with Pharisaism) as well as by his designation of the regulations pertaining to unclean things as "human commandments," to which Isaiah 29:13 applied (cf. also 1 Tim. 1:15 with Matt. 9:13). So then, the way in which Paul conducts his controversy with the Jews is clearly indebted to Jesus' call to repentance. Jesus' work did not yet consist in gathering his community; rather, he instituted the

---

2. The same train of thought can be found in Paul's letters to the Thessalonians, because the preservation of fellowship with Paul and the share in the gospel are there inextricably linked as well. See also the Pastoral epistles.

3. James, John, and Peter show that the instruction of the community regarding the obligatory will of God was everywhere distinguished from the "message," that is, the account of the divine work.

Twelve, among whom Peter, the "rock," was the first, with whom Jesus began the building of the new community. John is placed beside him, albeit in clear subordination to him. Since Paul says that Jesus authorized his messengers to receive financial support from their congregations, he knows that Jesus sent the Twelve to Israel and that he gave them particular instructions for their work. By this he further demonstrates that he is familiar with Jesus' stance toward wealth and poverty. He views him as poor and humble, not by compulsion, but out of deliberate renunciation. Jesus' will is love, love which he also requires from his own, unconditional love, which is unable to hate even one's enemy. For this reason his call to repentance included in itself the offer of forgiveness, proclaiming that "God does not reckon the sin of the world." For this reason is his message "the gospel," the good news of God, and it has power, because it not merely promises God's gift but also grants it. Jesus unconditionally promised this gift to faith when he attributed to faith the ability to move mountains. That Paul attributed to Jesus the power to do miracles is confirmed by the fact that he also attributes this power to himself and the other apostles. He would not expect to do miracles himself if miracle was absent from his view of the Christ. However, Jesus did not use miracles to exercise his judgment or to establish his rule; for he did not refuse to suffer. By this he proves his love for sinners, whose fallen state he does not take into account. For this reason he does not withdraw the good news on account of his rejection and crucifixion by Israel but rather sends his disciples to it again after his death in order to call it to himself. He bears the cross in obedience to Scripture according to Psalm 69, which was written for him, and for this reason he faces death freely and joyfully. For this reason he bid farewell to his disciples in the final night by giving to them his body and his blood. Thus he instituted God's new covenant with mankind. His death is the work of Israel, which thereby reveals its rebellion against God. Jesus dies on the cross, and thus by Roman verdict, judged by Pilate, before whom he testifies to his regal office, making the "good confession." But he was arrested at night, and thus certainly by the Jews. He is taken down from the cross and buried. Two days later follows Jesus' resurrection as recorded in the Easter account, and then the ascension to heaven, and only then, not already during their time of fellowship with Jesus, his disciples receive the Spirit. The promise of Jesus' return follows the same general pattern in Paul as in the Gospels.[4]

What does our Gospel tradition add to this portrait of the Christ? Concrete reminiscences are of great value; but what they reveal as Jesus' deed and will is nothing other than what is also expressed by the Pauline pronouncements. Just as he did not lose anything, he also did not add anything. Not even one of his statements regarding the history of Jesus is created freely out of a dogmatic motive. He does not provide even a single allusion to a saying or action of Jesus that may be considered to be a midrash on the Gospel tradition. Paul never enter-

4. Cf. Gal. 4:4; Rom. 8:3; 9:5; 1:3; 1 Cor. 9:5; Gal. 1:19; Rom. 1:3–4; 5:19; 2 Cor. 5:21; Rom. 15:8; 1 Cor. 7:10; Col. 2:21–22; Rom. 2:17–29; 1 Cor. 15:5; Gal. 2:9; 1 Cor. 9:14; 2 Cor. 8:9; Phil. 2:8; 2 Cor. 5:14, 19; Gal. 6:2; Rom. 12:17–21; 1 Cor. 9:14; Rom. 1:16; 1 Cor. 13:2; Rom. 15:19; 2 Cor. 12:12; Rom. 5:6–8; 2 Cor. 5:19; 1 Cor. 15:3; Rom. 15:3; 1 Thess. 1:6; 1 Cor. 11:23–25; 1 Thess. 2:15; 1 Cor. 2:2; 1 Tim. 6:13; 1 Cor. 15:4–7; 1 Thess. 1:10; Gal. 4:6.

tained the thought that he could provide illustrations created by his own imagination for his teaching regarding the Christ.[5] It is therefore impossible that Paul believed that he proclaimed another Jesus than the first disciples (2 Cor. 11:4; Gal. 1:6–9). Moreover, the occasional echoes of a rich Easter account and of the account of the Last Supper caution against the assumption that Paul's proclamation of the life of Jesus to his congregations was sparse (2 Cor. 15:1–7; 11:23–25). In any case, what is clear is that Paul did not transform the proclamation of Jesus' rule into a history lesson; rather, he placed Jesus' history before his audience as a unified work of God that was designed to reveal to them his grace and righteousness. Likewise, Paul did not conceive of Jesus as the Lawgiver who sought to determine his disciples' entire conduct with his rules, so that their actions received their correctness solely by appeal to Jesus' teaching or example. Jesus' pronouncement against oaths did not lead Paul to omit an appeal to the all-knowing God as a confirmation of his own statement. He did not use an oath merely when he defended himself against false accusations, but also when he spoke of inner processes which he alone was able to know. Jesus' warning against the "fathers" who were venerated by Palestinian Judaism did not prevent Paul from calling those he had led to faith his children and himself as the father of his community. Jesus' demand to leave everything and to hate wife and child did not cause Peter to condemn the marriage of Peter and the other apostles (1 Cor. 9:5). The prohibition of judging others did not curb church discipline, and the phrase used by Jesus for the unlimited nature of patience is not applied in such a way that church members were required to suffer all injustice. Rather, when consensus cannot be reached, a process of arbitration is to ensue (1 Cor. 6:5). The version of prayer stemming from Jesus is nowhere evident when Paul speaks of the worship of the community. But in all these instances Paul fully executed the will of Jesus as it found expression in the sayings preserved by the disciples. Lying is completely removed from believers' dealings with one another, and the principle of truth has absolute validity. Similarly, Paul completely liberated love for God from human encumbrances and selfish desire. Every believer must be prepared to suffer, and church discipline is placed completely in the service of grace. But by distinguishing his message from the knowledge of Jesus' history, and by not setting Jesus' commandment in the place of personal resolution, Paul did not pursue an independent path but rather was in agreement with the convictions of the entire church.

He also used as tools the particular proofs of divine power which provided help for others and the special revelations of the Spirit, since these attest to him

---

5. The statement that the living will not precede the dead at Christ's return Paul makes ἐν λόγῳ κυρίου (1 Thess. 4:15). If this indicates a quotation of a saying by Jesus, this would add a new element to our Gospel tradition, because the latter nowhere relates the second coming to the resurrection. But the statements are not framed in a way that suggests a quotation of a saying of Jesus. Paul either uses the term "Lord" to refer to God and to the contrast between human hope and divine promise—in this case he would assert that his message possesses the certainty of a divine promise—or he uses "Lord" to refer to Jesus, showing his conviction that Jesus taught both his return and the resurrection. This is the only instance where it is even possible to consider that Paul provides additional material not found in our Gospels.

as God's messenger (Rom. 15:19; 2 Cor. 6:6–7; 12:1–6, 12). Yet he never sought to effect a decision for God merely by a sign but rather considered it to be the purpose of divine grace to turn a person inwardly to God. Thus he calls it his task to commend the truthfulness of his message to everyone's conscience (2 Cor. 4:2).

Like the other apostles, he related his work to the divine activity by linking it with continual prayer (Rom. 1:8–9; 1 Cor. 1:4–5; 1 Thess. 1:2–3; 2:13; 2 Thess. 1:3; Phil. 1:3–5, 9; Eph. 1:15–16; Col. 1:3–4, 9–12; cf. the reference to sleepless nights in 2 Cor. 6:5; 11:27). Thus the community participated in Paul's ministry, because he incorporated its prayer into his work (Rom. 15:30; 2 Cor. 1:11; Eph. 6:18–20; Col. 4:3–4; 2 Thess. 3:1). He did not merely pray for others but produced prayer fellowship by which the community also interceded for him before God. Thus he realized the equality between himself and the community at an important junction. He readily made use of liturgical formulations for his ministry, because it has its final aim not merely in the salvation of men but in the glorification of God. His apostolic ministry becomes liturgical service he offers to God (Rom. 15:16; Phil. 2:17; 2 Cor. 4:15).

Thus it was impossible for Paul, as it had been for the first disciples, to develop some sort of technique as his special method to ensure the success of his message. After all, its success consisted entirely in those inner processes by which a person is brought into communion with God and which take place only when God himself performs his work in man. In the absence of technique, Paul's apostolic office provides as little impetus for legislation as does Peter's. This can clearly be observed by the manner in which Paul involved Timothy in his work, because he delegated the entire work necessary for the establishment of the community to Timothy as well. There is no trace of a distribution of powers. The means which provides the community with everything it needs is the divine message, which loses nothing of its power when someone other than Paul proclaims it.[6]

### d) The Apostle of the Nations and the Apostle of Israel

Paul's special office is his commission to the nations (Rom. 1:5; 11:13, 15–16; Gal. 1:16; 2:8–9; Eph. 3:1–12; Col. 1:25–27; 1 Tim. 2:7; 2 Tim. 1:11). He did not conceive of his commission merely in terms of individuals but of the totality of the ethnic units which constitute a religious entity by virtue of Israel's status in contradistinction to them.[7] Of course, he can only call the nations to Christ by leading individuals to faith, forming congregations by the personal conversion of many individuals. Still, his understanding of his office remains parallel to the self-understanding held by the Twelve regarding their commission to Israel in that he likewise relates the call to larger communities, by which individuals are assigned their religious position. But this does not cause him to

---

6. Notice the "we" in the Thessalonian epistles and in 2 Corinthians. This exactly parallels the impression given by the epistles to Timothy and Titus regarding the participation of Paul's associates in his work.

7. With the term "nations," which considered all other nations except Israel as a unity, subjecting them to the same verdict, Paul preserved an important legacy of Jewish tradition.

attempt the launching of a mass movement by external or political means, such as by influencing the authorities or by way of literature. Rather, his work consists in an effort to introduce individuals internally and personally to God. He is unaware of any other means by which man can receive God's grace than that he turn to him by his own repentance and faith. Yet he detects in these small individual processes events which have important implications for all, because they reveal how the divine grace is oriented toward the nations.

Paul's work required a larger amount of his own decisionmaking and spontaneous activity than the apostles needed in Jerusalem. They were able to fulfill their obligation simply by taking advantage of the opportunities presenting themselves to them without having to seek out the recipients of their message. Paul, on the other hand, did not simply wait for the pagan to come to him but rather pursued him, delighting in particular in seeking him out where he had not yet had the opportunity to hear Jesus' message (2 Cor. 10:14–16; Rom. 15:19–21). This corresponded to his own conversion, because he did not become a Christian by approaching the church himself but by Christ's reaching out to him while he resisted him. His current outreach to the Gentiles was facilitated by the grace of Jesus which calls that which is lost, the grace he himself had experienced. Still, his restless and energetic work is always based on the conviction that he was nothing without God and that he could not take credit for his success. To the contrary, he was able to be successful only when God was active on his behalf (1 Cor. 3:7; 15:10; 2 Cor. 1:9; 3:5; 10:13; 12:11). Even in his most ambitious or daring plans, he did not think that he could guide himself, always pointing to the fact, not reluctantly but joyfully, that he could not and did not want to carry out his entire work in any other way than how it was assigned to him by the course of events (Rom. 1:10, 13; 1 Cor. 4:19; 1 Thess. 3:11).[8]

Paul never thought that Israel's calling was nullified by the calling of the Gentiles; for he did not seek to replace Jewish particularism with a Greek one. In his relationship to Jesus, he saw nothing that placed him below Peter, because even in the case of Peter he considered the decisive element to be that he was sent by the Resurrected One. Whoever conceived of their position in Christ differently was charged by Paul with attributing to Christ the giving of arbitrary favors (Gal. 2:6). He was conscious of only one way in which he fell short of the Jerusalem apostles: his initial sin against Jesus. For this reason he was "the least" of the apostles (1 Cor. 15:9). Because for those who were under the Law no guilt became a thing of the past, making them unable to forgive, all those who thought in the terms of Judaism kept reminding Paul of his guilt. Paul for his part did not dodge these charges but rather responded that it was precisely his sin which made his apostolic ministry effective, because it revealed the patience and saving power of the Christ (1 Tim. 1:13).

The superiority of Jerusalem's apostles over Paul remained undisputed and evident to the entire church, because they had been "eyewitnesses and servants of the Word from the beginning" (Luke 1:2). For this reason Paul did belong

---

8. This is the continuation of Jesus' passivity, who desires his rule only because God gives it to him.

to the weighty and important personages on whom the eyes of not merely those who were personally connected with them rested but those of the entire church. But even this Paul did not consider to be a handicap for his ministry but rather a source of energy. For his commission proved that communion with Jesus, and Christian service, were not extended merely by natural means (2 Cor. 5:16: "to know Christ according to the flesh"). But there is no hint that it was ever charged that Paul's account of the words and works of Jesus was less rich or correct than Peter's.[9] He, too, did not lack a rich knowledge of Jesus' history, because for decades he had worked with men who had participated in the establishment of the Jerusalem church. And the entire church agreed that Jesus' messenger must show Jesus' rule by proclaiming his crucifixion and resurrection. But it was precisely this that made Peter's apostolate indispensable for Paul. It was indispensable due to the message's content: it was history and took visible form as witness. But a single witness was never a witness. Had Paul been able to name merely himself as a witness of Jesus' resurrection and glory, his message would have failed. Solely by the concurring account of all messengers was the message confirmed (1 Cor. 15:11).

Likewise, the necessity of an independent apostolic ministry arose for Paul not from some opposition toward the ministry of Peter. We have not a single statement by Paul where he attacks Peter's religious posture,[10] because Paul, like Peter, clearly advocated proclaiming Jesus to Jerusalem (Rom. 15:19; Gal. 2:7–9). But this led, with a necessity evident to all, to the conclusion that the Law could not be set aside by Peter, because a clear break with the Law would have made any contact with the Jews impossible. Jesus would have become the target of blasphemy, for he would seem to have advocated apostasy from God. This would have brought their apostolic ministry to the Jews to an end. Paul therefore also did not recognize a rightful rationale excusing those who lived among the Jews and worked for them from keeping the Law. Nevertheless, Peter's ministry in Jerusalem was an indispensable prerequisite for Paul's ministry among the Greeks and his ability to protect his churches from Judaism. His ministry in the Diaspora and among the Greeks was entirely impossible if at the same time Christ was not proclaimed in Judaism, and that not merely in a distant corner but in its very center, in the headquarters of the entire church, that is, Jerusalem.[11] If there were no "apostolate for the circumcised," there would also be none for the "nations" (Gal. 2:8). With equal certainty, Paul's congregations would have irredeemably lost their liberty if he had not at the same time extended it to other congregations. If the Jews must be Hellenized in order to become Christians, the Greeks must be Judaized if they want to become a part of

9. In Corinth, Paul was charged with poverty in spirit and lack of knowledge, not ignorance of the history of Jesus (1 Cor. 7:40; 2 Cor. 11:6; 1 Cor. 2:1).

10. Rom. 10:14–18 is directed primarily toward the Jerusalem apostles. The indicting verdict concerning Peter, Gal. 2:11–13, was aimed at his hypocritical compromise of liberty before the Jerusalemites, not his faithful discharge of his obligations to the Law for the sake of his conscience. Paul here used ethical judgments that were equally applicable to apostles and nonapostles, Greeks and Jews.

11. This is the appropriate point highlighted by Luke in Acts 13:31.

the church. Liberty was available only when it was extended to all, because in the community there were neither Jews nor Greeks, but all exclusively through the work of Jesus received the Law for their conduct (Gal. 3:28; 1 Cor. 12:13).[12]

Paul created the dual apostolic office solely because it was in light of Judaism's stance impossible to unite the work among the nations and that among the Jews. This was crystal clear to everyone from the very beginning and had already been foreseen by Jesus (Matt. 10:5). Since the Jerusalem apostles therefore limited their work to Jerusalem and the Jews as long the synagogue was still open to them and had not yet decisively rejected them, the church's unity was achieved by the subordination of the newly emerging Greek communities to the Jerusalem apostles and the recognition of the Jerusalem church as the mother church, for whose preservation they all contended (Gal. 2:10). Thereby the church's constitution followed existing conditions in Judaism, because it, too, ensured unity by allegiance to Jerusalem and those who ruled the church there. This resulted in James, Peter, and John possessing authority everywhere in Christendom, being the "pillars" not merely for the community in Jerusalem church but for the entire church (Gal. 2:2, 6, 9). Paul was not critical of this nor bore it grudgingly. He did not consider this condition to be a drawback for the independence of his congregations or his apostolic ministry. For the dual apostolic office resulted necessarily from the work that must be done not only in Jerusalem, but also among the nations, and not merely among the nations, but also in Jerusalem. If the first disciples accomplished the initial great work, the proclamation of the Christ for Israel, they were "the eminent apostles" (2 Cor. 11:5; 12:11). Paul saw in the dual form of the apostolic ministry the wealth of divine grace and instructed his congregations to draw from both to the enrichment of their lives (1 Cor. 3:22). But his churches had frequent difficulty dealing with his principle of liberty, as is evident from the wavering of the Galatian churches, which pondered whether to follow Jesus or Paul: they were ready to forgo their independence as well as Paul's own commission.[13] Paul resisted such tendencies; he never put up with contempt toward his commission, considering the churches' breaking of fellowship with him also to be their separation from the Christ, in the event they desired to turn away from him to Peter. He never claimed a special privilege among the apostles, but he fought resolutely against any contempt toward the divine grace that had been brought to the churches through him, when this arose by appeal to other disciples. He saw in the tendency of the Greeks to subject themselves to James, Peter, and John, to the extent of venerating men and connecting the divine activity with men, the end of faith bound to Jesus. Still, he did not counter this tendency by postulating a dictatorial edict on his part by which he sought to bind others to his own person. Rather, he placed the independence of his apostolic ministry on solid footing with brief yet masterful argumentation when it was questioned by the Galatians. Thereby he opened up for them the free, well-founded obedience which under-

---

12. The course of history completely vindicated Paul. When the congregations no longer tolerated Jews in their midst but assimilated them, their Judaization progressed irresistibly.

13. Similar deliberations went on in Corinth: see 1 Cor. 1:12; 3:22; 9:1–6; 15:8–11; 2 Cor. 11:2–6; 12:11.

stood his special place alongside the first apostles, and therefore grasped why he did not permit an appeal away from his apostolic office to another authority, seeing therein rather a violation of the faith and a sin toward Jesus (Gal. 1:11–2:21).

The experiences of the Greek congregations in dealing with synagogues aided vigorously in the preservation of ecclesiastical unity. The Greeks could easily understand that, by participating in the ministry to the Greeks, it would have been impossible for the Twelve to tell Jerusalem Jesus' message. For the Greeks had seen how the synagogues militated against Paul's preaching to the Gentiles. Thus both, Peter as well as Paul, provided for the church's unity by cultivating relationships simultaneously also with the segment of Christendom foreign to their ministry, as far as it was compatible with their ministry purpose. This aspect of Paul's work is not only highlighted by Luke; it is also manifest in Paul's epistles (Rom. 9:3; 10:1, 18; 11:14; 1 Cor. 9:20; 10:32–33; Rom. 15:25–27; 1 Cor. 16:1–4; 2 Cor. 9:12–14). That Peter's ministry is likewise not void of parallels can be seen by his stay in Antioch, which provides clear evidence of the vigorous collaboration of the Jerusalemites in the establishment of Greek congregations (2 Cor. 1:19; 1 Thess. 1:1; 2 Thess. 1:1; Gal. 2:1, 9, 13; 1 Cor. 9:6; Phlm. 24; Col. 4:10; 2 Tim. 4:11). Other evidence pointing in this direction would be the (perhaps purposeful) transfer of individual members of the Palestinian church to these communities (Acts 11:22; Rom. 16:7; cf. the events in Corinth and Galatia).

Since Paul lent visible demonstration to the universal scope of Jesus' rule by remaining God's messenger for Israel while fulfilling his ministry as the apostle to the Gentiles, his work took on a dimension, not merely by its expansion but also its internal depth, that far surpassed what the founders of the Palestinian church were able to accomplish in the early stages of their ministry. Paul entered into full communion (apart from which he could not have conceived his apostolic work) with both Jews and Greeks, not alternately, but simultaneously. He knew himself authorized to the liberty which he practiced in his communion with Jews and Greeks alike by the perfect grace of Christ. This grace elevated him above all existing differences and offered him sufficient grace for every need.

The similarity of his apostolic ministry to that of those who had walked with Jesus is also borne out by the fact that Paul concluded his ministry the same way the Twelve did: he had no notion of needing to appoint a successor. Neither Philippians nor Paul's second letter to Timothy provide any indication of how Paul's apostolic ministry could be continued. The connection between the apostolic office and the earthly life of Jesus, a fact that enables the apostle to testify to the sending of the Christ, rules out the possibility that it can be repeated. By establishing the church, it had fulfilled its purpose; now the church must by its own labor ensure the preservation of what it had received.

## 2. Paul as Thinker

### a) The Expansion of Knowledge

Paul's resolve to go to Rome and deep reflection on the work he wanted to accomplish there produced a complex of ideas answering to the intellectual grandeur of the epistle to the Romans. That he must not avoid Rome, despite considerations cautioning against working there, but must rather establish contact with Roman Christendom, results from the fact that it is through Paul's ministry that God reveals his righteousness to believers. This places his ministry in a most lofty context, which he now explores and extends in numerous directions. From one point of view, the earthly, it is necessitated by the ethical need of the Gentile and Jew; from another, the heavenly, by the completeness of God's grace in Christ. It is therefore in conformity with the establishment of Israel through the call of Abraham and with the beginning of human history through the fall of the first man. It finds its justification in the completeness of redemption, which grants to the believer, in the Spirit, life that has been liberated from evil. His ministry also coheres with the promise by which God has bound himself to Israel, because it, too, reveals both God's sovereignty over all Jewish claims and the unshakable nature of God's faithfulness. This promise is confirmed by the fact that love is now given free rein in Jesus' community. These lofty convictions provide both basis and firmness for his resolve to go to Rome and Spain. By this we see how soberly and successfully Paul carried out intellectual labor.

This is no less visible in those letters that serve pastoral purposes. Every one of Paul's answers given in response to the Corinthians' questions becomes the occasion of the impressive demonstration of Paul's doctrinal giftedness, as he provides principles for the community's actions that cannot merely be limited to the particular occasion but penetrate to the very foundation of their devotion and conduct. This invests Paul's injunctions with a necessity and practical relevance that comprehensively unifies their conduct and puts it on a firm foundation. When, responding to the disruption introduced by new preachers into the community's relationship with its teachers, Paul says, "Everything is yours; but you are Christ's, and Christ is God's." This provides the constitution of the community with a comprehensive framework which does not merely heal the present conflict nor bring unity between the ecclesiastical office and the community, but decisively determines for all relationships, including those the community sustains with the world, under which circumstances communion can be granted and where it must be refused. The discussion of the legitimacy of religious celibacy presents the proper motives for such a choice so diligently and fully that it becomes a perfect example of the development of an ethically right-minded will. The evaluation of different pneumatic activities ascends such heights that it develops the basic principles for every form of human fellowship. As far as doubts regarding the resurrection are concerned, Paul did not only prohibit them nor merely demonstrate the factuality of Jesus' resurrection. He rather at the same time also satisfied the just demand for intellectual labor by a comprehensive discussion of eschatology which unites the expectation of resurrection with statements regarding Christ in a unified viewpoint. This he did without in the least yielding to Greek rationalism, giving complete priority to fact over against the urge to use human reasoning.

### b) The Limitation of Knowledge

Paul's intellectual achievement achieved greatness only by circumscribing it with non-negotiable limitations. Since the community's aim is determined by its opposition toward its former sinful condition, he presents it in his epistle to the Romans with his thought regarding sin and demonstrates why the conduct of the Greeks and Jews is reprehensible and renders them guilty. Paul further shows that sin determines the condition of all of mankind even apart from the choice of individuals. Moreover, he contends that man's ethical impotence derives from his natural condition, so that no one can help but the Christ. But the numerous questions arising from such argumentation, such as how such inclusion of every individual under sin relates to sin's universal power, and how the flesh produces it even though it stems from Adam, are not discussed. Since he thinks so clearly and vigorously, why does Paul not press his thoughts further? He rather cuts them short. When he creates peace in the community by giving it authority over all because it, in turn, is ruled by Christ, this axiom remains at the same time a great mystery. After all, how is Christ's rule revealed in everything, making all things redound to the community's benefit? He sets forth various respective principles as guiding rules for its conduct, but beyond this it neither requires nor receives additional theories. Jesus' oneness with God is the presupposition for his entire thought, but he supplies only pronouncements that describe Jesus' general purpose, out of which issues his work in its renunciation and glory; but he never discusses how we should conceive of Jesus' simultaneous possession of divine and human life.

By expanding and limiting his knowledge at the same time, Paul subordinated his thought to the same principle and lent it the same characteristic as is revealed in Matthew's and John's treatment of Jesus' word.[14] Paul likewise did not view his conceptual work under the rubric of "explorer" or inventor but knew himself to be the witness who proclaims what has happened and protects it against any assault, the steward who manages what has been entrusted to him and makes it productive (1 Cor. 1:6; 2:1; 15:15; 4:1–2).[15] His assurance of God removes doubt, anxiety, and selfish thirst for knowledge as driving forces of his thinking. For this reason Paul is not troubled by the limitations of his knowledge. His own thinking is transcended by the perfect clarity and immovability of the divine activity. At the same time, looking at God becomes a source of energy for Paul's thought and renders clear, large thoughts indispensable, because without them he cannot act according to God's will. Focusing on God provides Paul with the assurance that he attains to genuine insight, because in Christ he has access to the treasures of divine knowledge. Thus his thinking also takes on enduring value, because through his knowledge of God he possesses convictions that must be applied to everything that happens and that prove themselves in real life.

Because his act of thinking is controlled by the assurance of God, Paul remains in close contact with his act of living. Paul did not place his conceptual work independently beside his conduct of life but rather practiced it as part of his service offered to God. Thus he performed it in the full energy of love that

---

14. Cf. pp. 127–29.
15. When gnostic teaching connected intellectual labor with the concept of "speculative exploration," Paul felt this to be contradictory (1 Tim. 1:4).

characterized his service of God, but only to the extent it was necessary for his practical actions. He never conceives of knowing as his highest possession, resting when he has come to know. To the contrary, he judged all insights, even those mediated directly by the Spirit, including prophecy, as ephemeral. He assigned penultimate significance only to the things that we know at the present time. Nothing but the fruit of God's work, as manifested in the realm of our will, will last. For the eternal possession given to man already now is love (1 Cor. 13:8–13). Thus it was that the greatest theological document to arise in earliest Christendom turned out to be a treatise dealing with the question why Paul desired to go to Rome.

### c) The Grounding of Knowledge in the Divine Gift

The aim assigned by Paul to his intellectual labor and his verdict regarding its grounding stand in close correlation. He never conceived of a kind of knowledge of God that was not the result of God's own work. What he wants to know is God's gift, and that he knows it is God's gift as well. Therefore the accomplished fact of the divine work is the subject of his thought, while he leaves undivulged that which is irreducibly transcendent. He talks about God's revelation, not his nature, about the gift of the Christ, not his communion with God, about the reality of sin, not its possibility and origin, about the effect Jesus' death has on us, not his reconciling power by which he moves God.

Paul was led to pronouncements that in their universal scope comprehend even transcendent elements, because the gnostic movement pushed the Jewish community's ideas, which transcended experience and brought human history into a close connection with the angelic world, into the foreground in the Christian congregations as well. Paul knew himself authorized to make such formulations, because, in the Christ, he has the knowledge of God which is the basis for judgments that are absolutely valid. These judgments Paul extends fearlessly to the entire universe, including the powers that remain hidden from us (Rom. 8:38–39; Eph. 1:21; 3:10; Col. 1:16, 20; 2:15; cf. 1 Cor. 2:8). But even in this regard there does not emerge a single pronouncement by which Paul makes these powers the subject of his own personal contemplation. His thought remains even now entirely attached to the work of God by which Jesus reached his fulfillment, and his statements regarding the transcendent apply to all realms of the world merely that which Paul learned to perceive via Jesus' history.

Paul likewise understands the true apprehension of the divine work as brought about by God. He did not attribute it to the human power of will but recognizes in the eruption of light the creative act of the one who created light in the beginning (2 Cor. 4:6). That is why we are given the wisdom of the Christ, in whom are contained all its treasures (1 Cor. 1:24, 30; Col. 2:3). This is experienced by Christ's operation in man through the Spirit, who does not leave men's consciousness untouched. Since the Spirit is in its essence the One who knows and searches all things in God, he also works in us as the agent of wisdom, so that the gift of the Spirit issues in the growth of knowledge that now truly agrees with God's thoughts, extending even so far as the final eschatological aim (1 Cor. 2:10–16). This corresponds to Paul's practice of tying the whole of his intellectual labor firmly to Scripture. Even the pronouncements that are original with Paul are always expressive of a thought drawn from Scripture. For his ultimate statements regarding the Christ, Paul used the scriptural terms "the image of God," by which creation took place, and "firstborn"; and his teaching on justification likewise was not developed without recourse to Scripture.[16]

Paul did not devalue human teaching through these pronouncements. After all, God creates the community, gifts individuals through the community, and makes them messengers of his word and bearers of his gifts for one another. Paul's concept of God is in no way intermingled with "quietism." Still, he was mindful in all his teaching that he could not inject knowledge into his listeners through the superiority of his technique or the perfection of his proofs. Rather, knowledge can grow in them only as part of their life act, which is grounded in the divine activity transcending the individual. Even when he spoke with the Galatians about Christendom's freedom from Mosaic regulations, a topic on which he had firm convictions, he did so fully aware that the rooting of this knowledge in his listeners required a birthing process transforming them into the image of Christ in their inner condition of life (Gal. 4:19). Paul's acknowledgment of knowledge as a divine gift leads him to respect the freedom of his readers. This respect does not claim to rule over them but rather understands the teaching office in all sincerity as service. In the outworking of Paul's teaching ministry, too, faith and love unite to produce a single thrust. Paul teaches for the purpose of providing the community with its own judgment, seeking to impart to it a faith that is their own, knowing its foundation. He wants to facilitate obedience that is free and joyful, fully aware of what it does. This is what invests his teaching with richness and flexibility. But for himself, as also for the community, Paul maintains that their relationship with Christ is not an achievement of their own thinking but of faith, and that all knowledge needed for faith is God's gift. This constitutes the boundary Paul never crosses in his teaching ministry.

For this reason Paul was separated both from Greek philosophy and from rabbinic scholarship by a contrast of will, not merely by the differing contents of their religious and ethical pronouncements. Paul detects in those systems a self-centered striving by which man seeks to elevate his thinking to the level of God. But this attempt to ascend intellectually to the divine "from below" is doomed to fail, because it cannot rise above the content inherent to man's natural constitution. The world's separation from God renders such effort futile, even when it seeks to satisfy a religious longing, and its futility corresponds to its impurity, the vain, arrogant manner that makes knowledge an occasion for man's glory. But as long as man receives that incentive and conceptual substance which determine his thinking merely from his "soul," his judgment regarding the divine is false (1 Cor. 1:17–24; 2:14; 8:1–3; 3:18–20).

16. Image in keeping with Gen. 1:26: Rom. 8:29; 1 Cor. 11:7, 15, 49; 2 Cor. 4:4; Col. 1:15; firstborn in keeping with Ps. 89:28: Col. 1:15; faith in keeping with Gen. 15:6 and Hab. 2:4: Rom. 1:17; 4:3–5; Gal. 3:6–12.

If, on the other hand, knowledge grows from God's gift, intellectual labor becomes filled with joy and confidence. Paul praises God as the perfect giver also in this respect. The one formed by the Spirit searches all things, is not put to shame by any of his requests, and is not turned back by any of his questions (1 Cor. 2:15; Rom. 15:14–15). This promise requires an external boundary just as little as the unconditional promise for prayer does. For it possesses its boundary in the fact that human striving and work is founded on the Spirit. This does not lead to irrelevant questions, but rather removes the craving for knowledge that serves nothing but the enhancement of one's own life. If someone focuses on questions that are out of his reach, this indicates that he is not led by the Spirit. Where union with Christ is preserved by the Spirit, there is no distortion of the message for the purpose of vain talk or theological strife (1 Cor. 3:3). Where God's call, on the other hand, leads to action, and where the question arises what love should and can do, Paul has unbroken courage for reflection, claiming God's unconditional promise which extends to him, because he has been placed through Christ into a communion with God.

Since this is the nature of Paul's thought, any creative procedure that goes beyond his statements is excluded in the presentation of Pauline teaching. Whoever shapes these into a Pauline system infuses Paul with his own rationalism and seriously distorts him. It is also hard to know how the ideas available to us relate to the entirety of his thought. Many a thesis may currently be present in his letters merely as an axiom providing a rationale for his command, while he may have developed the thesis extensively for himself. He called the water given by God to Israel in the desert a gift of the Christ, but this is hardly the only instance where he linked the preexistent Christ with God's revelation to Israel. He portrayed Christ's gift to us through his cross by way of the Passover lamb, probably also by the Ark of the Covenant, but hardly limited the comparison between the cult ordered by the Law with Christ's work to these instances (1 Cor. 10:4–5, 7; Rom. 3:25). But it eludes simple rational analysis how Paul compared Israel's ritual at the altar with Christ's cross or how he elaborated on the topic that Christ was the mediator of revelation to Abraham and Israel.

By construing his thought in such a way Paul remained faithful to his Pharisaic piety. For the Pharisee likewise was no philosopher but esteemed doctrine because it enables him to determine the correct work. But Paul now had a closer unity between his knowledge and his will than previously. The rabbinate ended up with a dualism between doctrine and works, because there doctrine approached man externally, so that he first must acquire knowledge of the Law and then act on what he had learned. In Paul, knowledge and will issue from the one central event of his life: his union with Christ in the Spirit. For this reason he is no longer confronted with two obligations, to learn what God said and to do what he commanded. He now has but a single will: to believe in Christ, to be in him, to preserve his gift, to follow his leading. This provides him with discernment and the will to do what is right. Thereby Paul's thinking also remains on the course mapped out for him through Jesus' own didactic labor, and by thinking in accordance with this pattern, he proves himself to be a Christian.

## d) Special Revelations

The internal intellectual labor done by Paul in the common forms of human consciousness was accompanied by the special experiences that he characterized as revelations, visions, or spiritual gifts. He did not brag about these experiences; we know about them merely by the polemic required in dealing with the Corinthians. Because others boasted of their miracle-working prayer and visions while despising Paul, who is alleged to lack such manifestations, he partially uncovers this part of his inner life; it had been unknown even to the Corinthians up to that point (1 Cor. 14:18; 2 Cor. 12:1–9). Parallel to this is the fact that Paul's epistles nowhere substitute mysterious words claiming to be revelation from above for argumentation aiming at his readers' understanding. Nowhere does Paul merely command without also appealing to the reasonableness of the apostle's injunctions, which are therefore also accessible to his readers' understanding.

This is not the result of doubt regarding the value of pneumatic processes. For Paul esteemed praying in tongues and visions as genuine experiences of communion with the Lord and of the Spirit's presence. These manifestations, however, were not set apart from the rest of his life as isolated details, as though he reached a state of grace only in those hours and only then experienced effective communion with Christ. Paul always clings to the totality of the divine grace, which is vouchsafed to him in his conscious, personal life. Thus these experiences elevate his entire being and confirm to him that his rational intellectual labor and his ministry carried out by natural means take place in Christ.

Paul is fully aware of the alluring appeal these kinds of experiences may exert, and how their extraordinary nature may enhance one's self-consciousness in a peculiar way. He therefore saw God's wisdom in the fact that these emotional and intellectual highpoints were balanced with low points filled with the pain and suffering characteristic of lurking satanic power. The result of those ups and downs of his inner life, which exceeded both positive and negative common human experience, is the simple condition of faith, which supplements the consciousness of one's own weakness by the assurance of Christ's power and thus is able to persevere.

This determines the extent to which Paul related the notion of inspiration to his own teaching activity. The fact that he does not claim his pneumatic experiences to be the source of particular words or doctrines reveals that he no longer applied the pre-Christian concept of inspiration with its notion of the obliteration of human consciousness and the will-less movement of man by the power of the Spirit. For this would have resulted in pneumatic experiences that constituted interruptions of the rest of his inner life. Paul, however, related his entire intellectual being and inner condition to God's gift, occurring in Christ and being effected by the Spirit. Thus Paul's concept of inspiration extends to his entire apostolic work, and he can note at any time—even when he explicitly distinguishes his word from Jesus' and calls it a word of advice designed to support rather than preclude his reader's own judgment—that he speaks as the one who has God's Spirit. His consciousness of his authority consequently encompasses his entire ministry; it does not merely extend to individual aspects of his work but extends to all he does (1 Cor. 2:12–13; 7:40; Rom. 9:1).

## 3. The Verdict against Man

### a) The Rebellion against the Truth

The following conclusion may suggest itself to a speculative reconstructive procedure: when Paul offered Jesus' word to the Greeks, he changed his purpose; for the Greek needed illumination, not a call to repentance. But Paul had the same goal for his dealings with the Greeks as for the Jews. He gave the message of repentance a universal formulation, so that it applied to man in every circumstance.

Thus he acted according to the conviction prevailing in the Jewish community and in obedience to the norms under which Jesus had placed his community. All of them, both the rabbinate and Jesus' disciples, connected with every reprehensible act the notion of guilt, which rejected sin absolutely and made it the basis for man's death. The universal validity of the attribution of guilt resulted for them directly from the concept of God. According to Paul, the Greek likewise needs the demonstration of divine kindness that seeks to draw him away from evil to God. He experiences this demonstration of kindness not merely by enjoying good gifts but above all by being able to desire and accomplish what is good. That gift of God which renders human activity righteous is the truth. Its indestructible presence in man results both in his ability to serve God and in his guilt (Rom. 1:18, 20, 32; 2:4, 7–8; 7:15–23). Because his evil constitutes disobedience to the truth, it is not merely a misfortune of which he is victim but his act for which he is responsible. Paul places full confidence in the concept of truth and expects that all people sense an obligation to it (Rom. 2:20; 2 Cor. 4:2; Gal. 5:7; 2 Thess. 2:9–13; 1 Tim. 6:2; 2 Tim. 2:25; 3:7; 4:4). Paul values the assurance of God as the centerpiece of truth, an assurance that is given to all, because all see God's works and because works reveal their creator and gifts their giver. Therefore an appeal is made to all to honor God as God and to thank him. And for this reason judgment is incurred by all, because man fails to obey the truth given to him and eludes its lordship by his perverse desire.

Thus Paul judged all evil, including that done to one's neighbor, according to a religious standard. Since truth is God's gift, the one opposing it and suppressing it enters into rebellion against God. Therefore his sin results in death (Rom. 1:32; 5:12, 21; 6:16, 23; 7:5, 9–13; 1 Cor. 15:56; 2 Cor. 3:7). Because sinful behavior does not do damage merely to the natural conditions of life or break mere norms given to man by himself, but because it constitutes an assault on truth, this becomes the occasion for the fall which leads to loss of life. Paul's terms for God's sin-opposing will is "wrath" (Rom. 1:18; 2:5, 8; 3:5; 4:15; 5:9; 9:22; 12:19; 13:4; Eph. 2:3; 5:6; Col. 3:6). When God's wrath is directed against man, this occurs for his life's sake. Paul strove to instill the certainty in Christendom that it is impossible for man and sin to coexist. If sin lives, man dies. For man to live, sin must die. He considers this Law to be indissoluble, because it results directly from the presence and rule of God. Man suffers the death which sin incurs not merely by seeing his life disintegrate, but already by his loss of divine gifts, which he needs in order to conduct his life. God responds to man's evil by giving him over to vain, dark thoughts and unnatural passions and drives (Rom. 1:21–32; Eph. 4:17–19).

### b) The Fall of Mankind

Paul does not attribute the rebellion against the truth which subjects man to God's wrath as something arising new in every single individual. For everyone partakes of the common condition of all, from which each receives his thoughts and will. The "world" concept also plays a role in Pauline thought; this world is evil, and the spirit of the world, who conforms the thoughts and desires of all to each other is not the divine Spirit (Gal. 1:4; 1 Cor. 2:12; Eph. 2:2, 12). But more strongly than the "world" concept, Paul's trademark affirmation is that sin has become the all-mastering might through the fall of the first man, whose act has determined God's dealings with each person since (Rom. 5:12–19; cf. 1 Cor. 15:21–22, 48–49). Paul initially calls death the thing the one man made to be the destiny of all. But since all have been born into a condition in which they are unable to live because death exercises regal power over them, all are likewise subjected to the power of sin. Through this separation from God, which issues in the loss of life, good becomes unattainable for all. Paul establishes the solidarity of all with Adam through God's decree which orders their destiny. Thus God has judged; his judicial verdict condemned all and placed them into a position of sin and death. The term "inheritance," designed to illumine the connection between the first man and the entire race, slightly exceeds Paul's explicit assertion, because it is supposed to designate the natural mediation which links our condition with Adam's conduct. With reference to Genesis 3 Paul, of course, also believed that men are sons of Adam, having been born through conception by him. But it is unclear whether he linked the notion of "inheritance" with this fact. He was moved solely by the thought that here God rules and reveals his judgment. God's judicial verdict assumed full force in the course of human history, just as God's verdict unifies the Christ with his community in oneness.

### c) The Struggle of the Flesh against the Spirit

While this train of thought grounds the sinful condition of all in the course of history, Paul also provides our sinfulness with grounding in the natural condition of our lives. He does this by his characteristic use of the term "flesh" (Rom. 7:5, 14, 18; 8:3–9, 12–13; 1 Cor. 1:26; 3:1–4; 2 Cor. 1:12; 10:2–3; Gal. 3:3; 5:13, 16, 24; 6:8; Eph. 2:3; Col. 2:11, 18). Thus sin becomes as much a fact of life for us as man's natural condition generally. Paul starts with the observation that our entire inner life depends on natural processes occurring in our body. The flesh, the body, and its members determine not merely our physical condition but also the capacity of our entire religious and ethical achievement (body: Rom. 6:6; 7:24; 8:13; members: Rom. 7:5, 23; Col. 3:5). Everything we bear within ourselves pertaining to our capacity to act, whether our worship or our service performed for others, whether our knowledge and love for God or our kindness toward men, is tied to our bodily organs. According to Paul, this dependence produces not the correctness but the weakness and corruptness of our actions.

The effects of the flesh which Paul has in mind do not consist merely in the difficulties caused for us by the sexual drive and perhaps additionally those disturbances issuing from our drive for sustenance. To be sure, the devastation caused by these drives serve Paul by providing examples for the power of the flesh to incite sin. Without these it would be unthinkable that man's belly becomes his god to which he sacrifices everything and by which he is completely enslaved (Rom. 16:18; Phil. 3:19).[17] Still, Paul saw the influence of the flesh on our internal lives not merely in the inciting and unnaturalness of sensual drives; he perceived it also in our loftiest actions. Harshness, selfishness, arrogance, prayerlessness, in short, godlessness in all its forms are no less caused by our dependence on natural provocations than the licentiousness of the demand for sex. All these result from flesh providing us with our thoughts and will.

By linking the ethical judgment with a statement describing our nature, Paul notably intensified the "flesh" concept. Since our nature turns out to be the ground for our evil desires, we must forgo any form of self-help. Man's reprehensible actions are thus rooted in an inescapable law, inescapable because it controls his members, which are indispensable for every life act and determine his entire conduct (Rom. 7:23; 8:2).

Thus the rebellion of the will against the divine commandment reveals at the same time the essential opposition separating us from God. For God and everything derived from him is of the Spirit. For this reason rebellion against God issues in us to the extent that we are aware of God's will. The constitution of our body results in the fact that we bear within ourselves an infinite number of passions, constantly having needs, constantly nurturing cravings, so that our lives and aspirations consist in the fulfillment of our desires. As soon as a clear view of God is granted us, however, and his law takes hold of us, our desire is prohibited. Thus the thought is rendered baseless that we have in that desire guidelines for our actions and that we are to seek the purpose of our lives in its fulfillment. We are now confronted with a higher will with which we are to concur, a will telling us that we must receive what is given to us and that we must do what we are told. The grounding of our passions in our physical nature, however, does not permit them to disappear; it is likewise impossible that the choices we make will be correct and that what we desire concurs with God's will. Rather, what we desire for ourselves is forbidden by the divine commandment, and our will, grounded in the flesh, militates against the things the commandment requires from us. This conflict leads to our ethical powerlessness, which disfigures our goodness into mere thoughts, wishes, or attempts, while we find ourselves unable actually to perform the good deed. With this discussion of the observed human condition Paul also linked an assessment of the makeup of the cosmos. That which is God's is revealed in heaven and possesses the heavenly nature; the flesh and its members, on the other hand, belong to the earth, from which and for which they were formed. Thus there persists a conflict between the longings incited by them and the divine will (Rom. 7:14; Col. 3:5; 1 Cor. 15:47–48).

---

17. Paul, however, expressed this verdict not regarding Greeks or Jews but regarding those Christians whose Christianity still failed to liberate them from their selfish drives.

Paul also related the mortality of our bodies to the influence they exercise on our conduct. Because our members are mortal and our body is a body of death, it is the realm where sin is master and the cause of our powerlessness (Rom. 6:12; 7:24; 5:12). This reveals our separation from God, because where death reigns, fellowship with God is broken. Thus we are given a body that is merely subject to decay and therefore not fit to serve as our instrument for God's service.

Owing to the corrupting influence of the flesh, our inner man is the better part of our being, for the renewing of which the divine grace works (Rom. 7:22; 2 Cor. 4:16; Eph. 3:16). Because truth provides us with our relationship with God, our ability to think is given particular dignity. With our minds we truly apprehend God's good will and sense the compelling power of his commandment; thus we are slaves, belong and are subject to the divine Law in our minds, despite the opposing law controlling our actions (Rom. 7:23, 25; 12:2; 1 Tim. 6:5; 2 Tim. 3:8; Titus 1:15).

The comprehensive condemnation of the entire condition of human life by Paul could be supposed to suggest that Paul sought to divert attention from particular ethical tasks. When the flaring up of sin is linked with the judgment, "I am dead," it is of no further consequence, it may be argued, how man conducts himself: what kind of evil can a dead man commit? He is already totally condemned. Thus, it may be said, Paul by his verdict regarding man greatly jeopardized the community's ethical condition. But his own thought never takes this course. By his verdict, he in no way sought to replace or curb diligent perception or evaluation of concrete individual cases. Rather, he used it to approach individual actions with full attentiveness and decisiveness. With his consideration of the human condition he does not devalue history, as if he had little esteem for action on account of essence. He proves this by the fact that the pronouncements regarding the power of evil over man do not lead to a condemnation of the entire content of human life as sin. Paul did not attribute to man nothing but evil, which would have caused him to embrace the inactive quietism of a hermit. Paul consistently distinguished between good and evil in all, be they Greeks, Jews, or believers, and always acknowledged the mixed character of the human will.

Because man perceives with his mind the good will of God and recognizes his compelling power, he concurs with and rejoices in God's Law. He is therefore able to hate evil and desire good, desiring good even while doing evil. That full compliance with the good proves to be virtually unattainable does not mean that the good will is deprived of deeds altogether, withering to a mere powerless wish. Genuine unwillingness can set itself against evil, and an earnest will can long for good (Rom. 7:15–23; 14:5). Parallel to this thesis, compelling power is attributed to the conscience, and unconditional obedience is required of it.[18] Paul assigned only secondary importance to the question of whether the views making up our moral judgments are correct. Even in their present condition

---

18. Cf. Rom. 2:15; 9:1; 13:5; 1 Cor. 8:7, 10; 10:29; 2 Cor. 1:12; 4:2; 5:11; 1 Tim. 1:5, 19; 3:9; 4:2; 2 Tim. 1:3; Titus 1:15.

they oblige man, as long as he has them.[19] No one else's conscience can assume the place of one's own; everyone must obey the truth he discerns. Therefore the mind provides us with a connection to the divine Law that cannot be severed. While the blinding of the thoughts formed by the mind causes a severe loss for man, created for him by Satan in order to prevent him from accepting the gospel, the preservation of thoughts in Christ is the indispensable and inestimable blessing God grants us because he keeps peace with us (2 Cor. 3:14; 4:4; 11:3; Phil. 4:7).

If Paul's thinking had been influenced by gnostic impulses, the question of how the flesh takes on its oppressive nature for us would have moved him deeply. But we find no statement by him in this regard. By linking the members of our body with the earth and contrasting Adam's earthly nature with Jesus' heavenly nature, Paul does not seek to derive the condition of the flesh, resulting in reprehensible lusts and rebellion against God, from God's creation. The pure and complete denial by which Paul rejected all he called sin barred him from theories that incorporate sin into the fabric of the divine work. To be sure, he extended the comprehensive rule of God even to reprehensible conditions, but only in such a way that he derived them from God's judicial activity that makes sin the sinner's punishment (Rom. 1:24, 26, 28; 9:17–18, 22; 11:7, 25). Because he ties the fleshly nature of man to his mortality, letting death enter the world through sin, one may suspect the first man's fall to be the process by which the body received its corrupting omnipotence over man. But even there we look in vain for a Pauline statement. We see here at a particularly crucial juncture how diligent Paul was, despite the fearless courage of his thought, in respecting the boundaries within which he saw himself granted insight. Daring formation of theories was not his style. He seeks to show Christendom what it now must consider in its particular circumstances in order to fulfill its calling. This includes that it not be unaware of the dependence of its inner life on its physical nature, not indulge in dreams as if it were not flesh. How this condition arose is a question that might profoundly affect the gnostic; Paul set it aside as dispensable. Here one may also find the reason why Genesis 6:5, a popular passage in Pharisaism, which created the phrase "the evil nature" for the human condition, is not found in Paul. Paul completely separated evil from God's creation. While the Pharisaic formulation describes what is reprehensible in man as a condition suffered by him against which he is powerless, the Pauline formulations never express our powerlessness in our struggle with evil in such a way that they become merely the basis of a feeling of weakness and pain. Paul rather always confronts us with our conscious, personal participation in evil in order to bring about a willful repentance that sees ourselves as the guilty party. The flesh enslaves us by moving us and controlling our thoughts and decisions. The flesh concept thus does not cause Paul to blame God, nor to develop a speculative dualism that holds the condition of the world responsible for our sin. He

---

19. Nothing in nature is unclean in itself; whoever considers something to be unclean, however, must avoid it (Rom. 14:14). The idol is nothing in and of itself; but whoever considers it to be a god sins, if he fails to give proper attention to it (1 Cor. 8:7).

simply views it as the occasion for the act of repentance and faith, an act by which we judge ourselves as guilty and understand Christ to be our righteousness. The Pharisaic depiction of the "evil nature," on the other hand, encouraged an immoral quietism that excused itself on account of its powerlessness.

### d) Pre-Christian Parallels to Paul's Struggle Against the Flesh

Greek thought had popularized the thought that there was a struggle between the natural and the personal, the bodily and the mental world. This led to the formulation of systems that were in part scientific and in part religious and that depicted and sought to overcome this dualism by the formulation of an abstract concept of God and an ascetic way of life. For this reason we find in Jewish-Greek theology too the opposition between what is discerned by sense perception and what is intellectually conceived, between the corporeal and pure reason. From all this, the practical result of such doctrine led either to the praise of the superiority of reason in Stoic terms and with this to the demand to control one's passions, or to a skeptical mood which sought to curb sensual imaginations and natural drives through an ascetic way of life in order to prepare thereby for the mystical experience of the divine activity.[20] According to one widespread theory, Paul patterned his condemnation of the flesh after these theologies, which he doubtless frequently encountered both in the Greek synagogue and with pagan Greeks.

In Paul, however, we find no trace of dualism by which nature or at least the physical world in its totality becomes the topic of reflection and critical judgment. While Greek thought always treated the relationship between the concept and the thing, between reason and matter, as a cosmological and cosmogonical problem, by which man is affected because he is part of nature, Paul makes no mention of the term "matter" at all. He nowhere speaks of the corporeality or manifestation characteristic of matter but solely of a particular kind of material, flesh, which clothes our bones and bears our blood. Frequently flesh is even discussed without any further distinction being made regarding its composition (Rom. 9:3; 11:14; 15:27; 1 Cor. 5:5; 7:28; 9:11; 10:18; 2 Cor. 3:3; 4:11; 7:1, 5; 12:7; Gal. 2:20; 4:14; Phil. 1:22, 24; Eph. 5:29, 31; 6:5; Col. 1:24; 2:1, 5; 3:22; Phlm. 16). If the term "flesh" is given a negative connotation, this is merely in reference to man. It is therefore mistaken to equate flesh and matter in Paul's pronouncements. Where he uses "flesh" alternately with "body" and "members," he makes clear that he conceives of the contrast decidedly in anthropological rather than cosmological terms. Paul's rejection of Greek ideas bearing a surface resemblance with his own constitutes a brilliant critical achievement. For Paul thereby lifted the problem from the speculative vagueness and idealism it possessed for the Greeks, limiting it to the point where it directly encounters our self-consciousness.[21]

---

20. The Stoic form of Greek-Jewish theology was closer to Pharisaism and thus was presumably the most widespread in Greek synagogues. Typical of it is the sermon about the autonomy of reason (4 Macc.). The other type of theological understanding is found in Philo.

21. The cosmological and epistemological portions of the theory no longer triggered serious interest already in the synagogue. Attention was given merely to its practical, ethical aspects.

The curtailment of thought used merely to understand our own conduct also immediately results in an essential difference from Greek religious thinkers and the theologians of the synagogue. For the logical question, that is, what was accomplished by sense perception and how concepts relate to it, was of no interest to Paul. His verdict regarding the flesh has merely an indirect bearing on epistemology. Since he describes by it human volition and action, it relates indeed to our thinking, which is, together with our will, connected to a unified life act (fleshly wisdom: 1 Cor. 1:26; 2 Cor. 1:12; fleshly understanding: Col. 2:18; know according to the flesh: 2 Cor. 5:16). The question of the sources for our knowledge, on the other hand, is entirely foreign to Paul. Thus a further important element of Greek teaching disappears, its opposition to our sense perception. It despised joy and hated pain, because our sense perception stirs passion with irresistible force. Paul, however, remains completely free from seeking to regulate sense perception for the purpose of keeping one's spiritual life from all fluctuation. He felt the depths of joy and pain without fear that they might corrupt him. But even where the comparison of Pauline pronouncements with pre-Christian ones is limited to ethical judgments, there remains a profound contrast owing to the fact that Paul did not combat the senses nor matter nor the flesh's natural condition by itself isolated from spiritual processes, but spoke of the flesh solely in terms of how it shapes man's self and produces and controls his thoughts and volition. Paul did not struggle with a "flesh" that stood in essential opposition to God owing to an alleged intrinsic quality. He rather combated the kind of flesh by which he himself is who he is, because he constantly experiences its operation within himself. Therefore his judgment is directed not against the external but internal, not against the natural but ethical effects of the flesh, which pertain not merely to a part of man, not merely to his lower, savage, natural half but to his entire condition of life, which Paul measured by another standard than the Greeks. He did not measure it by what he finds within himself as his higher form of being but by the concept of God. For the characteristic of God and the bearer of his activity is the Spirit; the flesh, on the other hand, is the characteristic of man in his difference from God. Therefore Paul used the notion of the fleshly nature of man also as a weapon against Greek strivings, because he denied together with the flesh also all the things those who followed Greek piety called their reason and virtue (cf. the dispute with the Corinthians in 1 Cor. 1:26; 3:1–4; 2 Cor. 1:12, 17; 5:16; 10:2–4; 11:18).

This is confirmed by the fact that the Pauline "spirit" is not the correlate to the Greek term "reason," because Paul did not conceive of it as the natural property of man nor as his higher nature that he contrasted with the lower nature. Rather, man receives the Spirit from Christ through his presence with him. Thus the alleged parallel between the Greek antithesis and that of Paul turns out to be invalid. The fact that Paul ties out fleshly nature to our mortality likewise shows that the category of matter does not belong here. Whoever was concerned about the material nature of the body considered death to be a desirable event and deemed the mortality of the body to be an advantage, because the prison of matter was thereby thrust open and the soul liberated from its bondage. Paul, on the other hand, linked the mortality of the body with the disorder and weakness of our will and longed for an imperishable body.

In Paul's Christology or eschatology one looks in vain for consequences that would necessarily result from a physiological dualism. The Pauline Christ is not conceived of in docetic terms and does not reject corporeality but rather lives in the flesh in such a way that he knows no sin (Rom. 1:3; 8:3; 9:5; Eph. 2:14; Col. 1:22; 1 Tim. 3:16). An interpretation of Paul's doctrine of the cross that based its effectiveness on the destruction of Jesus' body would clearly be wrong. The glorified condition does not produce a purely spiritual existence. Paul's ethic likewise knows nothing of such dualism; for he regulates his dealings with nature by the principle of liberty.

The connection established by Paul between the Spirit and glory and light does not warrant the conclusion that he thereby thinks of a contrast between the rough material of flesh and a fine, luminous kind of material he called Spirit who proceeded from Christ and entered believers. Where Paul juxtaposes Scripture and Spirit, claiming that Scripture kills while the Spirit gives life, we certainly distort his intention if we contrast Scripture that kills with a life-giving immaterial substance (2 Cor. 3:6). For the fatal effect of Scripture is not tied to a particular kind of material but comes into play because it expresses the divine will. Correspondingly, the Spirit gives life, because he, as Paul clearly states, embodies a law that seizes and controls man's internal condition (Rom. 8:2). Regarding Moses Paul states, according to the Pentateuch, that his face shone after his encounters with God. Here he thinks of a brilliance comparable to physical processes. Subsequently, Paul places himself above Moses as sharing in greater glory, because the Lord is the Spirit and therefore brings about liberty and because he reflects his glory with an unveiled face (2 Cor. 3:7–18). Did he thereby really describe a natural process, claiming that a miraculous substance of light streamed into him and then again out of him? One saw nothing of Paul's brilliance, and still it is argued that he described it as a physical process. We receive "invisible light," the theory runs; from Paul's perspective this surely was a confusing thought. True, Paul's glory will be revealed at the end, at the revelation of the Lord. But Paul's statement is not given an eschatological dimension but claims regarding his person and work that they possess a kind of glory that is greater than that given to Moses. Its higher value is expressed by locating its origin in the Spirit. Thereby he lifted the thought beyond a mere physical dimension. This glory is doubtless real for Paul and has its closest analogy in the term "light." But this does not bring us to the teaching of minuscule particles of light Paul called "Spirit."

The dualism used by Paul in his evaluation of man is inseparable from the dualism arising in God's reign through the sending of Christ and the Law. The Law and the flesh, and the Christ and the Spirit belong together. This contrast, however, was not a result of Platonic or Stoic asceticism which used nothing but a peculiar fine-tuned Law. Neither did it arise from contempt of coarse matter and admiration of fine luminal substance. It rather was rooted in the historical events that revealed to Paul the divine will.

For this reason the pronouncements of the apostles in Palestine regarding the flesh stand in much greater proximity to Paul's statements than any parallel in

Seneca or Philo. James assigns lust afflicting man its place in the members and calls ideas rooted in ourselves "natural wisdom." In dispute with the gnostics the question posed itself whether they had the Spirit or were merely controlled by their own nature, and they are rejected because they cultivate the lusts of the flesh. In John and Peter, fleshly lust is the characteristic of pagans and of the world; it is set in contrast to the worship given to the community which is of a spiritual nature (James 4:1; 3:15; Jude 8, 19; 1 John 2:16; John 3:6; 1 Pet. 2:11, 5).[22] These statements reveal the motif that lent decisive significance to careful deliberation regarding the deeds of the "flesh" for the evaluation of human conduct. Because "Spirit" and "flesh" express the difference between divine and human nature, Christendom received through the claim of having the Spirit and of God's operation in believers' inner being a strong incentive to pay attention to the contrast thus revealed in the internal process. The kind of thinking and desire that originates in man's natural condition differs sharply from the thinking and desire that is judged to be God's gift, and man's own thinking is characterized according to its source and value by being attributed to the flesh. Paul's "flesh" concept evidences a Greek element only in that he used it with whatever conceptual force he felt was necessary in the evangelization of the Greeks. This led him to direct attention to the dependence of our will on our natural condition, whereby he was able to formulate a doctrine of human need that comprised all men and everything in man and revealed the value of Christ's gift to all. In this respect there was a connection between Paul's mission to the Greeks and his depiction of the flesh as a universal incentive to faith.

### e) The Dispute with the Law

Paul significantly deepened his verdict on the human condition by seeing in the Law that divine will to which all are subject. The fact that God presents his will to us in the specific form of a divine commandment renders rebellion against God to be particularly culpable. Now sin becomes transgression (Rom. 2:23, 25, 27; 4:15; 5:14; Gal. 2:18; 3:19). While sin is dead without the commandment and thus remains ineffectual, it comes to life and thus becomes effective when the commandment comes to man (Rom. 7:7–10). Through the commandment, man's relationship with God is not confined to his own thinking, so that it remains up to him what he does with the truth revealed to him; God rather obliges his will through his commandment and calls him to obedience. Thus resistance against what is good turns into conscious, personal rebellion against God. The greater effect corresponds to the enhanced intensity of this process. That sin is dead without the commandment and that it produces no consequences is based on the fact that it is not taken into account without the Law (Rom. 4:15; 5:13). Once it counts as breaking of the divine commandment, however, it determines man's destiny: now it kills him, because he be-

---

22. The linguistic antecedent to the Pauline antithesis of flesh and Spirit can be found in the biblical and Palestinian contrast between flesh and Spirit. In Paul, circumcision occurs in the "flesh" (Rom. 2:28; Eph. 2:11; Col. 2:13): this is attested Palestinian usage. The same can be said regarding the phrase "flesh and blood" (1 Cor. 15:50; Gal. 1:16) and "all flesh" (Rom. 3:20; 1 Cor. 1:29; Gal. 2:16).

comes guilty of transgressing the divine commandment, and disobedience fanned into conscious rebellion brings condemnation upon man. The Law thus causes man to know sin, not merely in such a way that previously existing evil is exposed, but in such a way that the Law exacerbates man's rebellion against God and now also brings its calamitous consequences upon man. The two pronouncements, that sin kills him and that the Law kills him, are mutually explanatory. If the Law did not pronounce the death sentence upon evil, we would not die as a result of evil, and if sin did not destroy life, the Law would not assign us death. This yields the further insight that the Law produces God's wrath; for it kills, because God's displeasure falls on the one who breaks it. The word of wrath that terminates fellowship is the curse. So then, the Law pronounces God's curse, a curse understood by Paul not merely as threat but as everything that proceeds from God regarded as an effectual force. Because the Law subjects man to the divine wrath and curse, the hour in which he is confronted with the commandment is the hour in which he dies (Rom. 3:20; 4:15; 2 Cor. 3:6, 9; Gal. 3:13). The effecting of sin, death, and wrath constitutes the role assigned to the Law by God. Paul does not merely maintain that man transgresses the divine commandment but demonstrates the power of his God concept by understanding the effects of the Law as its God-given purpose (Rom. 3:19–20; 5:20; Gal. 3:19). What comes about through the Law is not a thwarting of its intention but rather a revealing of the purpose for which it exists, since it does exactly what it is sent for, as does every messenger of God. These pronouncements of Paul have nothing in common with denial of or contempt for the Law. The Law rather produces this effect, because it is holy and reveals God's good will. The calamitous nature of sin consists and shows itself in the fact that it makes good the occasion for evil, God's gift the ground of hostility against him, and what is designed to give us life the means of death (Rom. 7:12–13). Thus it is not merely the Jew who is shown how he must conceive of his relationship with God: the demonstration pertains to all. For the nations likewise have that God above them who desires what the Law stipulates. Paul did not speak of a purely Jewish Law; he rather considered the Law to be the power to which all are subject, because it reveals God's will. By speaking to the Jew, the Law instructs man regarding the things constituting righteousness before God. Paul's consciousness of God never permitted limited versions of the divine will and activity. For this reason his discussion of the Law likewise does not center on its national dimension. The Law is given to the Jew because he is man; it judges what is reprehensible in man's desires and actions, and makes known man's responsibilities before God. Because the Greek also does what is rejected by the Law, the Law's verdict regarding the Jewish sinner applies to him as well.

For this reason whoever sinned without the Law is not free from guilt and is not free from judgment but falls in accordance with his sin (Rom. 2:12). The statement that the reckoning of sin depends on the existence of the Law does not mean that the evil will only becomes blameworthy through the commandment of the Law. It is blameworthy in itself and is always and everywhere rejected by God, and this is also explicitly attested by the Law. The Law expresses the will of God that evil must not go unpunished. The fact that the Law judges the Jew's evil and exposes his rebellion against God enhances, of course, his inner misery. But the condition of the Gentile, whose sin increases unrecognized and unhindered, is utterly calamitous. Paul never saw an advantage in lawlessness, in anomie. Help can come to man not through flight from the Law into lawlessness but only through liberation from it by entering into fellowship with the Christ.

Thus the Law also has utmost importance for the pagan, because it separates him from Israel and signifies the barrier between the holy community and the rest of mankind. It makes pagans foreigners, denies them the right of citizenship in the holy community, and thus excludes them from any share in God's gifts. The Pauline pronouncements about the Law are inevitably distorted if we fail to understand the commitment Paul attributed to God in relation to the pre-Christian community. In Paul's view, nothing can separate God from his community; the community has God, and because the Law separates the pagan from it, he needs liberation from the Law in order to gain access to God's grace (Eph. 2:11–12, 14).[23]

A consequence of the theological orientation of Paul's teaching about the Law was that he was not particularly concerned to show analogies in the spiritual thought of pagans to the function of the Law for Israel. The main point remains that the Law's origin from God invests it with absolute authority. At any rate, this conviction finds confirmation in the fact that man's spiritual life is everywhere similar to that of the Jews. All sense the obligatory nature of ethical norms and know that evil is worthy of death, because evil deserves the total rejection that takes away the right to live from the perpetrator of evil (Rom. 1:32; 2:14). Thus everyone is able to understand Jesus' work on the cross. The pagan, too, is aware of the basic premise underlying it, that is, that God's righteousness categorically and irrevocably rejects sin and renders it worthy of death.

### f) The Power of Satan

The misery and danger of evil further consists in the fact that it subjects man to Satan and the spirits serving him (Eph. 2:2; 2 Cor. 4:4). The fact is instructive, however, that Paul did not elaborate on sin's relation to Satan in the didactic portions in Romans, either in his treatment of the pagan's guilt or when discussing the powerlessness of the flesh. By this he proved that he rejected intellectualism in his thought. If he had wanted to reveal sin in its full extent or even had sought to explain its origin, he would also have spoken of transcendent evil and its influence on the sinful condition of mankind. But Paul, in his treatment of sin, desires solely to effect repentance and faith, by which man rejects his evil will and submits to the righteousness of God. Thus Paul's profound apprehension of the condition manifest in his own consciousness does not occasion the exploration of mysteries resulting from the relation of mankind to the supernatural spirit world. Paul described death as a ruler and as the most powerful enemy of Christ (1 Cor. 15:26). But he nowhere pronounced death's

---

23. Whoever declares Judaism to be religiously worthless thinks so very differently than Paul that he will hardly still be able to understand him.

power to be identical with the accuser. He nowhere depicted Jesus' demise as a wrestling with Satan in order to reveal the salvific power of the cross. He related it solely to those powers which are visible to our own eyes, to death, the flesh, and the Law (on Col. 2:15, see p. 309). Paul thought of Satan particularly when evil took place in Christendom. He conceived of him as the adversary of Christ, who seeks to destroy his work (Rom. 16:20; 1 Cor. 5:5; 7:5; 2 Cor. 2:11; 6:15; 11:3, 14; 12:7; Eph. 4:27; 6:11; 1 Thess. 2:18; 1 Tim. 1:20; 3:6–7; 5:15). Thus he did not call attention to the seduction of the first man by Satan when Adam is depicted as the initiator of sin for mankind, but rather when the proud community needs to realize that it stands in danger of falling. That Satan is the god of this world is said not when the pagan needs to realize why he must turn believingly to Christ, but when gnostic arrogance despises the gospel. When forgiveness is to be granted, mention is made of the adversary, who will appeal to God's righteousness in the face of any instance of lovelessness in the community. If his inner life evidences disturbances capable of destroying his faith, he senses in this the hammer blow of an angel sent by Satan, and when obstacle upon obstacle mounts up against his work, he speaks of the invisible enemy.

## 4. The Dispute with the Jew

### a) The Jewish Predicament

When Paul entered the community of Jesus, the controversy between Judaism and Christendom was already well underway. Indeed, his conversion was itself part of this dispute, which he entered at once and which occupied him for the rest of his life. It was Jesus' own work that provided Paul with the seminal idea that guided him in this struggle, an idea Paul preserved faithfully: Jesus' disciple must call Israel to repentance. Criticism is directed not toward the Jew's beliefs; the main target is his conduct, his will. Paul did not make the question, "Judaism" or Christianity?" a question of doctrine. One additional, far more vital matter was determined already by Jesus' own ministry: Paul attributes guilt to the Jews not first of all on account of their rejection of Jesus and their persecution of the church but because of their already culpable Jewish piety. He considers the Jews' rejection of Jesus to be the result of sin committed toward God by the Jew as Jew.

The Jewish predicament, which makes it impossible for him to retain his Judaism and yet base his hope on the Law, arises from the fact that the Jew transgresses the Law, which reveals the Law's condemning power even in the case of the Jew. As at the beginning, when John the Baptist and Jesus brought the message of repentance to the community, Paul does not confront the Jews initially or solely with their religious aberrations; again, it is the second tablet of the Decalogue that is decisive. We do not have a single passage where Paul noted the difference between Jewish and Christian belief with regard to the concept of God or the understanding of God's rule or the conception of the Christ; the decisive fact causing Judaism to collapse is that it cannot keep the Jew from stealing or committing adultery (Rom. 2:21–22). Therefore the judgment pronounced upon all also applies to him. Paul also directs the message of repentance toward the Jewish community as a unity; he does not merely single out individuals in order to call them to repent. We have no passage where the rabbinate is considered particularly guilty or Pharisaism given particular responsibility for Israel's demise; nowhere is a distinction made between Hellenistic and Palestinian Judaism. The community is treated as a coherent entity. As the struggle against Jesus and Paul is not conceived as the deed of individual Jews but as that of the Jews as a whole, so the fact that the Jewish community has in its midst people who do what the Law judges contradicts the community's glory and its claim to righteousness. Paul assumes, of course, that every Jew has such discerning perceptions not merely regarding others but also with respect to himself. Still, for Paul, the validity of the call to repentance is not based on the fact that every Jew proves himself to be a sinner with equal clarity but that evil takes place within Judaism, even though its perpetrator is and remains a Jew, so that evil here unites with the knowledge of God, the possession of the Law, and confidence in God. A piety that does not put to flight the practice of evil deeds stands condemned.

This kind of argument has as its prerequisite Paul's confidence in being able to present Christ as the one who saves from evil. Without this confidence, Paul's argument would collapse. Paul is able to speak to the Jew in such a way solely because he knows himself to be the servant of righteousness, since God's righteousness is revealed in Christ.

Paul does not locate the reason for the Jews' demise in their national organization; he rather saw great value in the particular communion that linked fellow-Jews and always held it in high esteem (Rom. 9:3; 16:7, 11, 21). If Paul's opposition had been directed against Israel's constitution as a nation, this would have meant that he attributed responsibility for the Jew's demise to the Law, which provided the old community with its constitution. But Paul not only refrained from taking issue with all that came to Israel as the word and work of God; he rather venerated it as the glorious proofs of divine grace with most profound gratitude. When he thinks of what God gave to Israel, he finds words of highest adoration (Rom. 9:4–5). Therefore Paul does not make a single statement that denigrates Jewish worship. The verdict that the works of the Law are reprehensible is not Pauline. His statement that man is not justified by works of the Law must not be twisted to mean that works of the Law are sinful.[24] This statement would amount to antinomianism, while Paul always considers the Law as God's Law and therefore describes it as the authority that decides man's destiny and determines God's attitude toward him. For this reason Paul never disputed that the Jew was pious or zealous for God, and he described his own career in Pharisaism not as his sin but as conduct appropriate for his pre-Christian life. He spoke of his former service to God in the lofty consciousness which the Pharisee acquired by his resolute obedience toward the divine commandment (Rom. 9:31; 10:2; Gal. 2:15; 1:14; Phil. 3:5–6). What he had at that time

---

24. In Rom. 3:20; Gal. 2:16; 3:10; Rom. 9:32, it is not the "works of the Law" that are rejected as sin; the Jew's guilt rather consists in his effort to make his doing of works required by the Law into his righteousness.

was authentic Judaism, resolute and joyful service of God. This, however, was true of Jewish piety only when compared with the rest of mankind. If the Jew is placed, not beside other people, but before the Law and thus before God, it becomes evident that his service does not procure him justification. It is of no avail to him, because he incurs death through his transgression of the Law.

Paul substantiates this principle by pronouncing the Jew's hope that he might be able to atone for his sin by works done in obedience to the Law and in fulfillment of the divine will futile. He saw in this a contradiction against the Law and thus against God (Gal. 3:10, 12; Rom 2:1–11; 10:5). Because the Law rejects evil absolutely, man can never derive an excuse for his evil from what he does in fulfillment of the Law. He cannot cover his guilt by obeying the Law in other matters, as if he thereby could acquire the right to sin without being punished or procure a means of making his own evil palatable for God. If the Law is valid, it is valid in its entirety. If it is used to establish the Jew's righteousness where he obeys it, it establishes his guilt with equal certainty where he breaks it (Rom. 3:19). The rabbinate's theory according to which evil action can be compensated for by good action and God eventually calculates which side outweighs the other, Paul rejected, because it simultaneously invokes the Law as God's holy will when the work of the Law is supposed to count as righteousness, while devaluing it as peripheral when its transgression of the Law must not prevent justification. Paul refutes this theory by detecting in it a perverse will seeking to justify evil (Rom. 3:7). The Law here serves the purpose of facilitating sin, because what man has done in obedience to the Law is supposed to be sufficient to cover his sin. Through this rationale Paul placed his argument against Judaism on the basis of the absolute validity of ethical norms.

Whoever seeks to cover sin by his pious acts uses good works to glorify himself (Rom 2:17–20; 3:27; Eph. 2:9). Thus the Jew's piety turns into an inflated self-esteem which leads to mercilessness toward others. Himself he pardons; others he condemns (Rom. 2:1). In order to be able to praise himself he intellectualizes piety. He studies, preaches, and judges; this is his religion (Rom. 2:21). Therefore he places his confidence in what he is according to the flesh. The external characteristics of piety replace the internal service of God (Rom. 2:28–29; Phil. 3:3). Now his concept of God inevitably turns dark, since he now hopes in God's partiality rather than his justice. At the same time that he calls on God as the judge and thus as the one who brings about righteousness, he demands of him injustice and denies the thesis that there is no partiality with God. God is supposed to overlook evil in his favorites and assign merit to their works (Rom. 2:3, 11). The aim of divine goodness, that is, that it seeks to separate man from evil, remains unapprehended; the Jew hardens himself against it (Rom. 2:4). His internal opposition to God is revealed by the fact that he does not want to place his trust in God (Rom. 9:32; 10:3, 12–21). This is brought to light by his rejection of Jesus. But Paul derives the Jew's inability to faith (which is demonstrated by his rejection of Jesus' proclamation) from that kind of religious attitude which he already possesses as a Jew: that he injects into his worship a selfish will that fights for man's right against God instead of longing for the revelation of God's righteousness. As his selfish will induces him to break the love commandment of the Law and to do injustice to his neighbor, it also seduces him into glorifying himself on account of his piety and into attempting to subject God to himself. Thus God's promise is of no value to him. He views the Law as if a condition were attached to God's testament, and he considers himself to be a child of God merely by virtue of being a child of Abraham (Gal. 3:15; 4:21–28; Rom. 9:6–13). His strong confidence in God thus becomes arrogance. He demands miracles from God and refuses to believe in him apart from them (1 Cor. 1:22). Because he removes ethical norms from God's relationship with him, he refuses to permit God his work as Judge. And because God's judgment is executed upon him nonetheless, revealing also upon him that God's wrath falls on every act of ungodliness and unrighteousness, he murmurs against God (Rom. 3:5–8; 9:14–23). Paul concluded that the Jew must first learn the rudiments of true piety from Jesus: both obedience to God, which commits itself into his care without reservations, and confidence in God, which rests on his promise with certainty.

Paul's confrontation of Judaism with ethical norms is the reason why we do not have a single statement by him on the value of the Old Testament priesthood, sacrifice, or altar. This issue is not resolved by the fact that worship in the Diaspora had little share in the Temple, because Paul looked at Judaism as a whole, according to the commandments it was given by the Law. His view on the institutions by which the Law offered the community forgiveness of sins can be seen from his interpretation of Genesis 15:6 and Psalm 32:1, as well as from his verdict regarding circumcision, which he calls the seal that attests to the righteousness of faith (Rom. 4:1–18, 11; Gal. 3:6–9). He did not consider the Old Testament sacrifice and sacrament to be a work of man but the manifestation of divine grace. This portion of the Law does not produce *man's* righteousness; it rather proclaims *God's* righteousness. Whoever approaches the altar according to the Law does not obtain merit and does not appeal to his own work but seeks God's mercy. But Paul considers decisive in the Jew's turning away from the Law to the Christ, not the question of how much of the divine gift he already possesses, but how he acts in relation to God's good will. He therefore seeks to ensure that the Jew applies clear and undistorted ethical standards to himself. For the aim Paul seeks to attain through his dispute with Judaism is the establishment of repentance which removes evil, and of faith which sees in the Christ the God who gives.

The connection between the pronouncements with which Paul conducted his confrontation with the Jews and Jesus' message of repentance is obvious. Paul adopts Jesus' practice of moving the conflict away from the realm of religious theory, so that the Jew is rendered culpable not by what he thinks and teaches but by what he does. Like Jesus, Paul sees in the separation of doctrine from practice the pervasive corrupting cause of Jewish piety. Original with Jesus is, further, the universal formulation of the call to repentance which is directed toward the entirety of Jewry including its righteous ones, as well as the absolute conception of the ethical norm that categorically rejects all evil. Just as Jesus did not grant that the avoidance of the reprehensible deed excused the reprehensible will, Paul does not allow that the works of the Law cover transgressions of it.

Again like Jesus, Paul considers Israel's piety sin, because that piety is the source of its own pride. Both Jesus and Paul call the Jews unbelieving despite their proud confidence in God, confidence shattered by Jesus and Paul precisely because it is really arrogance. Paul also preserved Jesus' message in the fact that his dispute with the Jews did not weaken his love for Judaism but rather made it complete. Only now Paul has love for his people which is prepared for any sacrifice and even culminates in the wish to surrender, if that were possible, his own share in the Christ for Israel (Rom. 9:1–3). He does not retain his love for the Jew *although* he shattered the hollow pride of the synagogue in uncompromising commitment to the truth—his love and his message of repentance rather constitute for him an inseparable unity. Because his love belongs to Israel, he issues his call to repentance to it in the clearest form possible, and because he cannot spare it the call to repentance, he bears within himself ever-present suffering. For Paul's call to repentance has the form given to it by Jesus: it bears in itself the offer of forgiveness and calls to reconciliation with God.

The great commonality between Jesus' message of repentance and Pharisaic aims enabled Paul to retain a large part of his previous convictions in his dispute with the Jews. His message of repentance to the Jew is founded on the sanctity of the Law which must not be broken and which separates the one who breaks it from God. Paul attributes this power to the Law not because it contains doctrine but because it tells man what to do. This is the way the Pharisee thought of it, and Paul does not waver in affirming this conviction. Both the Pharisee and Paul also find doctrine in the Law, because it does not merely regulate man's work but also reveals how God acts. And Paul considers the Law's teachings to be inexhaustibly rich, so that he seeks its guidance in everything of concern to him. In the patriarchal narratives and the accounts of Israel in the wilderness, or in the Law's commandments regarding oxen, Paul gains direct and clear insight into the things that are his own and Christendom's duty (Rom. 9:6–13; Gal. 4:21–31; 1 Cor. 10:1–11; 9:9). In like manner, the Pharisee continually looked from present events to the Law and obtained from the Law an understanding of what must happen now. But both Paul and Pharisee concur that the healing power of the Law was not merely based on its teaching, as if it had been given exclusively for the purpose of instruction; this purpose is rather subordinate to the commandment, because the significance of the Law consists in the fact that it states God's claim on man's conduct. The point is not merely to learn it but to do it. The firm connection between the terms "Law" and "works" in Paul directly builds on Pharisaic thought, and he retains important parts of Pharisaic tradition through the phrases "good works" and "transgression" (which designates the worst, most reprehensible level of evil). Therefore the Law procures man's salvation only when it is done; only the doer of the Law is justified (Rom. 2:13). Therefore "Law" and "guilt" are corresponding terms for both Pharisee and Paul. The Law imposes judgment on every evil work. The pronouncement that everyone who does not keep the entire Law is cursed was the foundation of Pharisaic piety and at the same time Paul's weapon in overcoming it. For Paul applied this pronouncement in all its aspects to faith in Christ, as no Pharisee before him had done (Gal. 3:10).

Paul's refusal to make the sacraments of the Law the crucial issue likewise corresponds to Pharisaic thought. For while the Pharisee derives great confidence from these, he maintains that they do not replace the commandment directed toward man or rob it of its absolute validity. The healing power of the means of grace instituted by the Law depends on man's right conduct (Rom. 2:25–27). Even here, in the weight Paul places on the written form of the Law, he stays close to Pharisaic thought. As the Pharisee refers man regarding the question of what is good to the Holy Book, the terms "Law" and "what is written" are related with Paul. This, however, did not cause his teaching on the Law to approximate a superstitious veneration of the Book (Rom. 2:27; 7:6; 2 Cor. 3:6). Paul did not project the Law's omnipotence from God into the letters that testify to the divine will. Rather, he attributes to the Pentateuch power over man because it is there that people learn what God desires and there that God commits himself in his entire activity to his expressed will. The question of how the content of the Law was transferred from the Book into man's consciousness and how it there manifested its compelling power was not addressed by Paul. He rests content with the fact that God subjected his community to the Holy Book which rules it with divine authority. When he subsumes all the Old Testament writings, including the Prophets and the Psalms, under the term "Law" and quotes them as Law, Paul again does not depart from Pharisaic usage (Rom. 3:19; 1 Cor. 14:21).

The consciousness that he used in his dispute with the Jew not foreign standards, but without dilution or contradiction solely the convictions that were holy for the Jew himself, lent Paul assurance in his struggle. Everything the Jew champions as his own conviction remains upheld; for Paul's reproach takes the shape of a charge that the Jew denied his own assurance. In bringing the Jew to the Christ, Paul does not therefore tear the Jew away from Judaism; he rather makes him now truly a Jew, so that he is one not merely in appearance but in reality. This conviction was indispensable for Paul if he were to recognize in Jesus the Christ and to present him to Israel; for the Christ is the one who brings Israel to its consummation.

### b) The Weakness of the Law

Equally important for the acknowledgment of Jesus as the Christ was the recognition that Christ's gift reveals the Law's incompleteness. Paul demonstrated to the Jews, with the same fearlessness with which he taught the sanctity of the Law, what it is that renders the Law weak and ephemeral. This reveals his profound gratitude for Christ's gift. Because the Law brings about man's rebellion against the commandment, it makes him a mere slave subjected to God out of compulsion and fear even when he serves the Law zealously and piously (Gal. 4:1–3, 7, 25–26; 5:1; Rom. 8:15; 2 Cor. 3:16–17). The community produced by the Law is thus still denied God's heavenly and eternal gifts. Its mother is merely the earthly, not yet the heavenly, Jerusalem. It received through the Law merely elements destined for the world, not the fulfillment of divine revelation. That fulfillment is given, not to the world, but to those who are transferred out of mankind into God's community by God's love (Gal. 4:3,

9; Col. 2:8, 20).[25] Therefore Paul speaks of the symbolism inherent in Old Testament institutions: that circumcision occurred only in the flesh, not in the heart through the Spirit; that Israel's worship was a shadow prefiguring the later gift in Christ; that animal sacrifices were not the reasonable worship; and that tying formal corporate worship to certain days pointed to its preliminary nature (Rom. 2:28–29; Phil. 3:3; Eph. 2:11; Col. 2:11, 17; Rom. 12:1; Gal. 4:10; Col. 2:16). This incompleteness is evident also in the origin and form of the Law, because it was revealed as Scripture by angels (Gal. 3:19; 2 Cor. 3:3, 6; Rom. 7:6; 2:27; cf. 2:15). Regarding the angels who bring the Law one should not think of powers other than the ones who acted in God's service and by God's commission. But Paul also saw in the fact that the giving of the Law occurred through mediating powers a sign that the Law was not the final and sole word of God. For the perfect revelation takes place, not through angels, but through the Son. Likewise, the form of the Law indicates its limited validity. While Jesus gives the Spirit and indwells us through him, God at the giving of the Law inscribed his will in stone and onto a book. Thus he remains external to man, while the Law is man's personal possession and help only when it is written on his heart. God's legislative act does not yet achieve this; for it only provided Israel with a holy book. Akin to this is the emphasis on the imperative substructure of the Law, which exists in the form of commandments (Eph. 2:15; Col. 2:14). This reveals that God holds back in his giving, calls man to move forward with his own ability, and limits man to himself. The divine word brought by Christ is of a different nature. It is not merely a collection of commandments but the good news by which God's gift is proclaimed and granted.

Therefore the Law is also not the first word of God. Rather, it follows the promise only at considerable distance, because it has Christ as its fulfillment. The appointment of a pedagogue to rule the son does not put the tutor in place of the father forever. It was meant from the very beginning to last only for a certain period of time. The one who towers over it, that is, the Christ, was part of God's vision and counsel from the start. The Law was interposed. For the Jew who does not perceive this, the Law is veiled (Gal. 3:17; Rom. 10:4; Gal. 3:23–24; 4:1–2; Rom. 5:20; 2 Cor. 3:14–16).

However, all these verdicts directed against the content and form of the Law did not move Paul to divert the Jew from the Law or to exempt him from it. The Law may be poor and weak; yet as God's commandment, it possesses indestructible ruling power over man. Even the pedagogue has been appointed by the father, and the father's authority is transferred to him. When the son subjected to the tutor objects that the tutor's authority separates him from the father, this does not yet liberate the son from the tutor. Content criticism of the Law does not procure help for the one who is subjected to it.

---

25. The common interpretation of "the elements of the world" as a designation for (evil) spirits seems improbable to me. The moon's significance for the festive calendar led no Jew to call Jewish ritual "star worship," with "world" understood in terms of heavenly realms. If "world" is seen to denote mankind and "elements" invisible world rulers, another improbable notion results, because Paul considers paganism to indulge in spirit worship but not Judaism. That for Paul God is the one who speaks in Scripture is not to be doubted.

If Paul had derived the impossibility to adhere to the Law merely or primarily from the limited nature of its content, he would have transferred Jewish guilt to God and produced complaint rather than repentance, accusations against the divine way of working things. This Paul did not permit, because man does not merely rebel against the "limited" commandments of the Law but opposes what all recognize as holy and good. The Law becomes a heavy burden for man not because he stands above it and must stoop from his lofty spiritual position to the limited commandment: however limited the Law may be, the Jew is unable to keep it, and his opposition is directed toward the holy aspects of the Law. Thus Paul, when giving his final answer to the question of the Law, did not address ritual issues such as the value of the Sabbath or washings. Rather, he dealt with the commandment proscribing covetousness (Rom. 7:7). At this point, where the Law's sanctity is safeguarded against any objection, man's relationship with the Law is determined, because here it becomes evident that the Law does not exterminate sin in us but rather awakens it, so that we need to be set free from it. The desire for liberation arising at this juncture is pure and in keeping with God's will. It is fulfilled in Christ in such a way that we are not merely elevated above individual aspects of the Law but above the Law in its entirety. Rationalism thought that Paul sought to achieve by way of a complicated system what he could have won much more easily and surely through rational and historical deliberations: whoever reached the kind of inner liberty that is able to acknowledge the limitations of Mosaic ritual has all he needs to be free from the Law. But rational criticism of the Torah and its ritual, which was prevalent in the Greek world, did not produce liberation from the Law but merely lack of piety. This is illustrated not merely by the lax, semi-pagan forms of Hellenistic Judaism but also by Pharisaism, which was not closed to critical considerations regarding the value of legal institutions and which assigned merely symbolic value to the bath of purification, sacrificial statutes, and the localization of God in the Temple. But because Pharisaism's vigorous concept of God established the obligation to obedience, it always returns to the notion that God has commanded to do a certain thing, and this notion sufficed not merely to establish the abiding validity of the commandment but to evoke the movement toward increasing preoccupation with the minutiae of the Law which was never satisfied merely with the keeping of these commandments. True liberation from the Law could be attained without religious rupture or a profaning of the community not by obfuscation of the divine nature of the Law but only by the grounding of freedom from the Law in its divine purpose. It is not the phrase "elements of the world" that expresses the new element not already possessed by Paul during his time as a Pharisee; what was new was that he pleaded guilty to violating the commandment "Thou shalt not covet," while still knowing himself to be free from it rather than being condemned by the Law.

Moreover, the low esteem accorded to the Law by Hellenistic and rationalistic thought merely strove for the simplification and transformation of ritual while retaining casuistry for ethics and the concept of merit for religion. In contrast to this, Paul did not seek to liberate the Jew from ritual but from his religious misconceptions. The rational critics of the Law no longer had the ancient ritual, but they still had the old guilt, the old insecure conscience in relation to the ethical norms of the Law which turned out to be indispensable, the old uncertainty pertaining to their relationship with God which resulted from the elevation of human conduct above the divine activity. Even Paul's "enlightened" contemporaries, including a liberal Pharisee such as Josephus or a mystic striving for inner perfection like Philo, remained nomists, not in their treatment of the Sabbath or of purity, but in their ethics. In Paul's view, however, the Jew, particularly owing to his ethical condition, required liberation from the Law, because he needed liberation from guilt and humbling before the God who graciously gave. The elements of the service of the Law resisting faith in Christ were not removed in those elegant forms of nomism; to the contrary, they were intensified. They, too, forsook clear, upright opposition to sin, dressed up their evil, admired themselves for their religious greatness, and made God contingent on their own will. Therefore Jews who adhered to Greek rationalism were just as far away from faith in the Christ as a disciple of Gamaliel. In Paul's view, both were helped only by acknowledging without making excuses that their will was judged by the divine Law.

### c) The Promise of Scripture

Through his proclamation of Jesus as the Christ, through whom God grants his grace to the Jew, Paul derived the obligation to show the Jew that the promise of Scripture is fulfilled in the community of Jesus. Because he recognizes already regarding the commandment of the Law that he must not convert the Jew in such a way that he makes him an opponent of the Law, rather providing him access to Jesus by showing him that he now, as a Christian, for the first time understands and uses the Law according to its true meaning and purpose, he must prove with regard to the promise of Scripture that the Christian community corresponds to the future work of God described by the promise. It is instructive that not a single pronouncement of Paul is devoted to justifying his calling of the nations (Rom. 15:8–12 is hardly occasioned by an objection). This did not allow the Jew to raise objections against Paul, because all read in Scripture that God's purpose pertained to all of mankind and that the Christ will reign above all. The Jew did, however, take offense at the manner in which Paul gathered the universal church, that it came into being through faith. But Paul was entirely convinced that he acted thus according to the promise of Scripture and served its fulfillment through his work. He considered Abraham's call to be the decisive event in this regard, in which he perceived the same divine will that now provided the substance of the Christian message. What God gave to Abraham was the free promise of divine goodness, not a Law, also not a conditional promise that made God's gift contingent on Abraham's work and merit, but the assurance of complete grace by which God chooses his own. Therefore Abraham's task was to believe God, and this, as Scripture says expressly, was his righteousness before God. Circumcision was added to faith only later as a confirming sign. This is why all believers are sons of Abraham, and even among the Jews only believers are sons of Abraham. Thus for Paul the term "sons of Abraham" remained the suitable designation of the community chosen by God. The way in which Paul's thought differed from Pharisaic belief was merely his teaching on what constitutes Abrahamic sonship. For Paul, it is not based on ethnic origin. Rather, it arises as Abraham's faith also characterizes later believers, because God acts toward them according to the same grace by which he called Abraham. Therefore it is especially the Gentile church—which is based solely on faith—that is the fulfillment of the promise given to Israel through Abraham. All the particular Jewish institutions were thus given only subsequent to the promise and according to the Law of faith. They do not aid in the promise's fulfillment. They also do not provide an obstacle for it, as long as they are not used contrary to its true meaning and purpose but as seal of the righteousness of faith and thus of the true Abrahamic sonship, which is why they were given to Israel in the first place.

## 5. The Dispute with the Gentile

Paul was led to the Greeks not by a preference for the Greek way of life but in view of their guilt and need, for which Christ has the remedy. Paul's conversion did not diminish but rather exacerbated the contrast between his will and that of the Greeks in comparison with his time as a Pharisee. The relationship between the Pharisaic notion of merit and the Greek concept of virtue, and between Pharisaic theology and Greek wisdom, was indeed characterized by differences, but it had at the same time close commonalities. Just as the Pharisaism in him had died, Hellenism was also a thing of the past for him, and he stood, as a Christian and Jesus' messenger, at a vast distance indeed from the Greek way of life.

His conversion prepared him for his preaching to the Gentiles, because it completely shattered his Jewish piety, so that he no longer possessed anything other than his confidence based on Christ. This confidence, however, he possessed with such certitude that it guaranteed for him the boon of eternal life. He incorporated into his work among the Greeks nothing of Jewish pride or Jewish overscrupulousness. If the Greek had nothing Paul could consider righteous, he himself was in the same position. What he possessed—knowledge of the Christ and faith in him—the Greek could receive as well, and Christ's grace calling the Gentile was not greater than the one he himself had received. In such a way he stepped among the Greek as having become their equal, because he stood in the same guilt and grace as they.

### a) The Verdict against Gentile Religion

The Gentile's need arises initially from his religion whose reprehensible nature cannot be denied. Like all Jews, Paul called attention to the idolatrous image as that which refutes pagan worship, and along with it the Gentiles' worship of demons (Rom. 1:21–23; 1 Cor. 10:20–21; Gal. 4:8). When exhorting the Corinthians not to participate in Gentile ritual, he quoted the passage of Scripture that speaks of sacrifices for the spirits. As far as we know, he did not develop a theory from this passage, because he bases his judgment also regarding this issue not on what remains mysterious but on what is revealed. Paul considered it self-evident that God's glory is misunderstood and compromised when man offers his adoration to a human or animal figure. In the ethical realm he also stresses, in keeping with the general Jewish verdict against unrestrained expressions of sexual passion, the manifold evils perverting human intercourse with others (Rom. 1:24–32; 1 Cor. 6:9–11). The denunciation of wealth, on the other hand, retreats into the background in Paul's dealings with the Gentiles. What takes center stage is that among them one man destroys and shames the other. Paul does not excuse the Gentile's indulgence of his love of material things. But he regards it as a lesser evil beside the great guilt that is incurred continually in man's conduct toward others.

Because in his dealings with the Gentiles Paul fought also solely for the validity of ethical norms, everything pertaining to the normal conduct of life remains entirely untouched by the word of repentance. Paul himself evidences a strong Hellenistic dimension in his way of thinking. It is not a coincidence that we do not possess any sayings of Paul directed against the Greek's jurisprudence, the arts, crafts, or trade; this never presented a conflict for him. As little as he reproached the Jew for his national custom did he reproach Gentiles for theirs. Even in the ethical sphere, he shows equal esteem for the good done by the Gentile as for the things done by the Jew. He does not assign God's wrath to the Gentile and God's praise and peace to the Jew or Christian. After all, this is precisely what he considers to be the Jewish sin: presuming upon favoritism with God. God's rule stands above all in complete justice, and his praise extends to everyone who does what is good. Even the Gentile can do the words of the Law, because he can be his own Law and figure out for himself what is good or evil before God, so that he wants the good and rejects the evil. Therefore it is possible that a Gentile has a higher standing before God than a Jew: if the work of the Law is written into his heart, while, for the Jew, it remains written only in his Book (Rom. 2:6–11, 14–16, 26–27).

Much sophistry has been applied to these pronouncements. It is contended that Paul speaks of the Gentiles' good works only as an impossibility or that he thinks of Christians. This objection is substantiated by the thesis that thus the necessity of active repentance would be removed. But this argument departs from Paul by concealing the pure resoluteness of his ethical judgment and renews Pharisaic theory, according to which one can outweigh evil through good. For Paul, sin, where it is found, effects man's helplessness, because it subjects him to God's condemnation. He did not think that need only ensued when man finds in himself nothing but pure evil. In this case, the guilty person would once again venture to excuse himself, because he still has good apart from his sin. Paul did not excuse any sin, least of which by claiming that there is still good in man. For Paul, every sin, not only a descent of one's entire life into pure evil, renders its perpetrator to be in need of grace, and faith in Christ alone becomes his righteousness.

The Gentile's capacity to perform work that is good before God is rooted in the fact that God's rule reveals not merely his wrath but also his kindness upon man. In his being handed over to a dark religion and wild, destructive passions he experiences God's opposition to his evil will. But he is surrounded by divine works, too, which continually demonstrate God's greatness and goodness toward man and render truth indestructible. From it issues the possibility of ethically correct action, because man can allow truth to reign over him. The Gentile too has reason and a conscience, and his mind concurs with the divine Law. This train of thought, however, does not cause Paul to begin his dealings with the Gentiles with a "doctrine of conscience."[26] Just as the Jew could not be helped by becoming a rabbi and by studying the Law, the Gentile could not be helped by being given an explanation of the inner workings of the conscience. The factuality of his responsibility and guilt resulted from it and was met by Paul with the proclamation of the Christ.

Paul did not put together conglomerates of Jesus' word and Gentile efforts at piety. Because he based his work on the absolute validity of ethical norms, he did not acknowledge longing for happiness as a religious motivation. He does not want to satisfy man's selfish will but to turn him away from himself to God. Thus the question that occupied him regarding his trip to Rome was not that of happiness versus misery, or what was the highest good or the path to blessedness. Rather, he was concerned with righteousness versus unrighteousness, and in particular God's righteousness in contrast to unrighteousness and to the righteousness of man. Together with the eudaemonistic ethic, the conceptualities related to the Greek concept of virtue were completely eliminated by Paul, although he was confronted with them every time he encountered Greeks. Indeed, these ideas served only to promote the aggrandizement of their perceived autonomous power. Because Paul naturally considered any outworking of human industry as proper and valuable, the refutation of the doctrine of virtue became necessary only when virtue was transmogrified into glory. Paul adhered also in Gentile territories to Jesus' teaching that rejects craving for greatness (Phil. 4:8; 1 Cor. 1:29; 4:7; 8:1; 2 Cor. 11:1, 16–18, 21, 23).

### b) The Verdict against Greek Wisdom

The contrast between Paul's aim and the rationalistic leanings of the Greeks was most readily apparent, because these encountered him continually in the form of his listeners' claims and their responses to his message. In Paul's view, whoever wants him to be a preacher of wisdom expects him to deny his calling and remove Jesus' cross. His refusal to accede to the craving for wisdom is thus not solely rooted in his particular circumstances but arises from God's work. The proclamation with which he is charged heralds the fact that God has sent the Christ and given him over to the cross. The gift thus conferred on mankind by God consists therefore not in ideas revealing to it the divine wisdom. Rather, measured by the thoughts of men, the cross of Christ turns out to be foolish-

---

26. It can, of course, not be denied that Paul's statement in Rom. 2:14 is undergirded by a richly developed sequence of thoughts, similar to the way that the mental process preserved for us in Rom. 7:7ff. constitutes the background for 1 Cor. 15:56. Conceiving of Paul's "missionary preaching" as differing according to his audience, and as substituting in the case of the Greeks teaching on the conscience for teaching about the Law, distorts history by anachronistically injecting an intellectualism that only later came to prevail in the church. Paul's proclamation of God's message did not consist in religion lessons.

ness, because people are controlled by the selfish will which seeks to raise man to greatness and glory, and by which he also demands from God the proof of his greatness in terms of lofty intellectual concepts and striking acts. All this is contradicted by the cross of Christ. God here does not reveal to man the greatness of his own thinking but treats him as the guilty one who needs salvation and who receives it by being given justification. In its juridical aspect, God's revelation denies the achievements of human thought no less than those of human will. It utterly destroys all theories of man and shows him that he cannot unite himself with God by his own ideas. The corollary of this act of God in terms of its desired effect in man is not understanding appropriating divine thoughts but faith that relies on God's grace (1 Cor. 1:17–31). Faith, however, was rendered impossible for the Greeks by their rationalism, because they suspended agreement with his word until their thinking reached what they considered satisfactory results.

At the same time, Paul told knowledge-seeking Greeks that the divine grace which now turns to man in its completeness provided the loftiest content even for their cognition precisely because it is directed to man in sincerity and turns his will and thus also his thinking toward God. But only when the rejection of wisdom is fully realized, and Christ is recognized as the redeemer from evil so that faith in him is established, does knowledge has a place in our dealings with God. Paul therefore demonstrated also in the manner in which he carried out his teaching continually that man's relationship with God is engendered not through divine teaching and human comprehension but through divine love and human faith.

This led to the initially remarkable fact that he only rarely resorted to Greek forms of thought, despite the liberty with which he appropriated all kinds of means for his work.[27] Paul expected no help from such concepts in light of the contrast between the foundational concepts of his message and Greek thought. "Reason" and "conscience" are terms originating from Greek intellectual effort. Moreover, he made ample use of the idea of an athletic contest with the related images of "race," "prize," "crown," or "judge," because he needed terms that described the necessity and industry of Christian striving. In all Christian functions, be it faith, prayer, service, or suffering, Paul exhorts the community through images related to the athletic contest: it must exercise and reveal the power given to it and must devote itself to that task with a resolute will, in full sincerity that this is the condition of its salvation.[28] This series of images was valuable for Paul also because he thus could call believers to

27. Paul's worldview likewise does not reveal Greek influence. The only thing that may be noted in this regard is that he locates the spirits in the air (Eph. 3:2), which evidences an approach that distributes the different realms of the world to different kinds of beings. But even this saying does not go beyond concepts present in the synagogue. Regarding the contrast between flesh and Spirit, see p. 209.

28. The contest consists in the demonstration of faith (1 Tim. 6:12; 2 Tim. 4:7), prayer (Col. 2:1; 4:12; Rom. 15:30), the fulfillment of one's calling (1 Cor. 9:24–25), Christian conduct (Phil. 3:14; Gal. 5:7), the apostolic work (Gal. 2:2; Phil. 2:16; Col. 1:29; 1 Tim. 4:10), and suffering (Phil. 1:30). The preparation for application of this image was provided by the Greek synagogue.

exert all their energies without obscuring the rule of love. Rather, all of Christian activity was thereby related to the Lord's will. For in case of the athletic contest it was not the competitor who evaluated his own performance but the judge. Related to this "contest" motif is the use of the "honor" motif for the strengthening of the work. It sounds Greek when Paul calls it his ambition to make Jesus' name known where he was not yet proclaimed (2 Cor. 10:13–16; Rom. 15:20; 2 Cor. 5:9; 1 Thess. 4:11). When Paul's thought takes up the world's opposition toward the Christian, serving Jesus becomes military service and the community the army recruited by him (2 Cor. 10:3–6; Phil. 2:25; Phlm. 2; 1 Tim. 1:18; 2 Tim. 2:3–4; cf. ἀτακτεῖν, 1 Thess. 5:14; 2 Thess. 3:6–7, 11). The call for a sound mind and dignity also has a Greek ring to it (soundness of mind: Rom. 12:3; 2 Tim. 1:7; Titus 2:12; 1 Tim. 2:9, 15; 3:2; Titus 1:8; 2:2–6; dignity: Phil. 4:8; 1 Tim. 2:2; 3:4, 8, 11; Titus 2:2, 7). The former illumines the connection between right thinking and prudent action; the latter is sensitive to the difficulties in the church's interpersonal dealings and fellowship stemming from a violation of others' aesthetic sensibilities. Because the Greek was very sophisticated in this regard, it immediately became an important task for Christendom to avoid in its conduct whatever gave the impression of being ludicrous or crude.

## B. Christ's Gift

### 1. Justification

If Paul had merely been the critic of Jews and Gentiles, he would neither have been the proclaimer of Christ nor himself a Christian. The depiction of human sinfulness was not the purpose of Jesus' proclamation; it serves grace and takes place in order to help man. This also is the principle that fully controls Paul. His verdict regarding man has only a preparatory significance for him. Through it he leads man's perception and desire to the gift of Christ. For the one who concurred with Paul's verdict regarding man, however, the question of what Paul had to offer took on profound solemnity. Could he really elevate man above what he described as his misery? Paul replies: through his ministry God granted man justification (2 Cor. 3:9; Rom. 1:15–17).

#### a) The Meaning of the Term "Justification"

By the term "justification" Paul describes God as the one who exercises his juridical office in favor of man. This office Paul depicts as an essential part of the divine work. The principle established by Jesus, which had currency in the entire apostolic circle, that is, that the provision of salvation is one with the procurement of righteousness, thus remains fully valid also in Paul's thought. The concept with which "justification" is contrasted is "condemnation": these are the two corresponding acts of divine judgment (Rom. 5:16, 18; 8:1–4, 33–34; 2 Cor. 3:9).[29] Likewise, being given over to sin and justification are contrasted,

---

29. Thereby Paul departed sharply from Greek thought, which linked justification, in contrast to Paul, to punishment.

because being handed over to be punished is the act of the condemning judge (Rom. 4:25; 1:24, 26, 28). The strength by which the thought of the divine judgment moves one's consciousness corresponds to the power with which mindfulness of the Law determines one's consciousness of God. Both convictions express the inviolability of the norm that separates good from evil and makes solely what is good the object of the divine will. Because God wills that which is good, he is the Lawgiver, and he is therefore also the Judge, because his giving of the Law comes to fulfillment in his juridical work. After man is called to service through God's commandment and his relationship with God has imposed on him an obligation that must not be broken, a new divine act is thus generated that examines, evaluates, and commends or rejects human conduct. Behavior in accordance with the divine will results in man's justification, by which he possesses God's good pleasure.

Since justification makes ethical norms an essential part of the concept of God, the expectation of an arbitrary verdict, which would reveal only God's power, and the hope of a grace that would do away with ethical norms, are excluded. The judge's act is grounded in justice, and when God judges, no doubt remains whether his verdict is based on righteousness or not. Paul was completely certain that through justification the righteousness of God would be revealed (Rom. 1:17; 3:21, 25–26; 10:3; 2 Cor. 5:21). When he spoke of righteousness, he thought of that kind of conduct, in the case of God as well as man, that acts according to norms rooted in truth and required by goodness.[30] "Just" is that verdict by which God proves his total opposition toward lies and evil. But Paul does not stop there, because a merely defensive, merely negative will is inconceivable, especially with God. God proves to be the one who removes evil by bringing about what is good and by conforming man to his good pleasure. The negative will, the displeasure directed toward evil, Paul calls "wrath." He distinguishes wrath from righteousness, because wrath destroys what is untrue and worthy of rejection, while righteousness works what is good and true and thus well-pleasing to God. But Paul considered any conflict or dualism between these two elements an impossibility. Rather, both working harmoniously together— the revelation of the divine wrath and the divine righteousness—make up God's work in the world (Rom. 1:17–18; note the substantiation of 1:17 by 1:18).

Because God unites himself completely with the one he declares to be righteous, man receives, together with the justification awarded him by God's commendation of his conduct, complete fellowship with God, his entire love and gift (Rom. 1:17; 4:13, 16; 5:9, 18; 8:1–4, 31–34; Gal. 3:8–9, 24–26; 2 Cor. 3:7–9). Likewise, the one who stands guilty before God and is judged by him to be unrighteous is cut off from his grace and is dead (Rom. 2:12; 5:17; 2 Cor. 3:7–9). The proclamation of justification is therefore at the same time the proclamation of life and of God's love, and this in such a way that the one who knows himself to be guilty needs it. Through justification the question of guilt

---

30. Because Paul unites justice with truth and goodness, justice is for him not merely a formal category that merely determines the correctness of the will while leaving the thing that is desired out of consideration. This distinguished him again from the Greeks, who describe as just the establishment of equality. The hankering for equality is incompatible with both truth and goodness.

is expressly stated and denied. Paul tells the person who is condemned by the Law, and who finds in himself reprehensible passions through his fleshly nature, that the divine judgment by which God reveals his justice and works righteousness has turned out in his favor, so that he is granted the very highest prize: relationship with God.

### b) Christ's Procurement of Justification

Every doctrine of justification must indicate which kind of human conduct meets with God's favor to the extent that God becomes man's advocate. Without such clarification, the teaching of justification would merely pose a problem that would puzzle man or at most would express a hope that would also retain the uncertainty of mere hope. As hope, Paul possessed the concept of justification already as a Pharisee. But now he describes it in terms of what God did for mankind. These statements that describe the divine activity by which God justifies us, and which determine the human conduct that is awarded justification, constitute the new element in the Pauline doctrine of justification. The question of how man is justified Paul answers thus: God, in Christ, has justified those who believe in him.

Paul would never have spoken of past justification if he had merely thought of divine ideas. It is already true of human, and thus even more of divine, judgment that the judge does not merely think but also acts, because he determines, by his verdict, the destiny of both the justified and the convicted, rendering judgment according to their conduct. Without revelation of God, which makes him as the one who is active on behalf of mankind palpably visible, there is no justification. On this basis of justification, Paul discerned that it came about through the sending of the Christ, because God acts through him before the eyes of mankind, revealing to it his attitude toward it (Rom. 3:24; 5:9; 8:33–34; Gal. 2:17; 1 Cor. 1:30). Therefore Paul expects all of Christendom to concur with his affirmation that we are justified in Christ, because all recognize in Christ the one through whom God's grace and righteousness perform their work (Gal. 2:16). In his sending and work, the divine verdict concerning man is manifested and carried out. The concepts of justification and of the Christ were immediately linked, because the office of the Anointed One consists in the establishment of the holy community through the execution of justice. Because God's judgment is realized in Christ's judgment and God's rule is realized in Christ's rule, anyone accepted by Christ is justified.

The justification of the guilty can occur only through God's granting of grace to mankind; for through justification of the one who has sinned occurs the forgiveness of his sins, and this forgiveness is an act of grace. The aim of justification is the reconciliation of sinful man with God and the bestowal of the divine gifts on him. Even this prerequisite of the doctrine of justification, however, results from the sending of the Christ, because he is given to mankind by God's grace in order that people be called to God through him and receive the eternal gifts (Rom. 3:24; 4:4–5; 1 Tim. 1:15; Titus 3:7).

In order for the grace here shown to man to reveal God's righteousness and to procure righteousness for man, it is, further, indispensable that it prove its ethical nature, be entirely set apart from evil and produce all that is good. According to Paul, this prerequisite of justification likewise was met in Christ, because his commission is directed against sin and makes him its conqueror. Therefore he entered into death (Rom. 3:25; 4:25; 5:9; 6–7; 8:31–34; 2 Cor. 5:21). Because God made him the Christ through the cross, one and the same will resulted from grace and righteousness, one and the same work from the bestowal of grace and the working of righteousness.

Death results for Paul from the juridical activity of God, particularly the death of Christ, who as God's Son shares in God's life and is given to the world as the messenger of divine grace in order to bring life to it. That he is nevertheless subjected to death has its explanation in human sin. Because of it God surrendered him and thus executed his judgment upon man. Thus it is revealed by the cross what is sin before God, what sort of judgment befalls it. God's curse, by which he separates evildoers from himself, falls on him (Rom. 4:25; 8:1–4; Gal. 2:21; 3:13–14; 2 Cor. 5:21). Therefore it was of special significance for Paul that Jesus died on the cross; for his death thus occurs through a juridical act, not merely out of natural necessity.

However, this does not mean that Christ fails to fulfill his commission given to him by divine grace; rather, he fulfills it through his death. The purpose for which he is handed over is our acceptance. God did not spare him, so he might forgive us everything; he gave him over, that he might justify us; he made him sin and a curse, in order to bestow righteousness and blessing on us; he condemned him, in order to justify those who believe in him. Through his blood, Jesus provides the community with forgiveness of sins (Rom. 3:25; Eph. 1:7; Col. 1:20).

By placing Christ in the condition prepared for him by the guilt of mankind, with the purpose and result that he provides it with a share in what he himself possesses through his divine sonship and what he can grant it by his messianic office, God reveals both that he is against us and that he is for us, that he hates evil and that he forgives, that he does not want man and that he wants him, that he does not want him the way he is now but rather the way he makes him through the Christ. In each instance the former is revealed by Jesus' death, the latter by the fact that it is the grace of God that leads him into death, the grace by which he is the Christ. Paul bears witness to the ethical perfection of the grace thus manifested. It is suffused with the glory of righteousness and leads not to God's dethronement in favor of man, but rather to God's glorification in his separation from all evil. It issues not in the breaking of the divine will and Law but in its realization, with the result of effecting our reconciliation with God. Thus God's righteousness was manifested through the Christ (Rom. 3:21).

By linking the bestowal of grace with the working of justice grace receives its truth and fulfillment. The notion is foreign to Paul that a deficiency in grace requires the demonstration of righteousness. He did not want to, nor could, conceive of a divine grace that simply circumvented the ethical deficiency of man. Grace would be broken and profaned if given to man in disregard of his guilt, so that this guilt were concealed from man and God. Paul believed that this human desire dishonored God, because it considered him capable both of breaking the Law and compromising truth in order to do so. In this he detected the malicious lie latent in Jewish righteousness. Grace is the revelation and glorification of God only when it completely exposes man's guilt and brings full truth into his relationship with God. When man stands before the judging God as he is, and just as he is with guilt clearly laid bare receives justification from God, only then he has really been pardoned, only then been called to God; only then have his guilt and evil been removed. Because Paul had been brought to repentance and had to judge himself, and because he knew himself to be under condemnation as all others, and knew no one who was not guilty, therefore this form of the gospel was particularly significant for him. Now his own judgment by which he must accuse himself was countered by God's verdict which canceled out his self-condemnation and declared him not guilty. In the proclamation of justification, Paul saw that offer of divine grace which can be believed by the one who must judge himself.

Because the guilty person can receive justification only by being forgiven, the phrase initially customary for God's attitude toward sinners, "forgiveness of sins," retains for Paul its full significance (Rom. 4:6–8; 8:32; 2 Cor. 5:19; Eph. 1:7; 4:32; Col. 1:14; 2:13; 3:13). But he used the concept of justification with particular emphasis, because this enabled him to exclude the limited, incomplete conceptions of divine forgiveness that provide nothing but a negative aim for it and think solely of the removal of negative consequences arising from evil. The removal of guilt and of consciousness of guilt, the end of divine rejection, the liberation from corruption, all are conceptions that are insufficient and inconceivable by themselves, unless they are linked with their positive equivalent. Wrath comes to an end only with the bestowal of love, and guilt only through the awarding of righteousness. The evil conscience and the consequences of evil are overcome only when man receives what righteousness grants to him. Truth and the perfection of forgiveness, which completely restore fellowship with the guilty person, are given powerful expression through the doctrine of justification. Inadequate notions of forgiveness always suffer from the idea of arbitrariness, travesty of justice, and the partiality of God; but the fact that God's pardon in Christ is carried out through the execution of judgment manifests precisely in this forgiveness that God is in every respect set apart from evil.

Paul did not doubt that Jesus' cross-work was able to achieve its aim. He describes its success by using the metaphor derived from Jesus himself, that the Christ redeemed us through his death. We are justified through the redemption prepared for us by him; by his death, he paid the price by which he made us his own and bought us for himself (Rom. 3:24; 1 Cor. 6:20; 7:23; Eph. 1:7; Col. 1:14). Because his authority over us is based on his death, it is grounded in his obedience toward God. Because he is the one who practiced obedience, through his obedience the justifying verdict is available and has been established for all (Rom. 5:19; Phil. 2:8).

But Paul also described the power of Jesus' death that achieved its aim by way of new formulations. Through him we all died and put on the cross with him. That peculiar human nature that makes up who we essentially are is judged by his death, and our flesh is buried through him. Thus justification has been granted to us only in such a way that it is preceded by a dying that affects not merely individuals but all, and not merely individual parts of us but everything. Thus God extends his good pleasure not to the sinner who lives in the flesh but to a new creature come into being by Christ's subjection of human nature to death and by the resurrection of a new man who now lives eternally separate from sin through God and for God (2 Cor. 5:14–17; Rom. 6:3–11; Gal. 2:19–21; Rom. 8:1–4; Eph. 2:14–15; Col. 2:11–14, 20; 3:3; Gal. 6:14; Eph. 4:22–24; Col. 3:9–10).

Paul does not derive the pervasive power of Jesus' death from mystical processes arising in the believer through his own will-power but rather from Jesus' messianic office. It is his appointment as Lord of all that issues in the pervasive power of his death and life. Just as he, as the Christ, has life not merely for himself but for all, and just as Christ's life also means the life of his community, Christ's death has not merely occurred to him but constitutes a universal event. It reveals God's stance toward him to everyone and executes God's judgment over him, making known to all that we are judged by him, but in such a way that here life issues from death for us and righteousness from condemnation. The power of Christ extends just as far as the power of his death, through which he became the Christ, and the power of his life has equally far-reaching dimensions.

This is indicated by the fact that Paul depicts participation in Jesus' death as a secure and completed act rather than as a goal we still must achieve and must effect in ourselves. This participation is granted to us in baptism (Rom. 6:3–4) and is thus inherent in one's status as a Christian from the beginning rather than attained only on a higher plane of religious perfection. It is given to all rather than merely to the particularly religious or ethically advanced. Indeed, Paul does not even limit participation in Jesus' cross to the community but presents it as universal in keeping with the universal calling of Christ who is Lord, not merely of the perfect but of all believers, and Lord not merely of the church but of mankind (2 Cor. 5:19). All these affirmations are incompatible with a mystical interpretation that sees in them a self-produced conforming to Christ's death and life.

### c) The Mediation of Justification through Faith

But these considerations do not yet completely describe justification. What is further necessary is information telling a person how he must live now that he has been justified. Because justification determines God's stance toward us, it arises through two processes: a revelatory act of God, and a process within the human being by which God's act touches and influences him. The practical application of the doctrine of justification depended completely on this formulation. Because we are justified in Christ, it is completely identical with the question of for whom Christ intercedes and against whom Christ turns, to whom he grants God's grace and whom he denies it. Concurring with all of Christendom, Paul answered this question by affirming that all who believe in the Christ are his. Man's justification thus occurs through God's sending of the Christ and by God's surrendering him to death, and further by man's believing in him (Rom. 3:21–26; Gal. 2:16–21). If God's will were not revealed and effected through an act of God, there would be no justification. It also would not exist if no attitude were found in us for which the divine verdict intercedes. Without man's inner participation in Christ's work, God's power might perhaps be revealed through him, but not God's righteousness. His own will might become visible, but not his relationship to our will.

In sketching out the relationship between the faith that is our righteousness and justification itself, two kinds of formulations are possible, both true: that righteousness is the foundation of justification and that justification confers righteousness. Righteousness can and must be called what God's judgment of man commends and makes the ground of his favor.[31] Again, righteousness is what is granted to man through justification. It is conferred on him through God's verdict, because his conduct takes on the nature of righteousness only when God accepts it. Righteousness is ours not before the judge speaks, but when he speaks on our behalf.[32] Therefore imputation is linked with justification in every doctrine of justification, because the pronouncement of a verdict always depends on what is or is not imputed to man. Therefore Paul says that faith is our righteousness before God, that God imputes righteousness to the believer, and that he declares him to be righteous by his verdict. Thus he expresses that all guilt is removed through faith in Christ and all its consequences done away with, that God's favor has been attained and all its benefits gained.

Because faith procures our justification, it turns out that God's grace is the underlying motivation moving God to justify us. For not by exercising faith does man award himself value that provides the ground for God's favor and moves him to fellowship with us. As believer, man truly apprehends what God gives him, and because man's acceptance of the divine gift and grace is the behavior by which God's demands on us are met, his good will for us carried out, God's stance toward us is revealed as perfect grace. The concept of merit is thus completely removed from justification (Rom. 4:4–5; 10:9–10; 11:6). And still it is our own conscious conduct that draws God's praise, and we are placed in communion with God as persons with our knowing and willing. This is precisely what lends the divine activity the characteristic of grace that esteems man, leads him to God, and unites him with God. This is why, through justification, we receive divine love.

Moreover, because God justifies the believer on account of his faith, it is assured that nothing evil becomes the object of God's good pleasure. For thus he does not extend his favor to what man produces by virtue of his own will-power but to what God does himself. If a synergism arose from the fact that justification is based on Christ's death and man's faith, a synergism by which the working of righteousness was divided up between God and man, the doctrine of justification would be rendered impossible. But faith arises from what Christ is and does. It is based on Christ's conduct toward mankind. Therefore the me-

---

31. Faith is reckoned as righteousness: Rom. 4:5, 9; being justified by faith: Rom. 3:28; as a result of faith: Rom. 3:30; 5:1; Gal. 2:16; 3:8, 24; righteousness through faith: Rom. 9:30; 10:6; on the basis of faith: Phil. 3:9.

32. Righteousness is imputed: Rom. 4:6, 11; gift of righteousness: Rom. 5:17; hope of righteousness: Gal. 5:5.

diation of righteousness through Christ and through faith issues in a uniform act whose causal power is entirely attributed to God, and precisely on account of this it becomes possible to consider faith to be our righteousness. Now it leads not to a broken but a complete result, not an insecure success dependent on further conditions but a certain outcome. Because the doctrine of justification indicates what God does for us, it expresses certainty and does not remain mere hope but rather expresses what Christendom is to recognize as the possession given to it.

Faith has this certainty because divine grace is never invoked in vain. God never disappoints confidence in him, and Jesus proves himself to be the servant of divine grace by honoring every expression of confidence offered to him and giving to it his gift.

Thus divine grace remains free from any notion of arbitrary favor, because the same pure and perfect goodness that sent the Christ and surrendered him to death performs its healing work against evil with the same resolve in all who believe in him (Rom. 3:29–30).

The doctrine of justification is further based on the conviction that faith is the right conduct toward the manifestation of God that occurred in the Christ. No uncertainty attached to this part of Paul's train of thought. After God's love in Jesus has appeared, has called man, has forgiven him and granted him eternal life, faith is the proper consequence. It is established that faith is the attitude willed by God and established in man, an attitude that esteems his verdict as righteousness. By expressing the conviction that man acts aright when he trusts Jesus, however, Paul does not bring the notion of merit into play once again; rather, he removes it completely. For the spiritual process occurring in us through faith can never by itself provide the grounds for God's justifying verdict. It can do so only because it establishes our union with Christ. The believer's righteous status is based on the placing of his confidence in Christ. Because he has been laid hold of by Christ and clings to him and has been made his possession, the believer is justified. This is why the justification of believers pertains not to righteous but to godless persons, those who cannot attain to righteousness through their own works because they can obtain it only by being forgiven. Thus it is God's, not their own, righteousness that is manifested upon them (Rom. 4:5; 3:21; 1:17; 10:3; Phil. 3:9; 2 Cor. 5:21).

It would be impossible to describe faith as righteousness and as reception of justification if it did not effect man's separation from evil. But in Paul's view faith surely effects this for the sake of what Christ is and what he gives to believers. By turning their confidence away from themselves to Jesus, they pronounce condemnation both upon themselves and their sin and affirm God's Law over against themselves. They acknowledge that their own conduct renders them subject to condemnation and loss of life. They see the reason for the fact that they do not incur this result but the contrary solely in God's deed, solely in the Christ, solely in the fact that he died for them and now grants them what he acquired for them. Thus God's complete renunciation of evil is realized in us, so that we refuse to find any inherent righteousness in ourselves. We ground God's favor not in our own works but see ourselves placed in God's love because

Christ places us in it. Precisely because faith does not award to man his own, self-made righteousness, it is his genuine and true righteousness.

The negative act by which we judge our sin, however, cannot exist by itself but has its reason for existence in the positive will by which we adhere believingly to the Christ. This will is good, even completely good, because it seeks to receive what Christ promises: the perfect and good gift of God. By turning to Christ, the believer belongs to him, and Christ's work is performed upon him with all its power that overcomes evil and produces righteousness. This is why the notion was foreign to Paul that God's verdict clashed with reality by justifying the believer in spite of his sinfulness. For those who are united with Christ know him to be their Savior from evil. He never conceived of justification merely in terms of illusion and unreality. God effectively extends his favor to the believer because Christ effectively brings all sin to an end. In this, of course, present and future, present experience and promise, diverge. As long as our union with Jesus is brought about by faith, liberation from evil is not yet completed in the human life situation (Rom. 8:10, 23–25; cf. Gal. 5:5). But it is God's and Jesus' will to give us freedom from evil because and as certainly as he justifies us. Paul does not derive this will merely from conjecture but already envisions its final realization, not in himself or in other Christians but in what Jesus possesses, who will manifest his redemptive power through his final revelation. Doubt regarding the effective power of God's verdict coincided in Paul's estimation with doubt in the truth of the messianic name of Jesus. If the latter is affirmed, it is clear that his community is, and one day manifestly will be, what God's verdict attributes to it—although its current condition does not yet entirely reflect this—because God's verdict cannot be broken. His grace grants what it intends for us and in Christ produces the perfect community.

### d) Justification as Ground of Hope

The contrast between what is believed and what is currently experienced links the concept of justification with Jesus' promise and the longing for its fulfillment. If the divine verdict were already revealed to its full extent, the final judgment would already have occurred. But because our relationship with Jesus consists in trust, eschatology retains its full significance for Paul, turning the notion of judgment once more toward the believer, because he will stand before the judgment seat of Christ on that day and there be justified or condemned (1 Cor. 4:4–5; 2 Cor. 5:9–10; Rom. 5:9–10). But because the Christ has come, the concept of justification, together with all the other eschatological motifs, invades the present. For on account of Christ's finished work, God's verdict regarding believers did not have the effect of separating them from him but of uniting them with him, so that certainty flows into both their present and their future relationship with God.

Paul's religious conduct was significantly impacted by the eschatological import of the doctrine of justification. Otherwise, it could have entailed the same danger Jesus exposed in the Pharisees' righteousness. Paul is assured of God, has his favor, and has arrived; how does he protect belief from arrogance? For his righteousness consists solely in belief, solely in being given what Christ has provided. Yet faith for Paul is certainty and engenders complete thanksgiving. This is where eschatological considerations enter in and overcome the danger that the believer might become proud of himself in his righteousness. An encounter with Christ still lies in the future, and he must make sure that he passes Christ's judgment. Thus faith gives rise to that striving for righteousness to which Paul devotes himself with all his energy. As one who is justified he is now called to run for the prize (Phil. 3:12–14 in the context of vv. 8–11). He does not obtain power for his effort merely by mediating on his sinfulness, even less through doubting the validity of justification, exchanging the certainty of faith for the uncertainty of fear. Precisely for this reason he runs toward the goal with all his energy, because the grace that now justifies him grants him what is perfect, running, not plagued by doubt, but in the assurance that Christ's death and life are available for him.

For this reason Paul never linked the doctrine of justification with the idea that it reduced Christianity to mere faith and exempted believers from works. In order to protect justification from such notions, he confronts believers with the Crucified and Risen One, who will not let himself be used as a servant of sin, because it is beyond doubt that he died to sin and lives for God (Rom. 6:1–4; Gal. 2:17). Because this provides faith's aim with its content, the will to sin consequently cancels out faith.

### e) Love's Part in Justification

Will grounded in faith is love, by which we live no longer for ourselves but for God in Christ and thus for the brethren. It is no surprise that Paul linked with his doctrine of justification a conduct of life that is grounded in love, expressly calling love greater than faith (2 Cor. 5:14–15; Rom. 14:7–9; 1 Cor. 13:13). Paul saw man's guilt in that lovelessness which despises God and corrupts man. Christ freed him from such lovelessness by acting toward him in God's love as well as by creating love in him. How can he consider himself dead to sin if he persists in lovelessness, how prove to be alive apart from the goodwill that places itself in God's service? God's will and Jesus' impact occur in him with the appearance of this love. Through it he attains the fruit of faith and experiences that Christ rules him and that his Spirit moves him. Because love is that which faith desires and what Christ grants to it, it is greater than faith. But by the same token love is accompanied by a readiness to do the divine will.

The objection that Paul could just as well say that he is justified by love has no basis in a deficiency in Paul's statements. He said in all clarity why he turns us in the case of justification completely away from ourselves, basing it not on our good will but solely on faith. This he considered to be necessary for both religious and ethical reasons. Only thus does man truly treat God as God and honor him in the glory of his grace and in the truth of his lordship. This does not occur when man esteems his love as his righteousness, whether love is understood as purity of his disposition or as the greatness of his work. This would amount to man praising himself and to making himself the founder of his own religion. For he would be grounding his relationship with God in his own act, which God was now expected to praise and reward. By making faith our righteousness, God becomes the one who creates our connection with him, and this alone normalizes our relationship with him.

Paul thinks thus because he does not merely speak about love but has it and thinks within the sphere it creates. A love that parades before God while pointing to its value and demanding recognition from him, is not love according to the standard used by Paul. Selflessness is its essential ingredient, by which it has its aim not in its own but in God's greatness, not in its own but in God's justice. Because faith is our righteousness before God, boasting is excluded, and this Paul considers to be a goal that absolutely must be reached in order for us to possesses righteousness before God (Rom. 3:27). But it is reached solely through the Law of faith. Only now does our attitude toward God become love; as long as man boasts of himself, he does not judge or act according to love. Love praises the one to whom it devotes itself, and for Paul, this is God.

It is just as clear that repentance requires that we consider our righteousness to be our faith, not our love. Because man knows not merely the good but also the evil will, he would excuse his evil by appeal to his own goodness if he considered love to be his righteousness, expecting God to turn a blind eye to his sin. But he possesses righteousness only when he foregoes all excuses or rationalizations for his evil, acknowledging his guilt before God without reservation. Now there will never be a righteousness for him that consists in his own goodness. He has it merely because God in the creative power of his grace unites the believer with himself.

### f) The Importance of the Doctrine of Justification for Paul

The verdict against man and the doctrine of justification precisely converge in Paul, so that they perfectly complement each other and together establish what he calls faith. All that makes his verdict regarding man appear severe is removed, not through a later weakening or a hidden disavowal, but in such a way that the total condemnation of human conduct, the foregoing of any excuse and the complete humbling before God remain intact. They become effective, not on the grounds of weakness or desperation but in relation to complete thankfulness and joy, because Christ supplies human guilt with God's gift and human powerlessness with God's power, so that man is able to reach his ethical goal. Thereby Paul inoculated his community against both Judaistic and gnostic aspirations, which could entice the community only as long as the question of justification still remained open and their relationship with God thus appeared uncertain. The motive by which Judaism sought to influence congregations was fear that they still might have God against them and that they would be able to assure themselves of God's favor more perfectly by works of the Law. Where Paul's doctrine of justification was understood, such allurements lost all appeal. gnostic thought sought to influence congregations by praising the greatness of their Christian knowledge and freedom. This motivation, too, was extinguished when with Paul the community saw its righteousness in faith. For thus all religious pride dies, and any derailment of religious desire from its proper ethical aim was fended off.

However, the apologetic thrust of the doctrine that made it a useful weapon against all Paul considered to be corrupt Christianity does not support the notion that Paul postulated the doctrine of justification merely for apologetic reasons. It is simply untrue that he spoke about human guilt and divine righteousness, not because these were his greatest concerns and most serious aspirations, but because these pronouncements were useful for his ecclesiastical or personal purposes. The documents show that Paul's entire will and work were determined by the truth denoted in "justification." In the epistle to the Galatians, Paul made it the grounds for the legitimacy of Gentile Christianity and thereby designated it as the foundation for his entire work. He told the Galatians that he sought and found common ground with the Jerusalem apostles through the doctrine of justification. When he began dealing with the Roman church, he based his decision to go to Rome and thus his entire ministry on the doctrine of justification. Why he stands before all as a debtor who is obliged to them, he expresses through the doctrine of justification. Even if he was led to this by apologetic concerns, responding to objections to his ministry, the fact that his opponents attacked his teaching on justification reveals that they considered it to be the centerpiece of his preaching which set it apart from other forms of Christianity. To the Philippians, Paul presented it in his autobiographical review as the core of his Christianity, in order that they likewise might find in it the governing principle for their Christian conduct. Parallel to this, he concluded the section in which he revealed to the Corinthians his controlling motivation with the doctrine of justification, and in his instruction to his helpers he counted it among the certainties that order the church's ministry and keep it from any gnostic arrogance (Gal. 2:16; Rom. 1:15–17; Phil. 3:7–14; 2 Cor. 5:21; Titus 3:4–7; 2 Tim. 4:7–8).

This is not refuted or weakened by the fact that he kept himself admirably free from formalism. In light of his high esteem for clarity of thought and the long duration of his teaching ministry, it would not be strange if the doctrine of justification had become a fixed formula by which he uniformly and consistently repeated the gospel. But he always expresses it in different terms, according to the situation in which his ministry places him. He can also present it in its entirety and in its unabbreviated form apart from the doctrine of justification, so that he lends full expression to everything he possesses in the certainty of his justification. Therefore this doctrine still remains the particularly instructive and effective result of his work. The fact that it is found in his writings continually also casts light on the meaning of other formulations he chooses for his proclamation of Jesus.

### g) The Relationship of the Doctrine of Justification to Jesus' Call to Repentance

Since Jesus made repentance the prerequisite for entrance into God's kingdom, Paul proved himself to be Jesus' messenger by proclaiming Jesus' rule through the offer of justification. All the features of Jesus' call to repentance are present without attenuation in Pauline justification: the total rejection of all wickedness; the extension of repentance to all; the complete uniting of righteousness with grace, so that the call to repentance becomes the offer of forgiveness, finding its purpose not in the mere exposure of evil but in victory over it.

The Pauline formulation attacks neither mourning nor trust in God, neither God's opposition to evil nor his solidarity with us. Every major element of Jesus' call to repentance recurs in Paul, not via repetition learned by rote but in distinctive, new form that nonetheless leaves the original thrust intact. Other features of Jesus' call reflected in Paul's teaching include: the painful submission of man followed by his joyous elevation to God; the total subjection to ethical norms in connection with the liberty of love transcending those norms; personal experience of a spiritual relationship together with the universal scope of God's reign; the battle for justice, which is hallowed as unassailable, coupled with the bestowal of grace that becomes effective in the glory of divine kindness.

Still, according to widespread opinion, Paul's doctrine of justification led the community's devotion away from Jesus' message. This view takes issue in part with Paul's grounding of justification in Jesus' death, also objecting to the tying of justification to faith. The tie to Jesus' death, it is argued, is theologically damaging, because it complicates the picture of God. Instead of pointing to God's unmediated readiness to forgive, as Jesus did, it is objected that, for Paul, God is now using a complicated procedure to effect forgiveness, because justification is attainable only through the substitutionary death of Jesus. And tying justification to faith is ethically harmful, it is said, because of what it does subjectively. To value faith so highly as to see in it our righteousness runs the risk of intellectualizing religion. Here Paul starts down the path of salvific dogmatics, the argument runs; the constraint that he thereby places on the intellect is especially deleterious because faith is the condition for remission of sins. In all this Paul allegedly sinks below the level of Jesus' moral earnestness; he conceived of repentance in terms of turning from hostility to charity, granting his promise to simple demonstrations of love while refraining from making demands on the intellect.

Obviously such objections seem entirely justified if the historian interprets Jesus' call to repentance as moral illumination, viewing guilt as a melancholic abnormality of human consciousness, an abnormality healed by Jesus' placing the conception of God's kindness in the mind instead. But such theories are useless for historical analysis. Jesus placed evil under comprehensive condemnation that touches the whole person, not merely his thoughts. He imparted a new will and new works, not alternative conceptions of God's kindness. Just as he conceived of repentance as act, he knew of no forgiveness that was not God's doing, by which he preserved the forgiven slave in his service and received the wayward son back into his fellowship. Of the work of divine grace Jesus said: God brings it to pass. Jesus did not instruct the mournful to forgive themselves; they receive forgiveness from God as he grants them the Christ who calls them to himself. This is the common element between Paul and Jesus: Paul was convinced that God, through Jesus, has granted forgiveness to him and all mankind.

Nor does Paul distance himself from Jesus by conceiving of the cross as the demonstration of God's righteousness. When Paul steered clear of the false notion that Jesus revealed God's grace "in spite of" his death, he did not distort but understood Jesus' own intention. Jesus' prerogative to extend grace to those who repent was for Jesus no less than for Paul grounded in the conviction that the Father was leading him to the cross. For Paul, this connection shone in the bright daylight of fulfilled history, daylight permeating Christendom's entire relationship with Jesus. Paul regarded as untruth, as conscious rebellion against the word and work of Jesus, the attempt to conceal Jesus' cross and to seek the demonstration of divine grace exclusively in that which Jesus had previously said and done. Since Paul's following of Jesus was of necessity determined by the outcome of Jesus' life, Paul used formulations that highlighted the justification of the sinful world as the goal of Jesus' work on the cross.

Paul is not to blame for the later emergence of immoral distortions of religious life in Christendom that took their starting point from the Pauline version of the doctrine of justification. These distortions despised works in the name of faith, substituting faith with religious theory. But Paul never saw faith as a substitute for action. Faith rather enabled him to believe in Christ, so that he could perform good works through him. These kinds of distortions of Pauline teaching did not arise through his doctrine of justification but were the products of misunderstanding and misapplication. Of course, when a doctrine of faith is construed, according to which faith no longer seeks or receives righteousness from God, devoting itself to different aims instead, be it knowledge or blessedness, an immoral kind of "faith" will be the result. But Paul is not responsible for this. He was a servant of righteousness.

## 2. Liberation from the Law

### a) Liberation through Christ

According to Paul, whoever has truly apprehended what the Law produces in man, no longer sets his hope on the Law. Since man's resistance toward truth caused God to give him over, he can receive help only by being accepted by Christ, so that his rejection is replaced by his calling to God. Because Adam's fall led to the dominion of sin and death over the world, this dominion is not already broken by the proclamation of the Law to man; thereby it is rather confirmed and intensified. The consequences of disobedience are removed only by obedience, and condemnation only by justification, which is awarded to us, now that we have become sinners, as God's gift through Christ. Because our flesh renders us sinful, justification is impossible for the Law, because it does not remove our fleshly nature, so that man's encounter with the Law does not result in his innocence but his guilt, not in life but in death. This gives rise to the longing for liberation from the Law, because we do not want to remain in sin and because we are lost as long as we remain in death. The longing for freedom from the Law arises here thus not from sinful passion but from the will directed toward the Law, because we hate evil and fear God's wrath as we are instructed by the Law. It is a sign of a good will when we long to be free from the evil condemned by the Law. But after having become sinners, we can attain freedom only by being set free from the Law.

Therefore it is God's will to set man free from the Law, and this he made the calling of the Christ. Liberation can occur not through man, because he cannot abolish God's Law, certainly not through the Law itself that brings him death.

God, on the other hand, sets free from the Law through the Christ, because the Law which tells us what to do is transcended by God's grace which establishes his own work, and righteousness that kills on account of evil is transcended by forgiveness by which God reconciles the guilty person with himself. By making it impossible for man to achieve his own righteousness, the Law does not prevent God from revealing his righteousness toward man. The means for this is that now Christ is given lordship over mankind in place of the Law.

Paul recognizes the unity between the earlier and the new work of God in the fact that the Law's verdict, by which it punishes sin with death, is confirmed and carried out through the Christ by suffering the punishment himself. He was subjected to the Law, and this resulted in his cross by which he became a curse (because the Law curses sin) and by which he himself suffers the condemnation pronounced by the Law over the flesh. Now Christ brings the positive will of the Law to fulfillment, that is, its designated purpose for the righteous, because he carries out God's good will through his death and resurrection, effecting our separation from evil through his death and our life for God with his life. Because the Law does not contain merely the condemnation of evil but also makes known what is righteous before God and what he does for the righteous person, its purpose is carried out only through the Christ (Gal. 4:4–5; 3:13–14; 2:19; Rom. 7:4–6; 8:3–4). He overcomes the struggle between the Law and our fleshly nature by manifesting himself to his community as the giver of the Spirit. Those who walk in the Spirit have received love and thus obtained what the Law desires as that which is good before God (Rom. 13:8–10; Gal. 5:14, 18–23). Of course, Christ's gift is obtained not through works of the Law, because it is given to us not through the Law but through the Christ by his freeing us from the Law. But even the awarding of his gift to faith stands in accordance with the Law, because it does not permit anyone to excuse evil but subjects all to God's righteousness, destroying their confidence in themselves, so that they believe in the one whom God's grace has sent to them. Thus everything desired and effected by the Law attains its goal through faith. Where the Law requires us to judge ourselves, the believer concurs and acknowledges his guilt before God. Where the Law attests to God's righteousness, the Christ manifests it, and the believer truly apprehends it in him and recognizes in it his salvation (Rom. 3:19–22; Gal. 3:22–24).

This is why Paul possessed in his freedom from the Law an entirely clear conscience that rested completely assured when confronted with the Law. By keeping to the Christ in faith, he acts the way the Law requires it. He is not a Christian in that he conceals the Law with a cover; rather, while he was a Jew, a cover lay over the Law, as was the case for all of Judaism. The Law itself places him in the condition of death, which requires him to expect his justification not from the works he does for the sake of the Law but from his reliance on God's righteousness, and through the Law he has died to the Law. Therefore he answers the question whether he nullifies the Law through faith in the negative without any sophistry or ambiguity, because both the condemning and the justifying word of the Law is confirmed through the Christ and carried out on behalf of his community (2 Cor. 3:15–17; Gal. 2:19; Rom. 3:31).

Done away with through the Christ is the restriction of the community to Israel and thus all those ordinances of the Law that established Israel's peculiar separated existence. What reigns in Christ's community is his will alone, and its worship consists in obedience which is grounded in faith. Only what results from Christ's work and word has legitimacy in it and constitutes its obligation, not what can only be justified by the Law. When Paul told the Romans they must not hinder the singling out of particular days, he substantiated the appropriateness of such a celebration by contending that the worshiper gave thanks for his feast days and thus revealed that he celebrated by faith and to the Lord. And still, the Sabbath and Passover surely held first place among these special days. Nevertheless, Paul does not permit here any appeal to the Decalogue. The celebration is appropriate only when it occurs out of faith in Christ (Rom. 14:5–9). This portion demonstrates with particular clarity how completely Paul excluded nomistic ordinances from the legislation of the Christian will.

### b) Freedom the Antithesis of Lawlessness

Because freedom is Christ's gift, it is entirely distinct from human egotistic self-sufficiency. For Christ subjects the community completely to himself. Paul showed also regarding the false liberty man claims for his evil will that freedom can be attained through complete dependence, because freedom to sin can be achieved only by entering into a kind of slavery that renders evil a necessity (Rom. 6:16–23). Likewise, the believer's freedom is based on the fact that he does not belong to himself but to Christ and that he has surrendered his will and his life completely to him. He is at the same time both Christ's slave and his freedman, set free from the Law by having been bought for God (Rom. 7:6; 14:7–9, 18; 1 Cor. 3:23; 6:20; 7:22–23; Eph. 6:6). Therefore Paul used the term "Law" without reservation also for Christ's relationship with the believer, just as he always employs the term "service" for his communion with Christ. To fulfill "the Law of Christ" is the calling of the community, and it obtains its freedom through "the Law of the Spirit." Its connection with Jesus through faith is based on "the Law of faith" (Gal. 6:2; Rom. 8:2; 3:27). Because Christ carries out the divine will, the community's freedom is predicated upon the unshakeable and absolute authority of fixed norms. In this Paul saw no tension or antinomy, because he considered freedom to be not an achievement of the human will but a gift of divine grace. Through God man receives a will of his own, a work of his own, a life of his own. He does not possess these apart from God, however, but through God, whose will remains the controlling principle. He thus obtains his freedom by the fact that the Law of Christ becomes effective for him and in him.

### c) Perfect Freedom

Paul formulates his concept of freedom in equally absolute terms as the concept of justification and all those phrases by which he describes Jesus' gift. If divine grace turns to man, it makes him to be what God wants him to be. Now he is pure and everything is pure for him, now he is just and what he does takes place according to God's will. Now he may love and act, and every demonstration of his love for God meets with God's good pleasure. Therefore man is now completely free. The freedom granted to him is complete (1 Cor. 3:21; 6:12; 10:23; Titus 1:15; 1 Tim. 1:9). Thereby every claim by others for control over his conscience or faith is rejected. For connectedness to God in Christ is complete and does not permit other lords. Paul thus carried out the principle of freedom completely in the exercise of his apostleship and the organization of his community. It is protected against self-centered abuse as long as its religious foundation, which provides it with its substance and its limitation, remains visible. The believer can desire and exercise liberty only to the extent it is grounded in his relationship with God—to that extent, however, with immovable courage.

Likewise, the sovereignty of God, who rules all of nature, results in a relationship with nature for believers that placed them in a state of total inviolability and supremacy with respect to it. Thus Paul dealt with nature fully convinced that it contained nothing that could damage man internally. It does not render him unclean and does not touch his dignity or relationship with God. Nothing stemming from nature separates from God. Because everything serves him, everything also, when used properly, serves the community and contributes to its well-being. There no longer exists any evil for those who belong to God (Rom. 8:28; 14:14; 1 Cor. 10:26; Titus 1:15).

Thus arises the grateful assurance of comfort and security. We are saved. After the one grave danger, that of evil, has been removed from the believer, he is freed from the ravages of any other hostile power (Rom. 1:16; 8:24; 10:9–10; 1 Cor. 15:2; Eph. 2:5; 1 Tim. 1:15; Titus 3:5).

### d) Pauline Freedom and the Freedom of Jesus

Through his divine sonship, Jesus knew himself to be authorized to deprive the Mosaic Law of its obligatory power and instead to bind his disciples to his own word. He led them out of the Temple and away from the priest and tore down the barrier that surrounded the Jews. He did away with the old purity, the tithe, and sacrifices and subjected rest on the Sabbath to the love commandment. However, he did not present his freedom as contradiction to the Law but subjected himself to it with deliberate resolve and defended its holiness against all who broke it. For it is not the sinful will that sets free from the Law; rather, the Father's communion with the Son shows him and those he leads what his perfect goodness desires and how they serve them in a new way. All of this Paul kept intact through his freedom concept. Jesus' fidelity to the Law is kept unblemished, because the sanctity of the Law remains undisputed. Paul rather sees in it a crucial part of Christ's mission, because he can set someone free from the Law only by fulfilling it. At the same time, however, it is true that Jesus establishes in his divine sonship something greater than what the Law provided. The difference between the words of Jesus and those of Paul regarding the Law arises from the fact that Paul uses them to reveal his own consciousness of guilt and to show by his own example how the Law brought the fall and death to him and to us. Jesus, on the other hand, did not view the Law as a burden for his own relationship with God, but saw its oppressiveness in the fact that the community was weighed down by it. This provided a new form for the teaching on the Law, because now it was the one who had to gain and to show others freedom from the Law who had experienced the condemnation and the curse of the Law by his own experience. This led to the difference separating all of Paul's statements from those of Jesus. That difference stems from the fact that Paul obtained what Jesus had in the Father in no other way than through the Christ.

### 3. Reconciliation

#### a) The Accomplishment of Reconciliation through Christ

Paul chose to describe divine grace by way of several parallel phrases not merely out of pedagogical reasons, which prohibited the fossilization of the word that would have resulted from expressing it only in a fixed formula. Paul's use of varied language also derives from the fact that his assurance of God comprises convictions other than the concept of Law. It also provides us with the assurance of the divine love, and Paul demonstrates through the entire content of the concept of God that God has manifested himself through Jesus.

While being convinced of God's ability to love, man, owing to his guilt, is conscious of his own alienation from God. This awareness is mediated to the Jew and the Gentile not merely by his individual conscience—after all, he knows that he is afraid of God and grumbles against him and opposes him—it is imparted to them also through the condition in which the great human communions subsist, because Israel crucified the Christ and the nations serve false gods. Both prove not merely their ignorance but their dispute with God in open rebellion against him. Paul did not anticipate the objection that this struggle would remain without consequences for man. For he perceives the human condition in such a way that enmity toward God has an impact on God's attitude toward man. He observes this by noticing that God distances himself from him, resulting in humiliation and bondage; this, in turn, leads to vanity, malice, and death (Rom. 5:10; 8:7; Col. 1:21; Eph. 2:14–18).

The removal of this rupture through the restoration of fellowship takes place through God. Only he can effect this restoration through a new demonstration of his love, and he has done so through Christ, because Christ does away with sin, the flesh, and death in the service of divine grace, thus uniting us with himself in the Spirit, so that we are united with God in him. Because he carries out his ministry through his death, it fully takes on the characteristic of a reconciling work. For thus man's rebellion against God is exposed and given expression, and God's opposition toward the world's sinful way of life revealed. Yet at the same time, the love of God and of Jesus does not cease but holds fast to its goal, granting forgiveness and establishing fellowship. Therefore the message of Jesus' messengers now consists in exhorting the world to "be reconciled with God" (2 Cor. 5:18–20).

God thus reveals himself in the Christ as the God of peace, because he establishes peace between himself and us. Therefore his messengers proclaim peace, show man that God acts not against him but for him, thus ending his opposition toward God and providing him with access to divine grace (Rom. 15:33;

16:20; 2 Cor. 13:11; Phil. 4:9; 1 Thess. 5:23; 2 Thess. 3:16; Rom. 1:7 and par. 5:1; 8:6; 10:15; 14:17; Gal. 6:16; Eph. 2:14–18; 6:15). Therefore the peace granted to us by God is our shield against every corrupting influence and the principle that guides our activity according to God's will, conforming it to God's love (Phil. 4:7; Col. 3:15).

However, the notion of reconciliation does not bring into play the concept of restitution, which would cast Christ's work in terms of restoring what man had lost. Rather, the Pauline proclamation is once again shaped by the messianic message with its eschatological thrust, which consistently looks toward God's final aim and is thus elevated above all previous demonstrations of the divine government. That Christ does not merely restore man's former glory but brings it to completion is revealed with regard to reconciliation, in that it does not merely demonstrate already existing love but represents a new act of love, which is at the same time more profound and more lofty than anything God has done up to this point. Reconciliation overcomes the broken communion between God and sinners by being more powerful in effect and richer in gift than what had been forfeited and destroyed through man's enmity. Paul celebrates reconciliation not by proclaiming, "Old things have been restored," but "Now old things are done away with," not "the already existing creature is saved," but "a new creature has been created" (2 Cor. 5:17).

The concept of reconciliation is thus developed in precise analogy to that of reconciliation. God is both justifier and reconciler; in both cases, we are told not merely of a hidden internal disposition of God but an act of God providing us with a gift that changes and renews us existentially. The one by whom God justifies and reconciles is the Christ; both acts together constitute uniformly the substance of his messianic calling. They are completed in Christ, so that our part is not to effect them but to receive them. They therefore possess a universal scope and are given to the world, because they reach as far as Christ's rule extends. But since they do not become man's own as long as they remain transcendent and unconscious, they are offered to him for his personal appropriation which, because we are here confronted with a divine activity and gift, takes place through faith, and in particular faith in Christ, because justification and reconciliation are linked for us with Christ, and faith places us in communion with the Christ.

Therefore the two demonstrations of divine grace cannot be distinguished temporally, because neither their establishment for the world nor their appropriation by the individual takes place through processes that differ in time. Justification is accomplished by Christ through his cross; reconciliation occurs by faith. The enmity existing between God and man is removed immediately when man's relationship with God takes on ethical propriety, without any need for further mediation. According to Paul, it is solely sin that divides God and man. Therefore the demonstration of God's love consists in the extinction of sin, which places man as soon as it is effected in a position where he is the object of God's love. This concurs with the fact that Paul derives man's death solely from his sin, so that the removal of sin directly leads to the granting of life to man. Yet the dual phrase "justification and reconciliation" was indispensable for

Paul because both righteousness and love constitute the abiding characteristic of the divine will and thus are both manifested, and this in such a way that they are revealed and effective as a unity.

One can speak of a causal relationship between them only with reference to God's activity, because in Paul's view causal power is found solely with God. It can also not be established one-sidedly, but only in such a way that both acts provide the foundation as well as are built on the other, thus turning out to be of equal value. Paul could describe reconciliation as the major act and justification as its result. God's love is the creative motivating will producing the entire process. Because he wanted to reconcile the world with himself, he did not take its sin into account. Justification is the way reconciliation is mediated, because love preserves its perfection and truth only when righteousness is effected (2 Cor. 5:14–21). But Paul also could begin with justification as the first gift and describe reconciliation as the goal to which justification leads us. God's guilt-removing verdict, by which he turns his favor toward us, effects our inclusion into his love which is manifested upon us by the gift of the Spirit (Rom. 5:9–10).

### b) The Granting of Sonship

God's gift of inclusion in the sonship of God and our adoption as children by God relates closely to God's name as "Father" and Jesus' name as the "Son" (Rom. 8:14–17; 19:21, 29; Gal. 3:26; 4:4–7; Phil. 2:15; Eph. 1:5). Through our union with the Son of God we ourselves enter into sonship. It is brought about and made visible through the operation of the Spirit. Yet the term does not by this fact move away from Christ, because Paul closely links all pronouncements regarding the Spirit with those regarding the Christ. God assigned to his Son the many brothers who are to be conformed to his image. The idea of being conformed to his image is already used in the doctrine of justification and determines Paul's entire contemplation of Jesus. He took on our image, the image of flesh, bore in himself what sinners are according to God's verdict, and thus gave us his image, bringing us death and then life with him. The goal of his condescension to us and our metamorphosis into his image are achieved by the fact that we are now God's sons.

The appropriation of the legal metaphor "adoption" is based on the fact that Paul thereby consciously seeks to reiterate God's hostile disposition toward the human will. Therefore the notion of son is affected by the realization that we were not sons but became sons only through the free act of divine grace which makes a person a son who has not previously been one. This is why Paul preferred the forensic term "adoption" over the term "conception" derived from the natural realm. But this does not diminish sonship as if it were merely figurative or incomplete. The will of God that removes our alienation from him brings about what he desires.

### c) The Granting of Life

As Paul describes justification in terms of extirpation of guilt, reconciliation as removal of enmity, and adoption as the granting of sonship to someone who is not a son, he also presents the granting of life as awakening from death, as resurrection, given to us through the Christ, because his entrance into life from death makes us resurrected ones as well. Thereby Paul does not thereby describe a form of existence other than the one we possess through faith. For Paul, the status of resurrection, by which we are raised above the flesh and mortality, does not consist in an intrinsic power given to us but in the fact that Christ who has entered eternal life is united with us (Rom. 6:4–5, 11, 13; 8:6, 10; Gal. 2:20; 5:25; Eph. 2:5–6; Col. 2:12; 3:1–4).

Paul also expressed, through his use of the concept of Creator, that God's work upon man proceeds from God himself, that it reveals his glory, and that it thus is distinguished from man's previous condition as something entirely new. Its goal is accomplished swiftly and surely. Thus man is a new creature in Christ (2 Cor. 5:17; Gal. 6:15).[33]

## 4. Sanctification

### a) Justification and Sanctification

Along with others in the early church, Paul uses the concept of sanctification with particular frequency in order to designate what believers receive through the Christ. Their union with God separates them from what is profaned or stained and provides them with a share in God's integrity, purity, and majesty. It requires no further explanation why Paul also in the case of sanctification does not give first place to human achievement but that he assigns the act of granting us sanctification to God. Sanctification is realized by God's reconciling of the community of Christ with himself. Therefore Paul emphasized the passive phrase "you have been sanctified in Christ" (1 Cor. 1:2; 6:11; cf. 1 Thess. 5:23; 2 Thess. 2:13; this calling sanctifies: Rom. 1:7; 1 Cor. 1:2). Likewise, he used the metaphor of a "seal" to show that the community is God's possession through the Christ. The indestructible settledness of the church's union with him results from the fact that no one will be able to break God's seal (2 Cor. 1:22; Eph. 1:13; 4:30; 2 Tim. 2:19).

Paul's juxtaposition of justification and reconciliation with God's sanctifying work does not suggest that he conceived of the divine gift as divided in parts, such as that justification made help possible without actually granting it, so that it required sanctification as the second exercise of divine grace in order to make that grace effective. Paul sees in God's justifying verdict that divine will that removes everything that separates us from God and grants as our aim everything that is assigned to us. God gives to the righteous one his complete favor, so that he is made God's child and granted life. A holy person is not more than a righteous person, because there are no righteous persons whom God rejects and fails to include in his love, just as man cannot be holy without being righteous, since whoever is the object of divine wrath is profaned.[34]

---

33. He was given the phrase by language current in the synagogue.
34. The contention that Paul in Rom. 6–8 no longer discusses justification but something different, that is, sanctification, departs from his own train of thought. He expresses there what the community is given through justification. This is made clear by Gal. 2:15–21, where the same convictions are found in the identical combination as in Rom. 1–8.

In the theology of the community, the idea of sanctification predominated. This is already made clear by its designation, which it derives not from the notion of righteousness but that of holiness. In Paul's letters, too, the concept of holiness plays a more dominant role than the concept of justification. In this context it is not without significance that justification possesses the complete finality of a one-time decision, so that it describes how the community's share in God was established, while the community reminds itself of its continuing fellowship with God through the idea of sanctification. Because it is directed toward its aim in its thinking and willing, the term depicting its present condition is given first place. Yet no tension arose for Paul between the two terms by which he describes the divine grace. He considered both regarding justification and sanctification, that the completeness of divine grace is demonstrated in that it affects the concrete aspects of our lives, so that it results in the obligation to lead our lives in accordance with the divine grace. Therefore Paul can present sanctification as the goal to which the believer is brought by obedience (Rom. 6:19, 22; 2 Cor. 7:1; 1 Thess. 3:13; Eph. 1:4; Col. 1:22; 1 Thess. 4:3–7). At the same time, he sees also in justification the effective motivation for one's conduct of life, so that it produces obedience in relation to righteousness (Rom. 6:12–13, 16–23; 8:10; 14:17–18; 1 Cor. 6:9–11). Because the community's righteousness is based on faith, it determines its entire conduct, because Paul conceives of faith as a conviction that moves a man and provides him with his thoughts and will. The difference, even contrast, between the one-time, initial act of God that establishes our relationship with him and the changing, oscillating events in our history may move us deeply, so that we experience the encounter of the absolute, timeless, divine activity with our time-bound history as a profound mystery. In the case of Paul, on the other hand, it is not clear that this issue was significant for him. He never phrases his absolute pronouncements regarding our inclusion in the divine grace in abstract terms that circumvent the practicalities of what we experience and do. Likewise, he does not separate the evaluation of these processes from those foundational certainties. He rather links the revelation of divine grace with the wealth of all its consequences. He connects our individual experiences with the full depth of their source.

The terms "justification" and "sanctification" take on a particular content through the statements regarding God entailed by them. When reference is made to righteousness or unrighteousness, justification or condemnation, attention is drawn to the contrast of wills in which man stands against God, to the fact that man can subject himself to God's good will or oppose it and carry out his own will. Therefore God, who executes justice, who wants and works righteousness, pronounces his verdict against him, just as the believer, by recognizing his righteousness to be in faith, condemns his own unrighteousness as his demise, subjecting himself to the righteousness of God. In the case of the idea of sanctification, one is mindful of God's majesty, which humbles man before him who is perfect and eternal. God suspends this contrast, enters into communion with us, and makes us his own possession. But our conduct is thereby also given its controlling principle, because the New Testament certainty of God never views him merely in terms of the natural majesty of his substance or power but finds God's greatness always also in his purity and the goodness of his will. Thus the sanctified person is awarded not merely the benefit that God is not ashamed of him and bestows on him his own name, but also the obligation of avoiding what is unworthy of God, of not obscuring God's glory through his own conduct, and of not rendering himself incapable of being God's possession (to walk in a manner worthy of one's calling (1 Thess. 2:12; Col. 1:10; Phil. 1:27; Eph. 4:1; cf. 2 Thess. 1:11). The more profoundly felt the value of communion with God and the more clearly the image of God according to its personal nature in the glory of his love is placed before one's perception, the more pregnant with meaning the idea of sanctification becomes, both when it is used to express what God's grace has granted us and when it designates the means whereby we must honor God.

### b) Glorification

Because Paul, when speaking of God's grace, thinks of God turned to us indivisibly and in his entirety, he presents God's glory as it approaches us together with his righteousness, love, and holiness. This is why Paul also describes God's gracious act in terms of "glorification" (Rom. 8:30). But because in Paul's thinking glory always also entails the manifestation of the greatness of God, participation in it carries connotations of perfection, providing material for hope. Yet even at this point Paul showed how he conceived of our relationship with Christ in vigorous and effective terms. Because Christ is exalted into God's glory, our communion with him already provides us with access to glory, just as it grants us a share in eternal life (2 Cor. 3:18; 4:17; Eph. 3:16; 2 Thess. 1:12). Paul was capable of recognizing his preparation for glory in every aspect of his Christian destiny and therefore thanked God for everything.

## 5. Calling

Because Christ's relationship with the believer comes about through that word which proclaims him, the divine act of grace can also be presented thus: God called us (Rom. 1:6; 8:28, 30; 9:24; 1 Cor. 1:9, 24, 26; Gal. 1:6; 5:8; Phil. 3:14; 1 Thess. 2:12; 4:7; 5:24; 2 Thess. 1:11; 2:14; Eph. 1:18; 4:1, 4; Col. 3:15; 1 Tim. 6:12; 2 Tim. 1:9). Paul does not sever the proclamation of Christ from his sending or the word of the cross from the deed of the cross. His notion is not that God's revelation occurred at some point in the past, with it now being described; he rather considers the Word to be part and parcel of God's ongoing revelatory work. God's reconciling activity in Christ would not be truly apprehended in its entirety if we failed to consider that he established the Word of reconciliation and now brings it to man. Jesus' messianic office is acknowledged only when it is perceived that he sends his messengers, so that the world hears his grace and thus is able to believe in it (2 Cor. 5:18–20; Rom. 10:13–15). Because Paul considers the Word to be part of God's work, he thinks of the Word and the power jointly. God is with his Word; it speaks, not of the absent but of the present God and Christ, not of events that happened at some point in the past but of what he does and gives at the present time (Rom. 1:16; 1 Cor. 1:18;

2 Cor. 2:14–16). Therefore calling completely and effectively bears within itself the divine grace and is not merely its announcement or description. By calling us, God establishes communion with us and places us within the scope of his love. Therefore we are holy through his calling, and the ones he called are also those he justified.

As far as we are aware Paul did not discuss the fact that the offer of the Word and its acceptance are frequently separated in time. He speaks of God's grace-revealing call only where the offer of the Word elicited faith. What is clear is that man is rendered culpable when the Word is proclaimed in vain. Paul responded to the question of why Israel had fallen: because they did not believe, and this entails for him the weight of the attribution of guilt. He gave the same answer to the question of why he himself had fallen (Rom. 9:32; 10:16; 11:20, 31; 15:31; 1 Tim. 1:13; Eph. 2:2; 5:6; Col. 3:6). Apart from this, he bows down before the divine providence which is revealed both in the offer of the Word with faith-producing power and in the refusal of the same.

With justification and reconciliation, calling stands in a dual causal relationship. As far as our justification took place through Christ's death, it precedes calling, establishing it and being revealed in it (God's righteousness revealing itself through the gospel: Rom. 1:17). But because we participate in our justification by exercising faith, calling precedes justification and establishes it. For faith comes through the Word, which is given to us through our calling.

## 6. Election

### a) Eternal Grace

Calling and election have been aligned with each other ever since the establishment of Israel. For Paul, the concept of election became a particularly significant parallel term to justification or sanctification, because the idea of love, which God gives to us by making us the objects of his election, is linked with particular force with the recognition of God's majesty and sovereignty, by which he determines our destiny according to his own free will and authority (Rom. 8:33; 9:11; 11:5, 7, 28; 1 Thess. 1:4; 1 Cor. 1:27; Eph. 1:4; Col. 3:12; 2 Tim. 2:10; Titus 1:1). Election means that God himself according to his free, uplifting counsel establishes our relationship with himself. Thus it is linked with the idea of the eternity of the divine will (Rom. 8:28–30; Eph. 1:4, 11; 2 Tim. 1:9; cf. the "eternal house" prepared for us in 2 Cor. 5:1). What proceeds from God himself is not subject to temporal origins and destinies. The believer thus is not merely looking forward to a future in eternity but already has an eternal foundation for his communion with God. He has been foreknown by God; his image has always been within God's purview as an object of his love and a recipient of his grace.

Paul's thinking remains at a distance from intellectualism also at this point. This can be seen in the fact that he presents the concept of election in close connection with the condition of faith granted to us rather than separating it from the experience of fellowship with Christ, as if it were by itself the subject of an insight that seeks to explore the eternal source of our relationship with God.

Men who were predominantly occupied with the intellectual formulations were frequently led away from the perceptible foundation given to us for our thought and faith. Does not election name for us the primal, truly causal event? Do we not thereby lay hold of the course of history at the point where it steps out of its eternal origin and attains to temporality? If so, the pronouncement regarding our election becomes the primary doctrine and is given preeminence over all other statements regarding God. Such a use of the idea of election is foreign to Paul. He derives faith in God's deed from what occurred in time and on earth and is proclaimed through the Word. Only at the point where the received gift is said to be valued in its greatness does Paul introduce the thought that all which God wills and does did not originate in time and does not enter him from the outside but belongs to him and thus already existed before the foundation of the world.

Even more sharply than in Christology, the idea of eternity, when applied to our lives, stands in contrast with the fluctuating nature of our will and our resulting susceptibility to temptation. The believer, too, can fall. How does this relate to the eternal firmness of the divine counsel? Paul did not level the two pronouncements by a mediating consideration.

On the one side, he praised the unbroken firmness of divine giving as unconditional and indestructible. From predestination, it proceeds to man's glorification in the straight, secure course of the divine work. At the same time, he attached the attribute of guilt just as unambiguously to Christian sins and attested to their life-destroying power (Rom. 8:13; 1 Cor. 6:9–10; 2 Cor. 12:21; 13:5; Gal. 6:8; Eph. 5:5). How both coincide remains God's secret. God knows his own, knows whom he has chosen, and will lead and perfect them with unfailing justice (2 Tim. 2:10).

In practice, Paul saw the solution of the question in the fact that he merges faith and repentance into a perfect unity, so that every increase in faith comes to fruition in the defense of evil and likewise every experience of sinfulness gives increased incentive to faith. Together with the concept of election, he elevates faith to the highest degree of certainty attainable for him: eternal grace has chosen us! But the strengthening of faith also entails the strengthening of the will that yields itself to God, resists evil, and obeys in earnestness. Likewise, from his insight into our sinful and fleshly nature Paul does not infer a cause for doubt or unbelief; it rather leads him to renewed and intensified allegiance to God in whom alone we are given help in our dealing with our sin. The ups and downs of our will and the ethical dilemma plaguing us do not lead Paul to anxious deliberations regarding election or condemnation but to renewed allegiance to Jesus as the one who is our righteousness (Rom. 8:1 derived from 7:25; Rom. 1:18 providing the reason for 1:17; cf. Rom. 5:20–21).

### b) Reprobation

Election, similar to calling, indicates that God takes his own out of the world and separates them from the rest of humanity that is in bondage to sin and death. Every choice entails a dual will, which forms the basis for its decision. Reprobation is therefore the corollary to election. It corresponds to the clarity with which Paul works through the characteristic antitheses, considering in the case of justification our guilt and in the case of reconciliation our enmity with God, that with utmost seriousness he also contrasts election with reprobation with great earnestness (Rom. 9:6–24; 11:7, 15–25; 1 Cor. 1:18; 2 Cor. 2:15–16; 3:14).

He told Israel that God had rejected it. God in the liberty of his absolute power over man decides as the potter regarding clay, also preparing vessels for his wrath, by which he reveals how he judges. This cannot merely be limited to the Jewish community as a whole, so that Paul speaks only about the temporal priority of the Jews but not about the personal relationship of individuals to God or their eternal destiny. For such abstractions which designate the community without talking about its constituent members are not found in Paul. He does not speak of a reprobation of Israel that is not also the reprobation of Israelites, just as he does not speak of an acceptance of Israel which is not also acceptance and election of Israelites. "I, too, am an Israelite": by this he demonstrates Israel's election. What now happens to Israel is likewise not conceived in terms of a temporal disadvantage but is described as the work of divine wrath that brings about destruction, and this wrath is poured out against Israel's sin against God, against Christ, and against his community. Sin never merely causes temporal harm; it completely destroys the person it enslaves.

But Paul separated reprobation as little as he did election from the concrete conduct of a person as it makes up his history in time. His ideas never transcend reality and soar up into a preexistent, transcendent mystery. Those who now boast of their unbelief and resist God he confronted with God's omnipotence, which can be domesticated by no one, which even strengthens the resistance of those who oppose him, bringing out their corruption and thus achieving his divine aim while revealing at the same time the glory of his mercy. He does not detract from God's present relationship with human history and does not describe God as one who planned the punishment of the wicked from eternity. Paul's purpose is fulfilled when he brings about complete unconditional subjection to God's sovereign plan as it currently reveals itself to us, so that his absolute authority is acknowledged even when his judicial work effects hardening in evil and a consequent demise.

Paul did not consider this to diminish the gospel, because man experiences salvation precisely as he does not prevail against God but humbles himself before his judgment and his rule. If he commits himself into God's hands, he surrenders to the one who has mercy on him. Man's calamity does not result from God's rule and freedom but from his rebellion against God by which he inflates his own importance. Therefore Paul considers insight into our complete dependence upon God's will to be an essential component of the gospel.

He feared resistance or denial of the attribution of guilt on the basis of the guilt-pronouncing verdict as little as the foregoing of repentance or obedience on account of election. He told those who rejected the ethical judgment in whatsoever form and justified evil that their condemnation was just (Rom. 3:8). The firmness of the ethical Law that commands us to do good and prohibits evil he considers to be a sure possession of every person. Whoever dares to meddle with it is disobedient to the truth and acts in such a way that the revelation of the divine wrath upon him becomes necessary.

## C. God's Presence in Christ

### 1. Christ's Entrance into Humanity

#### a) The Preexistent Christ

Paul describes Jesus' divine sonship as Jesus' perfect communion with God. Christ is God's without limitation (1 Cor. 3:23). This is the root of all of Paul's thoughts, so that a breaking of this pronouncement also results in the destruction of all his statements. Therefore he always carries the idea of preexistence with himself when he thinks of Jesus, not in form of a formulaic usage and not in such a way that he sought to understand Jesus' divine nature apart from his sending, but in such a way that he reminds himself through the concept of eternity of the communion of the man Jesus with God (Gal. 4:4; Rom. 8:3, 29; 1 Cor. 8:6; 2 Cor. 8:9; Phil. 2:6–11). Thereby he preserves the sense in which Jesus himself spoke of his eternal sonship.[35]

It is frequently maintained that Paul conceived of the Preexistent One as a heavenly man. What is clear is that Paul never thought of God in other than human thought forms and that he likewise did not use material formulas, forces, substances, or the like to describe Christ. But he does not thereby blur the distinction between man and God, because he separates what he conceives of the divine activity from what man is capable of not by a fluid but a qualitative difference. It is characteristic of God that he creates, and this quality Paul attributes also to Jesus. He regards Jesus' communion with the Father as complete in that he presents him as Co-creator with God from creation. Everything exists through him. Therefore man's election takes place through him as well. Paul grounds the eternal grace turned toward man in the eternal love given to the Son by God. He never conceived of the Preexistent One's eternal existence in God in terms of rest; this is not permitted by the elementary terms by which he describes God's relationship to the world. If he had wanted to find phrases that depict existence without activity, he would have had to derive them from nature. But his conceptions of God are all taken from personal life. Here life consists in will and activity, and God's will is love which perfects communion by making the Son to be the one who accomplishes his works. Paul assigns to the Father the primary, initial activity that provides the Son with his will and power. Everything is from God; but the one by whom he acts is the Christ (1 Cor. 6:8; cf. the phrase "through Christ" in Rom. 5:9, 11; 2 Cor. 5:18–19; Eph. 1:5; Col. 1:16, 20; 1 Thess. 5:9; Titus 3:6; regarding eternal election in Christ, cf. Eph. 1:4; Rom. 8:29). Thus he proves himself to be his Father, by entrusting him with his works. The focus of all of God's heavenly and earthly activity on Christ also reveals to the community why the totality of divine grace

35. Cf. *The History of the Christ*, pp. 29–34.

coincides for it with Jesus' presence. Therefore Paul could also say regarding what Israel previously had received as divine gift through God's miraculous activity that it was given through the Christ. And therefore Christendom, when it wants to say who its God is, names not merely the one God and Father, but places Jesus beside him, whom it counts not among its own number and among what is created but worships as the one through whom everything that exists has received its share in God (1 Cor. 10:4; 8:6). Paul could therefore express with the divine name uniformly and completely what Jesus is in his relationship with God, and he did this especially when he reminded himself of his human manner and work by which he belonged to the Jews. The sonship Jesus possesses in relation to his Jewish ancestors determines only what he is according to the flesh; at the same time he also has another sonship which unites him with God so completely that he is worthy of the divine name and of worship (Rom. 9:5; cf. 1:3, 4). Therefore the doctrine of God takes on also in Paul a trinitarian form; Jesus is placed alongside the Father and the Spirit (2 Cor. 13:13; 1 Cor. 12:4–6; Eph. 4:4–6).

Phrases designed to elaborate on the Son's eternal inner dealings with the Father are not found in Paul. He did not sever the filial name from Jesus' human life and did not use it to speculate what God is in his eternal, internal divine nature. Perhaps he possessed in the term "image of God" a construct by which he conceived of the Father's eternal relationship with the Son (2 Cor. 4:4; Col. 1:15).[36] He uses it confidently, because he sees in Genesis 1:25 that God had his image by his side already prior to creation and that he created man through it. But the statements preserved for us use even the term "image of God" only to show the community what it has in Jesus. They do not say that the Father created his image in Christ but that Christ is given to us as God's image, by which we perceive what God wills and does. This phrase does not diminish Christ's personalistic character, as if he were thereby described as a divine force or nature; for participation in the divine activity is essential for Jesus' capacity to be God's image.

Paul does not dilute the clear contrast between what God is and wills and what man is and wills by contrasting two forms of human nature, that of the primal man and that of later men. He always places Jesus beside God as the one by whom God's will is accomplished. When he compared and contrasted Adam and Jesus, Paul called not Jesus but Adam the first man and Jesus the last or second man (1 Cor. 15:45–47). This statement does not provide an occasion for speculations why Paul called Jesus a man, because he describes here, as everywhere else, the work Jesus accomplished on earth. What the two men who are elevated above all other men share in common is that what they are is transferred to all others; they are different on account of what they became, and corresponding to this on account of what they were in the first place. Adam became a soul that had life, Jesus the Spirit who creates life, and he alone has this ability,

---

36. The term "image of God" could easily be used as a basic concept that comprises all of Paul's christological pronouncements. But one must not develop one's own hypothetical reconstructions in one's presentation of Pauline thought.

because, unlike Adam, he was not from the earth and of earthly material but from heaven. The fact that no reference is made here to the Preexistent One does not say anything about his kind of existence. Rather, it is said regarding the man Jesus that he received what he is not from the earth but from heaven because he comes from God, and that he is what he is through God. Moreover, by receiving his power and his office from heaven, he became the Life-giver and the Giver of the Spirit for all. Jesus' divine sonship is here described as possession of heavenly life in contrast to the earth to which the first man's existence was tied. The passage thus does not differ from Paul's other statements. He does not describe Jesus' entrance into his earthly existence in terms of a heavenly person's transformation into an earthly one but as the assumption of human form through the one who was in the form of God. Jesus' authority over all creation is grounded not in his alleged status as the primal man but in his possession of the fullness of deity (Phil. 2:6–8; Col. 1:19; 2:9). When he describes the Son as the one to whom God assigns and conforms those whom he foreknew as brethren (Rom. 8:29), he does not dispense with the fact of man's creation in the image of God but rather seeks to show the completeness and glory with which man is to become God's image. Even here Paul makes no effort to recall the condition of the Preexistent One, because he looks, in his discussion of our ultimate destiny, forward to the Risen One rather than backward to what was before the world began. This parallels his treatment of the second man whose image we will obtain by receiving a spiritual body (1 Cor. 15:48–49). Paul's persistent turning away from Haggadic, Alexandrine, or Platonic speculation is not compromised by the way in which he shapes the concept of preexistence. It rather reveals with particular clarity what Paul called faith and knowledge. Faith arises not from the divine mystery but from what we are offered as God's act and gift, and knowledge emerges not apart from the life-act but raises into consciousness what God has given to us.

It is not necessary to engage in speculation regarding the motivation for Paul's christological pronouncements; for he stated with perfect clarity the basis on which he based his faith, from which his entire theology takes shape. He possesses the foundation for his faith in the facts of Jesus' earthly life (1 Cor. 2:2). What he has in the Preexistent One or the Exalted One he knows because he saw what the Crucified One and the Risen One is. In him he sees God present and at work, and now he knows nothing of a demigod. In Jesus' love the entirety of God's grace appears, and in Jesus' kingdom all of God's authority. Because his relationship with the man Jesus was religion, he trusts him as he trusts God, that is, fully, and obeys him as he obeys God, that is, completely. Similar to Jesus' other disciples, he does not explain his communion with God in terms of natural processes, so that he attributed Jesus with possessing heavenly materials or pictured divisive powers as flowing down into him. This would not result in the Christ; this would not be the one who rules and thus wills, and who rules by grace and thus is able to love with God's love. This comes about solely through Jesus' personal union with God, and this is the basis for Paul's assurance that he is in Jesus dealing with the one who is to be venerated as Creator and Lord above all.

### b) The Beginning of Jesus' Human Life

From his participation in God's power to effect creation Jesus enters life in the flesh through God's will. God sent his Son in the likeness of flesh (Rom. 8:3; Gal. 4:4). Corresponding to the divine will is the will of Christ, who, in unity with God's will, was intent not on equality with God but on human existence: he emptied himself (Phil. 2:6–8). Paul derived the origin of Christ and his taking on human likeness not from a natural destiny or compulsion, to which God was subjected or to which he subjected Christ, but conceived of it in terms of a free act that occurs because Christ wills to be what we are, desiring human likeness and the position of slave as they characterize us. Therefore Paul views Jesus' life and death as a uniform act. Already his coming is based on his free identification with us; correspondingly, it is his goal and end that he steps freely into the position assigned by God to the sinner.

Paul did not arrive at a docetic version of Jesus' humanity, because he did not conceive of Christ's will as failed and frustrated by countervailing effects but as bringing about what he desires. He truly enters into the existence that he has chosen. After all, it is the will of the one who is given the form of God by his sonship and who carries out the Father's will. Therefore his decision effectively brings about the condition to which his sending corresponds.

No one who cherished the Christ concept in himself gave docetic inclinations a hearing, because these assign to man the office of glorifying God in mankind. That Paul finds in the Christ concept his all-controlling conviction we know from his doctrine of justification. That the man Jesus was obedient to God, that the man Jesus suffered, what man's destiny must be, that he surrendered his flesh to death, these are indispensable pronouncements for the doctrine of justification. They indicate that Paul had the strongest religious interest in the humanity and history of Jesus. Jesus' messianic office is based on his entrance into our form of existence, as are his representative activity and the significance of his death and his life for us. Paul portrayed Jesus' equality with us in stark terms when he attributed to him the "likeness of sinful flesh" (Rom. 8:3). Paul did not doubt Jesus' purity, his will and ability to bear the flesh in such a way that it did not become an occasion for sin for him, already because of the outcome of Jesus' life. But he considers it to be an essential characteristic of Jesus that he had his divine sonship in the same flesh that mediates to us our sinful passion and weakness and that he hung this same flesh on the cross, raising it to eternal glory at the resurrection. The fact, however, that he has the flesh not by natural compulsion but according to the power of his own will ensures that he possesses not merely equality with men but also that preeminence over them by which his regal status is established. Because through his will he possessed human likeness, he maintained over it an even loftier possession: he existed in the form of God.

It is commonly assumed that Paul said this merely regarding the Preexistent One and that he restricted his existence in the form of God to the time prior to his birth. In this case, the act by which he emptied himself would constitute a one-time renunciation, after which he was left with nothing but the form of man and slave. It is clear that Christ's deliberate entrance into human life does not rupture his relationship with the Father; even in the flesh, he is the Son who is known by the Father and who belongs to him. Yet this would still be compatible with the notion that he laid aside the form of God at the inception of his human life. But perhaps the other supposition is correct that Paul thought of the earthly Christ even when he stated that Jesus was in the form of God. For he follows up the statement "he emptied himself" through the second affirmation: "he humbled himself," and does not conceive of this as a one-time act that preceded Jesus' history but as his insistent will that determines his entire life up to the cross. He describes Jesus' lowliness that rendered him a slave who must obey, not as a condition but as a thing desired by him, and does not say, "he was lowly because he emptied himself," but sees in Jesus' weakness and subjection his free renunciation whose greatness he measures by Christ's possession of the divine form. Because Paul thereby included Jesus' will to the cross in the will that established his humanity, thus uniting his humanity with reference to his status as slave and his subjection (just as being God and being Lord belong together), he hardly condensed Jesus' will by which he seized not divinity but humanity, into a single transcendent moment. He rather conceived his full assumption of human servanthood to be the first act as the internal process that pervaded Jesus' entire history and lent it its greatness.

By this act of Jesus the community should realize its own task. Jesus' act establishes its love; therefore it also shows the community in what it consists and what it does. To this end, Paul hardly used the inscrutable mystery that exists prior to Jesus' human life. Of course, its result, Jesus' poverty and lowliness, are manifest to the community even when Paul thinks of the act of the Preexistent One, because he is proclaimed to it in his human form. But the passage stands in closer connection with the purpose which shapes it, as Paul describes in terms of self-emptying even that act performed by Jesus in his earthly existence. For the community, too, the selfemptying it must exercise in obedience to Christ does not consist merely in a one-time decision that evokes a transformation of its being. Rather, it issues in a persistent attitude that continually determines relationships with others. Free renunciation does not remove what one is entrusted with but orders its use. It does not render the more intelligent person a fool but means that he does not use his knowledge to shame and enslave others and that he retains fellowship with them. Whoever renounces his own privilege does not insist on receiving the honor due him, or does not exercise his authority, does not thereby become disenfranchised, devoid of honor, or weak. The passage's ethical import is not that Paul conceived of Jesus' self-emptying in terms of a loss of nature but that he thought of the selfless renunciation that did not exploit for himself what Jesus owned as his abiding possession on account of God's fatherly regard for him. If he thought thus, he predicated existence in the form of God and existence in the form of man as Jesus' simultaneous possession; yet not the former but the latter is made by him the determinative aspect of his experience and his actions.

In any case, Paul venerated in Christ an indescribable mystery, because he attributed to him both series of activity, that of divine operation and also the course of life and dying resembling us. The now common interpretation of the passage assumes that Paul sought to clarify for himself the coexistence of both attributes by way of a temporal scheme; previously he possessed deity, later humanity. But perhaps he attributed to him dual communion, upward to the Father and outward to humanity, at the same time.

The two natures subsequent ecclesiastical dogma assigns to Jesus cohere closely with the two forms attributed to Christ by Paul. Still, it is instructive regarding Paul's way of thinking that he did not use the phrase "nature" but "form." The term "nature" presented itself to all who allowed Greek traditions to influence their thought as the most meaningful and clearest category. That Paul avoided this term shows how little he was concerned to accommodate his thought to Greek conceptualities. By the phrase "nature," what is personal is traced back as a product or appearance to something impersonal which stands behind or above the personal. By using "form," an event is not placed behind the person but is conceived as that person's action; for the person provides itself with its form. For God and Christ, Paul exclusively utilizes personal categories. He considers their will to be the essence, the cause, from which their entire work originates.

The two forms assumed by Jesus are akin to the contrast of flesh and Spirit which Paul, similar to the other disciples, uses in describing Jesus. On one side, what he becomes depends on the flesh, on the other, on the Spirit. He was in the likeness of flesh and at the same time life-giving Spirit (Rom. 1:3–4; 8:3; 1 Cor. 15:45). But even through this formula, Paul does not inject a division into the Christ. As according to the pronouncement regarding Christ's two forms mankind is what is willed by deity and united with it, Jesus comes in the flesh because, not although, he is the Son of God, not against his will, but in the accomplishment of his mission. His assumption of flesh does not result in an obstacle to his revelation and rule but is the means by which he accomplishes his goal and establishes his lordship. Just as Paul does not dispute Jesus' cross but sees in it God's gracious act, he also raises no objection against Jesus' assumption of flesh but sees in it God's work. For Jesus' humiliation issues in his exaltation, and his poverty in his riches. Of course, whoever knows him merely in the flesh does not know him. For thus would be obscured what has been accomplished through the outcome of Jesus' life. After he has been raised, he is no longer in the flesh. Therefore knowledge of him likewise cannot be gained through the flesh (2 Cor. 5:16). Now he is assigned the position he has as the Son in the power of the Spirit.

Through the concept of preexistence the beginning of Jesus' life is rendered a miracle. But we have no statement by Paul regarding the event that attended his birth, just as he does not narrate a single miracle performed in the course of Jesus' ministry. This is not indicative of a critical stance toward the miracle story, because Paul indeed attributes to Jesus a divine-human ability and worships him as the one through whom everything came into being. Rather, the suppression of signs relates to the basic premise of Pauline Christology that Jesus himself is the miracle of divine grace. Compared to the miracle of his person no single element of his life possesses particular revelatory value. Of course, it must not be concluded from the epistles that what Paul related to others about Jesus was devoid of a birth or miracle narrative. We must not forget the portrait of Christ we have from Luke, the one who accompanied Paul. The supposition that Luke submitted to the church another Christology than the one he received also in his dealings with Paul dissolves the course of history into leaps of imagination.

## 2. Jesus' Human Activity

### a) The Phrases Explaining the Term "Christ"

In light of the novelty and unintelligibility of the Christ concept for the Greeks, one would expect Paul to provide parallel, explanatory terms. Indeed, some of his ideas can be subsumed under this perspective, although the formulations under this category are not numerous. That the simple and yet substantive phrase "our Lord" gained currency to explain Jesus' office was not merely a result of Paul's initiative. On the other hand, according to the available documents, the comparison of Adam and Jesus is original to Paul (Rom. 5:12–19; 1 Cor. 15:21–22).

If Paul's intention is read as seeking to portray Jesus as the ideal man and owner of all human perfections, it is distorted through modern ideas of a different orientation. Paul never used Jesus as a proof of human greatness, but viewed him solely as instrument of God and executor of the divine will. But Genesis 1–3 provides Paul with a parallel regarding Jesus' relationship with God and his resulting authority over mankind, because all of mankind depends on the first man who comes into being as a result of God's creative power, receiving its measure of life through his act. An additional and higher parallel to this is God's new creative act by which his Son originates in mankind, because his authority once again encompasses the world, renders it dependent on him, and determines its existence. The analogy thus deepens to a causal relationship. On account of what mankind became through Adam, it is given the Christ. Because Adam subjected all to sin and death, Christ is indispensable for them, and therefore he is given to them by God in such a way that he now places them in righteousness and life. But even in the comparison of Jesus with Adam, the idea of restitution is not given primary significance, according to which Christ restores what has been lost through Adam. Rather, also this train of thought is determined by the forward-looking aim of Jesus' lordship. The second man is the higher one; with a view toward him, Adam was already created and the condition arising from his fall ordained. Not only is Jesus rendered intelligible through Adam; Adam's history likewise only is illumined by Jesus' work. For it has its aim and thus its ground in Christ's mission. The first man is from the earth, because the second man will be from heaven; the first man is no more than a living soul, because the second will have the life-giving Spirit; the first man has power to subject all to sin and death, because the second will have the power to provide righteousness and life for all. The office of the Christ does not consist merely in the removal of the calamities having arisen through Adam but in the bestowal of those divine gifts through which mankind receives fulfillment.

The orientation of will and thought Paul receives through faith in Jesus resulted in a comparison of Jesus and Adam useful for the elucidation of the core tenet of the gospel. Conversely, this comparison could not become the primary vantage point that provided his preaching with its systematic framework. His longing is directed toward the coming Lord; this does not permit a mere backward look toward what was lost. Moreover, his thought has its sufficient ground of certainty in the fact of Jesus' history and does not require a higher principle above it that revealed a necessity for Jesus' mission, by which only now certainty regarding him can be had. His faith belongs to Christ because of what Christ himself is and creates and does not depend on an interpretive theory concerning God's plan for the world.

While the comparison between Christ and Adam adduces the course of history for the purpose of clarifying Jesus' office, with the designation of Jesus as the head that has preeminence over the body Paul provides a natural analogy for his messianic office. With the body metaphor, Paul did not illustrate merely the genuine interdependence between the community and its head, Christ; he rather also finds in this analogy rich material for Christ's authority owing to the head's preeminence over the body. Thus he expresses both the indispensability and indestructibility of his authority and its difference from all self-centered use of power. The head does not hinder the body's aliveness through its lordship; it rather brings it about. And still, the body's dependence on it is complete, both in that it gains by the head unity and aliveness, but also in that it works for the head and must carry out the command given to it. Christ's lordship is thus simultaneously depicted as providing blessing and obligation. That faith which lives by his grace and that love which does all for him equally find their ground in this illustration. Paul used it not merely for the community as a whole but also for individual members and instructs every believer to consider himself and his body as a member of Christ (the body of Christ: Rom. 12:5; 1 Cor. 10:17; 12:12–13, 27; Eph. 1:23; 4:4, 12; Col. 1:24; 3:15; individuals are members of Christ: 1 Cor. 6:15–16; Eph. 5:30; Christ as head: 1 Cor. 11:3; Eph. 1:22; 4:15–16; 5:23; Col. 1:18; 2:10, 19).

The difference in status between man and woman established by nature also serves Paul in explaining Jesus' lordship. He postulates a series of dependent relationships ordered by God in which one explains the other according to its ground and aim: the man stands above the woman as her head, Christ over the man as his head, and God above the Christ as his head (1 Cor. 11:3). From Christ's obedience and lordship, a man ought to learn both proper obedience toward what is over him and proper authority over what is under him. Likewise, Paul, by means of a widespread messianic simile, subjected the community as bride and wife to the Christ as her husband (2 Cor. 11:2–3; Eph. 5:22–33).

### b) God's Activity in Jesus

Paul describes Jesus' attitude toward God as obedience (Rom. 5:19; Phil. 2:8; cf. Gal. 4:4). In comparison with Adam, Paul summarizes what Jesus accomplished in the statement: he obeyed God. This is what renders Jesus' work the revelation of God. Here God's will is carried out, and God himself acts through him, not in such a way that Jesus thereby is condemned to passivity; rather, as the one who obeys, he himself is the one who acts. Therefore Paul develops two statements to describe the events constituting Jesus' history: one that presents God, and one that casts Christ as the one who acts. God sent him in the flesh, and the Christ emptied himself; God surrendered the Christ to death, and the Christ surrendered himself for us. Thereby God revealed his love for sinners, and Christ loved us while we were still sinners. God's glory raised him, and Christ rose. God will judge all, and Christ will be the judge (sending of Jesus: Rom. 8:3; Gal. 4:4; Phil. 2:7; death: Rom. 4:25; 8:32; Gal. 2:20; Rom. 5:6–8; 1 Tim. 2:6; resurrection: Rom. 4:24–25; 6:4; 8:11; 1 Thess. 4:14; Rom. 14:9; judgment: Rom. 2:16; 14:10; 1 Cor. 4:5; 2 Cor. 5:10).

Starting with Pharisaism, one could expect that the concept of merit is tied to Jesus' obedience, providing Paul with the formula by which he explained the value of Jesus' earthly ministry, in particular of his cross. His statements can easily be interpreted as saying that Jesus' task consisted in establishing merit on the basis of which God forgives the world. But this train of thought is absent from Paul, because he thinks of God even in his relationship with Jesus as the one who gives rather than as the one who receives. Nor does he consign him to passivity. The merit concept attributes to God initially a wait-and-see attitude; his servant acts on his behalf, albeit in keeping with his commandment and in love to him, but still in such a way that he must first complete his work, which God then rewards. This train of thought was not serviceable for Paul concerning Christ, because he does not become what he is, live, and die apart from God, and because he does not attain God's favor only after completing his work. The cross of Jesus is God's own act; he resurrected him in his righteousness, which condemns the world's sin, and thereby reconciles the world with himself. This is done in his own grace, which is not only elicited by the Christ but itself effects Jesus' sending and his death and exaltation. Thereby Jesus' activity takes on its orientation not merely toward the world but also toward the Father whom he loves and honors as his God and whose Son he considers himself to be even at the cross in complete filial obedience. Paul never forgets this active participation of Jesus in his mission; apart from it, the cross would not contain grace-bestowing power. But he did not separate Jesus' decision from God's decision and did not attribute the causal power given to Jesus by his royal status to Jesus alone but observes with Christ a ministry that is unified with the Father. Specifically, the Father assumes an initiating, determining function, proving the glory of his love by exalting the Son to perform his own work.

Therefore Paul made neither the concept of priest nor that of mediator the central term of his Christology and theology of the cross but used the concept of mediator to define the difference between Moses and Jesus (Gal. 3:19). While Jesus is the instrument through which God acts even at the cross, the Law stands above Moses and is not one with his will and his person but is received by him and given to him on behalf of the people. Thus Moses' role as mediator reveals that the Law is not God's final and perfect gift, because we obtain it only when God's messenger, through whom we hear God and see his kingdom, is one with him in such a way that he does not stand between God and the community but is himself God's revelation. In contrast to this, Paul, when deriving the pattern for the community's prayer from Christ's work, also used the concept of mediator for him, thus indicating that his grace possessed the same indispensability for all, but also the same salvific all-sufficiency, because one man effected redemption for all in accordance with the uniqueness of God (1 Tim. 2:5). Here Paul thinks of the distance in which people stand from God, which Jesus removed by surrendering his life for them. A similar train of thought causes Paul to subordinate Jesus' act at the cross to the notion of sacrifice when he makes it the basis for the community's unshackled love (Eph. 5:2).[37]

Because Paul extends Jesus' communion with God also to his cross, he saw in him not merely suffering but also a demonstration of divine power, not merely just the greatness of divine grace but also the profundity of renunciation and the gravity of suffering. These both lay in one and the same act, without Paul being able to detect or, according to the statements available to us, having detected in this an unevenness or contradiction in his thinking. He thus affirms both: that Jesus died our death and that we die through his death. At the cross, Jesus bears the human fate; but thereby he carries out God's will, and this provides his death with all-renewing, recreating power. Therefore the statements assigning to Jesus what is due us are transmuted in Paul to pronouncements that assign to us what belongs to Jesus. Both constitute the firmly linked elements of the same verdict that perceives God's righteousness accomplishing our salvation through Jesus' death.

It is commonly asked whether Paul's view of the Crucified One wavered in the midst of countervailing notions. Paul should, it is argued, deduce from Christ's taking man's place in death that man is set free from death and judgment through Jesus, but not that mankind is thus handed over to death. But by recognizing Christ's death as signifying the death of all, Paul indicates that Jesus' vicarious representation did not merely remain an attempt or wish, but that it accomplished its goal and procured help for mankind by which it becomes God's community. His vicarious representation would not have been able to accomplish this if it had merely led him into suffering but not into action, merely lowering him to our level without elevating us to his. That he assumes what is ours occurs from the start in the intention that he provide us with what he acquires and possesses himself. The transfer of his death and his life to us would be excluded only if his cross were grounded elsewhere than in our condition. But because he dies not because of his own guilt but because of that of mankind, his cross reveals God's verdict to mankind, and because he was sent into flesh not for his own sake but for ours, his death is the end of the flesh and the establishment of that communion with God that is brought about through the Spirit. An unevenness in Pauline thought was detected here only when a notion of forgiveness was used that was foreign to Paul. When forgiveness is thought to be effected merely by the suffering of punishment, whereby the measure of pain required for this is subject to arbitrary measurement, Christ's act is concluded with the suffering of punishment. But because Paul perceived in

---

37. The use of the Passover for the interpretation of the cross (1 Cor. 5:7) stands in close proximity to these pronouncements. But the Passover is sacrificed on the basis of divine instruction according to God's command.

Jesus a type of forgiveness that overcomes evil and establishes a new communion with God, a communion that was previously broken, he recognizes the atoning power of Jesus' death in its sanctifying power and finds it not merely in its having remitted punishment but in having effected judgment of sin. Moreover, he believes that this has truly been accomplished, because Christ's authority over the world also pertains to his act at the cross, which is why he killed and buried the sin of all at the cross.

Jesus' communion with God, which renders his act the act of God, also provides his word with abiding authority. Paul's Christology makes unmistakably clear that an issue which Jesus settled is no longer subject to debate in Christendom. The Lord prohibited divorce; nothing more need be said. Likewise, in the case of the Lord's Supper, what the Lord said is forever above dispute (1 Cor. 7:10; 11:23). Paul does not doubt that the word regarding the Lord's Supper embodied abiding divine authority both in its giving and in its obliging significance. The same christological rationale that renders Jesus' word holy for Paul also is responsible for the fact that we find in Paul only few appeals to Jesus' word. For the divine sonship and the messianic office, as Paul conceives of them, cannot be limited to the impartation of instructions or commandments but make Jesus' presence and lordship the substance of the gospel. Thus Paul, with the phrase "the gospel of Jesus Christ," designated neither merely the author of his proclamation nor merely its content but both at the same time (Rom. 1:9; 15:19; 1 Cor. 9:12; Gal. 1:7; 2 Thess. 1:8). In his attestation of Jesus' mission, which originates with him and through his messengers comes to the nations, Paul sees the means by which he brings about believing allegiance to Christ. In this, the memory of Jesus' own words also has an important place; but the decisive event remains that Christ's call reaches people through his messengers.

### 3. The Ministry of the Exalted One

#### a) Jesus' Resurrection

Theology of the cross is in Paul always also theology of the resurrection. Separated from the resurrection, Christ's death would result in the execution of justice that issues in our condemnation, not justification. Only the Living One can be Lord; yet Jesus is said to be the Lord through the name "Christ." Moreover, the name expresses his closeness to the community: death separates; communion arises through life. By rising from the dead, Jesus obtains the form of existence that constitutes the prerequisite for his regal activity. It also provides him with the gift through which he leads the community to its fulfillment. The resurrection thus provides Paul not merely with confirmation regarding what was effected by Jesus' life and death; it itself effects salvation, because neither a dead Christ nor a Christ caught up disembodied into transcendence would lend truth to the messianic name (1 Cor. 15:14–19). Through the resurrection, Christ is restored to the world in such a way that he now is with it with the benefit of his cross and thus as the one who grants the Spirit, life, and glory.

Paul saw in Jesus' resurrection God's work. That God acts here invests the event with universal significance and direct relevance for faith. Jesus' resurrection is tied to his death by a causal bond. Because Jesus proved to be obedient even unto death on the cross, God exalted him. Because he provides us justification through his death, he was raised (Phil. 2:9; Rom. 4:25). In the surrender of Christ into death and in his institution into eternal life, Paul sees a coherent divine will in which every step conditions the other. What Jesus gives to God through his will to face the cross provides the basis for what he receives from him through the resurrection, and the way in which he shapes his relationship with us through his cross provides the basis for the new relationship into which he enters with us through his resurrection. After Jesus has served to reveal God in the form of the cross, God now reveals himself to us as well through the form of Jesus' resurrection. Paul doubted the universal power of Jesus' resurrection as little as that of his cross. As the latter imparts to us our death with him, his resurrection provides us with life with him (Rom. 6:3–10; 1 Cor. 15:20–22; 2 Cor. 4:10; Gal. 2:20; Phil. 3:10–11; Eph. 2:5–6; Col. 2:12–13; 3:1–4; 2 Tim. 2:11). The mystical interpretation of the Pauline statements remains untenable also in this instance; for life is given to us because he lives, not because we ourselves awaken life in us that resembles his. Not the believer lives, but Christ lives in him, by demonstrating the fact of his own life upon the believer in that he confers life also on him.

Jesus' new kind of existence is characterized by the fact that he is now in his relationship to mankind the Spirit (2 Cor. 3:17). The renewal and glorification of his body is the work of the Spirit, so that now his body no longer prevents him from uniting himself with all in such a way that he controls their inner lives (Rom. 8:11; 1 Cor. 6:17). Therefore his resurrection brings us liberation from the flesh, because we are now connected with the one who himself no longer lives in the flesh (Rom. 7:5; 8:9). This, however, does not signify the beginning of a natureless and bodiless existence; for since we reach our goal through our resurrection, only what serves as the place and instrument of evil is removed in our nature. Thus man is guaranteed completion also with regard to his physical side.

### b) Jesus' Participation in God's Rule

In his elevated state, Christ acts in his dealings with the Father on behalf of the community by interceding for it (Rom. 8:34). This reveals that Paul did not view Jesus' entrance into heaven as a lessening of his personal life. He independently stands with the Father and effectively uses his filial relationship to benefit his own.

The Pauline notion retains its consistent unity, however, through the fact that even regarding the Exalted One his relationship to believers is portrayed much more frequently and definitively than his dealings with the Father. This is parallel to the fact that in Paul's theology of the cross it is not Christ's intercession for the world, not his dealings with the Father by which he establishes divine forgiveness for us, but his love directed toward the world and its sin-atoning power which become the main topic.

Utilizing the terminology of Psalm 110:1, Christ's participation in the divine world government is stated thus: he is at the right hand of God (Rom.

8:34; Eph. 1:20–23; Col. 3:1; Phil. 2:9–11). This sentence has greatest significance for Paul's state of faith, because on it Paul bases his confidence that the course of history does not harm us but everywhere provides us with valuable gifts. That everything belongs to Christendom results from the fact that it belongs to the Christ, to whom everything is subject, and the called ones for whom everything works together for good are those who are united with Christ (1 Cor. 3:21–23; Rom. 8:28, 35–39). But even here every tendency toward gnostic theories is cut off. The desire to distinguish God's government from that of Christ and to designate particular events in history as the demonstration of Christ's government in distinction from that of God did not arise from Pauline Christology, because that Christology is centered around Christ's perfect communion with the Father. Thus it is sufficient for the community to know that "the Christ is God's," whereby it also knows that nothing in history eludes his government or disturbs it.

### c) Jesus' Presence in Believers

Just as heaven as the place of God and his omnipresence stand side by side in the concept of God, Christ's presence with God in heaven and his presence with believers are linked. Paul did not sense any tension here; rather, it is precisely Christ's transposition into heaven that provides him with that participation in God's work which makes him present for all. This conviction possessed great power for Paul; the consciousness is always present for him that the believer is in Christ and acts in him.[38] The strength of this conviction must be noted also when we want to understand why Paul sees in the cross and the resurrection of Jesus that fact that controls the course of every person's life. The power of that history which is transferred to all is mediated through the fact that Christ places all in communion with himself and that he controls their internal and external history through his presence with them. Paul liked to use spatial imagery to express this: believers are in Christ, because he takes them in and surrounds them (Rom. 8:1; 16:7, 11; 2 Cor. 5:17; Phil. 3:9). The place provides us with the form; *where* we are determines *what* we are. Since we are in Christ, our thinking and willing is shaped and guided by him. The completeness of his communion with us finds expression in the reversal of the phrase: "Christ is in us" (Rom. 8:10; 2 Cor. 13:5; Eph. 3:17; cf. Gal. 4:19). Beside spatial imagery, Paul also used clothing metaphors, perhaps taken from baptism in which the one who is baptized puts on new clothes: "we have put on Christ" (Rom. 13:14; Gal. 3:27). This expresses that his communion with us determines our status

---

38. Regarding the origin of the phrase, see pp.28–29. The phrase "in Christ" occurs more frequently than "in God." The community is "in God and in Christ" (1 Thess. 1:1; 2 Thess. 1:1). "to rejoice in our God" (1 Thess. 2:2) alternates with "to rejoice in Christ" (Eph. 3:12). Paul frequently says ἐν κυρίῳ whereby it is not always clear which of the two completely related ideas, that of God or of Christ, stands in the foreground of consciousness. Work is done in Christ (Rom. 16:3, 9, 12; 1 Cor. 9:1; Col. 4:7, 17; 1 Thess. 5:12). Speaking and exhortation occur in him (Rom. 9:1; 2 Cor. 2:17; 1 Thess. 4:1; 2 Thess. 3:12) or through him (Rom. 15:30; 1 Thess. 4:2). Christians' dealings with one another take place in him (Rom. 16:2, 8, 22; Phil. 2:29; Philem. 16, 20; 1 Cor. 16:19; Phil. 4:21; 1 Cor. 7:39; Eph. 6:1; 5:8). Even suffering and dying occur in him (Eph. 4:1; Philem. 23; 1 Cor. 15:18). Thanks is given "through him" (Rom. 1:8; 7:25; Col. 3:17).

before God and in the world: we stand before God not separated from him but united with him; therefore we are justified and sanctified.

Christ's presence pertains to the individual and the community in such a way that it cannot be said that Paul preferred one thought over the other. Everyone is assigned his own, direct relationship with Christ, but Christ's care and lordship are likewise related to all of Christendom. Just as the individual's personal faith and entrance into the community are inextricably linked, so Christ's ministry to the individual and his connection with the community are one inseparable act.

## 4. The Presence of the Spirit

### a) The New Element in Paul's Theology of the Spirit

Paul significantly strengthened the common conviction of Christendom that the Spirit of God had been sent to it, far beyond what we otherwise find in the community. This progress does not consist in the fact that only Paul linked the ethical aim with the doctrine of the Spirit, conceiving of the Spirit as the author of the good will while previously only power was expected from the Spirit, so that one judged as pneumatic what appeared to be unintelligible and miraculous. Paul, too, conceives of the Spirit—because he is holy and God's possession—as a participant in the divine power and sees in miraculous experiences attestation of him, the value of which for the entire community is based on the fact that the miracle of the certainty of God always provides notable strengthening (1 Cor. 12:9–10, 28; 14:5, 8; 2 Cor. 12:1–4). On the other hand, that conception of the Spirit that solely desires miracles from him is nowhere evident in the documents stemming from the Jerusalem church, neither in James, where godly wisdom comes from above, nor in Jude, where the community prays in the Spirit, nor in John, where the Spirit gives truth.[39] Such ideas could not emerge in the community because it was always the Christ concept that provided it with the norm for the ministry of the Spirit. For Jesus was venerated as the one who possessed the Spirit. This guarantees that Christendom never spoke of the Spirit in terms other than that it expected from him the preparation for its work.

The new element that Paul provided for the community consists in the complete execution of the unity between the work of Jesus and the work of the Spirit. He concluded all of his statements regarding the ministry of Jesus by affirmations regarding the Spirit and provided immediate and effective substantiation for all of the former pronouncements through the latter. In Paul, the Spirit does not stand as an isolated gift of Jesus beside the other proofs of his lordship. Rather, he is Jesus' gift, which is why the doctrine of the Spirit incorporates the full wealth of relationships that result from Jesus' fellowship with us. This, of course, led Paul, like Jesus, to assign less significance to miracle than where the Spirit stands beside Christ's work as proof of the truth of the Christ. When proof takes on precedence in the ministry of the Spirit, signs carry strong

---

39. See pp. 57–58, 72–73, 83–84, 106. Regarding the term "enthusiasm," see p. 369.

weight, because they conduct proof most conclusively. For Paul, too, the Spirit reveals the Christ, but he does so by doing Christ's will in us and by providing us with his gift. Here the Spirit does not furnish further proof beyond Christ's ministry; he rather proves it by bringing about this effect. Thus the new acquisition of Paul, which he received from his faith, his repentance, and his doctrine of the cross and of justification, recurs in his doctrine of the Spirit.

Regarding the completeness with which Paul presents the unity of the Christ and the Spirit, his statement that we have drunk of the one Spirit through the Lord's Supper (1 Cor. 12:13) is instructive, because here Paul first directs attention toward the body and the blood, thus precisely to what is not Spirit, to how Jesus brought about redemption as a man. But because Paul knows of no encounter with Christ that is not also an encounter with the Spirit, we drink the Spirit in the cup of the Lord's Supper.

### b) The Fulfillment of the Gospel through the Description of the Spirit

Christ's unity with God does not result in Paul's positing a division, either for himself or for other Christians, in which he assigned one part of his thinking and willing to the Christ and another to the Spirit. By virtue of his unity with God, Christ has access to man's inner life, and man owes him all internal processes that prove to be true and good. What Paul does in the Spirit is not placed beside what he does in the Christ as a separate area. The Christ is God's; the Spirit is God's as well; thus there is unity between the effects of Christ and those of the Spirit (Rom. 8:9–10: God's Spirit indwells us; we have Christ's Spirit; Christ is in us; all three pronouncements describe the same state of affairs). The concept of God does not diverge dualistically, as if another divine will revealed itself in the Spirit than in Christ. The completeness of the work wrought by Christ in the community excludes that the effects of both are placed side by side, perhaps in a temporal scheme, according to which one follows the other. The community belongs to the Christ entirely and forever, and beyond him nothing exists for it.

Paul expresses the unity between Christ and the Spirit by linking their ministries through a complete and thus dual causal relationship. First God sent the Son, then the Spirit of his Son on the basis of what the Son brought to mankind. The Spirit's presence with mankind is grounded in the sending of the Christ. He is the foremost possessor of the Spirit, and therefore he is also given to believers according to the same Law according to which his death is their death and his life is their life. Thus it is the community of the Christ that has him, not the pagan, who is mindlessly driven toward dumb idols, or the Jew, who curses Jesus (Gal. 4:4–6; 1 Cor. 12:2–3; 2 Cor. 3:16–17). Once again, the work of Christ for the community has as its prerequisite the work of the Spirit, because the Spirit brings about the confession by which the community witnesses to Christ's lordship, effects faith by which it has his grace, and elicits love by which it lives for him and does God's will. He unites believers to a community and equips it with the powers by which it performs its service as the body of Christ (1 Cor. 12:3; 2 Cor. 4:13; Rom. 15:30; 1 Cor. 12:13; Eph. 4:3; Phil. 2:1).

This, however, does not render the doctrine of the Spirit a mere repetition of the pronouncements describing the presence of the exalted Christ. It would misrepresent the facts of the matter to say that Paul, when speaking about the Spirit, merely redesigned his statements regarding the Christ. True, what Paul says regarding the Spirit aims at praising solely the grace of Christ without leading him away from him or to a higher plane than him. But in his own view, he would not yet have expressed the gift of Christ, if he could not have referred us to the Spirit. The relationship remains similar to that of Paul's affirmations regarding God and Christ. Christ's grace is nothing other than God's love; with every word regarding the Christ, Paul merely describes what God grants us. But Paul does not consider his proclamation of the Christ to be merely a repetition of his teaching regarding God, developed merely in order to furnish religious language with a dynamic quality. According to Paul, one stands in a markedly different relationship with God depending on whether one knows Christ or does not know him. With Christ's presence, not merely religious imagination and language changes, but real participation in God. It is the same with his witness to the Spirit: he thus signals a marked change in his relationship with God.

The Spirit's importance for Paul arises from the fact that, through the Spirit, Christ's sending truly becomes the manifestation of divine grace. If he had attributed to Christ a self-centered will to rule, he would never have arrived at the doctrine of the Spirit. But he finds in Christ that will of God to be active which is directed toward us, which esteems us and draws us into communion with him. The sending of the Spirit is the realization of this and thus also its proof. Christ stands over the community as the Lord to whom the community must look up, and even when Jesus encompasses it, so that the believer is in him, he simultaneously demonstrates precisely through this his majesty. This is an essential characteristic of his office, not its obfuscation or lessening. God's grace condescends to man from his majesty and holiness. Whoever calls this imperfection or calamity does not think in Pauline terms. Nothing other than this is appropriate to the relationship between God and us. But grace really condescends to man and thus gives him a possession that comes from God (Rom. 5:9). God's giving is genuine and complete because he places his gift into man in such a way that he himself has it. The entrance of divine love into our own being, its presence and operation in us, by which it becomes the driving force of our own impulses—this is prepared for us by the Spirit; this is what the Spirit in us is. This is how Christ is experienced as the messenger of grace, and this is how faith in him takes on firm roots and conclusive completeness.

Thereby the vigorous development of the concept of "the flesh," which is the characteristic of Pauline devotion, finds its positive conclusion. The dependence on natural impulses characteristic of our spiritual lives is met by another power shaping us—the Spirit. For the one who has clearly understood what the will rooted in the flesh desires, a spiritual will is manifest that cannot arise from the flesh, because it does not aim at its preservation and cultivation but is directed toward God. Paul spoke of no other characteristic by which the operation of the Spirit can be distinguished from the human will. In his outlook, man perceives in what he thinks and desires which power moves him, whether his will belongs to him or is given to him by God. If a person has recognized and judged the fleshly nature of his will, he now also recognizes gratefully that he has been given, through God's effect on him, a will that is oriented toward God (Gal. 5:19–22; Rom. 8:5–8).

Thus justification, reconciliation, and institution into sonship find their completion, because now divine love proves to be not merely an attitude or promise or a preparation for our future salvation but moves on toward its provision, establishing fellowship with us which shapes our existence. In such a way believers truly appear as righteous persons and as sons (Rom. 8:4; 1 Cor. 6:11; Gal. 5:5). This also renders Christ's path to the cross completely intelligible. Because the community is to live through the Spirit, it is the office of its Lord and Creator to die for it and to be raised for it. As long as he himself still lives in the flesh, what is promised, that is, the Spirit, is not yet available. He becomes the community's possession, when Christ judges sin in the flesh and produces in himself heavenly humanity through his exaltation. Now he is the Spirit, and his entire dealings with the community are mediated through the Spirit, and what comes from him is characteristic of the manner of the Spirit. Through its connection with him, the community is no longer in the flesh (Gal. 3:13–14; Rom. 7:5–6; 8:1–9).

Thus Christ becomes the liberator of men. For through the Spirit he receives his own knowledge of God and his own love for God. In Paul, the grace of the Spirit becomes visible not as an individual human function but in everything, in knowing and in willing. To the former he assigns a share in God's thinking; to the latter a share in his love (2 Cor. 3:16–18; 1 Cor. 2:10–16; 12:4–11; Eph. 3:16). That is why the Spirit is the mark of sonship. For the son receives from the father a life and life force of his own. To have a life that originates from God and that is unified with God, that is what it means to have the Spirit.

### c) The Unification of the Divine Spirit with the Human Spirit

The connection in which the Spirit enters with us is complete. Paul thus never spoke of two spirits in the believer, a divine and a human one. What is present in us as the source of our inner life is conceived of as a unity.[40] But this does not result in separation from God for the Spirit who enters man; he remains the Holy Spirit, one with God. Paul searched for no particular expression to describe the mystery that arises here. Because it is essential for the doctrine of the Spirit that it conceive of the Spirit as an effective, productive power which provides insight and will and which shapes the person, statements that speak of him as of a power are inevitable. But one must not for that reason speak of the Spirit, according to Paul, as impersonal, as an invisible, fine substance or a kind of higher natural force.[41] For according to Paul, the Spirit does not separate from God but is God's Spirit, Jesus' Spirit, and thus elevated above any com-

---

40. When the Spirit operates through a number of prophets, the plural "spirits" is used (1 Cor. 14:12, 32). This further reveals that the Spirit is considered to be one with the person he influences.

41. For the argument that Paul did not conceive of the Spirit as a fine luminous substance, see pp. 210–11.

parison with powers or substances. At this point naturalism does not suddenly intrude into Paul's concept of God. His consciousness retains its complete personal clarity. Therefore the Spirit is the one who knows and desires, and his gift in us is life that encompasses thinking and willing in unity.[42]

This is borne out by the fact that Paul never taught a natural connection on the part of the human self to a Spirit that seizes him from above, as if an overpowering effect of proportions commensurate to natural powers elevated our human existence and merely evoked a divine impulse. It would have been the end of pneumatology for Paul not to subsume it under grace as the determinative generic term and to sever it from Christ. But in Christ, the Spirit produces true humanness. Therefore his presence also does not remove the necessity of ethical decision, of the susceptibility to temptation, and of the possibility of sin from the believer. Through the reception of the Spirit he is rather given the dual opportunity either to be in the flesh or in the Spirit, to order his conduct according to the flesh or according to the Spirit, to obey the one or the other. We can trustingly sow seed to both, with different outcomes. Here, too, an obligation arises from the gift. What matters is not merely possession of the Spirit but walking in the Spirit, to act and to live as the Spirit's guidance shows us. Paul did not doubt the correctness or clarity of this guidance. The joyfulness of his Christian life and apostolic office depends on the fact that the one statement "walk in the Spirit; live as the Spirit shows you to live" can express the entire Christian duty, the entire ethic, and all corollaries of salvation. Obedience to the Spirit provides complete protection against sin. And yet the Pauline doctrine of the Spirit knew nothing of a means of doing without the good will. To the contrary, with that doctrine Paul creates, together with the highest expression for divine love, also the most serious designation for our responsibility and for the importance of the correct use of our will (Rom. 8:13; Gal. 5:16–17, 25; 6:8).

The exploitation of the doctrine of the Spirit for boundless individualism and religious hermitism appears to be inevitable, because it portrays the divine as real and perceptible in the consciousness of individuals. Such distortions are, however, excluded in Paul, because he conceives of the Spirit in all sincerity as God's Spirit and thus also as Christ's Spirit. God's grace and work are corrupted when man strives for nothing but an enhancement of his own life. As little as the Spirit is available solely for man's happiness—it is there rather to enable him to participate in Christ's suffering and death—so little it is present in order for man to perfect himself according to a particular method and to fulfill his ego. Power and service are also here one, and the manifestation of the Spirit does not occur merely for its recipient but for all, because it must glorify the one who gave him. God's work retains its universal scope also in the sending of the Spirit and, by moving and guiding the many, produces, not religious egotists or heroes, but the community (1 Cor. 12–14; Eph. 4:3–6).

---

42. If the concept of power had had priority in the Pauline doctrine of the Spirit, Paul would not have developed trinitarian formulas. Paul did not juxtapose the Father, the Christ, and "a power."

Because Christ's promise aims at perfection, the doctrine of the Spirit is not the end of the Pauline gospel. Man's entire condition is not yet renewed by the internal process effected in believers by the Spirit. Paul retains his anthropology without distortion, which includes not merely spirit but also body, not merely internal processes but also nature and appearance. This dimension of our being still remains untouched by the Spirit: the body is dead, simultaneously with the fact that the Spirit is life. What is internal still lacks form; the treasure given to us by God is found in earthen vessels. The Spirit is thus no substitute for hope; he rather establishes it, the kind of hope that longs for Christ's coming, whereby those who have in the Spirit the firstfruits of God's gifts will be given the revelation of their identity as children of God, because their bodies will experience redemption at that time as well. In this direction, too, the Spirit works closely with Christ and establishes his work, not only by guaranteeing it as a downpayment, because the gift already received by us secures its completion, but also by evoking in those who suffer from the pressures of the world sighs that appeal for God's help. He also intercedes for the saints before God (Rom. 8:10, 23–27; 2 Cor. 4:7; 5:5, 7; 1:22; Gal. 5:5).

## 5. The Work of Christ in His New Revelation

### a) The Goal of Jesus' Rule

Paul's statements regarding the return of Christ use the same axioms that exist for the unified coalescence of wills between the earthly and the exalted Christ and the Father. Christ even then acts on his own initiative, but in such a way that he is the revealer of God, because he accomplishes God's work. Then he will do away with all powers that currently rule the world, both those who stand in opposition to God and those who administer an office assigned to them. But even this regal activity of Christ Paul described as obedience by which Christ executes the commission given to him. Because he will assuredly attain his aim in the power of God, his rule will come to an end. Subsequent to his return, Jesus will reign as king until death has been abolished, and when God has subjected all things to him, the wonderful conclusion will follow that Paul lends expression in his prophecy: Christ's adoration of God, the subjection of the one who is King over all to the one who subjected everything to him, including the universe of the living, to whom he brought liberation from guilt and death. Now God will be all in all (1 Cor. 15:24–28).

Were the critics of Paul correct, who saw here an inconsistency in his Christology? Elsewhere, they contend, Paul sees in Jesus the one who reveals God, because God works through him; but here he is placed in a position of independence in relation to God that requires a subjection to God in order for God's domain to extend to all men, and he places all persons in a condition in which they are completely God's work. Paul, however, never applied the notion of fusion to Jesus' relationship with God. He always conceived of it as love, and love is for Paul just as completely distinguished from the suspension of one's own life as it is distinct from a self-centered exercise of power. Because Jesus received his office from God's love, he performs it through his obedience. This is how

Paul conceives of him even at the final, highest stage of his vocation, at his eschatological mission, when he does not walk the path of death but operates in the sphere of all of creation as the giver of life. Even then, his rule is service, execution of an office given to him by the Father, and his service does not remain a vain, inconsequential effort but accomplishes his goal. This goal, in turn, does not consist in binding mankind to himself but in leading it to God and in uniting it with God in such a way that there no longer stands anything between God and humanity. Therefore, according to Pauline Christology, when Christ has fulfilled his commission, there can be no result other than the glorification of God, who is the author of all the authority and glory of Christ and of all of life's creation in union with him.

The concern that this dethrones Christ is not a Pauline thought, because he does not express concern for the Son when he bows before the Father. Paul looked with concern at all arrogance by which man elevates himself, fearing that such boasting would corrupt man; but he was never concerned for the one who subjects himself to God. For his God is not an abyss into which one might sink or a primal being in which one could lose oneself, but the Father of love with whom the Son who glorifies him can be perfectly secured. Nevertheless, Paul does not address what will happen then. He accompanies Christ in his prophecy to the completion of his office. Once he stands there, he lets the Son celebrate the greatest moment, an act of adoration such as the universe has not yet known, and breaks off.

## b) The Expansion of Jesus' Rule

One may call Paul's expectation chiliastic, if the essential element of chiliasm is seen in the distinction between Jesus' return and the final consummation. For Paul expected both from Jesus' return and from the conclusion of his regal activity a manifestation of his life-giving power. The second coming brings resurrection to those who belong to Christ. Before the conclusion of his rule comes the removal of death as the final adversary and destroyer of the divine work. The removal of death creates life. After this life has attained complete manifestation through the Christ, God is now all in all (1 Cor. 15:24–28). By not only bringing resurrection to his community but also removing death in an even more far-reaching sense, Jesus is conceived of as the giver of grace even in his eschatological office.

This form of hope also appears in the statement that Christ fulfills not merely the hope of Christendom but all creatures' longing for freedom. While now waiting and longing extend persistently throughout all stages of life, since creatures still must sigh and wait for a liberty that is yet future—even though they, as creatures, already possess a relationship with God as those who came into being through the will of God—and since Christendom also waits and sighs, and since even the Spirit participates in this sighing, the revelation of the Christ brings this entire suffering to an end and brings the gift for all this hope (Rom. 8:19–27). Thus the life that he brings about in his glory transcends Christendom, which is distinguished from that which is created by already possessing the Spirit and thus only needing to wait for the redemption of their bodies. Because Paul profoundly felt the misery caused us by our bodies, he perhaps perceived a painful bondage in the entire realm of nature, whose end he expected at the appearance of Christ. And yet his statement cannot be limited to the material part of creation. Suffering, waiting, hoping is primarily a function of being human, and to human beings belongs first of all the name "creature." Paul promised fulfillment for the longing of mankind.

The extension of grace beyond the small currently gathered community of Jesus did not result for Paul in consternation but constituted a confirmation of the doctrine of justification that was predicated upon faith; for it directly substantiates everything revealed by the salvific power and majestic greatness of Jesus. Paul would never have recognized as faith an envious insistence on the church's privilege, thought to be jeopardized when Jesus' lordship created life beyond its sphere. The thought: If Jesus saves those who have not yet been reached by his good news or who have not yet been brought to him during their earthly sojourn, it is unnecessary to believe in him, would be foreign to him. For Paul saw in faith not an arbitrary achievement of man which he would have preferred to do without but which he now accepts out of some form of compulsion. Rather, he recognizes in faith the only right attitude toward what the Christ did and is. Not to believe is sin, and thus completely out of the question. The one who has been brought to faith can only be thankful, and the more gloriously Christ's grace is revealed, the more he knows whom he believes and how great a gift he has received through his faith.

### c) Christ's Judgment

Paul describes the judging work of the Coming One not merely as the granting of reward to those who served God but also as the exercise of divine wrath upon those whom he rejects (Rom. 2:5–10; 2 Cor. 5:10). He placed the dual outcome of his judgment beside the absolute statements regarding the life-bringing impact of Christ that overcomes all of God's adversaries, does away with death, and sets creatures free. For he was at the same time certain of the eternal validity of justice that rejects wickedness and of the sovereignty of divine grace that fulfills its will. Beyond this he does not search for insight, so that one cannot speak of a particular teaching of Paul at this point beyond the norms valid in the entire community. No break in confidence in Jesus resulted for him from the fact that Jesus' renewed appearance brings about the execution of justice; for he did not view the activity of the Returning One as opposition toward the grace demonstrated by him toward mankind. Its offer is accompanied even now by the execution of justice, and when Christ exercises his judgment at the appointed time ahead, the community will experience him as its Savior in the utmost sense, because it will at that time not only perceive the power of his death but also the power of his life (Rom. 5:9–10). Paul here forms an escalating conclusion that expects much more from life than from death. At that time the community will perceive in Christ not only God's righteousness but also God's glory, which grants to it glorification.

Christ's juridical authority encompasses both the angels and human beings, and his community's closeness to him shows itself also in the fact that it participates with him in the execution of justice (1 Cor. 6:2–3). Paul thus used for Christ's eschatological activity the same perspective that shapes his verdict regarding his cross and his resurrection: Christ provides his own with a share in what he is. As he will be judge and king, so will they. The fact that Paul also assigns to the community a part in the judgment of angels may constitute an expansion of the earlier eschatological picture, in connection with the fact that he related the history of Christendom as a whole closely to the supernatural spirit world. Yet Jesus' words had already provided the community with the idea that Jesus' disciples would be active with him also in his judicial function.

Still, Paul thereby did not diminish the conviction that Christ's judgment extends to the community itself. The community must not think of itself as merely executing judgment; it must be mindful of the fact that it must pass through judgment itself. The benefit it should derive from this expectation is the elimination of all self-exaltation, which dares to justify itself, and of all elevation above others that seeks to anticipate Christ's verdict (1 Cor. 6:2–3). The simultaneous validity of both statements, that the community is judged by Christ and that it judges with him, is made easier through the applicability of a temporal distinction. When Christ comes, his own come to life first, which is linked with their judgment, because the circle of his own is thus determined and revealed. Subsequently, they will judge with Christ and rule, just as they live with him.

### d) The State of the Resurrected

Paul included in his hope everything that he prized in earthly circumstances as God's work. He will stand before the judge as the apostle of his congregations, and his congregations as those called by Paul, and he hopes that they will at that time be occasion for each other's glory. The same can be said regarding all who are related to each other by the word of Christ and the community of faith. All relationships between believers receive through this an eternal significance. The one who is related to his slave as brother stands in an eternal fellowship with him (2 Cor. 1:14; 1 Thess. 2:19; Phil. 2:16; Phlm. 15). But Paul does not abandon that word of Jesus which elevates the state of the resurrected ones above their present condition. He does not merely cast eternal life as a continuation of one's earthly existence but made it clear to the community through the idea of transformation that it must not merely hope for restoration of what death took away from it but was to long for a higher life (1 Cor. 15:35–36). Therefore he rejected all pronouncements regarding the present condition of life that were derived by way of inferences from the present form of existence. As little as one may judge from the seed what the growing plant will look like, so little can the resurrection body be described from looking at our present bodies. Paul strengthened this idea by uniting it with Christology and pneumatology. Jesus is a new human being, not limited to the image of Adam, but placed into a relationship with God that made him heavenly. By linking the community's longing to himself and by promising it to be conformed with himself, he lifts its hope beyond what it already sees and has in its present condition. Subsequently, it experiences with the possession of the Spirit the sharp, painful rupture between spirit and body and has its life as an internal treasure still resisted by dead corporeality. It is to recognize in its lack and need what it may hope for. Instead of the body that serves as a house and instrument of the soul, it will receive a body that is able to serve the Spirit. Among the things that distinguish the present from the future body is particularly the belly, in view of the misery arising for mankind from the passions emerging from it (1 Cor. 6:13). Paul lent clear expression to this conviction through the statement that even those who are alive when Christ returns will not enter the eternal community the way they are but will be changed. Thus he states that all have their aim not merely in the preservation of their present life but beyond this in a higher form of life, however their life story relates to the revelation of Christ.

As he retains in this regard the equality of the goal for the living and the dead, he also maintained that death does not shortchange the dead in their participation in Christ's new revelation. Rather, they will first be raised and translated to the Lord in the air (1 Thess. 4:13–18). This is one of the few features of Paul's image of the future by which he provides a description destined for imagination, beyond the terse, serious designation of the aims forming the will. But after he pictures the multitude of those raised from the dead reaching Christ, so that they do not only meet him on the earth but already in the air, he breaks off his presentation. We do not hear what happens thereafter, whether Christ remains with them in the air and orders earthly matters from there or whether he descends with them to the earth. An anticipatory presentation of eschatological conditions is missing.

The same kind of reservation can be observed in Paul when he deliberates on what kind of fate death will deal him. It may be expected that he feels compelled to develop a doctrine that seeks to link the state resulting from death with resurrection; but he does not have it. He was clearly aware of the possibility that he might die through the increasing bitterness with which the synagogue conducted its battle with him. In view of this possibility, he maintained that the greatest gift he could receive was that translation into eternal life which he calls "being clothed," the transformation of those who see Christ come. Yet, even the other possibility, that his tent would be taken down and his clothes removed, is not a terrifying prospect, because the house in which he will live is prepared for him in heaven by God's eternal grace, not at some point in the future but immediately. However, he does not assign primary significance to his reflection on God's eternal buildings and the heavenly city of God but elevates above this thought the one that dying will bring for him union with Christ. Thus it became for him an object of longing that competed with his will to live (2 Cor. 5:1–9; Phil. 1:20–24).

The connecting line between this form of promise, which promises to the individual a heavenly house with Christ, and its orientation toward the perfection of mankind, which is expressed by the concept of resurrection, was not drawn by Paul. This is one of the most peculiar proofs of the power with which he kept his conceptual work subject to the rule of faith, so that he extended it only to the extent that he needed it to substantiate the correct will. He must be able to die in peace and be ready to die daily. Therefore he reminded himself of the perfection of Christ's grace that did not allow him to be orphaned in death but prepares a dwelling for him. But he must be able to believe not merely for himself but also on behalf of mankind, for the sake of Christ's universal office, for God's sake, whose rule makes the earth his possession. For this he needs the assurance of resurrection, and it remains the basic message of his eschatology.[43]

### e) The Promise for Israel

Paul instructed the community to expect prior to Christ's arrival the rule of the man of sin, and it appears that he related the Antichrist to Jerusalem and that he saw in the Roman emperor the power that still hindered Judaism's opposition toward the Christ (2 Thess. 2:1–12; cf. 1 Cor. 10:13; 7:26–31). Thereby he hardly introduced new ideas into the community's expectation; by this interpretation of Daniel's prophecy and by the conviction that the near future would bring the severe struggle with the most wicked outbreak of sin, he presumably was in agreement with prophecy current in the community. It did, however, take on particular significance through his dispute with the Jews. Nevertheless, the consideration that Israel's sin moved toward the final, worst revelation of evil did not weaken his confidence in the divine promise for Israel. He saw its confirmation primarily in the fact that Christendom did not arise through a completely new beginning but that it was linked with Israel through the first group of believers. Moreover, he found in Scripture a promise for Israel that had not been completely fulfilled through the calling of the remnant that had now been brought into the community, particularly in prophetic words that promise Israel the forgiveness of her sins. At first, of course, the complete break with the synagogue is inevitable, and the church's independence the only proper goal. But it must not forget that God is connected not only with it but also with the Jews through a communion which he invested with his unfailing faithfulness (Rom. 11). But even at this juncture, he did not use prophecy to construe a system. When divine aid for Israel would enter the series of final events, whether before or by means of Jesus' appearance, and how the national, natural element in Israel's constitution related to the transcendent manner of life beginning with the resurrection, and whereby Israel's separation from the nations would be revealed—these are questions Paul did not entertain. Thus his statements regarding Israel's future differ widely. According to one verdict, Israel, on account of her resistance toward God, finds itself close to the final, worst revelation of satanic power and human arrogance; according to the other verdict, Israel's election through God's perfect grace is irreversible. Paul expects the worst from the sin of the Jew and the greatest from divine mercy, and both expectations are based on the cross of Christ. From its vantage point any anticipation of the future is difficult, because Christ's death made clear that the struggle unfolding in world history ends in an absolute contrast that reaches

---

43. Second Cor. 5:1 does not constitute a change of 1 Cor. 15 or even a contradiction of the confidence expressed there. Paul never promised himself or others that they would see Christ alive without dying. Rather, he always considers the possibility that he lives or dies unto the Lord, that life or death may befall him.

into the afterlife. At the same time, however, Christ's cross reveals the glorious grace that ends the old order with creative power and produces a new beginning that is able to renew even dead Israel and to fulfill the promise made to her. The contrast between those two expectations served Paul as a measure for the greatness of the riches and the wisdom of God.

## D. The Church

### 1. Faith

#### a) The Genesis of Faith

By showing the community that faith is the foundational act of its devotion, Paul protects it against the understanding that it provides itself with its own godliness by way of self-effort, so that its religiosity constitutes its own product. For faith receives its content and its salvific power through God's work. To be sure, Paul never spoke in detail about faith arising in man through God and how this happens. He maintains that God has given faith to the community; that the Spirit is the Spirit of faith, who engenders faith not merely in those upon whom Christ's life becomes manifest, but also in those who must die with him; and that God's righteousness reveals itself for the purpose and with the result that faith comes about (Phil. 1:29; 2 Cor. 4:13; Rom. 1:17). That the idea is not expressed more pointedly results from the fact that faith's dependence upon the faith-producing message already makes the believer the recipient of the divine gift, and regarding this dependence on the part of faith Paul placed a major stress on man's dependence on the divine activity. Apart from hearing there is no faith; but for them to hear requires the sending of messengers, which is God's act. Faith came as a result of Christ's coming (Rom. 10:13–17; Gal. 3:2, 23–25). It arises from the true apprehension of his greatness and goodness rather than from the exertion of the human will. Moreover, by placing faith and work in antithesis, Paul already ensured that it cannot be derived from our activity. The application of the merit principle to it was excluded because Paul removed it from the sphere in which it was considered particularly legitimate, that is, in the area of works.

The affirmation that faith is God's gift has nothing to do with the idea that it can be in us apart from our perception or volition. Assurance is predicated upon knowing, and confidence on one who trusts. That faith is a decision by which a person apprehends God's word and desires God's grace, Paul vividly emphasized in the description of faith that Abraham exercised in God. In being seized by God, we seize him in faith (Rom. 4:17–21; Phil. 3:12). Because the proclamation of Jesus brings about faith, the community's devotion takes on two characteristics: it foregoes any attempt of concocting religion, and it simultaneously moves man personally, and thus with his entire thinking and willing, to God.

Paul provides no discussion of the processes engendering faith, as far as they take place within the life of the soul. There is thus no instruction concerning how one makes oneself or another person believe, which method most assuredly evokes faith, which internal processes facilitate or prevent its emergence. The only thing Paul has to say about this is the statement that faith can arise only— but there certainly—where the assurance of God is united with the proclamation of Jesus. Whoever accepts his word as the word of God believes. When something else is substituted for the events that manifest themselves to the consciousness as divine, when, for example, rhetoric or speculations are used to replace Spirit and power, then the emergence of faith is hindered (1 Thess. 2:13; 1 Cor. 2:1–5; 1 Thess. 1:5). The certainty of affirmation and the completeness of surrender, which are the essential characteristics of faith, are possible and legitimate only in relation to God. Therefore faith is made difficult or impossible through everything that obscures the revelation of God in the community's word and work and that directs attention toward man rather than toward God.

The supposition that Paul seeks to evoke faith through a strong emotional appeal is not a result of observation but of the exegete's need to make the emergence of faith intelligible for himself. It cannot be demonstrated that Paul himself ever had this need. The only thing that is clear is that he sees a perfect correspondence between the content of the message and its faith-producing effect, and further, that he counts in his proclamation on the activity of God that neither requires nor is capable of analysis or description. What Paul considers mysterious is not that faith arises from the call that issues from God's grace, but rather that unbelief opposed it. Even this turns out to be an entirely transparent fact, when he remembers the god of this age and his blinding of the minds of unbelievers (Gal. 1:6; 2 Cor. 4:3–4). Because faith always entails obedience, not in such a way that it results as its consequence, but such that man subjects himself in faith to the truthfulness and righteousness of God, man is free at any time, through his false attitude of the will, to prevent faith in himself and to be unbelieving (Rom. 1:6; 10:3, 16; 16:26).

### b) The Individual Determination of Faith

Paul demonstrated the integrity of his faith by heeding the individual parameters of faith and by teaching the community to respect this. Faith is said both to be one and the same for all and thus to unite the community, and to have its particular form in everyone. The former results from the fact that everyone's faith is devoted to the same giver and the same grace; thereby it produces equality in the community. It receives its distinctness from the fact that the believer must turn to Christ with his own perception and volition, that is, in an individual determination (on the one hand, Eph. 4:5; Gal. 3:26–28; Col. 3:11; on the other hand, Rom. 12:3; 1 Cor. 12:9; Rom. 14:1, 22–23).

Paul did not merely attribute these differences to human handicaps and did not view them as abnormalities which distorted the community; he rather sees in them God's sovereignty, which assigns to everyone his own measure of faith, which is why there can also be those in the community who have received faith in special measure as the grace gift characteristic of them. Of course, lack or weakness of faith is also caused by the sinful conduct of believers, so that they fall foul of an ethical verdict. Moreover, growth in faith is made the task of all, and the unity of faith is, similar to knowledge, the aim to which the community is to aspire (1 Thess. 3:10; 2 Cor. 10:15; Eph. 4:13). Deficiencies in faith can be the result of confused thinking; in this case, they are overcome through instruction. Or they can be related to deficiencies in the conscience that stem from false practice and produce fear of God and Christ instead of confidence; in this case, growth in faith is effected by the exercise of ethical sincerity.

Paul expressly defended the contention that those who are weak in faith must not be pushed out of the community but be allowed to live in it undisturbed by attack or contempt, albeit under the condition that they also do not impose their own measure of faith on others or judge them because they do what their own faith does not allow the "weak" to do. The assumption that can and must speak of faith, albeit of weak faith, rather than of unbelief, consists in the fact that even weak faith relates a person's entire life to Christ. Even weak faith must subject itself to the principle that no one lives for himself. If this principle is rejected and self-centered desires are given free rein, faith has been denied and one's rightful place in the community has been forfeited (Rom. 14).

Paul's profound interest in the individual diversity of measures of faith issued from the fact that he gained from faith the boundary between sin and proper action and thus the verdict regarding everyone's proper task. This was a result of the fact that he rooted our righteousness in our faith; thus man does not sin if he acts in faith and has the conviction that he is authorized to his act by God and does it in communion with the Lord. When he exceeds his confidence in the divine guidance and aid granted to him, on the other hand, religious arrogance sets in, and when he ignores his inner sense of right and wrong, disobedience takes place. Each can find the controlling principle for his actions in faith only when he keeps himself free from the imitation or illusion that belongs to an alien faith, and when he adopts circumspect sobriety regarding the extent of his own confidence (Rom. 12:3; 14:23).

### c) Resistance against Evil

The confidence with which the believer knows himself to be given righteousness and childhood of God by Christ does not cripple the resistance against ethically reprehensible allurements, which continually arise from within ourselves and from our dealings with others. Rather, the believer receives through the absolute pronouncements "dead to sin, alive to God" the norms for his conduct by which he makes his decisions (Rom. 6:11–23; 8:12–14; 12:1–2; Gal. 5:16–25). The doctrine of salvation thus issues in all of its statements in Paul in formulations denoting obligation, although it does not consist of them exclusively or begin with them. The community's devotion is grounded in the work of God effected by Christ, through which it is completely removed from what God rejects. Thus it remains in fellowship with Christ only when it becomes obedient to the grace granted to it by a continually ongoing decision of the will.

On the other hand, it is equally clear that the believer's confidence is not shaken by his deficiency and impurity of his will, because his confidence does not come by the purity and perfection of his will but by the condemnation of his own conduct and the true apprehension of the divine will and work. What has taken place within him to this point is not its entire content. Divine grace transcends our present, and its verdicts and promises extend to our eternal goal. The believer affirms in the flesh that he is not in the flesh, for Christ's sake; he remains conscious of his sinfulness even in his justification and certain of his resurrection in the midst of experiencing his mortality.

It is a mark of Pauline devotion that Paul developed both series of pronouncements with equal precision: the absolute statements regarding the grace of God that praise its completeness, and the statements that perceive and assess the believer's susceptibility to temptation, defilement, and powerlessness. This fact cannot be explained through an illusionism that dreamily wavered between both assessments and forgot one while lingering over the other. This theory fails to recognize that Paul derives his absolute pronouncements regarding the believer's righteousness, aliveness, and holiness, as well as the no less absolute statements that pronounce the death of the sinner and the lostness of the unbeliever, not from self-observation but from the certainty of God. The substance of this certainty he gains from Christ. These pronouncements take on the characteristic of faith through Paul's complete affirmation of them, which attributes determinative power over us to what God thinks and does. Because these statements are valid apart from us, they do not disturb self-assessment; to the contrary, they provide it with a basis in reality and sobriety, because those who are certain of God's grace no longer excuse themselves. They no longer need rationalizations or illusions, while they have an unlimited interest in truthfulness.

This makes Paulinism vulnerable to objections that ultimately faith attains nothing much different from the previous ethical condition. Both stages have a mixed character: the pre-Christian one, because it did not contain anything but sin but also reflected goodness owing to the divine truth and goodness that are always present in man; the Christian one, because it does not reflect anything but righteousness, for faith does not suspend the continual existence and operation of our fleshliness and sinfulness. Why did Paul nevertheless see in the change effected by faith not merely relative progress, not merely a lessening of the reprehensible element in man and an increase in what was good in man, but rather a new beginning, which made something qualitatively different out of man, the old man becoming subject to death together with Christ? This assessment resulted for him from God's changed relationship with us that arises through the emergence of faith. Through allegiance to Christ, God's grace becomes for Paul the potency that determines human existence. The gift of grace entails the power of shaping man completely in soul and body, in spirit and nature, according to God's will. On the other hand, if someone remains separated from Christ, Paul considers sin to be the element that controls his position toward God and thus the outcome of his life.

## 2. Love

### a) The Establishment of Love through Faith

Because rejection of justification through our works is based on the fact that we recognized ourselves to be sinners, and because faith in Christ is based on the fact that we acknowledged him to be the redeemer from evil, it was unthinkable for Paul that faith could be linked with an antipathy toward action or an unethical quietism. Whoever seriously does not want evil, wants what is good. Jesus' entire rule and gift are aimed at setting us free from sin and making us obedient toward God. His death brings about our exoneration from guilt and therefore excludes that will which constantly recommits and heaps up sin. His resurrection and lordship provide us with our share in his life and ministry, our calling and the ability to live for him and thus for God. Faith is thus of necessity the end of selfish desires and the beginning of that love by which we live our lives in the way Jesus intended. Paul did not acknowledge the validity of a love-less faith; for where lovelessness is, there is no understanding of Jesus and no possession of his gift. The statement, "none of us lives for himself, everyone lives for Christ," expresses merely what faith produced in all. Where this result did not occur, faith was not present.

Paul related love to Christ and God with the same determination that he did faith. Love's desire is to live for him. It is erroneous to consider only faith to be the decisive religious phenomenon in Paul, while assigning love to ethics. To the contrary, Paul entirely preserved Jesus' concept of love, which is character-ized by the fact that love directed toward God cannot coexist with a desire to corrupt men. In Paul, too, love determines a person's entire conduct both to-ward God and toward one's neighbors. If self-centeredness is broken, it is bro-ken entirely. The one who does not live for himself serves God and, because he serves God, serves also the brethren.

Just as the spiritual processes by which faith comes into being do not become the subject of investigation for Paul, the spiritual connections between faith and love which thus lead to action did not attract his focused attention. At least, no treatment is available to us where Paul indicates that he devoted specific reflec-tion to this kind of phenomenon. From his perspective, the community is given everything it needs when it acknowledges that the content of the gospel, that Christ, brings it help against sin and places it in the new service of God that it carries out through love. Thereby it is granted protection against every tempta-tion that is attached to faith, inasmuch as grace can be used as authorization to evil. Yet grace is not rendered ineffective by evil but rather rises through sin to ever greater power and fullness (Rom. 5:20–6:3; 1 Cor. 13:2). However, the perversion of faith into unethical confidence is impossible, because such a con-clusion denies what is granted to the believer already through baptism as Jesus' gift through his death and his resurrection. Such faith would actually repudiate Jesus' gift, would cancel out allegiance to him, and thus would cease to be truly faith in Christ. It would turn into opposition toward him.

### b) The Liberty of Love

As with faith, Paul also with love paid attention to the special characteristics it takes on through man's individual nature. He does not merely develop com-pelling formulations that are valid for all, as if everyone's task were the same. For love has not yet achieved its goal when duty is done. For everyone, the ques-tion arises what he personally is empowered to do. Therefore Paul spoke about what is permitted, not because he desired to allow us to shrink back from universal normative injunctions and to draw close to evil, but because he supplies us together with love with our own voluntary will, so that everyone can exercise his desire to give all to the Lord and to do everything for him according to his own judgment and ability. For this reason Paul does not merely work with the contrasting terms "sin" and "righteousness" but sets above what is good what is even better. He considered his apostolic office to be his obligation, because it was placed upon him apart from his will. Above this he placed the freeing of his ministry from any imposition of the community as his own, free gift, by which he expresses that he serves the Lord not out of compulsion but with complete love (1 Cor. 9:4–18; 6:12; 10:23; Rom. 2:18; Phil. 1:10; 1 Cor. 7:32–38). He was, of course, aware of the fact that the free, voluntary decision to act that he thereby grants us involves dangers; no "self-serving pseudo-worship" must arise (Col. 2:23). The freedom given to us does not allow us to tackle whatever we want and to choose our goals arbitrarily. The basic rule remains for every use of freedom that it arise from the gift given to us. A decision that goes beyond the ability given to us leads to sin, and the goal freely chosen by us must be valuable in itself. When Paul preaches the gospel free of charge, he removes a potential stumbling block for many, because now no one can charge that he uses his apostolic office for his own benefit.

### c) Renunciation

Because he saw in love the will desired by God, it does not come as a surprise that Paul placed a high premium on the capacity for renunciation; for love and sacrifice belong together. He lived in voluntary celibacy and poverty, since he did without the support of his congregations; he watched with joy when others emulated him (1 Cor. 7:7; 9:18; 2 Cor. 12:14–15; 1 Thess. 2:7–9; Phil. 4:11–13). Renunciation results in a secret battle against faith as little as any other work does. Of course, every achievement of love presents the believer with the task of viewing his share in God not as the merits of his work but as God's grace. He must turn away from the industry and greatness of his own work to God who enabled him to do his work (1 Cor. 15:10). But this demands from him nothing other than that even in the midst of renunciation he remain a believer who depends not on himself but on God and remains in Christ. In this he is aided by renunciation if it truly originates in love for God, because love does not glorify itself and does not promote but slays self-will. Paul did not fear that anyone would be tempted by love to unbelief; faith that is assured of divine grace is jeopardized only through lovelessness. Likewise, renunciation does not violate the freedom given to the believer; for this is the way he exercises and uses it. Paul did not use the statement that all things are lawful for us to promote the cultivation of self-centeredness or of sensual passions. He possesses and uses his power even in renunciation, not merely in enjoyment; in the ability to be poor, not merely in the ability to be rich; in suffering, not merely in the avoidance of suffering (Phil. 4:11–13).

Paul made ascetic actions a duty when they serve to remove an obstacle in one's dealings with others and to prevent sin. The difficulties resulting from the Pharisaic shunning of meat and wine used in pagan ritual, Paul overcame through his readiness to every kind of renunciation (1 Cor. 8:9–13; Rom. 14:13–21). Those kinds of ascetic resolutions that initially only regulate one's own conduct, such as celibacy or poverty, require sober attention to the ethical power given to the individual. Thereafter they also require subordination to a positive aim by which they become fruitful. These achievements are not yet justified merely by their difficult or painful nature. Paul counseled others to forego marriage not merely because such renunciation itself constitutes a vigorous, rich achievement, nor even because marriage brings woes of its own, but because such forbearance freed a person to serve Christ with all his strength (1 Cor. 7). These statements reveal that Paul was entirely free from the notion that love stood in conflict with faith and must be hindered, so that faith alone might be our righteousness.

### d) The Value of Good Works

The same fearlessness is seen in the manner in which Paul attributes a causal power to human good will and works in the context of relationship to God, so that they establish God's good pleasure and love for us and procure for us his grace. Paul's doctrine of justification frequently is taken to imply that, for Paul, our actions are immaterial for God's relationship with us. This is false, because Paul very definitely attributed corrupting power to Christians' sin and because he related the verdict of the judging Christ, by which entrance into eternal life is opened up to us, to our actions. The eschatological formula, however, necessarily also applies to the evaluation of events occurring in the present, because it has in view both the reception of salvation in its perfection and likewise the loss of salvation in its ultimate terribleness. Whoever knows that Christ will judge his actions must not act with the intention that he will receive his praise. Paul expressly demanded the application of the eschatological formulation for the regulation of present conduct. He did not merely postulate it as the theoretical conclusion of a system but provides it with the seriousness of a motive that must determine our conduct (Rom. 2:6, 16; 1 Cor. 3:8, 14–15; 4:5; Rom. 14:10–12).

Thus Paul retains his verdict regarding the Law with faithful consistency. The principle is unwavering that God's praise belongs to the one, and solely to the one, who works what is good. The idea that he thus violates faith and enters into conflict with justification could not arise with him, because his faith is directed toward liberation from sin and the granting of a kind of life that becomes fruitful for God. Once placing his confidence in Christ because he found in himself the inability to do good, he cannot separate Jesus' verdict from his own works, because he would thus forget that he sought and received righteousness from him, and recognized in him the one with whom evil has passed away and good has appeared. He thus does not depart from faith with his joy in work and with the will to receive God's praise for it. That Israel does not come to faith on account of its works is based solely in the fact that it seeks to prove its own righteousness by them, because it recognizes nothing but the Law. Whoever has been brought to faith, however, is free from selfish arrogance in the evaluation of his own works and thus experiences the greatness of the divine grace, in grateful joy at the work entrusted to him. At the same time, however, he knows that God's grace is never separate from God's justice. For this reason whoever does not merely know God's will but also does it will never cease to believe in Christ, from whom, after all, he has received everything he owns. It was only sin, not good works, that Paul saw as rendering faith difficult or even destroying it.

Still less does Paul think of a change or a wavering in God, when he now makes faith at the present time, but works on the last day, to be our righteousness, and when he attaches to Jesus' cross that justification which is based on faith but to his coming regal revelation a justification that is based on works. Owing to the fact that our faith in Jesus is our righteousness, the grace in Jesus' sending is revealed in a way appropriate to us as guilty ones who live in the flesh. Thereby God's gift is directly brought to bear on the need which the earthly state places on man. At his new revelation, Christ judges those who lived in him and served God; now the fruit of their faith becomes manifest before him. At the cross, Christ took the judgment upon himself, so that from him the word goes forth that calls all people to faith. At his new revelation, he executes justice upon mankind, both upon the world and upon his community, and thus judges what it did. His work upon it would turn out to have been in vain and futile, if he had not established a community whose works are good before God. The justification granted to faith proves to be divine, true, and just, because it brings about the kind of union with God by which his will is done. Paul did not fear that this assurance could produce a proud or fearful assessment of our work, because the grace in whose commission he died remains visible to the believer when he directs his view toward the verdict of the Coming One. Therefore the community anticipates his coming with joy, because it gains from the received grace the assurance of perfect redemption. What it needs for this redemption is nothing but its faith, nothing but its justification in Christ's blood. But it needs this because it thereby receives that pattern of conduct which it requires for the attainment of its goal.

Thus Paul's Christian life is infused with a mighty striving (Phil. 3:8–14; 1 Cor. 9:24–27; 2 Tim. 4:7; 1 Tim. 6:12; 2 Cor. 4:1, 16). He did not merely find rest in what was accomplished and had been received. He also received a goal, and he set on its achievement the entire will granted to him. This is effected by Christ's mandate of bringing about fulfillment. Paul's striving thus arises at the same point as does his faith, at the perfection of divine grace. The receptive attitude by which the work of the one who has come intervenes in his own life and the striving that reaches for the future aim converge, because in both he requires nothing but Jesus, who effects at the cross and at his coming appearance that revelation of righteousness which is grace (Phil. 3:8: to gain Christ). Paul believed in the righteousness of Jesus' deed at the cross, because he also believed in the righteousness of his judging activity. He desired the Judge's praise for his work, because he believed in the grace of the One who forgives. If striving energy arose in Pauline devotion merely through the consciousness of his incompleteness and sinfulness, then, of course, a secret contradiction between it and the absolute statements of faith would come to light. The persistent conflict in us between the flesh and the Spirit, sinfulness and righteousness, mortality and life, actually reveals that we have not yet received the full portion of Christ's grace. But this does not cause Paul to doubt and to set forth fear and remorse as incentives for action. His notion springs from what Christ is, from his calling to reveal God, to effect righteousness, to give life. Thereby he presents Paul with a goal on which he sets his hope. But just as he did not transform his faith into a theory, he also does not pervert his hope into a fantasy. He sets his will upon his hope and longs for the completed act of Christ, and because he desires, he acts and renders his Christian life a race for the prize which awaits him through his calling to God.

## 3. The Community of Believers

### a) The Completeness of Community

The terms by which Paul describes God's grace provide the personal life of the individual with its greatest escalation. The concept of guilt places the decisive event by which our relationship with God comes into being or is broken within the depth of the individual life. As the agent of justification, Christ turns to the individual as the one who gives; "he loved me and gave himself up for me" (Gal. 2:20). The individual is granted God's love in such greatness and glory that his Spirit moves him. He has become free. That the Pauline community does not merely not hinder, or grudgingly overlook, or just tolerate this rich and strong emphasis on the individual life but that it rather produces it, provides it with its peculiar greatness. Only the community that truly is the community of Christ, that represents his body, that becomes God's temple, can consist of such vigorous and free members.

The closeness of its communion comes about through the fact that the awakening and strengthening of the life given to the individual is effected by God and thus takes place for everyone only with all and through all. Christ is Lord of all and offers his gifts to all. Paul gives no grounds for establishing a distinction in rank or time between personal Christianity and the existence of the community. He does not suggest that justification is first given to the community and only in a secondary sense to the individual through allegiance to the community, as if the Spirit was initially "common spirit" and only later became the possession of individuals. Neither did he hold that the divine activity initially takes place in the hidden realm of individual life; only later was what had been acquired added up and elevated to the community's possession. For Paul, there is here no sequence one way or the other. There is no community before there are Christians; likewise, there are no Christians apart from the existence of a community. Knowing Christ means having the community, because Christ's work consists in the establishment of the perfect community. Fellowship with him is therefore also fellowship with the brethren.

Believers' communion with one another is not based merely on the fact that all live in the same God and the one Lord; after all, this would merely result in that kind of community that is based on pleasure in sameness. Rather, there are dependent relationships among individuals that render people dependent on one another, and this again not merely in such a way that only problems and difficulties require others' help and that the struggle against evil makes brotherly strengthening and discipline necessary, but also in such a way that we experience God's government and gifting through mediation of others. Christ does not move believers merely from within but also speaks to them through the brethren. The Spirit does not work the same thing in all, but a Spirit-given word may come to one and through him reach another. Therefore Paul liked to point to the body as an apt metaphor for the community, because it depicts not merely the unity of the group but also the special nature and peculiarity of members. Not all members are eyes, not all are ears. Thus members need one another, and this bond cannot be broken apart without resulting in the death of isolated members (Rom. 12:4–8; 1 Cor. 10:17; 12:4–31; Eph. 2:19–22; 4:3–16; Col. 2:19; 1 Tim. 3:15).

As soon as the concept of love becomes the central term of ethical instruction, the community's indispensability is secure. In the isolation of the individual, love would lose its sphere of operation and wither to an empty attitude. If it truly comes to permeate the human will, a union of giving and receiving arises for which the recipient is as indispensable as the giver. By recognizing God's will to be love, the community receives irreproachable sanctity.

### b) The Goals Shown to the Community

Paul vividly felt the mutual responsibility arising from the incorporation of all as members in the community. It first of all pertains to those who assume an office in it. For them, the performance of their service and the gaining of their own salvation converge entirely. Paul permitted neither himself nor his associates to separate between the divine grace and faithfulness in service, as if they could possess one without the other. By saving others, he saves himself. Whoever builds the community in such a way that he incorporates people who do not belong to it does not merely labor in vain; he also jeopardizes his own salvific state. He will be saved though as by fire. But if he becomes entirely the corrupter of the community, this is a sin that provokes the judgment of God (1 Cor. 9:23–27; 1 Tim. 4:16; 1 Cor. 3:12–17).

In Paul, concern for one's own obligation and work is accompanied by patience that does not despair in view of the problems and sins in the congregation. A large house contains all kinds of vessels, not merely precious but also worthless ones, and the removal of the latter is not within the sphere of authority of those who lead the congregation. It is placed in the battle brought about by the world's opposition against God, in which God's patience, his righteous judgment, but also the perfection of his grace, are revealed. All this is also manifested within the congregation. Joy in ministry despite failure and humbling imperfection arises from the fact that God knows those who are his possession and that he renders his building indestructible. Also in view of the congregation Paul did not permit friction between the comforting conviction that affirms the flawlessness of divine activity, on the one hand, and the fluctuating conviction that reflects on one's own collaboration with God's work. For after all, both arise from the glory of the divine government and grace. From that glory results both the possibility of accepting the limitations of one's work and the seriousness that understands the responsibility involved (Gal. 4:19; 1 Cor. 4:8–15; Phil. 1:15–18; 2 Tim. 2:19–21).

This responsibility, however, does not remain limited to those who are given a special commission but extends to all in light of the powerful connection of all members of the community with one another. Paul called causing others to sin through the reckless use of one's own freedom sin against Christ, and he charges this attitude with contempt of what the dying Christ acquired for the brothers. This means that the one who harms another ethically destroys his own possession of salvation (1 Cor. 8:11–12; Rom. 14:15). Conversely, he confirms it by helping others in the preservation of their Christian lives.

### c) The Christian Community's Relationship with Natural Institutions

Paul did not render the Christian community indifferent toward natural institutions but rather acknowledged these as the indestructible foundation of all our activity. But this immediately resulted in the fact that the new acquisition of love, by which Christian communion was gained, also entered the old community and provided it with a firmness and completeness that far transcended the previous fellowship. By basing the community on the family, Paul did not merely preserve it; rather, the relationships between husband and wife, parents and children, masters and slaves, now are subject to the rule of Jesus. The service to be performed in these relationships becomes an aspect of worshiping God and embodies the completeness of love offered to God. The husband now loves his wife as he saw love exhibited by, and received through, Christ; the wife shows her husband obedience as she offers it to the Lord. The master is now related to the slave as Christ unites brothers, and the slave serves the master as he serves Christ. Through the parents' sanctification, the children are sanctified as well, and a wife is sanctified through the sanctification of her husband. A special test was imposed on the esteem of natural institutions when the gospel initially separated between their members and, for example, only the husband entered the community. But even then the Christian is not profaned by fellowship with the one who resists the gospel. It is not that the Christian spouse becomes unsanctified, but rather the non-Christian spouse is sanctified on account of the fact that God has sanctified the spouse related to him or her. In this, however, it is recognized that natural fellowship may become impossible if it can be preserved only if the Christian foregoes his convictions. In that case, obedience toward Christ has priority over any other form of dependence. The obligation and power to dissolve any relationship for God's sake is not diminished in Paul (1 Cor. 7:10–24; Eph. 5:22–6:9; Col. 3:18–4:1).

Paul also provided the community immediately with a positive relationship with the state, which frees the conscience of the community to share in its well-being and thus makes the power of its love fruitful for it. In light of the raw, violent form of the Roman state, of course, this participation in the state on the part of individuals was still extremely limited; it consisted primarily in paying taxes. The thought by which Paul established not merely a negative but a fruitful participatory relationship with the city was that the norms by which civic order is established among the nations are rooted in God's justice. It therefore appears as a divine act of mercy that there are authorities to punish evil and to protect and honor what is good, so that obedience toward them became one's duty not merely because of benefit or harm but for conscience's sake (Rom. 13:1–7). The priority given to one's own Christian possession over what creation order grants to all is simultaneously expressed by the fact that congregations exempt themselves from the state regarding their own concerns. Thus Paul prohibited them from calling on pagan or Jewish judges (1 Cor. 6:1–6). This independence, however, does not establish enmity toward the state nor give rise to efforts aimed at its destruction. That the government also has the task of hindering evil and of promoting good is not obscured by the fact that the community ensures Law and order within its own circle.

Because only those who dwell close together are able to live with one another, the congregation is initially a local congregation. If a house is larger, perhaps through having numerous servants, a special congregation is established whose leader is the father of the household (1 Cor. 16:19; Rom. 16:5; Col. 4:15; Phlm. 2). Nevertheless, the church concept continues to transcend all temporal or spatial limitations, because the congregation, no matter how large or small, belongs to Christ. It is therefore united with all who belong to him. Therefore there is only one community, and all Christian groupings comprise one communion arising from their common bond with Christ (1 Cor. 12:28; 15:9; Gal. 1:13; Phil. 3:6; Eph. 1:22; 3:10, 21; 4:5–16; 5:23–32; Col. 1:18, 24; 1 Tim. 3:15).

The priority of the divine gift over all natural values places dealings in the community under the principle of equality, which Paul upheld for slaves and free, Jews and Gentiles, men and women. He never conceived of this in terms of a destruction of gender, social, or national differences; after all, he seeks to preserve natural institutions. But within the community, he set people's dealings with one another free from the limitations issuing from these differences (1 Cor. 7:17–24; Gal. 3:28; Eph. 5:22–6:9; Col. 3:11; 3:18–4:1). That the implementation of the equality of all in Christ constituted a lofty task for the community that did not succeed without struggle was evident to all. Differences in economic status gave way most readily, in view of the superior value of the possession given to all in Christ. But even in this regard Paul had to warn the Corinthians not to shame the poor by exposing them to painful reminders of their desperate situation (1 Cor. 11:22). More difficult was the regulation of relationships between the sexes, because these dealings must be protected against the intrusion of sensual impulses. Paul was here prepared to exercise great caution for the purpose of protecting purity of relationships. That the woman keeps the veil on her head even during prayer as a sign of her subordination to her husband takes on serious importance for him, and for the same reason women are not permitted to administer the word in the congregation (1 Cor. 11:3–16; 14:34–35; 1 Tim. 2:8–15). It is not evident that Paul considered the woman as less gifted than the man as far as her natural abilities are concerned. The decisive issue for him, from which he establishes custom, is that erotic impulses be excluded from the congregation. As gifted as a woman might be, even when she is a prophetess, she remains a woman, and it is dangerous when she or the congregations wants to forget this.

The unification of born Jews and born Gentiles in the same congregation was particularly difficult, because Jews were able to have full dealings with Gentiles only by transgressing the Law. A Jew's conscience must therefore become sufficiently free from the Law that he no longer viewed his transgression as sin. Similar to the Jerusalem apostles and already Jesus, Paul saw in table fellowship the sign and means of complete communion that overcame all separation. He therefore called for its practice among both parts of the community, rejecting refusal of it in the name of the Law as sin against the community (Gal. 2:11–14). How diligently he honored the Jewish conscience even in this question, however, is seen in his instruction to the Romans, which must not be portrayed as a later concession for peace's sake but as instruction regarding the way he everywhere regulated conduct (Rom. 14). He did not make membership in the community contingent upon everyone's participation in another's table fellowship with no misgivings. He expressly ensured the share of those in the community who refused to eat meat. That table fellowship is what is desired is evident here, because the refusal of meat is subsumed under "weakness of faith," and strong faith is what is desirable for all. But the absolute verdict "sin" is not applied to this behavior; rather, space is reserved in the community also for those who consider a particular diet indispensable. Likewise, Jewish Christians retain the celebration of the Sabbath and of certain feasts as well as circumcision (Rom. 14:5–6; 1 Cor. 7:18–19; Gal. 5:6; 6:15). For inhabitants of Palestine, this principle also included participation at the service of the Temple altar. While such conditions shortly appeared to the congregations as an unbearable violation of ecclesiastical unity, Paul's treatments clearly reveal the high regard he had for the positive value of these difficulties for the congregation. It is thereby required to establish its unity from within, not by trivializing established practice, not by the tyranny of a ruling party, but through the inviolable preservation of esteem for another's conscience. Indeed, unity is to be established based on the fundamental act of the community's devotion: faith and the divine grace that faith receives.

## E. Conditions Affecting Pauline Teaching

### 1. Jesus and Paul

#### a) The Aim of Devotion

Jesus' regal will was based on his divine sonship; Paul's apostolic ministry was rooted in his knowledge of Christ. In light of this the difference between these two figures is vast. Paul continually made this clear, as he renders any comparison of his calling with Jesus' work impossible. He thus did not entertain the thought that he could or should possess the certainty of God in the same immediacy that is revealed by Jesus' words. Paul's entire religious thought and desire were rather grounded in what he knew about Jesus. From his perspective, the human will has no part in this difference; for it has been determined by God; and by continually acknowledging this and by considering Jesus truly as Lord, Paul proves his status as believer. But when this fundamental distinction is observed—and it is reflected all across the full range of statements made by both men—it also becomes clear how completely Paul's devotion was dependent on Jesus' religious conduct.

The grounding of Jesus' regal will in his divine sonship had as a consequence that he linked his relationship with God and his relationship with mankind to form a firm unity. This is echoed in Paul in that he also receives his office on behalf of mankind through God's calling and that he cannot separate his share in God's grace from the performance of his work.

As a result of the sonship Jesus enjoys with God, his idea of God also included reminiscences and hopes, yet did not receive its content solely from them, because he possessed a communion with God that filled the present. In his view, God manifested himself long ago to the patriarchs and will reveal himself again soon through the fulfillment of his kingdom. But Jesus did not base his work on this fact alone; rather, he proclaimed God's kingdom as present, because in him God provided the community with the Christ. This is continued in Paul in that his religion also consisted not only in reminiscences of Jesus' history and the prophecy of his coming appearance but also fills the present. In Paul's view, God reveals himself in that he demonstrates his grace and righteousness to mankind through the message about Christ.

In his fellowship with God Jesus located his entire will in the conviction that God too gives his entire grace to men. This resulted in the fact that Paul likewise does away with all limited versions of the religious aim, which place it merely in blessedness or knowledge or merely in partial ethical improvement. He rather employed exclusively absolute terms both for God's gift and for man's obligation.

Jesus derived his consciousness of power from the currently unfolding revelation of God's kingdom. But because it arises from God's kingdom, it remained unpolluted from all selfish desires and included complete self-humbling before God. Therefore the consciousness of power which corresponded to Paul's office likewise is accompanied by the renunciation of any selfish exercise of power. Being a Christian meant for him at any level the complete removal of pride and of one's own praise.

Jesus incorporated ethical norms in his idea of God and therefore uses his power to remove evil and to establish the community that is obedient to God. By the phrase "righteousness of God," Paul expressed the highest truth he knew of God and recognized the completeness of the divine grace in the fact that it brings about righteousness. For this reason his description of what it means to be a Christian consisted in his doctrine of righteousness, and the community he gathers is characterized by the fact that it has died to sin and does what is good. To be sure, Jesus' word of repentance took on a new dimension in Paul, in that he inaugurated the concept of original sin in the church, speaking in collective terms. He retained consensus with Jesus, however, in that he did not therefore compromise the complete renunciation of evil will but rather thereby carried it out. Jesus likewise was not afraid of the fact that his verdicts also affected what we must call our nature. But this did not lead him to transform the message of repentance into a meditation that deplored the irreversible sinfulness of the human will and issued in a dualism that destroyed man's ability to act. For he upheld the truth of God's gracious presence with man. Paul likewise upheld it and provided it with a concrete form through his statements regarding Christ and the Spirit. Therefore he also was able to bear in himself the verdicts that confront man's reprehensible nature in such a way that they produced turning away from evil and joyful readiness for the good work.

### b) The Church

Because the basic shape of religious thought reaches seamlessly from Jesus to Paul, the relationship of both to the Jewish community converges as well. The manner in which Jesus was a Jew and simultaneously judged the Jews recurs without alteration in the way in which Paul was a Jew. The existing community with its Scripture, its Law, and its national constitution is honored as God's work. The separation results from the word of repentance, because the ethical norms are hallowed completely. The Jewish sin likewise is not rationalized but rejected. For Paul, the new element in his pronouncements regarding the Law did not entail the consciousness that he thus changed the aim of Jesus. In his view, his statements regarding the Law only expressed what had become evident through the outcome of Jesus' life. Israel had fallen; in this fact, Paul saw God's will and the means to perfection of his lordship. But because Israel's condition is determined by the Law, the interpretation of its fall becomes teaching on the negative purpose of the Law. The contemplation of Israel's destiny was linked with that of his own history. In contrast to Jesus, he had the opponent whom he must overcome also in himself. His verdict regarding Israel was a judgment concerning himself, and he executes it through the confession that he, like all, did not become innocent through the Law, but guilty.

With his establishment of a community that was open to all, Paul did not enter into conflict with Jesus, because the aims "kingdom of God" and "rule of the Messiah" had always included the nations. Jesus himself shattered the contrast "not the nations, but Israel," because his work was determined by a different contrast, that is, that between God's good will and man's godless will, which he rejected in the Jew no less than in the Greek. Paul's "universalism" is placed on the same exclusively religious basis. He did not elevate the Greek above the Jew or the barbarian but placed the divine grace above the guilt and misery of all.

Paul did not see any departure from Jesus' aim in the fact that now a new community came into being beside the Jews and the Greeks. The charge against Paul that he corrupted Jesus' godliness into "churchianity" overlooks that the religious aim retains, in the community established by Paul, the completeness it had with Jesus. To be sure, a distinction of the religious aim from man's natural concerns emerged owing to the fact that now the church was placed beside and over other institutions. But its isolation also constitutes an important goal of Jesus' work. Through his founding of the church Paul did not bring about a separation of the religious function from the other tasks of human life, because in his view the community unites its members in all their concerns. One does not enter the Pauline community in order to satisfy an isolated desire but with the entire will, not merely as soul but as person, not merely to practice ritual but to conduct one's life. The completeness of community into which Paul brings believers with one another proves that it does not break with the liberty Jesus gave to his disciples. Paul did not permit the enslavement of individuals through the community but made the awarding of complete liberty to all its high purpose, because it must administer the divine grace to all. For this reason he did not abandon Jesus' battle against lack of religious authenticity and hypocrisy, even though he united believers in one church. As the place of liberty, the Pauline community was also the place of authenticity.

### c) Faith and Love

Part of the unification of the community is the development of a body of established belief, the acquisition of convictions that unify all and grant them the basis for common activity. As significant the difference between Jesus and Paul is in their thought and ministry, when it comes to the striking contrast existing between the ideals of Greek philosophy and Jesus' teaching, Paul aligns himself perfectly with Jesus. His thought does not serve selfish motives, which desire the enhancement of one's own ability, but love that magnifies the divine work because it desires to serve God.

By highlighting faith as the process that establishes fellowship with God, Paul, in the context of his verdict regarding the reprehensible nature of man, yielded to neither an intellectualistic nor an unethical craving. He would have obeyed the former only if he had sought to establish communion with God exclusively through thinking, and the latter if he had tried to do without action. But because Paul, by elevating faith above all functions, expressed God's and Christ's sovereignty over all other human circumstances and achievements, deriving from the perfection of divine grace the independence of faith from all human accomplishments and man's all-sufficiency, he thus preserved Jesus' devotion. For Jesus assigned priority to the divine activity and perfection to divine grace. The goals Paul set for man's activity were determined by the rule of love. This is Jesus' commandment, and Paul never formed formulas of obligation other than those derived from Jesus' rule of love. He preserved the perfection of love in all directions of activity, in personal interchange with God, with others, and with nature. Thus Jesus' carefreeness reappears undiminished in Paul, and for the same reason that Jesus had it, because all events are ordained by the good God. Because Paul too gains carefreeness through faith, he did not consider it unnatural, but related to the statement that there was no evil for those who are called, the incisive observation of reality and the courageous use of the power given to him. For this reason carefreeness did not harden him toward pain, as little as we observe this with Jesus. It does not lead him to apathy but to the resolve that is willing to suffer. As curious as this phenomenon may be in itself, it is found with Paul no less than with Jesus. Therefore Paul likewise possessed the ability to die together with the will to live. Paul, too, proves his love for God through the ability to surrender all natural goods. The term "asceticism," however, is as unsuitable for him as it is for Jesus, because he likewise does not take a negative view toward material things. In his work for people, he proves their grounding in love by portraying his self-imposed restriction to small things not as a burden but as a value. He thereby preserves Jesus' idea of humility without attenuation. Further, he demonstrates the origin of his ministry in love by making its goal the liberation of others. Notions of power do not entice him. Thus he did not develop a heteronomic ethic, no ethic that imposed its will-shaping norms upon man from the outside. His entire ministry was aimed at encouraging the community to act in its own certitude and to possess and exercise the good will as its own. Because the unity of love with the justice-producing norms remains intact, Paul, like Jesus, was able to get angry without violating love. For his love does not cultivate evil but produces the battle against all evil in others in complete truthfulness. This battle, however, is conducted in peace, because the ability to forgive is always present.

From love for God, Paul also received ritual, which he kept free of symbolism as well as magic. He prayed, just as Jesus was a man of prayer, and he did not doubt the value of sacrifice, by which he yields his will to God. His will was completely open to proper ritual, yet still protects it against the perversion that arises if it absorbs all other functions. Jesus' characteristic practice of rendering his entire activity as his worship of God is also characteristic of Paul. From love he derived man's right to present to God everything he has. But this does not resurrect the merit concept which had been removed by Jesus; it remains completely dead in Paul. He has full and clear consciousness that the first mark of love is obedience, and that love profanes its liberty when it is not based on accountability to divine norms.

### d) Evaluation of the Cross

The event which serves Paul as the norm for all his judgments regarding faith and love is the outcome of Jesus' life. By conceiving it as the revelatory act by which he perceives God's stance toward man, he aligns himself with Jesus; for Jesus, too, accepted his cross from God. When Paul saw in this God's judging will, which removes whatever forms man's inner possession apart from Christ, he thereby continues Jesus' verdict, who derived his cross from sin, from man's rebellion against God and his consequent rejection by God. Paul had been personally confronted with this conflict, which lends his words regarding the cross a novel, unique form. In the fact that Christ's cross brought him condemnation, Paul could not see merely an individual experience. The one who dies on the cross is the Christ, and this provides the judgment of God that was executed there with universal validity. Still, he remains one with Jesus in placing God's judging activity within the sphere of his grace. Just as Jesus clung to the messianic idea in his death, seeing in the cross the means by which God made him Christ, Paul perceives in Christ's cross the divine grace, because he considers the removal of what separates man from God to be the highest blessing and the demonstration of God's love.

From his death, Jesus expected life. For this reason Paul likewise views the Crucified One always at the same time as the Living One and knows himself to be in a communion with him that embraces his entire internal life. This conforms his inner life to that of Jesus, though not as a copy, as if he could imitate Jesus' divine sonship or repeat the work he did. From Paul's standpoint this would be consummate madness. But from the divine grace, Paul derives the certainty that he has Christ, and therefore God, with him in such a way that he thinks and acts in him. He owes to Jesus the fact that the conflict between God and him is entirely removed, so that the human element in him no longer obscures what is divine, while what is divine does not destroy what is human, either in his contemplation of Jesus, or in the way in which he views his own life and carries out his office, or in his verdict regarding the community. Paul's reconciliation with God and Jesus' dealings with God as his Son cannot be viewed as two completely independent facts. Jesus' divine sonship is here the primary and causal fact, and the way in which he made his fellowship with the disciples to become God's revelation for them is the historical basis from which Paul's reconciliation with God was effected through Christ.

For this reason Paul was able to hold fast unwaveringly to the offer of reconciliation, which is the goal of Jesus' message of repentance, through his doctrine of justification. The union of Law and grace, which is characteristic of Jesus' concept of God, is also the mark of Pauline justification, and the perfection of divine forgiveness is expressly attested by both the removal of guilt and the establishment of a will that is subject to God.[44]

### e) The Spirit

The concept of the Spirit, who is presented by Paul as the foundation for his own and the community's spiritual service, introduced a new element beyond what was previously present among the circle of Jesus' disciples. But the link between Jesus' work and Paul's aim is not broken even at this point, because Jesus bound his disciples to himself internally through faith and love. Fellowship with him was accomplished not by compulsion or religious forms but by those kinds of processes that are now described by way of the term "Spirit." Now that Jesus was no longer with the community, the fact that he united the disciples internally with himself became the new proposition that he moved them through his Spirit. When speaking of the Spirit, Paul thought expressly of the Spirit of Christ. This resulted in the fact that the new phenomena in the community leave intact the basic form of devotion which had come into being through Jesus' dealings with his disciples. As in Christ divine and human elements are not played off against one another but the divine becomes the ground for what is human, so the Spirit's work in Paul consists of producing people who live from God and for God, placing their entire energy in his service.

### f) Hope

None of the deliberations regarding the riches of the divine gift now offered to mankind, according to Paul, replaces the hope Jesus gave to his disciples. Paul bears it in himself just as Jesus' disciples did, as genuine hope that is will, not merely as eschatological theory; as longing directed toward God, thus completely separated from merely self-centered passions, and not intermingled with a sensual desire that strives only for well-being. His longing is directed toward

44. Cf. pp. 239–41.

the revelation of Christ, which will bring fulfillment for individuals and the entire world. Thus he gains through his hope the energy for the work that must now be accomplished. It awakens him to clear vision, renders him ready for action, because he hopes for the one in whose fellowship he currently lives and in whose service he stands. As for Jesus, hope extends also for Paul to the execution of judgment and nonetheless remains joyful, because the execution of righteousness upon all lies in the hands of Christ, in whom divine grace has been manifested. The evident connection linking Paul's hope with Jesus' promise reveals how completely Paul stood under Jesus' authority. It was no bizarre distortion of his consciousness when he considered himself to be a Christian and explained that he had been given his intellectual possession by Jesus.

The transfer of forms of thought and will from Jesus to Paul is not a function of literary means; it occurs through the community, through the fact that Paul's history in all its stages, already during his Pharisaic opposition to Jesus and even more since his baptism and since his serving as Jesus' messenger, took place not alongside but in the community. It is precisely because of Paul's independence that his Christianity constitutes particularly clear evidence for the vigor with which the Christian community engaged its members internally and brought them under Jesus' influence.

## 2. The Relationship between Paul's Convictions and His Conversion

Paul's ideas never lead us away from his history to constructs that developed as abstractions by way of imagination that is able to invent by the use of terms. His new pronouncements rather sustain clear relationships with his history. To understand him, we must always remember that he was initially a Pharisee, with such resolve that he was at the forefront of the battle against Christianity. Then Jesus' appearance produced his sudden and complete conversion, and he effected through the exercise of his apostolic office with increasing vigor the universal establishment of the church among the Greeks, thus overcoming Christian Pharisaism and Christian gnosis.

### a) The Law

As a Pharisee, Paul considered the divine Law to have the authority to determine man's relationship with God, and this remained his unshakable conviction. Without Christ, mankind is subject to the Law. The Law stands above it as its master which instructs it regarding its relationship to God. Paul never accepted the rationale suggested to him by every Greek, that the Jewish Law did not apply to him because he was not a Jew. For he saw in it God's commandment, binding on all. Therefore he maintained even against gnostic thinking that the Law judged every instance of lawlessness or disobedience even in Christendom. Because the Law's authority constitutes a parallel to the authority with which Christ stands above mankind, the relationship between the two must be made crystal clear, both for the Jews and no less for the Greeks. All receive their relationship with God either through the Law or through Christ, and all must be told that God's grace sets them free from the Law through Christ. The attempts of Christian Pharisaism to subject the church to itself intensified this need; but it existed also apart from it. The history of Paul's own life already indicated that he saw in the presentation of how Christ is the end of the Law an essential link in the universal doctrine of salvation.

His conversion did not change his verdict regarding the content of the Law or its origin from God, but it did change what he thought the Law achieved. Because he had become the persecutor of Christ and his community, his effort to do the Law and thereby to attain his own righteousness turned out to be a failure. Once he realized this, he considered the Pharisaism in himself dead and his confidence entirely separated from the Law.[45] He always believed that he alone was to blame for his opposition toward Christ. He did not charge God with it nor claim that the Law was false or sinful. Rather, he maintained that, through the Law, he became a sinner. His conversion did not consist in a shift in theory but in repentance, judgment of his own desires and activities, attribution of guilt to himself. This was determined directly by his Pharisaic piety, which forbid him any accusation of God and instructed him to condemn sin as the act of man. The circumspectness and resolve of his conversion continues the sincerity of his Pharisaic piety. Therefore he steered clear of antinomianism, no matter how courageous he is in his application of his freedom from the Law in word and deed. The contrast characteristic of his train of thought relates to man and does not have its source in God. From God's perspective, the Law and Christ serve his holy grace together in harmony. Both come from God, both carry out his will and serve his goal. The dilemma arises merely in man, who perverts what is good into damage and death by resisting the Law.

### b) Jesus' Cross

Even when Paul combated Christendom, he had much in common with it: he too awaited the Christ, fought against godlessness in Israel, and likely had appreciation for Christians' piety. He was separated from them by Jesus' cross, not merely because the Crucified lacked power—had this been the case, the conflict would have rested merely in an egotistic craving for happiness and splendor and thus to that which Paul judged as impious and sinful even according to his Pharisaic conviction—but because he saw in Jesus' cross the end of the Law, because Israel's righteousness was obliterated and the whole of its pious activity judged as worthless, if it indeed had rejected the Christ. This provided Paul's wrestling with Christendom its profundity and continuing fruitfulness: that Paul's piety rebelled against Jesus, not what was within him that he condemned as fleshly but that which he considered to be good and holy. As a Pharisee, he maintained that doubting the Law's salvific power amounted to doubting God himself. But when he recognized Jesus' lordship, he reversed, to-

---

45. Paul's break with Pharisaism did not merely remove its entire legislation but affected Paul's view of narrative (haggada) as clearly as is the case elsewhere in the New Testament writings. To be sure, Paul used Jewish concepts almost exclusively; but there is little rabbinic exegesis: the rock wandering with Israel (1 Cor. 10:4); the heavenly city of God (Gal. 4:25–26); the participation of heavenly rulers in human history (1 Cor. 15:24; Eph. 3:10; 6:12; Col. 2:15; 1 Cor. 2:6, 8 [?]); the names for the Egyptian magicians (2 Tim. 3:8).

gether with his verdict regarding the Law, also his verdict regarding Jesus' cross. Now he perceived in the removal of the Law through Jesus' death God's own act. Now he was convinced that Christ through his death was the end of the Law. Just as guilt arose from the Law, now righteousness was established through the cross. His fear was confirmed that the cross demonstrated Israel's guilt; thereby God's condemning verdict was indeed placed upon all. But because it is the cross of the Christ, he expresses the grateful certainty that through it man is granted justification.

### c) Justification

The special nature of his conversion provided the negative verdict which the individual pronounces against himself at repentance with particular vigor. From it issues the sharp contrast reflected in his train of thought: not the Law but Christ, not works but faith, not the flesh but the Spirit, not man but God— such contrasts dominate this thought. He is lifted above this contrast and reconciled with God, but he reaches this goal by apprehending the contrast in all its profundity. When he was persuaded of Jesus' messianic glory at his appearance, he saw himself compelled to a complete denial of self. His confidence in his own work and knowledge was shattered. He experienced a dying that smote him in his highest aspirations and works. What saved him was solely the grace of Christ, who presented himself to him as the giver of divine grace. This grace now stood before him so powerfully, so completely, that it revealed God to him as the one who had mercy (1 Cor. 7:25; 2 Cor. 4:1; 1 Tim. 1:13, 16). God's mercy saved him. Thus Paul, through his conversion, becomes a believer. He received through it nothing but faith, because it is solely in Christ that he has everything, that is, God with his righteousness interceding for him and his life granted to him. From now on, he recognizes a clear contrast between Christ and the Law. For he came to see the Law as the occasion for sin, condemnation, and divine wrath, through which Christ brought grace, justification, and service well-pleasing to God. As a result, faith and works are separated, and an intermingling of both became inconceivable for him. Because faith was the only thing that was required and effected in him at his conversion, it also provides the aim of his entire ministry to others. He understands his commission as helping others to believe in Jesus as well.

In this no work could collaborate with faith. What he did before Christ called him was sin. He received Christ's grace apart from the Law and works of the Law. Likewise, faith could not be transmogrified into gnosis. If he had transformed faith into a theological theory about Jesus, he would have distanced himself from the beginning of his Christian life. For the turning point in his life was not produced by an act of thinking, nor by stories about Jesus with which he was amply supplied in his battle with Christians. Paul considered his conversion to be the act of the one who had authority to be gracious, and his grace did not consist in providing him with instruction but with certainty regarding his regal commission. This is what overcame Paul's opposition toward him.

Paul required forgiveness when Jesus called him, and he received forgiveness when he called on Jesus. His conversion furnishes the reason why, of the two messianic works, redemption from evil and redemption from death, the former became the center of his thought and the focus of his message. What he experienced as Christ's act was that sinners are justified in him. But this did not cause Paul to neglect the concept of life. Rather, just as when a Pharisee he expected Christ to establish the community of the resurrected, he now saw in Jesus additionally the one who ultimately did away with death and brought life to light. Jesus achieved this by conquering sin.

His conversion to Jesus was a call, the establishment of communion through the word. He did not experience fusion of his essence with Christ, nor an infusion of heavenly power into his inner being. He rather heard Jesus' call. Thus the word always remains for him the means by which Jesus' grace reaches man. He conceives of his task in terms of uniting people with Jesus by bringing his call to them. Hearing comes through faith, and the foundation of the Pauline community is the word.

### d) The Church

Imaginative presenters of Paul's history claim that his conversion must have drawn him away from religious community and transformed his piety into that of a self-sufficient hermit. This is allegedly borne out by his statements in the Galatian epistle which express his independence from other people and assert his exclusive dependence on God and the revelation given to him through Christ. He was converted not by the church but by Christ apart from it, not by men but God, as result of direct miraculous intervention. What did he still need people for? Now he sketched out his dogmatics himself as a contemplative hermit in Arabia and established his own church as a visionary who considers himself to be the bearer of revelation. This interpretation of events considers Paul to have experienced at his conversion the passing away of the world, which indeed "was crucified to him" at that time. His own self, however, was exempt from this death. This interpretation conceives of his conversion in self-centered terms as an enhancement of his own self. It is thought to have provided him with the satisfaction of not needing anyone and of creating his theology and church from the things he found in himself. However, this conception is historically useless. The death through which Paul passed hit him first of all, not merely others; it rocked his own thinking and willing, his own wisdom and righteousness. Of course, he also perceived in his experience God's universal verdict, but he maintained with equal sincerity that this verdict also applied to him. Thus he was prevented from any self-centered interpretation or use of his conversion. He does not become the founder of a religion, because he receives his relationship with God through divine grace rather than acquiring it himself; he does not become the creator of a new dogmatics, because his thinking proved to have been foolishness that brought him into conflict with God, and because his knowledge of God had come about as a result of God's shining light into his darkness. What he had recognized was the Christ, and he is for Paul as for all the one who establishes God's community. For this reason Paul did not recognize the legitimacy of the thought that he could have fellowship with Christ apart from the church, even at junctures when he found himself distanced from other disciples. His Christian life began, as it does for everyone else, when he entered the community through baptism.

## 3. Internal Struggles in Christianity

### a) The Surmounting of Pharisaic Christianity

Jesus' word disputed Jewish piety, because it strengthened the selfish desires of the Jew through the assurance of God, while the disciples wanted to administer faith and love in such a way that his attitude toward God and man received its ground in them. But it can come as a surprise to no one that this struggle continued in Christendom, because in it, too, there were men who linked knowledge of Christ not with faith and love but their selfish desires. The ally to whom they looked was Pharisaism, which was during the first few years not the most violent but the most dangerous opponent of the community, because it combined its opposition to Jesus' rule with vigorous piety. Those who contend that allegiance to Pharisaism was possible only where zeal for Jesus' regal privilege was weak need to take a closer look at the facts. Of course, there were occasions where Christian convictions faltered; but these led to a withdrawal back into the synagogue, not to Judaism, not to the effort to establish a community of Jesus against the apostolic office and the word of Jesus, a community that was to have as its mark the defense of Jewish privilege. What was required for this was that the pronouncements describing the call to Jesus as the participation in God's kingdom be stressed vigorously, but now in such a way that Christ's commission was seen to confirm the divine approval of Judaism. Had it not just now been revealed in new glory through the advent of Christ what it meant to belong to Israel (consider Rom. 9:5)? Christ had come for the fulfillment of Israel, and those to whom it was granted to recognize him were fulfilled Jews. From this perspective, and for a selfishly determined will, the struggle for the Jew's privilege easily appeared to be a Christian duty. But then one also reverted to the Pharisaic stance toward the Law. There could not be two means of salvation. As Jew, the Jewish Christian received his relationship with God through the Law, whose fulfillment is his righteousness. It leads him to God's grace and thus at some future point to eternal life. As Christian, he considered Jesus to be the mediator of salvation, from whom he receives reconciliation with God and eternal life. While these two positions remained unreconciled, this position was unbearable; a harmonization of these two convictions was indispensable, and such could be attained only by assigning priority to one aspect over the other. Jesus' disciples placed his mediatorial office above the validity of the Law. Not because of the Law but because of Christ, not as reward for kept commandments but as Christ's gracious gift, they now possessed, and will possess in the future, their communion with God. The opposite set of priorities between the two ways of salvation, on the other hand, must be represented by all who maintained that the glorification of the Jews was the goal of the messianic work. In that case, the Law determined one's relationship with God, and Christ confirmed the teaching of the Law, explained and expanded the obedience required by it, and fulfilled the promise given by it. Thus what it emphasized regarding the fulfillment brought by Christ is what is fulfilled, not the One who fulfills, and thus man is once again placed above God in the Jewish manner, whereby piety was transformed into a struggle for Jewish greatness.

Now the Gentile mission must be rejected as false, if it did not bring about the nations' conversion to Mosaism. Fellowship with non-Christian Jews was here valued more highly than fellowship with Gentiles who believed in Christ. The disappearance of paganism through Christian preaching was considered less valuable than the preservation and glorification of Israel. Therefore the universal establishment of the church incited Judaistic circles to sectarian movements, because the resulting practical question could not be avoided but required action and thus also a consensus view. Now there appeared both in Palestine and in the Diaspora those who denied fellowship to the Gentile church and therefore also separated from the apostles in the name of the Law, which for them stood above the Christ.

Yet it was not only the ecclesiastical question that resulted in separation; the internal reason was that Judaism evaded faith in Jesus. According to its view, Jesus had nothing to give that was perfect, which makes it impossible for a conclusive, complete confidence in him to arise. What Judaism sought transcended him and extended rather to the alleged goal of his ministry, that is, the Law. Now trust finds its support in the religious achievements of man. Therefore Judaism considered all forms of the proclamation of Jesus as false that sought to establish complete faith in Jesus. A doctrine of justification, as expressed by the Pauline pronouncements, was rejected here, not because faith must not be separated from works, but because such faith was considered impossible and incorrect, because it was judged to lack a proper basis and content. Here Jesus does not reveal the divine righteousness and grace in such a way that man's confidence must turn to him.

Paul's conversion had prepared him to perceive sharply the internal aspect of the religious contrast that thereby entered Christendom. He did not encounter faith in those who were from the Law. He therefore placed the question of faith, that is, whether Christendom places its confidence in Jesus and has God's grace through faith in him, above the ecclesiastical question, that is, who should be called and how the constitution of the community should be designed. It is probably to a large extent Paul's work that the question of mission merged completely with the question of faith and that the former was resolved by answering the latter.

The Judaistic conviction could easily result in a christological formula that equated Jesus' relationship with God with that of God's Old Testament messengers. The more his religious possession conformed to theirs, the clearer it was that he was united with them merely as a link in the chain of God's revelation to Israel, albeit as the final and greatest in the series that granted religion, while all statements regarding Jesus' communion with God describing it as complete and eternal stood in opposition to Judaism. For Paul, the contrast with Judaism did not yet present itself as a battle for Jesus' divine sonship, and the statement attributing to the community the possession of the Spirit did not become part of the conflict. Pharisaic Christianity that sought to disturb Paul's work thus also upheld the Christ concept in the magnitude it had received through Jesus' end, and it acknowledged Israel's glorification precisely in the fact that Jesus ruled in the glory of God and gave his Spirit to the community. On the other hand, Pharisaic Christianity parted ways with Jesus by pushing his cross aside as a forgettable episode, a calamity that had been compensated for by Jesus' exaltation. It did not view Jesus' death as the manifestation of the divine verdict that reveals Israel's guilt nor as the offer of divine grace that grants reconciliation to the community. This opposition confirmed Paul in his conviction that he must gather the community around Jesus' cross and that he must show the community in it the event that judges and gives grace to all. According to Paul, selfish will dies before the cross of Christ; now and here man's faith turns to God.[46]

The efforts of the Judaizers to redirect the Greek mission in such a way that it aimed at the conversion of Christians to the Law emerged in two forms, since two different tendencies could also be discerned in Pharisaism. Alongside the committed defense of the Law that rigorously rejected any deviation from it and thus could increase to fanaticism, there stood the rule that the Law must be accommodated to the circumstances of the people and man's ability and be worded in such a way that it was possible to fulfill it. Likewise, one group among the Judaizers viewed the Law in such a way that it retained its absolute validity; this group claimed that those who rejected the Law were lost despite their faith in Christ. This is the verdict of those who began to oppose Paul in Antioch (Acts 15:1; thus Paul's verdict: "false brethren who had sneaked in," Gal. 2:4). They considered even the baptized Greek to be a sinner, because he did not accept the Law. The other group placed the Law above the Christ in such a way that both forms of piety stood beside each other as a higher and a lower stage; according to this view, the Jew is closer to God and favored by God over the one who merely had faith in Jesus; the Gentile Christian attained perfection when he was circumcised. Thus the result of the Gentile mission was accepted, but merely as an initial stage that took account of man's weakness (Gal. 1:10). God's complete blessing and perfect obedience were reached by the one who added to faith adherence to the Law. In this form we know Judaism from the epistle to the Galatians. Paul saw also in this form a complete surrender of the faith. He judged that full trust was also here not directed toward Christ. It was rather placed on the Law and the work of man.

On the other hand, Paul did not speak of heresy when the Christian Jew practiced communion with the church that was free from the Law but himself sought wherever possible to avoid the transgression of the Law that could arise from this and to order his own conduct as much as possible according to the Law. This Paul called weakness of faith but not sin (Rom. 14; 1 Cor. 8:13).

Because Paul gave Jewish Christians not just in Jerusalem but also in the congregations he had established complete freedom to retain Jewish custom, Jewish Christianity was not distinguished from the Judaizers through an external characteristic such as Sabbath observance or the practice of circumcision. Paul did

---

46. Regarding the exaggeration of this observation, to the effect that Paul used the doctrine of justification merely for polemical purposes, see pp. 238–39.

not seek to evade this internalization of conflict. To the contrary, he considered solely the inner process as significant. The question was whether faith was placed in Christ or man praised himself, whether the flesh or the Spirit was the basis for confidence. Through this intensification of contrast Paul lent the conflict its magnitude and fruitfulness. He did not fear that the boundary between authentic and counterfeit Christianity would thereby be blurred. For Paul assumed that faith would be manifested by a man's actions. The occasion at which it must be shown whether the Jewish Christian served the Law or Christ presented itself when he was confronted with the Greek Christian (Gal. 2:3). If he refused him fellowship despite his faith, he proved that his own devotion was something other than faith in Christ. For this reason Paul for his part withheld fellowship from those who refused fellowship to the Gentile church (Gal. 1:8–9; 1 Cor. 16:22).

### b) Gnostic Christianity

Even easier than the blending of Christianity with the principles of Pharisaism was the merger with gnostic forms of piety. How quickly self-centered piety could take on gnostic traits even in a Pauline congregation is seen by what happened in Corinth, when the congregation came under the influence of new teachers who had come to it from the Orient. Now God's revelation was understood as the impartation of his wisdom, and an effort was made to move beyond Christian faith as an immature initial stage. Ethical norms were accorded little esteem, intercourse with prostitutes was defended as harmless, and marrying one's mother-in-law was seen as a splendid demonstration of Christian liberty. By appeal to it one also softened the contrast with Greek religious practice. At the same time, religious celibacy was celebrated. Regarding pneumatic processes, the mysterious and spectacular were esteemed and made the occasion for self-admiration. Thus these elements were also displayed before the congregation. The leaders of the movement pointed to their own spiritual greatness while at the same time praising that of Jesus' companions, especially of Peter (1 Cor. 9:1–6; 15:8–11; cf. 2 Cor. 11:5; 12:11). For themselves, they created a paid teaching office, destroyed the congregation's freedom, ruled, and thus did not tolerate Paul's apostolic office. Because they praised and enjoyed the religious state they had attained, hope withered. While they had not yet compromised the expectation of the manifestation of Christ, but the pronouncement guaranteeing resurrection, which promises to everything, including the dead, a share in Christ's kingdom, hope was threatened. This constituted the beginning of a transformation of prophecy into an eschatological doctrine that is no longer able to command man's will but merely provides fulfillment for the contemplation of the world and occupies the imagination.

Similar processes can be seen in Colossae, where a form of wisdom was found that sought to produce interchange with heavenly powers and thus to develop a method of sanctification, in part by using Mosaic commandments, in part by ascetic regulations, by which one sought to effect religious perfection. The Pastoral epistles make clear that Paul considered his entire ministry to be jeopardized through his movement. Now the Christian scholar comes into being, who considers his task to be the discussion of religious problems and allows himself to be paid for it. Because it is speculative, his research immediately gives up the difference between truth and fiction. The contrast with Jewish legend is thus surrendered, and myth is esteemed. With this faith ceases to function as the central process of Christian piety. Rather, knowledge is viewed as the essential characteristic of communion with God, and gatherings are used for theoretical discourses and disputations. Hope in the resurrection dies in view of the proud consciousness of attained religious greatness, because new life has already been received. Because the rule of love no longer determines the will, man's perfection is sought through ascetic regulations. The leaders surround themselves with followers that are slavishly subservient to them, while Paul's apostolic office is not tolerated.[47]

But even these developments did not cause Paul to surrender the congregation's liberty as unattainable and to look for a foundation other than faith for it. He therefore did not reject and prohibit individual gnostic ideas regarding God, Christ, or man. He barred these theories from the congregation only when they undid what happened in Christ (1 Cor. 15:1; 2 Tim. 2:18). He did not permit any doubt regarding the truthfulness of the historical affirmations that make up the gospel. At the same time, he did not counter these theories with corresponding ones but rather postulated the preservation of faith and love as the aim in the conflict. When faith in Christ is robbed of assurance by contact with other mediators of salvation, and when it is to be replaced with a theory, religious efforts fall under condemnation. This condemnation retains force when the gospel's relation to the good will is loosened and when other regulations are put in effect than the one that requires the congregation to love and makes it fruitful in every good work.

## 4. Stages in the Formation of Pauline Teaching

The effort to discern distinct periods in Paul's thought and ministry may be encouraged by the fact that his epistles can be divided into groups according to their content. Both Thessalonian letters stand together. The four major epistles are linked by a great common theme, while Ephesians and Colossians,[48] as well as the letters to Timothy and Titus, constitute respective separate groups. The supposition that Paul completely expressed the religious property he had at the time of gathering the Corinthian community in the epistle to Thessalonica results in the thesis that he arrived at the convictions which he expresses for the first time in the major epistles only in the Ephesian period. But this would suggest that the peculiar content of Colossians and Ephesians and of the Pastoral epistles represents later teaching, which would then more appropriately be attributed no longer to Paul himself but to later followers who sought to preserve his legacy.

47. The movement reached far beyond Pauline congregations and the Pauline period; cf. the epistles of Jude (pp. 103–6) and John (pp. 120–21).

48. In contrast, the letter to the Philippians has more definite ties both to the Thessalonian as well as to the four major Pauline epistles.

### a) The Similarity between the Thessalonian Correspondence and the Major Epistles

The construction of a preliminary form of Pauline theology from the Thessalonian epistles, to which the pronouncements of the major epistles are subsequently added, is opposed by the confirmed fact that the overcoming of Judaism preceded Paul's ministry in Greece. But because we do not find the principles by which Paul established the Law-free order of community in the Thessalonian epistles, these would have been acquired by him, according to this theory, only when the decisive events had already occurred. This conjecture is not merely improbable by itself; it also contradicts Paul's statement that he represented the convictions that are developed in Romans in Antioch and that he based his relationship with the Jerusalem apostles on them (Gal. 2:15–16 summarizes the train of thought developed in Rom. 1–3 in one single sentence). It also contradicts Paul's claim regarding his ministry in Corinth, according to which he considered his ministry there to consist exclusively in the proclamation of Jesus' cross (1 Cor. 2:2; cf. Gal. 3:1). But this is inconceivable apart from Paul's characteristic interpretation of Jesus' death; only through it does the proclamation of the cross become the whole gospel.

The major epistles likewise show that statistics counting the affirmations of an epistle do not yet provide us with a complete knowledge of the body of theological understanding that Paul bore within himself at that time. No one can deduce the doctrine of justification which is presented to us by Galatians and Romans from the Corinthian epistles. Only from the former epistles do we learn what passages such as 1 Corinthians 15:56 or 2 Corinthians 5:21 meant for Paul. Despite the large overlap between Galatians and Romans, however, Galatians would not suffice to justify the supposition that the idea of God's predestination has the significance indicated by the epistle to the Romans. But this does not warrant the conclusion that Paul arrived at this conviction only during his second stay at Corinth. Paul perceived from the history of the patriarchs that God created free men rather than slaves and that he did not act toward mankind according to human merit but according to his own will. Only the former affirmation is made in Galatians, the latter only in Romans; but both of these conclusions regarding Israel's beginnings grew jointly and were not separated by many years (Rom. 9:6–13; Gal. 4:21–31). The manner in which Paul makes the gospel to be a teaching about the resurrection in 1 Corinthians 15 does not have any close parallels; but it would be to misunderstand the summing up of the gospel in the concept of life if Paul's resurrection teaching were judged to be new, unprecedented when Paul propounded it, and forgotten after Paul expressed his views. For the statement that life appeared through Christ is a basic component of messianism and extends not merely to but even prior to the beginning of the church.

Through the epistles to the Thessalonians Paul continues his relationship with them even subsequent to his departure. This initially leads him to remind them of the ethical norms that regulate Christian conduct. But even those would reveal a clear difference if the teaching of the major epistles had still been missing, because strong changes in one's faith result in new ethical goals. But the Thessalonian epistles take the same position regarding ethical norms as the later epistles. According to them, Christian piety consists in the following three actions: faith, hope, and love (1 Thess. 1:3; 5:8). Nothing ranks beside these in value. But the seriousness with which Paul directs the community's attention to its own conduct does not lead to an obfuscation of the perfection of the divine gift. The community received through the proclamation of Jesus God's calling, election, and sanctification from which its glorification grows.[49] Thereby God demonstrated his perfect love for the community, love that comes to its completion through his faithfulness (1 Thess. 5:24; 2 Thess. 1:12; 2:13, 16; 3:3). The relationship between faith and works is thus cast in the same way Paul always does. The demand for the community's obedience is not based on a deficiency in the divine gift and therefore does not negatively affect the certainty of faith. Rather, because perfect grace is offered to the community in Christ, the absolute demand is made of it that now claims its love and its obedience for God. God's gift is given to it through the word, through which Christ and the Spirit are with them.[50] The community's inclusion in Christ and the manifestation of the Spirit in it is described in the same manner as in the other epistles. The congregation has prophets in its midst; yet the Spirit's work is not limited to these special functions, for he provides them with love, gives them sanctification, and grants that they suffer joyfully for God's sake. Therefore intellectualism and the Law are rejected in these letters as completely as in the later epistles. Paul's capacity for serving as God's messenger and of speaking his word is not grounded in his theological thought, as if he was able to exercise his calling as messenger through theoretical instruction. Rather, because he brings to man his calling to God, Paul's apostolic office reached its goal only when he could subject man with his will and actions to God. Therefore the Thessalonian epistles also place no restriction whatsoever on the Pauline rule of liberty. There is no trace of legislation. Both believers' fellowship with one another and their dealings with their prophets and elders, even their subordination to the apostles, occurs freely, even though the community has just been gathered and is still inexperienced. Nowhere do the later epistles lead the community beyond these norms; they merely reveal more completely Paul's rationale and why he assigned absolute validity to these norms. But it is highly improbable that Paul only subsequently concocted a rationale why he instructed the congregations in this way rather than in another.

### b) Jesus' Divinity in Colossians and Ephesians

The epistles to the Colossians and Ephesians tell the congregations that they possess complete communion with God through Christ, whereby any religious striving that seeks religious benefit apart from Christ, such as through dealings with heavenly spirits, is proven to be false and sinful. The fullness of deity dwells

49. Calling: 1 Thess. 1:12; 4:7; 5:24; 2 Thess. 1:11; 2:14; election: 1 Thess. 1:4; 2 Thess. 2:13; sanctification: 1 Thess. 3:13; 4:3–7; 5:23; 2 Thess. 2:13; glorification: 2 Thess. 1:10; 2:14.
50. Word: 1 Thess. 1:5–6; 2:13; 2 Thess. 1:8; 2:14; Spirit: 1 Thess. 1:5–6; 4:5, 8–9, 19–20; 2 Thess. 2:13; in the Lord: 1 Thess. 3:8; 4:16; 5:12; 4:1; 2 Thess. 3:4, 12.

in him, not merely a limited gift or power, not an isolated grace, but God with his whole strength, his entire wisdom, his complete will (Col. 1:19; 2:9). Allegiance to Christ thus brings communion with God and full possession of the benefits of fellowship with him. The one who is united with Christ is "filled," does not suffer from deficiencies or powerlessness, but has everything he can obtain through the possession of divine love (Col. 2:10; Eph. 3:19). These statements are statements of faith akin to the absolute judgments of earlier epistles. For the verdict that the community possesses complete union with God is not grounded in human accomplishments. It is based neither in mental achievements by which the community raises itself to a knowledge of God, nor in an exercise of its will, whichever work it might seek in order to establish communion with God. Paul's negative verdict regarding everything man could consider his own piety returns here undiminished, and the positive verdict that unites the possession of divine grace with faith is represented in no less vigorous terms. Nevertheless, the state of faith reflected by the older epistles is not merely copied in these discussions but is developed in a new direction. For here it is not the Law that provides the occasion for a striving that elevates itself above faith and distances itself from Christ, and therefore the subject of discussion is here not the antithesis between guilt and righteousness, works and faith. Rather, here the question arises regarding the completeness of the Christian possession, in light of the contemplation of the immeasurable greatness of the universe with all its mysterious profundities and the multitudes of rulers and thrones that are in heaven, beside which Jesus, who bears witness regarding himself through his blood and cross, appears small. But just as Paul rejected any appeal to the Law because thereby confidence in Christ is broken and the perfection of his messianic office is disputed, he rejects here attempts to ensure oneself of the services of other bearers of divine grace and revelation. He does so through the same affirmation that the union with Christ established through faith includes everything we need, whereby any movement away from Christ and beyond faith becomes sin. But no historian will claim that Paul discovered magic religious formulas expressing a desire for the attaining of heavenly spheres only in Colossae but not earlier, such as in Antioch or Asia Minor. And it is certain that Paul never provided an answer other than the one contained in the Colossian epistle that responds to human longing for the knowledge of God by presenting the uniqueness and all-sufficiency of Christ, who possesses the fullness of God's wisdom and authority.

In this context, Paul emphasizes that Christ's majesty is grounded already in his participation in God's act of creation. Everything has been created in him, thus also has its abiding subsistence and aim in him, and everything is created for his sake in order that it be his possession and receive life and glory from him, thus manifesting his sonship (Col. 1:15–17). These pronouncements do not primarily refer to nature, even though, in their universal scope, they also derive it from Christ's creative activity. But they should primarily be applied to the spiritual realm, because the confusion of the congregation arose not from the contemplation of nature but from the realization of hidden heavenly powers. Paul did not portray their dependence on Christ merely as a future prospect that will be reached only in the course of history, be it through a new appearance of Jesus or at his exaltation. Rather, he describes it as already essentially and irreversibly grounded in the act of creation. The spirits also received life through Jesus and for this reason have him as their head. This now also provides Jesus' earthly work with its universal scope. Through Jesus' cross, God removes the spirits who act as rulers, displaying their powerlessness, and celebrating his triumph over them. Likewise, the positive impact of his cross, his reconciling power, encompasses not merely those on earth but also those in heaven. Precisely at the point where the community experiences God's love and where its enmity with him comes to an end, every objection vanishes also in the heavenlies. Now every conflict with him ceases, and they are placed in his love. Thus the wisdom of the divine government, which provides the community with its history, is revealed to the heavenlies as well (Col. 2:15; 1:20; Eph. 3:10). It is impossible to determine when Paul first conceived of this thought, because we know that he framed Jesus' divine sonship already earlier in a way that made him the executor of the divine will at the beginning of all things, and because we also know that the authority delegated to the spirits already earlier had significance for Paul's cosmology, because he brought them into connection with the contrast between the present age and the age to come, with the misery and darkness of the present world (1 Cor. 15:24).[51] But clearly discernible is that these affirmations regarding the Christ reiterate the major contours of Pauline Christology, while at the same time deepening them in a powerful way.

We know through the earlier epistles that Paul did not consider Christ's ministry to be a substitute for God's activity but rather grounded Christ's power in God's working through him. A different hand would then be visible in the later presentation if the invisible universe's dependence on Christ were grounded in an abstract concept of God that removes any contact with the world from God and replaces the divine activity with that of Christ. But in this regard the message of the epistles is authentically Pauline: through the crucifixion of Christ God celebrates his triumph over the spirits, and by the same means he reconciles it with himself, exercising his rule by making Christ the head. God makes the world his possession and the place of his revelation by having created it for the sake of Christ. Moreover, we know from the major epistles that Paul spoke of God only insofar as he is dealing with God's revelation. Christology would be lifted out of its Pauline form if it appeared as a description of God apart from his relationship with us, which would certainly have occurred if these pronouncements had received their universal scope through Greek or gnostic influence. But regarding Jesus' relationship with the Father, we receive only phrases which we already know from Paul anyway. Among these are "Son of God" and "image of God." Further, regarding Jesus' participation in the divine activity, we have no other statement than the one contained in 1 Corinthians 8:6, taken by Paul directly from Scripture, that Christ was the agent of God's

---

51. Whoever takes 1 Cor. 2:6–8 to refer to heavenly princes thus finds a close parallel to the pronouncements of Colossians.

creation as the image of God.[52] For an imagination stirred by gnostic ideas, however, this was not the only way in which the Preexistent One could implement his ministry. Here, too, Paul does not explain his statements in speculative terms. No sentence seeks to explain how the Father conceived the Son, and not even the idea of "image" is placed in a direct causal relationship with "sonship of God." The verdict regarding the Christ is also here based solely on what is manifest as God's work in the condition of the world and the community.

The conviction that the spirits take part in human history and therefore are also comprehended in Christ's work that brings humanity to completion is confirmed Pauline material. The day of Christ becomes the day of judgment also for the angels, and the community will pronounce judgment over them together with its Lord. When the community approaches God in prayer, it must be careful not to give the angels any occasion to bring a charge against it. The inviolability of the community through all power of height or depth is part of Christ's grace, and his regal activity brings an end to their rule and thus provides humanity with direct and complete communion with God (1 Cor. 6:3; 11:10; Rom. 8:38; 1 Cor. 15:24). The new pronouncements remain consistent with these ideas, because not one word makes the angels in themselves the object of description. Paul also here does not speak as the one who was charged with the issuing of revelations regarding them, even though he wants to assure the community that God's glory and love shines from the cross through the entire world. We go beyond the text if we say that Paul thinks, in speaking of the reconciliation of the heavenlies, merely of fallen angels, or that he describes them as the recipients of reconciliation because they stood before God as the accusers of mankind until the cross, making common cause with his wrath and bringing about death in the world. We go beyond the text if we say that Paul leaves God to a certain extent hidden for all creation prior to the fulfillment of Christ, concealing insight into his counsel for it, while now God's ways are displayed in broad daylight for the heavenlies. We do the same if we claim that Paul thinks, regarding God's triumph over the powers, of Satan or the death angel, or that God relates the triumph to the removal of the charge of guilt issuing from the Law, so that the angels are conceived of as mediators and keepers of the Law; or if Paul is viewed as thinking of the triumph of grace that provided salvation for the world of sinners not through glorious heavenly spirits but through the dying man Jesus—with all these deliberations we have already gone beyond what is explicitly stated in the text.[53]

The manner in which Paul criticizes gnostic theories provides a clear analogy to his discussion of the question of the Law. He says that he has no confidence in the gnostics' knowledge; for it works with traditions of men and originates from fleshly reason, which arrives at such ideas because it is ruled by pride (Col. 2:4, 8, 20–22, 18). However, he does not substantiate his criticism by concrete reference to his opponents' individual theories; for he gains his principal con-

---

52. It is improbable that Paul ever interpreted Gen. 1:26 differently than by identifying Christ with the image of God.

53. The passage retains its Pauline character in that it does not transform Jesus' end into a wrestling with spirits, much less with Satan in the singular.

clusions from the certainty issuing directly from faith in Christ. Analogously, Paul engaged in material criticism of the Law only after deriving freedom from the Law from the basic act of Christian devotion, that is, that by faith we are united with Christ. In both instances, Paul invests this basic consideration with profundity by providing a complete exposition of the truth of the opposing pronouncement. In the same way that he affirms the authority and validity of the Law as seriously as any Jew, he does not withhold recognition of the authority of the heavenly powers. He understands and acknowledges the motive at work in these pious efforts; for he too considers the mystery with which regions hidden to us present us to be solemn and profound. But because he answers the question exclusively from the vantage point of Christ, he arrives in both instances at a true resolution that would not have been attainable by rational considerations alone. The community knows what it has in Christ, and thereby it gains complete assurance that does not allow it to look for other mediators of salvation. Thus the discussion does not end in doubt, with the deliberation of possibilities or probabilities, but in a definitive verdict, precisely because it is gained not through theories but through faith arising from Christ.

An important connection with the earlier epistles, and one that can hardly be attained by a third person in this way, arises through the verdict of these writings regarding the flesh. Also to the Colossians, Paul describes as the benefit they receive from Christ that he set them free from the body of flesh and thus granted them the true, effective circumcision (Col. 2:11). The denigration of the flesh appears to open the way for a Christology that views Christ's flesh exclusively as part of his humiliation, and that understands it solely in terms of the concealment of his sonship and prevention of his lordship, particularly if he is simultaneously described as Creator and Lord of the spirits who shows the Father's love also to them. But Jesus' greatness consists in the fact that the fullness of God dwelt in him in bodily form (Col. 2:9). Paul refers those who wander into transcendent domains to the one who represented and manifested God to them in human form and thus also in visible bodily reality. Thereby Jesus' corporeality is assigned a positive value as the means of the divine revelation and rule, while our own flesh simultaneously becomes the object of complete renunciation. This was always the way Paul thought. For this reason Christ's blood is designated as the means of reconciliation and the ground of faith also in these epistles, without any noticeable difference from earlier statements regarding Jesus' blood (Eph. 1:7; 2:13; Col. 1:20).

### c) The Church in the Epistles to the Colossians and Ephesians

Through the statements regarding Christ's heavenly rule, the pronouncements regarding the church also take on a new dimension. While Paul's teaching on justification and the categories of guilt and righteousness used there result in individual faith strongly emerging as the goal of preaching and the condition for the church's existence, here Christ and the church are combined in such a way that the establishment of the church is the aim of Christ's commission and death and Christ exercises his rule through the church's ministry. Christ's union with the church as the head of the body does not merely indicate the church's subordination to Christ but also portrays the value it has for him as "his fullness," which is his possession and his glory (Eph. 1:23). Accordingly, the contrast between the Law and Christ is seen in the fact that the Law prevented the emergence of the one great community, because it separated Jews from Gentiles and established enmity between them, so that it had to be dismantled to make room for the community that is God's temple. The idea that the Law renders the transgressor guilty and prevents his access to God is not absent from Ephesians but does not constitute the primary emphasis (Eph. 2:11–22; on the other hand, Col. 1:21–22; 2:13–15 aligns more closely with the earlier epistles). Correspondingly, what is stressed as the most significant element in Paul's ministry is that through it the mystery of God has been revealed that the nations are called as well (Eph. 3:1–12; Col. 1:24–29).

But in individualizing piety and the apostolic ministry, Paul never intended to erect a dichotomy between the individual and the community, so that the latter was added merely as an addition to the salvation of individuals. The basic pattern of the messianic idea that assigns to Christ the task of perfecting the community remains the foundational axiom for all of Pauline thought. It is therefore once again impossible for conjectures to measure how he showed his congregations the greatness of divine grace in the emergence of the church, which unites mankind, and how he instilled gratitude in them for their incorporation into it.

We would stray outside the parameters of Paul's epistles to the Colossians and Ephesians if we inferred that in them faith is directed away from Christ to the church, so that individuals received their salvation through the church's sacrament, office, and doctrine. But their pronouncements regarding baptism, office-bearers, and the gospel remain identical with the distinctive and often surprising Pauline statements we find elsewhere in his writings (baptism: Eph. 4:5; Col. 2:12; office: Eph. 4:11–13; Col. 4:17; gospel: Eph. 1:13; 3:6; Col. 1:5, 23, 25). The community comes into being through Jesus' message; because this message comes from him, it provides the community with communion with Christ and thus also the Spirit, and thus the community is sanctified. Through this portrayal of the church, faith is placed solely and indivisibly in the Christ. But that Paul was able to stress emphatically the establishment of the church as being among the gifts of Christ by which he reveals himself to mankind and brings about faith among men—this was determined by the actual outcome of early Christian history.

If the concept of church changed in Colossians and Ephesians compared to Paul's other letters, this would need to find expression in the ethical instruction that constitutes a major theme of these epistles. But their distance from Paul cannot in fact be demonstrated solely from this vantage point. These letters know nothing of particular characteristics by which a Christian can be identified or of methods of sanctification by which religious success can be achieved. Through ethical categories evident to all, such as chastity and impurity, love and wrath, truth and lie, that which constitutes sin is separated from what Christendom does. But these requirements are invested with the resolute sincerity of a complete will, because the perfect divine gift has been obtained in

Christ. From this ethic it becomes immediately clear that complete Christian virtuousness is demanded not merely for the religious community but also for natural forms of community that coexist in a complete family, such as marriage, children, and slaves.[54]

All instructions are grounded in the love commandment, which determines what is said both regarding the religious ritual of the community and regarding what Christians owe one another in their dealings with one another. A need to supplement the love motif through other ethical norms can be detected here as little as in the ethical portions of Romans or Galatians. The community is expected to resist sin in the conviction that its share in God depends on this; but repentance is not separated from faith. Through union with Christ, the ethical question has already been determined, and the believer now must apply the decision in effect regarding his entire existence to his particular tasks. He put off the old man and thus puts to death sinful lust within himself (Eph. 4:22–24; Col. 3:9–11).

Thus the concept of liberty is expressed here as completely as elsewhere. This becomes evident in the treatment of the ascetic question, which presented particular difficulties because both the virtues and the shortcomings of ascetic aspirations must be exposed. All ascetic regulations are rejected as unchristian, but as in 1 Corinthians in such a way that the ethical norms that are summed up in the condemnation of the flesh remain in full force (Col. 2:18–3:6). It is precisely on this condemnation that Paul bases the community's freedom from ascetic legalism. The community is free, because it has its life no longer in the world but in Christ. It is thus separated from all evil and engaged in a persistent struggle against desires originating from the members of the body. Thus the epistles reiterate the Yes and No given by Paul to passions issuing from the body, not merely by quoting earlier statements but in new formulations with distinct creative force.

#### d) The Office in the Pastoral Epistles

The Pastoral epistles present us once more with the question of whether they reveal stages in the formation of doctrine, perhaps stages that transcend Paul's thought in the major epistles, because they differ not merely in formal respects but also in matters of substance. But while one may detect in the prison epistles a conscious interaction with gnostic thought owing to the emphasis given to Paul's "mystery," the Pastoral epistles deal exclusively with the work required for the community's preservation. Here speaks a worker who is engaged in the fulfillment of his ministry and who knows of no more pressing need than to complete it; and his ministry serves not gnostic or ritual aims that are to be realized in the transcendent sphere but rather draws its substance in interaction with people by means of a discerning and courageous involvement in the world.

The answer to the question of whether these writings indeed present us with Paul's final words is significantly influenced by the picture we make for our-

---

54. That the state is missing in this list does not present a difficulty in light of Paul's stance elsewhere.

selves regarding the attitude of early Christianity. Moreover, even if these texts are separated from Paul owing to the difficulties presented by them in form and content, this does not mean that their importance would be diminished. For since they stand in close relationship with Paul's ministry in any case, the fact is instructive that their testimony regarding Paul's aims arose in his circle and was accepted by the congregations as an authentic picture of the apostle.

The new element in these epistles is that they present the ecclesiastical office as indispensable for the functioning and health of the community. Its normal activity does not arise virtually by itself from its union with Christ. Rather, it is only through the faithful, continuing ministry of those who hold an office that communities are preserved and fulfill their obligation. The office is accentuated already by the fact that the epistles are directed not to the congregations as a whole but to Paul's co-workers.[55] It is through them that the apostle relates to the congregations. Above them, Paul himself stands once again with his expressly stated authority that transfers also to his co-workers a distinctive authorization and responsibility. Thereafter they are charged with the important task of selecting office-bearers. The congregation's well-being to a large extent depends on the successful completion of this task.

It is equally clear that the epistles retain the community's unity rather than dividing it into clergy and laity. For we hear nothing of a division of the labor to be accomplished by the community into individual, mutually exclusive functions. The apostle's co-workers do not receive a distinct mandate, separate from the congregation's ministry, which would exhaust the scope of their specific responsibility. Rather, there is nothing in the community for which they are not responsible. Doctrine and financial stewardship, overseer and widow, the reading of Scripture and congregational prayer, but also the conduct of individuals and their temptations and sins—they are given charge of all of these. The epistles thus stand in complete contrast with everything later called canon law, because canon law exists only when individual spheres of authority are delimited over against others. The separation between the responsibilities of office-bearers and the community, and between what both are charged with in separate areas, is essential for canon law; but this perspective is foreign to the Pastorals. This is already indicated by the fact that there is no designation for the office of their recipients. They administer neither the apostolate nor the episcopate. Their ministry lacks institutional permanence, and its lack of designation and delimitation is not felt to be a hindrance. The epistles do not reflect the view that the divine government established forms which subsequently led to the search for a man to fill them. There is no indication that a job description was designed prior to the concrete situation, a description which then had to be carried out by someone. Rather, the Pastorals indicate that God's government so guides and forms conditions in the community and the men ministering in it that the divine message is proclaimed by them and the fulfillment of the divine will is facilitated. Accordingly, the sections regarding the selection of overseers and

---

55. The epistle's content accounts for this only in the case of 2 Timothy, but not in the case of 1 Timothy or Titus.

deacons are silent regarding their functions, rights, and duties; mention is made solely of what kinds of men may be entrusted with the work needing to be accomplished on behalf of the community.

The absence of legal provisions in the presentation of ecclesiastical calling does not imply that the apostle's co-workers do the whole work themselves and take over the community's entire task. For the epistles speak clearly of the participation of all in the work of the community. Likewise, they do not infringe on the community's right to order its affairs according to its own judgment. They contain virtually nothing in terms of statuary regulations that are grounded not in generally valid ethical norms but in expediencies.[56] The instructions regarding prayer, offices, discipline, and dealings with pagan fellow-citizens demand only what Paul always considered necessary, because it follows directly from God's revealed will. That the bishop must not weaken the community's ethical vigor through sin or bring contempt on the ecclesiastical office is an absolute, normative requirement; how many overseers there should be, one or several, how they are to be elected, how they are to order their affairs and to delimit these from deacons and the rest of congregational matters, and particularly the many other issues that must immediately be dealt with for the orderly fulfillment of the office—regarding these matters, the epistles do not provide an apostolic injunction (1 Tim. 3:1–13; Titus 1:5–9). Paul charges his representative to ensure that prayer is kept free from sectarian self-centeredness, which fanatically closes itself off from the world, and is not limited solely to Christians but rather issued for all men; how often prayer meetings should be held, how they are to be used for the word and prayer, and whether or not prayer is regulated liturgically—we hear nothing of this sort; for this is subject to the community's discretion, because the community knows its needs and must act in the best interests of its own piety (1 Tim. 2:1–8).

The treatment of sacraments has particular importance in this regard, because their free observance places high demands on the spiritual maturity of the congregations, which is why sacraments have always been the starting point for the formulation of sacred orders. Baptism is considered to be one of the means by which divine grace is dispensed to the community. This corresponds to the Pauline concept of baptism. The expression by which baptismal grace is described, that is, that is grants rebirth, is new, but concurs with the earlier epistles by linking the entire gift of divine grace rather than only part of it with baptism (Titus 3:5). *Palingenesia* designates everything Christ grants to the believer, including eschatological fulfillment. But the epistles are in agreement with Pauline teaching on baptism also in that they do not contain anything regarding the performance of baptism, for example, the question of infant baptism or baptismal confession. Nor do they regulate the celebration of the Last Supper. Ordination is accentuated in the exhortation directed to Timothy. He must remember that prophecy caused his entrance into ministry and

---

56. At the most one may here refer to some of the regulations pertaining to the church's care for widows (1 Tim. 5:3–16). But even those are explained by the opposition to the gnostic movement, which drove women to join the widows already received by the community.

that it occurred through the laying on of hands of Paul and the elders (1 Tim. 1:18; 4:14; 2 Tim. 1:6). This serves the establishment of faith in the epistles, not merely for Timothy, who gains assurance and courage in his struggle with the boastful new teachers (because these events ensure that he entered his ministry not by his own choice but in obedience to God's call and with his promise), but also for Paul, because he, too, strengthened his confidence of fulfilling his work through remembrance of the distinct call of God which gave Timothy his ministry, for his own gain and that of the community. Therefore Paul also warns against the premature laying on of hands, because it loses its inner value if it is given without certainty but merely on the basis of a vain supposition (1 Tim. 5:22). Nevertheless, the epistles do not contain a single word regarding legislation concerning ordination.

Because the freedom of congregations remains intact, the difficulties this freedom creates for the leadership of these communities come to the fore as well. Those who "teach differently" cannot be silenced merely by issuing a decree or by removing them from the congregation (1 Tim. 1:3; Titus 1:10–11). They must be combated with internal means, because nothing can be done— or should be done—against them apart from the community's conviction that the instructions these false teachers provide it for its conduct are foreign to Christian ethics and harmful. Therefore the epistles face the church's future with serious concern and expect its demise (1 Tim. 4:1–3; 2 Tim. 3:1–9). The repeated "do not do this" is instructive as well, as is the exhortation for Paul's representatives not to allow themselves to be despised and for the congregation to honor its elders (1 Tim. 4:7; 5:11; 2 Tim. 2:23; Titus 3:10; 1 Tim. 4:12; 5:17). Protection against such difficulties is sought not in the instituting of a legally established ruling office. The challenge posed by the congregation's liberty cannot be removed; it must overcome the difficulties resulting from it through the administration of the word in the power of the Spirit. That the congregations' freedom could be curtailed is a thought completely missing from the scope of the epistles. Nor is the freedom of Paul's co-workers compromised in his dealings with them. Paul does not merely issue commands requiring their obedience; he rather illumines the relationship in which his instruction stands to the gospel, even though this is partly done for the sake of the congregation, to which Paul's co-workers must justify why it must not act differently than Paul and his co-workers call for.

Paul's co-workers are not presented as his disciples. The epistles cast bright light on the fact that the apostles have no disciples and thus also no successors. The relationship of Paul's co-workers to the apostle is grounded in the fact that they are his children on account of faith (1 Tim. 1:2, 18; 2 Tim. 1:2; 2:1; Titus 1:4). They are therefore not merely to repeat what they learned but are responsible for their own ministry, and Paul supports them in their work by showing them the guiding principle for their work in the gospel. The authority assigned to Paul is derived exclusively from the fact that he serves Christ. Therefore his conversion makes clear forever how Jesus brings God's grace to sinners, and his commission to the Gentiles indicates that prayer and the church's work must remain free of any self-centered limitation. Paul's suffering challenges even his co-workers to be concerned for more than merely their own well-being; his pattern of conduct serves them as an example of a pure life (1 Tim. 1:12–16; 2:7; 4:10; 2 Tim. 1:11; 2:9–10; 3:10–11, 14). None of these pronouncements suggests that their dependence on Paul is that of a student. Independence is indispensable for them, because their participation in eternal salvation is, as for Paul, contingent on the fulfillment of their ministry (1 Tim. 4:16; 6:11–14, 20; 2 Tim. 2:22). They remain united with Christ only by serving the community and would forfeit their Christian status through unfaithfulness in their office. Because they have their goal to which they aspire still before them, Paul's word to his sons is not just a thanksgiving, praising God for the great ministry they received and the great men they have become, but takes on the form of an exhortation that is only intensified by their fellowship with Paul and the greatness of their calling.

The simultaneous existence of liberty (expressed in the congregation's constitution) and authority (on which the concept of office is based) is here substantiated in the same way as everywhere else in the apostolic writings. The workers' authority is not attached to their person but extends beyond them to the God who called them. This is explicitly stated regarding Paul and thus also applies by extension to those he sends (1 Tim. 1:1, 11; 2:5–7; 5:21; 6:13; 2 Tim. 1:1, 8–11; Titus 1:1–3; man of God: 1 Tim. 6:11; 2 Tim. 3:17; the Lord's bond-servant: 2 Tim. 2:24). Therefore their office does not deprive the community of its responsibility, because it is not the purpose of divine grace, which is the source of their office, to restrict the congregation or to weaken it but rather to enliven and strengthen it. Its own share in God's grace also provides it with the authorization for its own, God-pleasing work.

The derivation of the office's authority and the congregation's liberty from God does not occur on the basis of an enthusiastic train of thought, such as that to every person is granted a personal source of revelation in his inner life. The community's foundation is rather the word passed on to it, which is perpetrated in it through teaching. Paul's co-worker has confidence, because he knows Scripture and the apostle; this provides the foundation for his ministry forever, and it is his duty to preserve what he has received (1 Tim. 1:10; 4:6, 16; 6:3, 20; 2 Tim. 1:13–14; 2:2; 3:14–17; 4:3; Titus 1:9; 2:1, 7–8). Nevertheless, the concept of Spirit is not absent and is used not merely with reference to the particular manifestations of the Spirit in prophecy (1 Tim. 4:1; 1:18; 4:14; 2 Tim. 1:6). Rather, God's rich distribution of the Spirit is the factual reality which provides the basis for every important decision and the entire conduct of office (Titus 3:5; 2 Tim. 1:7, 14). But the standard by which spirituality is measured and the means by which the congregations continues to possess the Spirit is the word passed on to it which attests to it the Christ.

If we judge these epistles' concept of office by the earlier letters, it is immediately evident that the exclusion of canon law is a Pauline feature. The earlier epistles deal with congregational concerns in equally and exclusively pastoral terms as the Pastoral epistles treat problems in the Ephesian or Cretan church. That the congregations gathered by Paul have overseers or deacons is nothing new (Rom. 16:1; Phil. 1:1). No less Pauline is the fact that the epistles' scope extends to all of the congregations' concerns. What Paul's co-workers must accomplish according to his instructions is highly reminiscent of the things Paul himself does for the community in the first Corinthian epistle. In both instances, boundless love expresses the standard of the work which neglects nothing that impinges on the community's well-being. The use of office and authority for the establishment of freedom and its regulation through faith is also Pauline; the Corinthian epistles provide telling testimony in this regard. But the sincerity which renders the fulfillment of one's calling the condition for participation in salvation is Pauline as well; for Paul always made his participation in Christ's eternal kingdom contingent on the faithful fulfillment of his ministry according to the Lord's will. Precisely in the major points constituting Paul's concept of office it can therefore not be said that the Pastoral epistles introduce a further development or even constitute a change of direction.

### e) The Boundary between Authentic and Gnostic Christianity according to the Pastoral Epistles

The piety that Paul opposes is rejected by him because it conceives of its goal in intellectualistic terms and because it evokes vivid mental deliberations producing only vain words, myths, questions, and explorations (1 Tim. 1:3–4; 4:7; 6:4–5, 20; 2 Tim. 2:14, 23; 4:3–4; Titus 1:10–16; 3:9–11). This results in instruction of the congregation that is unhealthy, because it postulates false aims and subjects the community's conduct to reprehensible norms. This led to attacks on the core tenets of the Pauline message. In any case his doctrine of resurrection came under fire; targeted also was probably his presentation of the significance of the Law. This means that ideas were held that Paul calls blasphemies against God (2 Tim. 2:18; 1 Tim. 1:8–11, 20). Paul confronts imaginative and speculative constructs with the principle that only those words which are characterized by truth are to be accorded validity in the community. This also designates his purpose: for since truth reveals God's work to us and provides us with the knowledge of God, the true word postulates as the community's aim that it offer honor and service to God; it makes man godly (truth: 1 Tim. 2:4, 7; 3:15; 6:5; 2 Tim. 2:15, 18, 25; 3:7–8; 4:4; Titus 1:14; godliness: 1 Tim. 3:16; 4:7–8; 6:3; 2 Tim. 3:5; Titus 1:1).

In the context of this contrast, these epistles reveal more than earlier ones that the community's discipline is to be directed not merely toward sin; it also must judge emerging ideas and the word it is offered. But even this perspective is not foreign to earlier epistles, because Paul obliged congregations from the beginning to examine even the message of their prophets (1 Thess. 5:19–21; 1 Cor. 14:29). This reveals that Paul was never amenable to the idea that what could be heard in his congregations was exclusively the wisdom and truth of God. He held the community responsible if an attack on the gospel arose in its midst (1 Cor. 15:12, 33–34). But now it becomes all the more the task of those who work in the community to preserve it in the word passed on to it and to defend it against opposing ideas. This also leads to the stronger emphasis on office, particularly the Pauline apostolic office, which was treated with contempt by the representatives of gnostic perfection.

In contrast with theological work that is merely innovative and exhausts itself in words, the epistles present works as the goal of Christendom. But this is not presented as a novel insight but as self-evident truth that is now merely represented with particular seriousness. The conception reflected in the epistles is not that Paul's friends had up to that point worked as theologians but that from now on they should also not neglect practical application; rather, they have no other duty at all other than to help the community to right action and to instill love in it together with its prerequisites without which that love remains impossible for man. They know of no other aim, because Jesus' commission and cross have as their purpose the establishment of the community that accomplishes good works, and for this purpose it is also given the Scriptures (1 Tim. 1:5; Titus 2:14; 2 Tim. 3:17). The close connection between love and faith, albeit genuine, unhypocritical rather than merely illusory faith, is demonstrated even by the opponents, because love is unattainable for them, once they only profess to have faith without actually possessing it. Because their piety nourishes religious pride, it results in numerous despicable acts that cause the congregation to fragment (1 Tim. 6:4). They proudly separate from those who do not belong to the community, do not believe that Christ wants to save them as well, and therefore have no desire even to pray for them (1 Tim. 1:12–16; 2:1–7; 4:10; Titus 2:11; 3:2–7). They despise the natural institutions of life; therefore they divide slaves and masters, wives and husbands, and refuse to engage in friendly dealings with their fellow-citizens (1 Tim. 6:1–2; Titus 2:9–10; 1 Tim. 2:9–15). While they make ascetic achievements the mark of holiness, they know no bounds in the selfish craving for ministerial pay and in the evasion of suffering.[57]

Genuine piety, on the other hand, proves itself in the right ordering of natural relationships. The woman is directed away from spiritual accomplishments to her motherly work. If her husband dies, she is not to crowd her way into the circle of widows who are supported by the congregation and take part in its religious activities. This is fitting only for the woman who cannot be provided for by her family or a second marriage (1 Tim. 2:15; 5:3, 9, 14–16). The congregational office and the circle of elders are protected against lack of honor and accusations, as long as suitable men are chosen as office-holders. Their suitability is assessed primarily by how they discharge their natural responsibilities (1 Tim. 3:1; 5:19; 3:1–12; Titus 1:6–9). Asceticism is contrasted with that liberty which enables one both to make use of life's natural benefits and to renounce them. At the same time, the epistles refrain entirely from cultivating sensual passions that crave for material happiness. They describe the surrender of one's life for Jesus' sake as a clear Christian duty and show no evidence of a soft stance toward martyrdom. The rich must recognize their honor and true wealth in being rich in good works, and slaves are obliged to double service through their Christian dignity. But renunciation must take place in obedience toward the obligation assigned to the individual and therefore remains a free decision based on an indi-

---

57. Asceticism: 1 Tim. 4:3–4, 7–8; 5:23; Titus 1:15; money: 1 Tim. 6:5–10; suffering: 2 Tim. 1:15; 2:11–14; 3:12.

vidual's inner conviction. In contrast, if asceticism is commanded and recommended as means of sanctification in and of itself, this is condemned as an attack on what has been divinely created. It is judged to be an indication that the sinful will is powerfully at work in man, that his relationship with God is unclear and his consciousness impure. Opposition toward nature is considered to be opposition toward God, and the attempt to sanctify oneself by way of asceticism is viewed as inability to exercise faith. If ascetic tendencies arise not from love but fear of guilt, they do not accomplish their purpose, because what corrupts a man is found within him. First man must become clean; then everything is clean for him. The clean man, however, comes into being not by subjecting his dealings with material things to regulations but when he subjects himself to God in faith on account of the truth (Titus 1:15–16; 1 Tim. 4:1–4).

Does this mark a change away from Paulinism? Whoever knows the earlier writings will not expect Paul to use the religious undertakings of those who developed Christianity along gnostic lines for the purpose of demonstrating his theological mastery in their refutation. Paul never developed his thought for a purpose other than serving the ethical goal. His greatest intellectual achievements, such as the epistle to the Romans, stand completely in the service of the ethical will and provide an answer to the question of how the church can become free from evil and do good. Whoever declares himself impoverished (as Paul did) because he fails to do good cannot think differently from the way Paul does, because his misery is not removed by Christ's making a theologian out of him but by being liberated from his inability to do good. From Paul's refutation of Jewish and Christian Pharisaism through the message of repentance it follows naturally that he also measured the gnostic movement exclusively by its ethical performance.

The epistles do not speak of an activity that is intellectually lazy and cognitively indifferent; they rather apply the entire scope of Pauline affirmations regarding the Christ in order to demonstrate the validity of the pronouncement that good works are established by the gospel. Also according to these epistles, Jesus possesses complete unity with the Father. But the idea of preexistence does not become by itself the object of reflection (2 Tim. 1:9–10; 1 Tim. 3:16). At the same time, it is considered to be an incontrovertible fact that Jesus became man, and believers' share in God is expressly grounded in Jesus' historical work which he accomplished as man, in contrast with the gnostic tendency to separate Jesus from mankind as a heavenly being (1 Tim. 2:5; 3:16). The condition of faith distinct to Christendom is based on the sending of the Spirit to the community; but there is no discussion of the way in which the divine activity is manifested in internal experiences and how it unites itself with the conscious, personal life act. On the other hand, great emphasis is laid on the undiminished applicability of the ethical verdict rejecting human desire and activity; if this essential characteristic of Christian devotion is missing, the conscience cannot be pure and faith cannot be present. Thus any self-glory is rendered impossible for Christendom, and the foundation for the universal scope of love is laid; now it can engage in friendly, kind dealings with all. For through the ethical verdict, by which the community judges its own will, it is prohibited from the exercise of any arrogance or harshness toward those who still sin at the present time (1 Tim. 1:13, 15; Titus 3:2–3). Their plight is transcended by the certainty of justification and election, together with the offer of perfect, eternal grace to all (2 Tim. 1:9–10; Titus 3:4–7; 2 Tim. 2:10; Titus 1:1). The Law is then used according to its true meaning and purpose, if both the condemnation of all evil and freedom for everything good arise from it (1 Tim. 1:8–16). The realization is thus confirmed in the community that the Law cannot be placed beside or above Christ but that it has a negative purpose, because it serves as means for the divine justice by which God judges sinners. But the Law must not be looked down upon because of its judging function, because its role receives ample substantiation by the magnitude of human sin. But those who are righteous and do what is righteous are not placed under the Law. The perfection of divine grace that deals with man not according to the Law is demonstrated in Paul's conversion, which makes clear for all times how Christ relates to sinners. Because Paul is the visible demonstration of Jesus' patience with sinners, he received his universal apostolic office.

Just as Paul did not confront gnostic theories with his own theological knowledge, he also does not counter their lofty spirituality with the wealth of his own inner life. What may be called Pauline mysticism, the consistent full involvement of his inner life in communion with Christ that is so palpable to Paul, appears in these epistles only in the statement that faith is in Christ (1 Tim. 1:14; 3:13; 2 Tim. 1:13; 3:15; cf. 3:12). Thereby man is united with him, and the condition for fruitful labor and Christian communion is established. Because the granting of faith occurs here as everywhere in Paul through the word, faith is kept by the passing on of the received word, by the remaining in what has been learned. This occurs not exclusively yet still necessarily through right action, because the one whose conscience is not pure also cannot believe. This is no deviation from Paulinism, because Paul never conceived of the Christian solely as believer but always also as the one who loves, knows, works, suffers, and hopes. Paul expected from faith that it would establish all activities of man and thus prove that faith truly unites him with the Christ and that it is his righteousness. Nevertheless, the distinction between faith and knowledge and works is nowhere blurred in these writings. For they do not contrast gnosis with a faith that itself was transformed into gnosis, neither in the proud consciousness that it was better theory nor in the skeptical mood that we are merely given "faith" while knowledge remained unattainable. The causal relationships that make right thinking, which truly apprehends what is true, and right conduct, which does what is good, the condition of faith do not deny faith a basis and value of its own. For it arises from Christ and therefore provides man with what Christ gives him. One can speak here neither of a further development nor of an impoverished version of the Pauline conviction. Rather, it could perhaps be said that all these formulations consciously and vigorously serve the intention of conceiving of Christian ideas in as definite and simple terms as possible, because the power of guiding Christendom's conduct depends on their simplicity and intelligibility. The wealth of ideas found in earlier writings here issues in formulations that serve everyone in ordering his conduct.

In contrast to gnostic perfection, hope is placed emphatically beside faith, because the community's justification and salvation is completed only with Jesus' appearing, by which he becomes visible for it (1 Tim. 1:1; 4:10; 6:14; 2 Tim. 4:1, 8; Titus 1:2; 2:13; 3:7). But any theoretical or imaginative portrayal of the eschatological event is absent; the emphasis on the final goal primarily serves the purpose of providing the community with complete sobriety in its perspective on the religious possession to which it has attained.

The form of these writings coheres with their overall disposition insofar as they employ Greek vocabulary somewhat more frequently than the earlier epistles. While every gnosis produces an artificial theological language, seeking to impress by the choice of unusual words, the vocabulary of these epistles differs from the earlier ones by its more frequent use of popular language conventions. Yet certain boundaries remain in effect regarding the adoption of Greek terms, first in that formulations of Greek science are entirely avoided, and second in that traditional religious language is excluded, because it is characterized by Greek tendencies that constitute a contrast with the Christian faith. It is therefore no coincidence that "godliness" is frequently used while "virtue" and "providence" remain excluded. Also in this respect the epistles do not depart from Paul's general orientation, because the formation of a particular ecclesiastical or didactic language was not part of his aims. The use of available linguistic resources, even when he expresses most profound truths in words he considers to be "taught by the Spirit," constitutes an important trait of his didactic labor; he was not derailed from this course even by his opposition to gnostic thought.

# The Share
# of Apostolic Associates
# in Doctrinal Formation

## A. The Simplification of the Gospel by Mark[1]

### 1. The Primacy of Jesus' Works over His Word

The form and content of the second Gospel confirm the church's claim that it was composed by a man who originally belonged to the Jerusalem church. At the same time, it clearly indicates that it was written for Gentile congregations. Its parallelism with Matthew permits the observation that the account of Jesus changed only little when it was transferred from the Palestinian to the Gentile region of the church. Yet, the conclusion may seem to be warranted that the account underwent a substantial transformation. The texts, however, show that this conclusion is not borne out by the actual evidence.

The most important difference between the two texts consists in the fact that Mark preferred the second of the two components of the Gospel account, if we think of the first as reiterating Jesus' words and the second his works. Even this presentation of Jesus is based on the conviction that God's rule over men takes place through his word; for Christ's means of operation is the word even in Mark (1:14–15, 21–22, 38–39; 2:2; 4:1–20, 33; 8:35, 38). But Mark perceives the characteristic of Jesus that reveals his commission and his aim to be Jesus' works. After a drastically shortened mention of the events that brought about the beginning of Jesus' ministry, we are told about Jesus' activity in Capernaum, not by being introduced to the new teaching by which he instructed the local community, but by a presentation of his gracious acts through which he pro-

---

1. In studying Mark one cannot hope to attain a high level of precision in defining Mark's guiding convictions. This is more true for Mark than for Matthew. In abbreviating Jesus' words, Mark left out precisely the material that would have directly clarified his convictions. And there is no certain knowledge, only numerous conjectures, regarding the sources of information Mark used in his presentation of Jesus.

vided help for the needy. In place of the Sermon on the Mount, Mark reports only the act of Jesus which took place during that stay in the Galilean hill country and which provided the lasting foundation for the church: the appointment of the Twelve. At the occasion of their commissioning to Israel, it becomes clear also in Mark that this commission entailed the memory of rules by which Jesus regulated their work; but in the case of Mark, this discourse consists of only a few sentences. The depiction of God's rule by way of parables is indeed presented as an important element; but we receive only the three parables taken from the growth of seed, while the account of the events Mark associates with this discourse considerably exceeds the concise formulation it has in Matthew. The denunciation of Pharisaism which concludes Jesus' work is documented by Mark with only a single saying; at the same time, he portrays Jesus' verdict regarding Jewish worship by a narrative that depicts, by the offering of the poor widow, why Jesus rejected the boastful temple worship and what he considered to be the mark of true worship. The text received this shape not because it had already become impossible at that time to gather Jesus' teachings in the form of discourses; for Mark presents Jesus' prophetic speech in a form similar to Matthew. Thus Mark allows Jesus to speak to the church himself about how he promised to realize his regal aim through his new revelation by combining a longer series of sayings into a discourse (Mark 1:21–22; 3:13–15; 6:7–11; 4:1–34; 12:38–40; 13:1–37).

This portrayal of Jesus is based on the Christ concept. If Mark had wanted to portray Jesus as teacher, he would have made fuller use of the tradition regarding his word. But the community gains confidence in Jesus' regal name not because of his ideas but because of his works, by which it perceives that his actions reveal God's omnipotent grace which liberates from every dire need. This is followed by the Passion and Easter accounts, by which the community learns how Jesus became its Lord, just as it learns from the Easter miracle account that he truly bore the cross as the Christ.

But because the designation "Christ" entails the absolute appreciation of Jesus' word—just as Mark always reiterates that Jesus' work consisted in the offer of his word—lack of its repetition is intelligible only when Mark presupposes the identity of the word proclaimed by Jesus and the word available in the community. He did not believe that the community had remained ignorant of the word Jesus had proclaimed. It, too, had been told the good news by which Jesus brings God's grace to man; for it is one with the gospel by which Christendom came into being and which is proclaimed at every one of its gatherings. Likewise, Jesus' commandment, by which he told the disciples what was their obligation, was alive in the community; for it is audible in every piece of instruction that directs its members to right action. Insofar as Jesus' call to repentance was aimed at denouncing sins of which certain Jews were particularly guilty, it need not be reiterated, because Pharisaism no longer threatens the community,[2]

---

2. The only portion in which Mark shows in detail that Jesus rejected Pharisaism if for no other reason than because of what it viewed as piety, is the dispute regarding the washing of hands (7:1–16). This portion had great practical importance for the early church because it expressed Jesus' concept of purity. But even here no mention is made of the harm caused Judaism by Pharisaism

and it should not be tempted to elevate itself above the Jews and rejoice in their demise. We are again faced with the distinction between "doctrine" and "message," which places the message above teachings regulating man's conduct, because it proclaims God's work and grants knowledge of God. Similar to John, Mark adhered to this distinction in the case of the most important aspect of "doctrine," Jesus' own commandments. From the man who was made a particularly effective proponent of Christian proclamation on account of his provenance from the mother church and his acquaintance with the first apostles, the community expected, not instruction regarding its own worship and the work it must accomplish or "doctrine," but the visualization and confirmation of that portrait of Christ that places Jesus before mankind not as the one who commands but as the one who gives and dies.

Thus that kind of interpretation of Mark is rejected which traces his account back to "popular" piety, supposedly impressed mainly by Jesus' miracles rather than any ethical knowledge. Granted, the new element that Mark desired to impart to the church consists in the account of those miracles performed by Jesus which reveal his regal privilege. In these miracles his crucifixion is demonstrated as the Jews' grave guilt, and his exaltation is prepared and rendered credible. But miracle is the centerpiece of the message here, not because it is marveled at as an end in itself, but because it is the Christ who performs it. This portrayal of Jesus became possible only because Jesus' messianic claim was considered to be the actual meaning and content of his word. This is borne out also by the form of the discourse material. Of the pronouncements grouped by Matthew in the Sermon on the Mount, Mark includes only small portions; on the other hand, he at least provides sketches of the content of the discourses that describe for the apostles their authority and obligation, also showing how Jesus reveals God's rule through his ministry and providing an extensive account of Jesus' return. Of the parables by which Matthew portrays Jesus' call to repentance to Jerusalem, Mark includes solely the one that speaks directly of Jesus' work and destiny. He portrays Jesus' conflict with Pharisaism to the extent that it is occasioned by Jesus' grace and liberty, and parallel to this he selects from among John the Baptist's words solely the word that promises the Christ.[3]

The corollary to the manifestation of the Christ in his gracious power is the community's faith. Through his narratives, Mark seeks to show which conduct was considered to be "faith" by Jesus and how it arose and achieved perfection despite all obstacles. The pronouncement summarizing Jesus' entire message designates not merely repentance but also faith elicited by the good news as the thing Jesus desires. The bearers of the lame man, the woman with the flow of blood, Jairus, and the father of the epileptic boy serve as examples of how Jesus led those who sought his help to faith. In the case of the disciples, it is their in-

3. In the shaping of his text, Mark also made allowance for the fact that Jesus' words originated from the concrete condition of Palestinian Judaism, so that they are not intelligible and applicable for believers later in the church without explanation (cf. Mark 3:4 and Matt. 12:11–12; Mark 2:27 and Matt. 12:5–6; Mark 7:15, 18–19 and Matt. 15:11; Mark 10:2 and Matt. 19:3; Mark 7:24–30 and Matt. 15:21–28; 8:5–13). The Greek thought that Jesus' word revealed a timeless wisdom which stands in no relation to his history is completely absent.

ability to believe that is denounced with strong words as what separated them from Jesus. The new parable portraying the divine rule serves the same purpose, lending the entire discourse a coloring different from Matthew; it expresses solely the calmness with which Jesus expects the completion of his work and which he also imparts to his disciples. Thus Jesus establishes faith in them (Mark 1:15; 2:2–5; 5:30–34; 5:35–36; 9:20–24; 6:52; 8:17; 4:26–29).

## 2. The Relationship of the Gospel to the Gentile Church

The grounding of the name of the Christ in the grace offered to all, to which corresponds faith as the community's devotion, is given to us by that Gospel by which the Gentile church came into being. Accordingly, Mark's account of Jesus is set apart from Israel's history. He recounts it as a self-contained whole. Jesus' work is grounded in his divine sonship, manifested at his baptism, and aimed at the rule realized at his return. Israel's rejection is presented as a fait accompli already in the first discourse of Jesus provided by Mark (4:11–12). Only in this way can the account begin without any information regarding Jesus' birth or youth, while a narrator who describes Jesus as an Israelite will indicate somehow which place in Israel he was assigned by his birth. The community addressed by Mark is sufficiently informed if it learns how he was shown to be the Son of God.

There is no antagonism toward the Jews or Scripture. The connection between Jesus' sending and previous divine revelation is illumined in the introduction when the work of John the Baptist is presented as the fulfillment of the prophecy regarding him. Accordingly, Moses and Elijah stand beside Jesus at his transfiguration, and the obedience to Scripture shown by Jesus in his suffering is clearly portrayed (1:2–3; 9:4, 13; 14:21, 27, 49; 15:28). But by distancing Jesus' work from Judaism, that work, which Jesus himself and thus also the earliest proclamation interwove at every point with Scripture, is extricated from it, and faith is shown to be rooted exclusively in what Jesus did. The Gentile church was no longer shaken by the conflict of Jesus' history with Jewish expectation. Therefore the demonstration of its agreement with Scripture no longer had the same weight as it did for Jewish Christendom. Mark considers it certain and requiring no particular substantiation that Jesus' aim was the universal church. He must not be burdened with the notion that, by portraying Jesus as having come for the Gentiles, he injected this consciousness as a foreign element into Jesus' history. The universal scope of Jesus' proclamation is for Mark directly tied to the Christ concept. His depiction of Jesus is completely immune from any gnostic influence. No account provides less information than Mark about Jesus' dealings with God, who grants him sonship, and the manner in which he now manifests his rule in the community. He is different from the first form of tradition only in that he accommodates the imagination that desires a visual, impressive picture of events more than Matthew does. In the Gentile church, the book was no longer composed as a memory aid but becomes itself the basis for the tradition passed on in the church. This made a visual, intelligible depiction of the narratives desirable.

What distinguishes Mark from Matthew—the separation of the message from doctrine, which produced the summation of Jesus' word in the form of his own self-witness and the reduction of the message that confronted Jewish sin; the relating of Jesus' ministry to the establishment of faith; the final verdict of rejection of the Jews; the universality directly attributed to Jesus—all this provides common ground with John. John applies these convictions in the presentation of Jesus more boldly and independently than Mark, who reiterates the materials available to him. But these prove neither in the case of Mark nor John that the evangelist did not originate from the Palestinian community; at the same time, the events that influenced the portrayal of Jesus at the transition of Christian proclamation to the Gentiles are confirmed and sharpened through the agreement between both texts.

# B. The Enrichment of Recollections of Jesus through the Witnesses Consulted by Luke

## 1. The Grace of Jesus

Because the portions that Luke combined with the text of Mark, without drawing them from Matthew, stand in a clear linguistic and thematic connection with one another, they reveal to us an evangelist that Luke esteemed, as did Mark, and whom he clearly preferred over Matthew.[4] Because the text's character confirms its provenance from the Jewish church, its repetition by Luke becomes part of a series of events that attest to the connectedness of the Gentile and the Jewish church.

This narrator made the perfect nature of the forgiveness given by Jesus to the guilty a centerpiece of his presentation. Jesus begins his work in Nazareth by proclaiming to the community the forgiveness it is granted by his word, and Peter's fellowship with him is put on a firm foundation when Jesus responds to Peter's confession that he is a sinful man by issuing his call. The woman anointing Jesus receives forgiveness, and the parable of the two debtors formulates the principle according to which Jesus grants it. Jesus' intercession for Israel is portrayed by the example of the fig tree, and his reconciling work is richly described by the shepherd and the two sons. Jesus proclaims justification to the repentant tax-collector, and he brings salvation to Zacchaeus. An important saying expresses the greatness of the forgiveness received by Peter when he denies Jesus, and at the cross Jesus opens paradise for the one who is crucified beside him. The Resurrected One confronts the hopeless disciples with their inability to understand and their unbelief, not in order to reject them but to grant them his forgiveness. For even as the Resurrected One he remains united with them, and he commands the reunited disciples to proclaim repentance for the forgiveness of sins to all nations (Luke 4:16–19; 5:8; 7:36–50; 13:6–9; chap. 15; 18:9–14; 19:1–10; 22:31–34, 61; 23:42–43; 24:13–31, 47).

---

4. Luke 1:5–2:52; 3:10–14, 23–38; 4:16–30; 5:1–11; 6:20–38; 7:1–6, 11–16, 36–50; 8:1–3; 9:51–56, 61–62; 10:1–12, 17–20, 25–42; 11:1–8, 27–28, 39–54; 12:13–21, 32–38, 47–50, 54–59; 13:1–17, 23–27, 31–33; chap. 14: chap. 15; 16:1–12, 14–16, 19–31; 17:1–23; 18:1–14; 19:1–28, 39–44; 21:20–28; 22:13–19a, 24–38, 47–48, 61, 66–70; 23:1–12, 27–31, 34, 39–43, 46; 24:4–53; the delineation of these texts in relation to Matthew is not seldom difficult to determine.

These materials cannot be interpreted as free inventions of Luke which supposedly depict his conception of faith as determined by Paul. Faith that produced its own material by free invention would constitute such a distortion of Paulinism that this term would no longer be applicable for Luke. However, these materials are connected in both form and substance with other elements that cannot be derived from the particular aims of Pauline devotion. The portrayal of Jesus' dealings with the sinful woman belongs to Jesus' polemic against the Pharisees and draws on the Palestinian antithesis between the righteous, who have only few sins, and the fallen ones, who have many. The parable of the fig tree is connected with Jesus' word of repentance that is occasioned by the execution of the Galileans. This word of repentance, in turn, shows with strong local coloring how Jesus suffered in the anticipation of Jerusalem's destiny. Again, the shepherd and the woman looking for her penny as well as the two sons reflect Jesus' conflict with Pharisaism and divide the community into fallen ones and righteous ones who do not need conversion. Here we find a portrayal of the righteous person (without conflicting with Jesus' absolute verdict elsewhere), so friendly toward Pharisaism and so ready to recognize its privilege, that the formation of this piece is hard to imagine apart from contact with Pharisaism on part of the Gentile church. The two men at prayer, whom Jesus uses as examples for God's condemning and justifying acts, stand in formal parallel to the other freely formed examples by which this narrator illustrates Jesus' verdicts (the Samaritan: Luke 10:30–37; the rich farmer: 12:16–20; the steward: 16:1–9; the hardened rich man: 16:19–31). The material added to Mark's Passion narrative all but adds up to an independent account characterized by a strong emphasis on Jesus' concern for Jerusalem's destiny. The demise of the holy city and of Israel is offset by the salvation of individual persons, particularly those who bear a heavy load of guilt. In addition to this, the piece regarding Zacchaeus emphatically stresses the value of membership in Israel, because Jesus uses him to demonstrate what is given to a son of Abraham, and the promise to the man crucified beside Jesus uses the term "paradise," which tradition amply attests as Palestinian. Here Luke reiterates material passed on to him, and his Paulinism influences it only to the extent that it helps him realize the exceeding value of these vignettes for the entire church.

These portions stand in the Lucan account at the place where they originally took place; for they constitute the final element in Jesus' call to repentance, which never had any other purpose than inviting the guilty to return to God. These sections document the significant fact that the proclamation of the call to repentance as gospel persisted undiminished in the Jewish church. Beside Matthew's concise sincerity and Israel's final condemnation in Mark and John, the witness of this account has great value.

This narrator did not obscure the conflict in which Jesus was engaged with Judaism through his call to repentance; he brings it to light both in portrayals of Jesus' grace and in sections peculiar to him. He sets forth the words of Jesus that pronounce judgment on Pharisaism and the rabbinate in his own distinct form. While Matthew uses these words to express Jesus' final judgment over Jerusalem, this narrator portrays through them how Jesus confronted individual religious persons in personal encounters. The parable of the guests who were invited in vain, which shatters the Pharisees' presumptuous confidence, serves the same purpose as does the prophecy regarding Jesus' return, which is a reply to the Pharisees' longing for the messianic age (Luke 11:13–52; 14:15–24; 17:20–21). But this narrator assigns great significance also to Jesus' national aim, his wrestling for Israel. Prior to describing Jesus' ministry, he presents the messianic hope, through the brilliant light of the Christmas story, in the national conception which it had before Christendom. Through the genealogy, Jesus receives his place in Israel, and although it is traced back to Adam, the son of God, Jesus' connection with Adam is nonetheless mediated through the fact that he is son of Abraham and son of David. The warning and condemnation of the nation is depicted in independent sections. At Jesus' entry into Jerusalem, at the proclamation of his return, and at his final departure from the city, he predicts and deplores its demise (Luke 19:41–44; 21:20–24; 23:27–31). This constitutes a valuable confirmation of the religious attitude which can be observed in Matthew. For Jesus' will to save Israel as a nation was also not considered by this evangelist to be antithetical to Jesus' universal salvific will. This will results from the fact that Jesus' work, in light of Israel's unwillingness to repent, consists in the calling of individuals. In Matthew, Jesus' universal intention is explicitly portrayed in the final sections of the account. For Jesus' work for Israel even to the point of the cross is followed by the commissioning of the disciples to the nations through the Risen One (Luke 24:47).

## 2. Jesus' Love Commandment

A second group of the passages received by Luke provides Jesus' warning against riches with a particularly impressive form. Already John the Baptist demands from those who have an abundance that they sacrifice for the sake of those who suffer lack. The Sermon on the Mount begins with a promise for the poor and a woe against the rich. The parallel to Matthew 6 is introduced by the indictment of the one who sought to secure his inheritance with Jesus' help and by the story of the rich farmer. Two parables, effective on account of their strong coloring, impressively portray the consequences of the correct and improper use of possessions. Jesus calls the poor the proper guests at the festive meal, sets Zacchaeus free from his wealth, and even in his final words leaves a reminder that he sent the disciples out in utter poverty (Luke 3:11; 6:20, 24; 12:13–21; 16:1–9, 19–31; 14:12–14; 19:8; 22:35; cf. 10:4).

This group of passages cannot be separated from the one that describes the grace of Jesus. The brief conversation that provides the introduction to the discourse against worldly concern has several parallels in other pericopes (with Luke 12:13–14 cf. 10:25–29; 11:1, 27–28, 45; 13:1, 23, 31; 14:15; 17:5, 20). The rich farmer, the steward, and the hardened rich man equally serve as examples for Jesus' pronouncement in the same way as do the Samaritan and the justified tax-collector. The reminder of the disciples' carefree poverty resembles the word directed to Peter so closely that a derivation from different sources appears improbable, and the account of Zacchaeus combines the portrayal of Jesus' grace with liberation from the power of possessions. This is confirmed by the fact that Luke's Sermon on the Mount, which begins with the blessing of the poor, because they are poor, and with the rejection of the rich, because they are rich, contains nothing but the love commandment, which is as in Matthew free from all restrictions. But the proclamation of divine grace and the calling of the disciples to love are inseparable. The struggle against the popular esteem of wealth is thus a major tenet of the gospel for this narrator, and obedience to Jesus' word in this regard is considered to be an essential mark of Christendom. This fits with other indicators which point to the author's provenance from the Jewish church, because we also know from Matthew and James that the Jewish church understood the call to repentance to have the continual implication that the community of Jesus must be different from Judaism by protecting itself against godlessness arising from possessions.

The connection between Jesus' verdicts regarding wealth and his love commandment is not missed by this narrator. The pronouncements of John the Baptist do not render the possession of food and clothes to be sin; what is sinful is rather the manner in which the one who owns them uses them exclusively for himself. After all, when John tells the tax-collectors and military mercenaries to return to their profession, he does so demanding that they exercise it justly. There were no ascetics who promised the customs officials a share in God's rule by the exercise of their profession. The introduction to the Sermon on the Mount treats poverty not as a virtue but as abject need, juxtaposing it with weeping and being put to shame or hated. It is treated as a burden imposed on the disciples, not as perfection chosen by them. It therefore receives the promise because such need occasions help and suffering stirs divine mercy. The promise given to the poor is not intended to render it unnecessary for him to turn to God with his love and his obedience, as if he already possessed a guarantee of salvation through his poverty. This would have been to cast aside Jesus' entire message given to us by this narrator and to destroy everything that he tells us about man's personal, internal subjection to God. In the description of the farmer who rejoices over his harvest, the selfish craving that amasses only for itself is graphically depicted. Jesus' opposition toward the customary way of inviting guests creates the same effect. Parallel to this, in the pair of parables regarding blessing and curse of possessions, it is the use of wealth that is the decisive issue. To give or not to give, to keep for oneself or to use for others, this is the constitutive antithesis of these parables. Here, too, poverty is cast as utter need, not virtue, and wealth is considered to be comfort and good fortune, not sin (Luke 6:24). Blessedness turns into calamity when it leads to selfish hardening. This is confirmed by the fact that the rule teaching a proper assessment of wealth is said to be found already in Moses and the prophets. But there Christendom did not read ascetic rules but the love commandment (Luke 16:29).

It corresponds to the resolute, courageous glorification of renunciation in which love proves its power that this narrator, in his version of the Sermon on the Mount, makes love the central commandment of Jesus even more strongly than does Matthew. For he portrays in exclusively positive terms what love accomplishes without contrasting what Jesus commands with the Mosaic commandment. He does not dwell on what is sin and, in the final portion of the discourse, derives even the disciples' teaching ministry from the rule of love (Luke 6:39–45).[5] Likewise, the narrator emphatically stresses love in the accounts of the Samaritan and of the slave who is not exempt from service by his work in the field but is still required to serve his master. The indefatigability of love and the impossibility of completing all that it demands, so that the work it performs never suffices, is strongly expressed through the verdict "worthless slaves." The same can be said regarding the word that illustrates the absolute nature of love by the obligation to hate one's closest relatives and one's own soul. Love proves its authenticity by being able to transcend all other bonds (Luke 17:7–10; 14:26).

More than Matthew, this narrator seeks to clarify for the community the positive aims to which Jesus points them in their work. He does not merely call for it to resist evil but describes for it the good upon which Jesus' good pleasure rests. Therefore the concrete example had greater significance for him than for the other narrators. One Samaritan is the example for the way in which one acts toward one's neighbor according to the rule of love, and another for how one thanks Jesus for his help. As examples of repentance, this narrator presents the sinful woman, Zacchaeus, and the praying tax-collector in the Temple, while Mary of Bethany serves as an example of faith. But the opposition of the gospel tradition against legalistic regulation of conduct is thereby not compromised. The narrator clearly expresses Jesus' will in particular episodes, but he maintains that the work of love cannot be legislated.

Not just the pronouncements regarding love, but the entire account is characterized by strong emotion. Jesus comes to Jerusalem weeping, and when he leaves the city burdened by his cross, his address to the women is filled with the highest pathos. Jesus' prayer at Gethsemane is cast by this narrator as an intense struggle, and Jesus' empathy with the despair now descending upon the disciples finds strong expression through the exhortation to obtain swords at all cost. The Beatitudes of the Sermon on the Mount are considerably intensified by the addition of woes, and the welcome for the returning disciples reflects profound emotional response. In the depiction of the repentant sinful woman, in Jesus' encounter with the weeping widow, in Jesus' look at Peter during his acts of betrayal by the fireside, and in the thief's request lie powers that grip the emotions, powers to which the narrator is not oblivious but which he rather uses deliberately. The Christmas story is told in the bright colors of complete joy; his Easter narrative, with the two disciples from Emmaus, is given the same coloring; and the picture of the widow in need is provided with intense force by the passionate longing for the coming Lord. The depth of events is also stressed by the reminder that transcendent powers are at work. For the angels in heaven rejoice; Satan fell from heaven as lightning and accused Peter and made Judas his instrument (Luke 15:7, 10; 10:18; 22:31, 3).

This distinguishes this narrator from all other types of gospel narrative: from Matthew, for whom all internal processes are subordinated to the obedient will;

---

5. It remains doubtful to what extent the linkage of these pronouncements with the love commandment was already accomplished by Luke's source.

from John, for whom the entire attention is directed toward faith; and even from Mark's effort to offer the reader easily understandable and colorful images. Yet the difference reaches perhaps beyond the narrator's spiritual orientation to the religious attitude of the community of which he is a part and for which he writes. Strong emotions arise from the greatness of the tasks with which that community is confronted: the avoidance of evil, the perfection of love, and the hope that longs for Jesus' return. If these emotions are intense, they aid in the accomplishment of the Christian goal. In the solemn peacefulness of the other texts the Christian will is portrayed as the possession owned by the community. It knows what it wills and wills it with complete resolve. But this does not result in calm ownership; this possession must be won through struggle. It emerges from the intense pain evoked by Jewish sin, from trembling anxiety in view of the present and imminent crisis, and from profound joy in the perception of divine grace.

The account knows nothing of any tension between love and faith. One Samaritan shows how the love commandment is carried out, the other, how Jesus' help leads its recipient to thanksgiving and thus also to faith. After portraying the service to be done to one's neighbor by way of the Samaritan, it is demonstrated in probably deliberate sequence by the example of Mary what Jesus demands from the disciple: not that he serve him but that he hear his word. The pronouncement regarding the indefatigability of love stands beside the unconditional promise to faith, because faith and love are destroyed by the same process, that is, that the disciples turn their attention to their own actions and find in them the grounds for the extension of divine grace (Luke 17:5–10). If they measure the greatness of their faith and fearfully look at its smallness, they have lost faith; if they admiringly measure their own work and derive from its greatness the right to cease serving, claiming on the basis of their work joy and blessedness, they have destroyed love. Because love liberates the will from self-interest, it combines with the confidence which expects from Christ the riches of divine grace apart from any appeal to one's own accomplishments as the basis for his grace. Therefore this narrator also draws attention to the mighty fact that Jesus desired no adulation for himself but rather referred those who rendered it to him to the divine word. Not the one who serves him but the one who desires his word receives his praise (Luke 11:27–28; 10:38–42). The inner contrast between adulation that celebrates Jesus' greatness and faith turned toward his grace was clear to this narrator.

In its theoretical aims, this account does not transcend Matthew. The concept of preexistence is only hinted at but not developed (Luke 1:78). The orientation of Jesus' ministry toward Israel stands beside the universal office of his disciples, without the narrator surmising that this required a theoretical resolution in order to show the compatibility of both aims. The concrete nature of Jesus' didactic labors is not felt to be a difficulty. Rather, it is particularly stressed through the conversations by which this account likes to introduce Jesus' pronouncements. He allows Jesus to speak when an occasion calls forth his teaching, and then Jesus speaks as is fitting for the occasion. Because the similarity of this portrayal of Jesus with that provided by Matthew cannot be traced to literary dependence,[6] the commonality between both reveals the work of the community, which singled out from Jesus' history these particular events and thereby gained forms for its uniform thought and will as its common property. At the same time, the diverse nature of the accounts shows the community's inner freedom. It did not create a didactic law that stipulated which of Jesus' words and which events from his history it should know. As much as it esteemed the memory of Jesus, the distinction between the divine message that grants the calling to God and historical instruction regarding Jesus was in effect.

## C. The Incorporation of Careful Regard for History into the Church's Body of Conviction through Luke

For the historical record, it is a big advantage that we know Luke to be a follower of Paul. From Luke we can apprehend what came into being from Paul's compatriots through their interaction with him.

### 1. Luke's Paulinism

#### a) Paul's Work

If the Lucan account put Paul on the same level as Jesus, this would prove its inauthenticity, because thus all those convictions would be denied that led Paul and that he presumably instilled as unshakable convictions in his co-workers. Rather, for Luke the apostles' message consists in the proclamation of Jesus' lordship. He already makes this clear by the form of his account. The first account is devoted solely to Jesus, who reveals himself as the Son of God from his birth to his resurrection and ascension to heaven. The community should know his word as he told it. This is followed not immediately by the account regarding Paul but the one about Peter and Jesus' other first disciples. Regarding these Luke also states expressly that their entire work took place through the word, and he submits its content to us; this, however, is accomplished not by a series of pronouncements by which the words of Peter or Paul are passed on to the church, but by discourses shaped by Luke. That we find in the Gospel no discourses of Jesus composed by Luke and in the book of Acts no sayings of Peter or Paul that constitute parallels to the pronouncements included in the Gospel is based on the different kind of religious relationship Luke has with Jesus and the apostles.

Luke also had a religious relationship with Paul, because he describes him as God's messenger by whose work God reveals himself. The account does therefore not turn into a biography of Paul, or into the narration of his ministry in individual selected accounts. Rather, the issue addressed is what Christ commanded, how he showed himself to be mighty and how he used Paul in his ser-

---

6. The birth narrative, the genealogy, the account of the calling of the first four disciples, the form of the Lord's Prayer, probably also the account of the Last Supper, then also the Easter narrative including Jesus' appearance to the Twelve in Jerusalem—all of these sections in Luke both supplement and intersect with Matthew. In any case, connections with the material provided by Matthew are not made clear.

vice and gathered the church through him. Luke sees Paul's significance in the fact that he called those to whom he traveled to God, so that they, by accepting his word, received God's grace (Acts 13:43, 46–48; 14:15, 27; 16:14, 20–21; 26:18). Thus he proves to be a true follower of Paul; for this thought provided Paul with the understanding of his office, which is portrayed undiminished in Luke. His Paul confronts everyone, Jew as well as Gentile, with a decision for or against God. If they accept his call, they are sanctified and saved; if they refuse the apostle, they have resisted God (sanctified: Acts 20:32; 26:18; saved: 16:31; 13:26; 28:28). For this reason Luke, in apparent deviation from Paul, makes miracles one of the centerpieces of his narrative not merely in his account of Jesus but also in that of the apostles, because these signs show that the Lord is on Paul's side and that he supports his word by his mighty works. He speaks not of miracles performed by the church but solely of those done by the apostles. For him, miracle is a function of the apostolic office.[7]

This meant that Luke did not portray Paul as the hero whom he wanted others to admire. This Paul gravely forbid his co-workers to do, and the example of Luke shows that Paul was truly successful in this. Luke's portrayal of Paul indeed evidences a vivid sense of his greatness; but it remains entirely subordinated to the thought that Paul's work is service, carried out according to the Lord's will and in the Lord's strength. Therefore Paul's dependence on supernatural divine guidance is intentionally brought to light. He cannot choose his work for himself; he is bound in the Spirit, whose glory consists in the fact that he obeys (Acts 13:2; 16:6–11; 18:9–10, 20–21; 23:11; 27:23–24). The exclusion of the ideas encapsulated by the term "hero" came about only as the result of a persistent and determined struggle with Greek thought. It is a great achievement that Luke kept himself free from the tendency to glorify man in his treatment of Paul, even though he originated from the Gentile church and had contact with Greek literature.

He also does not venerate Paul as a great thinker. Luke entirely grasped Paul's opposition to Greek intellectualism and brought it out in his presentation. He did not seek to present Paul's significance in the fact that he imparted new or profound insights to the church. The greatness of his word, as that of the other apostles, consists in the fact that it proclaims to his listeners the same divine message as did the preaching of the apostles. The distinction made by Paul between the gospel and doctrine remains in effect in Luke. He also points to the differences that existed between the teachings of the apostles by portraying the congregations' freedom from the Law as Paul's work and by emphasizing the very different stance of James and the Jerusalemites (Acts 15:21, 18–25; 10:14). In a Pauline sermon before a Jewish congregation, Luke depicts the doctrine of justification as Paul's characteristic version of the Christian message, by which Paul presented Christ's gift to Jewish need (Acts 13:38–39). But the purpose of the account is not to present the reader with a Pauline theology whose discovery

---

7. At the same time, Paul's sea travels provide Luke with the opportunity to show the superior sobriety and energy with which Paul mastered everyday challenges with which he was faced. Thus the miracle account does not introduce an element of strangeness into his picture of Paul.

and dissemination were Paul's achievement. He identified, not the particular insights of individual apostles, but the invariably uniform factual content of their message as what gave rise to the church. It is already apparent in the form of Luke's account that he does not conceive of or portray Paul as a thinker. Such a presentation would have made Paul's epistles to be its most important source, while Luke shows no signs of use of the letters (only Acts 9:25 shows a verbal parallel with a Pauline passage, 2 Cor. 11:33). He produced his account of Jesus differently than his account of Paul. Regarding his account of the Lord, the written Gospels are indispensable; Paul's epistles, on the other hand, are for the circle of his co-workers not yet canon in the sense that they drew their information regarding him from them and quoted them when reiterating his word.

Luke portrays Paul not as the thinker who arrives at knowledge but as the worker who in God's service does the work by which God's grace presents itself to mankind. Thus he is one with Paul's aim. He describes him as the wise master builder who laid the foundation for God's building among the nations. Regarding the work he did in Christ's service, he is not merely put on the same level as Peter but is placed above him, because Peter's work, as indispensable as it was, was unable to overcome Jerusalem's resistance, while Paul's work achieved notable stature in Gentile territory. Therefore the account leaves Peter and moves from him on to Paul, because what Peter had accomplished in Jerusalem received its continuation and completion in the work of Paul. Thereby Luke reiterated the Pauline pronouncement regarding the dual apostolic office, and the weight he attributes to it is revealed in the fact that he makes the equality of the two apostles assigned to them by Christ's service a theme that pervades the entire account. For he intentionally demonstrates, both in the case of their word and in the case of the signs done by them, that both men's apostolic office possessed the same power and was administered in the same fellowship with Christ. Thereby Luke proved to be a true follower of Paul at a place where a sick Paulinism could easily have developed, one which might have denied the privilege Peter received through his commission to Jerusalem and despised his work as a bust, acknowledging nothing but the superiority of his own apostle, whose ministry was crowned with success.

### b) Paul's Fellowship with the Church

Because Luke rejected the selfishness of sectarianism as sinful, he is fully conscious of the significance of the fact that Paul's ministry took place in communion with the church. He did not portray him as a loner, as one exalted above the rest of the church, but as its member who achieved his particular effectiveness only through his connection with it. Already Paul's conversion and the early ministry for which he comes to Antioch are placed in the context of the history of the entire church. Subsequently, his commission takes place through the church of Antioch, and Paul is shown to cultivate diligently his contact with it and with Jerusalem (Acts 9:10–30; 13:1–3; 14:26; 18:22; 20:16, 22). The share of the Jerusalem Jewish Christians in the planting of the congregations in Asia Minor and Greece, in particular Barnabas and Silas, is expressly emphasized. The account portrays how Paul only gradually achieved that premier authority which made him Jesus' foremost messenger to the nations. Because this authority emerges from the greatness of his work, any appearance of arrogance or arbitrariness is excluded. Thus another major element in Paul's understanding of his office is preserved, because he did not separate the office from the community but located it within it.

The personal orientation of his work, which is directed to the individual, comes to clear expression in Luke. The account insists that there is no way by which the decision with which the individual is confronted can be circumvented. The effect desired by the Lucan Paul is faith, and this faith arises in individuals. But this does not mean that his ministry is merely the conversion of many individual persons; to the contrary, it is striking how few conversion stories are recounted by Luke.[8] The aim of the work, devoted as it is to individuals, transcends them; for they are led to Christ in order that they may be brought together to form his community. Not the conversion of many Gentiles but the establishment of the Gentile church was for Luke the work which Paul completed in the power of Christ.

### c) Paul's Fellowship with the Jews

The great event that rendered this possible was for Luke the church's parting of ways with Judaism. This established the universal scope of the church and its rootedness in the soil of faith in Christ. Regarding Paul's recruitment of his co-workers, it is instructive that the description of this struggle contains no elements of bitterness. Not only is there no bitter comment in the portrayal of the Jerusalem apostles, which is inaccessible already because Jewish and Gentile Christendom are united into one church; there also is no trace of a description of Judaism's conflict with Peter or Paul. In this regard, the account of Peter is a lofty achievement, and the account of Paul is no less grand. The call to repentance comes to the fore in all its seriousness. By persecuting the apostles, Israel rebels against God; but this struggle produces neither hatred nor a fanaticism of self-defense in Jesus' messengers. The intercession of the dying Stephen together with the fearless indictment of Israel's leaders illumines the motives guiding the community's conduct toward Israel at a particularly moving event (Acts 7:51–59); but beyond this, they determine the book's entire way of thinking.

Therefore it is completely out of the question for Luke to attack or demean Israel's religion. Scripture is considered to be God's word, and the Old Testament community in its pre-Christian form to be God's work, including its national constitution and its resulting exclusion of the Gentiles.

The overcoming of hatred which makes it possible to conduct the difficult battle without resentment is grounded by Luke in Jesus' will, which brings God's grace to Israel and from which also the apostles receive love. They demonstrate it also to Israel, for the sake of what Israel obtained through God's revelation.[9]

8. Only the narratives pertaining to Philippi, of Lydia and the Philippian jailer, may be mentioned in this regard.
9. Luke portrayed Jesus' love commandment in strong terms in his Gospel.

How faithful Paul was in his effort to spare Israel any offense, how he made this his life's major aspiration, becomes a major emphasis of the account.[10] A Gentile with no understanding of Paul could readily detect in this a contradiction with Pauline conviction represented elsewhere. Even if he were not to scold Paul's Jewish actions nor call them incompatible with his liberty, they would have lost religious interest for him. What was edifying in the fact that Paul had Timothy circumcised, paid for Nazirites' sacrifices in Jerusalem, and persistently turned first to the synagogues? Luke still sees Paul's greatness in these actions and narrates them in the opinion that Paul thus left a legacy for the church which showed her for all times how it kept a pure conscience in relation to the Jews, regardless of the intense hostility with which the Jews caused its suffering. In this the Pauline church concept operates in tandem with Jesus' instruction regarding the fundamental condition for the fruitful execution of his office as messenger. Luke still knows what distinguishes the church from heresy: not merely differences in thought, but whether a community lives and fights for itself and thus lays hatred in its conflict with others—or whether it acts in love. And this is how it must act if it truly is the community that has been called to God and has become obedient to Christ.

### d) Opposition toward Magic and Paganism

While every concession is made for the Jews, as long as it does not affect the essence of the gospel, Luke absolutely separates the church from gnostic forms of religion. Simon the sorcerer and also Elymas are sinister counterparts to the messenger of Jesus. In this it is not their theories that are identified as the ground for separation, but the combination of this religiosity with perverse aspirations of the will. Gnosis produces a priesthood that wants to sell God's Spirit for money. If it makes its way into the community, it shatters its unity, because the gnostic teacher chains his followers to himself and oppresses them (Acts 8:18–24; 13:6–12; 19:13–19; 20:29–35). These verdicts of Luke are Pauline, as is his opposition to religious activity involving the acquisition of money and his fear that gnosis might ravish the Pauline congregations. But Luke's verdict quickly became unintelligible to the Gentile for the same reason that caused them to take offense at Paul's Jewish actions. In later Gentile understanding the sorcerer becomes a heretic because he was a teacher of false doctrine.

With equal clarity, Luke retains Pauline principles in his assessment of the relationship between the church and paganism. Here the battle rages fiercely. Mockery in Athens, antagonism on the part of artisans deriving their livelihood from Ephesian Artemis, the Jews' incitement of the Gentiles, the use of Jesus' regnal name for the purpose of charging Christians as enemies of the state, the insecure legal situation which casts doubt on the extent to which the rights granted Judaism also extend to Christendom—all these things reveal the powerful elements emanating from Gentile quarters and resisting the church (Acts

10. Acts 13:14, 44; 14:1; 16:3, 13; 17:2, 10, 17; 18:4, 18; 19:8; 20:16; 21:20–26; 22:17–20; 23:6; 24:14–17; 25:8; 26:6–7; 28:17–20.

17:18, 32; 19:24–28; 13:50; 14:2, 19; 17:5, 7; 24:10–21; 25:8; 26:6–7, 22). What this motif has in common with Paul is the low regard Luke expresses for the intellectual power invested by Hellenism in its religion. To be sure, in the portrayal of Athens reference is made to the fact that popular Stoic and Epicurean philosophies oppose the church. But the gravity of the incipient intellectual struggle is not yet felt. Luke writes in the joyful assurance of intellectual superiority over all that the Greek has to say. Luke's confidence is grounded in the fact that the Greek god needs no refutation but immediately falls apart when confronted with Scripture's concept of God. He therefore considers it to be the primary task of preaching to the Gentiles to unfold the Christian concept of God as it is summed up in the Creator concept (Acts 17:24–29). This creates the prerequisite for the call to repentance directed toward the nations, a call that confronts them with the reprehensible nature of their religious conduct (Acts 17:30; 20:21; 26:20). The reference to the positive elements of Greek religion, such as the longing for the unknown god and the Stoic notion of man's kinship via nature with God, likewise serves the call to conversion. This call holds even the Greek responsible for his religious aberrations.[11] But because victory over the sinful will proves to be as difficult in the Gentile realm as in the Jewish one, Paul's ministry is successful only because God calls a limited number of elect out from among the nations.

In agreement with Paul, Luke also does not emphasize the Roman emperor or Rome's rule as the dangerous opponent that rendered the struggle difficult in the conflict with paganism. To be sure, Rome's importance for the pagan nations, and thus also for the church which is to extend God's calling to it, frames the entire presentation, since Luke accompanies Paul all the way to Rome. But no element can be detected that might be interpreted as, say, influence of Johannine prophecy on Luke's view of history.[12] Grateful appreciation is expressed for the Roman state's benevolent, protective function, which is why Paul as an advocate of Christendom demonstrated before Judea's Roman administrators that it had a justified claim on the state's protection. The church's condition is judged as serious, but it is viewed with calm courage. The community must be prepared to suffer and to die, and the apostles' service of Jesus continually issues in their persecution.[13] But no fanatical veneration is attached to martyrdom. Because it is part of believers' obligation, it is accepted with the same determined calmness as any other duty (Acts 14:22; 15:26; 20:24). The outcome of the struggle is guaranteed for mankind and the church through Jesus' second coming (Acts 17:31; 3:20–21). The persecution of the apostles, which seeks to undo their successes, provides renewed strength to hope longing for Jesus' return.

---

11. Originally, Jewish apologists used these quotations from philosophers and poets, including Aratus's words, in order to justify the merger of Judaism with Hellenism. Now these quotations serve as indicting truths for the purpose of effecting repentance in light of the condition of Greek religion. Thereby Luke remains entirely in step with Paul.

12. In the assessment of gnosticism likewise no Johannine influence can be detected.

13. Luke understood why Paul boasted in his weakness.

## 2. New Material in Luke

### a) History as Proof of the Divine Government

Luke's work differs from Mark, who portrays only Jesus' ministry, or from John, who adds hortatory discourses and prophecy to his presentation of Jesus, in that Luke possesses an understanding of the effective power of those processes that we refer to by the term "history." This was an important new dimension which, to be sure, did not arise from an intermingling of Greek thoughts with Christian ones but which nonetheless was not without connection to Luke's Greek education.[14] What was proclaimed in the congregations as God's message had everywhere a historical dimension. But this did not mean that attention must be directed toward history in and of itself, in the same way in which the concept of God always also entails a statement regarding nature, without implying that nature should captivate one's entire reflection. For after nature has served the purpose of revealing God's power, one's thought can rise above nature in possession of this revelation apart from reflection on how nature brought about this revelation. Similarly, historical processes can be used for the purpose of producing and fulfilling the assurance of God without one's reflection being captivated by the course of history itself. In this case what history achieves for the concept of God would be something heeded and hankered after, not history's intrinsic content. Luke went beyond this; for he directs the community's attention to the chain of events because he sees in them God's sovereign providence. Regarding Paul's work, he pays attention to the progressive movement that makes Paul the founder of the church in a continually growing territory until he gets to Rome. As short as Luke's narrative is, it reveals with great insight what aids Paul in this process and which obstacles confront him. No less clear are the connections that Luke works out between the first and the second half of the book of Acts. The reader is to see how the church grows from its beginning onward toward becoming a Gentile church, and what supports or hinders it in this development. But the apostle's work and the church's development are predicated upon the fact that Jesus' ministry to the Jews and with his disciples took place and ended the way the Gospel describes it.[15] At the same time Luke provides a rich and impressive account of the connection that leads from Jesus' history to the Old Testament. This he accomplishes by illustrating devout Israel with its messianic expectation by means of those in whose midst the birth of Jesus took place.

Here the movement of events in itself becomes the subject of perception, not because a lesson is drawn from them or because they serve as examples for a

---

14. Regarding Luke's ability to observe a longer series of events as a unified process one may be reminded of Luke's medical training. This is more important than the small echoes of medical terminology that may perhaps be demonstrated in his writings.

15. Luke also proved his sound wisdom in not deviating far from the older gospel presentations even though he desired to record the constitutive events of Jesus' history "in sequence." For he realized that the tradition rendered it impossible to bring Jesus' words and actions into an assured chronological order. His most important alterations of the older presentation is that he arranges the pronouncements according to material considerations and transposes these to the time after Jesus' ministry in Galilee had been concluded.

given principle or because they revealed humanity's guilt and misery merely as a foil for the divine grace, but because they took shape through God's sovereign providence and revealed his will, thereby taking on a profundity that makes them unforgettable.

This enabled Luke to illumine the differences that separated consecutive periods. The expectation of those who are gathered around the newborn Christ is not corrected or supplemented in light of the outcome of Jesus' life but retains its pre-Christian form. To be sure, Luke did not edit these accounts himself; but he also did not rewrite them and did not take offense at the fact that the angel Gabriel proclaims the one who rules on David's throne. He also did not supplement the tradition of Jesus' words from apostolic or Pauline preaching, although a great deal of insight was necessary for a follower of Paul to realize the agreement of his convictions with the word of Jesus as this is provided by Luke. Likewise, no accommodation takes place between the apostles' ministry and that of Jesus, and two periods are clearly distinguished: the first period, in which Jesus' proclamation takes place only for the Jews, and the second, which produces the church which is open to all. The church is compelled to remember how it was shaped by God's sovereign providence into a form that no one could have foreseen at the outset.

Thus Luke critically evaluates his material with discernment and resolve, not in a destructive manner that domesticates the facts according to his own judgment, but based on observation that truly apprehends the limits by which successive periods of history are distinguished from one another. The intellectual independence required for this coheres with the principle by which Jesus ordered his disciples' dealings with Scripture, enabling them to unite esteem for Scripture with openness for what was revealed to them as God's work in the present. The same liberty was exercised by the Christian prophet with regard to his prophecy and by the community regarding the prophecy passed on to it. Therefore Luke likewise did not consider it inappropriate or unseemly that in his Christmas account Gabriel, Mary, and Zechariah reiterated prophecy as it was available prior to the end of Jesus' earthly ministry and that Peter needed new compelling revelation so that he could enter a pagan household as an evangelist.

Luke reiterated the account of Jesus shaped by Mark; but where his other sources made clear that the account received its form only from Mark, he reverted to the original account (cf. Luke 6:5 with Mark 2:27–28; Luke 9:3 with Mark 6:8–9; Luke 9:24 with Mark 3:35; Luke 18:29–30 with Mark 10:29–30). The doubt is hardly justified that he also took from Matthew words of Jesus in order to supplement his major sources. That he uses Matthew only in the third instance may probably be explained by the fact that he was keenly aware of Matthew's connection with the Palestinian church, both in the form of his narrative and regarding the content of the sayings, and that he rejected the contention that the entire church was tied to the particular nature of the Palestinian church and the presentation of Jesus by Matthew. He thus exercised the Pauline principle of liberty upon the loftiest possession of the church: all of its teachers should be used, but none should be granted preeminence.

Thus Luke in no way detracted from the supernaturalism of Jesus and Paul. The history he conveys to us presents itself to him as God's work and is recognized as such through the particular demonstrations of God that manifest themselves in the miracle and the Spirit-effected guidance of his messengers. But for Luke, God's supernatural sovereignty does not destroy history but is foundational for it, and his perception and actions are turned to the historical process by his assurance of God. For this process is the means by which God brings the nations to a knowledge of himself.

The next preparation for the thought developed in the Lucan work is the contemplation of Israel's history from the patriarchs until Christ as a uniform divine work. This concept of history was present in Matthew, and this is also how Luke conceives of history, because in Stephen's speech he grounds Jesus' history in Israel's history, both in how God had acted toward Israel up to that point and in how Israel had resisted God up to that point. But it nonetheless constituted a significant further development of this idea when now the work of Jesus and of his messengers and the church were conceived as an interconnected process by which God's rule is realized.

Luke's interest in history is fueled not by doubt but by gratitude for what it brought about. He describes it not in order to furnish an apologetic or a theodicy but in order to demonstrate by it the work of God. Thus he preserves his communion with Paul, who conceded no one the right to call God to account for what he did. There is not a single statement that suggests that Luke placed Jesus' ministry beside that of the apostles, or Peter's work beside that of Paul, or the years in which Paul's ministry unfolded and grew freely beside the years Paul spent in prison, for the purpose of overcoming doubt about God or Jesus or Paul and to write an apologetic. In his view, the facts speak for themselves and do not require any defense by the narrator; for they possess the characteristic of divine provenance and of divine purpose, because they came about only because man here acted in the service of God. Luke's account is shaped by faith; he expressed this himself by expecting faith to be strengthened as a result of his presentation. In his judgment, the historical account enables the community to recognize the certainty of the word given to it (Luke 1:4).

### b) The Hiddenness of Internal Dynamics

The religious appreciation of history reveals a distinction between Luke and Paul that is visible everywhere. The Pauline epistles turn readers' attention inward to the present manifestation of Christ which takes place in their inner lives, to the effect brought about upon them by his Spirit, that is, the renewal of their will. One should not conceive of this as Luke's protest against this grounding of faith; but he gave first place to a different idea in his own presentation. He directs attention outward to God's manifestation in history and uses the way in which the church came into being to confirm faith. If we had nothing but the Lucan account of the apostles, we would not derive from it the profundity of their inner lives. How completely Paul lived in Christ and in the Spirit and included himself in Jesus' death and life, how resolute the denial was that he directed toward the human will, and how completely he appropriated grace as the power controlling him, all this is portrayed by Luke only indirectly, only in that he portrays Paul as the untiring worker who carries out his ministry until the end, but not by portraying the internal roots of his power by themselves. The concealment of the inner life has the result that even the individual element, which provides individuals with their personal characteristics, is assigned second place. According to Luke, the church's unity is based on that all-encompassing history, whose self-evident factuality provides everyone's faith with certainty and harmonious uniformity.

This led to the result that must surprise every historian: Luke is in no way found to imitate Paul. What is missing is not merely the reduction of Paul's words to formulas repeated by students, but also conformity to his will and imitation of his religious experience. The epistles could give the certain impression that Paul evoked in his co-workers a strong mystical tendency, so that in any case faith would have become the subject of their and others' continual observation; a follower of Paul would therefore be continually aware of his guilt, see forgiving grace in Jesus' death, and experience how it issues in confidence in Jesus. Luke shows that a focus on faith as the decisive event did not result in a preoccupation with their internal circumstances on the part of Paul's followers. For there was for them a still greater concern that overrode attention to their spiritual states and experiences: the service that gave them a share in God's work by which he called humanity to himself.

No Pauline document is closer to Luke than the Pastoral epistles. Both portray Paul as the worker who gives absolute priority to his ministry. The fulfillment of the work given to him and to his co-workers is the great concern that transcends all other aspirations. The cultivation of one's own religious life is the means to this end, but not an end in itself. The yields of knowledge are formulated in the intention of making them fruitful for all and of providing all with right conduct. No furtive listening for the Spirit's activity in one's inner life, no focus on divine mysteries for knowledge's sake, is permitted. The church's future is viewed with concern on account of the threat of gnosticism; it faces internal struggles. One cannot say that Luke evidences jubilant joy regarding great experiences or achievements, just as this can also not be found in the Pastorals. But the opposite, despondency, likewise is absent from both documents. The weighty challenge arising from the course of events is felt; but the basic resolve is determined steadfastness; for the disciples' original aim, Jesus' future work, is not yet shaken.

# D. Resistance to a Return to Judaism through the Epistle to the Hebrews

## 1. Doubts Regarding the Value of Christianity

The teacher speaking to us in the epistle to the Hebrews likewise does not receive his topic merely from theoretical deliberations, removed from the condition of the community, but rather from the religious relapse he perceived in a segment of Jewish Christendom with which he had contact.[16] The retrogressive movement from which the author wants to protect his readers arises from the contrast between the actual condition of Christendom and the absolute content of the messianic idea, which separated the religious condition of Christendom entirely from that of Judaism through the proclamation of fulfillment. But whether this contrast was borne out in reality and the inner separation from Judaism was necessary, this became the issue for this group within the church. The sacrifices required from them on account of their separation intensified such concerns (10:32–34; 12:3–4; 13:23), and the manner in which the epistle lays out its argument, in particular its treatment of Melchizedek, suggests that it was further intensified through the gnostic idealization of Judaism (1:3–4; 2:5; 7:1–3; 13:9).[17]

### a) Stages of Revelation

The verdict regarding the relationship between Christendom and Judaism is replaced entirely by the empirical condition of both communities. What is considered is not whether the Jew or the Christian is superior; God's work alone is presented in its former and present distinctives. It is not human achievements that are compared with one another but the stages of revelation. This reveals the community's state of faith with instructive clarity. A conflict regarding who was superior, the Christian or the Jew, was rendered impossible on account of the grounding of the church in faith. Thereby the value of Christendom was placed in what God gave to the community, and only from this arise the absolute pronouncements by which Christendom describes its relationship with God. However, it cannot praise God's gift in its own case while criticizing the Jew's conduct in the case of the Jew. In the case of Judaism, too, the verdict is exclusively grounded in what it has received from God.[18]

Thus we hear in this epistle nothing of the Temple, of priests or sacrifices as they existed at that time, nothing of the manner in which the Jew or the Pharisee actually intends to fulfill the Law. The author considers his topic to be entirely in the realm of theology, in knowledge regarding the divine government. This meant that the basis for the verdict regarding Judaism is Scripture, not the present condition. Scripture reveals what God granted to the old community; it illumines the imperishable possession of Judaism, because God's promise cannot be broken, however the Jew acts. Separation from Judaism is enacted with

---

16. The writing's place of destination is unknown; the only thing that can be determined is that it is directed to a group of Jewish Christians; the author worked together with Timothy in Paul's mission field (13:23).

17. Whoever questions whether the treatment of Melchizedek is based on the fact that the author used Ps. 110:4 together with Gen. 14 as exegetical evidence for Jesus' superiority over Aaron, will assume that gnostic speculation regarding Melchizedek was used to level the difference between Old Testament revelation and Jesus. Confession of Jesus constituted no grounds for separation from Judaism, in this view, because there was already one who possessed an eternal priesthood without father or mother in the old covenant.

18. This calls attention to the epistle's strong affinity with Matthew, who, to be sure, shows the Jews what is sinful in their conduct, but who simultaneously confronts Christendom with equal seriousness with possible judgment.

justification only when what Scripture assigns it is transcended by the religious possession given by Jesus to his community.

For this reason the epistle starts by stating that God revealed himself to the fathers through angels and that he gave them the Law through them; for the fact that heavenly beings were mediators between God and Israel remains the permanently valid characteristic of the relationship into which God enters with Israel. Likewise, the vocation assigned to Moses by God forever provides the standard by which the religious power of Judaism is measured, and the same is true regarding the appointment of Aaron and the furnishing of the Tabernacle. The ritual instituted for Israel by the Law reveals for all times wherein consists the gracious gift that is theirs by virtue of being Jews.

Thus faith is here compared with faith in such a way that it is not the experience of faith of the communities that is judged but the ground and substance of the faith given to them by God. Thereby the distinction between both states of faith is completely removed from all selfish strife or sectarian glorification of one's own church. The verdict regarding the difference existing here can rather be reached only by revealing the privilege granted to Israel in all of its greatness. Thus this epistle likewise contains not a single bitter word against the Jews or even a negative evaluation of their religion; the limitation inherent in God's former attestation can rather be recognized only where its positive value was realized without being diminished. Therefore the epistle does not begin with the human but rather with God's heavenly messengers. It portrays Moses as receiving God's entire praise and as being put in charge of God's entire house as his faithful servant, describing the priest according to his divine appointment and as carrying out his ministry as the mediator of forgiveness through the sacrifice which provides the community with its relationship to God. The aim of the argument now lies in the demonstration that Christendom did not lose anything of Israel's entire endowment; in fact, everything is not only preserved in Jesus but is rather fulfilled (1:5–14; 3:1–6; 5:1–10; 7:1–10, 28).

This determines the particular perspective from which here the Mosaic Law is viewed, not as the legislation regulating human conduct but as the ordering of ritual which provides the nation with divine blessing. This does not indicate that the author or his readers strongly adhered to Aaronic priests or cherished a vivid desire for the Jewish altar or animal sacrifices; these are mentioned because Scripture mandates them as the means by which reconciliation with God is obtained in the Old Testament period.

### b) Objections to Jesus

From the Christian side, nothing stands in contrast to Jewish possession but Jesus' work. This fact gives rise to readers' desire to look backward. It cannot be demonstrated that their eschatological hopes wavered, because the epistle does not attempt to provide support for Jesus' promise by affirming, for example, the imminence or possibility of his second coming. The readers know that at some point in the future the course of history will be completed and God will reign in glory. For this reason the comparison with Judaism is not undertaken from the perspective of weighing which of the two religions provides better guarantees for participating in future salvation.

To be sure, the readers' hope must be strengthened, but not because eschatological expectations are disputed, but because their religious present seems unsatisfactory to them (3:4; 4:1, 11; 6:11–12, 17–20; 10:19–23). Because weariness of faith results in disintegration of hope, strengthening of hope takes place through a presentation of the gift granted by Jesus to his community.

The thrust of the entire investigation is directed toward the religious status attained through Jesus. Christendom is in the right only if it is now given the perfect good through Jesus. The question is not whether fulfillment will occur at some point in the future but whether it *has* occurred through Jesus and the readers have it. It is whether the relationship with God given to them justifies absolute messianic statements, and whether therefore a qualitative difference over against the pre-Christian period has truly been reached. For this reason the term "perfection" becomes the most important term for the epistle: Jesus is the Christ, if he himself is perfect and if he has perfected his community (Christ as the one who is perfect: 2:10; 5:9; 7:28; the community as perfected: 7:11, 19; 9:9; 10:1, 14; 11:40; 12:2).

Because faith is that attitude by which the community is united with Jesus, however, what is perceptible falls far short of what is expressed by Christian affirmations. Christ's advent ends with his death, and his exaltation to God translates him into the invisible realm. The theology of the epistle thus turns exclusively into Christology, particularly teaching regarding his cross and his exaltation. His death constitutes the fruit of his earthly ministry, and his heavenly exaltation provides the basis for the community's present relationship with him. Is this perfection? From a Jewish point of view, allegiance to Jesus, whose greatest deed on earth was his death, falls seriously short of what the Old Testament community received, as it was given visible manifestations of God and abiding sacramental salvific ordinances. But in the view of the author, everything conferred by the Old Testament means of grace has also been given to the community by Jesus. What is more, he grants it God's perfect grace, which fulfills what remained incomplete for the old community.

What unites Christendom with the deceased and exalted Jesus is solely faith. But even faith is affected by the question which the epistle seeks to answer, because it appears to be a contradiction against Jesus' identity as the Christ that he does not grant his community to see but obliges it likewise again to believe. Thereby, of course, it is placed in the same relationship with God in which everyone has always stood. It must therefore be made clear what faith is and what it receives. Apart from it, no other process that is part of Christian devotion is affected by controversy. No issue that is characteristic of Christendom in the realm of Christian ethics or ritual or organization is discussed, such as what is the significance of the Sabbath or the Lord's Supper or the office of overseer. Nothing rivals Jesus and faith directed toward him. This is where the author locates the characteristic that determines a man's or a community's Christian character. Whatever the community accomplishes itself in its religious conduct, he considers irrelevant, if it does not possess in Jesus the entire gift of grace.

Otherwise, it would no longer stand above, but beside Judaism, and the ground for separation from it would be removed.

This reveals that separation from the Law must not still be effected; it has already occurred. The readers' task is to preserve the freedom that has long been won, not to first achieve it. The fact that freedom already exists and that separation from Judaism has already taken place leads to the backward look by which the legitimacy of the completed separation is once more reconsidered and its indispensable necessity is demonstrated.

That only the legitimacy of faith is discussed from among all elements of Christian devotion results from the fact that the community does not possess anything other than what Jesus' perfection has provided; its allegiance to Jesus is thus its entire religious possession. Conversely, the singling out of faith does not mean that Christian devotion is limited to it alone. The importance of its accompanying features, such as fear, hope, love, works, knowledge, is acknowledged. The author shows how he assesses knowledge by providing a detailed investigation regarding the difference between the religions and by providing a careful rationale for the verdict through which believing allegiance to Jesus takes place. All of the community's activities, however, receive their Christian character from the fact that faith in Jesus provides them with their foundation and goal. If these were to disintegrate, his reader's piety would be no more valuable than Jewish faith.

## 2. The Gift of the Christ

### a) Jesus' Priesthood

The all-surpassing value of knowing Jesus is based on the perfection of his divine sonship. Through it he is mediator of revelation in a higher sense than the angels and still more so than Moses. It is also the basis for the salvific effect of his death. Thereby the epistle uses the convictions known to us through Paul and John. It does, however, break new ground by drawing on priestly terminology in its interpretation of the outcome of Jesus' life. Offense at Jesus, arising from his descent into death and his ascent to heaven, has been overcome by the epistle only when Jesus' end can be presented as the demonstration of perfect grace, and this is achieved when it is presented as providing the basis for his priestly office. Jesus is assigned priestly character not only in a single moment, such as merely in his suffering; rather, Jesus' entire work—his entrance into humanity, his suffering and death and his exaltation to God—is subsumed under the concept of priest (2:17–18; 4:14–16; 5:5–10; 6:20; 7:24–28; 9:11–14, 24–28; 10:12–14, 19–21). Through his entrance into humanity, the Son of God enters into that fellowship with it which becomes the prerequisite of his priestly office on its behalf. Thus Jesus' death, too, becomes an essential aspect of his office, because the role of priest consists in the offering of a sacrifice. As the Dying One he offers this sacrifice to God through the shedding of his blood. He renders his death a sacrifice because he yields himself to God as the Dying One. It is required of him on account of the sin of man who can receive access to God only when he is forgiven. But Jesus dies in the throes of a will intent on providing man with forgiveness. This sacrifice is complete, because there is nothing greater a man could give to God than his life. By offering his blood, Jesus offers himself, with everything he is and has, to God (5:7; 9:12–14, 25–26; 10:12, 19; 12:24; 13:12). But it is also part of the priestly office that the priest has access to God and draws near to God on the basis of the sacrifice he offered. Through this the separation that distances the community from God is overcome. For this reason Jesus' cross is followed by his exaltation to God, and his priestly office is complete even in this respect, because Jesus' destiny entails not merely his ascent into heaven but even beyond heaven to the throne of God and because he has perfect communion with the Father. Thereby his priestly service takes place in the true heavenly sanctuary (4:14; 6:20; 7:26; 8:1–5; 9:11, 24; 10:12). The anticipation of Christ's return follows from this without tension, because the priest returns to the community after having entered the Holy of Holies, now as the bearer of the blessing he acquired for it through his reconciling activity (9:28).

Through the priest concept, the epistle orients Jesus' ministry first of all toward God, so that his gift to the community is grounded in what he receives for it from God. This constitutes for the epistle the didactic value of the phrase that Jesus is the High Priest. After all, he seeks to show perfect divine grace in Jesus' death and exaltation; but Jesus' death and exaltation do not immediately bring about a change in the course of the world, because they separate him from humanity and subject him to suffering. Jesus' activity at his death is oriented toward God, and the epistle secures the illumining analogy for the work he accomplishes together with the Father by linking it with the work of the priest.

This train of thought leads in the contemplation of Jesus to a sharper differentiation of his participation in humanity and divinity than is found elsewhere in the New Testament. Jesus becomes a priest as man, because the priest must belong to the community on behalf of which he holds his office. But Jesus derives the ability to accomplish his work through his communion with God. The epistle therefore attributes to him simultaneously divinity and humanity, each of which has in its own way a part in his priestly activity. His participation in human nature provides him with the authority to be merciful. By resisting temptation, he becomes the helper of those who face temptation. By making his blood the sacrifice by which he yields himself to God, he procures forgiveness for the community. By being inaugurated into heaven and elevated to the throne of God by his priestly vocation, Jesus provides the community with its calling to God (2:17–18; 4:15; 5:7–8; 9:11–14). All of this is possible for him, however, because he comes from God and, as the Son, stands in complete unity with him. This lends Jesus' human deed its comprehensive effect; therefore it renews relationship with God forever and for all. Apart from statements regarding Jesus' eternal and perfect sonship, the pronouncements regarding his priestly activity could be understood along the lines of the pagan concept of sacrifice, according to which God is the recipient of impulses which are projected onto him by mankind. But now Jesus' entire work is grounded, both in its origin and in its outcome and success, in the share in God given to him, whereby it remains completely comprised by the divine will and operation and has its presupposition in him. His blood is the sacrifice offered to God, because he gave it to God through the eternal Spirit.

For this reason the epistle was able to use the legal analogy implied in the idea of "testament"; for Jesus' entire work is based on the divine stipulation by which God himself in his grace determines man's relationship with him. Because a testament goes into effect only when the testator dies, Jesus renders his will, which is rooted in God's stipulation, unchanging by dying. Now his testament is enacted (9:16–17).

### b) The Result of Jesus' Sacrifice

Because divine sonship makes Jesus' priesthood complete, there arises not merely a relative but a complete difference between the old and the new community. All limitations are removed from the grace given to it by Jesus' priestly service. Now it is no longer man's flesh that is cleansed, not merely what is external and natural in him, but man's inner condition becomes new, and he receives a pure conscience. Now sacrifice has its purpose and result not merely in effecting remorseful remembrance of sin but in reconciling the guilty person with God. It also does not merely atone for individual sins but makes us perfect and completely removes our separation from God. It also does not merely cleanse us from what clings to us as stains and guilt but makes us holy, united with God, able to approach him, so that his throne is for us a throne of grace. Thus that community comes into being which is able to worship God and to serve him with all its will. Now believers are placed into the communion that encompasses heaven and earth, for which God is the eternal king (9:8–14; 10:1–22; 12:18–29).

This is why faith is perfected through Jesus' priestly service, and because he is the perfecter of faith, he can also be called its author, although the devotion of all whom God united with himself consisted always and necessarily in faith (12:2). Faith is also for Christendom the attitude to which it is led by Jesus, because God's gift and work rises above what is visible and what is present (11:1). An assurance that lays hold of what is invisible is not seeing but faith, and because it guarantees for us what is perfect and thus turns our longing toward the future, we are not yet provided with our possession and experience; we still believe. But because the Son of God became a priest for us, our faith is complete. It is perfect assurance and full confidence. For he provides us with perfect grace.

### 3. Hebrews and Paul

The epistle's train of thought stands in profound harmony with Paul, because it gains a part in God solely in the Christ, but in him completely, desiring no religious possession other than the knowledge of Jesus which is provided for the community by faith in him. This eliminates any possible combining of Judaism and Christianity. Separation from Judaism is complete. For both authors, union with Christ is accomplished through faith, and because the epistle derives the verdict on man's relationship with God solely on the basis of Christ, it considers all of devotion to be grounded in faith in Christ. At the same time, the epistle stands beside Paul with such independence, both in individual passages and in its entire shaping of thinking and willing, that an imitation of Paul or a relationship of a disciple with his master is inconceivable.

The contemplation of the Law from which Paul derives all of his pronouncements regarding the Law, that is, that it reveals God's demands for man's works and thus judges the sinful work and condemns man, is not found in Hebrews. Here the Law determines to what extent and in what way Israel has received the divine grace. Thus the stipulations regarding ritual are the centerpiece of the Law, while Paul interpreted the Law from the vantage point of the Decalogue. Therefore the relationship between Christ and the Law does not issue in an antithesis. The community must be redeemed from the transgression of the Law, but not from the Law itself (9:15). The Law and Christ both serve the same will of God, but in such a way that the Law carries it out only to a limited extent while Christ does so perfectly. The Law, too, provides forgiveness, but only a limited kind; Christ, on the other hand, provides it completely. The Law also provides cleansing, but only for the flesh, while Christ also cleanses internally, that is, one's conscience.

Thus Pauline formulas regarding the impact of Jesus' cross lose their usefulness for the teacher speaking in Hebrews, because they are based on the fact that the verdict of the Law regarding man is executed through Christ's death, whereby Christ's death becomes the death of all and Christ's resurrection the resurrection of all. Because this teacher depicts Jesus' death as the act of the priest who makes himself the perfect sacrifice for God, he also conceives of the impact of Jesus' death as universal, extensively as well as intensively; but he mediates its applicability to all by showing how Jesus is exalted to God on account of the fulfillment of his priestly office and is thus enabled to extend the benefits of his priestly activity to the community. Because Paul subsumes Jesus' death under the concept of Law, it was important for him that Jesus died at the cross as the Condemned One. In Hebrews, the cross is mentioned only a single time as the antithesis of the glory Jesus had by virtue of his sonship, a glory which he yielded in exchange for the shame of the cross in the fulfillment of his priestly office (12:2; cf. the allusion in 6:6). The Pauline teaching on the cross is always also teaching on the resurrection, because Christ's death becomes the demonstration of saving grace by his being raised from the dead. Hebrews refers to Jesus' resurrection only in the concluding statement (13:20). To be sure, it continually presupposes it, because it lets Jesus' death be followed by his exaltation to heaven. But it does not achieve an understanding of Jesus' death by way of the concept of resurrection, because it is not this concept that expresses what arises from his death in relation to God. On the contrary, this is described through Jesus' arriving at God's throne subsequent to his death. Imitation of Paul is inconceivable when the trademark significance that resurrection had for him is absent.

This is also why the Pauline contrast between flesh and Spirit is not found here, either in such a way that the concept of flesh served the purpose of depicting the human condition apart from Christ; or in such a way that Christ had his distinguishing characteristic in the Spirit; or in such a way that the greatness of the church's possession was described by the fact that it had the Spirit and acted under his guidance. To be sure, the Spirit concept is not absent here, just as it is not absent elsewhere in the New Testament writings (9:14; 2:4; 6:4; 10:29). By it the divine operation is described as it takes place in Christ and in the community. Thus Jesus offered himself to God through the eternal Spirit, and the distributions of the Holy Spirit to the community attest to him. But it is characteristic of the epistle that the Spirit's presence with the community does not serve the purpose of demonstrating its superiority over the synagogue but to reveal the greatness of guilt incurred by the rejection of Christ after he has been acknowledged. If the community had wanted to boast of the Spirit, this would have become its demise. But it must fear, because he is with it; for thus it is entrusted with the perfect gift, and when it forfeits it, has nothing to look forward to but judgment.

Thus the epistle also does not present faith as the distinguishing mark separating Christendom from Judaism. That Judaism now proves to be faithless is doubtless true; but the Jew's actual conduct is not even the subject of debate, and thus also not how unbelieving and disobedient the readers were toward God when they previously resisted God. What is certain is that the fathers believed in God. While Paul portrays faith as the new element that cannot arise from the Law because it judges sin, but which rather arises through Christ, the present epistle shows that Christendom, by believing, does the same thing everyone did who came to God and who was attested as pleasing to him. For any manifestation of God at any time obliged people to faith. And faith was heard at these occasions and was rewarded with the receipt of divine gifts. Therefore the epistle lacks the occasion to expose the contrast between faith and works. Rather, it is the remarkable quality of faith that it provides man's entire conduct with its rightness, because it grounds it in the divine activity. Therefore it gives rise to insight that perceives God's creative activity, separation from the world that rejects its conduct and sanctifies God's will, obedience that does God's commandment, hope that longs for the promise, patience that suffers and dies for God's sake. Fear likewise is not presented as antithetical to faith by the epistle, because it is seriously concerned to awaken in the readers fear of the divine execution of justice (2:1–4; 6:4–8; 10:26–31; 12:15–29). Also in this respect the operation of the Law forms a unity with that of Christ, except that Christ's impact is more thoroughgoing and powerful. He calls us to fear before God even more than the Law, even though he did not step before humanity in the terrible nature of the old revelation of God but guides it into communion with God's heavenly kingdom. But precisely because he grants the perfect gift, perfect fear arises through him as well.

The epistle does not address the contrast between Israel and the Gentiles. The purpose of Jesus' sending is not discussed in terms of the church's universal scope, and his death is not tied to the calling of the Gentiles to God. The discussion remains limited to Israel. The only subject of discussion is whether or not the Jew has received a grace through Jesus that he did not receive before and that he could not obtain, because it can be granted in its perfect form solely through the Son.

The new thought of Hebrews stands in a clear connection with the absence of convictions required for Paulinism. In Paul, Jesus' regal status is the centerpiece of his message; the one who is designated as the Lord of the community dies and lives for it. The significance of his death and his life for us issues directly from his messianic office, as does his communion with God, because the Son alone is the Christ. Thus in Jesus' activity Paul sees God's activity. God judges and forgives through what he does for and through Christ. For this reason Paul does not portray Jesus as a priest, even though the thought was not far from him, because he also saw in Psalm 110 one of the most important biblical testimonies regarding Christ's aim. By describing the manner in which Jesus reveals God in priestly terms, however, the teacher speaking to us in the epistle of Hebrews relates him to us as the one whom God makes our representative before himself. Thereby Christ's union with God and with believers is no longer assigned the same immediacy as is the case with the Pauline formulations regarding the cross and faith. With the concept of priesthood the epistle parts ways with what may be termed "Pauline mysticism."

Of course, it must not be forgotten in this comparison, as in the entire work of New Testament theology, that we possess only a small number of writings. We do not have from Paul any discussion of the Old Testament priest and his sacrifice; the deliberations we receive from the author of Hebrews likewise do not constitute a complete presentation of his religious thought. We do not hear how he confronts a Jew who boasts of his own righteousness with Jesus' word or repentance, but only how he seeks to remove the thoughts now burdening his readers. They are hard-pressed to confess the Crucified; Jesus' death and his messianic office appear to stand in contradiction to each other for them; in order that they might see that Jesus' death was the prerequisite for his rule, he incorporates the priest concept into the presentation of his office. How he would have portrayed Christ in response to different concerns for different needs we are not told here, and the mere fact that we possess only this discussion from him does not support the conclusion that he did not possess any other concepts by which he would have been equally able to express the value of Jesus' gift as he does through use of the analogy of the priestly office. In view of the situation as it presents itself to us it must be said, however, that the teacher who here speaks to us arrives at independent judgments concerning so many issues essential for Paul that the phrase "follower of Paul" cannot be applied to him.

## 4. The Relationship of Hebrews to the Synagogue

The differences between this epistle and Paul do not come about through the influence of Greek conceptions. None of the ideas that served as the basis for Greek piety features prominently here. No Greek influence can be detected in the fact that Jesus' resurrection is not stressed here as the foundation of faith; for its lack of emphasis is not coupled with doubt regarding it. The epistle reveals unwavering confidence regarding the fact that Jesus is alive. If Greek sentiment or thought had overshadowed the resurrection, the author would have expressly substantiated and defended this confidence. The fact that he does not consider the community to be the means by which Jesus reveals and glorifies himself likewise does not reveal Greek influence. Greek thought can indeed lead to an individualism which separates individuals' religious concerns from the church. But the epistle relates Jesus' commission always to the community, to the "nation," to "us" who are united to a religious community. If the church had become for him grounds for astonishment on account of Hellenism, we would receive a working out of this train of thought that relates the church to the divine aim. Instead, the readers' incorporation into the community is the fact that is consistently presupposed but whose significance does not constitute the subject of extensive discussion.

The conceptualities and injunctions of the epistle are, on the other hand, clearly related to synagogual tradition. If a Gentile spoke here about the advantage of Christianity over Judaism, it would remain a peculiar mystery that he devotes no space to the national limitation of Judaism, which was palpable enough to the Gentiles and was why they considered the Christian community's liberation from ethnic boundaries to be an essential difference between the two religions. For a born Jew, on the other hand, the national form of the community was a given, which as a self-evident condition needed no further discussion. The separation of the question from any consideration of the present condition of Judaism also points to the synagogue. The synagogue formed its opinion regarding the nature and benefit of its religion by using the same method.[19] It thus adheres to the same principle that also guides the epistle, that is, that the Jew's relationship with God does not issue from what the community does but from what God has commanded it to do. For the Jew bases his share in God on Scripture; what it says regarding him provides him with his standing before God.

The epistle also remains aligned with the synagogue when it finds the injunctions that regulate God's relationship with Israel in the Pentateuch. One finds here a clear preference for the Pentateuch over the rest of the Bible, not as extreme as in the case of Philo, for whom the remaining writings entirely vanish from sight. The epistle rather contrasts the Son with the long series of prophets through whom God has spoken in a variety of ways, and the review of the faith of Old Testament believers conceives of the entire community as a unity that reaches from Abel to the present. The scope of the canon used by the epistle does not differ from what is known to us through the rabbinate and Greek translations. But the significance of what is given through the later prophets is clearly subordinated to the Law; the Law makes completely clear what God granted to Israel. Prophecy adds to this the messianic promise. But Judaism is fully contained in the Law and does not experience any significant alteration in the period between Moses and the present.

His topic and his perspective meant that exegetical work had greater significance for this teacher than for the other New Testament writings. Because one learns through the interpretation of the Law what Judaism is, exegesis also directly affects the assessment of Jesus. For Jesus' work brings fulfillment to what

---

19. The rabbinate, Josephus, and Philo all determine simply by the commandments of the Law what Jewish ritual is, without discussion of whether it was still practiced.

the old community has and is thus to be measured by what Scripture says regarding Israel's share in God. Thus the conclusion gained through exegesis becomes the indispensable foundation for the pronouncement regarding Christ, and for this reason the epistle consists of a series of reflections on Old Testament texts which he now uses to reveal Christ's all-surpassing supremacy. One must not say that a Gentile could not have used this kind of study of the Old Testament as a means for the knowledge of Jesus. But the epistle's train of thought primarily aligns itself with the tradition that so strongly determined Jewish piety, for which exegesis was the most important means of establishing the assurance of God and the knowledge of his will.

The exegetical function loses significance in Christian doctrine when Jesus is separated from Israel's history and, as independent agent of a new divine work, becomes the ground of faith that is based solely on him. But when the unity of the divine will, which establishes the old and the new community, and the unity of faith, by which all are united with God from the beginning, become the primary guiding principle of thought, exegesis becomes an important function without which this contemplation of the divine rule cannot be obtained. Then the unity between Judaism and Christianity is recognized on account of the fact that the unity between Scripture and Christ is revealed. The position thus taken by the epistle is that of Jewish Christendom. Among the ritual acts which make up Temple worship, the Day of Atonement with the high priest's going into the Holy of Holies is stressed as the most important; this corresponds to the Palestinian esteem of the Day of Atonement. The affirmation that the Mosaic sanctuary has its prototype in heaven is based directly on a saying of Scripture and is thus not relevant merely for a particular group in the community. However, the heavenly sanctuary did not fit the Greek conception of heaven and the universe, while Palestinian tradition emphasized that Temple worship resembled the heavenly worship of God. At this juncture the author says of the Cherubim that they provide the occasion for thorough instruction (9:5). The interpretation of Ezekiel's theophany was considered in the synagogue to be one of the greatest theological achievements. Moreover, interpreters devoted particular attention to the divine oath; its importance is emphasized also in the epistle, both in the case of Abraham and in the interpretation of Psalm 110:4 (6:13–18; 7:20–22). That God said of the blood of Abel that it cried out is a feature of Palestinian interpretation; the epistle likewise conceives of the speaking of Abel's blood subsequent to his death as still present (11:4; 12:24).

By grounding faith in Christ in the fact that the value of the salvation procured by him is recognized, the epistle occupies common ground with Greek and Hellenistic-Jewish theologians who saw in one's dealings with God the means by which man gained blessedness. But the supremacy of the will originating in the consciousness of God over all selfish passions is never in doubt for the present teacher. When he causes the community to tremble in view of the final loss of life and kindles its hope by the thought of the greatness of the coming help, he does not place human longing above the divine aim; for he grounds everything man receives in God's work. The way by which he arrives at freedom from passions that seek one's own happiness is none other than the one the disciples, according to Jesus' instruction, walked from the beginning: faith renders man subordinate to God.

There are only a few concrete connections with the Alexandrian form of Jewish theology. The two images, "ray" of light by which light is revealed and "pattern" by which something is recognized, are used by the epistle for the description of Jesus' ministry when it brackets together simultaneously the ministry of the Preexistent One and the one who became man (1:3). Through the same images the Alexandrian Logos doctrine discusses the share in God's eternal wisdom at the creation of the world. Through it light shone into the world, and it shapes things by giving them their purposeful form. This provides a clear connection; but that it is to be explained by the reading of Philonic books was a premature conclusion, because the essential characteristics of Philo's thought and piety are completely absent. Whoever learns from Philo will first of all appropriate his method; the epistle does not contain allegory but belongs in its exploitation of literal meaning directly to the milieu of Palestinian interpreters.[20] Moreover, Philonic influences produce mystical tendencies. The epistle does not even contain what may be called mystical in the case of Paul or John, much less the Philonic efforts to produce a process in the soul by which union with the deity can be achieved. There is nothing of Philo's ascetic principles, nothing of his cosmological theories. Whoever combines the superiority of the heavenly sanctuary over the earthly one and of the heavenly priest over human priests with Philonic ideas opens the door to confusion. Even the terms applied to Christ, "radiance" and "pattern," are removed from their Philonic form in that they do not serve cosmogony here but elaborate on how Jesus revealed God to mankind. The interest of the epistle is oriented solely toward God, not toward the explanation of the course of the world, but on how God's relationship with man comes about. And because God becomes manifest in Jesus, the author calls Jesus the radiance of divine glory and the mark of divine existence.

Nevertheless, the use of these phrases renders probable that not merely the first readers but also the author belonged to the Greek branch of Judaism, which is also confirmed by the epistle's entire terminology. This also coheres with the fact that his view of the Law is not the Pharisaic one. While Pharisaism considers the Law to contain commandments that compel man's obedience—even though it also regulates ritual acts—but in such a way that they receive their significance by providing man the opportunity for obedience by which he submits to God, the extant Alexandrian literature shows that a concept of religion developed in the Greek portion of Judaism that was significantly shaped by the institutions of God, by which he raises man to himself and unites him with himself. The same concept of religion also determines the religious formations of gnosticism; one of these, speculation regarding Melchizedek, is mentioned even in the present epistle. He does, however, thereby not yield to gnostic impulses, because he does not make Melchizedek the subject of his discussion for his own sake. He says of him only what Scripture says; for since

---

20. That the epistle in 7:2 translates the terms "Melchizedek" and "Salem" has several parallels in Palestinian tradition.

Christ is said to become an eternal priest like Melchizedek, the epistle attributes to Melchizedek likewise an imperishable priesthood. But any extension of discussion beyond biblical statements, whereby Melchizedek's provenance and the manner of his priestly ministry would be transposed to the supernatural realm, is omitted. The entire treatment is designed solely to show Jesus' calling in its incomparable greatness. The community has Jesus, not Melchizedek, as its priest, and it knows this because he is placed not merely above Aaron but also above Melchizedek by virtue of his divine sonship.

## 5. Hebrews and John

The epistle to the Hebrews constitutes an instructive parallel to John, because it shares with John the Jewish foundation of piety and at the same time has significant common ground with Paul. Both men share the centering of their entire thought on Christology, a move which has its presupposition in the fact that they view the unfolding of the entire revelation of God, from the creation of the world until its perfection, in the Christ. In both documents, Jesus' complete oneness with God does not lead to docetism or to the depreciation of history. The Son concept remains in the framework given to it by Jesus, for it remains related to his human, personal life, so that his work on earth yields the revelation of God which provides for humanity eternal communion with God. For this reason it is for both writers faith, viewed from the subjective side, which is singled out from all other aspects of piety as that process that unites us with God (the assertion that the epistle to the Hebrews was written in the first century while John belongs to a later period is completely arbitrary).

The use of the term "word" for the interpretation of Jesus' oneness with God is also close to the epistle to the Hebrews. For the designations of the Christ as the radiance and the express image of God derives from the Logos doctrine, and Hebrews likewise completely merges the divine word with the divine power, whereby the divine word is given mediation of all divine works (1:3–4; 12:13). Also parallel are therefore the connections between Christology and the teaching regarding the Spirit, as well as eschatology. The distance between the epistle to the Hebrews' pronouncements regarding the Spirit and the Pauline statements resembles those we find in John. Both find in their relationship to Jesus everything they need for the assurance of their salvation. This does not result in their loss of hope, which rather receives its power and assurance through Jesus' perfect sonship of God. For Hebrews as for John, however, following Jesus does not arise from a preview of the last things but from the way in which Jesus determined the community's standing before God. Similar is the lack of emphasis on the church concept and on the task given to the church regarding the world.

The difference between John and the epistle to the Hebrews arises at the same point where John differs from Paul. What is missing is what one might call "Johannine mysticism," that is, the immediate envelopment by Jesus in which John lives. This injects into the piety of Hebrews more tension and struggle than one finds in John. In the epistle to the Hebrews, the struggle is not merely directed against the world but against one's own will. The will wrestles with doubt and with Christians' weariness and reluctance to suffer, envisioning the danger of final apostasy. What keeps the believer dwells above him, that is, the heavenly Christ, and what gives him assurance is especially the Scriptures. This does not, however, effect a transformation of the concept of faith in the sense that faith in Hebrews signifies the appropriation of scriptural teaching. Its object remains the divine testimony, which brings that which is invisible and future to the individual. Because this occurs for Christendom through the Christ, faith here, as in John, consists of certainty regarding the Christ and the work accomplished by him for the community. Stronger than in John, however, is the thought that the individual is moved to faith by a longing for the things offered to him by God. In John, likewise, Jesus' message draws the person to him by granting him life. But the relationship between faith and the human longing striving to move from darkness into light and from death into life renders the basis for faith not what man perceives in himself but that he recognizes God in Jesus. In the description of faith in Hebrews 11:1, however, hope and faith are united more closely, since hope becomes faith when it strives for the things it hopes for with persistent resolve.

# E. The Renewed Determination of the Church's Goal in the Name of Peter

## 1. The Apostolic Office

By writing not in his own name but in the name of Peter, a Christian here indicates that the weight of the apostolic word transcends all that is owned by the present community. No message of a contemporary possesses similar authority. This reveals a certain amount of the community's despair of its own vigor remaining after the death of the apostles, as well as the realization that nothing the community produces can be compared with the apostolic word. By seeking to remind the community in the name of Peter of what it has received, the writer calls the memory that continually draws on the apostolic word the condition for the church's existence (2 Pet. 1:13).

The preference given to the apostolic work over that of later believers is based on the eyewitness character of the disciples, which provided them with assured knowledge of Jesus. Thus nothing appears more suitable for the writer in his effort to reveal the greatness of the apostolic office than the account of the transfiguration (2 Pet. 1:16–18). Peter heard the voice of God which provided Jesus with God's witness. The value of the apostolic ministry is sought not in individual traditions regarding Jesus but in the fact that the apostle can attest to Jesus' sonship and lordship on the basis of his own experience.

Peter's martyrdom likewise lends particular significance to his work. As in John, it is considered to be assigned to him by the Lord. Nevertheless, no veneration of martyrdom can be detected that deviates from the rest of the New Testament, and the memory of the severe sufferings of the Roman church does not evoke in the community a demoralizing unease that would have required particular strengthening. The martyrdom assigned to the apostle merely provides the basis for concern regarding the expansion and preservation of the word (2 Pet. 1:13–14).

The epistle's comment regarding the Pauline epistles provides a material parallel to its use of the apostolic name. Paul's epistles likewise provide an opportunity for the church to preserve the apostolic word; for this reason they are to be used continually and carefully, although they provide an occasion for misinterpretation on account of their profundity (2 Pet. 3:15–16). The comment is probably occasioned by the zeal with which men involved in gnosticism interpreted the Pauline epistles, whose pronouncements they reshaped according to their own theories. Still, this abuse of Paul's epistles must not prevent the church from using them as its canon. For they provide it with indispensable contact with the word that establishes it. To this may be added that the writer invested Jude's epistle, whose preservation he desired, with apostolic authority by reworking it.

Along with the Petrine and Pauline epistles, the writer calls the Old Testament canon the foundation of Christian devotion (2 Pet. 1:19–21). It is not regarded as Law but exclusively in terms of prophecy, whose use is limited by the stipulation that it must not be made the subject of arbitrary interpretation. Because God's Spirit speaks in it, it is also God's Spirit who alone can explain it. The writer acknowledges that Old Testament prophecy cannot be directly transferred into the present but that it requires renewed appropriation, which the community can draw only from the same source from which prophecy came to be. Still, it is valuable as prophecy, as long as night covers the world and even the community living in it. Prophecy is likened to the lamp which remains indispensable as long as day has not yet dawned. The day comes with Jesus' appearing, which will provide the community with perception of the divine glory and works; with it light will enter the ears of those who receive a share in his rule.

## 2. Christianity's Aim

Jesus' proclamation turned the author from the world to God. The mark of the world is the passion that is fatal to it. Through Christ, on the other hand, man receives God's gifts which are of a divine nature and which place that nature into the individual. This results in a calling that spans the entire will (2 Pet. 1:3–7). Thereby the author appropriated the fundamental ideas of the apostolic proclamation without alteration. He does not transform knowledge of God into an abstract term or speculation but conceives it of the true apprehension of the divine work which is realized by Christ's rule. This internalization of God is life. One's religious possession is not separated from the act of seeing that apprehends God; it is inseparably linked with the process by which God reveals himself to man. For this reason knowledge of God is set into a forceful causal relationship with the attitude of the will (2 Pet. 1:8–9). One's ethical capacities enable perception of God, and the epistle arranges them in a sequence by which it achieves a certain overview over moral tasks. The process that is considered to undergird everything else is faith. It establishes virtue, because it moves man to use and to form his strength. Virtue leads to knowledge, not because knowledge is considered to be a preeminent human faculty but because it pertains to the divine will and thus is awarded only to the one who does away with reprehensible passions. Knowledge provides man with clarity and firmness of ethical judgment, by which he is able to control his sensual desires, and control over these also provides the power to steadfastness, which bears and overcomes external pressures. Now, if he does not shrink away from any opposition man can be godly and offer worship and service to God. Because he is godly, he now is also able to render love to his brethren, by which he lives with and for them free from selfish desires, and with his ability to brotherly love he also attains that love which serves everyone.

But internal growth to a good and strong will does not arise merely through a natural process but requires persistent, perceptive attentiveness and resolute devotion. The prerequisite for it is that the struggle with reprehensible impulses and circumstances arising from one's pre-Christian life continues to be fought. Cleansing from formerly committed sins continues to be believers' abiding obligation.

These aims completely separate genuine Christendom from the gnostic movement, whose reprehensible nature is attested by the writer through the incorporation of Jude's epistle. Jude, too, urges congregations to decisively reject the notion that all religious processes cropping up in their circles are pure and Christian. False prophecy operates within them as well, and internal discipline is the indispensable means for the community's preservation.

### 3. Christendom's Hope

The way in which the author speaks about hope reveals the influence of Greek ideas on his church; for he names the unchangeableness of nature, which had remained the same as long as mankind has existed, as the argument that gave rise to mockery of Christian hope (2 Pet. 3:4). The idea should probably be attributed to gnostic thought, which used it to substantiate the rejection of Christian hope; but the epistle presupposes that it had also entered the community and that it had the possible effect of crippling its hope. In the remainder of the New Testament writings, the alteration of nature through God's omnipotent will is always considered to be axiomatic, without devoting any major reflection to this fact. Here, on the other hand, the expectation of a renewal of the world is considered to be a figment of imagination in view of the stability of nature. This consideration is supported by the fact that the time that had transpired since the promise had first been made far transcends the expectations given rise to by the original promise. The fact that an evaluation of nature stirs here that eludes the control of the concept of God injects a new and powerful idea into Christian thought. The means available for the epistle to refute such an idea likewise demonstrates the novelty of this idea, because it knows neither a word of Jesus nor a teaching of the apostles which denounced these opponents but appeals to an idea that belongs to synagogual tradition (2 Pet. 3:5–7). The synagogue juxtaposed the flood of water by which the first world perished and the flood of fire which makes an end to the present world. The comparison of the end with the start of the flood, of course, goes back already to Jesus' word (Matt. 24:37–39); but in his case it serves the ethical purpose of guarding against careless presumption. Here it is used to suggest the possibility, even certainty, of a new catastrophe; just as the first world perished in water, the present world will come to an end through fire. Thus the concept of a burning of the world moves from synagogual apocalypticism into the conceptions of Christendom. But at the same time the notion is retained, according to the promises of Scripture and of Jesus, that the world's demise merely furnishes the means for the establishment of the new heaven and the new earth (2 Pet. 3:13). The doubt that arises from the uncertain fulfillment of the promise is dealt with by the epistle by pointing to the greatness of the divine perspective, for which human measurements of time are immaterial. This again draws on an idea from synagogual tradition (2 Pet. 3:8).

More assured and more original is the epistle in the ethical sphere, where ideas are used for the purpose of making the continued existence of the present condition fruitful for the establishment of will. The greatness of the end expected by Christendom renders the time still given to it precious and excludes that impatience which demands the end right now. It must view the extension of time not as a delay or hardship in their salvation but as an aid that provides it salvation, because it may use the available time to prepare for the end of all things (2 Pet. 3:9–15).

Mention is made solely of the community's completion, not of what Christ's return brings for mankind, even though reference is made to the dissolution of elements. In this respect the epistle does not preserve the initial form of hope. No reference is made to the community's work among the nations in the portrayal of the task arising from its Christian convictions, and the suffering resulting from the struggle with the nations does not affect the exhortation. The events under Nero become visible only because allusion is made to Peter's execution. Christendom appears to live in a quiet period, is occupied with itself, and sees its most important task in the congregations' defense against gnostic attacks. This also colors its hope. It has not yet vanished, nor has it become a mere theory. Rather, it still represents sincere longing which determines one's conduct. But the process that transforms it into the guarantee of eternal blessing for individuals and transforms it into a theory to the extent that it still speaks of the end of the world is already in full swing.

# The Knowledge Possessed by the Early Church

## A. The God of Christendom

### 1. The Creator of the World

All the recipients of apostolic instruction viewed nature and history in light of its Creator and Ruler. The Greeks were immediately directed to do this as they were told the message about Jesus. When presenting Paul's labors among the Greeks, Luke indicated that the appropriation of Jesus' message was impossible if the Creator God was not acknowledged (Acts 17:22–29; 14:15–17), and his account is confirmed by Paul's epistles. To be sure, they do not directly deal with the Creator concept, but they continually affirm God as the one who effects all things. Thus the entire theology formulated in the epistles would disintegrate if the Creator concept were not present.

Regarding its concept of God, Christendom thus decidedly took the side of the Jews and rejected polytheism, which made God part of the world, as completely as Judaism did. The entire multitude of gods vanished, without particular theoretical or apologetic substantiation, because the picture of multiple idolatrous deities which signified separation from God and veneration of myth paled beside the Creator concept. For this reason the differences between the nations' rituals—those of Asian, Egyptian, and Greek religion; the worship of Zeus and Aphrodite; the veneration of stars and of gods resembling humans; both public cults and mystery religions—all these different modes and objects of worship were seen in the church as amounting to one thing. Differences existing between them did not weaken the validity of the uniform formulas "the nations" and "the world," because they all turned out to be equally meaningless beside the Creator God. The nations' religious condition rather proved their intrinsic similarity and substantiated the rejection of human common life implied by the Christian term "world."[1]

---

1. Already in the synagogue, the awareness of the fundamental difference between the Creator God and all other divine figures constituted the most pronounced factor in the formation of the a "world" concept.

Now magic was done away with (Acts 19:19). The early church used no particular protective devices against foreign gods or evil spirits, for example, amulets or the like. It was protected by being God's community and his possession. Therefore it also did not consider the removal of all Greek and Jewish, rabbinic and Mosaic purity regulations as a deterioration into a weakened or vulnerable condition; for its free dealings with nature were grounded in the knowledge of God and took Scripture's pronouncement seriously that the earth is the Lord's and all that is in it.

The community proved with equal sincerity that it worshiped the Creator when it came to miracles, which the apostles esteemed as an important component of their work and which appeared in conjunction with the Spirit concept also in the realm of their internal experiences. Here resistance to nature, had it attached to miracle, would necessarily have had entirely destructive effects and led to self-destruction. By the way in which the community knew itself to be under the control of the Spirit it also maintained that God is greater than man and nature. Therefore the Spirit is greater than reason and capable of revealing what no eye is able to see, and to teach what no mind can grasp apart from him. It also is greater than the human will and can give power that man does not have apart from the Spirit. But because at the same time regard for the Creator also sanctified the natural condition of life, miracle did not produce any dualism in the realm of the Spirit nor effect an attack on nature, and the pronouncements regarding Jesus and the Spirit remained in precise agreement with one another. The community rejoiced regarding both Jesus and the Spirit in all those things wherein it detected God's omniscient hand; but it was not ashamed of Jesus' humanity and did not view the Spirit's operation as obliterating human consciousness or will. It considered God's operations to be good gifts that heal and strengthen man rather than destroying him. Thus a drunken immersion into the stream of the Spirit was never praised or aspired to as Christian perfection. It was rather always the sanctification of one's personal life that was recognized as the gift granted to us by the Spirit. The certainty of God given to the church by the apostles encompassed the supernatural as well as the natural realm.

The carefreeness with which the disciples began their work in view of the God who was in charge and who cared for them did not disintegrate, although it now became a continual battle with the entire world. This is why the theme of suffering is given particular attention in the writings of the early church (Matthew; John [13:36]; Acts; James; Peter; Paul; Luke; Hebrews). But these discussions show clearly that the church lived in the confidence that God's grace was revealed in everything that happened. This was achieved by the community not by efforts at interpreting individual events teleologically[2] but by giving attention to the connection between its suffering and its communion with Jesus. Thus it no longer resisted its conviction that God's grace was revealed in all its experiences, because everything that takes place in communion with Jesus takes

---

2. To be sure, the prevalent understanding of Judaism that sufferings constitute discipline continues unabated, but it no longer led to the interpretation of individual destinies according to the principle of retribution, because the Christian understanding did not single out individual actions as reprehensible: the entire human condition was under judgment.

place for the sake of grace. Now suffering itself is taken to be proof of the community's participation in God, because it arises from the work of Christ, and is made fruitful by being viewed as an occasion for the exercise of faith.

The seriousness with which the church appreciated the natural order of our lives and thus cared for the external circumstances of its members attained pronounced expression through the fact that it produced in every community a particular office for the procurement of daily necessities which issued in the division of the community's office in two levels. Thereby the community stated effectively that its most important work lay in the administration of the word but that it also extended its communion to natural concerns, since the lower office was instituted in order to secure the provision of these services for all (Acts 6:1–4). Thus a vigorous movement arose in the initial stages in Jerusalem that sought to ensure the functioning of the community by the surrender of individual property (Acts 2:44–45; 4:32–5:4).[3] It was, however, limited by the strong sovereignty of the divine grace over all natural goods, with which the principle of freedom was inseparably linked. This principle had validity also for the community's greatest concerns, that is, the administration of the word and of prayer, and thus regulated also the use of property, not permitting any compulsory incorporation of personal property into the possession of the community. It did not allow any unnatural devaluation of economic values within itself, nor could make it its first priority to secure favorable external circumstances for its members. For the requirement for believers to be able to deny themselves pertained not merely to the rich but also to slaves. And Jesus' word remained in force that the poor were given, not property, but God's good news. When the gnostic movement incorporated the liberation of slaves and the emancipation of women among its aims, the apostles opposed these efforts (Peter, 1 Corinthians, Ephesians, Colossians, 1 Timothy, Titus).

The protection of marriage was an even graver matter in the internal life of the congregations than the preservation of personal property. When the gnostic movement attempted to challenge the principle of chastity and viewed marriage as confinement which it sought to break, the community rejected it and ensured that Christian fellowship had a strengthening rather than destructive effect on the family. The emphatic manner in which Paul makes wives subject to their own husbands is aimed at the protection of the family in view of the supremacy of the communion called for by the church that is conceivably able to replace and thus dissolve it (1 Cor. 14:35; Eph. 5:22; Col. 3:18; Titus 2:5). Because the family is considered to be God's work, it is also able to serve as a means of divine grace. Therefore the calling granted to the man also includes his household, because it is not directed toward an abstract human being but places that man in his concrete circumstances, that is, as husband and father, in God's grace (Acts 16:31). The personal, free manner of Christian devotion in repentance and faith is thereby not violated, and Jesus' saying legitimizing the foregoing of family and the rupture of all natural relationships remains intact. The

---

3. The obligation of all the Greek congregations to ensure the well-being of the Jerusalem church (Gal. 2:10; 2 Cor. 8 and 9) is due to this same consideration.

husband's will cannot convert the wife, the father's commandment cannot make Christians out of his children. Only God's grace working inside a person can make these natural relationships fruitful for the religious aim of man. But Christendom acted in the confidence that the one who brought about natural communion would also fill it with his grace. Thus there arose from the establishment of the community no "women's" or "children's" issue; Jesus' pronouncement was carried out, according to which women and children were both granted a share in the community, just as was the man.[4]

Because the community's religious possession separated it from the Gentiles no less profoundly than from the Jews, the question regarding its relationship to the Roman state arose as soon as there were Gentile congregations. In Palestine, the incorporation of Christendom into the Roman state was still facilitated through the fact that it was a part of Judaism; this is also the argument made by Paul before the Palestinian authorities. These arguments maintained the right of Christendom within Judaism, whereby it was guaranteed the protection of the state. But this train of thought was no longer sufficient in the case of Gentile Christendom, because Judaism passionately denied any connection with it as entirely foreign to it, denying it not merely participation in its privileges but using magistrates to its destruction as much as possible. Because Gentile Christendom thus existed as an independent entity, it must arrive at a new definition of its relationship with the civic and federal regulations and authorities. That this would be a severe confrontation was immediately clear for the leading men. When Jesus described the work of his messengers upon Israel in terms of martyrdom, this perspective quickly extended to Israel being replaced with the world. The connection between idolatrous worship and the state and in particular with the emperor permitted no delusion regarding the seriousness of the situation. We must not imagine that the appraisal of the situation presupposed by John's prophecy constituted only an isolated or even late phenomenon. But the community's consciousness of God prevented its relationship with the state from turning into enmity that sought to destroy it. The nations are also governed by God and are not merely under the power of Satan, and the law governing their lives stands in close connection with God's good will (Rom. 13:1–7; 1 Pet. 2:13–14, 17). Thus a similar evaluation of the state was reached as was applied to marriage; an effort was made to distinguish between what the state does according to divine law in the fulfillment of its calling and where it moves away from its calling, using its power to protect evil and becoming an instrument of Satan's power rather than acting in the service of God. This is why mission on Greek soil took the same apolitical stance as in Jerusalem; as it did not join forces with revolutionary efforts despite its absolute rejection of Judaism, it was here not intermingled with political motives, and just as custom was preserved there when it did not force one into conflict with God's will, Christendom was also here provided with the rule that it should enter into effective com-

---

4. Therefore baptism could become the baptism of entire families from the beginning; to what extent this also involved the baptism of infants eludes observation. All arguments pro and con are but conjecture.

munion with its neighbors, the city, and the state, as long they called it not to an evil but a good work (Titus 3:1; 1 Pet. 2:15–16).

## 2. The Christ Who Reigns in God's Manner

The aim of the apostolic message, that is, the apprehension of God in Jesus, vigorously determined the entire life of the new community. Allegiance to Jesus was everywhere religion, access to God. This becomes clear in view of the community's prayer. For its hallmark was that it called upon the name of Jesus (1 Cor. 1:2; 2 Tim. 2:22; Rom. 10:13; Acts 9:21; 22:16; 7:59). Faith directed toward him finds its closest, most simple result in moving man to request his grace and help. The thought that Jesus could be called upon without calling also upon God did not arise in the early church. It directed its adoration, its thanksgiving, and its petition to God.

Historians who do not find sufficient grounds for the disciples' conviction in Jesus' history conjecture that the community's religious relationship with Jesus came into being only through the impulse of foreign ideas that blended with the memory of Jesus, such as under the influence of Oriental speculations regarding a divine primal man; or Persian, Babylonian, or Indian gods or heroes that were conceived as saviors; or, in order to remain near the series of concepts in closest proximity to the New Testament phenomena, emperor worship, since after all the emperor received divine veneration as "Lord."

This theory is at the outset refuted by the fact that the received memory of Jesus was not even reconfigured where new convictions demonstrably developed in Christendom. Paul's new verdicts regarding Jesus' work did not produce a single piece of information regarding him that did not already exist independently of his doctrine of justification.[5] It is no different with the epistle of Hebrews, which bound together a new, significant pronouncement with Jesus' history by describing him as priest for humanity. But the data regarding the historical course of his life are not affected by this. They are the same in Hebrews as everywhere in apostolic proclamation. The Johannine statement regarding Jesus' communion with the Father is based on the same perspective on his earthly ministry that the proclamation of Jesus used elsewhere.[6]

This theory considers the gnostic movement to be the way by which the myth reached Jesus' disciples and gained power over them. It is, however, refuted by the fact that the contrast between gnostic ideas and Jesus' aim is clearly portrayed in the New Testament. All accommodations of Christ to myth lead inevitably to a contradiction against the fundamental tenet of the Christian confession that the man Jesus stood in communion with God. That a God appearing in human form is something other than the man Jesus who is the Son of God—this was recognized especially at the community's earliest stage with particular clarity, because the monotheism inherent in Judaism resisted the proliferation of a plethora of gods. Moreover, the memory of the genuineness and humanity of Jesus, who was closed to all gnostic theories, rejected such notions.

5. See pp. 190–91.
6. This was demonstrated in *The History of the Christ.*

That the Gospels derive their basic ideas from gnostic tradition while at the same time expressing Jesus' opposition toward everything pertaining to it in all its vehemence is a historical impossibility.

The parallelism existing between gnostic speculations and Christian preaching became immediately apparent once it went beyond Jerusalem.[7] First and foremost, gnostic religions were rejected by the disciples especially because the will grounded in them was reprehensible according to the norms of Jesus; but the portrait of Christ available in Christian documents shows that the contrast between one's own convictions and gnostic conceptions was also clearly felt. gnostic religions destroy consciousness of God, because according to their theory a spiritual being separate from God, equal or subordinate to him, appears as man or in man, thus forfeiting God's uniqueness. At the same time man's personal life is destroyed, because God here does not turn into a man, but, if a human being is left at all, he is invaded by a transcendent being which thus creates in him a dual self. In contrast to all such speculations, the disciples' Son of God completely retains the natural manner of human life and is united as a human being not with an inferior god or a divine force—such does not exist for the apostles—but with the Father. There are no parallels with New Testament Christology, however many divinized human beings or anthropomorphic gods are known to the history of religions. Its originality furnishes historical proof that the roots from which it developed are not found outside of the community; the disciples' claim rather reveals the true course of events in that it points to Jesus' dealings with God as what grounds all its statements regarding the divine sonship. This is not rendered doubtful by the fact that the terms by which they explain Jesus' share in God, that is, Spirit of God, image of God, Word of God, radiance and glory of God, imprint of God, were also used by Jewish teaching to describe the divine activity. That the then-present shape of understanding of God helps shape the statements regarding Jesus' divine sonship is a process that is so simple that it does not require any further explanation.

The independence of New Testament teaching over against mythological developments is confirmed by the fact that the statements regarding the eternality of the Son mention nothing but his participation in creation, while any speculative or mythological portrayal of the eternal Christ's communion with the eternal God is absent. But Christendom did not derive the Creator concept from the Roman emperor or from Krishna or Mithras. It is the exclusive domain of Israel's concept of God, and the New Testament speaks of the eternality of the Son only in this particularly Jewish form.

In the interpretation of Jesus' work the contrast emerged forcefully that separated apostolic from Greek thought. While the Greeks turned their thinking away from reality toward the realm of possibility, the thought of the apostles remains tied to historical events and is directed toward the obligation arising from these events. Therefore the church did not receive from them any "Christology" concerning itself with some Person of Jesus arrived at through quiet mental contemplation. Rather, the entire instruction regarding Jesus was focused on his

---

7. Luke expressly emphasizes this; see p. 337.

work, by which he establishes the community and by which he will bring it to completion. Moreover, the course of apostolic teaching reveals that the community concurred in its verdict regarding Jesus' relationship with the Father. Where anyone did not agree with this, he was not permitted entrance into the church. Doubt regarding Christ and polemic against him were of course widespread even then; but they are found with the community's opponents, not within the community itself. Thus christological formulations that created turmoil in the community can be found only late in the epistles. The epistle to the Romans does not indicate that people in the church differed in their views of Jesus' share in God. In refuting those opponents who might disturb the Philippians, only the soteriological concept surfaces (Phil. 3).[8] In instances where gnostic aspirations championed their own christological tenets, fellowship was immediately denied them.[9] When assessing these facts, of course, we must remember that Christian communion was grounded not in a didactic formula but in faith in Jesus, in that everyone subordinated himself to Jesus with a resolute will, not by describing Jesus' nature with an unobjectionable formula. Nevertheless, the discussion of christological questions would not have been absent if at this point there had been weighty disagreement among teachers, because this has considerable ramifications for the faith. The visible unity of the community's faith presupposes that its statements regarding Jesus were uniform, and this is confirmed by the portrayals of Christ available to us.

Those called to Jesus praised with overflowing gratitude the perfection of divine grace operating in him. But its devotion was pervaded just as powerfully by the assurance that God's grace is completely one with his righteousness. Thus there existed within Christendom no worship other than the one which considered ethical norms sacred and carried them out. Christ's office thus also entails the execution of judgment; the sanctity given to the community by the Spirit also includes victory over evil; faith also involves the sin-judging message of repentance; and love unifying the community also requires discipline. When gnostic Christians broke ethical norms in the name of grace and of the Spirit, the community broke fellowship with them.

The statement that God's perfect gift was granted by Christ to faith did not merely lead the community beyond the level that disciples enjoyed prior to the end of Jesus' ministry; it rather placed them continually into an ongoing movement. The first thing Christendom cultivated were reminiscences and hopes the disciples had received from Jesus. It subordinated itself to what he had said and done and waited for his return. Even so, its present was not empty; for Christ and the Spirit are with it. The community's task in the early stage of Christendom was, however, that it preserve what it had received and that it prepare itself for the future.[10] But then the conviction grew in connection with the burgeoning work that it already has the perfect gift in the Christ of God.[11] The terms

8. Phil. 2:5–11 also speaks out against the sectarian division, spiritual arrogance, etc., within the community; but there is no indication that Jesus' communion with God was disputed.
9. Cf. Colossians, the Pastorals, the epistle of Jude, and the Johannine epistles.
10. This is the stress found in Matthew and James.
11. This can be perceived in John, Paul, and Hebrews.

describing present participation in Christ took on increased vividness and power. Eschatology did not become dispensable; to the contrary, precisely the growth of the work performed by the church lent additional power to the realization that the church would never be able to reveal God's rule to mankind. Jesus' goal would be realized solely by his own return.[12] But the community also grew continually in its awareness of what God had already granted to it. Not merely its work and its suffering were on the increase; God's gift grew as well. The community understands how much it possesses already now in Christ.

This furnishes the reason why the apostolic word came alongside the word of Christ and also explains why Christ's absolute authority over the apostles did not issue in a condition in which the entire proclamation consisted solely in the preservation and repetition of Jesus' words. All saw that the community had become something other than Jesus' circle of disciples, so that the question of how God acts upon it and what it must do for him cannot be answered merely by sayings of Jesus. This did not lead to estrangement from Jesus' word, so that it was assigned to the past and judged to be merely a beginning which now had been left behind. Thereby the community would have compromised the Christ concept and foregone Jesus' rule. The fact is evident that the community saw in Jesus' word the complete revelation of divine truth and grace by which Jesus fulfilled his calling and made it known to humanity. But this does not yet exhaust its task; rather, it must also realize what the implications of its communion with the exalted Lord are.[13]

Therefore the new canon in Christendom consists of both Gospels and apostolic writings. The verdict of the early era is expressed in this. A retrospective reviving of apostolic documents was inconceivable. Only that was preserved which had always been valid, while the things that were no longer read during the gatherings of Christendom and no longer used to regulate its message or actions quickly sank into oblivion.[14]

## 3. God's Work in the Spirit

By including the statement that God's Spirit was at work in believers as part of the disciples' message, believers were shown a high aim. If it was contradicted by the actual condition of the congregations, this could result in severe tremors. These surface again and again in the later church and profoundly determine its history. In the New Testament, these doubts do not appear. Even when the congregations wavered, so that their entire Christian identity became questionable, as happened in Galatia, Paul did not doubt that they had life in the Spirit. The Corinthians' conduct toward him gave him reason for concern, but not the

---

12. For this reason the phrases describing the greatness of divine grace go hand in hand with negative assessments regarding the church's condition (Matthew, Pastorals, Revelation, Acts).

13. Many historians could not conceive of any other movement in Christendom than one that constitutes falling away from Jesus.

14. We would not have a collection of Pauline epistles if these had not been letters that determined the community's conduct from the time they were written. The Book of Acts was preserved together with Luke's Gospel, the Johannine epistles together with the Gospel.

question of whether God's Spirit indwelled them. He did not know the lives of Roman Christians from his own observation; but it was clear to him also regarding them that they were led by God's Spirit (Gal. 3:2; 5:16; 1 Cor. 3:16; 6:19; Rom. 8:15). After all, doubt regarding the Spirit would amount to doubt regarding Christ and would cast doubt on the Spirit's presence in the congregations. It would also render questionable whether faith in Christ provided believers with union with Christ. As certainly as they were Christ's possession, they were also led by the Spirit.

For the one who derives the community's religiosity from pre-Christian religious conditions, the supposition takes on compelling strength that what happened in the congregations subsequent to Pentecost bore an affinity with mantic features in pre-Christian religions and should therefore be called "enthusiasm." This theory maintains that the community saw the divine in conditions that suppressed the natural course of one's inner life, that is, in irrational and will-less tendencies, which either nearly or completely suspended normal rational consciousness. The unusual and mysterious nature of these events, it is alleged, gave rise to strong religious gratification; they intensified the certainty of God, because the person thus considered himself to have been transferred into God's possession and to be taken hold of and moved by God. The basis of this theory are those kinds of events that disappear again after the first generation, particularly "tongues-speaking," and whatever was counted among the "powers." Thus processes were attributed to the divine Spirit that had suspended the reasonable exercise of one's intellect or will. The pathological nature of these processes, it is argued, did not prevent the emergence of a wave of strong, immediate sensations inundating one's consciousness, so that they became a source of power and enriched the conscious course of one's life.

However, there arose in the community strong elements opposing a conception of the Spirit in terms of enthusiasm. For one thing, it was opposed by Jesus' word. For love for God, of which he spoke, makes man with his will a doer of the divine will. For Jesus, the locus of religion is the realm of our lives which is comprised of our knowledge and which we freely control. If instead emotion-laden conditions are thought to produce or demonstrate union with God on account of their incomprehensibility, the community then obeys a desire that was rejected by Jesus. But we know Jesus' aims exclusively through the community, solely because it preserved Jesus' word and acted accordingly. It did not part with his word. The disciples considered Jesus to be the bearer of the Spirit par excellence. They looked first and foremost at him in order to see how God's Spirit manifests itself and what he gives to men.

The preservation of Jesus' word coheres with the fact that the apostles' statements regarding the Spirit nowhere indulge in enthusiastic ideas. Paul begins his discussion of the pneumatic events taking place in Corinth by pointing to the contrast between pagan piety and possession of the Spirit. He sees it not merely in the fact that pagan worship is rendered to material images, while God speaks in the person through the Spirit, but also in the fact that it consists in being moved in a way that defies all human explanation of its reason or purpose (1 Cor. 12:2). He also considered mantic processes to stand in express opposition to the Spirit, as a mark of separation from the Spirit, not a parallel to him.[15] This verdict did not arise by coincidence; it rather grows from fundamental Christian convictions. Enthusiastic piety limited the concept of God to the notion of power. The vigor of the impulse is supposed to attest by itself to its divine origin, and the peculiarity of the effect is thought to show its sanctity. No demands are made on the content of experience, only that man behave passively and feel himself given over to a superior power. But the assurance of God had a different content in Christendom. It is certain that it viewed God as the giver of light and love and that it did not separate its knowing and willing from him but rather referred his grace to its personal condition of life rather than merely to nature. Therefore the Spirit whom the apostles desire from God and whom they know to have been given is always the one who illumines and sanctifies, the giver of truth and love, the root of that kind of thinking that obtains the knowledge of God, and of that kind of will that does the will of God. The New Testament does not contain a single statement regarding the Spirit that evidences a different orientation. But we cannot construe an alleged practice of the community that denies the doctrinal norm present in it.

To be sure, it is clear that the sign was highly esteemed even in the realm of emotional experience on account of its arresting, astonishing power. When Paul, for example, recalls his pneumatic experiences, he realizes how strong the internal power was that moved him, so that he did not know whether he was still in the body or outside of the body. He was unaware how distant or holy the place was to which he was translated, into the third heaven, into paradise, and how mysterious the words were that he heard, inexpressible words (2 Cor. 12:2–4). But already the tender, reserved manner in which he speaks of these things reveals that he did not consider the value and purpose of these events to lie in their peculiar nature but that he rather focused on the fact that he thus received a revelation of Christ that attests itself to him as such through its content. For Paul, the manifestation of the Spirit does not consist in just any miraculous transposition from one place to another but into the exaltation to heaven and into paradise, the places where God's glory and grace are manifested. And the heart of the experience is the fact that he saw Jesus there.

All enthusiastic motifs express the unreconciled consciousness of man which knows itself to be in dispute with God and thus describes his relationship with God in dualistic terms. What is natural is rejected as incapable of receiving God's revelation and of being used in his service; God's work begins, it is alleged, only where nature ends, and man must vanish in order for God to be revealed. If the disciples had begun such a dispute with the natural condition of human life in the name of religion, this would have had major consequences. If at a certain point self-emptying is held up as religious aim, and a struggle against one's

15. Paul's practice of identifying the word that curses Jesus as the mark of the Spirit's absence likewise does not imply the use of mantic criteria, as if Paul sought to separate those who do not have the Spirit from those who have him. For Paul, the criterion is rather one's conscious attitude toward Jesus, whether Jesus is loved and believed or hated and rejected. Paul's pronouncement maintains that the Spirit is obtained solely through subjection to Christ whose work consists in commending Christ to man's faith.

own existence is entered for God's sake, this has significant ramifications. But apostolic teaching remains entirely free from dualism and considers man's dispute with God to be superseded by the certitude of his reconciliation with him.

Any piety that seriously opens itself to enthusiasm gives up the personal nature of God and of human consciousness. The diviner yields himself to the deity, which, because one can lose oneself in it, is not conceived of as a person, not as conscious of itself and as controlling itself. But the apostles never spoke of a divine "something" but of the personal God, in whom one does not lose oneself but whose grace consists in the fact that he places man as a person in his love and completes him through it. If this had not been preserved in the statements regarding the Spirit, they also would have destroyed Christology and would have transmuted the Son of God into the vessel of a divine power. But it is historically certain that the apostles did not formulate their thought contrary to the gospel in this decisive, central issue, but that they rather lived in and by the gospel.

Enthusiasm thus never has its goal and success in the establishment of faith. Before the mantic condition is achieved, it rather produces a relaxed state, the passive anticipation of a divine operation, and it might perhaps attain to a lofty sense of union with the deity when such divine operation has taken place. Both passive waiting for God and man's being seized by God while being emptied of self stand in direct contradiction with New Testament faith. But it is a historical fact that the apostles' religion consisted in trust in God in Christ.

Enthusiastic piety necessarily requires information that describes the inner processes it calls spiritual according to their nature and the patterns they follow. The difficulty of portraying psychological processes and of verbalizing sensory experiences cannot prevent attempts at describing this exceedingly lofty experience to all. The New Testament contains not a single description of the psychological characteristics of a pneumatic event. When the Spirit is the subject of discussion, reference is never made to particular spiritual processes that differ from the rest of one's inner life through peculiar characteristics; rather, it is expressed that man is turned toward God through the Spirit. What we find is not the exercise of a new way of thinking; rather, God is approached with assurance and confidence. What is experienced is not a new form of willing; rather, a love is received that lives for God. If the process is experienced in the awareness that it is received rather than being produced by one's own self and one's own will, this strengthens the conviction that the Spirit here manifests himself. But this does not mean that merely the form of the event becomes what is esteemed and enjoyed as divine gift; otherwise, it would be described. The New Testament words, however, focus solely on the content and aim of these internal movements. Because they take place according to God's will and have their aim in him, they are also accompanied by the verdict that they are not the product of one's own will power but God's gift. In view of the power with which the concept of God manifests itself at this point, this verdict takes on great clarity.

Enthusiasm of necessity results in methods prescribing how the transposition into an enthusiastic state can be achieved. While it is conceived purely in passive terms, as descending upon man, there must nonetheless be means through which this condition can be brought about. But the New Testament contains nothing on methods to produce a pneumatic condition. A spiritual condition into which someone would transpose himself remains for the community a self-contradiction and an ethical impossibility. This is not obscured but rather confirmed through the exhortation to "strive for the gifts of the Spirit" and through the connection in which the special manifestations of the Spirit stand with prayer and thus also with fasting (1 Cor. 14:1; Acts 13:2; 10:9–10). For because the Spirit's ministry relates to man's personal functions, the believer's conduct toward him falls under ethical norms. His effects are thus not merely experiences but acts that stand in a causal relationship with the believer's desire and prayer. Therefore there can be no doubt that the manifestations of the Spirit are "gifts of grace."

The prayer called "tongues-speaking" that attracted attention through its form can be used as evidence for enthusiasm only when the account of Paul, who himself practiced prayer in this form and through whom it thus entered into his congregations, is removed. He expressly affirmed its inner value, not on account of the processes that rendered it spectacular, not because it remained unintelligible and did not occupy the intellect—this is rather what Paul considered to be the limitation of this kind of prayer—but because of the internal turning to God that accompanied it. Paul knew nothing of a partial or complete removal of a person's will or consciousness during these processes; he fully expected those who prayed in this way to control themselves and to remain quiet when this seemed called for in light of the situation of the congregation. He amply exercised this form of prayer without the Corinthians having learned anything about it (1 Cor. 14:14–19, 27–33).

That he was not alone in this assessment but that he concurred with the entire community is attested by the community's language on this subject. If we detected in it the tendency to esteem the unintelligible in and of itself as spiritual, this kind of "Spirit" would inevitably have gained influence on its terminology. In that case, we would find mysterious words, technical formulas, ecclesiastical language unintelligible for the uninitiated, and lofty rhetoric. None of this took place. Terminology developed naturally in close association with the words and ideas found in Judaism and Hellenism. For the word current in the community sought to establish faith and obedience and thus wanted to be understood. But word and Spirit cannot be separated. As the word is conceived, so also is the Spirit. Every word of the apostles shows that they esteemed the Spirit as the giver of the true knowledge and of the good will.

## B. The Task to Be Accomplished by the Church

### 1. The Church's Leadership

#### a) Jesus' Messengers

The church's unity becomes visible and effective in that the apostles possess authority that is obeyed by all believers. Even Luke described Peter's work for the church with the notion that Peter established the church that exists in all places, not merely the one in Jerusalem, in the exercise of his apostolic office.

The accounts of the Gospels, including John, regarding Peter and the Twelve proceed from the same basis. The Pauline epistles likewise show this to be the firm conviction of all congregations. Even the way in which Peter and the other apostles ordered their personal affairs determined for all teachers, including those in Corinth, what was to be accorded them (Acts 1–12; 1 Cor. 9:5; cf. Gal. 2:14, 5). All segments of Christendom sought guidance for their thoughts and actions from Jesus' messengers.

Nevertheless, their work proceeded exclusively through the means of personal contact and never took on forms that transcended it. This set boundaries for the apostles' realms of ministry. They were apostles for those to whom they gave the word: Peter for Judaism, Paul for the nations (1 Cor. 9:2; Gal. 2:7).[16] This corresponded with the fact that the written instruction of the congregations took place not through the book but through the epistle which is directed to certain portions of Christendom. John did not immediately send his vision to the entire church but to the churches of Asia, to the part of the church with which he sustained a personal relationship. Not even the Christians in Rome, who were particularly affected by the content of the prophecy and whose severe destiny is assuredly in the apostle's mind, is included among the original recipients.

The apostles' right to govern the church was never derived from their individual giftedness or greatness but grounded solely in their relationship with Jesus, which continued in that he now ruled them through his Spirit. The early church did not engage in a contemplation of the apostles that attributed their religious power to their greatness or that venerated them as heroes of action or of suffering or of knowledge. Several of the Twelve were never the subject of any tradition, because the church's desire was not directed toward being instructed regarding the work and success of every apostle, as if his calling was rendered uncertain if he did not distinguish himself through an outstanding achievement. And yet the Gospel record maintains, and parallel to it Luke's narrative regarding the replacement of the twelfth apostle, that the Twelve retained a position superior to the other disciples and that their office constituted the foundation for the entire church. They carried out their work, however, by being the ones through whom the church possessed Jesus' word and was instructed in obedience to his commandment. As far as the congregations were told about their ministry, they were described solely as God's instruments by which God revealed the Christ. It is significant that the church did not even receive an account regarding either Peter's or Paul's martyrdom. The fact that the apostolic office remained free from any glorification of the apostles reveals how genuine the church's obedience was that it rendered to Jesus' word.

This resulted in the fact that the community's faith was directed solely toward Jesus rather than being attached to an apostle. Apostles were viewed as those who spoke and acted in Christ's name, so that faith in Christ is shown when their word is accepted and their commandment obeyed. This is why there never arose a conflict between the apostles' authority and the church's freedom; the former rather served to establish and protect the latter, because the apostles

---

16. This motif controls the structure of the Book of Acts.

subjected the congregations to Christ by their own faith. Therefore there never existed an apostolic dictatorship. While we know Paul also in this regard the best—the care with which he strove for his congregations' agreement in his committed teaching ministry; the patience with which he bore even malicious opposition for a long period of time, though he never gave up the complete consciousness of the authority of the apostolic office of Jesus' messenger—the same observations can be made regarding the work of the other apostles. The decision regarding the issue of the Gentile mission was not merely a decision of the apostles: a gathering of the brethren was imperative. James's rejoicing in Paul's presence and his successes among the Greeks did not already resolve the matter. For the offense taken by the remaining brethren was not yet removed merely because James had been pacified. They formed their own judgment; therefore "it is necessary for the assembly to come together." John complained of malicious opposition, despite his considerable reputation in Asia, which was mounted by the one who found satisfaction in being "first" in the congregations and whom John could not humble even by a letter (Acts 15:5, 22; 21:22; 3 John 9). The apostles' authority was always substantiated intrinsically and never turned into compulsion in the manner of the government exercised by the state.

The task of honoring the apostles' authority as grounded in God with voluntary obedience was one of greatest ethical profundity, and it is not surprising that we also encounter tensions. It can be observed that the apostles' authority burdened the congregations. Paul feared in Antioch that a misstep on the part of Peter might further confuse the congregation. By speaking of those "of repute" or of those "who are superapostles," Paul indicated that a false veneration of apostles could be observed in the congregations that became a snare for them (Gal. 2:14, 6; 2 Cor. 11:5, 11). He expressly reminds the community that the apostles, too, are "flesh and blood." Where a clear divine commandment exists, it would constitute a breach of obedience, if even then an apostle's agreement would still be solicited. This is how Paul acted subsequent to his conversion, and he tells this to the community in order that it might understand in the case of a particularly significant and clear instance how it must use its freedom in all of its relationships, and how it is protected from any pressure that the prestige of the apostolic office might exert upon it (Gal. 1:16–17). An appropriate relationship could be gained only by serious ethical effort and was obtained only when the congregations' faith was fully developed. It requires no explanation that this led to tensions, both as a result of insubordinate obstinacy and of lackluster readiness to submit.

This conception of the apostolic office excluded the possibility that a sanctity was attributed to the apostles that covered up their humanity. The Gospels focus not only on their faith but also on their unbelief with regard to Jesus' cross and resurrection, and it is of course no coincidence that the unbelief is shown by the example of the foremost apostle, Peter. The community had before it always the memory of a Peter who had denied the Lord. Conduct such as that of Peter and Barnabas in Antioch is rejected as hypocrisy, because the application of ethical norms must not be foregone merely on account of veneration for the name of an apostle. Alongside the term "apostle" there also develops the term "false apostle." The community thus assumed the right and the obligation to distinguish between legitimate and illegitimate offices and did not exercise blind submissiveness on account of the mere title. Paul did not spare the "false apostles" in Corinth and thus subjected himself to the same open and serious scrutiny. In Ephesus, false apostles were rejected also at a later point (Gal. 2:11–13; 2 Cor. 11:13; Rev. 2:2). The dealings between Paul's co-workers and Paul do not evidence a trace of veneration of saints. The admiration and reverence with which Luke viewed Paul did not issue in the effort to isolate him from the rest of the church and to elevate him above all others, including Peter. The thought with which Paul himself ordered his relationship with Peter, that is, that it was Christ who had granted Peter and him their position and their success, controlled the whole of Christendom, and the apostles' holiness developed in the same way as that of the entire community, namely in that God calls sinful people to himself, unites them with himself in his Spirit, and places them in his service. In this the disciples prove themselves to be obedient to the word of Jesus, who judged his disciples' sin the same way as he did that of the people.

The fact that the apostles' work had its aim in the establishment of faith resulted in a situation where they could not create any method or technique for the performance of their vocation, either for mission work or for the leadership of the established communities. Also in this regard, Jesus' own conduct remained the abiding norm for the disciples.[17] Luke portrayed graphically the significance a given opportunity had for the apostles' work. They speak when they are given the opportunity. The obligation to confess the Lord at that time in open testimony is fully accepted and carried out at the risk of one's life. But the opportunity is not forced. That the apostles' will remains focused solely on the desire to recognize their Lord's sovereign providence, and to be completely obedience when it is manifested, amounts to a continuance of the calm waiting by which Jesus himself committed his own revelation and exaltation to God. As he could not bring about his rule by his own authority but received it from God, his messengers likewise knew themselves in the fulfillment of their commission completely dependent upon the things granted to them by God's rule.

It corresponds to the disciples' overall conduct that the apostolic name did not fossilize into a title which was reserved exclusively for the Twelve, but which was also used in a broader sense for all who were enabled by their contact with Jesus to collaboration in his proclamation (Acts 14:4, 14; Rom. 16:7; 1 Cor. 15:7). As late as during John's time there appeared in Ephesus apostles who were condemned, not simply because they used a title that was not due them, but because they did not in fact possess the commission that they claimed to have been given (Rev. 2:2). Thus it would not have been impossible in itself for the apostolic office to have continued beyond the death of the Twelve. However, their role as witnesses was such a major part of their office that a continuation of the apostolic office beyond their death was inconceivable. That the apostles could expand their circle by including others was completely out of the question. To congregations in which none of the old apostles spent time, there

17. Cf. *The History of the Christ*, 113.

cannot be given an apostle by retroactive commissioning. The final portion of the Johannine Gospel indicates that the idea was prevalent in the congregations that the Lord would not take the last apostle away from them before he would come. This hope is rejected; but this rejection is not linked with a positive command providing a replacement for the last apostle (John 21:21–23). Paul judged no differently regarding the apostolic office. The community for whose sake it has been instituted has now come into being. It lives, knows its Lord, and has received the apostolic word. Beyond this, everything is committed to the lordship of Christ, which will be manifested in the course of history.

### b) Pneumatics

Among the men in whom the Spirit revealed himself in a particular way, the prophets occupied first place.[18] They did not alter the gospel's aim to call, not merely to knowledge, but to action according to God's will. For prophecy provided particularly instructions that guided the actions of the community, while no mention is made of doctrinal knowledge that was proclaimed by a prophet. The Antiochian community heard from Agabus that years of famine would plunge the Christians of Jerusalem into misery; this directly affected them too, because they had to play a part in the preservation of Jerusalem's church. The same community heard from its prophets that it should send Barnabas and Paul to the Greek regions. Prophets told Paul what his resolve to go to Jerusalem would entail and identified Timothy for him as his co-worker. If a stranger enters the community, prophets show him what God's will for him is by revealing what he secretly harbors within himself. Prophets proclaimed it as the will of Christ that the nations be called; they also predicted the increase in the ascetic movement (Acts 11:27–28; 13:2; 20:23; 21:4, 11; 1 Cor. 14:24–25; Eph. 3:5; 1 Tim. 1:18; 4:14, 1). John's prophecy confirms the accounts of Paul and Luke, because it supports the community in its great work, its struggle with the Roman world.

Alongside ideas that dealt directly with the last things the convictions that transcended experience and that constituted the mystery believed in by Christendom were likewise strengthened by prophecy. The certainty with which the community clings to Christ's invisible presence and rule, and the close connection into which it brought human history with the spirit world, were confirmed by the prophet, who saw, albeit only in a vision, what the physical eye does not see: the open heaven and Christ in his glory and the spirits at their work. The prophet also occupied an important role in the interpretation of Old Testament prophecy, because it had undergone at the same time a confirmation and a thoroughgoing transformation through the outcome of Jesus' life. Now it required inner renewal through new prophecy that linked the Old Testament word with the knowledge of Christ and transferred it to the present.[19]

18. In Jerusalem, the prophets were, according to Luke's account, the leading men after the apostles, and Paul placed them above the other pneumatics. For Jerusalem, see Acts 11:27; 15:32; 21:10; outside of Jerusalem, 13:1; 20:23; 24:4, 9; in Paul, 1 Cor. 12:28; 14:1; Eph. 2:20; 3:5.

19. The prophets' exegetical achievement is underscored by the Book of Revelation.

But the pneumatic did not exercise his worship merely through the things he told the community; his possession of the Spirit also equipped him in particular ways for the priestly function which turned upward to God through the exercise of prayer. The Spirit asks for Christ's return and produces those final forms of prayer that reach even past the boundaries of our knowledge (Rev. 22:17; Rom. 8:26). Therefore the community also had grateful appreciation for that manifestation of the Spirit that it was given by those who prayed "with the new tongue." Because these acts of prayer praised God in a peculiar way that was perhaps likened to the adoration of the heavenly ones (1 Cor. 13:1), they possessed intrinsic value even apart from what the community learned through them.

The value pneumatics had for the community never consisted merely in particular services that they performed at certain occasions; at the same time, they provided ever new confirmation for the assurance that the Spirit of God had been given to the communities. This assigned to them a position that was similar to that of the apostles. They too were witnesses of Jesus, not of his earthly life, but of his exaltation to God in glory. Therefore experiences that initially moved only individuals, such as "tongues," also took on significance for the entire congregation. The fact that not the pneumatics but the apostles remained in charge of the congregation reveals, however, what can already be observed in the Easter account: that all experiences that revealed the exalted state of Christ did not distract Christendom from the fruitful outcome of his earthly life but rather increased understanding and appreciation for him. Congregational leadership stayed with those who had been eyewitnesses of his life. In this regard the form and substance of the New Testament canon mutually confirm each other; prophetic writings did not become canonical, only those which were at the same time apostolic.

### c) Teachers

Teachers occupied a position similar to that of prophets, because their ability to provide answers to the questions arising from the community's calling was likewise based on an illumination that was not accessible to every member of the community (Acts 13:1; 1 Cor. 12:28; Eph. 4:11; James 3:1). But the particular power of the teacher was more strongly conditioned by natural factors than in the case of the prophet. What he had to offer was based on his learning and depended on whom he had as a teacher, in whose community he previously lived in such a way that he took over from him his word as clear and confirmed knowledge. But because his service also required a peculiar gift and orientation of his spiritual life as prerequisites, a teacher could be chosen as little as a prophet; the community either did or did not have one. If the Lord gave a teacher to a congregation, he must serve the entire church with his gift according to the same principle by which each person fruitfully exercised whatever gift he had.

### d) Exegetes of Scripture

Part of the holy possession of the old community which the disciples preserved was most of all Scripture, which was entirely set apart as holy for them through Christ's commission and through the obedience Jesus had rendered to it. The conviction that they themselves were gifted with the Holy Spirit did not weaken their allegiance to Scripture. In the gnostic movement, of course, the idea can be found that confidence in the presence of the divine Spirit with the community actually required the removal of the canon, because the believer needs nothing but his own share in the Spirit (1 Cor. 4:6; 2 Tim. 3:15–17). But this train of thought remained foreign to the apostles, because they did not tie any selfish aspiration to the possession of the Spirit. They did not conceive of him in terms of enhancement of their own lives with the result that man was self-sufficient and did not require any instruction or help from others. The church led by the disciples was protected against this use in that they sincerely honored him as God's Spirit. But they know nothing of a communion with God that operated in a self-centered manner, nothing of a divine gift that rendered man self-sufficient. In this they perceived the abuse of divine grace by which it is forfeited. Because God's Spirit turns man to God, it also connects him with everything by which God reveals himself and does his work. Through the Spirit, man receives an ear for those who speak in the Spirit and obedience toward those whom God uses as his messengers. The early church thus had Scripture as its canon, not despite its possession of the Spirit, but because of it. In this regard, Scripture is no different than Christ or the church. The Spirit does not separate the one who has it from Christ but leads him to him, and it does not separate him from the brethren but unites him with them. So also, through the Spirit, the church's Scripture becomes intelligible and holy rather than unnecessary.

The disciples' confidence in Scripture was not shaken by the fact that Jewish objections against Jesus' regal status likewise appealed to Scripture. In their view, the opponent refers to individual details of Scripture rather than to the whole, renders his understanding and his obedience narrow and small, and falls short of what Scripture promises to and requires from him. The Law he obeys is not the perfect Law; rather, he only adheres to parts of it, namely, the small things satisfying his human nature. But this only provided Christendom with its actual calling, that it now believed and obeyed the fullness of the divine word as Scripture told it (Matt. 5:18; James 1:25; Rom. 3:31; 2 Tim. 3:16). Therefore the Gentile Christian congregations also received the canon immediately at their establishment, and a great deal of mental effort was expended on its understanding, which took place in their gatherings and through their teachers.

Jesus' own use of the Bible showed the disciples where their use of Scripture must remain one with the rabbinate and where it must remain separate from it. The Christian use of Scripture remained one with the Jewish in that it also adhered to the principle of inspiration; for the desire of Christendom was directed solely toward hearing God in Scripture, and Scripture granted this to it because its word has been produced by the divine Spirit. On the other hand, Jesus departed from the rabbinic use of Scripture by not using Scripture for the establishment of casuistry and thus not as a book of Law by which man's conduct receives external regulations. The disciples followed Jesus in this regard in complete obedience. For there is nowhere a use of Scripture in which rabbinic legislation is imitated, either in prayer or at the celebration of the sacrament or in the case of the love to be granted to the brother, and not even at the place where every historian would expect it most of all: in the manner in which Jesus is considered to be the example by the community. Nowhere is Scripture used to develop a heteronomous ethic, which cites Scripture in order that the notion of Scripture replace one's own knowledge or the commandment of Scripture one's own will. In this regard, all New Testament documents are distinct from the use of Scripture practiced by earlier theology by a complete change of perspective. Because Jesus effected faith in his disciples, their use of Scripture also become believing and thus free. They did not use it because they themselves did not know God but merely heard him through Scripture, or because they had no will of their own but merely received it through the commandment of Scripture. Rather, they used it in order to obtain through its teaching their own assurance of God and to render their own will obedient to God through its commandments.

This is also evident from the fact that textual issues were handled without overscrupulousness. No Hebrew schools were erected in the Greek congregations, on some assumption that it was Christian duty to read the holy text in the holy language. Rather, they were given the Greek text, in the conviction that they would be able to find out from it what they needed to know. Neither do the apostles coming from Palestine, such as Matthew, John, or Paul, evidence a commitment to the Greek text that prevented their deviating from it. Their use of Scripture was rather clearly influenced by the Hebrew text, yet in such a way that this was not accompanied by the concern that this would disturb the congregations' use of Scripture.

The same calmness is retained in the question regarding the delimitation of the canon. The epistles do not contain any statement in this direction. The centerpiece of Scripture is considered to be "the Law and the Prophets" (Rom. 3:21; Matt. 5:17; 7:12), to which are added a not yet clearly delineated circle of more recent writings. Jude quotes from the book of Enoch and from the Assumption of Moses; Paul and James likewise refer to sayings with the customary introductory formula for Scripture whose provenance is unknown to us (Jude 9, 14–15; 1 Cor. 2:9 [Isa. 64:3]; Eph. 4:8 [Ps. 68:19]; 5:14; James 4:5–6). But there were no objections against this, because the major writings were relied on to gain insight as to what is the divine commandment and the divine promise.[20] Thus it is not their gripping novelties or miracles (of which there were plenty) that are lifted out of the extracanonical documents that were used, but pronouncements that are also accredited as firm truth by the canon: that the Lord comes in judgment for those who yield to sin, that even the angels did not themselves assume the right to judge, that Christ illumines the one who turns to him, that God's gift is the Spirit whom he allows to dwell in us. None of these pronouncements adds materially to the religious scope of Scripture. Christendom was protected against those dangerous tendencies which are not absent from this later literature. It was given the standard for evaluating all Scripture not merely by the old form of the canon but, beyond it, by Jesus' word and work.

---

20. Paul may have read and meditated upon the Greek "Wisdom of Solomon," but he did not quote from it. But reading of a book does not amount to considering it canonical.

Together with casuistry, Jesus also removed legend, together with slavish subjection to Scripture, which suspends one's own knowing and willing in the place of mere quotation. He even removed the arbitrary transformation of the words of Scripture which accommodated it through conjectures and poetic supplements to one's own spiritual condition and made it subservient to one's own desires. The disciples followed in Jesus' footsteps also in this regard. Nowhere do we receive the rabbinic school's legend of Abraham or Moses as described by Akiba; we only receive the Abraham and Moses of the text, resolute attention being given to the statements of Scripture. Imaginary postulates are removed, and one detects a vivid sense for the irreplaceable significance of facts. This can be observed with particular clarity in the segments that reiterate larger portions of Old Testament content, such as Stephen's speech or the depiction of the ancients' faith in Hebrews 11. Evidential value is here attributed to the existing condition of the biblical pronouncements, not to their arbitrary use or embellishment. Of course, once the basic separation from Pharisaism had occurred, complete liberation from Pharisaic Law could be realized more easily than the elimination of legendary material from tradition. They were interwoven with the text to a uniform narrative, and a distinction could be made here only incrementally and with difficulty. For this reason several legendary notions still enter from exegetical tradition into the historical picture of the New Testament; but these do not cast doubt on the thoroughgoing turning away from the school to the text.[21]

Because the community needs Scripture in order to hear God's word through it, its entire use is ordered by the axiom that it must fully reconcile its statements with its Christian convictions. In the refutation of the low esteem awarded Scripture by the gnostics, the aim determining its use took on precise and profound formulation that proved itself in the entire exegetical work of the first period (2 Tim. 3:15–17). The wisdom sought in the Bible has its aim not in a theory, not merely in the knowledge of divine wisdom, but in salvation; Scripture is read for the purpose of perceiving God's salvific will. It reveals this will by leading to faith through its manifold content and its punishing and encouraging words, but not in such a way that now faith is related to Scripture, but rather so that faith has its ground and substance in Christ. By its instruction in that faith which unites the community with Christ, Scripture proves itself to be the means of grace and the work of the Holy Spirit. Also in this positive principle that regulates their relationship to Scripture, not merely in their opposition to Jewish interpretation, the disciples preserved what they received from Jesus. Because Jesus was simultaneously guided by Scripture and his own divine sonship, his disciples likewise approached Scripture with both accountability and liberty. They obey it; however, they are not merely exegetes, but rather know Christ and therefore appropriate with gratitude whatever Scripture grants them. For their faith in Jesus is faith in God, who already gave his word to his ancient messengers.

Therefore it became an important task for the Christian use of Scripture to explain how Jesus' cross and his heavenly reign cohere with the Old Testa-

---

21. Traditional statements include Rahab's marriage with Salmon (Matt. 1:5) and the allusion to the rock accompanying Israel (1 Cor. 10:4); cf. pp. 296–97.

ment message. However, the facts are not observed correctly when it is said that interpretation grows solely from an apologetic motive, exclusively from the desire to prove Jesus' work through Old Testament sayings. For those possessed independent value for the apostles. They are read by them as the valid, eternal revelation of the divine will, beside which Jesus' history now stands as an independent, self-disclosing revelation of God. The motifs issuing from the interpretation of Scripture therefore arise both from Scripture and from Christ, and attention shifts back and forth between them. Scripture facilitates understanding of Christ; only Christ opens up the meaning of Scripture. What the Old Testament word means and what is the aim of God's previous acts—this is recognized in Christ. The New Testament interpretations of scriptural passages thus consistently have dual substantiation, because they arise from who Jesus is and from what the biblical verse says. From the coherent combination of both aspects, the community gained an instrument that produced certainty.

It would be false to derive Paul's doctrine of justification only from Habakkuk 2:4 and Genesis 15:6; it is based in the outcome of Jesus' life, in the fact that he becomes the Christ through his death and unites the community with himself through faith and thus sets it apart from all evil. However, this did not render the fact that Scripture likewise links righteousness and faith a mere cosmetic addition or a ready-made insight for Paul; rather, by viewing Jesus' history and the pronouncement of Scripture as identical, his knowledge was confirmed. Likewise, the application of the priest concept to Jesus in the epistle to the Hebrews did not originate merely from Psalm 110:4 but was grounded in the actual result of Jesus' work, in the things constituting the religious possession of his community. Because the pronouncement in the psalm provides a phrase that coheres with Jesus' work, the epistle develops a thesis by which it interprets Jesus' impact and Scripture (which says that the Christ was made an eternal priest) at the same time.

Thus it was not that selected portions of Scripture, such as a collection of messianic passages, became Christendom's canon; rather, the entire Old Testament without alteration, "all Scripture," was esteemed as "given by the Spirit" (2 Tim. 3:16–17). For the entire course of Old Testament history was connected to Christ and to his community as preparation effected by God, and all were convinced that the objective course of events at large also proved in the details that every pronouncement could serve in its own way to prepare a person belonging to God for every good work.

Thereby the Christian use of Scripture took on again a resemblance to the Jewish one, because the apostles likewise united their own conviction with the words of Scripture, free from doubt and with complete confidence, so that they understood even individual passages of Scripture without reservation as the attestation of the divine will revealed in Christ.[22] But the breakthrough re-

---

22. The promise was made not to many, but to a single seed of Abraham: Gal. 3:16; because Hagar's name is also used with reference to Sinai, she symbolizes the spiritual reality that the physical sons of Abraham are subjected to slavery by the Law: Gal. 4:25.

garding the exegetical traditions of the rabbinic school remains in effect, even in Paul's allegories and in the meditations on the Old Testament texts in the epistle to the Hebrews and in the repetitions of prophetic images by John. When Paul transfers Israel's wilderness wanderings to the situation of Christendom, which looks back to Jesus' earthly ministry behind it and forward to his return, or when he illustrates God's free election by the birth of the sons of Abraham and Isaac, or when he discusses the struggle now existing between the two kinds of sons of Abraham by the two sons of Abraham, the one born according to the flesh and the other born according to the promise (1 Cor. 10:1–11; Rom. 9:6–13; Gal. 4:21–31), his use of Scripture remains essentially distinct from Alexandrian allegory and its transmutations in the Palestinian school. For he did not transform the persons and stories of texts into ideas which take on an entirely separate character, and did not seek an allegedly higher or more fruitful insight behind the text, but turned his attention exclusively to what Scripture said. The similarity between his procedure and the Jewish one resulted from the fact that also for him both divine acts and human nature are revealed in what happened then in such a way that he draws norms from these events for the present. But this present took on its content, for him and for the entire church, in that they saw God's activity in Christ, and therefore they also interpreted God's earlier work from the vantage point of the Christ.

## 2. The Sacraments of the Church

### a) Baptism

Because Jesus' name determined the meaning of the act of baptism, it provided the one who was baptized never merely with the realization of his guilt but at the same time with the assurance of forgiveness. This fact resulted directly from the outcome of Jesus' life. Thus Paul assumes that everyone who gets baptized, not merely those instructed by him, understands his baptism in such a way that he is baptized into the death of Christ. For not merely the convicting but also the reconciling part of the baptismal preaching is grounded in Christ's death. This ensures that baptism is administered and received as sacrament, that is, as an offer of divine grace, not as a portrayal of human effort that seeks to effect liberation from evil by way of repentance or asceticism.

The benefit it granted to the one who was baptized did not consist in an individual grace gift, not in a particular religious state, but rather in union with Christ, by which God's perfect gifts are obtained. Therefore baptismal preaching used the entire gospel to interpret baptism in uniform completeness. Guilt and grace, Jesus' cross and his messianic glory, forgiveness of sins and the Holy Spirit, the personal faith of the individual and his entrance into the community—all these things were affirmed by the act of baptism in a uniform act. It was understood as the proclamation of Jesus' entire, indivisible will, not as the impartation of a single, isolated gift, but rather as the offer of God's grace which encompasses all the benefits of Christ's work as a unity and totality in the present and the coming world. This never changed during the apostolic period. There is no gift or power that the apostolic documents do not attribute to baptism. Through it, people are planted into Christ; whoever has been baptized "has put on Christ." It subjects the baptized person to the effect of his death; it grants the right to become a child of God, rebirth, renewal of will through separation from sin. It grants the baptized person Christ's love, provides him with identification with his life, procures for him a good conscience as well as the washing of the body which sets him apart for God (Gal. 3:27; Rom. 6:3; John 3:5; Titus 3:5; 1 Cor. 6:11; Eph. 5:25–26; 1 Pet. 3:21; Heb. 10:22).

Such a baptism cannot be described in terms of metaphor. It was administered and received as a meaningful and effective event by which the relationship with Christ was effected in vigorous reality. Equally excluded, however, are notions regarding baptism that sought in it a material means of grace in which the divine operation was tied to and located in the water. If such notions could be observed in New Testament baptismal practice, this would furnish proof that the disciples developed a Christendom by their own independent religious production that arose not from Jesus' work but entered into an internal conflict with him. For material mediators of the divine operation, which are salvific apart from the personal participation of their giver, that is, Christ, and of its recipient, would represent a new development, not the preserving of a tradition instituted by Jesus but an alteration of it. No grace could be reconciled with Jesus' word and deed that was anything other than God's giving will, and no entrance into grace was conceivable that occurred in a way other than by a person's believing conversion to God. The concept of religion characteristic of Jesus is uniformly, consistently, and in all its dimensions conceived in personal terms and thus rejects material means of salvation. But such interpretations of apostolic baptism are excluded because no specialized effect was attached to it that could be separated from Christ's other manifestations, while this was the inevitable consequence of those notions of baptism that understood it to be analogous to pre-Christian consecrations of a material nature. By consistently identifying the totality of divine grace as the benefit of baptism, the apostolic pronouncements indicate that they consider Christ to be the one who is at work. He calls people to himself through his messengers and accepts those who repent by providing baptism for them. He extends to them forgiveness through baptism and enters into fellowship with them. Because for the apostles the gospel and baptism granted the same thing and had identical content, any understanding of baptism is excluded that brings it into conflict with the train of thought that expresses the value of the gospel.

This observation is confirmed by the fact that there is nowhere a trace of legislation regulating the external administration of the sacrament. It would exist, however, if faith had been based on it and had considered it as the means of grace. In that case, what is external regarding the sacrament would itself be what is holy and would require that complete diligence and correctness with which what is holy always must be treated. Thus the external process of the sacrament would need to be protected from violations through a system of rules and to be brought to its salvific effect. The New Testament evidences no tendency toward such legislation; rather, it begins immediately in the later church and attains extensive control over it.[23]

Another fact stands in close connection with this: no other sacrament comes to the fore in the community other than the acts originating with Jesus, that is, baptism, with which the proclamation of heavenly rule had started, and the meal, with which Jesus began to move toward death. Conversely, the community turned completely away from the Old Testament sacraments, which used a natural substance as sign of election and grace—circumcision, sacrifice, and washings of purification. The inner shake-ups that threatened the unity of the church did not arise from the wish to continue the sacraments that had been practiced up to that point but from the Law. For many found it objectionable, indeed completely unthinkable, to transgress God's laws. But that the community had produced analogous salvific means while simultaneously its faith severed itself from all available holy objects, being grounded solely in Christ—this would be a remarkable process that could only be confirmed through hard evidence. Where elsewhere the notion appears that the divine grace was communicable through natural processes, such processes are regularly repeated, because an effect conceived of in terms of natural processes can be enhanced only when these processes are repeated frequently and in a variety of ways. However, the community did not detect the effective or permanent bestowal of divine grace even in the Old Testament sacraments, although it acknowledged these as divine institutions. In fact, through baptism in Jesus' name, it moved away from them rather than merely adding baptism to them. This shows that it found in baptism something different, that is, the attestation and realization of Christ's will, who grants forgiveness and grace to the sinner.

If the supposition were correct that baptism was administered in Corinth according to 1 Corinthians 15:29 not merely for the living but also for the dead, such as deceased family members or friends—with which I do not agree—this still would not demonstrate the existence of a magical theory in Paul that attaches faith to water. For water did not extend to the dead but only to the one who received baptism in his place. In the case of effects conceived according to the analogy of natural processes there is no representation; this arises in the realm of love and intercession. If such occurred, the event was related to baptism of an entire household and took place in the confidence that the love found in the natural fellowship was also holy and powerful before God, so that, for example, the son who had been converted to Christ could also name the name of his deceased father before him and was permitted to include him in Christ's grace at his own baptism. Such a process presupposes, of course, the idea that baptism produces contact with Christ that is powerful and vital; but even here it is not separate from Christ's will or tied to natural means.[24]

---

23. The oldest document regarding the development of legislation regarding the performance of baptism is "The Teaching of the Twelve Apostles."

24. In my opinion, the passage deals with the offering up of one's life for Jesus' sake, which becomes meaningless apart from the hope of resurrection. The phrase "being baptized" is used for martyrdom. Thus it does not refer to individual dead but to "the dead," into the circle of whom the martyr enters as the bearer and messenger of Jesus' grace.

Because Christ's entire gift is linked with baptism, it did not lead to different levels of Christianity, a preliminary, still searching kind of Christian state and beyond this a complete one which partook of the entirety of divine grace. For baptism assigned equal value to the Christian state of all. However, this did not lead to an effort to postpone it. The vigorous faith characteristic of the early church is shown by the fact that baptism was administered immediately upon confession of Christ (Acts 8:16; 16:33). A regulation or practice comparable to later catechism does not appear,[25] although something similar was foreshadowed by the result of the Jewish mission, which created two kinds of proselytes, those who entered the community completely and those who accepted only its word but not also its sacrament. That baptism was frequently administered not by the apostles themselves but through other Christians (Acts 10:48; 1 Cor. 1:14) indicates that the act's effectiveness was not derived from the person who performed the baptism. Rather, the faith of the person baptized was directed solely toward Christ. This also indicates that things did not proceed according to passionate excitement, with baptism immediately following the initial proclamation, but that the listener was rather given time, so that a confirmed decision might arise in him that took place subsequent to sober deliberation. But once a hearer arrived at a clear verdict regarding Christ's message, Jesus' principle, "Let it be to you according to your faith," applied and the correspondence between God's gift and faith remained unbroken. The believer is the Lord's, who now assumes his care, and he is given without reservation what the Lord has prepared for him. This practice was made possible by the fact that the strong mutual bond of the brethren ensured the preservation and consolidation of the state of faith that had been achieved and, if this remained unattainable and insurmountable conflicts surfaced, it possessed in discipline the means of rejecting foreign elements. It is understandable that the church rapidly created another practice, although this development constituted a considerable departure from the lofty nature of the original state of faith.

### b) The Lord's Supper

The Lord's Supper, with the partaking of the body and blood of Jesus through bread and wine, became an established part of worship in all congregations, because they considered this to be Jesus' own deed. This is indicated by the fact that we never find the idea of the Lord's Supper as the center of personal devotion, worked by the writer's own originality, in the epistles. Because Christ made it the expression of his will and provided content for the most important celebration of the community, it self-evidently remained protected against any doubt; but it retained an isolated position beside the convictions moving the community. Of the new formulas developed by Paul to express the effective power of Jesus' cross and the fullness of his grace, none took its departure from the eating and drinking of the body and blood of Christ. Nowhere in the Jo-

---

25. In Luke 1:4, catechism is posited by some, but without reason. Rich written instruction regarding the history of Jesus showed every Christian, not merely the one who was catechized, the reliability of the word he believed.

hannine or Petrine epistles, in Luke, in the epistle to the Hebrews, or in the Apocalypse does a formula appear that arose from a meditation on the words at the Lord's Supper.[26] A strong sense regarding the conflict of the celebration of the Lord's Supper with the human sentiment not merely of the Greeks, but even more so of the Jews, who were extremely offended by the thought of drinking blood, does not yet explain the nature of the formation of New Testament thought. For where the Lord's Supper is discussed, it becomes clear that the community has overcome this obstacle, viewing Jesus' act as faith must view it. It eats his body with gratitude and drinks his blood in the conviction that it thereby is united with him. At the same time, this formulation regarding the salvific value of his death and the aim of his sending occupies an isolated position beside its own thinking elsewhere. This reveals that it was given to it already in completed form. One can perhaps speaks of a certain measure of mystery from the beginning of the apostolic work with which the Lord's Supper was veiled and guarded.[27] The term "breaking of bread" in Luke does not express the ritual act at all. In the Pauline epistles it comes to the fore only in 1 Corinthians, because Paul must organize its celebration anew. What is particularly curious is that it nowhere surfaces in the Pastorals; also, that the detailed discussion of the salvific power of Jesus' death in the epistle to the Hebrews does not take its point of departure from the Lord's Supper, which is only alluded to in a single expression. In the older Gospels reference is made only to what Jesus did, not to the fact that the community now eats his body and drinks his blood. John speaks in his first epistle of Jesus' blood in such a way that no one outside of the community learned anything regarding the Lord's Supper. John's Gospel admittedly grounds Jesus' decision to suffer death explicitly in terms of providing eternal life for believers by their eating of Jesus' flesh and drinking his blood; but that the community appropriated this promise by observing Jesus' supper and by receiving his body with the bread and his blood with the cup—this was not even revealed by the Johannine discourse to anyone who was not part of the community. This reserve may be occasioned by the fact that those who did not understand the community slandered it on account of the Lord's Supper. But this further confirms that we must not interpret the Lord's Supper as the proper, free development of the disciples; rather, they observed it in obedience to Christ.

The church's gaze in the Last Supper's celebration was directed unwaveringly to the salvific power of Jesus' death. This is revealed not merely by the Passion narratives of Matthew and Mark but also by the unique Lucan account of the celebration of the Lord's Supper (Luke 22:15–19a). If according to this account Jesus actually gives to the disciples only the bread as his body, this lends a certain probability to the supposition that it can be traced to a variation in the celebration of the Lord's Supper, which consisted merely in the offering of the bread.

26. John 5:7 speaks of the witness of the blood, not of what the blood that has been drunk by us brings about. Heb. 13:10 reminds one of the priests' privilege to eat from the altar, which had been superseded by the altar possessed by Christendom. Behind the idea of "eating from the altar" probably stands the fact that the community ate Jesus' body.

27. In any case is baptism mentioned more frequently and with greater clarity.

That the celebration was held also in this simplified form is not inconceivable on account of its connection with the common meal, because the cup of wine did not constitute a component of the daily meal but is characteristic of a feast. Perhaps the congregations, when lacking wine, did not therefore forego the celebration but conducted it in that case with the bread. In this case the Lucan text would indicate that the early church was free from any legislation arising from the sacrament, not viewing the means of grace to be the external aspect of the act. But the inner substance of the celebration would not have varied. For at this Lord's Supper, too, Jesus gives to his disciples with the bread his body, because he faces death for them.

John, while not referring to the Lord's Supper itself, developed in view of it the notion of feeding from the vantage point of the concept of life, so that he portrays everything Christ grants to his own. The one who gives them life becomes for them the bread they must eat. But this would result in a celebration of the Lord's Supper which deviated from that of Matthew and Paul only if Jesus' life-giving effect would have resulted independently from his death, such as through the impartation of supernatural powers or through the pneumatics' material union with the Exalted One. Such interpretations are foreign to John, because he expressly designated Jesus' flesh and blood as the life-giving agents. But these are surrendered by Jesus in his death. Because the reference to Jesus' death cannot be removed from the Johannine words, we arrive at a train of thought that is parallel to the celebration described by Paul.

The community's celebration of the Lord's Supper was at the same time vividly determined by the anticipation of the new meal Christ would celebrate with his community at the occasion of his return. Bread is eaten in God's kingdom, and the community does this already now by observing the meal prepared for it by Christ. But the celebration could never become merely the symbolic anticipation of the eschatological meal as long as the element to be consumed was called Jesus' body, which he surrendered to death. The movement in the devotion of the initial period, which on the basis of eschatology increasingly realizes the possessions given to the community already at the present time, proved anything but irrelevant regarding the celebration of the Lord's Supper. The supposition may have some merit that in the first few years, and perhaps permanently in Palestine, at mealtimes the promise that assures the eschatological meal with the Christ of the second coming was strongly emphasized. But thereafter, reconciliation, justification, and new life arising for the community from Jesus' death constituted the reason for thanksgiving. No conflict developed at this point in the apostolic period. For the grateful remembrance of Jesus' death was instilled into the celebration by its institution and possessed particular power during the beginnings of the community when the memory of the cross still had its full force. Also, the hope of the completion of union with Christ through his parousia was united with the celebration even in the Greek church through the Pauline proclamation.

Baptism and the Lord's Supper must approximate one another on account of their content as the two acts by which Jesus revealed and effected his relationship with believers. Both were set apart from all other acts of the community by the fact that it was here touched by Jesus' own deed, so that through them the entire gospel was gathered into one act that provided those who participated in it with Christian character. The grouping together of both foreshadowed the emergence of the concept of sacrament. It is not yet fully developed in the New Testament. But the Pauline and the Johannine words which juxtapose baptism and the Lord's Supper show that it is in the process of being developed (1 Cor. 10:1–4; 12:13; 1 John 5:6). By reminding believers of the baptism that has been received by all and of the cup that has been drunk by all when describing the congregation's unity, which despite the diversity of its independent members is linked to a harmonious communal life, Paul indicates that the importance of the sacraments for the establishment of ecclesiastical unity has been felt from the beginning.

But it was of utmost importance for the community's entire devotion that neither of the two sacraments used by it gave rise to a badge by which its members could prove their Christian identity. Baptism, which was filled with the sincerity of repentance, was unsuitable for this, and so was participation in the Lord's Supper, although it became the characteristic of believers on account of its constant repetition. For the act proclaimed exclusively the reconciling power of the Crucified One. Despite, or rather precisely because of, the Lord's Supper, the fact remained that there existed in the early church no external object or action that were by themselves sufficient to prove the Christian identity of a man. Everything depended on the internal, personal relationship with God in Christ.

## 3. The Church's Unity

### a) Faith

Because completeness of communion can only be attained by those who live in the same location, the visualization and application of Christianity initially became the task of local congregations, and the epistles show how independently and energetically individual communities tackled their Christian calling. But this never led to an isolation of local congregations, which would have severed them from the remainder of Christendom. Even in the Jerusalem church, which claimed a—generally acknowledged—preeminence over all other churches, the idea never arose that they could separate from the other communities. When congregations formed in Samaria, Damascus, Antioch, and many other places among the nations, Jerusalem did not claim that it was not affected by these developments because these were foreign congregations; rather, the extent of brotherhood reached immediately as far as confession of Christ had spread. When a baptized Ethiopian returns to Ethiopia, he belongs even there to Christ's community. Peter wrote assuming that the congregations of Asia Minor constituted a single church even though they lived at a distance from one another. The conflicts pertaining to the validity of the Law, too, rested on the impossibility of dissolving Christendom into a multitude of independent churches; the question of the Law took on its importance from the fact that the church, even though it now comprised both those obedient to the Law and those free from the Law, was still a unity.

Because believers' association resulted from their faith, all participated in the community of their own accord, and as long as Jesus' disciples led the community, no substitute was sought for this. No one doctrine was put in the place of the one faith, nor were Law and righteousness understood to produce fellowship in place of the common act of believing. The brothers were united with one another because all had come to Christ. "Faith" was conceived of as trust in him, not merely as a doctrinal affirmation regarding him. Trust was placed in Christ, not in Christology.

But just because it was faith that united Christendom, this did not mean that its desire for knowledge was hindered or that the importance of the work of faith was depreciated. Because it could not place its confidence in Christ without engaging in a struggle with human sin, works were of course made its first priority, and it was prohibited from seeing its task merely in the development and cultivation of doctrine; for sin is overcome not by ideas but only by obedience. But because it directed a committed, complete will toward action on account of the sanctity of ethical norms and the gloriousness of the desired aim, its practical orientation also set its thinking into the most dynamic motion. Christendom's vision became clear, because the goal of its thought consisted in the understanding of God's will, not merely for its own sake, but for the community, and in the communication to the community of what is right before God. No other aim stretches the ability to think with equal vigor. The doctrinal formation of the apostolic period remains a closed book if the ethical energy of the message of repentance, and the circumspectness of its didactic labor as it wrestled to arrive at sure knowledge, are considered to be in conflict or to be unconnected processes. The vigor with which evil was repudiated and the vigor with which the divine word was appropriated were mutually productive. For the community directed its attention toward Christ because it separated itself from evil, and it separated itself from evil because it knew Christ.

But faith also generated, in a very direct way, impulses that produced vigorous thinking. For the community comes to a realization of the basis and content of its faith—thus strengthening it—by the attainment of firm concepts. Therefore growth in insight is considered to be valuable and fruitful for faith, and there is no trace of any fear of knowledge, as if vigor of insight could weaken faith and faith thereby cease to be faith. This holds true even when it became necessary to combat illusory knowledge. It was recognized that no progress in understanding can raise one's relationship with God and Christ above that confidence that results from understanding without seeing, but that even faith cannot afford to do without knowledge, because it must know in whom faith is placed. The intensity of intellectual labor and the plethora of formulations it produced in the early period is, when compared with the later doctrinal labor of the church, which bears the mark of lazy verbosity, proof of the vigor of its faith.

Despite all the joy in clear thoughts and expansive formulas, the community's foundation, that is, faith, did not waver, nor was it replaced by salvific theology. Because of this, there was no effort to effect an external uniformity of doctrine. A formulaic version of Christian doctrine, which renders it usable for all, even apart from one's own intellectual labor and without internal grounding of a given formulation in the individual, is nowhere to be found. All New Testament documents bear the stamp of surprising originality. The thought emerges in a fresh way from the writer as his own achievement that grew within him through his internal and external history. Even the writings by one and the same person, such as Romans when compared with the epistles to the Corinthians, or Philippians when compared with Colossians, as well as John's Gospel when compared with the epistle or the book of Revelation, demonstrate with unusual power how original and fresh were the thoughts that emerged from the challenge presented by a given situation. No fear is apparent that the unity of the congregation could be harmed, because it has the ground of its unity not in men but in the undergirding presence of Christ. Into this presence all are placed, as long as they abide in the faith.

As evident as the stimulating effect of faith, which provides the material, orientation, and courage for thinking and allows it free movement, is faith's limiting effect regarding doctrinal formulation as a whole. Such limitation is revealed by the fact that any merely theoretical or speculative problems are rejected. The knowledge-oriented labor of the community was stirred by the questions that arose from its experienced history or the service it must perform. This subjected the formulation of questions and the answers provided for them to clear limitations that arose not from an external confinement of the word but from the inner impulse that controls the entire movement of thought. Where the apostles' calling, life, and activity end, there their investigation and questioning also are restrained. The prerequisite as well as the result of this doctrinal development was firm allegiance to Jesus' own word, which desired to stimulate repentance and faith and rejected any mere intellectual dealings with God. No New Testament document violated this common characteristic of all the writings. None sought to develop theological pronouncements that strive to achieve nothing but an expansion of knowledge. Such restraint and focus were indispensable if faith was to remain the community's foundation.

The pronouncements that are furthest removed from experience furnish the most powerful proof for this, because even they never lose connection with the kind of knowledge the community must have in order to act rightly. The assumption of the epistle to the Hebrews, that Melchizedek lives forever and holds an eternal priesthood, could easily denigrate into expansive speculation; for what is a high priest who operates at a heavenly location, and why does Melchizedek hold this office? But the thought remains strictly subjected to the epistle's practical aim, because it seeks solely to reveal what the community is granted through Jesus' priesthood, through his death and his exaltation. The idea does not evolve into speculation regarding Melchizedek but remains entirely in the realm of Christology. When Peter speaks of Christ's ministry among the spirits in prison, he expresses a thought that could easily mushroom into a major system, because there was considerable interest in the universal scope of Jesus' commission, which encompassed the living and the dead. But the idea in Peter's usage is limited to the purpose of strengthening; this component of his teaching serves to assure the community that it can confidently give itself over to suffering, because Christ likewise suffered and acquired through suffering his saving power, through which he touches even the dead. Through God's contact with human history, what is eternal becomes the ground of temporal history, and the resulting mystery had a profound effect on both Paul and John. But the New Testament does not contain any theory regarding the relationship between God's predestination and the temporal nature of our lives. Christ's unity with God was the foundation of the apostolic faith on which it rested with all its consequences; but there was no New Testament pronouncement that strove to establish more than that the completeness of Jesus' communion with the Father became a certainty for the community. No effort was made to explain Christ's form of existence, whether in his trinitarian relationship with the Father or in his human form.

More recent historical scholarship has been influenced by the question of whether the truth value of the community's tradition is jeopardized by the fact that its entire intellectual life took place under the control of faith. The observation, amply attested to by the New Testament, is psychologically accurate that any faith, whatever content it may have, as long as it takes hold in us with the force of certainty, serves as a comprehensive framework for subsequent thought and determines the inferences we draw. But this, it is alleged, amounts to the destruction of thought, because it now deems itself, under the influence of faith, to be a productive force that no longer requires reality but is satisfied with even figments of the imagination. Jesus' disciples are convinced, it is alleged, that Jesus is the Christ and must be proclaimed as such. But because Christ is inconceivable to them apart from miracles, and a crucified Christ unthinkable apart from resurrection, Jesus, by necessity of the inherent logic of his disciples' belief system, performed miracles and experienced resurrection, without these claims requiring any substantiation other than the disciples' faith.[28]

However, this theory uses a concept of faith that was at all times foreign to the disciples and that was completely rejected by them. The kind of faith that arrogates for itself the power to equip Jesus with the characteristics of his commission, such as miracles or resurrection, would not have been called faith but foolishness and sin by the disciples. For such faith would have completely moved away from the consciousness of God and would have denied that Christ comes only through God's commission and that he can reign only by God's will. But this is to give up what the disciples consider to be the essential characteristic of faith (1 Cor. 15:15; 2 Thess. 2:10; 1 Tim. 2:7; 1 John 1:1). In their view, the fundamental relationship between God and man would thereby be reversed, because man thus would create his own religion, conceiving of God's relationship to himself in the manner desired by himself. But for them faith is the certainty that man must relate to God in a receiving manner and therefore be tied to the divine testimony and the divine deed. If the community had surrendered this principle, it would have severed itself from the norms of Jesus' word

---

28. This argument is given added power by the fact that pre-Christian religiosities offered a plethora of examples and instruction regarding the interference of thinking in "faith." Hellenism spawned myth, and the synagogues spun legends.

of repentance. If, in the historian's view, the Christ of the apostles is a construct of their faith, he must not close his eyes when confronted with the fact that he is not here describing the apostles' consciousness and the state of affairs as they themselves perceived it. He has had to inject into his historical calculations a shift in apostolic consciousness that did not exist in their own perception, a shift alleging that they considered their own construct to be reality and their own invention to be history. The fact is that as soon as the apostles recognized a legend to be such, they unmasked it at once.

The sincerity with which the portrayal of the Christ remained subjected to the truth principle is evident in the fact that the accomplishments of apostolic ministry are not interwoven with it. How is the kind of faith that is allegedly capable of creating its own Christ supposed to be able to arrive at this distinction, if its Christ is alleged merely to mirror its own religious condition? But Jesus did not take on the traits of the apostles, and the characteristic manner of his ministry as it issued from his own situation is not destroyed. As far as we can observe the history of tradition, it confirms the disciples' claim that faith can be grounded solely in truth. Paul's vigorous faith did not make him the creator of messianic legends; rather, he consistently and in an unwavering commitment to truthfulness distinguished between what he had received from tradition and what he himself said. The Synoptic texts clearly reveal the condition and orientation of their authors; all accounts reflect originality, so that they are never mere carbon copies of one another. But where tradition is used, this is done faithfully, so that it is all the same regarding the portrayal of Christ, whether we proceed from Matthew or Luke, although the former was a Pharisee, the latter a Gentile follower of Paul. Even in the case of John, material identical with the Synoptics outweighs by far what may be considered to be new material in John. Anyone who deems it necessary to postulate the free development of legends in analogy to Midrash must do so out of the vacuum that exists prior to the history of the Gospels known to us. But from a historical perspective it will never turn out to be probable that the formation of Gospels in the first period took place along entirely different lines than it did where we can observe it, particularly since our witnesses, foremost of all Paul, but Matthew and John no less, reach back into the early genesis of the church.

No evangelist feared the intrusion of imagination into the depiction of Christ. Rather, he awakened it for himself and his readers, not only because no one can recount past events apart from imagination, even while being most soberly committed to truthfulness, but also because both narrator and listeners actively engage in these narratives with their will, and the moving of the will always takes place by confronting our desire with a visual image. The development of poetry stirred up by the picture of Christ is as old as evangelization, and we possess in many Gospel portions shining examples of early Christian poetry, through the graphic clarity given to the narratives and at the same time through the tenderness of presentation which knows how to direct attention to the things that are of greatest value for the observer of a particular event. In few cases we may no longer be able to determine the exact boundary between reminiscence and poetry or between the graphic depiction of an event and the actual event itself. But the greatness of early Christian poetry taking Christ as its inspiration derives largely from the fact that the imagination, together with the obvious graphic nature of its depiction of Jesus, remains subject to powerful discipline. Within the restraint of this discipline, the portrayal of Christ was not severed from faith, so that it never forgot the difference between myth and reality.

The manner in which the work to arrive at knowledge was carried out indicates in what sense we may speak of doctrinal formulation during this period. Closure regarding insight in terms of confirmed results is desired and achieved to the extent that the intellectual life of the community does not remain on the level of wavering searching but produces convictions that have the status of truth for both thinking and conduct. We therefore encounter terms that constitute the constant and secure possession of the apostles and congregations. At the same time, however, it is clear that the subject of their thinking and teaching transcends any set formulas, so that all concepts are given great flexibility, because every set formula contains a dimension that renders it incomplete. Thus the consciousness of knowing and telling the truth combined with an aspiring intellectual industriousness that did not grow weary but continued to be ready for a new glimpse of the glory of God.

If the organizational significance of doctrine for the community is considered, the term "doctrine" is applicable for the apostolic teaching ministry only in part. The community as a whole takes part in the knowledge of Christ; this knowledge is not made the possession of a privileged few. Apostolic teaching was addressed to all; it sought and produced consent and could not forego this aim, because the rightness of practical behavior and the health of the community depended on the condition of its knowledge. Its knowledge of the divine gift did not merely serve as window dressing but represented the indispensable equipment for its calling and constituted itself an essential part of the gift granted to it. But because it remained evident that the community's unity was not brought about merely or even primarily through the uniformity of its terminology, but that it had a deeper foundation, that of its common faith, the community sought in God's presence and Christ's lordship what united it and did not make Christology the substitute for Christ. For this reason it also resisted the temptation to make the church's knowledge a surrogate for the insight of individuals. One knew that knowledge can never be produced merely by learning and teaching but that it must arise from the personal history of the knowing subject; only what is established in us internally is true knowledge. The community's doctrinal labor and its tradition thus became aids in helping stimulate personal perception and judgment. Teaching could stir up, support, and guide this process but never replace it. Despite their unique office by which they knew themselves to be the bearers of divine revelation, the apostles' efforts to aid the congregations and every individual in them to arrive at their own verdict and personal assurance show how successfully the idea was rejected that doctrine itself was sufficient for the production of ecclesiastical unity. It could find its purpose nowhere else than in subserviently helping everyone arrive at knowledge of his own.

## b) The Common Struggle for Ethical Norms

By knowing itself to be united with God and thus capable of overcoming all evil, the community did not replace fear of God with arrogance. It rather expressed man's ethical dilemma and the intricate connection of his perverse will with his nature and the world in a measure previously unprecedented. But it was not merely mindful of its slavery to sin but also of the presence of God, whose forgiveness blotted out its sin and who grants to it help in dealing with its ethical dilemma and liberating it from evil. These convictions confront us in the apostolic writings everywhere at the same level, both the orderly neatness of opposition toward perverse desires and the assurance of victory over all that is reprehensible.

However, because separation from evil arises from union with God, Christendom did not conceive of it in terms of external preservation or natural separation but remained mindful of the personal nature of believers' relationship with God. This finds expression in the vivid hortatory nature of a large part of the apostolic message. Jesus' word remained unforgotten which confronted his disciples with the danger and guilt of apostasy with increased seriousness. It therefore became an important task of the community to assist all its members in their struggle against sin, initially by keeping them from falling, then when somebody fell, by helping him up again.

In this effort the community retained the state of faith that provided it with the consciousness of being holy by protecting its dealings from all timidity and all enslaving pronouncements. Even the brother is included in one's trust in the perfect divine grace, because the Lord intercedes for him with the same forgiveness, help, and guidance as for all (Rom. 14:4). In this way discipline never led to a violation of that liberty which constituted the foundation for the community. We therefore do not receive any enumeration of things that are intolerable for the community, no list of prohibitions that had legal character, no institution of penance that was compulsory for the members of the congregation. The value of confession for the turning around of those who had fallen was awarded full respect. Already baptism included the confession of guilt, and confession was also practiced in the dealings of Christians with one another (James 5:16; 1 John 1:8–10). Only through confession did the extension of communion to the ethical realm became possible. By confession, the guilty person attained truthfulness and avoided a heaping up of sin by lying and pretense. By accepting the consequences of his sin as part of his confession, he preserved the sincerity of his repentance and received at the same time forgiveness and the help found in the community, because his own condemnation of evil was grounded in and confirmed by the verdict of others, his faith in forgiveness by the faith of others, and his resistance toward sin by the intercession and care of others. All the power inherent in community thus was made fruitful for the ethical aim. Still, the community's practice of confession had as its aim not the revelation and public exposure of sin but the overcoming of sin, not in the shaming and punishment of the guilty person but in his liberation. Therefore it did not relieve the individual of the right and obligation of treating his ethical concerns as his own; it rather instructed him explicitly that he acted correctly only when he severed himself from his sin in complete uprightness and by his own will, showing him that this was the condition for his own access to the Lord who alone forgives and himself restores and sanctifies his own. Thus the community remained free from distorting repentance into faithless scrupulousness.

These convictions made clear that acceptance into the church was not irrevocable. Membership in it was not considered to be an external or essential guarantee of salvation. Relapse into sin, revoking one's faith, hardening against church discipline remained possible and occurred and resulted in the breaking of fellowship (1 Cor. 5:3–5, 11–13; 2 Cor. 2:6–11; 12:20–13:2; 2 Thess. 3:6, 14; 1 Tim. 1:20; Titus 3:10–11; 1 John 5:16–17; Rev. 2:20–23). Therefore even entire congregations can fall away again. It depended on their ethical stance whether they remained in communion with Christ or he "removed the lampstand again" (Rev. 2:5; 1 Thess. 3:5).

The practice of church discipline took place first in God's own judgment of the sinning one. In this category may be placed the cases where the apostles exercised a pronouncement of judgment that resulted in loss of life for the guilty person. The hypocritical Ananias collapsed dead before Peter, and Paul handed the immoral Corinthians over to Satan. In this the apostles acted in the same consciousness of power that they exercised toward the believer. The realm of Christ's authority is contrasted with the sphere of Satan's and the world's influence, so that the one severed from Christ and the community is thus handed over to the power of Satan. Therefore it is said regarding those who left the community that they had followed Satan (1 Tim. 5:15). This should not be interpreted as denoting a condition akin to demon possession. Paul expected in the case of one who was judged the destruction of his body, similar to the way in which he linked the sins accompanying the Lord's Supper to the expeditious deaths of many in Corinth (1 Cor. 11:30). The story of Job exerts a clear influence on this: Job was handed over to Satan with the result that he was afflicted with severe diseases. But even then, the execution of justice, as far as the will of Christendom was concerned, had grace as its aim. It must exercise no judgment other than the one whose final purpose is the salvation of the spirit.

As everywhere, God's activity did not obliterate man's responsibility to serve, but pointed it out to him and supported him in its execution, while not exempting him from taking his own action. Therefore the expectation of the manifestation of God's judging activity upon the community was accompanied by the rule "remove the evil one from your midst," and it results in reproach for the community when it did not refuse fellowship to the one who took his mother-in-law as his wife or tolerated a Jezebel in its midst.

That the community's dealings with one another were based on the principle of liberty facilitated the exercise of discipline because in most cases people voluntarily left the church when an ethical dilemma arose. When excommunication from the community became necessary, it was part of the overseers' responsibilities to effect it (3 John 10). However, such a decision on part of the overseer was conceivable and successful only in agreement with the community, because the execution of the verdict could be carried out only when all withheld fellowship from the guilty person. This was also stressed by Paul in his verdict regarding the Corinthian, when he said that the Corinthians were gathered together with his own spirit at the pronouncement of this verdict, even though he was absent (2 Thess. 3:6, 14, 15; 1 Cor. 5:4).

### c) Uniting the Community in Love

One can observe a uniform will in the congregations, because the epistles continually use an inclusive "you," which describes the community as capable of united action. If this "you" were found only in the Pauline epistles, one might conclude that this is characteristic of the particular closeness in which Paul united believers he had gained. But the same address is used in Peter's and John's epistles as well as in the epistle to the Hebrews, and the book of Revelation likewise describes congregations as moral units. The expectation of a common will was directed toward congregations not merely when they had been presented with an outline of Christian ethics, but also when concrete decisions must be made. If those who claim to speak in the Spirit of God must be examined and those who do not speak in the Spirit of God must be denied faith, the exhortation goes, "you" must not believe every spirit; the congregation arrives at the verdict that refuses to listen to such words allegedly received by the Spirit. If the celebration of the Lord's Supper or a custom in the gatherings must be regulated, the "you" formulate a decision. If a brother falls, it is the "you" who mourn or do not mourn; the community continues to have fellowship or denies fellowship to him (1 John 4:1–2; 1 Cor. 11:20–22, 33–34; 5:2, 12–13, etc.).

The common will did not arise in the congregations by compulsion. That custom and law are indispensable to produce joint action was clearly perceived. In developing such customs, the congregation drew from the institutions existing in the Jewish community, and when certain agreements became necessary, it acted in the conviction that it arrived at its decisions in communion with the Lord and that it was guided by him in them. There thus arose stipulations like the decree of the apostles regarding the question of Gentile Christians, stipulations binding on all (Acts 15:28–29). But even in the formation and exercise of customs it remained the continual aim that the participation of all in the community must be borne by their personal conviction, which could never be replaced by law or custom. A decision such as the one made in Jerusalem regarding the question of the Gentiles did not obviate the principle that no one acted correctly unless he acted according to his own conscience. Paul instituted the principle in Corinth that the Greek must avoid meat sacrificed to idols as well as prostitutes; but it was at that point still the subject of discussion whether these regulations were actually valid, and, in arguing for them, Paul does not cite a pronouncement by which he transposed the decision from the insight of the individual to an authority foreign to him. Whoever concludes from this that Paul never issued this decree does not understand the liberty of the first Christians. Equally inaccurate would be the supposition that the decree thus remained inconsequential. How the apostles and the brethren associated with them assessed the matter constituted for all a guiding authority, not merely for the sake of the apostles but for the sake of the Christ who reigns over them. But no one in the community could receive guidance for his conduct merely from the outside; everyone had his own internal connection with the Lord. Each thus possessed responsibility for himself and attained assurance only through his own knowledge regarding the divine will which he must obey.

This is how the community received its great possession: complete communion together with complete liberty for all. The community was raised beyond the secret or open dispute between one's own life and the community. Here the individual was given his own internal possession, which was secured and strengthened but also used entirely for communion. The reason for this was that all subjected themselves in faith to the One as their Lord. Because they are tied exclusively to the Lord, they are free in relation to one another, but thereby also free from their own selves and united with one another. With faith came love, and it has the ability to establish a liberating communion. The simultaneous existence of liberty and communion reveals that the community did not merely command love but also possessed it.

Those who have their highest social ideal in the Roman state charge that the apostles, by establishing the community on the basis of their own assurance and individuals' own love, failed to recognize the importance of law. But as far as their natural ties and associations are concerned, the congregations integrated themselves into the existing systems of the state, which remained completely undisputed. In those circumstances regulated by existing law, such as rights of citizenship, trade, marriage, and inheritance law, current legislation was gratefully utilized. Paul skillfully used the existing forms of legislation to his advantage when he fought for his life; he even defended the property rights of slave-owners and valued the reign of the emperor as an instrument of the divine government. Even the specialized work of the community, by which it fulfilled its own new task, does not reveal any opposition to the use of existing norms (Acts 16:37; 22:25; 24:10ff. 25:10; 1 Cor. 7:21; Philemon; Rom. 13:1–7).[29] But it was maintained regarding the communion existing between the brethren that everyone must participate personally and thus with his own assurance and his own love. In the free communion of wills that was thus established, the vigor and health of the community was clearly visible.

The same power of love that made it possible for the community to provide its communion with closeness and completeness without resorting to compulsion enabled it to apply ethical norms with resolute seriousness to all and in every circumstance. It did this without succumbing to the tendency to shame those who succumbed and without scolding or rejecting the weak. For the community possessed the ability to forgive as only love is able to.

Its love finds equally clear expression in the resoluteness with which it performed its thinking free from dogmatism or intellectualism. Doctrinal formulation did not absorb or weaken other functions, transforming the community into a school, be it a school of exegetes studying Scripture or a school of Gospel writers meditating on the mystery of the Christ. As Jesus established the circle of disciples in order that they might participate in his work, the church remains

---

29. Principles such as the one that the community must support those who administer the word or that two witnesses are necessary for bringing a charge against someone retain their validity.

a group of workers that furthers God's work among mankind. It confronts everyone with the question of salvation in such a way that it is addressed to him personally, so that his entire strength is exerted toward the gain of personal salvation. But this must never become his sole concern, because he produces his own salvation only by serving the divine grace through his caring concern for others. The community does not attain blessedness by being concerned for nothing other than its own salvation but in such a way that it carries out its ministry which renders it merciful toward all. Even the persistent power of that hope which, not weakened by the passing of time, desires Christ's return with intense longing, flows to the community through love.

Love also becomes visible in the community's worship. Because love is first exercised toward God and Christ, the community sees its highest vocation in common worship. The documents make entirely clear that its fellowship was also prayer fellowship. Thus it became perfect. Every experience became an occasion for community thanksgiving, and in prayer, the community saw the means by which it sanctified all of its dealings with nature. Its entire ministry was based on petition. The norms the disciples had received through Jesus' prayer thereby remained in effect and provided worship likewise with its principle, that is, the love of God. The community's worship practices would have departed from love if they had become magic, claiming to subject God to the authority of the one who prays. But there is not a single word that introduces magic into the formal structure of Christian worship. Moreover, the community's worship practice would have been loveless also if they had been exercised merely as a show to exhibit piety. In this way its thought and will would have centered even in prayer only upon itself, consummating in self-contemplation and self-admiration. The community, however, sincerely called upon God in the expectation that its thanksgiving and its petition would be pleasing to him and be answered by his grace.

Because norms rooted in love shape worship practice, that practice had a strengthening rather than distracting effect on the other functions. The phrase "fellowship of cultic practice" is historically useless for the early church. It was not merely gathered for common prayer but served every human need, being concerned as seriously for the provision of food as for prayer. Even love for the brethren attained vigor and intensity by the application of sacrificial terminology to brotherly love (Phil. 4:18; Heb. 13:16).

How was the community set free from selfishness? It held to Jesus' word, and Jesus had been able to demonstrate that his will was good and not subject to selfish motives. He also awakened the good will in his disciples. Thus the core of the community consisted from the beginning in men who did not merely talk about love but who thought and acted in love. The baptized person therefore entered a community in which love was the common will and where everyone who became a part of it was touched by and united with love. In this regard as well it was of utmost importance that the community continually understood its relationship with the Christ and with God in terms of the cross. There it saw the selfless will which yields everything to God and to men, and in it it saw God's grace which gives Christ for the world, even though it rejects him. Because it believed in the one who died for humanity, it gained freedom from selfish motives.

A common will is accompanied by common feelings. Because the freedom concept shaped the community of believers, we cannot expect to find events or methods that are designed for the purpose of leveling everyone's emotions, and indeed there is no evidence for such a phenomenon in the New Testament. Nevertheless, the New Testament is pervaded by a strong commonality of feeling. Luke says regarding the early church that it cherished great joy, and this joy finds expression everywhere in the epistles. Peter expects the church of Asia Minor to be a rejoicing group; John instructs his congregation with a view to completing their joy, and Paul is able to describe his ministry by claiming that he is the one who facilitates the community's joy (Acts 2:46–47; 13:52; 20:24; 2 Cor. 1:24; 13:11; Rom. 15:13; Phil. 1:25; 4:4; 1 Pet. 1:8; 1 John 1:4). That the community consisted of those who exercised repentance and persevered in continual resistance against all evil did not inject into it a lugubrious mood, because it did not transform repentance into a meditation over ethical wretchedness. Liberation from evil remained what it was in Jesus' proclamation: a joyful work, for it was grounded in the fact that God's grace is given to man.[30]

But joy is united in all documents with a profound seriousness that is open to pain. After all, the community's ministry occupied it continually with people's deepest needs, with difficulties that pressed upon them in the ethical realm. To this was added the struggle in which the community found itself with its surrounding environment, and it did not cover up its gravity by shining hope. Therefore communion did not merely consist in the brethren's rejoicing with one another but also in their weeping with one another. The book of Acts is no jubilant song of triumph about the great things that have been achieved through the work of Paul; it rather brings to strong expression the gravity of the situation. Its view turns back to dying Israel and at the same time looks forward to Rome, fully conscious of how difficult the task was that Christendom faced there. Luke thus shared the Pauline perspective. For Paul, it was his joyful wish to come to Rome; but he grounds it in the somber picture of Gentile and Jewish need. The idea that his stay in Rome will bring him nothing but pleasure is out of the question; he wants to produce fruit, because man's need makes him his debtor. John gives as the reason for his perfect joy that he helps the community recognize the contrast between walking in the light and walking in darkness.

Thereby the community remained closed to an eudaemonistic version of the notion of blessedness. It did not tolerate a will that desired nothing but pleasure; it rather opened itself up to pain. Its ability to have at the same time both joy and pain was achieved by the community's refusal to allow feelings to rule over it. Emotions, be they of joy or pain, never became an end in themselves, to be lingered over contemplatively. Not even the strong feelings linked with pneumatic processes may be allowed to crowd onto center stage. For the community never redirected the aim of its devotion into its own circumstances but saw it above it-

30. Dour repentance entered the church only when God's kingdom had been eliminated from Jesus' message and repentance alone remained.

self in the glorification of the one whom it served. Therefore it was not controlled by its moods, rejoicing as if it did not rejoice and weeping as if it did not weep (1 Cor. 7:30). For it must do the work of the Lord. Whether the community performs it with joy or with pain was not its foremost concern. This vigorous emotional control belongs to the inner commonality that becomes the characteristic of the community. It considered its will to be the decisive aspect of its devotion, and its will was not selfish. It was rather love, which wants God's good will.

### d) Common Hope

Faithful to Jesus' word, the community kept the prophecy given to it by him until the end of the apostolic period. The only substantial expansion received by the community's vision of the future beyond the things already contained in Jesus' words is Paul's and John's teaching that Christ's return will be preceded by the rule of the antichrist. Through this the vision of the future reveals the profundity of the contrast existing between the world and God, between sin and God's rule. Thus a sentimental, eudaemonistic use of a hope that seeks to manufacture merely joy was rejected, and an impatience that was unable to wait was resisted. But the surrender of hope was thus rejected with equal resolve, hope that indulged in complacency on account of the religious successes that had already been attained and that no longer raised longing beyond the present. Because the most severe battle was still future, there was no room for illusions regarding the success already achieved by the church or yet to be achieved through further progress. But this did not hinder the joyful and believing appropriation of the promise which gains assurance of salvation by it. Neither in Paul nor in John can such an effect of the notion of the antichrist be observed. The explanation of this at first striking fact is that regarding its entire hope the community thought not merely of its own happiness and fulfillment of desires but of God's great plan, which is opposed by all forces of evil. If these unfold first, this does not cast doubt on the manifestation of divine glory.

In subsequent generations, harmful consequences attached to the hope of the early church, because believers, now without apostolic hope and thus sensing a chasm between the New Testament and themselves, relied in part on contrived imitations of apostolic expectations. But if the New Testament community is considered by itself, it can hardly be demonstrated that abnormal results arose from its hope.[31]

Paul strengthened his dynamic ministry with hope. Because the Lord is near, he sought to go all the way to Spain and to the emperor and was not already satisfied with his large ministry to the Greeks. It would be an abnormal effect of hope, if the expansion of his work had hindered its deepening, say, if he had traversed the world with a loud proclamation of the imminent parousia. But Paul devoted great diligence to the internal aspect of his work that impacts the personal lives of individuals. He remained free from artificialities or contrived

---

31. gnostic distortions did not arise from an exaggeration of hope. To the contrary, they stand in connection with the fact that hope became unattainable for later generations, so that the present was supposed to be enough for the absolute claims of the Christian message.

situations. In James, attention to ethical concerns is strengthened by his conviction that the Lord "stands already at the door." But attention to the ethical process provided James's message with its incomparable fruitfulness. In the Johannine conception of Christianity, the assessment of the history of the world that realizes the absolute contrast between God and the world and sees its solution in the imminent revelation of Christ results in a certain distance from works, because John does not speak of Christendom's missionary labors and even less of its participation in culture. But the same limitation is characteristic of Johannine thought also in John's Gospel, where one cannot speak of the priority of hope over all other functions but where rather faith placed in Christ shapes the entire train of thought as the dominant motif. At any rate, the turning away from concrete formulas of obligation is thus based in John's case not solely on eschatological ideas, and he richly substituted for any omission in this regard by not merely describing—and doing so with vigor—the form of will that produces all fruitful activity, that is, love, but by also exercising it, which made him forever one of the greatest teachers of true action.

## 4. Differences within the Church

### a) The Office Established for the Congregations

The community initially can be divided according to the Jewish model into the old and the young; the old were responsible to care for the community in word and deed (Acts 5:6; 11:30; 15:2; 1 Pet. 5:1–5; 1 Tim. 5:1, 17, 19). But because every community that seeks to accomplish serious work needs men who can act on its behalf, it provided itself with the office that comes into being through election and commission and that entails particular functions. The only account referring to the emergence of office is Luke's regarding the appointment of those caring for the poor in Jerusalem (Acts 6:1–6). It clearly indicates that the office was understood as service, as it was carefully tailored to fit the purpose of the community. In Luke, the apostles do not speak of a divine right or of Jesus' commandment that regulated the office in one way and not the other; they act in the conviction that the community has the authority and the obligation to order its affairs in such a way as would serve the fulfillment of its task. Even in the creation of offices, the community was borne along by the conviction that it acted in conjunction with God. Therefore the office was linked with an act of ordination that was conceived as valid and effective before God (Acts 6:6; 13:3; 1 Tim. 4:14; 2 Tim. 1:6). Significant was the division of the office into two levels, the episcopate and the diaconate, of whom one cared for the community's internal well-being, the other for the external well-being (Rom. 16:1; Phil. 1:1; 1 Tim. 3:13). Through the institution of the lower office, the respective value of both branches of labor was clearly indicated and confirmed in the consciousness of congregations. The office of overseer should be freed from external concerns, in order that he can devote himself fully to the community's highest calling.

Later church history suggests that for it the formation of office had its point of departure in the administration of the sacraments, because particularly strong holy statutes develop later from the sacrament, and its administration becomes the essential characteristic of offices. But the New Testament does not provide any information in this regard, and in later legislation a concept of sacrament was used that is foreign to the early period. The apostles do not appear as the uniquely privileged baptizers; likewise, Paul's account regarding the Corinthians' Lord's Supper mentions nothing regarding official office there.[32] The data provided by the book of Acts and the Pastorals regarding the office nowhere tie to it regulations regarding the celebration of the sacraments. Regarding baptism as well as the Lord's Supper, the congregation turns exclusively to the Lord, so that the external form of the celebration is not important in and of itself. Therefore the celebration of sacraments provided no particular occasion for the establishment of office. Baptism did not require a designated baptizer, because it becomes effective through the name of Christ, not through the one who baptizes. The need for the office rather emerged where a man was called to act for all according to his own mental faculties, with his wisdom and love. In the case of such actions, it was not unimportant who performed the service; rather, the one to be called was selected with diligence, and the selection is not repeated each time need arises but is rendered into a permanent mandate.

It also does not correspond to the foundational will that determined the community to think of the establishment of office exclusively or primarily in terms of the financial assets whose orderly administration required the appointment of office-holders. To be sure, the need for the office, without which no unified or equipped community can arise, surely also became rapidly and clearly evident. The significance that an unobjectionable, clear financial administration has for the trust and peace of the community was not overlooked by the apostles. But they always attributed to the community's financial resources only subordinate significance, considering them to be a means to be used for ends that are truly valuable. Its great, essential possession was the word, and Luke says explicitly that the office came into being for the administration of the word: the diaconate in order to release the men called to the administration of the word, and correspondingly the office of overseer in order that the men gifted for the administration of the word may at any time be ready to serve the community and to be supported in their work by an authority that was expressly assigned to them.

The inner formation of office was produced by the same perspectives that guided the apostles' conduct. Because the entire community is encompassed by God's rule, and because it enjoys Christ's presence, its office is likewise not grounded in a train of thought that is severed from God but is acknowledged as desired and used by God. The relationship to the office-holder is thus religious (1 Cor. 3:9; Heb. 13:17). God's government is operative through him in the congregation and upon the world, and God's word is through him told to the

---

32. The deaconate is confirmed by Rom. 16:1, which sheds light on the Corinthian congregation of that time; but it is improbable that there ever was an office of deacon without there also being the office of overseer.

believer as well as to the one who is urged to repent. This lends the office its greatness.

Another idea is inseparably linked with this, that is, that the office must not depreciate the community or hinder its activity. It is therefore not exercised as rule in the sense of pagan rulership. The mandate given to the office and the calling issued to the community do not stand in conflict with one another but are carried out simultaneously through unified collaboration. The overseer's obligation to ensure proper proclamation therefore does not render the community silent; it retains the right to speak the word freely. Its missionary mandate is based not only on the office-holder; every believer has a part, as he is given the opportunity by his life circumstances (Col. 3:16; 1 Tim. 2:8; 2 Tim. 2:2; 1 Pet. 3:15). The community's sinking into passivity, consoled by the fact that the office-holder had been called to do the work, could arise only when the community itself did without its share in God's Spirit and eliminated the messianic conception from Jesus' commission. As long as he was sincerely believed to be the Lord of all, relationship with him issued in the obligation for all to serve, and as long as the Spirit was considered to be the gift given to all, all participated not merely in terms of receiving but also in terms of giving energetically to the work of the community.

Therefore in the apostolic period no limiting effect was entailed with the mandate given to the office, so that an office-bearer was restricted to a certain function or a given function to an office-bearer. The deacon initially had to care for concerns assigned to him, but this does not mean that he was kept from preaching. Even as a deacon he retained his full Christian privileges, which he could exercise now with particular effectiveness because he was honored as a valuable member of the community through his appointment to office (Acts 6:8; 8:5).

It is more difficult to lead a community awarded a considerable degree of flexibility than one that is bound by regulations and established custom. The documents point not infrequently to these difficulties (1 Cor. 16:15–16; 1 Thess. 5:12–13; 1 Pet. 5:5; Heb. 13:17; 1 Tim. 4:12; Titus 2:15). But this never gives rise to the idea that the carrying out of one's office may be made easier by taking over the work of the community from it or by relegating it to mere passivity; for thus truthfulness and love would be removed from the community. It is therefore maintained that the appointed offices with their various functions do not rupture the community's unity but rather are designed to strengthen it. It is curious how exclusively the documents address the community as a unity, even though one might have expected a discussion of how its circumstances had been produced by the conduct of its various members and how the commands given to them are to be carried out through the working together of its members. But the writers' thoughts never turn in this direction; they operate under the presupposition that the community finds its way easily in this regard. As one entire organism it sees its task in maintaining a clear vision of its obligation. Apart from this, the office would depend merely on compulsion and external influence. This would render the community's goal unattainable.

The selfless nature of the office is also apparent from the fact that it is unpaid. Of course, one who works for the congregation has the right to receive its sustenance from it, and the congregation's ungratefulness in this regard would amount to mockery of God (1 Cor. 9:4–14; Gal. 6:6–7). But when gnostic teachers charged for their religious services, Paul saw in this a major sign of degeneration (1 Tim. 6:5–10), because he feared that now the pollution of work through selfish motives could no longer be prevented and the incomparable nature of the divine gift in relation to natural goods was obscured.

The community received great flexibility for all of its tasks through this constitution. It determined the means by which it could attain its aim in particular circumstances, not according to a fixed rule but on a case-by-case basis through reasonable considerations. The shaping of the office in relation to the community also indicates that it was subject to Jesus' rule of love. Its constitution was based on the fact that all self-exaltation at the expense of others' humiliation was abolished and the well-being of all was sought with all one's strength.

The pneumatics were distinguished from the bearers of the congregational office in that they were set apart from the community by an experience that remained independent from human decision. Prophecy did not arise through election or ordination; here authority was attached directly to God's gift, which determined the prophet's internal experience. Therefore there was no expectation of dispute between the pneumatics and the bearers of the congregational office, because opposition toward the pneumatics would in effect result in opposition toward the Spirit and toward God, and opposition toward the overseers would divide the congregation. The overseer can only wish that the gifts of the Spirit are amply manifested in the community, and his own work attains its purpose with all the more certainty the richer the community is in pneumatics. Only the interference of a selfish passion that gives rise to false notions of rulership rendered the pneumatics a danger for the community in Corinth and later led to the overseer turning against the prophet (2 Cor. 11:20; 1 Tim. 3:1; Titus 1:11; 1 Pet. 5:3). If enthusiastic conceptions were attached to pneumatic processes, tensions between the pneumatics and the bearers of the word and thus also the bearers of the office, which was first and foremost engaged in the preservation of the word, were inevitable. For the overcoming of the conscious life through mantic excess stood in contradiction with its preservation and strengthening through the obedience and faith offered to God in voluntary love. Hence arose the apostle's dispute with the gnostic "spirit."

In relation to the pneumatics, too, equality in the community was preserved by requiring the community to examine and sift the prophetic words (1 Thess. 5:19–21; 1 Cor. 12:10; 14:29–33; 1 John 4:1–3). If the prophet has the Spirit, the congregation has him as well, and as it honors God in him, so he honors God among them. This passage is particularly instructive regarding how foreign a self-centered notion of authority was for the early church. The community is rather expressly reminded of the fact that temptation ensued from the strong elevation of the self-consciousness that accompanied prophetic experience. Out of this, deep rifts in one's inner life easily arise. Thus mention is frequently made of false prophets. Matthew already makes warning against false prophets part of the Sermon on the Mount, thus including it among Jesus' basic message, which is as much a part of the obligation of a disciple as the warning against worthless faith or mere hearing of the word. The gnostic movement created numerous processes that were judged to be false prophecy by Paul and John (Matt. 7:15–20; 1 John 4:1; Rev. 2:20; 2 Cor. 12:1–9). The tendency toward arrogance that can emerge from a sense of union with God became particularly dangerous when it was heightened to the consciousness of being set apart to a prophetic calling. The boundary between artificial excitement and genuine impulse, between imitation and experience, between selfish desires and subservient listening to divine instruction, was easily transgressed and remained preserved only when an essentially pure will guided the prophet internally in a pure state of faith. He, too, was subject to Paul's requirement for the office-holder: that he administer the mystery of the faith in a pure conscience (1 Tim. 3:9; cf. Rom. 12:7).

It was not required of the office-holder that he be a pneumatic. For the gifts and abilities which the pneumatic was granted served particular purposes and were of limited value; they were not part and parcel of what it means to be a Christian. Thus they superseded on the one hand the functions that must be fulfilled continually, so that Paul here applied a kind of order in which he put those who were gifted to govern the community at the end of the list (1 Cor. 12:28; Rom. 12:7–8). But this did not constitute a violation of the principle that the congregation required particularly an instruction regarding those activities which make up the state of everyone's Christianity. Therefore its office-holders were selected from Christians, not from those who brought to it particular revelation. It is clear, then, that these gifts were not continually present. To be sure, once a prophet had received prophetic illumination, he was expected to receive it again at a later point. The designation of prophet was attached to the person, not merely to individual processes, consistent with the fact that the Spirit's activity pertained to the conscious, personal life of his recipient. Nevertheless, the liberty of the divine will was continually kept in mind, and the conception did not exist that charisma consisted in an uninterrupted sequence of uniform experiences. Regarding the prophet, it was not presupposed that everything he uttered was prophecy; now the Spirit moved him, but later he might not. Whoever received the gift of healing did thereby not receive the ability of healing always and everywhere. Now it was granted him to bring help, another time it was not. But congregational leadership required what constituted its continual possession and its persistent work.

### b) Those Who Renounced Possessions or Marriage

Another group that stood out in the community through particular actions were those who renounced their possessions and gave them to the community, living in voluntary poverty or foregoing marriage (Acts 4:34–5:5; 1 Cor. 7; Matt. 19:12). But no privileges ensued from this in apostolic times, by which those who renounced their possessions or marriage were exalted above the community. It goes without saying that the one who gave his possessions to the community was thanked and that his gift was always remembered. But beyond this, he could not demand anything further from the community; it was rather part of his decision that he would from now on live from his work and that he would not now himself count on the community's welfare.[33] The one who avoids marriage likewise will be honored by the community like anyone who separates himself sincerely from evil.

This esteem for renunciation suggests that the merit concept had been entirely removed from the community. The path had been cleared for any sacrifice that repentance and love will to offer. There was no desire for a uniform average conduct, and therefore a courageous deed, incapable of being imitated by others and certainly not expected of all, was still acknowledged in its own right and the principle of liberty dealt with seriously. This, however, did not jeopardize the community's unity. The same basic principle applied to those with and those without possessions, to the unmarried and the married: in Christ, they had their relationship with God, and this relationship consisted in faith in him. This resulted in the rule that regulated the use of material possessions for each individual: whatever strengthened or hindered the state of faith which had been entered and made fruitful by works became blessing or curse for a man. This is why the generation that heard, with an obedience second to none, Jesus' word to the rich young ruler and his praise for the widow who gave her all for God nonetheless did not produce any ascetic regulations.[34] And it placed the renunciation of marriage, along with national and social differences, Jewishness or Hellenism, slavery or citizenship, all under the rule of liberty (1 Cor. 7:17–24, 29–31).

The absence of veneration for those who renounced their possessions, a veneration oriented around the merit concept, prevented them from being placed above or beside the rest of the community as a separate group of people. Such an order is nowhere apparent.[35] This did not preclude, however, that their influence on the community as a whole was profound. Events such as Ananias's renunciation under pretense illustrate this influence and show how it could be observed already in the example of the pneumatics. The variety of religious developments found in the community confronted it with a major challenge that could be met only through the utilization of all ethical faculties. Fictions and imitations come to the fore; it becomes a serious obligation to protect what is genuine. The beneficent effect flowing from those who renounced their possessions to the whole community consisted in the liberating incentive they imparted to all, strengthening their ability to do without certain things. Regarding outsiders, the courage to renunciation exercised by the community acted as a deterrent, as far as they were materially oriented. That the poor made up a large portion of the Jerusalem church hardly can account for their willingness to sacrifice, because it would have caused the economic circumstances of the community to deteriorate. It likely had more to do with the fact that the rich shied away from entering a community that viewed wealth as danger rather than a blessing.

Hope for Christ's return strengthened the zeal for renunciation; this is also evident in Paul's discussion of the unmarried state. But the movement is misin-

33. Whoever renounces in the appropriate fashion "is poor and makes many rich": 2 Cor. 6:10.
34. An ascetic law did not exist even for the apostolic circle: 1 Cor. 9:5–6.
35. I do not agree with the interpretation of 1 Cor. 7:25–38 that views the young women and those who marry them as ascetics.

terpreted in the same way as Jesus' call to repentance[36] if it is conceived as the pessimistic converse of eschatology, as contempt of the present and its goods on account of the imminent transformation of the world. The apostles' hope increased the significance of the present for them rather than lessening it, and it produced activity, not apathy or passivity. The community did not sink into a despondent waiting for the end, because the present time was evil. That it resisted those tendencies in the assessment of sexual passion and of material possessions is due to the clarity it arrived at regarding the ethical dilemmas linked with these. Its renunciation stands in connection with the word of repentance. This is also confirmed by the tradition regarding the ascetic pronouncements of Jesus, which are all tied to the notion of repentance. The living nature of hope provided strength for defense against evil and facilitated the foregoing of earthly goods in the same way it provided strength for all of the community's works.

### c) Martyrs

The community's verdict regarding martyrs coheres precisely with what can be observed regarding the position of those who renounced their possessions or marriage. The longing for voluntary death for Jesus' sake, by which love to God is rendered complete, strongly comes to the fore, and its value is increased when it is linked with a public confession of Jesus' regal status which urges the hearers to a decision. Whoever fulfills this calling is honored by the Lord and the community (Acts 7; Rev. 2:13; John 21:19; cf. Phil. 2:30). But this did not lead to two classes of Christians, martyrs and ordinary Christians. Believers live unto the Lord as they die unto him, and the work done for him during their lifetime is not made lower than the confession that is sealed by death. The community did not pray for Peter's "completion" through martyrdom but for his release, and Paul was considered Jesus' chosen instrument not because he was beheaded but because he became the teacher of the nations. The notion that martyrdom is the best guarantee of salvation is never what gives rise to Christian longing for death; martyrdom is not based on the depreciation of life but rather is united with a strong sense of the severity of death. This sense is not only characteristic of the account of Jesus' crucifixion; it also comes to light in the disciples' anticipation of their own martyrdom. In view of his execution Paul reminded himself and his friends of the highest ground of faith in order to gain from it calm composure. For this reason also all means of defending one's life are circumspectly used, as long as this can be done without violating one's conscience.

This situation likewise reveals the perfect faith that guided the community in all its judgments. If its faith had been unsure of itself, martyrdom would have been esteemed as a valuable sign guaranteeing the receipt of salvation. But no such attention was paid to the hour of death in New Testament devotion, because faith was not gained by individual signs designed to provide the community with an assurance of divine grace. It gained this assurance by Christ, and because it possessed faith through him, it also had the obligation and the ability to die for him, because it cannot deny him. But it did not ground faith only in

---

36. See *The History of the Christ,* 171.

particular experiences in the moment of death but possessed joy that was ready to die, because it had faith and preserved it until the end.

### d) Jewish and Gentile Christianity

Jesus' verdict regarding Judaism remained the rule which the disciples obeyed in directing the message of repentance to the Jews. Because of this, their message did not confront the Jews merely with their enmity toward Jesus but primarily with their sin of rebellion against the testimony of God given to them. By rejecting Jesus, they resist the divine work that provided their community with its existence, combat the Christ promised to them, refuse faith in the Scriptures given to them, and break the Law given to them. They destroy with their hands the existence of the holy nation that had been established through God's previous revelation. The stance of this call to repentance, however, demanded from Christendom that it give clear expression to and continually cultivate its fellowship with the Jewish people's devotion. It adhered to this obligation by considering itself to be the true Israel not despite its condemnation of Judaism but because of it, apart from any improper calculation or accommodation. The dual verdict regarding the relationship between the old and the new communities[37] remained therefore in effect throughout the entire apostolic period. When Paul provided the community with the metaphor of the olive tree into which believing Gentiles were grafted, he directly conceived of the Christian community as a unit together with Israel; it is the true Israel led to righteousness whose founding occurred not only through Jesus and even less only through the Gentile mission. At the same time, he gave vigorous expression to the newness of the community, which came into being because Jesus created a new man who is neither Jew nor Gentile (on the one hand, Rom. 11:17–24; Eph. 3:6; on the other hand, Eph. 2:15). Similarly, John sharply expressed the separation of Christendom from the synagogue, which now had become a community of Satan, at the same time portraying the unity of the community which reaches beyond Jesus' work into God's earlier revelation. For through that revelation the perfect community of the twelve tribes came into being, and the sanctuary in Jerusalem belonging to God has been rendered indestructible. This explains why the heavenly Jerusalem shows the names of the twelve patriarchs to be linked with those of Jesus' twelve disciples (on the one hand, Rev. 2:9; 3:9; John 8:44; on the other hand, Rev. 7:4; 12:1; 11:1; 21:12, 14).

The consideration of whether or not the disciples rendered their own work more difficult by failing to free their opposition to Judaism from all limitations has no room in a historical analysis of events. One may attribute a certain amount of probability to the theory that it may have had greater success if it had completely broken with the synagogue, eliminating any possibility of mediation, because a protest accompanied by respect weakens its thrust. But for the disciples, there were in this question no considerations that made a first priority out of success. Their relationship with Judaism could not be determined by calculations regarding how the success of Christian proclamation might be en-

37. See p. 41.

hanced or lessened, or how the preservation and victory of their community might become easier or more difficult. They were bound by the truth. They must not deny the God of Israel, must not denigrate his work upon the old community or throw away Scripture, and likewise must not obscure the point at which Jesus' dispute with Judaism arose. They must not permit Judaism the illusion that it served God in obedience and that it had what made a Jew truly a Jew. What thereby became of the church was not the disciples' concern. If they were no longer truthful in their judgment, no longer exercised righteousness, no longer honored God in all his works, and no longer showed love to all whom Christ had told them to love, the greatest success became a fall into corruption. If now Judaism rejected Jesus for Moses' sake, this corresponded to Jesus' prediction that new tenants of the vineyard would be appointed. He could produce true and eternal success only through the manifestation of his rule.

Of course, an internal weakening or loosening of the kind of fellowship that Christendom cultivated among itself was possible if it simultaneously also participated in Jewish worship and continued fellowship with Judaism.[38] That Christendom nonetheless existed as a separate fellowship reveals how deliberate and resolute it was in its appreciation of its relationship with Christ as of utmost and decisive value for the destiny of man. For this reason it was able to believe in Jesus without judging Judaism in an unbelieving way, to praise him without abusing those who rejected him, to love those united with them as brothers in the name of Jesus without despising their opponents. They were enabled to exercise a love that did not require hate to be strong, and to remain firm in their own circle even though the community was not clearly delineated for those outside.

In firm allegiance to Jesus' own ministry, the disciples addressed the calling to the entire nation, albeit in the assurance that fellowship with Christ brought about the "separation from this perverse generation" and the establishment of a remnant from it. But conversion is preached to the whole of Israel, to the community in its entirety. Thus thousands are baptized in rapid succession (Acts 2:41; 4:4). It was therefore considered indispensable and produced a major turning point in the community's history that and how the testimony regarding Christ was brought before the great Sanhedrin, how thus the leaders of the community viewed Jesus (Acts 4; 5:17–18; 7; the same idea controls the account of Paul in chaps. 23 and 26). Not merely one Jew or the other must convert but all Israel is urged to turn to the Christ. The same view of ministry is expressed by the declaration of Peter and Paul that Peter was sent to the circumcised (Gal. 2:9). Individual Jews are not juxtaposed with individual Gentiles, but the old community, which is described according to its dignity as the possessor of divine election by circumcision, is considered to be the field of ministry the disciples cannot afford to dispense with. Paul's principle of always directing his preaching first to the synagogue likewise did not arise from the consideration that individuals may be found there who might be receptive to his word; he rather honored the community as a whole as the one that had first been called to Christ.

38. James reveals such conditions: see pp. 92–93.

Regarding Judaism, mission was not limited to certain groups in the nation. No one was charged with unforgivable guilt, no one judged as not in need of conversion. Rather, the universal scope characterizing Jesus' own work was continued by the community, so that it accepted and united the Pharisee and the tax-collector within its ranks. In light of the outcome of Jesus' work it would not be surprising if the disciples had rejected Pharisaism, considering it condemned and excluded from Christ's calling. But such a break with the universal scope of the attestation of divine grace was completely avoided. To be sure, the Gospels, particularly Matthew, but also the narrative preserved by Luke as well as John, reveal how diligently the disciples remembered Jesus' dispute with Pharisaism. But they show no less that they sought to evangelize the Pharisees among all Jewish groups with particular urgency, demanding nothing but that they forsake what was sinful in their sect. The principle of liberty which was granted to all, as long as they acted in faith toward Christ, was not violated even with regard to Pharisaism. It received the right and the space in the community to tithe cummin and scrupulously to clean the outside of its cup, as long as it submitted to Christ. Pharisaism was therefore for the apostolic mission at the same time the place of its greatest successes and the scene of its most intense controversies (successes: Acts 15:1; 21:20; controversy: 7:57). The same universal dimension in the presentation of the gospel to the entire community subjected to the Law manifested itself in the fact that the disciples were able already at the very beginning to overcome the separation of Jews and Samaritans and to unite both parts to one church (Acts 8:5–17).

But the call to repentance could not be continued indefinitely; it called to decision. In the end, the Jews' conduct made it clear that as a nation they rejected the disciples' message. When Paul wrote the epistle to the Romans, this was an assured fact (Rom. 9–11; similarly Luke: see Acts 28:25–28). The disciples in Jerusalem may have clung to hope for the old community a bit longer, James perhaps until his death. But the Gospels and the Apocalypse indicate that regarding Israel even the Twelve judged that Christ had been proclaimed to it in vain and the time of Jerusalem was now past.

That the way to the Gentiles was opened up for the church through the battle regarding the Law reveals once again the lofty heights to which Jesus elevated his disciples. In keeping with customary analogies of history it might have been expected that national self-centeredness fought vehemently for Israel's privilege. Of course, only omniscient eyes can be certain whether these motives were secretly at work in the struggle regarding the Law. But we are confronted in the New Testament documents with the fact that the question was never asked in terms of what lay in Israel's interest, how the primacy of one's own nation could be secured and its honor and power be increased. The question was only: What is right before God, and what does his Law require (Acts 10:14; 15:1)? It becomes clear also at this moment that the disciples' repentance did not consist in words but that it sincerely subjected them to God. The love of God did not free them merely from personal but also from national self-centeredness, providing them with readiness to obey God in everything.

Up to this point, the Gentile had been separated from the community and from God through the Law. Could this separation be lifted without the Law taking effect for him? Was there a lawlessness other than lostness, another conversion to Christ than one that subjected the baptized person to the Law? And if it was possible for a law-free community of believing Gentiles to exist, could Jesus' messengers have dealings with them? Without transgression of the Law it was impossible to embark on a Gentile mission. Could a Jewish man enter complete fellowship with Gentiles—apart from which he cannot bring them the gospel—without committing sin? If the result were not to be two separate churches, the community living under the Law must be set free from it as well, and in such a way that dealing with law-free Christians did not become sin for it.

The solution to this question was found in Jesus' cross and in the repentance that issued from it for all of Christendom. This also constituted a turning away from the Law, a negative verdict regarding the value of the worship service rendered according to the Law. Such worship was, according to the judgment of Christendom, no longer righteousness, no longer merit. Salvation was found for all solely through faith in Christ, even for those who kept all statutes of the Law in complete obedience. Early Christendom did not effect a separation from Judaism or the obliteration of its custom, but it was clear that participation in God and his grace could be gained by nothing other than commitment to the Christ alone. Thus the concept of mediation, which determined God's relationship with man, had become new; this mediation is now exercised by Christ and no longer the Law. The more this conviction gained currency, the more easily and assured was the transition to the Gentile mission. Righteousness confers on man the will of Jesus, not the will of the Law. Herein lay the ability to do Jesus' will even when it transcended the Law, leading to the formation of a community that was based solely on him.

For this reason the need to experience Jesus' will through his own testimony was great, and this was made possible through experiences of the apostles that imparted to them in particular cases the command to the Gentile mission. It was of particular importance for the entire community that Peter had received such a command (Acts 10); but Paul likewise possessed the determined consciousness of being sent to the nations (Rom. 1:5; 15:18; Eph. 3:1–8; Acts 22:21). The natural course of events was not ignored in this regard; even in this question Christendom knew nothing of a postulate that divine guidance must occur exclusively by supernatural means. When persecution expelled the Christians of Jerusalem who were of Gentile origin and thus brought them in contact with Gentiles in Greek cities, the divine guidance was recognized also in this with gratitude and full assurance. But the community was thereby confirmed in its certainty that it did not lack prophetic experiences that confirmed this evaluation of events and expressly placed its overstepping of the bounds of the Law (as understood by current tradition) squarely within God's good pleasure.

From Hellenism, Israel had borrowed the conceits of sages, the concept of righteous merit, nationalistic fanaticism and the presumption that God would raise Israel to world rulership. Out of this milieu arose Jesus' cross, and thus this mixture of devotion and lack of piety, glorification of man and glorification of God, was judged. Now the possibility of proclamation to the Gentiles that could truly be successful had been created, of preaching that bore effective testimony of Israel's God to the Gentiles. Through the cross of Christ the struggle against Jewish and Gentile sin alike got underway, so that preaching to the Gentiles no longer resulted in a mere mixture of Gentile and Jewish elements, and God's judgment regarding Gentiles and Jews at the same time revealed God's grace to all. Moreover, the cross of Christ made possible a faith that sincerely grounded the life of both in God's grace. Thus Jesus' cross became a turning point in history, and the penetration of the Jewish world by Hellenism was now followed by the church's penetration of the Gentile world.

But even when it was given to the Gentiles, the gospel remained the calling to repentance. The entire Gentile exercise of religion was thereby not merely rejected but rejected as sin. The Gentile drew near to the Christ only by doing away with whatever he had thought about God and gods up to this point and by submitting to a new God who had thus far been unknown. This turnaround to which he was led, however, was never considered to be a mere progress in knowledge that brought an end to previous ignorance; rather, it took on the seriousness of repentance. The previous condition was condemned as straying from God and as judged by God, while in Christ's call God's reconciling grace also turned to the Gentile. For this reason the conversion of the Gentiles had immediately also a definite ethical connotation, because he thereby rejected whatever he recognized to be sinful, gaining a new will by following the Christ.

But it lay in the nature of the Gentile mission that faith must be identified clearly as the goal of proclamation, not merely by Paul, but everywhere among the Gentiles (Paul, John, Luke, Peter, Mark). This became necessary already because the Gentile, in contrast to the Jew, did not yet know faith in his relationship with the deity. Frequently, he had no conviction whatsoever regarding God; his conception was determined merely by custom, without any opinion or will of his own, or he fell into doubt in view of the manifold, varying traditions of his religion. He must be told that faith is the goal of the proclamation of Christ. It seeks to form the conviction in him that grows into certainty, and where faith is, there is grace; through faith, he has been placed in communion with God.

The act by which a person entered the community thus remained in the Gentile realm the same as in Jerusalem: baptism in the name of Christ, through which repentance received its fulfillment by forgiveness and by which faith obtained its confirmation through the pledge of communion with Christ and the Holy Spirit. This made Christendom, whether Jewish or Gentile in origin, a unity. All were converts, that is, converts to faith in the Christ, who recognized by faith in Jesus that experience which was decisive for God's relationship with them.

That the community was able to overcome the opposition between Jew and Gentile provided faith in Jesus' lordship with strongly felt confirmation. With visible clarity this lordship inaugurated in the present a process which hope had up to this point relegated to the end times. Christ brought an end to the separation between the two previously utterly disparate religions and nations, and the "new man" arose who was neither Jew nor Gentile but received his life principle from Christ. This was the fruit of faith and thus its affirmation and confirmation.

The condition for the unification of the Gentile congregations with the Palestinian church was that they completely reject Gentile ritual. When in earlier times culture or philosophy had replaced ancient religion, religious forms were generally retained, because Gentile ritual made no claims whatsoever on the faith of those who participated in it. If Christians had still occasionally taken part in sacrifices, this would have met with numerous precedents in the religious history of the Greek cities. But any ritual held in common with Hellenism was rejected from the beginning. The decision in Jerusalem regarding the stance to be taken toward the Gentile church maintains that whoever eats meat sacrificed to idols has departed from Christendom (Acts 15:28–29; Rev. 2:14, 20; 1 Cor. 10). From that point on, the basic principle that Christianity brought an end to the exercise of Greek religion possessed the firmness of an unshakeable axiom, although it entailed severe struggle with the Roman state, eventuating in martyrdom.

The Lord's Supper made a powerful contribution to Christendom's complete separation from pagan religions. It is no coincidence that Paul showed the Corinthians by it the impossibility of participating additionally in some sacrifice (1 Cor. 10:14–22). The Lord's Supper had this effect not merely because it provided the church with a ritual act comparable to the sacrifices of other rituals, providing it with a characteristic that distinguished it from these and closely united it within its own circle. Rather, the act was suited also on account of its internal content to provide the community with self-contained independence, because it describes Christ's fellowship with believers as total, so that it does not permit room for any love other than to Christ. Whoever ate the body of Christ and drank his blood belonged to Christ alone. Therefore it becomes an unshakeable principle that whoever participates in Jesus' table says farewell to all other rituals, while whoever still participates in these has no access to Jesus' table.

The Gentiles thus received a completely new religious custom through their entrance into the community. It was in all its aspects consciously and exclusively Christian. The danger of a sliding into sectarian decline that accompanied the uniting of believers into a firm association was overcome here with the same means by which Jewish Christendom had eluded it. The universal aim of divine grace is retained in the church's dealings with all, prayer is offered to God for all men, and natural contact with Gentiles is not forsaken. While relationships in the community are entirely subject to ethical norms, they are not applied in the community's dealings with outsiders; their sin must be borne patiently and overlooked. The Christian husband remains married to the Gentile, the Christian slave continues to serve the Gentile. Regarding believers' dealings with the state and the city, the principle applies that Christendom is prepared for every good work (1 Tim. 2:1–7; 1 Cor. 5:9–10; Titus 3:1).

In the ethical arena, Christendom laid decisive emphasis on the purification of sexual morality. Intercourse with a prostitute amounts to separation from

Christendom (Acts 15:29; Rev. 2:14, 20).[39] The implementation of the rule of chastity required a hard struggle against Oriental and Greek conventions. These surface also in the gnostic movement, which sought to solve the problem either through asceticism or the removal of ethical regulations altogether. The community evidenced a high degree of wisdom in the formation of custom. In the assessment of pagan marriage it remains free from Pharisaic exaggeration, which does not recognize any real marriage in the case of Gentiles. The marriage of Greeks likewise is honored as marriage and traced back to the divine creation order, which cannot be destroyed by human sin. With similar caution existing law is not set aside regarding the issue of slavery, while in people's personal dealings the slave's equal status with the master is affirmed.

The new ethical challenges were also accompanied by changes in the state of faith. The Hellenization of Christianity began already with the beginnings of the Gentile mission, and it would be foolish to call it (as some do) a calamity that happened to Christianity. The apostles called Gentiles to God as Gentiles, just as they called the Jews as Jews, and they condemned the Gentiles' sin, not their being Gentile, just as they also condemned sin in the Jews, not what made them Jewish.

A strong emphasis on doctrine was inevitable in the Gentile realm, already because more must be learned and taught here than where Jesus was added to Moses and the prophets as the greatest of God's messengers. The Gentile had to be introduced to the Old Testament canon, which the Jew already knew full well, and the entire conceptual world of which the gospel consisted, that is, God's kingdom, Christ, the Holy Spirit, which already possessed rich content for the Jew, must be corrected and confirmed solely through the knowledge of Jesus. This required considerably more intellectual labor from the Gentiles. All Christian terms must be newly conceptualized here from scratch and be communicated within the framework of existing conceptual categories. This extended to the simplest decisions of conscience. The epistles show how successful this work was, because they attest in the congregations to a level of knowledge that by far exceeds that of subsequent generations. What contributed to this result was that the congregations everywhere during the initial period still had a Jewish component, which provided a firm core for doctrine and custom. This appears in the canon in the fact that Luke is the only born Gentile among the New Testament authors, and the same fact is also evident in that not only the Pharisaic but also the gnostic adaptation of Christianity was initially undertaken by Christian Jews. Moreover, the internal nature and completeness of the community's fellowship was of great significance for its doctrinal labor. Instruction was not just meagerly doled out and sought; rather, the fellowship of believers rendered the exchange open and complete. This resulted in the possibility of providing all rapidly and successfully with what the community had to offer and to preserve and multiply it. In the Greek cities, the cultivation of teaching was of particular

---

39. The third point of the apostolic decree, the prohibition of the drinking of blood, is important primarily because of what it allowed rather than what it prohibited. Now there were no other food laws for Christendom.

significance, because in their population the desire to understand, the habit of doubt, and the effort to acquire a large, systematic way of thinking were more widespread than elsewhere. Moreover, a powerful rationalistic tendency still prevailed, which judged and explained everything by the few ideas that were available. In these communities, faith could be neither established nor guarded from confusion apart from the ability to impart material and help for knowledge. The significance of theology within the sphere of ecclesiastical functions grew.

Much in early Christian preaching remained foreign to Greek thought. While the phrase "the anointed king" immediately revealed to the Jew a concept whose value he did not doubt, because he received his entire religious heritage through his ethnic identity and expected God's greatest gift only by its fulfillment, the messianic thought remained empty for the Greek. Already Paul and more clearly John indicate the way by which the fundamental element of the Christian message gained significance for the Greek. If he saw in Jesus the Son of God, Jesus gained significance also for him; then Jesus' messianic identity received also for him the importance of a divine act that revolutionizes the course of the world. On the other hand, what belonged to Jesus' national identity, his concern and work for Israel, this required an explanation for the Gentile. Even with explanation it always remained only half intelligible to him. Even the strong influence exercised by the explanation of Jesus' work in terms of priesthood in the Gentile church is connected with the difficulty posed for the Gentiles with the Christ concept.

While in the Jewish realm hope was directed toward the end of world history, longing for the completion of the community called by God, the Gentile church had to take great pains to begin to learn to view human history as a unity and to identify its goal. In contrast, it resonated with the promise given to the individual, the promise of immortality. But when the community's hope changes, its entire devotion is altered.

Moreover, completeness of the fellowship that had been established among believers by the confession of Christ in the early church was loosened in the Gentile sphere. Already in the Pauline congregations, the bearers of gnostic devotion gave higher priority to their individual aims than work for the community, and in this they were supported by the strong traditions of Greek ethics. Yet, for Greeks the Hellenistic *polis* served as a model for how a community could be established. Here, however, community was grounded not in the faith or love of its members but in the authority of its leaders and in the law that ordered doctrine and ritual from the outside.

Finally and especially, in the Jewish realm the idea of a personal God was the fundamental conviction that controlled everyone's consciousness. In contrast, Greek tradition and science led to the tendency to explain the content of Jesus' message through natural analogies—to conceive of God as substance, the Spirit of God as a power, and the conversion of man to God as a natural process. Thereby theology, which produces knowledge of these processes, became the means of redemption, and the church became a salvific institution, granting redeeming teachings and powers to mankind. The sacrament then came to be presented as the chief means of conveying these blessings.

Thus new challenges arose with the community's taking root among the Gentile peoples. This serves as the clearest and richest explanation of the fact that the work of the next generation did not follow that of the early church as a straight line but transitioned into different paths with notable divergence. From the tension existing between the original proclamation of Jesus' lordship and Hellenized Christianity there resulted, right up until now, both the weakening of the church and the perpetual impulse driving it forward to new formations.

# Modern Reception of Schlatter's New Testament Theology

## Robert W. Yarbrough

To assess current reception of Schlatter's New Testament theology, first of all several misconceptions need to be identified. Otherwise, present consideration may be hampered by past misunderstanding. A number of commonly encountered opinions about Schlatter are somewhat skewed. For example, George Ladd linked Schlatter directly to the Erlangen school. But this view has almost nothing to commend it.[1] Leonhard Goppelt rightly notes that connections between Schlatter and Erlangen are formal and not genetic.[2] James Dunn and

---

1. *A Theology of the New Testament*, rev. ed. (Grand Rapids: Eerdmans, 1993), 4. Cf. D. A. Carson, "Current Issues in New Testament Theology," *Bulletin for Biblical Research* 5 (1995): 21 n. 15. Carson claims that J. C. K. von Hofmann's "influence on Schlatter was significant." Hofmann (1810–77) may be regarded as the founder of the so-called Erlangen school. Carson may be following a recurrent and ill-founded Barthian charge that thinkers like Cullmann, Schlatter, and Hofmann are tainted by an illicit philosophical idealism, a charge epitomized in K. G. Steck, *Die Idee der Heilsgeschichte: Hofmann—Schlatter—Cullmann*, Theologische Studien 56 (Zollikon-Zurich: Theologischer Verlag, 1959). Underscoring the distance between Schlatter and Erlangen-style conceptions of *Heilsgeschichte* is e.g. E. Güting, "Zu den Voraussetzungen des systematischen Denkens Adolf Schlatters," *Neue Zeitschrift für systematische Theologie* 15 (1973): 132–47, esp. 147 n. 80. It is telling that "Hofmann" does not even occur in the index of the new and massive Schlatter biography by Werner Neuer, *Adolf Schlatter: Ein Leben für Theologie und Kirche* (Wuppertal: R. Brockhaus, 1996). This underscores the lack of any direct connection between Schlatter and Hofmann, even if features of their work vis-à-vis more secularly minded scholars are comparable. Schlatter evenhandedly criticizes both the (liberal) Ritschlian and (conservative) Erlangen theologies in *Rückblick auf meine Lebensarbeit* (Stuttgart: Calwer, [2]1977), 158.

2. Leonhard Goppelt, *Theology of the New Testament*, vol. 1, trans. John E. Alsup, ed. Jürgen Roloff (Grand Rapids: Eerdmans, 1981), 278–79.

James Mackey seem to imply that Schlatter's distinctive is that he used the New Testament to "do" conservative theology.[3] This is a distortion, not least because "conservative" is at best a vague and crude characterization of Schlatter's theological outlook.[4] Moreover, it overlooks the fact that the majority of Schlatter's major scholarly works were rigorously philological and historical, not theological as Dunn and Mackey use the term. To imply that Schlatter primarily exploited the New Testament for conservative theological purposes suggests unfamiliarity with the full Schlatter corpus.

The only English-language monograph yet to appear on Schlatter tries to depict him as postmodern before there was such a thing, "the great 'proto-narrative' theologian of the late 19th and early 20th centuries."[5] The mind boggles at the attempt to enlist Schlatter, a critical realist who insisted that the historian could see with his eyes and not just through self-tinted glasses,[6] for the postmodernist cause. Gerald Bray writes that Schlatter defended J. T. Beck and was a follower of Hermann Cremer.[7] Neither of these claims can really be sustained.[8]

There is need to reconsider Schlatter's place in the history of scholarship, especially as it relates to recent New Testament theology. In some ways this is already taking place, for as we will see below, Schlatter's name and thought have influenced an astonishingly diverse set of New Testament theologians right up to the present time in spite of common misrepresentations of his heritage and views. This fact, combined with the availability of an increasing number of his works in English, suggests that Schlatter will be a significant, if behind-the-scenes, force for some time to come.

In the interest of bringing clarity to this rethinking, we will explore below how Schlatter both figures into and defies Bultmann's monumental treatment of New Testament theology. Next we will comment on other ways that Schlatter has continued to play a role in methodological discussion that is foundational to current New Testament theology. We will conclude with a few observations on his future importance.

## Schlatter and Bultmann

Reginald Fuller notes that "Bultmann had a high regard for the theological side of Schlatter's exegesis, though he was poles apart from him in matters of his-

---

3. *New Testament Theology in Dialogue* (London: SPCK, 1987), 3.

4. As Peter Stuhlmacher, among many others, has recognized; see *Historical Criticism and Theological Interpretation of Scripture*, trans. Roy A. Harrisville (Philadelphia: Fortress, 1977).

5. Stephen F. Dintaman, *Creative Grace: Faith and History in the Theology of Adolf Schlatter* (New York: Peter Lang, 1993), xii–xiii.

6. Note the anecdote recounted by one-time Schlatter student Otto Michel, *Anpassung oder Widerstand* (Wuppertal/Zürich: R. Brockhaus, 1989), 25–26.

7. Gerald Bray, *Biblical Interpretation* (Downers Grove: InterVarsity, 1996), 331, 339.

8. Schlatter makes his distance from Beck clear in *Rückblick auf meine Lebensarbeit*, 44–48. He concedes (ibid., 46) that he resembled Beck, but only in that he lived openly as a Christian in the university setting. See also Schlatter, "J. T. Becks theologische Arbeit," *Beiträge zur Förderung christlicher Theologie* 8, no. 4 (1904): 25–46. Schlatter was in no sense a follower of Cremer; as colleagues at Greifswald (1888–93), they made common cause.

torical criticism and NT introduction."[9] Bultmann agreed with Schlatter's rejection of the "doctrinal concepts" approach to New Testament theology used, for example, by Bernhard Weiss and Theodor Zahn.[10] He also agreed with Schlatter's criticism of the history of religions reductionism that replaced the New Testament's "theology" with "religion." Bultmann believed in theology—of a sort. But it was here that he parted company with Schlatter, who believed that Jesus was the Messiah promised by God in the Hebrew Scriptures, and that historical evidence centered in the first century, of which the New Testament documents are primary examples, supported this assertion.[11] Accordingly his New Testament theology affirms the conviction that the earthly Jesus actually possessed and exhibited what can only be termed divine prerogatives—an impossibility for Bultmann's philosophical naturalist commitments, which inclined him to affirm that Jesus became the Christ only in early church preaching. And this exaltation-through-proclamation was the effect of Hellenistic influence, according to Bultmann, whereas Schlatter saw the primary background of the four Gospels' presentation to be real events and reminiscences rooted in the Jewish soil of Galilee and Palestine.[12] In Bultmann's words, Schlatter was oblivious to "the importance of Hellenistic syncretism." For Schlatter's part, he found documentary evidence lacking for the theory that the early church was syncretistic. And he felt that scholarly aversion to acknowledging the plausibility of Jesus' messianic claims pointed to an obduracy of modern scholars directly analogous to "the teachers of Capernaum and the theologians of Jerusalem" in Jesus' earthly days.[13] Bultmann also lamented Schlatter's "peculiar inhibitions" in "all questions of historical criticism, especially where literary-historical investigation of the gospels is concerned." This is itself a peculiar side-stepping of the massive and cogent weight of critical argumentation comprised by Schlatter's linguistically rigorous commentaries on each of the four Gospels, especially when seen in the light of Schlatter's numerous historical monographs. Bultmann simply refused to see much

9. "New Testament Theology," in *The New Testament and Its Modern Interpreters*, ed. Eldon Jay Epp and George W. MacRae (Philadelphia/Atlanta: Fortress/Scholars Press, 1989), 575.
10. References in this section are to Bultmann's *Theologie des Neuen Testaments*, in which he comments explicitly on Schlatter. We cite the 8th edition (essentially unchanged from the first), ed. Otto Merk (Tübingen: J. C. B. Mohr [Paul Siebeck], 1980). The relevant pages are 585–99, especially 597–99. For the English translation, see Bultmann, *Theology of the New Testament*, vol. 2, trans. Kendrick Grobel (New York: Charles Scribner's Sons, 1955), 237–51.
11. The importance of Schlatter's conviction that Jesus was the Messiah is underscored in the opening pages of Peter Stuhlmacher, *Jesus of Nazareth—Christ of Faith*, trans. Siegfried S. Schatzmann (Peabody, Mass.: Hendrickson, 1993).
12. Schlatter well understood, and in fact anticipates, the point underscored generations later by Martin Hengel that Hellenism impinged on Judaism in Palestine already long before the New Testament era. This point is palpable in numerous passages of both volumes of Schlatter's New Testament theology. See Hengel, *Judaism and Hellenism*, 2 vols. (Philadelphia: Fortress, 1974).
13. Schlatter, "Der Zweifel an der Messianität Jesu," in *Zur Theologie des Neuen Testaments und zur Dogmatik*, ed. Ulrich Luck (Munich: Chr. Kaiser, 1969), 158. Stuhlmacher expands on this point (*Vom Verstehen des Neuen Testaments*, 2nd ed. [Göttingen: Vandenhoeck & Ruprecht, 1986], 174): "Schlatter insisted that the earthly Jesus was already the messianic son of God and charged all opponents of his outlook with deficient capacity for historical perception. Since his opponents counter-charged that Schlatter lacked powers of critical discernment, and since no direct scientific discussion ensued, the dispute remained unsettled, as it remains to this day."

historically accurate reportage in the Gospels, while Schlatter insisted that the historically constrained exegete was bound to acknowledge a great deal. Where Bultmann followed Schlatter was in his refusal to separate the *Denkakt* (act of thinking) from the *Lebensakt* (act of living). Schlatter saw, correctly in Bultmann's view, that the New Testament documents and their message are both a product of and an appeal to the will, not just a reflection of ancient intellectual processes of possible interest to modern intellectual agendas. The New Testament is not just about thinking and ideas: it is about living, about decision. While Schlatter did not push this in the direction of the existentialist *Entscheidung* (decision), which for Bultmann was the act of faith itself, Bultmann saw in Schlatter's work a nascent legitimation of his program.

Heikki Räisänen correctly notes that "Bultmann's *Theology of the New Testament* still stands as the unrivaled classic in its field. There is hardly a shadow of a challenger in view."[14] Some New Testament theologians, like Jeremias[15] and Goppelt (see below), reacted against Bultmann, while others, like J. M. Robinson[16] and Räisänen,[17] have sought to go beyond him. But it would be foolhardy as yet completely to ignore him, and he will certainly be of central importance in the history of the discipline as long as it endures in anything like its present form. Since Bultmann's importance persists, and given that he took his bearings in some respect from Schlatter, Schlatter's effect is still very much with us in the current discussion. It is with us particularly in the willingness we see in Stuhlmacher, Hans Hübner, and Alfons Weiser, for example, to continue to pursue theology in their historical analysis when Wrede, J. M. Robinson, and Räisänen have called for mere religious history instead (see below). This theological focus, whose existence in twentieth-century biblical studies is often traced to Barth and neo-orthodoxy, may owe at least as much to Schlatter, whose defense of theological sensitivities precisely on the part of the New Testament historian kept theology alive in his New Testament work, and Scripture at the core of his dogmatics, a full decade before Barth published his Romans commentary.[18]

## Schlatter in More Recent Discussion

### Robert Morgan, Otto Merk

Schlatter's current importance for New Testament theology extends back to the early 1970s. By that time Bultmann's hegemony in the discipline had given way to at least a mild form of methodological chaos from which there has so far

14. Heikki Räisänen, *Beyond New Testament Theology* (London/Philadelphia: SCM/Trinity Press International, 1990), xi.

15. Joachim Jeremias, *New Testament Theology: The Proclamation of Jesus* (New York: Scribner's, 1971).

16. James M. Robinson, "The Future of New Testament Theology," *Religious Studies Review* 2 (1976): 17–23.

17. See n. 14 above.

18. Cf. Peter Stuhlmacher, "Adolf Schlatter als Bibelausleger," *Zeitschrift für Theologie und Kirche* Beiheft 4 (1978): 104 n. 37.

been no clear recovery. In 1973 Robert Morgan translated and published William Wrede's classic essay on New Testament theology from a history of religions viewpoint, pairing it with an equally formidable treatise on method by Schlatter.[19] Morgan's accompanying sixty-seven page essay rounds out the volume. There Morgan makes his Wredian sympathies clear. But his respect for Schlatter is apparent, too, as he says he "can be rated in the same class as [F. C.] Baur, Wrede, Bousset, and Bultmann."[20] Morgan also wisely comments, "In a state of methodological confusion it is generally wise to look to history to find one's bearings."[21] Schlatter is a giant in that history, and Morgan shows why Schlatter has continued to inform at least background debate regarding New Testament theology over the years.

Also in the early 1970s there appeared Otto Merk's landmark treatment of biblical theology's rise and early history.[22] Merk grants Schlatter's monumental importance as forerunner to Bultmann and as continuing the tradition in New Testament theology stretching back to J. P. Gabler. This trajectory, says Merk, tends to stress "interpretation," the relevance for today, rather than "reconstruction," the analysis of past reality in itself as determined by application of modern historiographical tools and canons.[23] But for Merk, Schlatter's implication in this line of analysis marks Schlatter's fatal weakness as well; quoting Kümmel, Merk writes, "The historical task, which Schlatter undertook to address, cannot be carried out using *this* approach."[24] In the end Merk accuses Schlatter of arriving at a "purely theological understanding of New Testament theology" and of "sacrificing reconstruction for the sake of interpretation."[25] This harsh verdict reflects the fact that Schlatter's historical results, which see as factual and concretely true the New Testament's so-called theological claims like Jesus' divinity and resurrection, are anathema to the "historical" approach called for by Merk. What Schlatter thinks he has made sense of and given a coherent account of historically, Merk dismisses as not "historical" at all. At issue here is Merk's confidence that Enlightenment historical criticism has destroyed the notion that New Testament documents like the four Gospels are historically credible largely as they stand. Schlatter, in contrast, argued that there were no compelling historical reasons for setting aside the documents' prima facie claims to be describing space–time phenomena as experienced and later recalled by direct or secondary eyewitnesses. But for Merk, Schlatter's approach to New Testament theology is a line of inquiry without a future in the modern setting, where the New Testament documents must be read first in the light of contemporary, ultimately anti-creedal certainties. Merk's clearly modernist sympathies show no sign of losing strength in the discipline despite the arrival of "post" modernism.

19. Robert Morgan, *The Nature of New Testament Theology*, SBT 2/25 (London: SCM, 1973).
20. Ibid., 27.
21. Ibid., 28.
22. Otto Merk, *Biblische Theologie des Neuen Testaments in ihrer Anfangszeit* (Marburg: N. G. Elwert, 1972).
23. Ibid., 252.
24. Ibid., 249.
25. Ibid., 250.

### Leonhard Goppelt, Peter Stuhlmacher

Yet this negative verdict on Schlatter has not prevented others from assessing his program positively and even taking their bearings from it. Leonhard Goppelt saw Schlatter as an important forerunner of his own New Testament theology, noting the continuing importance of Schlatter's essay "Atheistic Methods in Theology" and praising Schlatter's "immense and superior history of religion/ philological investigation of the New Testament."[26] Goppelt likewise followed Schlatter in keeping dogmatics per se separate from biblical theology and defended Schlatter against Käsemann's charge that Schlatter was a "theological pietist."[27] Goppelt accorded Schlatter respect not least because of the way Bultmann acknowledged common ground with Schlatter. Also much like Schlatter is Goppelt's approach of seeking to bring historical-critical consciousness into respectful dialogue with New Testament claims rather than woodenly privileging modern consciousness over and above those claims as contemporary scholarship is wont to do. In other words, whereas most modern New Testament scholars have let their methods be dictated to them by the current largely secular world view,[28] Goppelt did not, at least not to the extent that Bultmann did. Goppelt's major precursor and ally in this politically incorrect strategy was Schlatter.

Peter Stuhlmacher has long championed a return to Schlatterian insights in New Testament theology. Partially in reaction to reactionary south German Pietism, Stuhlmacher has invoked Schlatter's name to underscore "the rigor and necessity of historical criticism in theology."[29] Yet his appropriation of Schlatter serves to check, not abet, the theologically caustic "criticism" championed by Franz Overbeck and Ernst Troeltsch.[30] Stuhlmacher's "hermeneutics of consent," which undergirds his approach to New Testament theology, is heavily informed by interaction with Schlatter.[31]

Stuhlmacher's New Testament theology makes sparing but strategic mention of Schlatter.[32] At one point Stuhlmacher is openly critical, disagreeing with Schlatter on the meaning of κτίσις in Romans 8:19–21.[33] But at a dozen other junctures he affirms Schlatter's interpretive tack. Schlatter has rightly seen that "intellectual and existential understanding must coalesce" and has contributed to a proper understanding of the method and construction of a New Testament theology.[34] Stuhlmacher follows Schlatter's rejection of an adoptionistic reading of the opening verses of Mark's Gospel.[35] He affirms at a number of points

---

26. Leonhard Goppelt, *Theology of the New Testament*, vol. 1, 278.
27. Ibid.
28. Cf. Morgan, *Nature of New Testament Theology*, 27.
29. Stuhlmacher, *Historical Criticism and Theological Interpretation of Scripture*, 44.
30. Ibid., 44-48.
31. Stuhlmacher, *Vom Verstehen des Neuen Testaments*, passim. While Stuhlmacher cites e.g. Luther, Schleiermacher, Bultmann, Barth, Fuchs, Gadamer, Ricoeur, and others extensively, the index of this book refers to Schlatter more times than to anyone else.
32. *Biblische Theologie des Neuen Testaments*, vol. 1, *Grundlegung. Von Jesus zu Paulus* (Göttingen: Vandenhoeck & Ruprecht, 1992).
33. Ibid., 271.
34. Ibid., 4, 11.
35. Ibid., 63.

Schlatter's interpretation of δικαιοσύνη θεοῦ (righteousness of God), an interpretation picked up by Käsemann and seconded by Stuhlmacher.[36] He also agrees with Schlatter's insistence that Paul did not view obedience to the law as itself sinful; the law in Paul has a certain redemptive as well as condemnatory function.[37] Most significantly, Stuhlmacher sides with Schlatter's contentions that "the earthly Jesus was none other than the Christ of faith" and that Paul was indeed "the messenger of Jesus" and not the founder of some new religion that made illicit use of the real Jesus.[38] In both its general conception and in numerous specific positions adopted, Stuhlmacher's New Testament theology probably reflects Schlatter's exegetical toughness and hermeneutical sophistication more fully than any comparable study written since Schlatter's death.

### Donald Guthrie, Gerhard Hasel

It is understandable that Schlatter has loomed large, at least in name, behind the scenes of conservative works on New Testament theology like those of Gerhard Hasel and Donald Guthrie. Guthrie endorsed Schlatter's theological openness[39] and his critique of overemphasis on history of religions parallels.[40] He likewise called for reconsideration of Schlatter's conviction that the New Testament is fundamentally a unity, not a monument to disparate diversity.[41] He states that "Schlatter's retention of the idea of revelation as an essential factor for a genuine understanding of NT theology has not been given the weight it deserves."[42] He endorses Schlatter's shrewd insight that "historical criticism is never based on fact alone, but always has its roots in the critic's own dogma,"[43] a truth still dawning on some who are currently underscoring this insight as if they were the first to discover it.[44] Guthrie also follows Schlatter's reasoning regarding the centrality of the canon for New Testament theology.[45] Yet he appears to distance himself from Schlatter regarding "righteousness of God" in Romans,[46] confirming that he did not simply become Schlatter's unthinking disciple.

Hasel, perhaps influenced by Ladd here, too facilely blends Schlatter in with the Erlangen school.[47] He is on firmer ground when he follows Robert Morgan in seeing Pannenberg's similarity to Schlatter in his critique of an ahistorical "theology of the Word."[48] He sides with Schlatter and against Morgan on the

---

36. Ibid., 238, 335.
37. Ibid., 341, 379.
38. Ibid., 157, 233.
39. Donald Guthrie, *New Testament Theology* (Downers Grove: InterVarsity, 1981), 24–25.
40. Ibid., 24 n. 11.
41. Ibid., 31.
42. Ibid.
43. Ibid., 34.
44. Cf., e.g., Daniel Patte, *Ethics of Biblical Interpretation: A Reevaluation* (Louisville: Westminster/John Knox, 1995).
45. Guthrie, *New Testament Theology*, 41.
46. Ibid., 100 n. 68.
47. Gerhard Hasel, *New Testament Theology: Basic Issues in the Current Debate* (Grand Rapids: Eerdmans, 1978), 69. On Schlatter and Erlangen see n. 1 above.
48. Ibid., 42.

plausibility of Schlatter's "conservative" conclusions regarding the date and apostolic authorship of most New Testament documents. Hasel concludes, "Schlatter stands before us as a giant who has carefully considered the nature of the whole enterprise of NT theology but whose views have not received the attention they deserve."[49] He rejects the claim that Schlatter was a biblicist,[50] a charge that Schlatter himself pondered and rejected as both inaccurate and peculiar. Schlatter's professor J. T. Beck might be called a biblicist, but Schlatter was fundamentally at odds with Beck's ahistoricism.

### Brevard Childs, Hendrikus Boers

Additional recent "conservative" interpreters like Ward Gasque and Gerhard Maier could be cited as explicitly supportive of Schlatter,[51] and others like N. T. Wright and Markus Bockmühl as at least implicitly supportive,[52] but it is important to note that New Testament theologians of other stripes have wrestled profitably with Schlatter as well. Brevard Childs would be an example here. He notes Schlatter's importance in the history of the discipline.[53] He observes that Schlatter is an example of how "much of the most profound and critical reflection on the Bible operated with various philosophical and theological categories, often as a vehicle for the critical, descriptive task."[54] He praises Schlatter's "remarkable study of faith"[55] and says that in terms of theological reflection on biblical narrative, "Schlatter's handling of the life of Jesus in his New Testament Theology (*Die Geschichte des Christus*) is another excellent model of Biblical Theology."[56] Much could be written on points of contact between Schlatter and Childs, but this suffices to show that Schlatter has positively influenced Childs' important work.

Hendrikus Boers is another notable scholar who in devoting extensive attention to Schlatter pays tribute to his importance. He notes that the principles discussed so insightfully in Schlatter's treatise on New Testament theology "remain influential in all subsequent attempts at theological interpretation of the New Testament, even where the influence of Schlatter himself is not recog-

---

49. Ibid., 43.
50. Ibid.
51. Note the works cited in Andreas Köstenberger, "Translator's Preface," in Adolf Schlatter, *The History of the Christ* (Grand Rapids: Baker, 1997), 12 n. 9.
52. Note references to Schlatter in the index of N. T. Wright, *The New Testament and the People of God* (Minneapolis: Fortress, 1992). In addition, Wright's critical realism, which informs his work across the board, has more affinities with Schlatter's hermeneutic than Wright seems to realize. See also Markus Bockmuehl, *This Jesus: Martyr, Lord, Messiah* (Edinburgh: T. & T. Clark, 1994), 218 n. 1, who calls Schlatter "brilliant but widely ignored." Bockmühl's careful attention to Jesus' and the Gospels' setting within the first-century Jewish world is an extension of Schlatter's historical and hermeneutical focus.
53. Brevard S. Childs, *Biblical Theology of the Old and New Testaments* (Minneapolis: Fortress, 1993), 3.
54. Ibid., 12.
55. Ibid., 15. Childs refers to Schlatter's landmark *Der Glaube im Neuen Testament* (Leiden: E. J. Brill, 1885).
56. Ibid., 708.

nized."[57] Boers rightly presents Schlatter as a pioneer among twentieth-century scholars who have been aware of the necessary connection between New Testament faith and other first-century religious outlooks. In other words, Schlatter conceded in principle the validity of history of religions research. But unlike Bousset Schlatter rejected the reductionism into which history of religions analysis of the New Testament too often fell. Conceding the ties of New Testament writers to their religious milieu, Schlatter never lost sight of their many points of difference, an insight that had profound impact on the church historian Karl Holl.[58] Boers seems to agree with Schlatter that "historical" inquiry of the New Testament cannot be "neutral."[59] The view that it can and must be was the claim of William Wrede and is commonly repeated today, recently in Bart Ehrman's New Testament survey.[60] Boers appears to agree with Schlatter that this conviction is mistaken. And he agrees with Schlatter that a New Testament theology undertaken with an eye to the New Testament's possible congruence with historic Christian orthodoxy is not necessarily invalid "historically," contra Troeltsch and all who have followed his lead at this point. Boers also praises Schlatter's "sharp but correct" insistence that "representing the New Testament writers as if they thought in the abstract way of Greek thinkers leads to a distorting theology of the New Testament."[61]

Yet Boers faults Schlatter, claiming that he separated New Testament history from its temporal nexus, a charge refuted even by Paul Tillich.[62] And he complains that Schlatter allows "present-day dogmatic concerns to predetermine the outcome of historical inquiry."[63] Here Boers seems to forget what he earlier praised Schlatter for: the insight that modern "historical" inquiry inevitably is informed by its own de facto dogmatics. That means that *all* historical inquiry is to some extent conditioned by present-day dogmatic concerns. (Schlatter remained convinced, however, that by humble observation the object of understanding itself could ultimately be normative for observation, not subjective preunderstanding.) The question then becomes: Whose dogmatic formulations can make the best claim to account for, evaluate, and where called for appropriate the affirmations of the relevant ancient evidence? Boers' conclusion that Schlatter's New Testament theology is "a dogmatic theology and should be appreciated as such,"[64] while meant as a criticism, is actually just as true of any New Testament

---

57. Hendrikus Boers, *What Is New Testament Theology?* (Philadelphia: Fortress, 1979), 92.

58. Schlatter's impact on Holl is brought out in Neuer, *Adolf Schlatter* (see "Holl" in index). Cf. Goppelt, *Theology of the New Testament*, vol. 1, 262 with n. 14.

59. Boers, *What Is New Testament Theology?*, 73

60. Bart Ehrman, *The New Testament* (New York/Oxford: Oxford University Press, 1997).

61. Boers, *What Is New Testament Theology?*, 74.

62. Tillich wrote that his own theology emphasized "that God is related to the world and not only to the individual and his inner life and not only to the church as a sociological entity. God is related to the universe, and this includes nature, history, and personality. May I add that Martin Kähler and Adolf Schlatter were also in this line of thought. They stressed the freedom of God to act apart from the church in either its orthodox or pietistic form" (*A Complete History of Christian Thought: Perspectives on 19th and 20th Century Protestant Theology*, ed. Carl E. Braaten [New York/Evanston/London: Harper & Row, 1967], 235).

63. Boers, *What Is New Testament Theology?*, 75.

64. Ibid.

theology ever written. It is no grounds for setting Schlatter aside but is rather a testimony to the mainstream relevance of his modus operandi, even if many of his critical conclusions and doctrinal convictions have been rejected by the hegemony of twentieth-century university theologians.

## Heikki Räisänen

The weightiness of a thinker can be measured not only by those who support him but also by those who oppose him. Heikki Räisänen finds plenty to oppose in Schlatter. He brackets him with Barth and sets both aside disparagingly as "spiritual masters."[65] "Spiritual" is a negative term for Räisänen, as is "theology" if used to refer to the New Testament, which he views as containing none. Räisänen writes dismissively that Schlatter's New Testament theology "remains in the fetters of dogmatics."[66] He does not deserve to be ranked with Bultmann, is wrong about the unity of the New Testament, and has little to offer because he is "unmistakeably . . . a figure from a bygone era."[67] He accuses Schlatter of biblicism, disputes his focus on the canon, and concludes that "Schlatter's New Testament theology is, in essence, his (systematic) theology, opaque in construction of its argument and often presented in a rather meditative manner. If the work is understood in this way, it can even be appreciated."[68] Räisänen's polemic extends to Peter Stuhlmacher, whom he criticizes for his affinities with Schlatter and for suggesting that "atonement" is at the center of biblical theology.[69] Räisänen rejects this because "this notion is rarely mentioned in, say, the Synoptic Gospels or Acts,"[70] thereby perhaps tipping his hand regarding the anti-confessional loyalties that give rise to his impatience with Stuhlmacher and Schlatter.

Might Räisänen be correct? As for his insistence that New Testament theology must follow Wrede in moving beyond New Testament theology, which historical criticism allegedly shows is at best myth and fantasy, it is worth noting that even nonevangelical New Testament scholars continue to turn out synthetic treatments of the New Testament—New Testament theologies—that focus on (Christian) beliefs and not just "religion" as Wrede, Räisänen, and others have called for. Alfons Weiser's treatment of the four Gospels could be mentioned here, which explicitly repudiates Wrede and by implication Räisänen.[71] Hans Hübner passionately rejects Räisänen's program, denying that it is necessary to be hostile to the church and to the kerygmatic dimensions of the results of New Testament theology for the church in order to perform historical-critical analysis of the New Testament.[72] Räisänen's rejection of Schlatter on the

---

65. Räisänen, *Beyond New Testament Theology*, xiv.
66. Ibid., 25.
67. Ibid.
68. Ibid.
69. Ibid., 80.
70. Ibid.
71. Alfons Weiser, *Theologie des Neuen Testaments* II (Stuttgart/Berlin/Cologne: Kohlhammer, 1993), 13–14.
72. Hans Hübner, *Biblische Theologie des Neuen Testaments*, vol. 1, *Prolegomena* (Göttingen: Vandenhoeck & Ruprecht, 1990), 27–28 n. 60.

grounds that prolegomena to New Testament theology is essentially meaning-less when compared to the actual results of that discipline's labors is countered by Robert Morgan, who notes the irreducibly theological nature of the disci-pline and states, "The theological orientation of N[ew] T[estament] T[heology] as a theological as well as biblical discipline means that it is largely concerned with theory."[73] Räisänen's assurance in attempting to marginalize Schlatter may have less to say for it than he realizes.

## Schlatter and the Future of New Testament Theology

### Continuing Promise

Recent studies reveal deep sympathy for Schlatter on the part of some but serious aversion to him from others. This aversion is largely restatement of ob-jections already raised as long as four generations years ago, as documented in the Köstenberger essay earlier in this volume. These criticisms were offset at the time by positive reviewers and by Schlatter himself. Despite weighty charges against Schlatter and obvious imperfections in aspects of his work, it seems jus-tified to conclude that he has hardly been discredited overall—there still re-mains a great deal to be learned from his hundreds of publications. And since this corpus is largely terra incognita today, the harvest from rediscovery of his work could be considerable indeed. After all, points at which some criticized him, such as his coherent vision of the entire New Testament so disparaged by Holtzmann, are points that others feel are his great strengths. Perhaps Schlatter *was* deluded and pulled many conservatively blinded readers down with him. On the other hand, few read Holtzmann anymore, while some thirty books by Schlatter are still in print in Germany. And it is not only his "theological" but also his historical corpus that is proving to stand the test of time.[74]

Since Schlatter's death in 1938 there has never been complete neglect of his writings in German-speaking Europe, as commemorative volumes, doctoral dissertations, monographs, and various critical articles have appeared, albeit with some irregularity. Schlatter has been a discussion partner over the years in both older commentators such as F. Büchsel, H.-D. Wendland, J. Schniewind, H. Strathmann, O. Michael and K.-H. Rengstorf, as well as in the work of more recent exegetes such as R. Riesner and M. Hengel. A milestone was reached in 1996 with the appearance of the first critical biography of Schlat-ter,[75] an impressive work that quickly precipitated some three dozen reviews in Germany, nearly all of them positive. In North America Roy Harrisville has re-cently honored Schlatter with a careful discussion of Schlatter's many similari-ties to Bultmann. Harrisville's playfulness outruns credibility when, evoking Paul's ode to *agape* in 1 Corinthians 13:13, he concludes, "Now Schlatter,

---

73. Robert Morgan, *ABD* 6:483.
74. See, e.g., Roland Deines, *Die Pharisäer*, WUNT 101 (Tübingen: Mohr Siebeck, 1997), 262–99, who points to Schlatter's significant contribution to Jewish studies in relation to New Testament times.
75. Neuer, *Adolf Schlatter.*

Barth, and Bultmann abide, but the greatest of these is . . . ," but he succeeds in demonstrating that if Barth and Bultmann are still valid discussion partners, so is Schlatter.[76] (We may leave to one side for now Harrisville's failure to pay attention to the profound differences between Schlatter and Bultmann, differences so vast that in private correspondence Schlatter spoke of Bultmann's atheistic tendencies.[77])

### New Translations and Studies

In the United States various translations of works by or about Schlatter, including the present volume and its predecessor, have appeared. Among these are his Romans commentary[78] and a short biography containing several key Schlatter essays, among them his renowned "Atheistic Methods in Theology."[79] It seems that in English-speaking circles, at least, the coming years may see Schlatter acquire a significance not previously enjoyed as new translations overcome former language barriers.

To be noted recently is the richly ironic appearance in Germany of a lengthy article by Fritz Neugebauer, "Wer war Adolf Schlatter?" (Who Was Adolf Schlatter?)[80] It is ironic in that it appeared in *Theologische Literaturzeitung*, the same journal in which Emil Schürer in 1893 bid fair to wreck Schlatter's budding academic career with a devastating review of Schlatter's monograph on Palestinian geography.[81] The irony is rich in that whereas Schürer was exquisitely dismissive, Neugebauer is soberly appreciative, not only of Schlatter's past achievement but of his future promise. But Neugebauer homes in on Schlatter's enduring philosophical,[82] hermeneutical,[83] and historiographical[84] importance. What about his contribution, if any, to New Testament theology and theologies yet to come?

A new monograph on New Testament theology by Peter Balla in the WUNT series, *Challenges to New Testament Theology*,[85] vindicates at least some of Schlatter's assumptions about New Testament theology and the history

---

76. Roy A. Harrisville, "Translator's Introduction," in *What Is Theology?*, ed. Eberhard Jüngel and Klaus W. Müller, trans. Roy A. Harrisville (Minneapolis: Fortress, 1997), 13–17 (quote on 17).

77. Neuer, *Adolf Schlatter*, 656, 658.

78. Adolf Schlatter, *Romans: The Righteousness of God*, trans. Siegfried Schatzmann (Peabody, Mass.: Henrdrickson, 1995).

79. Werner Neuer, *Adolf Schlatter*, trans. Robert W. Yarbrough (Grand Rapids: Baker, 1996). "Atheistic Methods in Theology," translated by David Bauer, appears in ibid., 211–25.

80. *Theologische Literaturzeitung* 122, no. 9 (1997): 770–82.

81. The story is told in Neuer, *Adolf Schlatter*, 280–84.

82. No study on Schlatter's impressive philosophical works has ever been published, but a recent Marburg dissertation on Schlatter's philosophy by Jochen Walldorf is in press; *Realistische Philosophie. Die philosophische Konzeption Adolf Schlatters* (Gottingen: Vandenhoeck & Ruprecht, 1999).

83. Schlatter receives considerable attention not only in Stuhlmacher's *Vom Verstehen des Neuen Testaments*, but also in Gerhard Maier, *Biblical Hermeneutics*, trans. Robert W. Yarbrough (Wheaton: Crossway, 1994).

84. See, e.g., n. 74 above.

85. WUNT 2/95 (Tübingen: Mohr Siebeck, 1997).

within which it arose. These include the relationship between history and theology, the priority of orthodoxy to heresy in earliest Christianity, the canon, and the unity of the New Testament. While Balla chooses not to interact with Schlatter directly, many of his contentions are strongly supported by articles and books in the Schlatter corpus. We have here, then, something of a Schlatter *redivivus* in Balla's arguments taken as a whole, which is not surprising in light of the fact that Balla is seeking to refute above all the Wrede–Räisänen insistence that New Testament theology is both a misnomer and an impossibility. A major difference between Balla and Schlatter is the former's rejection of revelation as relevant to a *historical* approach to New Testament theology. This marks Balla as a "historical-positive" rather than a "salvation-historical" interpreter[86] and may explain why Balla omits Schlatter from his study, an omission lamentable for how considerably it impoverishes his discussion.

There is also the rumor of a new edition of Robert Morgan's *The Nature of New Testament Theology*.[87] It is likely that this would give considerable impetus to continued discussion of Schlatter's proposals and example, in particular in conjunction with appearance of both volumes of his New Testament theology in English.

## Enduring Strengths

The intent of this essay thus far has been to characterize, not advocate, Schlatter reception. But in conclusion, three distinctives of Schlatter's approach to New Testament theology bear commendation for the sake of encouraging future interaction with his writings by those interested in the study of New Testament theology.

First is his determined focus on the original language sources as we have them in their historical setting. Without resorting to Childs' canonical strategy, which while admired has drawn criticism from many sides, Schlatter's model encourages painstaking interaction with the text—not some hypothetical source behind it, religious absolute allegedly beneath it, or *Religionsgeschichte* oblique to it. Robert Morgan grants that this is one of the strengths of what he calls biblicism: "it allows the text to challenge the interpreter."[88] In Schlatter this is not some sentimental loyalty to Scripture, much less hermeneutical naiveté. It is rather a rigorous historical-linguistic mission to make sure that the interpreter *sees* what is *there*. Observation must precede judgment. Neuer calls attention to Schlatter's "'*theology of facts*,' not biblicistic but biblical, not confessionalistic yet indebted to the Reformation heritage, the knowledge of which facts is not found in 'pious consciousness' but in the reality of salvation history and creation that has independent existence apart from consciousness."[89] If synthetic explication of the historical manifestation of earliest Christian belief is a goal of New Testament theology, and if painstaking observation of the primary

86. See Goppelt, *Theology of the New Testament*, 272ff.
87. See n. 19 above.
88. Robert Morgan, *ABD* 6:477.
89. Neuer, *Adolf Schlatter*, 167–68.

sources is the perennial order of the day, Schlatter is probably one of the more suggestive mentors in the recent history of the discipline. The precedent he sets strengthens both sides of the task that New Testament theology presents, the historical as well as the theological, by modeling first of all rigorous and re-sourceful exegesis.

A second promising dimension of the Schlatter corpus is its attention to the importance of method.[90] His masterful theoretical reflections are at points even more valuable than his two-volume New Testament theology proper. These re-flections, because of their hypothetical scope, provoke and liberate the careful reader to many fruitful insights. Morgan comments that nowadays "the con-texts of both text and interpreter so complicate the question of the theological meaning of the Bible that biblical scholars can be pardoned for retreating to their own specialist tasks and leaving theology to the theologians."[91] But this is a sorry state of affairs, for at the same time many theologians would like biblical scholarship to provide solid guidance regarding the Bible's message. It is no wonder that some theologies drift farther and farther from organic connection with Christian Scripture: Who is doing historically rigorous work on the Bible with an eye to the theologians' questions and calling? This is part of today's cri-sis of method in the discipline. Schlatter's extensive deliberations on both his-torical and dogmatic method are a rich source for gleaning insights and gaining resolve to execute the full gamut of the biblical theologian's task. What Neuge-bauer said of Schlatter's biography is also true of the Schlatter corpus in general: it is not so much a quarry to be mined as a treasure chest to be dipped into.[92]

A third strength of Schlatter's approach is his recovery of Jesus as *prima causa* for the early church's faith.[93] Neugebauer notes that modern scholarship's focus on the life circumstances of the early church and what it allegedly confessed makes it the *prima causa*, Jesus only the *causa secunda*.[94] Of course in many ap-proaches to New Testament theology, Bultmann's typical among them, this is not seen as a weakness but a necessary corollary to the modern secular impulse. What is there besides man? In any case Jesus was no more than a man, from the standpoint of post-Christian scholarship.

But Schlatter saw things differently. In a memorable dispute involving the Berlin faculty where Schlatter was teaching in 1895, university theologians were criticized for their hostility to confessional Christian belief in a statement issued

90. Schlatter's most important reflections are his "The Theology of the New Testament and Dogmatics," in Robert Morgan, *The Nature of New Testament Theology* (see n. 19 above; the same essay is reprinted in Neuer, *Adolf Schlatter*, n. 79 above, 169–210). For a briefer statement on ex-egetical and theological method, see Robert Yarbrough, "Adolf Schlatter's 'the Significance of Method for Theological Work': Translation and Commentary," *Southern Baptist Journal of The-ology* 1, no. 2 (1997): 64–76.

91. Morgan, *ABD* 6:475.

92. Neugebauer, "Wer war Adolf Schlatter," 778.

93. Although Schlatter is not cited in Richard Bauckham, ed., *The Gospels for All Christians* (Grand Rapids: Eerdmans, 1997), the proposals of the essays resonate deeply with Schlatter's views on Jesus' primacy, and the function of apostolic traditions and eventually writings, in the early Christian communities.

94. Neugebauer, "Wer war Adolf Schlatter," 780.

by churchmen at the annual Protestant assembly. Schlatter supported this measured but pointed protest statement. When attacked in print by university colleagues for his stance, the charge being that siding with conservative Christians against the university endangered the freedom of theological science, Schlatter was quick to reply. At issue, he said, was not science's freedom but the open unbelief of the church's ostensible teachers. The question was simple: Who was Jesus? Schlatter expressed joy to be able to identify with common believers. "If colleagues force the decision between faith in Christ and their 'science,' between the faculty and the church, the church being those who do not deny Christ, then in my view the apostolic word still applies today: 'I regard it all as refuse.'"[95] Schlatter concluded: "As long as God's grace guides me, I will join the church in kneeling before the slumbering child in the manger and the God-forsaken figure on the cross, confessing: My Lord and my God."[96] To some this may sound like melodrama. But to any who lament the loss of gospel belief in the Western world, whether in the form of the desolating effects of scholarly movements producing the likes of Robert Funk's *Honest to Jesus*[97] or the insipid nominalism and traditionalism afflicting too many Bible-believing churches, Schlatter's determination to live out Christ's lordship precisely as *an academician and churchman* could serve to both challenge and reform.

The fact is that like few scholars since the Enlightenment, Schlatter holds promise at multiple levels and in several areas for the wide range of concerns that converge when the question of New Testament theology's methods, goals, and practice arise. When Don Carson lists "five stances essential to biblical theology," it is hard to imagine the publications of a single scholar who better fulfills these desiderata than Schlatter.[98] As New Testament theologians continue to review the scholarly ideals and theological promise of their discipline, many sense that it could and should yield more constructive fruit in the next century than in the somewhat muddled previous two. Schlatter might be of assistance in any reformation that gets underway.[99]

95. Neuer, *Adolf Schlatter: Ein Leben für Theologie und Kirche*, 319.
96. Ibid.
97. San Francisco: HarperSanFrancisco, 1996.
98. Carson, "Current Issues," *Bulletin for Biblical Research* 5 (1995): 27–32. Carson lists these essential features: Biblical theology 1) "is a discipline necessarily dependent on reading the Bible as an historically developing collection of documents," 2) "must presuppose a coherent and agreed canon," 3) "presupposes a profound willingness to work inductively from the text—from individual books and from the canon as a whole," 4) "will not only work inductively in each of the biblical corpora but will seek to make clear the connections among the corpora," 5) "will transcend mere description and linking of the biblical documents, and call men and women to knowledge of the living God."
99. The author is grateful to Andreas Köstenberger, Werner Neuer, and Robert Morgan for constructive remarks on earlier drafts of this essay.

# Modern Author Index

# Subject Index

# Scripture Index

**Adolf Schlatter** was born August 16, 1852, in St. Gallen, Switzerland. He died May 19, 1938, in Tübingen, Germany, at the inception of the Second World War. His teaching career spanned more than forty years, with his most mature years spent at Tübingen. In an age when liberal scholarship carried the day, Schlatter stood firm in his advocacy of a conservative approach to biblical interpretation and theology. He was convinced that biblical exegesis was the only proper foundation for systematic theology, and in this respect anticipated and influenced Karl Barth.

**Andreas J. Köstenberger**, Ph.D., is associate professor of New Testament at Southeastern Baptist Theological Seminary in Wake Forest, North Carolina.